The Lure of the Transcendent:

Collected Essays by Dwayne E. Huebner

Studies in Curriculum Theory
William F. Pinar, Series Editor

The Lure of the Transcendent:

Collected Essays by Dwayne E. Huebner

Edited by
Vikki Hillis

Collected and Introduced by
William F. Pinar

LAWRENCE ERLBAUM ASSOCIATES, PUBLISHERS
1999   Mahwah, New Jersey   London

Permission to reprint the poem on pages 103–104 is gratefully acknowl-
edged: "Oh sweet spontaneous," copyright 1923, 1951, © 1991 by the
Trustees for the E. E. Cummings Trust. Copyright © 1976 by George
James Firmage, from COMPLETE POEMS: 1904–1962 by E. E.
Cummings, Edited by George J. Firmage. Reprinted by permission of
Liveright Publishing Corporation.

Lawrence Erlbaum Associates, Inc., Publishers
10 Industrial Avenue
Mahwah, NJ 07430

Cover design by Kathryn Houghtaling Lacey

Library of Congress Cataloging-in-Publication Data

    Huebner, Dwayne E.
    The lure of the transcendent : collected essays by Dwayne E. Huebner /
edited by Vikki Hillis; collected and introduced by William F. Pinar.
        p. cm. — (Studies in curriculum theory)
    Includes bibliographical references and indexes.
    ISBN 0-8058-2533-9 (cloth : alk. paper) — ISBN 0-8058-2534-7
(pbk. : alk. paper).
    1. Education—Curricula—Philosophy. 2. Curriculum planning—Phi-
losophy. I. Pinar, William. II. Hillis, Vikki. III. Title. IV. Series.
    LB1570.H82   1998
    375'.0001—dc21   98-35222
                                                CIP

Books published by Lawrence Erlbaum Associates are printed on acid-free
paper, and their bindings are chosen for strength and durability.

Printed in the United States of America
10 9 8 7 6 5 4 3 2 1

For my daughters
Morley and Gillian

In memory of
Virgil Herrick, mentor
James Macdonald, colleague and friend

With gratitude to
William Pinar for his foresight
Vikki Hillis for her committment

Contents

Preface

It is difficult to find just the right words to address, indeed, to honor the essays that follow. Powerful and evocative come to mind, charged with beauty and wisdom, yes, but what continues to strike me, is the prescient vision of Dwayne Huebner—his ability to sensitively identify and explore so early on, those topics which continue to occupy and engage the field of curriculum theory today. These essays tell, not only a certain history of the field, but continue to point, most generatively, toward other possible stories and renewing visions.

My work as editor of this manuscript began in the Spring of 1997 while I was Bill Pinar's graduate assistant. The essays had already been collected by Bill and my initial task was a largely technical one. Each chapter was scanned using optical character recognition software and then checked for errors and put right again. The scanned versions of some chapters more closely resembled old English than anything else and required careful line by line editing. If there are any discrepancies, I must accept responsibility for them.

It was during this more technical phase of the process that Huebner asked me to take on the more traditional task of editor, to revise and edit some of the unpublished essays and in particular to address his use of gendered language in the essays written during the sixties and seventies (see note on gender and language). To the extent that any of these essays have been altered, the majority of changes were made to the first seven chapters of the collection. As Huebner recalls, these essays were written during a summer on Martha's Vineyard in preparation for course lectures. In a letter, he describes these essays as "sketches," never intended for publication, and in need of "much more elaboration."[1] With editorial responsibilities shared by both Huebner and myself, the changes to these essays were largely grammatical and not substantive. The generative flow of these "sketches" remains intact, and what evocative "sketches" they are, addressing wonder and awe, laughter and rhythm.

Ultimately the greatest task in editing involved tracking down citations, verifying quotes and adding content notes for references that might prove elusive to the contemporary reader. This work was assisted by Huebner through his patient replies to my numerous inquiries and his keen ability to recall publication facts and point me in the right direction. As editor, my work is most evident in the notes. The attention that I have brought to the details is ultimately but one expression of the deep admiration I have for the work of Dwayne Huebner.

Many have offered support and encouragement during the year that it has taken to bring this manuscript to completion. My thanks go to the amazing women whom I am privileged to call my family, Beth, Jeri, and Zandy-Marie. Thanks also go to Molly Quinn, Elaine Riley, Anne Pautz, and Honyu Wang, my sisters in spirit, dialogue, and curriculum. Thanks also to Kevin Daigle for his knowledge of those infinitely fine points of the English language and its contemporary usage, and to Naomi Silverman, editor at L.E.A. To William E. Doll Jr., I owe much, not only did he introduce me to curriculum theory, and to the work of Dwayne Huebner, but ever he inspires through his vision and his teaching. To William F. Pinar, thank you for your scholarship and kindness, and for the invitation to assist in bringing forth this manuscript. My deepest thanks to Dwayne Huebner for the myriad blessings that are the gifts of his thinking and the spirit of his scholarship. He shares generously through his work. Thank you Dwayne.

—Vikki Hillis
Louisiana State University
April 1998

NOTES

[1]Dwayne Huebner, personal correspondence, November 4, 1997.

A Note on Gender and Language

In *Babel: A Reflection on Confounded Speech*, Dwayne Huebner acknowledges and affirms the critical task of recreating "the heritage of symbol and language, to make it a more fitting vehicle for women's stories."[1] He states that "There is healing work to be done, as there always has been and will be."[2] It was in the spirit of this "healing work,"that Dwayne Huebner asked me to edit the masculine gendered language used in the early essays in this collection. However, ultimately, the changes—s/he for "he," humankind for "man," self and other for "man," among numerous others—proved not only awkward, but also challenged the historical nature of the collection—meanings specific to the historical context and climate were being lost as contemporary discourses erupted in their place.

The chapters entitled *New Modes of Man's Relationship to Man* and *Curriculum as Concern for Man's Temporality* were particularly difficult. Here, my proposed revisions yielded that disconcerting feeling one has when viewing colorized versions of old black and white films. In a letter Huebner sent to me during this phase of the project, when we were confounded by the proposed changes he phrased it quite simply "bringing [the early essays] up to date would mess up the historical aspects of the collected writings."[3]

It is this aspect of the historical, confounding and otherwise, that Huebner refers to when he quotes the work of Michael Edwards "Languages even die, through disappearing from use, and they half-die by altering, and so alienate us from their, and our own, pasts."[4] In this spirit, we invite the creative understanding of the reader in regard to the masculine gendered language. As evidenced in the essays that follow, Huebner's keen sensitivity to the transformative and healing powers of language are parallelled only by his equal awareness of its oppressive and enslaving capabilities.

"There is healing work to be done, as there always has been and will be."

—Vikki Hillis
Louisiana State University
April 1998

NOTES

[1]See Chapter Twenty-four, 317.
[2]Ibid, 315.
[3]Dwayne Huebner, personal correspondence, November 3, 1997.
[4]Michael Edwards, Toward a Christian Poetics (Grand Rapids: Wm. Eerdmans, 1984), 11, quoted in Chapter Twenty-four, 317.

Introduction

During the autumn of 1969 I was privileged to study with Dwayne Huebner at Teachers College. It was a long ride from Port Washington, Long Island, where I was teaching English at Paul D. Schreiber High School, first via the Long Island Railroad to Manhattan, then the subway uptown to Teachers College. But what an event it was. In a large room with seventy others, I watched an extraordinary figure in the distance speaking a tongue few of us grasped, but which we all found compelling. We knew we were in the presence of a most remarkable and learned man.

Paul Klohr, in whose class I had been introduced to curriculum theory the summer before, had advised me to study with Dwayne Huebner. One of the most important figures in the field, he had said. Twenty-five years later, now that I know the field, I realize how right Paul was. In the fall of the 1969, Dwayne Huebner became a central figure in my "field," my stumbling, eccentric but determined efforts to find my way intellectually at the end of a revolutionary decade. Politics had led me to high-school teaching, but I had no faith left in SDS or a second American revolution, and little in the country, a country, I concluded after the Kent State murders, I had completely misunderstood. In this distressed state of mind, I met Dwayne Huebner.

It was the combination, I suppose, of his quiet, intense, undefeated manner and breathtaking scholarly scope that first heartened then inspired me. Huebner became central to my field; more importantly, he became central to *the* field. This fact is, I think, still under appreciated today. Philip Jackson has performed the extraordinarily useful and important service of writing a short history of curriculum studies in his introduction to the 1992 *Handbook of Research on Curriculum*. In it he discusses the "giants" in the field: Bobbitt, Dewey, Tyler, Schwab. Missing, I contend, is Dwayne Huebner. Consider the following: a decade before political issues would consume a wing of the field, Huebner was writing about the importance of political theory to curriculum studies. Fifteen years before phenomenology would emerge as an important discourse in the field, Huebner was studying Heidegger and Jaspers. Nearly a decade before Jo-

seph Schwab judged the field moribund, Huebner declared the field lacked vitality. And twenty years before religious and theological studies would
constitute a major sector of curriculum scholarship, Huebner was studying
transcendence while teaching courses at the Union Theological Seminary in
New York. In 1982 Dwayne left Columbia's Teachers College for Yale's Divinity School to focus upon religious studies more specifically, but he has returned to us, first in 1993 in his powerful analysis of spirituality and curriculum,
and now in this collection.

In *Understanding Curriculum*, I situated Dwayne's work historically, emphasizing the ways it foreshadowed the reconceptualization of the field in the
1970s. Now that I have been collecting and introducing his work, it has become
clear to me that Jackson's short history of the field is too short. It is now clear to
me, and I am confident you will agree as you work your way through this volume, that Huebner's importance to the field is great. It is greater, for instance,
than Schwab's. His influence on and significance for what would follow positions him alongside Tyler, although one must be quick to add that Huebner's influence is altogether salutary. Additionally, the intellectual character of the
contribution is altogether more complex and provocative than either Tyler's or
Schwab's. While it will seem to some audacious or unnecessary to make such a
claim, it needs to be made. Someday, I feel confident, Huebner will be recognized as more important than Tyler in the history of the field. Let us turn our attention, albeit in an introductory way, at what—over a thirty-five year
career—Dwayne Huebner has accomplished. Remarkable is only the first word
that comes to mind.

As early as the 1950s, Huebner was challenging the hegemony of the Tyler
Rationale, published only a few years earlier (Tyler, 1949). At Teachers College, Columbia University, Huebner taught a course in curriculum theory (with
Arno Bellack) which relied on non-Tylerian foundations. First offered in 1957,
this course on curriculum theory was part of the doctoral core in the Department
of Curriculum and Teaching at Teachers College, not only the first department
in the field [established in 1938], but at this time probably the premier department as well. Bellack approached curriculum problems through analytic philosophy; Huebner worked through phenomenology and political science. [Ten
years later Huebner would introduce phenomenology to the field at large
(Huebner, 1967a). Phenomenology and political theory now comprise two major sectors of curriculum scholarship: understanding curriculum as
phenomenological and political text.] Huebner's and Bellack's collaboration
would surface in print: in 1960 the two men reviewed the research on teaching.
Their conclusion pointed to the agenda Huebner would undertake in the years
to follow: "Too few of the studies referred to here move from empirical data to
an evaluation of the concepts used to organize these data" (Bellack & Huebner,
1960, p. 254).

The fundamental rethinking of concepts toward which this conclusion points would begin to appear two years later. In a collection entitled *Curriculum Crossroads*, Dwayne Huebner wrote "Politics and Curriculum" (1962a/chap. 9)[1], in which he discusses the value of political science in the study of curriculum problems. His examination of curriculum in terms of democratic ideology, control of resources, power, and slogans sets his paper apart from the others in the collection; it foreshadowed what would become a major scholarly initiative in the field. But in 1962, in the midst of the structures-of-disciplines movement, mainstream curriculum scholars must have read Huebner's essay with disbelief. Huebner seems to understand the naiveté of his audience, their need for him to explain himself. He asks: why make the move to political science in the first place? He begins his answer by noting, seven years before Schwab would make the same claim famous, that "the attempt [to look at curriculum with concepts from political science] seems justified by the present inadequate state of curriculum theory which is overwhelmed by problems, and suffering from a lack of intellectual vitality" (p. 15). Such insight must have seemed heresy to many readers, still smiling in a false security that the field was fine. Did Huebner's analysis escape the attention of his colleague at the University of Chicago? While Huebner was saying, in effect, that the field was moribund, Schwab was busy working on the structure of the disciplines. "Certainly the educational enterprise," Huebner says with uncharacteristic understatement, "is loaded with political action" (p. 15). The structure-of-the-disciplines movement was itself, needless to say, a testimony to that fact.

At this early date Huebner (1962a/chap. 3) understands that all the hoopla at ASCD meetings (for instance) regarding the democratic character of education was mostly that: hoopla. Always sensitive to this constituency, however, he puts the matter pedagogically:

> The democratic ideology used by educators, however, falls into the never-never land of wishful thinking. On the one hand, it approaches, never quite reaching but often replacing, a religious ideology .... On the other hand, the prevailing democratic conception never quite realizes the dimensions of a political ideology, for it fails to deal with conflict and struggle and the phenomenon which resolves both—power. (pp.15, 16)

Note that Huebner employs the notion of power—fifteen years before a succeeding generation of education scholars would eagerly seize upon the concept—referring to the work of Arendt, Merriam, Tillich, and Lasswell. There is as well a discussion of "educational elites" and "educational ideologies," buzzwords among leftist curriculum scholars in the 1970s.

---

[1]Page numbers for citations have been changed to reflect the pagination of this volume for those essays included in the collection as indicated by reference to a chapter number. *Ed.*

Power circulates it is not possessed, as Foucault has taught us. Recalling Albert Schweitzer, Martin Buber, Erich Fromm, Nicholas Berdyaev, Jose Ortega y Gasset, and Ernest G. Schachtel, Huebner (chap. 8) discusses intersubjective "circulation," i.e. "forms of relating to others." For him the central question is "what may transpire?" (p. 75). Half a dozen years before Freire would popularize the "dialogical encounter," Huebner explicates such encounter; he suggests it involves "a form of transaction which maintains the maximum freedom of each [person]" (p. 76). And years before Rorty (1989, 1991) would make it a centerpiece of his philosophy of culture and politics, Huebner dwells upon "the nature of conversation" (p. 78). Also in this early essay he foreshadows his later interest in language, discussing the "limitations of functional language" (p. 87), and the importance of "valuing religious and aesthetic language" (p. 88). Then he moves to the work of Karl Jaspers who recognized the centrality of communication for the development of "selfhood" (p. 89). Lest his reader think he is advocating a form of political quietism or social withdrawal, he points out that the educator must become "aware of his limited, and limiting, thought patterns and language systems for shaping value and legitimizing action" (p. 90). It is a landmark paper, well in advance of scholarship which would dominate the field in the 1970s.

Next Dwayne turns his attention to the "art of teaching" (1962b/chap. 4). Several years before Elliot Eisner (1971a, 1971b, 1972) would popularize art (specifically connoisseurship) as a metaphor for curriculum evaluation, Huebner understood that curriculum and teaching were aesthetic text. Also during these early years of the decade he was working on Heidegger, long before that name became known to curriculum students; he sketched phenomenological notions of knowledge, curriculum, and the classroom in three powerful papers (chaps. 5, 6, 7). His phenomenological interest was developed and extended in papers that would follow, culminating in his important 1967 "Curriculum as Concern for Man's Temporality."

In his 1966 "Curriculum as a Field of Study" Huebner advanced four radical propositions. First, he observed that conceptions of curriculum tended to be tied to "technique." They are not linked to the human spirit. Second, the field suffered from an overdependence upon values conceived as goals or objectives. Relatedly, the field suffered from an overdependence upon learning as the primary expression of human temporality. Third, correction of this primitive and simplistic conception of curriculum could be achieved partially by the design of an educative environment conceived as valued educational activity. Fourth, Huebner insisted that curriculum design was inherently a political process by means of which the curricular worker sought to attain a just environment. Extending the work he had done earlier, Huebner (1966a) endorsed art as a model of curriculum theory and design:

Is it possible, now that we are partially freed from vision-hindering busywork, that we can begin to make efforts to grasp the overall design of curriculum and to see how man's evolving techniques can be made subservient to man's evolving spirit? Educational environment and activity in the schools are symbolic of what man is today and what he wants to be tomorrow. The design of these symbols is a great art. The study of curriculum should be a preparation for this artistry. (p. 112)

One might think a career had been capped at this point. After all, he had scooped both Schwab and Eisner, declaring the field moribund in 1962, and introducing art, as well as political and social theory, by 1963, and theology and phenomenology by 1967. Realizing perhaps that he had swept away the traditional field of curriculum development, at least as Tyler understood it, he moved to outline the elements of what would become the new field.

In "The Tasks of the Curricular Theorist" in which Huebner (1975d, chap. 18) made three important points which would be developed further in the decade after the Reconceptualization. First, he noted that curricularists operated in human history, with other human subjects, in actual human environments. This complexity can be seen in the individual biographies of students and educators. Second, the curriculum theorist is responsible through language and through environmental design to generate new language and environmental forms. Huebner's notion of environment included the school building, materials, and people—all structuring "elements" of educational experience. Third, he argued that it is in praxis, through political engagement and pedagogical work in the world, where education takes place. Huebner wrote:

What are the tasks of the curriculum theorist? As is true of all theorists his task is to lay bear the structure of being-in-the-world and to articulate this structure through the language and environmental forms he creates. His responsibility is for the forms he creates and uses, that they may be controlled by him rather than controlling him. (chap. 18, p. 228)

Here Huebner is anticipating other sectors of contemporary curriculum scholarship, twenty years in advance of their maturation. Note that years before Kliebard's influential scholarship Huebner is calling for curriculum history. History is expressed in individual biographies, and in one breath he has pointed simultaneously to efforts to understand curriculum as historical and biographical/autobiographical text. His concept of environmental design is material—including architecture and artifacts—as well as social and intersubjective. He grounds educational experience in the world, at once an ontological and political concept. And a decade before it would become a buzzword, Huebner calls for *praxis*.

The political interest indicated in the last sentence is developed further in his tour-de-force "Poetry and Power: The Politics of Curricular Development" (1975e/chap. 19). In this gripping statement, Huebner asserted his view that educators are lost, that they will remain lost as long as they accept the promise of a "quick fix" through slogans and bandwagons, as long as teachers do not act to change the educational world. Such action, he pointed out, requires risk-taking. Huebner (1975e/chap. 19) advocated three rights: 1) there must be "unconditional respect for the political, civil, and legal rights of the young as free people participating in a public world" (p. 235); 2) the student has "the right of access to the wealth in the public domain—I mean primarily the knowledge, traditions, skills that shape and increase a person's power in the public world" (p. 236); and 3) the right of "each individual, regardless of age, to participate in the shaping and reshaping of the institutions in which they live" (p. 238). Huebner concluded: "The school is but a manifestation of public life. As educators we must be political activists who seek a more just public world. The alternative of course is to be school people—satisfied with the existing social order—the silent majority who embrace conservatism" (pp. 238–239).

Huebner's rejection of the traditional role of curriculum developers in favor of politically inspired actors engaged in seeking "a more just public world" inspired an entire generation of curriculum scholars. Efforts in the late 1970s and 1980s to understand curriculum politically, phenomenologically, aesthetically, and theologically can be directly traced to Huebner's groundbreaking scholarship in the 1960s and early 1970s. In 1975 Huebner reflected on his own journey:

> Throughout this contact with diverse philosophical and theological traditions, the basic operating assumptions of curriculum thought bothered me. How could one plan educational futures via behavioral objectives when the mystical literature emphasized the present moment and the need to let the future care for itself? The thread that ran through my questions and my searching was an intuition that an understanding of the nature of time was essential for understanding the nature of education .... The journey has been lonely at times, but the direction feels right even though it seems veiled in a "Cloud of Unknowing." I am convinced that the curriculum person's dependency on scientific thought patterns, even though they have not found their way into practice as they should, has broken the linkage with other very great and important intellectual traditions of the East and the West which have profound bearing on the talking about the practice of education. (Huebner, 1975a, p. 447)

Among the traditions upon which Huebner called were phenomenology and theology. Huebner's (1970a) earlier assertion of self-definition would thematize the reconceptualized field. He embraced the concrete, institutional interest Schwab had claimed: "I am a curriculum person. I happen to be concerned with the nitty gritty of schooling: what goes on in classrooms" (p. 169). Second, he points to language and discourse, both of which would preoccupy the contemporary field, when he wrote: "We have oversimplified the relationship between the design of educational environments and the language with which we talk about them" (pp. 178–179). Huebner's work would lay the path for contemporary studies, a path partly in the practical everyday life of schools and partly in theoretical issues of language, discourse, and textuality.

In 1982 Huebner left Teachers College, Columbia University for the Yale University Divinity School. That is not the end of our story. Just as his educational theory is important for students of theology, his essays in religious education speak strongly to students of education. He defined his interest in the religious and the spiritual broadly. In a 1985 paper on spirituality and knowing for the 94th Yearbook of the National Society for the Study of Education, he begins with the OED, where he finds that "spirit" is derived from the Latin word for breath and breathing … "spirit refers to that which gives vitality" (1985b, chap. 26, p. 343). Noting that this idea has broad significance, he stresses that: "Talk of the 'spirit' and the 'spiritual' in education need not, then, be God talk …. Rather, the talk is about lived reality, about experience and the possibility of experiencing" (p. 344). "Various modes of knowing," he points out, "are suffused with the spiritual" (p. 348). Indeed, "Education is only possible because the human being is a being that can transcend itself" (p 345).

In second provocative essay which also appeared that year, Huebner (1985c/chap. 28) explored the relationship between education and religion. They are, in his view, inseparable. He explains that:

> Religious language could be used as metaphor to look at speak about educational events and phenomena …. In fact, that very process of transferring religious language to education strikes me as being foreign to what I am about, and in part would distort the story of my own life as educator …. Most of my professional career has been a search for more adequate and powerful ways to describe education. (1985c, chap. 28, p. 358)

Religious or theological language helps one to do just that. He acknowledges that: "Over the years I have been led more and more directly into studies of and work in theological and religious education" (p. 358).

It is not only religion and education that are intertwined. Later in this essay he suggests how the political, the phenomenological, and the theological all inhabit what is educational:

> Education is the lure of the transcendent—that which we seem is not what we are for we could always be other. Education is the protest against present forms that they may be reformed and transformed. Education is the consciousness that we live in time, pulled by the inexorable Otherness that brings judgment and hope to the forms of life which are but the vessels of present experience. (1985c, chap. 28, p. 360).

In what seems to us today a brilliant Lacanian move, he says: "Content is otherness" (chap. 28, p. 362). But Huebner has theology not psychoanalysis in mind. Content he understands very broadly; it includes the pedagogical practice of encountering otherness, even that most transcendent of Others, God. In a 1987 essay on religious education and the presence of God, he writes: "In the minds of some, religious education is a time set-aside. It has become a place, such as Sunday school .... However, it need not be time ... set aside .... Religious education can be a way of practicing the presence of God" (1987, chap. 31, p. 388). What does that entail? "Practicing that presence," he explains, "requires more or less constant awareness of or reference to God in our life" (p. 389). What is religious education? In statements which echo his earlier work on the significance of human encounter and relationship as well as transcendence to educational experience, he answers:

> Here, then, is our agenda for religious education. It is one of scrutinizing the fabrics of relationships that we have, those of intimacy and those of community, and of asking how God is present or absent in those relationships. And then, with the help of our religious traditions, imagining how we can practice the presence of God in these relationships of intimacy and community. (chap. 31, p. 392)

He concludes by returning to the interrelatedness of his life-long interests:

> The religious part of the religious educational work before us is to help ourselves and others practice the presence of God in all our doings in this world. The educational part of the religious educational work before us is to overcome those habits—whether they are habits of mind, of language, of social convention—that substitute our diverse idols for God's presence in our midst, and to establish new habits more adequately grounded in God's realm and God's covenant with us. (chap. 31, p. 395)

In May 1993, a 70-year old Dwayne Huebner returned to the field in an importantly synoptic essay focused on the spiritual in curriculum. Huebner's paper was in response to an invitation to speak in New Orleans to a seminar on spirituality and curriculum, sponsored by three near-by universities, and organized by William E. Doll, Jr. In a powerful reading, Huebner returned to many of the themes that had preoccupied him—and the field—over a life-span. Huebner appreciates that the problem of the field remains one of language. He acknowledges that, while not dominant in the scholarly field, technical language remains embedded in the schools, i.e. in the talk of school people. To some extent he blames the field he left for the present predicament of educators, lost in the technical, pseudo-scientific language of bureaucratic legitimation which erases not only the spiritual but the imagination as well. In a "we" that includes educators and especially educational psychologists, he reminded us that: "We have forgotten or suppressed that imagination is a foundation of our givens" (1993c/chap. 33, p. 401). Evoking a notion of educational journey that he had employed over two decades ago (1975a), he dismissed once again the language of educational psychology, and especially that of learning theory: "'Learning' is a trivial way of speaking of the journey of the self" (chap. 33, p. 405). It is this pseudo-scientific and profoundly distorting language that had led Huebner to become skeptical of mainstream research: "Several years later I began to question the educator's dependency on the research enterprise" (p. 402). In part, it is that pretense of certainty associated with the social and behavioral science fields which is so reprehensible. It is awareness that there is a "beyond" to our knowledge that is the beginning of the theological: "It is a 'moreness' that takes us by surprise when we are at the edge and end of our knowing" (p. 403). What other damage has technical language done as he looks back at thirty years? Huebner (1993c/chap. 33) answered:

> Similarly, the significance of the word "study" has been destroyed. Students study to do what someone else requires, not for their own transformation, a way of 'working' on their own journey, or their struggle with spirit, the otherness beyond them. Just as therapy is work—hard work—but important for the loosening of old binds and discovering the new self; so too should education as study be seen as a form of that kind of work. (p. 411)

Next moves to teachers and teaching. Sounding not only theological but , Huebner (1993c) reminded the audience that: "teaching is a vocation .... A vocation is a call" (chap. 33, p. 411). Indeed, the vocation of teaching, he continued, involves three aspects: "Three voices call, or three demands are made on the teacher. Hence the life that is teaching is inherently a conflicted way of living. The teacher is called by the students, by the content, and by the institution within which the teacher lives .... Spiritual warfare is inherent in all vocations" (p. 411). Given the complexity of this calling, Huebner understands that: "The pain of teachers, unable to respond to the call of some students, is often too much, and they seek relief by hardening their hearts" (p. 413). How can teachers respond to the demands of their profession? Huebner tells us:

> It is also quite clear to me, that it is futile to hope that teachers can be aware of the spiritual in education unless they maintain some form of spiritual discipline. This needs to be of two kinds. Given the inherent conflicts involved in teaching, and the inherent vulnerability of their vocation, teachers need to seek out communities of faith, love, and hope .... The second discipline is a disciplining of the mind, not in the sense of staying on top of all the educational research and literature, but in the sense of developing an imagination that has room for the spiritual. When teachers examine the educational landscape we should see what is there and hear the call to respond with love, truth and justice. We should also see the principalities and powers, the idols and

the spiritual possibilities hidden behind all of the forms and events that are
taken for granted. (p. 415)

Here Huebner has pointed to the center of understanding curriculum, especially as theological text. He enables us to appreciate that finally our struggle to
teach and to study with others and with God is precisely that: a call for labor, for
discipline, sustained by faith, love, and hope. The effort to understand curriculum as theological text is not a separate specialized sector of scholarship; it is
the call to live with others morally and transcendentally: "The need is not to see
moral and spiritual values as something outside the normal curriculum and
school activity, but to probe deeper into the educational landscape to reveal
how the spiritual and moral is being denied in everything" (Huebner, p. 414). In
seeing how the moral is denied we glimpse how we might work toward its realization.

Dwayne E. Huebner returned to the curriculum field November 20, 1993, on
the campus of Loyola University in New Orleans, but it was clear he had never
left us. As this abbreviated and overly simple introduction to his work makes
clear, he and a very few others—such as his friend and colleague James B. Macdonald (1995)—helped create the world contemporary curriculum scholars
now inhabit and labor to recreate as educators and theoreticians. His generative
influence has been evident in many discourses, including the political, the
phenomenological, the aesthetic as well as the theological. Huebner may have
left the field partly in grief over what has happened in the schools, perhaps
partly because he was unable to find solace in the emerging scholarly field
which his own work had made possible, and certainly in order to focus more ex-
clusively on religious education. His journey has been remarkable, highly significant for two fields of study. Clearly one of the most important minds the
field of curriculum has known, Dwayne Huebner may well be judged by future
historians of the field as *the* most important. It seems so to me. And after you
have studied what follows, I think you will agree.

ACKNOWLEDGMENTS

Many many thanks to Dwayne Huebner for allowing me to collect and introduce his work. Rereading his remarkable essays has given me great satisfaction. But corresponding and meeting with him regarding the project has been
especially memorable and gratifying. I wish to thank Vikki Hillis, who agreed,
rather at the last moment, to edit the manuscript. She has done so with conspicuous sensitivity and care. I wish to thank Ted Aoki for generously allowing me
the use of his comprehensive collection of Huebner papers. Thanks as well to
Toby Daspit, LSU Ph.D. student, for obtaining permissions. Thanks finally to
my superb editor at LEA Naomi Silverman, and to Lawrence Erlbaum himself,
for supporting a project of such size and significance.

BIBLIOGRAPHY

Bellack, A., & Huebner, D. (1960, June). Teaching. *Review of Educational Research*, XXX (3), 246–257.

Eisner, E. W. (1971a, May). How can you measure a rainbow? *Art Education*, 24, 36–39.

Eisner, E. W. (Ed.). (1971b). *Confronting curriculum reform*. Boston, MA: Little, Brown.

Eisner, E. W. (1972). *Educating artistic vision*. New York: Macmillan.

Huebner, D. E. (1959a). *From classroom action to educational outcomes: An exploration in educational theory*. Madison, WI: University of Wisconsin, School of Education, Ph.D. dissertation. 218 pp. Abstract: *Dissertation Abstracts* 20: 968–969; No. 3, 1959.

Huebner, D. E. (1959b). *The capacity for wonder and education*. Paper presented at the All College Lecture Series (Summer). 15 pp.

Huebner, D. E. (1961a). *Is the elementary school curriculum adequate?* Paper presented to the New York State Teachers' Association. 11 pp.

Huebner, D. E. (1961b). *Creativity in teaching*. Paper presented to the Conference on Creativity and Teaching, 13 pp.

Huebner, D. E. (1961c). *Today's child builds self worth in the world*. Paper presented to the ACEI meeting, Omaha, April 7. 13 pp.

Huebner, D. E. (1962a). *Politics and the curriculum*. In A. Passow (Ed.), *Curriculum crossroads* (87–95). New York: Teachers College Press.

Huebner, D. E. (1962b). *The art of teaching*. Unpublished manuscript. 22 pp.

Huebner, D. E. (1962c). *The complexities in teaching*. 14 pp.

Huebner, D. E. (1962d). *The child as man*. 25 pp.

Huebner, D. E. (1962e). *Knowledge: An instrument of man*. 13 pp.

Huebner, D. E. (1962f). *Knowledge and the curriculum*. 38 pp.

Huebner, D. E. (1962g). *Classroom action*. 11 pp.

Huebner, D. E. (1963a). New modes of man's relationship to man. In A. Frazier (Ed.), *New insights and the curriculum* (144–164). Washington, DC: ASCD.

Huebner, D. E. (1963b). Challenges today and constructive action. *Childhood Education* (November), pp. 115–117.

Huebner, D. E. (1964a). *A reassessment of the curriculum*. New York: Bureau of Publications, Teachers College, Columbia University.

Huebner, D. E. (1964b). Politics and curriculum. *Educational Leadership* (November), pp. 115–129.

Huebner, D. E. (1964c). *Curriculum as a guidance strategy*. Paper delivered at elementary Guidance Workshop.

Huebner, D. E. (1964d). Cooperating teachers' dinner. March 9th, 14 pp.

Huebner, D. E. (1965). *Moral values and the curriculum*. Paper delivered at the Conference on the Moral Dilemma of Public Schooling. Madison, Wisconsin (May 12), 26 pp.

Huebner, D. E. (1966a). Curriculum as a field of study. In H. Robison (Ed.), *Precedents and promise in the curriculum field* (94–112). New York: Teachers College Press.

Huebner, D. E. (1966b). Curricular language and classroom meanings. In J. Macdonald & R. Leeper (Eds.), *Language and meaning* (8–26). Washington, DC: ASCD.

Huebner, D. E. (1966c). *Facilitating change as the responsibility of the supervisor*. Paper delivered at the Annual Supervisors' Conference, "The Changing Role of the Supervisor," Florida, Galt Ocean Mile Hotel, Fort Lauderdale, October 31, 1996.

Huebner, D. E. (1966d). *Reflections on the curriculum of two elementary schools in Washington*. 16 pp.

Huebner, D. E. (1966e). Review of Herbert Marcuse's *One-Dimensional Man*.

Huebner, D. E. (1967a). Curriculum as concern for man's temporality. *Theory into Practice*, 6(4), 172–179. Reprinted in W. Pinar (Ed.), *Curriculum theorizing: The reconceptualists* (237–249). Berkeley, CA: McCutchan.

Huebner, D. E. (1967b). Today's challenges. *Childhood Education*, pp. 252–258.

Huebner, D. E. (1968a). Implications of psychological thought for the curriculum. In G. Unruh & R. Leeper (Eds.), *Influences in curriculum change* (28–38). Washington, DC: ASCD.

Huebner, D. E. (1968b). *Teaching as art and politics*. 21 pp.

Huebner, D. E. (1968c). Curriculum and teaching. Lecture to TI 3003, Creative Arts in the Curriculum, Teachers College. May 7th. 21 pp.

Huebner, D. E. (1969, February). *Language and teaching: Reflections in light of Heidegger's writing about language*. Paper presented at the Union Theological Seminary, New York.

Huebner, D. E. (1970a). Status and identity: A reply. In C. Bowers, I. Housego, & D. Dyke (Eds.), *Education and social policy* (169–179). New York: Random House.

Huebner, D. E. (1970b). *Curriculum as the accessibility of knowledge*. A paper presented to the Curriculum Theory Study Group, Minneapolis, Minnesota, March 2nd. 15 pp.

Huebner, D. E. (1971a). The leadership role in curricular change. In M. R. Lawler (Ed.), *Strategies for Planned Curriculum Innovation* (133–150). New York: Teachers College Press. [Originally presented on May 22, 1966, at the Kenwood Conference on Curriculum Leadership held at the University of Wisconsin, sponsored by the Wisconsin State Department of Public Instruction.]

Huebner, D. E. (1971b). *Elementary education in Englewood: A model for planning*. New York: Institute for Field Studies, Teachers College, Columbia University.

Huebner, D. E. (1972). Education in the church. *Andover Newton Quarterly* (January), pp. 122–129.

Huebner, D. E. (1974a). Toward a remaking of curricular language. In W. Pinar (Ed.), *Heightened consciousness, cultural revolution, and curriculum theory* (36–53). Berkeley, CA: McCutchan.

Huebner, D. E. (1974b). *Curriculum "with liberty and justice for all"*. A paper presented to the Conference on Craft, Conflict, and Symbol: Their Import for Curriculum and Schooling Tennessee Technological University. April 25–26. 12 pp.

Huebner, D. E. (1974c). *Humanism and competency: A critical and dialectical interpretation*. Paper delivered to the Conference on Humanism and Competence, Teachers College, Columbia University, October 5th. 10 pp.

Huebner, D. E. (1974d). *The thingness of educational content*. Paper presented to the Conference on Reconceptualizing Curriculum Theory. Cincinnati, OH: Xavier University. October 18th. 13 pp.

Huebner, D. E. (1975a). Autobiographical statement. In W. Pinar (Ed.), *Curriculum theorizing: The reconceptualists* (213–215). Berkeley, CA: McCutchan.

Huebner, D. E. (1975b). Curricular language and classroom meanings. In W. Pinar (Ed.), *Curriculum theorizing: The reconceptualists* (217–237). Berkeley, CA: McCutchan.

Huebner, D. E. (1975c). Curriculum as concern for man's temporality. In W. Pinar (Ed.), *Curriculum theorizing: The reconceptualists* (237–249). Berkeley, CA: McCutchan.

Huebner, D. E. (1975d). The tasks of the curricular theorist. In W. Pinar (Ed.), *Curriculum theorizing: The reconceptualists* (250–270). Berkeley, CA: McCutchan.

Huebner, D. E. (1975e). Poetry and power: The politics of curricular development. In W. Pinar (Ed.), *Curriculum theorizing: The reconceptualists* (271–280). Berkeley, CA: McCutchan.

Huebner, D. E. (1975f). The contradiction between the recreative and the established. In J. B. Macdonald & E. Zaret (Eds.), *Schools in Search of Meaning* (27–37). Washington, DC: ASCD.

Huebner, D. E. (1976). The moribund curriculum field: Its wake and our work. *Curriculum Inquiry, 6*(2), 153–167.

Huebner, D. E. (1977a). *An educator's perspective on language about God*. Paper prepared for the Consultation on Language about God, Louisville (KY) Presbyterian Theological Seminary, October 3–4. 43 pp.

Huebner, D. E. (1977b). Toward a political economy of curriculum and human development. In Alex Molnar & John Zahorik (Eds.), *Curriculum Theory* (92–107). Washington, DC: ASCD.

Huebner, D. E. (1977c). Dialectical materialism as a method of doing education. 13 pp.

Huebner, D. E. (1977d). *Libraries and socialization.* Paper delivered at the School of Library Science, Columbia University. April 30th. 18 pp.

Huebner, D. E. (1979a). The language of religious education. In P. O'Hare (Ed.), *Transformation and Tradition in Religious Education* (87–111). Birmingham, AL: Religious Education Press.

Huebner, D. E. (1979b). Keynote Address at the Curriculum Symposium "Perspectives for Viewing Curriculum." Vancouver, BC: British Columbia Teachers Federation. 13 pp.

Huebner, D. E. (1979c). *Developing teacher competencies.* A paper presented at the Western Canada Educational Administrators Conference, Edmonton, Alberta, Canada, October 19, 1979.

Huebner, D. E. (1980). Humanism and competency. *The Reading Instruction Journal, 23*(3), 81–82.

Huebner, D. E. (1982, July-August). From theory to practice in curriculum: Interview. [By William Bean Kennedy, with reflective responses by fourteen others.] *Religious Education,* 77(4), 363–374.

Huebner, D. E. (1985a). The redemption of schooling: The work of James B. Macdonald. *JCT, 6*(3), 28–34.

Huebner, D. E. (1985b). Spirituality and knowing. In the *84th Yearbook of the National Society for the Study of Education, Part II* (159–173). Chicago: NSSE.

Huebner, D. E. (1985c). Religious metaphors in the language of education. *Religious Education, 80*(3), 460–472. [Also printed in *Phenomenology + Pedagogy, 2*(2)].

Huebner, D. E. (1985d). *Education in the congregation and seminary.* Prepared for the Project on the Congregation and Theological Education, Candler School of Theology, Emory University, Atlanta, June 3–5, 1985. 24 pp.

Huebner, D. E. (1985e). Babel: A reflection on confounded speech, *Reflection 82*(2), 9–13.

Huebner, D. E. (1986a). Christian growth in faith. *Religious Education, 81*(4), 511–521. [A paper read at An Ecumenical Conference sponsored by Delmara Ecumenical Agency, Saturday, October 12, 1985, Newark, Delaware.]

Huebner, D. E. (1986b). *The ministry of teaching.* New Haven: Yale University, the Divinity School. 6 pp.

Huebner, D. E. (1986c). *Given the realities of teaching, why choose to be a teacher?* Paper presented at Teachers College, Columbia University, July 7, 1986. 12 pp.

Huebner, D. E. (1987a). Teaching as a vocation. *The Auburn News* (Fall), 1–7.

Huebner, D. E. (1987b). Practicing the presence of God. *Religious Education, 82*(4), 569–577.

Huebner, D. E. (1987c). The vocation of teaching. In Frances Bolin & Judith Falk (Eds.), *Teacher renewal: Professional issues, personal choices.* New York: Teachers College Press.

Huebner, D. E. (1991, 1963). Notes toward a curriculum inquiry. *Journal of Curriculum and Supervision, 6*(2), 145–160.

Huebner, D. E. (1991a). *Educational activity and prophetic criticism.* New Haven: Yale University, the Divinity School. 5 pp.

Huebner, D. E. (1993b). Can theological education be church education? *Union Seminary Quarterly Review, 47*(3–4), 23–38.

Huebner, D. E. (1993c). *Education and spirituality.* New Haven, CT: Yale University, The Divinity School, unpublished manuscript. [Presented to the Seminar on Spirituality and Curriculum, November 20, 1993, on the campus of Loyola University in New Orleans, sponsored by Louisiana State, Loyola, and Xaiver Universities. Printed in *JCT, 11*(2), 13–34.]

Huebner, D. E. (1996). *Challenges bequeathed.* Paper read to faculty and students, Louisiana State University, November 22, 1996.

Huebner, D. E. (nd). *Elementary education.* Paper presented to the Conference on the Use of Printed and Audio Visual Materials for Instructional Purposes. 29 pp.

Jennings, F. (Ed.). (1971). Curriculum: Interdisciplinary insights. Special issue of *Teachers College Record, 73*(2).

Jennings, F. (Ed.). (1971). Curriculum: Interdisciplinary insights. Special issue of *Teachers College Record, 73*(2).

Macdonald, J. B. (Ed.). (1995). *Theory as a prayerful act: The collected essays of James B. Mac-donald.* [Introduction by William F. Pinar.] New York: Peter Lang.

McClintock, R. (1971). Toward a place for study in a world of instruction. *Teachers College Record, 73*(20), 161–205.

Pinar, W. F., & Reynolds, W. M. (Eds.). (1992). Appendix, section one: Genealogical notes on the history of phenomenology in curriculum studies. *Understanding curriculum as phenomenological and deconstructed text* (237–244). New York: Teachers College Press.

Pinar, William F., Reynolds, W. M., Slattery, P., & Taubman, P. M. (1995). *Understanding curriculum.* New York: Peter Lang.

Pinar, William F. (Ed.). (1997). *Curriculum: New identities in/for the field.* New York: Garland.

Plantinga, D. (1985). *Dwayne Huebner's curricular language model revisited.* Edmonton, Alberta, Canada: University of Alberta, Faculty of Education, Department of Secondary Education, unpublished master's thesis.

Rorty, R. (1989). *Contingency, irony and solidarity.* Cambridge, MA: Cambridge University Press.

Rorty, R. (1991). *Essays on Heidegger and others. Philosophical papers, Volume 2.* Cambridge & New York: Cambridge University Press.

Tyler, Ralph W. (1949). *Basic principles of curriculum and instruction.* Chicago, IL: University of Chicago Press.

White, K. (1980). The work of Dwayne Huebner: A summary and response. *JCT, 2*(2), 73–87.

Publication History
of the Collected Essays

Permission to reprint previously published articles
is gratefully acknowledged in the following list.

Chapter One

"The Capacity for Wonder and Education." Paper presented at the All College Lecture Series, Summer, 1959.

Chapter Two

"Is the Elementary Curriculum Adequate?" Presented to the New York State Teachers' Association, October, 1961.

Chapter Three

"Politics and the Curriculum." In *Curriculum Crossroads*, ed. A. Harry Passow, New York: Teachers College Press, 1962, 87-95.

Chapter Four

"The Art of Teaching." Unpublished manuscript, 1962.

Chapter Five

"Knowledge: An Instrument of Man." Unpublished manuscript, 1962.

Chapter Six

"Knowledge and the Curriculum." Unpublished manuscript, 1962.

Chapter Seven

"Classroom Action." Unpublished manuscript, 1962.

Chapter Eight

"New Modes of Man's Relationship to Man." *In New Insights and the Curriculum*, ed. A. Frazier, Washington, DC: ASCD, 1963, 144-164.

Chapter Nine

"Politics and Curriculum." *Educational Leadership* 22, no. 2 (November 1964): 115-129.

Chapter Ten

"Curricular Language and Classroom Meanings." In *Language and Meaning* ed. J. Macdonald and R. Leeper, 8-26. Washington, DC: ASCD, 1966.

Chapter Eleven

"Facilitating Change as the Responsibility of the Supervisor. A paper delivered at the Conference "The Changing Role of the Supervisor," Annual Supervisors' Conference, Florida, Galt Ocean Mile Hotel, Fort Lauderdale, October 31, 1966.

Chapter Twelve

"Curriculum as Concern for Man's Temporality." *Theory into Practice* 6, no. 4, (1967): 172-179. Reprinted in *Curriculum Theorizing: The Reconceptualists*, ed. W. Pinar, 237-249. Berkeley, CA: McCutchan, 1975.

Chapter Thirteen

"Language and Teaching: Reflections in the Light of Heidegger's Writing about Language." Paper presented at the Union Theological Seminary, New York, 1969.

Chapter Fourteen

"The Leadership Role in Curriculum Change." In *Strategies for Planned Curriculum Innovation,* ed. Marcella R. Lawler, 133-150, New York: Teachers College Press, 1971. [Originally presented on May 22,1966, at the Kenwood Conference on Curriculum Leadership held at the University of Wisconsin, a conference sponsored by the Wisconsin State Department of Public Instruction].

Chapter Fifteen

"Education in the Church." *Andover Newton Quarterly* (January 1972): 122-129.

Chapter Sixteen

"Toward a Remaking of Curricular Language." In *Heightened Consciousness, Cultural Revolution, and Curriculum Theory*, ed. William F. Pinar, 36-53. Berkeley, CA: McCutchan. 1974.

Chapter Seventeen

"The Thingness of Educational Content." Paper presented to the Conference on Reconceptualizing Curriculum Theory, Xavier University, Cincinnati, Ohio, October 18, 1974.

Chapter Eighteen

"The Tasks of the Curricular Theorist." In *Curriculum Theorizing: The Reconceptualists*, ed. W. Pinar, 250-270. Berkeley, CA: McCutchan, 1975.

Chapter Nineteen

"Poetry and Power: The Politics of Curricular Development." In *Curriculum Theorizing: The Reconceptualists*, ed. W. Pinar, 271-280. Berkeley, CA: McCutchan, 1975.

Chapter Twenty

"The Moribund Curriculum Field: Its Wake and our Work." *Curriculum Inquiry* 6, no. 2 (1976): 153-167.

Chapter Twenty-one

"An Educator's Perspective on Language about God." Paper prepared for the Consultation on Language about God, Presbyterian Theological Seminary, Louisville, Kentucky, October 3-4, 1977.

Chapter Twenty-two

"Toward a Political Economy of Curriculum and Human Development." In Curriculum Theory, ed. Alex Molnar and John Zahorik, 92-107. Washington, DC: ASCD, 1977.

Chapter Twenty-three

"Developing Teacher Competencies." A paper presented at the Western Canada Educational Administrators Conference, Edmonton, Alberta, Canada, October 19, 1979.

Chapter Twenty-four

"Babel: A Reflection on Confounded Speech." *Reflection* 82, no. 2 (1985): 9-13.

Chapter Twenty-five

"Education in the Congregation and Seminary." Prepared for the Project on the Congregation and Theological Education, Candler School of Theology, Emory University, Atlanta, June 3-5, 1985.

Chapter Twenty-six

"Spirituality and Knowing." In *Learning and Teaching the Ways of Knowing*, The 84th Yearbook of the National Society for the Study of Education, Part II, ed. Elliot Eisner, 159-173. Chicago, IL: NSSE, distributed by University of Chicago Press, 1985.

Chapter Twenty-seven

"The Redemption of Schooling: The Work of James B. Macdonald." JCT 6, no. 3 (1985): 28-34.

Chapter Twenty-eight

"Religious Metaphors in the Language of Education." *Religious Education* 80, no. 3 (1985): 460-472. [Also printed in *Phenomenology + Pedagogy* 2, no. 2 (1985)].

Chapter Twenty-nine

"Christian Growth in Faith." *Religious Education* 81, no. 4 (1986): 511-521. [A paper read at An Ecumenical Conference sponsored by Delmara Ecumenical Agency, Saturday, October 12, 1985, Newark, Delaware.]

Chapter Thirty

"Teaching as a Vocation." *The Auburn News* (Fall 1987): 1-7.

Chapter Thirty-one

"Practicing the Presence of God." *Religious Education* 82, no. 4 (1987): 569-577.

Chapter Thirty-two

"Educational Activity and Prophetic Criticism." New Haven: Yale University, The Divinity School, 1991.

Chapter Thirty-three

"Education and Spirituality." New Haven, CT: Yale University, The Divinity School, presented to the Seminar on Spirituality and Curriculum, November 20, 1993, on the campus of Loyola University in New Orleans, sponsored by Louisiana State, Loyola, and Xaiver Universities. Printed in JCT 11, no. 2 (1995): 13-34.

Chapter Thirty-four

"Can Theological Education Be Church Education?" *Union Seminary Quarterly Review* 47, no. 3-4 (1993): 23-38.

Chapter Thirty-five

"Challenges Bequeathed." Paper read to faculty and students, Louisiana State University, November 22, 1996.

1

The Capacity for Wonder and Education

(1959)

I suppose it is strange that an elementary educator should concern himself with such an esoteric topic—it seems more appropriate for a psychologist or philosopher to be discussing this than for a curriculum worker. But perhaps it is only a person who is psychologically or philosophically naive who would either conceive of such a topic or feel the need to speculate about it. Furthermore, I do not expect to provide you with information—facts, but I hope with something to think about. However, as I have thought about why I should do this, two reasons justify such boldness on my part. First, as an elementary teacher and educator I have had opportunity to witness the gradual change in children from the spontaneous, curious, poking, exploring, questioning, wondering child—a child full of awe in pre-school, kindergarten, even first grade to the stodgy, accepting, pliant, unresponsive student in the fifth grade, in the freshman year in college, and, indeed, in graduate school classes.

Only as a result of unusual teaching do we break through this mask formed by the repressive requirements of education to again see glimpses of the spark, the curiosity, and the wonder and awe of the young child. Frequently only at the doctoral level and sometimes not even then, where the student can explore on his own, seeking out newness and strangeness, going down dark paths alone and without fear, urging his major professor to follow along—is the pre-school spirit of joy, of curiosity, and wonder regained. What happens? What do we do in our educational program to snuff out the spark of curiosity and wonder and awe—indeed, kill the child for the sake of conformity and functional performance in this world of technical proficiency? This is one reason why the capacity for wonder should be probed and the influence that education has on this capacity looked into.

1

But I have another reason. I am not satisfied with our existing knowledge about the educational process. I am sure I am not alone. We need better knowledge in order to operate in the schools more effectively. To get this knowledge we have associated ourselves as professional people with the behavioral sciences. We have been led to believe that through the scientific study of behavior, institutions, and society we will eventually produce the needed controlling and predictive knowledge. I believe that this is so, otherwise, I would not be here.[1]

But we are in a curious position in education, for we must run the schools—we must educate the younger generation and ourselves. To do this job we need to use all available knowledge and more. We cannot postpone the educational task until we have the results of the "scientific" knowledge.

But this is where, I think, a problem exists. Because of our desire to have better knowledge and our dependency on the behavioral sciences, and because of our need to operate in the best fashion that we can right now—we have turned largely to one channel of information about human beings, and neglected some others. We have become overly dependent on the behavioral science channel. Though the information coming through is incomplete, charged with static, we nevertheless accept the picture we receive as the real representation. Yet during the next ten - twenty - or one hundred years that picture may change considerably. This, dependency would not be bad, if we, as practicing school people would recognize the transitory, incomplete, static-filled nature of the pictures. Of course, we can build educational programs around this incomplete and perhaps inaccurate picture. The difficulty is that this is not the only channel of information about human beings available to educators. It is not adequate that we base educational programs on psychological or behavioral science models. Behavioral scientists are not the only ones who speculate about and know men, women, and children. True, the behavioral scientist has perhaps the most communicable empirically valid model. But scientific validity is not the only kind of validity. In the existential situation in which we must plan for and act with boys and girls, we must bring all of our knowledge and creative powers to bear, not just those provided by the behavioral scientist.

In our concern to make the study of education scientific we have ignored other channels. The philosopher studies and formulates knowledge about humankind. So does the theologian, and indeed, the poet, the novelist, and the playwright. But I am content for now with the philosopher. As educators we frequently assume that the only contribution that the philosopher can make to education is epistemological (the study of knowledge) or axiological (the study of value). Our educational philosopher is so busy playing with the meaning of meaning and the problem of value that the metaphysical role of the philosopher in the study of the nature of being—of existence itself has been ignored. We forget that the present behavioral science conception of human beings seems to be rooted in one metaphysical tradition. But there are other traditions. And it is with one of these other traditions that I wish to concern myself.

I have found the writing of certain existentialists extremely thought-provoking. I have been reading casually, unsystematically, and perhaps without real comprehension, some of the writings of Gabriel Marcel, Buber, Berdyaev, Kierkegaard, Jasper, and Heidegger. They have something to offer not found in behavioral science. Here is a channel of information about human being to which we as professional educators have not been attuned by the producers and users of educational knowledge. As university people we do an injustice by not making these notions available to the educator. Some ideas or concepts may lack socially verifiable, empirical support. But such a lack does not indicate that the concepts or ideas are false or useless, only that the idea and concept have not been fed into the empirical world of the behavioral sciences as rapidly as they might have. The work of some European existential psychologists brought together by Rollo May in his book *Existence*,[2] is beginning to bridge the gap between European philosophy and the behavioral sciences.

The idea of the capacity for wonder helps me organize some of the reflections derived from this reading—and makes transparent, to some extent, some problem areas in education. Let me try to communicate to you the meaning I have in mind when I use the word "wonder."

Wonder has at least two meanings. Frequently we associate it with the feeling of doubt, curiosity, inquiry. We say "I wonder if" or "he wonders whether"—and we associate with it such synonyms as speculate, conjecture, ponder, theorize, question, surmise, imagine. Certainly this is a common meaning, but I have in mind the other sense of the word. The meaning which is more clearly associated with such synonyms as astonishment, amazement, surprise, fascination, awe. I think that it is akin to what Goethe might have had in mind when he said that the "very summit of man's attainment is the capacity of marvel." Its meaning seems to be conveyed by this poem of Christina Fraser Tytler.

> Sometimes, as in the summer fields
> I walk abroad, there comes to me
> So strange a sense of mystery,
> My heart stands still, my feet must stay,
> I am in such strange company.
> I look on high—the vasty deep
> Of blue outreaches all my mind;
> And yet I think beyond to find
> Something more vast—and at my feet
> The little bryony is twined.
>
> And turning suddenly away,

Grown sick and dizzy with the sense
Of Power, and mine own impotence,
I see the gentle cattle feed
In dumb unthinking innocence.
("In Summer Fields," Christina, Catherine Fraser-Tytler)[3]

A master of Zen Buddhism captured it with these words, "Have you noticed how the pebbles of the road are polished and pure after the rain? And the flowers? No word can describe them. One can only murmur an 'Ah' of admiration."

Wordsworth expresses the sense in this verse:

My heart leaps up when I behold
A rainbow in the sky:
So it was when my life began;
So it is now, I am a man;
So be it when I shall grow old
Or let me die![4]

Flaubert gets at this same kind of thing when he writes,

Often, appropo of no matter what, a drop of water, a shell, a hair, you stopped and stayed motionless, eyes fixed, heart open. The object you contemplated seemed to encroach upon you, by as much as you inclined yourself toward it, and bonds were established.

Wonder seems to be related to the sense of mystery that Schweitzer describes in his memoirs:

After all, is there not much more mystery in the relations of man to man than we generally recognize? None of us can truly assert that he really knows someone else, even if he has lived with him for years. Of that which constitutes our inner life we can impart even to those most intimate with us only fragments; the whole of it we cannot give, nor would they be able to comprehend it. We wander through life together in a semi-darkness in which none of us can distinguish exactly the features of his neighbor; only from time to time, through some experience that we have of our companion, or through some remark that he passes he stands for a moment close to us, as though illumined by a flash of lightning. Then we see him as he really is. After that we again walk on together in the darkness, perhaps for a long time, and try in vain to make out our fellow-traveller's features.[5]

It is the strange fascination that you feel as you watch the butterfly circle over the milkweed plant in the meadow. You recognize it as a swallowtail and your mind goes back to its caterpillar stage, to its life in the cocoon, to an awareness that it doesn't have too long to live, and you ask how it is ever able to locate the flowers and the milkweed as it flies yards away but circles back for a perfect landing. You know all these things or can find out more, but still you look and come eventually to the awareness: yes, there it is, and here am I. You go from what Buber calls an I-It relationship to an I-Thou relationship. The butterfly and the fellow traveler and the rainbow and the pebble are no longer just objects and you a subject. They too become subjects which cannot be completely grasped. They have an existence alongside your existence. They too occupy this world and are independent of you, not related to you or your needs. They will continue to occupy the world until their time comes, just as you will continue to occupy it until your time comes.

You encounter these phenomena as other existents and if they have sensory powers they encounter you as another existent. Then the two of you are in relationship, participating in life together, journeying down through time, side by side, together, yet apart.

The educator has accepted too readily the logical division of the world into subjects and objects. He identifies too easily with Descartes, "I think, therefore, I am," deriving existence from thinking. But it is this encounter with the world, not as an object but as another subject existing independently of a thought, which produces the feeling of awe and wonder. We have this capacity for wonder. It is possible for us to meet this world and the other subjects which make up this world and to stand face to face with them—to feel wonder, amazement, a sense of mystery.

But do we? In general, we don't. The capacity for wonder seems to have eluded us. It is either underdeveloped or suppressed. Why? What is there about our life which inhibits the functioning or the development of this capacity for wonder?

The reasons, perhaps, are many. Some existentialists seem to have a common core of meaning which hints of the cause. Buber would identify the cause as an over-emphasis on experience and the resulting I-It attitude, to the neglect of relationship and the corresponding I-Thou attitude.

Berdyaev would perhaps label the basic factor for this lack of wonder as our tendency for objectivism—placing everything out before us, in front of us to be grasped, instead of beside us; our making of everything an object to us, rather than a subject with which we communicate. Jaspers would look askance at the emphasis on technique and mass-need meeting by rationalized production. Marcel suggests that the spirit of abstraction, and the tendency to place function uppermost might be the cause. Let me try an interpretation of the possible cause. It is an oversimplification, but will point to what I mean and perhaps what they mean.

We tend to be an extremely anthropocentric if not egocentric people. Our concern is naturally enough for our own need meeting. Hence, the focus of many of our activities and experiences is in terms of what the experience can

provide for us. This is not bad, and is certainly natural, but coupled with this is
an orientation to the future and the neglect of the present. We focus on the process of becoming rather than on being. We miss the wonder of the here and now
for the expected glory or fullness or richness or security of the future. But the
struggle for that future and for the betterment of the present in that future makes
us less sensitive to the immediacy and wholeness of the present. Rather, we are
forced to become selective, to analyze the present to see what can be abstracted
from it for later use. Hence, we do not focus on the totality and uniqueness of the
phenomena that we encounter. We do not meet it as a subject beyond us, over
against us. We see only those objective aspects which have significance and
meaning for our need meeting or for the future. Henri Bergson, I think, states
this very well in his essay on laughter.

> I look and I think I see, I listen and I think I hear, I examine myself and I think I am
> reading the very depths of my heart. But what I see and hear of the outer world
> is purely and simply a selection made by my senses to serve as a light to my
> conduct; what I know of myself is what comes to the surface, what participates
> in my actions. My senses and my consciousness, therefore, give me no more
> than a practical simplification of reality .... The individuality of things and of be-
> ings escape us, unless it is materially to our advantage to perceive it.[6]

The basic problem may be one of conceptualizing the essence of being as
learning, of conditioning ourselves to our environment to meet our needs and
drives, whether primary or secondary. We learn more or less stable patterns of
behavior which guarantee reasonable adjustment to the world, reasonable satisfaction from the world, and reasonable security for the future. We tie ourselves
to the environment with our learning, through our habit patterns, our knowledge, our functional behaviors and attitude; and in so doing we lock ourselves
in a prison made up of that which we have abstracted from the past. We have
turned in upon ourselves. We are self enclosed. We are blinded by our knowledge and by our own being, which instead of liberating us confines us to our
past or to our needs, abstractions, and concepts. In essence we have given away
our freedom by tying ourselves to our environment via our needs and abstractions, through the process of learning.

We maintain our freedom only to the extent that we go beyond our learning,
our abstractions, our need meeting. Indeed, as Marcel states in his *Metaphysical Journal*, "unconditionality is the mark of freedom."[7] We are free only to the
extent that our responses go beyond the past, the abstractions, the learnings. We
are free to the extent that we meet the world with wonder and awe. The response
of awe and wonder essentially is going beyond our abstraction of the phenomena and our objectification of it, to an awareness of its individuality—its subjectivity, its existence, and consequently our existence. Wonder is a form of

participating with the time and being of the other. We are free only to the extent that we maintain and develop our capacity for wonder.

What does this mean for education? In the profession we continue to struggle to find better ways of thinking about children. We struggle, I think, to include in our thinking some metaphysical concerns, but our dependency upon science and the behavioral sciences has placed us in some strange, almost absurd, positions. We know that we work with the uniquely unique, the individual, who has being, an existence with us, whom we can never really comprehend, but only, as Schweitzer said, "walk on together in darkness." Yet we find ourselves in the strange position of having to put the child back together after tearing him apart—so we speak of the whole child. Intellectually we have taken apart the child. Intellectually we put the child back together, forgetting that this is impossible. How absurd. We work with the uniquely unique, the individual, and because of our functionalizing of education, our concern with technique and efficiency, we are forced into the insane tautology of talking about individual differences, when individuals are individuals only because they are different. This is the sad state that we have come to by overemphasizing the mechanical study of education via behavioral science to the exclusion of the philosophical, the metaphysical.

The concern for existence, for being, creeps into education again when we talk about the need for moral and spiritual values in education. We become concerned with values only when we have indeed lost something in our awareness. In education we have lost the eaning of being—of living—by over-emphasizing learning and abstraction. We insert into our thinking a concern for value, which becomes another abstraction, something objective to use. These examples, I think, illustrate the tremendous struggle we are having trying to realign education with the philosophical traditions of today. They suggest the difficulty we have in finding new concepts to deal with the phenomena which concern us.

A concern for wonder, or some other such phenomena, seems to facilitate this search for new concepts to deal with problems of education. We might really ask whether our curriculum provides opportunity for wonder—indeed is it full of wonder? Or is it dry, cut and digested, filled with abstractions and the future. We must struggle to keep the young open to the world about them—available to new, yet unknown phenomena. We must be sure that when students meet parts of the world about them, they do not lock that part up in a prison of knowledge or conditioned responses. Students need to have opportunities to approach parts of the world in many ways, to cognize it for control and production, to symbolize it via art and the aesthetic disciplines in order to increase sensitivity to its uniqueness, to contemplate and respond to it from as many points of view as possible; and yet constantly to keep it in the realm of "no knowledge,"[8] a subject which is ultimately beyond comprehension, but not beyond living with.

We must be sure that in this day of science we do not help the student completely functionalize and, if I may use a strange word, scientize his world and self. The young must learn to approach the world through art, literature, music, and even religion. Although we may need to (and I doubt this) start with children's needs and problems for reasons of involvement, we should not stop there but move students beyond their own egocentric concerns to an interest in the whole world. There is a world of excitement, of mystery, a wonderful world—which we may deny the child unless we see our task more broadly than preparation for life. If school is not a place for mystery, wonder and thrills, the young will find these elsewhere.

But to do this and more we must change our ways as teachers and educators. We cannot hope to help the child enlarge the capacity for wonder if we respond to him only in terms of our intellectual analysis, or psychological knowledge, if we help bottle his own being into a self concept. We can help the child only if we respond to him also as a subject of mystery—producing wonder and awe in us. We can help only if we walk together with children, through time, with faith and love, made more effective through knowledge, but not replaced by knowledge.

We cannot foster the capacity for wonder if our whole educational program is completely functional—conceived of as serving predetermined ends—rather than creating new, previously unheard of or unthought of interests. Even at the doctoral level we make this mistake when we focus the doctoral program toward turning out proficient supervisors or college teachers rather than curious people filled with the feeling of awe for the complex, incomprehensible task of education, and for the world about us.

The approach to the world through the intellect, through knowledge and learning, makes us more powerful by providing more control and prediction. But it may also lead to new enslavements—enslavement to the known, the abstract, and consequently to the past. This approach to the world, to education, leads to greater freedom, greater creativity, only if it is embodied in, and subservient to wonder, and filled with awe. Knowledge and learning alone lead to manipulation and control—wonder and knowledge and learning lead to the possibility of faith and love.

NOTES

[1]This lecture was written during the Summer of 1959 when Dwayne Huebner was teaching in the Department of Curriculum and Teaching, Teachers College, Columbia University. *Ed.*

[2]Rollo May, *Existence: A New Dimension in Psychiatry and Psychology* (New York: Basic Books, 1958).

[3]Christina Catherine Fraser-Tytler, In "Summer Fields," in *The Oxford Book of English Mystical Verse,* ed. D.H. S. Nicholson & A. H. E. Lee. Oxford: Clarendon Press, 1921, 375.

[4]William Wordsworth, "My heart leaps up when I behold," in F. T. Palgrave's, *The Golden Treasury: Selected from the Best Songs and Lyrical Poems in the English Language* (New York: Macmillan, 1929), 365.

[5]Albert Schweitzer, *Memoirs of Childhood and Youth.* New York: Macmillan, 1955, 68–69.

[6]Henri Bergson, "Laughter" in *Comedy: An Essay on Comedy*, ed. Wylie Sypher. Garden City, NY: Doubleday, Anchor Books, 1956, 158–159.

[7]Gabriel Marcel, *Metaphysical Journal*. Bernard Wall (Trans.). London: Rocklift, 1952, 42.

[8]The term "no-knowledge," is to be found in R. G. H. Siu, *The Tao of Science* (New York: John Wiley and Sons, 1957).

2

Is The Elementary Curriculum Adequate?

(1961)

Permit me to move directly into the topic at hand and say that, No! the elementary curriculum of today is not adequate.

But let me also quickly absolve you, the classroom teachers, from blame. For I am not saying that your teaching is inadequate. I have no doubt that there is really much fine teaching in the elementary classrooms. The blame, the responsibility, rests rather with those who are responsible for the over-all design of the elementary curriculum, those who develop the tools which the classroom teachers use as they work with boys and girls, and who seek more effective ways to organize the programs.

Your teaching is not inadequate, but the over-all design is. The intellectual tools with which you work are inadequate. Those of us who work in the college, or in administration are responsible, for we are failing to respond to today's challenges. Our concerns with TV, with educational technologies, team teaching, tracking, grouping, foreign language in elementary schools (F.L.E.S.), are important. They are also escapes, for the challenges of today require ideas, not merely administrative shuffling and technical manipulations. We are either suffering from the after effects of the McCarthy era or the forebodings of a possible John Birch Society era, for we seem unable to deal with the ideological struggles of today. Our problems in education stem from the broader social problems we face and the corresponding inadequacy of educational thought.

The world is obviously not the rosy picture we paint it to be in education. On the one hand we talk of educating the child to live in the world, to use his constructive creative talents to make the world of tomorrow, and to live and work with others with respect and dignity. On the other hand, we talk of a life after death, for which we prepare by secretly building fall-out shelters, and discuss the moral right to shoot our neighbor if he should try to occupy our shelter and

10

to share our food. We try to bridge this gap between the rosy picture and the tragic reality of today by inferring that we need more knowledgeable people, more skillful workers, and greater understanding of the world. Today's inadequacy is not a lack of knowledge about the world, although our knowledge is far from sufficient, but a lack of responsibility for the world. It is not a deficiency of skill or skills to make a living, but a lack of feeling for the life we have made and a lack of compassion for the lives that others have made. The question is not whether another world war will be avoided, or how we will survive nuclear destruction, but whether we who are living, you and I and the children we work with, love the world, the people and the beauty in it, enough to assume responsibility for it and to maintain it in some form of wholeness and to increase its wonder, productivity, and incomprehensible beauty. Responsibility comes not from a sense of burden or a sense of guilt. Responsibility comes because we have become so curious about the world, so excited by our participation in it, so involved with those who share our space and time, that we wish to continue our existence, the existence of those who share it with us and indeed to continue the world itself. Responsibility derives from enthusiastic, joyful participation in the world, in our world.

If I were to characterize the elementary curriculum in a few easy over generalizations, I would say that it is, frequently, a program by which we filter out the child's curiosity toward and love for the world, and hence filter out the responsibility for it. We replace curiosity with a more or less objective, stereotyped, unenthusiastic understanding of the world and its people. Enthusiasm, excitement, curiosity, love, all qualities which lead to responsibility, are too frequently considered dangerous emotions because we don't know how to help form them. We prefer the neat, well organized, controlled response which we associate with the objective scientist. Yes, the scientist is objective, but also excited and not aloof. Only a machine remains calm, organized, always controlled.

Ernest Schachtel describes this gradual early change from interest, discovery, and excitement to the controlled unenthusiastic response learned, in this fashion:

It is safe to assume that early childhood is the period of human life which is richest in experience. Everything is new to the newborn child. His gradual grasp of his environment and of the world around him are discoveries which, in experiential scope and quality, go far beyond any discovery that the most adventurous and daring explorer will ever make in his adult life. No Columbus, no Marco Polo has ever seen stranger and more fascinating and thoroughly absorbing sights than the child that learns to perceive, to taste, to smell, to touch, to hear and see, and to use his body, his senses, and his mind. No wonder that the child shows an insatiable curiosity. He has the whole world to discover. Education and learning, while on the one hand furthering this process of discovery, on the other hand gradually brake and finally stop it completely. There are relatively few adults who are fortunate enough to have retained something of the child's curiosity, his capacity for questioning and for wondering. The average adult "knows all the answers," which is exactly why he will never know even a single answer. He has ceased to wonder, to discover. He knows his way around, and it is indeed a way around and around the same conventional pattern, in which everything is familiar and nothing cause for wonder. It is this adult who answers the child's questions and, in answering, fails to answer them but instead acquaints the child with the conventional patterns of his civilization, which effectively close up the asking mouth and shut the wondering eye. Franz Kafka once formulated this aspect of education by saying that "probably all education is but two things, first, parrying of the ignorant children's impetuous assault on the truth and, second, gentle, imperceptible, step-by-step initiation of the humiliated children into the lie."[1]

The closing of the asking mouth and the shutting of the wondering eye lead eventually to the hardening of the responsible heart.

About 70 years ago, Nietzche asked this question, which I think we can use to evaluate the elementary school curriculum in action. He asked, "what have you really loved 'till now?" We don't usually like to tie education to such soft words. "Love" is more appropriate in the home or the church or even in cheap movies than in educational thought. But if love is tying one's self to the rest of the world—caring enough about it, interested enough in it, curious enough about it—to establish permanent responsible bonds with it, then we can ask this question of the boys and girls as they pass through our homes, our classrooms, on their way into their world of tomorrow.

The world is fresh and new to the child. He is only beginning the process of meeting and making friends with other people and the animals and plants and man-made things in the world. The child has only ties to and through the family when he comes to school "What has the child loved 'till then?" Nothing? Only his family? His dog? His friends in the neighborhood?

And when you get this child in the fourth grade or the fifth or sixth grade, what has he really loved till then? The adults in the school, his peers, the flowers and birds of the air, the crossing guard, the buildings of New York? The symbols and myths man has created? And what has the child really loved when he leaves your room? The mountains and people of Tibet? The people of Moscow? of Peking? of Accra? The ocean and the life in it? The planets and the stars? The scientists that he meets and the explorers of then and now? Or does the child only know of them—without feeling, without interest, without concern, and leave without a feeling of responsibility for the world and its wonders? Archibald MacLeish in *Poetry and Experience* claims that "The crime against life, the worst of all crimes, is *not* to feel."[2] Is our elementary curriculum an instrument for this crime?

Again, let me emphasize that you as individual teachers may be helping your students love this world and your world and hence eventually assume responsibility for it. If you do, it is because you are you, and not because of the elementary school curriculum. For we who have given verbal form to teaching and curriculum have not yet found adequate ways to emphasize and to maintain the love and excitement that children have for the world. We talk of understandings, of knowledge, of skills, and give token support to vague things like attitudes and appreciations and values; but these are only meager psychological pointers to the profound feelings of love and responsibility as they have been characterized in great writings and traditions.

You think that I am far-fetched—that I am speaking an esoteric language. I don't think so. I think Nietzsche's question is a valid one for those of us who teach. It is a form of educational criticism that we have not used, but could: "What have you really loved 'till now?" What have your children really loved 'till now, as a result of their experience in your classroom? What will they really love when they leave your classroom in June?

The content of our curriculum should be the vehicle by which we help the child establish ties to the rest of the world. A curriculum focusing only on the child's interests, on individual needs, is a curriculum which fosters egocentricity and selfishness. A curriculum focusing only on skills, concepts, and understanding is one which fosters estrangement from the world and schizophrenia. Children find themselves only as they explore their worlds, discovering its wonders and comedies and tragedies, reaching out to it with curiosity, and embracing it with joy and concern. Macmurray, a Scottish philosopher, has said that "all significant knowledge is for the sake of action, and all significant action, for the sake of friendship."[3] We usually stop at the knowledge level and do not go beyond to the action which establishes friendship.

There are two parts of the curriculum which are the primary vehicles for fostering love. The other parts make this love possible, more encompassing, and deeper. The first is the realm of social studies. Here we should be introducing our children to the people of the world, to their diversity, their similarities, their uniqueness, their wonderful- and awe-ful-ness, their creativity, their struggles. We like to think that our job in social studies is to help children understand other people and their way of life. But let's give up such grandiose ideas—for who ever understands another? As Albert Schweitzer poses it, "is there not much more mystery in the relations of man to man than we generally recognize?"[4]

What we can do in social studies is to help children discover and be curious about other people, that they live and breathe and converse, or did live, breathe, and converse. We can help them to be excited by their way of life, to wish to reach out to them, to exchange ideas with them and perhaps gradually feel for them. When they leave your classroom—what people have they really loved till then?

The science program should do the same for the world of nature. Through the sciences we are introducing children to scientific ways of thought, to the wonderful world of nature, this unknowable world of beauty and design, of comedy and tragedy. It is a world that the scientist explores and tries to explain and that the poet and painter also explore but never really completely encompass. Do you remember these wonderful lines of Tennyson?

Flower in the crannied wall,
I pluck you out of the crannies,
I hold you here, root and all, in my hand,
Little flower—but *if* I could understand
What you are, root and all, and all in all,
I should know what God and Man is.
                          (Lord Alfred Tennyson, "Flower in the Crannied Wall")

The science program is not that time of day when we box in the world of nature and give it to the child ready made. We can but point to it and say, "Here friend, here is a world I enjoy, I love. Reach out to it! Find your joys and your loves and care for it so others may also enjoy it and love it."

The skills of language, numbers, and the arts play their role in this adventure, for it is through language and number that the child becomes more powerful to reach further, see more, embrace more, love more. It is through the skills of the arts that the child establishes permanent ties remembering the loved world, discovering and transcending the growing self. Only if the skills help the child feel more powerful to explore, to create, to show his feelings do they add to the child's stature and make it possible for the young to assume responsibility for the world which we pass on to them.

NOTES

[1]Ernest G. Schachtel, *Metamorphosis: On the Development of Affect, Perception, Attention, and Memory* (New York: Basic Books, 1959), 292-293.

[2]Archibald MacLeish, *Poetry and Experience* (Cambridge: Riverside Press, 1961), 66.

[3]John Macmurray, *The Self As Agent* (New York: Harper and Brothers, 1957), 16.

[4]Albert Schweitzer, *Memoirs of Childhood and Youth* (New York: Macmillan, 1955), 68.

3

Politics
and the Curriculum

(1962)

In this discussion the curriculum field will be looked at using some concepts from political science, an action undertaken with some hesitation for the writer is no more than a neophyte in the political science realm. However, the attempt seems justified by the present inadequate state of curriculum theory which is overwhelmed by problems, and suffering from a lack of intellectual vitality. Any attempt to introduce new ideas or analytical schema into curriculum thinking would seem to have some value, if no other than to provide a target for more criticism. Furthermore, the attempt is justified by the fact that almost no one else has made a systematic effort to do the same. This is a task which would more effectively be undertaken by an educator who was also a trained political scientist. There are educational historians, psychologists, sociologists, anthropologists, but no educational political scientists. Certainly the educational enterprise in the United States is loaded with political action, and should be easy pickings for political scientists who wish limited data for analysis.[1]

DEMOCRATIC IDEOLOGY

A possible reason for the lack of attention to political science as a vehicle for exploring the curriculum is that curriculum workers for years have been accepting and operating under a pseudo-political ideology of substance, a simplified conception of democracy. The democratic ideology used by educators, however, falls into the never-never land of wishful thinking. On the one hand it approaches, never quite reaching but often replacing, a religious ideology. It gives form to, and affirms man's action with, and responsibility for, his fellow man, which is a component of most religious teachings. Furthermore, it has a conception of heaven—a future state of affairs, worldly of course, which man

15

may reach by good works, and of salvation—the proper use of reason. It never quite reaches the fullness and richness of a religious ideology, however, for it fails to give form to man's confrontation with the mystery and awe of the universe and it has no conception of hell or of sin except to its opponents. In spite of these shortcomings it has had its converts who have accepted the ideology with a passion which would please any missionary. This is unfortunate, for the curriculum worker has been led to believe that his responsibility to his fellow man exists because he is an educator, whereas he must assume that responsibility because he is a man sharing the tragedy and comedy of human life. By explaining his responsibilities to his fellow man via a simplified democratic ideology he no longer needs to turn to the great humanistic literature, to philosophy, or to theology for symbolic forms to guide action or thinking. The curriculum worker confuses responsibility as educator with his responsibility as man.

On the other hand, the prevailing democratic conception never quite realizes the dimensions of a political ideology, for it fails to deal with conflict and struggle and the phenomenon which resolves both—power. Conflict over educational values is theoretically resolved by argument, discussion, scientific research, and intellectual agreement. Of course such resolution is possible and desirable. But it is in the arena of human action that decisions must be made; social policy cannot wait for agreement among dissident groups. Political action, the wielding of superior power, is man's other acceptable means of resolving value differences.

Educators have shied away from power and from politics in their thinking, perhaps because of unfortunate connotations connected with both words. The politician is too frequently assumed to be a selfish, immoral individual living as a wealthy parasite off the honest, hardworking non-politicians. To engage in politics is to engage in sneaky behavior, unworthy of the greatness of which man is capable. The stereotype has out-lived its usefulness, and we must accept, with Hannah Arendt[2] that politics is one of the great arts of mankind. Indeed, it is only in the realm of political action that man realizes his freedom.

The concept "power" carries the same negative connotation. Charles Merriam offers an optimistic defense:

> There are those who fear power, as there are those who fear life itself; who dread organization and even association in any form—perhaps from temperament; from some sad social experience; from some lack of aptitude in inter-relations. But power may also be regarded not as a foe, a tyrant, an oppressor, a brutal hand upon the shoulder, a prison cell, the lash, but as a friend and guide, a companion, a special service, an instrumentation of personality, just as association may be the great flood into which one throws himself and rushes along in breathless delight perhaps, toward a goal not individually directed.
>
> The power of the creative and constructive type is slowly being ground out with infinite pains and with vast and widespread accompaniment of effort, of-

ten with temporary disillusionment. Power functionally fitted to life is not oppression but release, not a limitation but an expansion of opportunity, a wider
way to achievement, both for group and for individual. Power is positive
rather than negative, creative rather than destructive.[3]

Paul Tillich claims that

In any encounter of man with man, power is active, the power of personal ra-
diation expressed in language and gestures, in the glance of an eye and the
sound of the voice, in face and figure and movement, expressed in what one
is personally and what one represents socially. Every encounter, whether
friendly or hostile, whether benevolent or indifferent, is in some way, unconsciously or consciously, a struggle of power with power.[4]

Power and politics cannot be separated, for politics is the form that power in
action assumes. Lasswell acknowledges this: "When we speak of the science of
politics, we mean the science of power. Power is decision making. A decision is
a sanctioned choice, a choice which brings severe deprivations to bear against
anyone who flouts it. Hence the language of politics is the language of power. It
is the language of decision."[5] Elsewhere Lasswell states that "the study of politics is the study of influence and the influential."[6]

While refraining from discussions of power and politics, educators nevertheless engage in the same, as the reaction to criticism and changes imposed on
the field suggest. Furthermore, they hide their mobilization for power under the
legitimate but self-righteous concept of professionalization. The bid for power
and influence need not be so legitimized—for the search for professional status
is too easily interpreted as a move for prestige rather than a desire to assume
greater responsibility.

I have neither the space nor the competency to explore all the implications of
political science for the curriculum field, so the remainder of this discussion
deals with three major ideas: decisions and actions; educational elites; and educational ideologies. The primary sources for the concepts used are Lasswell and
Kaplan.[7] The intent is to do no more than to offer some ideas for discussion, reflection, and possibly future exploration. The formulations are only tentative
and suggestive. Briefly, the conception is concerned with those decisions or
acts influencing or taking place in the classroom. These decisions or acts are determined by the group among all interested groups with the power to make the
decision or to sanction the acts. These power groups may be called educational
elites.[8] The elites have or produce an ideology which (1) contains demands, expectations or values that determine decisions; (2) legitimizes acts; and (3) has
within it symbols permitting identification among the members of the elite or
the group it leads. This formulation ignores the problem of defining the word
curriculum, which is a rather fruitless task after all these years anyway.

DECISIONS AND ACTS

The basic referent for any discussion of curriculum would seem to be the individual classroom with one or more teachers or other resource people having various competencies or skills, a student or group of students with identifiable characteristics, resources of various kinds, and limited time. The interactions among teachers, students, and resources within a given duration of time constitute the acts which can be controlled and sanctioned. Decision must be made concerning the competencies, skills, or characteristics of the teacher, the characteristics and number of students, the types or kinds of resources, and the time element. Conceptions of purpose, objectives, or learning, if they are needed at all, are components of an ideology, not of the acts in the classroom, although of course a teacher can introduce such notions into the interactions if he wishes.

At this point it becomes obvious that the curriculum worker has not provided good descriptive tools for identifying and categorizing the variety of action or interaction patterns which can exist in classrooms. He acknowledges that there are actions loosely identified around science, language, social studies, art, or mathematics; or problem-solving, self-expression, reporting, or studying; or teacher-centered action, student-centered action, or group-centered action; but, except for the efforts of Smith,[9] there are really few efforts to develop classification systems of classroom action.

For the purposes of this discussion the deficiency of such description schemes is not crucial. The important fact is that the form these classroom actions assume is determined completely by (1) the control of resources going into the classroom, including materials and ideas; (2) the skills and competencies of the teacher; (3) the number and characteristics of the students; and (4) the available time. Furthermore, the form of action can be negatively or positively sanctioned by anyone who has influence over the actions in the situation. If someone wishes to change the form of action in the classroom he can withhold or add materials, select the teacher or change the present teacher's competencies or skills, alter the composition of the student group, change the time limits, or reward or punish any of the classroom actions. If Congress makes available money for obtaining science equipment or new science personnel, and a school system takes advantage of the offer to introduce new materials or personnel into a classroom, then Congress has exerted power to change classroom action. If the parents persuade their children to respond negatively to the teacher, then those parents have exerted power to change classroom action. If a principal negatively sanctions a teacher for arranging the desks in a given way, then that principal has exerted power to change classroom action. If a teacher refuses to permit a music teacher to come into the room, then she has used power to influence classroom action. And so on. The control of classroom action is multifaceted, with certain decisions controlled completely by the teacher, but other decisions controlled by anyone who can influence the input of resources, skills, ideas, or personnel into the classroom.

Educational Elites

Of course the individual teacher, student, principal, or parent has some power over the acts in a single classroom, or the classrooms directly under their influence. The extent of influence probably varies directly with the amount of power and, as Merriam states, "Power is first of all a phenomenon of group cohesion and aggregation."[10] Hence, the range and depth of power are increased if individuals sharing something in common can act in concert. If a group can find a basis for cohesion, and exert power enough to influence a number of classrooms in a community or other sociopolitical units, then such a group might be labeled an elite. Powerful elites may act to alter the availability of resource materials for classrooms; the education of teachers, and hence their skills and competencies, or the sanctions applied to a group of teachers by a community or administrator. These elites may consist of teachers, other groups of educators, parents and community members, or other occupational or interest groups.

As an aside, could it be that the ideology which legitimized lay participation actually weakened the cohesiveness and, hence, power of the teacher groups or administrative groups, thus inhibiting the formation of educational elites, weakening the power of the "professionals," and increasing the power of outside elites? Elites or potential elites need to communicate with each other and may try to convince others of their point of view, but they may do so from a position of power and need not dissolve to form a more inclusive control group. The functions of an elite are facilitated by their ideology.

Educational Ideologies

The term "ideology" is one of many that could be used. McClellan and Komisar[11] and Scheffler[12] use the terms "slogan" and "slogan system." Mannheim[13] distinguishes between an ideology and utopia, and others use the word "myth." The functions of the ideology are several. It includes symbols which facilitate the identification of members of the group with each other and with that which they have in common. It provides a set of expectations or values which give direction to decision-making and, finally, it provides a framework which justifies or legitimizes various courses of action. To oversimplify with examples, it is possible that the phrase "educating the whole child" enabled people with like sentiments to recognize their similarities; to plan for snack periods in school in order to facilitate good eating habits; or to justify complete freedom of expression during physical education or art periods.

Obviously, ideologies are complex symbol systems containing a variety of prescriptive and descriptive elements. Because they provide direction for decision-making and goal-setting they necessarily contain prescriptive elements. If they are to legitimize certain classroom actions, then they must contain the accepted, warranted assertions produced through the process of scientific inquiry. If they are to function effectively as identification symbols, then they should also contain art symbols or vehicles which permit the organization of feeling and sentiments. The producers of educational theory have frequently failed to recognize the multi-purposiveness of educational ideologies and have moved, hook, line, and sinker, into the search for truth, as defined by scientific criteria. Thus, the identification symbols are neglected and groups of educators lose their cohesiveness and their contact with, and/or differentiation from, other groups; or legitimation for classroom action is relegated to scientific generalizations, and the whole body of philosophical, theological and humanistic knowledge is forsaken for a weak social science substitute.

Implications

This brief examination of action, elites, and ideologies leads to several possible explorations, and in the space available oversimplification is necessary. Assume that at one time there existed a prevailing ideology which contained a concern for the education of the individual for maximum self-realization, and emphasized the need for occupational self-sufficiency, social adjustment, adequate family living, and worthy use of leisure time. Assume furthermore that another ideology existed which proposed developing the necessary intellectual disciplines and the need of the society for skilled scientists, other intellectuals, and technical workers. Assume also that the ideologies were complete enough to give some direction to the selection of resources (personnel and materials) and determination of the classroom action. The existence of differing ideologies leads obviously to public debate, and in some cases modification of classroom action, favoring the most powerful elite. Several different explanations for these two different ideologies could be offered. However, only one possible explanation will be explored here.

Talcott Parsons has proposed that there are three levels in the hierarchical structure of an organization: the technical system; the managerial system; and the community or institutional system. He suggests that the classroom is at the technical level; the general administration and school-community relations, at the managerial level; and board activity, at the institutional level. He describes the output at the technical level as change in the "character, knowledge, and skill levels of individual pupils;" the output at the managerial level as a "contribution to the general performance capacity in the community; and the output at the institutional level as "greater integration of the community."[14] In other words, the classroom has as its focus the development of the child; the administrative and managerial functioning has as its focus the growth of the community; and the board or institutional level has as its focus the integration of the various activities and functions in the community. Now with a different major focus or concern at each level, it would seem that a different ideology would be needed at each level. The people who function in the classroom must focus on the individual student, hence need an ideology which has as its major focus the student and his growth. There are other elements in the ideology, of course, but they assume a subservient position. The ideology for the managerial level must have as its major concern the performance capacity of the community, and other elements become subservient. It seems then that the two ideologies mentioned earlier need not be opposed, for they might serve different functions. The teacher's ideology must keep central the development of the individual, and in the educational political wars the teacher elite is the student's protector. The elite united by, and pushing, the other ideology, protects the community from its own downfall as it grows or competes with other societies, and protects the community from its self-destruction. Hence, in curriculum several conflicting ideologies could well exist side by side as different elites are united by, and push, different ideologies. The political struggle which evolves is probably necessary, and it behooves the educator to maneuver in the political arena more skillfully.

One consequence of this line of thought is to look again at the function of professional organizations. They would seem to be ideal vehicles for the political infighting. National meetings could be times to reaffirm solidarity by symbols of identification, planning political strategy, training local people for political tactics, and discovering how to sanction individuals or groups who support or oppose their ideological struggle. At the present time, educational conferences seem inadequate training grounds for political activity, functioning somewhat inadequately as opportunities for reaffirming solidarity ties, and gladly usurping the responsibility of the colleges and local school systems for resource development by feeding new ideas and materials to participants. A quick and easy division of responsibility among people and institutions responsible for curriculum improvement is not possible, but a political analysis of the curriculum field might help redefine roles and locate new questions to direct curriculum inquiry.

There is certainly no one road to wisdom in the curriculum field, and curriculum workers cannot depend only on educational research, psychological knowledge, or philosophical disciplines for insights. They must be open to all thought systems which provide any analytical power. By utilizing concepts rooted in political science, the curriculum worker may find new questions for dealing with age-old problems.

NOTES

[1]Two examples of such endeavors are available: York Willbern, "Education and the American Political System," *Teachers College Record* (February 1958): 292-98; and Neal Gross, *Who Runs Our Schools?* (New York: John Wiley and Sons, 1958).

[2]Hannah Arendt, *Between Past and Future* (New York: Viking, 1961).

[3]Charles E. Merriam, *Political Power: Its Composition and Incidence* (New York: McGraw-Hill, 1934), 322-23.

[4]Paul Tillich, *Love, Power and Justice* (New York: Oxford University Press, 1954), 87.

[5]Harold D. Lasswell, Nathan Leites, and Associates, *Language of Politics* (New York: George W. Stewart, 1949), 8.

[6]Harold D. Lasswell, *Politics: Who Gets What, When, How* (New York: Meridian Books, 1958), 13.

[7]Harold D. Lasswell and Abraham Kaplan, *Power and Society: A Framework for Political Inquiry* (New Haven: Yale University Press, 1950). See also Lasswell, *Politics: Who Gets What, When, How.*

[8]Lasswell and Kaplan, *Power and Society*, 201.

[9]B. O. Smith, "Concepts of Teaching," in *The Language and Concepts of Education*, ed., B. O. Smith and R. H. Ennis (Chicago: Rand McNally, 1961).

[10]Merriam, *Political Power*, 16.

[11]James McClellan and B. Paul Komisar, "The Logic of Slogans," in *Language and Concepts,* ed., Smith and Ennis, 195-214.

[12]Israel Scheffler, *The Language of Education* (Springfield, Illinois: Charles C. Thomas, 1960).

[13]Karl Mannheim, *Ideology and Utopia* (New York: Harcourt, Brace, 1936).

[14]Talcott Parsons, "Some Ingredients of a General Theory of Formal Organization," in *Administrative Theory in Education*, ed. Andrew Halpin (Chicago: Midwest Administration Center, University of Chicago Press, 1958), 40-72.

The Art of Teaching[1]

(1962)

A teacher may wish to reduce the complexity of teaching, but it cannot be greatly reduced. He must live with boys and girls in a classroom containing furniture, books, machines, and other materials. He must be ready to incorporate special teachers, visitors and other wandering individuals into the classroom activities. The teacher faces a situation complex as only life can be—filled with doubts, conflicts, humor, pain, frustration, bleakness and beauty, pathos and love, anger and laughter. He needs to be able to live and work with inconsistencies, opposites, and fluctuations. His task is to scrutinize this mass of people, feeling, things, and ideas; to foresee what it can become. He has to transform the everything into a valued something before it becomes a wasted nothing.

One way to make this complexity transparent is to use the methods of science. Teaching is amenable to scientific research, and the process of analysis and, hopefully, synthesis. As it has in industry, the analytic-synthetic process of research may identify elements by which the teaching process can be ordered and controlled. Certainly the development of programmed materials and teaching machines is a natural, and valuable consequence of such analysis. The teacher needs analytic skills to abstract from the complexity of the classroom components which may be manipulated and controlled. He needs to know the parts which make up good teaching. But more significantly, the teacher needs to know how to put the parts together. Somehow the teacher must transform the potential everything into classroom experiences which channel and compress existence. The teacher needs to synthesize the parts into a wholeness in which the children can perceive with heightened sensitivity the meanings and values of life.

This is a function of art—to heighten the participant's awareness of the significance, meaning, and beauty of life. It is done by abstracting and recombining bits of the chaos into unique, aesthetically satisfying patterns. Browning has said it this way:

> ... you've seen the world
> —The beauty and the wonder and the power,
> The shapes of things, their colours, lights and shades,
> Changes, surprises,—and God made it all!
> —For what? Do you feel thankful, ay or no,
> For this fair town's face, yonder river's line,
> The mountain round it and the sky above,
> Much more the figures of man, woman, child.
> These are the frame to? What's it all about?
> To be passed over, despised? or dwelt upon,
> Wondered at? oh, this last of course!—you say.
> ... we're made so that we love
> First when we see them painted, things we have passed
> Perhaps a hundred times nor cared to see;
> And so they are better, painted—better to us,
> Which is the same thing. Art was given for that;
> God uses us to help each other so,
> Lending our minds out ...
>
> (Robert Browning, from "Fra Lippo Lippi")[2]

In a way, that's what the teacher does. The children have passed parts of the world "Perhaps a hundred times nor cared to see." Teachers are there, living with the children, lending their minds out, that the children might love that which the teacher "paints." Of course, the elementary school teacher has an advantage, for the children may never before have passed "The beauty and the wonder and the power / The shapes of things, their columns, lights and shades, / changes and surprises." The teacher has the rare opportunity to help the child dwell upon and wonder at the detail and vastness and the awe-fulness of the world. It is important that the teacher "paint" a classroom of superb beauty; a classroom which can hold the child with fascination and which the child can leave with new power to view and comprehend the beauty of the world.

To do this the teacher must live with the intricacies, absurdities, and dissonances of life, without seeking to reduce them to neat formulae or maps. The teacher needs what Keats calls the quality of " ... Negative capability, that is, when man is capable of being in uncertainties, mysteries, doubts, without any irritable reaching after fact and reason ... "[3] Science encourages the "reaching after fact and reason." It deals less well with moods and mysteries. These belong to the domain of art. Art can deal with life in its fullness, its emptiness, its beauty and its ugliness. It can bring together the conflicts, the opposites and make sense out of them. The function of art is to discover sense and meaning in a world that at times seems senseless and meaningless; to create value where it is non-existent.

The teacher needs the skills of analysis and synthesis, of observation, of fact-finding, of forming hypotheses, and making generalizations. The teaching profession desperately needs more than warranted assertions about the teaching process, produced only by scientific activity. Teachers need an exact language, semantically clean, for communicating with others about their teaching. Teachers do have recurring problems for which there can be more or less standardized answers. To discuss teaching as an art is not to dismiss or deny these needs or that teaching can also be a science, or studied scientifically. Both approaches are needed, for new ideas are desperately needed in education. However, the prevailing mode of studying teaching is the scientific.[4] Most discussions of teaching proceed from within a scientific framework. An interest in the art of teaching needs to be revived. Education must apply aesthetic as well as scientific modes of comprehension to the phenomena of teaching. Whether teaching is or is not an art—is not an issue. The question is whether interpreting teaching as an art leads to new insights, new ways of acting, thinking, perceiving, or feeling about life in the classroom.

Approaching teaching as an art has value in a society moving toward automation but crying out for individuality. To use only scientific knowledge to think about teaching is to assume that the teaching situation can be more or less standardized. Existing studies of children and of the learning process suggest that there is a best way of working with children. If a teacher can master the principles of learning and child development; if objectives can be clearly delineated and carefully stated, objectives and lessons planned accordingly—then the crank can be turned—and teaching will be effective. Textbooks, some educational authorities, and administrators frequently assume that the teaching process can be, or is, standardized, and that teachers can be interchanged. This is possible, perhaps, but undesirable. Teachers, like children, have common characteristics. But they also have unique characteristics. Some teachers are shy, quiet, withdrawn; others boisterous, aggressive, extroverted. Some teachers show excitement and enthusiasm about teaching; others are sober and quietly dedicated. Being different, teachers cannot be expected to teach in the same manner. Considered only as the facilitation of learning, as a mirror image of the principles of learning, teaching may be assumed to have a common pattern; a pattern imprinted by a learning theory. Teaching approached in terms of scientific knowledge only, via principles of learning or teaching, does not take advantage of the teacher's significant idiosyncrasies. But art does, for art deals with differences and idiosyncrasies.

Furthermore, to think of teaching as an art may encourage the teacher to feel differently about himself, his life in the classroom, and the children with whom he works. Words or labels carry nuances which creep into thought and which may unconsciously structure a teacher's attitudes, feelings or actions. If called a technician, the teacher may think primarily of routines and the application of more or less standardized principles to situations which seem similar. Labeled a scientist, the teacher may be influenced by the attitude of detachment, objectivity and control. Identifying teachers as artists is to call to mind a host of interrelated notions. The label may create a feeling of impossibility, for few people are successful artists. Yet teaching is almost an impossibility, really, when all of the complexities and difficulties of teaching are enumerated. The word "artist" also carries with it the notion of a person continuously reaching out into the world and becoming a skilled creator of beauty and meaning; being disappointed and sad as expectations are not achieved, but feeling intense joy and accomplishment when they are. Teaching is also this constant search for perfection, for satisfaction, and in a sense, for beauty. It is the frequent disappointment and sadness of visions unrealized, and the joy and contentment of occasional success. As an artist, the teacher must think of maximizing his own individuality, of becoming a unique person in the world; for artists must stand out as individuals if lending their minds out is to have value. A master teacher maximizes his individuality, stands out as a person, and continues to search for his own meanings and significance.

THE NATURE OF ART

What is an art? Are there some things that can be said about it which may help teachers think and feel anew about teaching? There are, of course, many notions about it. Usually to think of art is to think of the painter with colors, the sculptor with stone, the writer with language or the musician with sounds. The artist turns out and displays canvases or statues or poems or musical scores. The artist's curiosity is apt to lead down numerous paths, and the artist's life is frequently interpreted as non-conventional. But these are stereotypes—and the picture needs broadening. Lu Chi, writing in the third century, A. D., expressed some ideas about poetry which can be applied to the other arts as well. He said:

> Taking his position at the hub of things [the poet] contemplates the mystery of the universe;

> He feeds his emotions and his mind on the great works of the past. Moving along with the four seasons, he sighs at the passing of time;

> Gazing at myriad objects, he thinks of the complexity of the world.

> He sorrows over the falling leaves in virile autumn;

> He takes joy in the delicate bud of fragrant spring. With awe in his heart he experiences chill;

His spirit solemn, he turns his gaze to the clouds. He declaims the superb works of his predecessors;

He croons the clean fragrance of past worthies. He roams in the forest of literature, and praises the symmetry of great art. Moved, he pushes his books away, and takes the writing brush, that he may express himself in letters.[5]

The image to be emphasized is that, on the one hand, is the poet or other artist, and on the other, the whole wise mysterious world before him. The artist is at the hub of things, with the awe, the complexity, the sorrow, the joy before him. He contemplates it, and then expresses his own feelings, his knowledge of the world. Lu Chi says further that, "The poet is one who 'traps Heaven and Earth in a cage of form'."[6] MacLeish continues: "It [the poem] cages the world with all its complexities upon it. It takes experience as experience stands there. It closes the cage of form on heaven and earth and makes them mean....[7] "The poet's labor is to struggle with the meaninglessness and silence of the world until he can force it to mean: until he can make silence answer and the non-Being BE."[8]

The following points from Lu Chi's poetic statement and MacLeish's commentary are convenient guideposts to look at teaching as an art.

1. The artist stands at the "hub of things," confronted by the wonder of the world.
2. He responds to or partakes sensitively of the world with strong, sincere and varied emotions—joy, sorrow, and chill.
3. He knows thoroughly and sensitively the great art created by others, not to imitate it, but to be inspired and to declaim, croon, and praise it.
4. He turns solemnly inward and struggles to compose the meaningless silence of the world into meaningful form.
5. He pushes all else aside to trap "Heaven and Earth in a cage of form."

The Artist Stands at the Hub of Things

The artist does not spend all his time in the studio, or at the typewriter. He gets immersed in the world; the mysteries, the seasons, the ants and the machines, the flowers and the buildings, the foibles and arguments, the wars and the rituals, the beauty and the ugliness, the love and the hatred, the sorrows and the joys, the securities and the chills of adventure. The whole world is his, to be poked, felt, tickled, tasted, served, smelled, and whatever else his physiological and cultural conditioning permits or facilitates. He is in the midst of life—at its hub. The immensity of life demands that he be on the go, experiencing the world of nature, of people, of ideas, and man-made things either directly or vicariously. Adventure, participation, involvement feed his art; they are indeed, the source and content of that art.

And so the teacher. The teacher must stand at the "hub of things," making and destroying the world with others, beholding the brilliant intensity and drab monotony of nature, living life amidst the cheapness and selflessness, and the comedy and tragedy of all life. It is this involvement which makes him an alive, exciting person; which quickens his teaching with life, with demand and compassion, enthusiasm and serenity, adventure and significant repetition. Through his own aliveness, his own standing at the hub of things, the teacher is able to find the wherewithal to channel experience, to compress it and to heighten its significance and value for the boys and girls with whom he lives. "Taking his position at the hub of things," must be the characteristic of the elementary school teacher even more than the secondary and college teacher, for he brings to his students not simply one set of experiences, but experiences in most areas of life. The teacher must experience life on many fronts, not as a narrow specialist.

The Artist Responds with Strong, Sincere, and Varied Emotions

MacLeish, elsewhere in the same book, *Poetry and Experience*, has said that, "The crime against life, the worst of all crimes, is *not* to feel."[9] Whitehead has drawn the parallel that "intellect is to emotions as our clothes are to our bodies."[10] Both statements imply the importance of affect, of feeling, in human life. Obviously neither Whitehead nor MacLeish could be accused of downgrading the intellectual component and upgrading the emotional, or of placing affect above intellect. They recognize, however, that a creative life is not simply an intellectual life. A life of emotion, of strong, vivid, and varied feelings, is necessary if the artist, or indeed any other person, is to be attuned to life around him. Feeling heightens perceptions, helps one select from among all stimuli those most crucial. Cox, in a wonderful, sensitive, and stimulating guide "for those who want to write," has said,

> In general, good writers are not flighty or obviously excitable. They are not "emotional people;" not as those who care little about words say "emotional." And yet the capacity to feel is one gift you must conserve and cherish if you want to be a writer. To feel intensely, sharply, exquisitely, variously, and far beyond the periphery of your private skin. To feel many kinds of feeling, and, more important still, not to check or muffle feelings, but to feel them to the limit. Including ugly, dangerous, and extremely painful feelings....
>
> Writers get their power from the much that they have felt, and they get their subject matter from perceptions made vivid by emotion.[11]

In this age when intellectual virtues are being stressed for the schools, how very important is this advice for a teacher. He, too, must sorrow "over the falling leaves" and "take joy in the delicate bud of fragrant spring." Engagement with the world is less human without the tinge of excitement or remorse, guilt or anticipation. The world compressed and channeled by the teacher for the children must be a world he loves, and perhaps at times hates. The teacher's feelings for the world he encounters and brings to the children makes that compressed and channeled experience "reverberate"[12] with significance for him and the boys and girls. The teacher's emotion cannot be left in other arenas of life: awe and mystery to religion, compassion and love to his home life, and his overflowing laughter and tears to the theater or television. Brought into the classroom, these feelings and emotions of the teacher spark the children to respond with heightened awareness and intensity. As the children see the teacher respond with feeling, they find freedom to express their feelings and accept them as significant aspects of human life.[13] Even the principles of science and the formal relations of mathematics have a beauty to which one can respond with a deep "ah" of admiration.

The Artist Knows and is Sensitive to the Great Art Created by Others

No artist works in a cultural vacuum. The artist's work is usually a part of a continuing sequence of art problems, forms and styles.[14] He works within a tradition influenced by media, style, or problems of the time. A few artists, geniuses perhaps, originate new traditions, or new sequences of style. They recognize that the current tradition has solved most of the outstanding problems of style and expression, and they create new styles, expressive forms, and perhaps new problems. But they know the past and can operate within its traditions. Picasso experimented with cubism after demonstrating proficiency with the art styles of the times. Keats' letters are filled with references to Shakespeare, and Proust was not only a novelist, but a critic of French literature. Lu Chi's words are perhaps most expressive of the artist's attitude toward other works of art. "He feeds his emotions and his mind on the great work of the past." "He declaims the superb work of his predecessors; he croons the clear fragrance of past worthies. He roams in the forest of literature and praises the symmetry of great art." This is not blind homage, or cultural reverence. Prior works are not "studied" simply for style and form, or because the artist must know the tradition as a condition for joining the guild. The artist engages the work of others because it nourishes, inspires, and challenges. It has a significant message which stimulates and reorders some aspect of the world. Through the art of another a mind is borrowed and the world seen and heard and felt anew.

An aspiring teacher is fortunate to be able to behold an artist-teacher at work. From the master teacher, the aspirer gains more than technique. He borrows the other's mind and senses to see anew the world important in teaching. He may be inspired and challenged to develop his own unique, satisfying classroom style. From viewing several artist-teachers, he may become more aware of the crafts necessary for or common to teaching. He may see more clearly the continuities and discontinuities in teaching traditions, and thus readily recognize whether his teaching is appropriate to that time or place, or an anachronism. There are two differences between beholding other teachers, and imbibing past art products. The teacher is lucky to be able to observe three or four master-teachers, but the artist beholds hundreds of paintings, or reads in a forest of literature. Few have tried to capture the art of a great teacher in written or visual form.[15] Plato introduces the modern teacher to the style and art of Socrates, and the New Testament to the teaching of Jesus. In a few novels, such as Sylvia Ashton Warner's, *Spinster*,[16] the reader is able to glance at a fine teacher in action. In a few films, such as *Passion for Life* and *Near Home*, a teacher may witness a teacher in selected actions. Great teaching has not been "declaimed" or "crooned" or preserved. It is too frequently behind a closed door and is lost to time as a symphony was lost before recordings, and as plays and dance were lost before film. A teacher has few opportunities "to feed his emotion and his mind" on the art of others or to roam into the classrooms of great teachers.

The other difference is that teachers have been conditioned to observe as scientists, not as artists or art critics. Both modes of observation, of course, are necessary. The aspiring teacher has only the analytic-synthetic model of science to follow. As a scientist, the aspiring teacher tries to identify and understand the characteristics of good teaching, or the dimensions of the teaching act. The analysis of teaching is usually a cause-effect or means-ends analysis: if the teacher does such and such, then these consequences follow ... Educators have not yet provided aesthetic models or guides for beholding or observing teaching. Teachers do not look at the teaching of others and ask questions such as: "How does this make me feel?" "What is the artist saying about the world?" "As I look through his eyes what do I see?" Nor are they given the skills to look at the teaching of others as an art critic would: "Is it balanced? Harmonious? Each act and word significant? Does it build and resolve tension?" Aspiring teachers visit other teachers to pick up techniques and emulate practices. Perhaps they could also visit to observe design and composition, and to identify craft and style. From these observations they could declaim the superb work of other teachers and praise great art, for it is this which develops tradition and a heritage which helps shape, without determining, the future.

The Artist Turns Inward to Compose

Participating in the world or expressing that which he knows and feels are not the only activities of the artist. There is a transition stage of composition which may occur while participating or expressing, or independently. Both Ortega y Gasset[17] and Macmurray[18] discuss a rhythm of involvement and withdrawal; a withdrawal when the abstracted elements are manipulated, composed, and re-arranged. From this composing activity—during withdrawal—ideas are formed which may then be expressed either in the artistic creation or in new experiencing.[19] The artist needs time away from the struggle and excitement of participation to let sensations and feelings and ideas be shaped, combined, dimmed, and intensified by his own memories, desires, purposes, or other conscious and unconscious processes. In this process a self is formed. The artist's own individuality is interwoven into the very matrix of that which is being composed.

The teacher, too, withdraws to compose. The teacher's own mundane and vividly profound experiences are brought into juxtaposition and put up against his memories, purposes, and idiosyncrasies until the compressed, channeled and heightened experiences are gradually composed into a seemingly workable plan. This stage of the art process corresponds with the planning process which is accepted as an essential aspect of the teaching process. Too frequently, however, teaching is assumed to begin with planning. Assuming that teaching is an art, the beginning of the teaching act must be when one is "standing at the hub of things," prior to the planning act. The composing process is not simply a logical process, which the analytic means-end scheme of the scientific model presupposes about teaching. It is an intuitive process, fed by all that a person is and has felt—mixed with previous interests, his weltanschanung and knowledge of what others accomplished using similar media. Composing need not begin with purpose or clearly stated objectives. They may arise out of the composing act or be but a component of the composition; they do not determine it completely.

The Artist Pushes All Else Aside to Trap "Heaven and Earth in his Cage of Form."

Each art has media which determine or limit the characteristics of its "cage of form." The visual artist uses canvas and patterns of color and texture to trap "Heaven and Earth." The composer uses sounds and rhythm; the sculptor clay or stone or metal. The choreographer traps the world in a cage of formed movement and spatial arrangements, while the dramatist uses words and movement and spatial arrangement. The architect's forms are building materials and space. The scientist, as an artist, traps the world in a cage of theories and logical structure of symbols, while the engineer does the same in bridges or processing plants. The difference between the unique art product and the mass-produced product is that the first carries with it some of the creator's heightened responses to the world, his feelings and sensuous perception of the world in which he lives. A bit of the artist lives in each of his created works, a bit of his life which can be perceived by the beholder.

With what media does the teacher work? What is the teacher's cage of form? Using the words creating or forming, it would be easy to answer that the boys and girls are to be formed, transformed, or created by teaching, or that they are the media. But the analogy is too simple; for the children are never media, they are never to be formed. They are to be lived with, and perhaps influenced; to think otherwise is basically a denial of the fellowship of life. They share this world with their teachers. They are not equals of the teacher, for they are of greater worth; less conditioned, freer. Potentially they are able to give more to the world than the teacher, for they have more energy and fewer fixed, uncreative ways. They may become more than the teacher is. To control them, to think of creating or forming them, to manipulate them as media is to deny their fellowship with the teacher.

The media controlled and manipulated by the teacher are the words, acts, and the materials with which he works. The classroom and classroom activity make up the cage of form. The teacher's "Heaven and Earth" are trapped with the teacher's language, the books, charts, and maps used, the available displays and specimens, and in the teacher's movements. In the classroom and through classroom activity the teacher, the artist, reveals how he sees and feels about his world, and how he composes it, makes it mean. Classroom activity is a telling expression of the sensitivity and awareness of the teacher, of the depth and breadth of the world at whose hub he takes his stand. The compressed, channeled, heightened experiences made available to the children are the teacher's "cage of form," the teacher's art product.

The Craft of the Artist

In a few words, Lu Chi summarizes the whole craft of writing; the poet "takes the writing brush, that he may express himself in letters." The physical skill of using the writer's brush can be expected of most literate people. To "express himself in letters" requires consummate skill; a skill which differentiates the person who "expresses himself" from those who express the sayings and thoughts of others. The non-artist is more apt to be used by the language. The artist must bend language to give verbal structure and form to his feelings and thoughts. Murray states that,

> Every work of enduring literature is not so much a triumph of language as a victory over language: a sudden injection of life-giving perceptions into a vocabulary that is, but for the energy of the creative writer, perpetually on the verge of exhaustion.[20]

So it is with all the arts, for the artist is the master of his medium. He urges and forces the medium to perform at the limits of, or beyond its potential, as Shakespeare kept "this overcharged, exploded, tense, swollen language supple under his fingers so that it will follow the contours of the most ethereal emotion."[21] As the writer shapes words to his meanings, so the sculptor shapes clay or stone, the painter pigment, and the composer sounds. Not simply a matter of physical control over the instruments of the craft, the brush, typewriter, chisel, piano; the artist has cognitive control over the media, knowing immediately and almost intuitively the possibilities of various stones, the blending and glazing characteristics of the pigments, and the harmonious qualities of the strings. Furthermore he is a master of the abstract knowledge about the craft: metrics, plot and character development, perspective, balance, melody, counterpoint, and other aspects of the lore and science of the craft.

Mastery in a craft develops slowly and requires the concentration, patience, and practice which goes with any discipline. The characteristics of the medium must be discovered both by testing out or playing with them and by more or less systematic study: reading, talking, or through apprenticeship or formal study. The characteristics are not identified once and for all; the artist continues to discover new properties of the medium, new awareness of what it can do. The characteristics and properties of the medium must become second nature to the artist, internalized so completely that they are subservient to the composed experiences and feelings which are to be expressed. To stop and think about the characteristics of the medium detracts from the process of giving ideal form to the composition. However, the artist may be challenged to withdraw from the expressive act to experiment and play with the medium, to discover new properties of the medium and to find new ways to work with it.

If teaching is considered an art, then it too must have a craft side. But not a single craft, for teachers use language, movement, color, materials, space and time. Using many media in this "cage of form" teachers must become virtuosos in the use of these media. Consequently, teachers need opportunities to discover the properties and characteristics of the media through experimentation and playing around with them, and through concentrated systematic study until the craft aspects of the art are internalized and become second nature. As in all arts, the source of the discipline, patience, and concentration required to master the media of the teaching art is a dedication to and love for the art.[22]

The Crafts in the Art of Teaching

The art of teaching partakes not of one craft but of many. To trap in his cage of form—in his classroom and in his acts—a compressed, meaningful, selection from the world with which the children can participate with heightened awareness and sensitivity, requires a mastery of language, of materials, of color and design, of stage setting, of movement and the flow of events. Teachers might become more proficient artists of teaching if they master to some extent, or at least are conversant with, the crafts in the art of poetry, the visual arts, drama and dance. Only mention of them is possible, for the implication of each for teaching deserves a full study.

Language is a prime vehicle of expression and exchange in the classroom, and is used in many ways: commands, descriptions, storytelling, unstructured conversation, and expressions of feelings or attitudes. For any language usage, precision is required; a precision determined by the use. In some situations the language is used as a scientist would use it, with clear and unequivocal referents, agreed upon usage, and an objective emotional content. Other situations demand exact communication of emotions stirred by environmental contacts which may require more equivocal referents and unique usage. The poet excels in the precise use of language, for he exerts control over his language to make it mean his meanings rather than the meanings of established usage. Certainly, if the teacher is to be an artist in the classroom, then he must be in command of his language, a master of it, rather than a slave to it. He must be able to create the mood, the awareness of the world that he has selected as significant. These are functions of poetry. The teacher should have a chance to discover the possibilities and limitations of language by playing with it and studying it, until he can do with it what he wants and not be confined by it.

The teacher is also concerned with the rhythm and flow of events in the classroom. He determines pace, the building and reduction of tension, the cross play of emotions and actions among people. The teacher needs to be aware of the shape of the movement of the experiences created during the day or over a period of several days. The staging and flow of events; the control of the passage of time, its compression and extension; the handling of tension among people, belong to the craft of drama. Movement is the province of dance. These are neglected elements in most classrooms though, for the flow of events tends to be a mechanical rhythm determined by purpose and its accomplishment, which may not be the best means of handling time and duration in a classroom. The teacher also depends on space and visual factors of color and design which are the province of the visual arts. Again, skill in these crafts might be used by the teacher as he becomes master of his art of teaching.

The crafts of teaching have only been hinted at, for this is an infrequently explored area. The uses of language, space, movement, time, tension and other components of the crafts essential to the various arts may be fruitful fields for educational search and eventually research.

Whether teaching is or is not an art, is not an issue, and will never be a question with a single answer. Teaching is complex. Education needs to follow many roads if teachers are to find greater comprehension of and satisfaction in teaching. Postulating that teaching is an art opens roadways of exploration which could lead to new horizons.

NOTES

[1]The writer is indebted to Professor Leland Jacobs for his stimulating discussions about art and the art of teaching, and specifically for the notion of composition and craft.

[2]See Robert Browning, *My Last Duchess and Other Poems* (New York: Dover, 1993), 43–44. *Ed.*

[3]John Keats, Letter to the Brothers George and Thomas Keats, Dated 21 December, 1817, Hamstead, England. Published in *The Selected Letters of John Keats*, selected and edited by Lionel Trilling (Garden City, New York; Doubleday, 1956), 103.

[4]See B. Orthanel Smith, "On the Anatomy of Teaching," *Journal of Teacher Education*, December, 1956; "A Concept of Teaching," *Teachers College Record*, February, 1960, and Marie Hughes, *Assessment of the Quality of Teaching in Elementary Schools*, mimeograph (University of Utah, 1959).

[5]Quoted in Archibald MacLeish, *Poetry and Experience* (Cambridge; Riverside Press, 1961), 4–5.

[6]Ibid., 7.

[7]Ibid., 8.

[8]Ibid., 9.

[9]Archibald MacLeish, *Poetry and Experience*, 66.

[10]Lucien Price, *Dialogues of Alfred North Whitehead* (Boston: Little Brown, 1954), 188.

[11]Sidney Cox, *Indirections for Those Who Want to Write* (New York: The Viking Press, 1962), 7.

[12]Louise Brogan, speaking to the young writer, said, "Remember, if you are a young poet, that you are endowed with emotion, that makes your work reverberate; with intellect, that gives your work form; and that you have another endowment as well; a spirited ingredient that has not yet been isolated." From "Popular and Unpopular Poetry in America," in *The Writer and His Craft,* ed. R. W. Cowden (Ann Arbor, MI: The University of Michigan Press), 189.

[13]John Macmurray, *Reason and Emotion* (New York: Barnes and Noble, 1962), 67–91.

[14]George Kubler, *The Shape of Time* (New Haven: Yale University Press, 1962).

[15]Houston Peterson, ed. *Great Teachers* (New York: Random House and Rutgers University Press, 1946).

[16]Sylvia Ashton-Warner, *Spinster, A Novel* (New York: Simon and Schuster, 1959).

[17]José Ortega y Gasset, "The Self and the Other," in *Dehumanization of Art and Other Writings on Art and Culture* (Garden City, New York; Doubleday, 1956). See also Ortega y Gasset, *Man and People* (W. W. Norton, 1957), chap. 1.

[18]John Macmurray, *The Self as Agent* (New York: Harper, 1957).

[19]"The act of composition is performed by all. Every time we make up our minds we compose. We change the composition of ourselves and the world. Where there is life at all there is constant forming. And the fun and joy of living comes when we make incompatibles unite." S. Cox, *Indirections*, VIII.

[20]J. Middleton Murray, *The Problem of Style* (London: Oxford University Press, 1922, printed as Oxford Paperback, 1960), 85.

[21]Ibid., 98.

[22]Erich Fromm, *The Art of Loving* (New York: Harper, 1956), chap. 4.

5

Knowledge:
An Instrument of Man

(1962)

To become a fully responsible, contributing person in a society, the child must take on the preferred ways of exploring, making and using symbols, and encountering others; engaging in the necessities of labor and work; and building and rebuilding society within the freedom of existing limits. Society has various ways to influence the young to accept these preferred and required modes of existence. The child's acts may be directly influenced by physical sanctions of influential persons or authority figures, but ways of perceiving, thinking, and feeling are more subtly influenced through the communication of knowledge. The schools are the major social institutions for influencing the neophyte's ways of perceiving, thinking and feeling, and thus, must be concerned with knowledge and its significance in the life of man.

THE POWER OF KNOWLEDGE

Knowledge is supposedly an instrument of man, although he is frequently placed in the unfortunate position of serving it. It is a tool to enrich man's existence, and as such, must be subservient to his existence. Like all tools, it provides increased power for the activities of life. In the exploration of the world, knowledge is an instrument of great penetration. It helps make transparent that which seems opaque. It relates events and phenomena which seem unrelated to the unknowledgeable eye. Its vocabulary and rules say to the newcomer, "Look, here is a world to explore. Others have explored it before you and left this map. Go forth and find the same wonders and joys, and eventually the same perplexities." To the sophisticated it offers charts which point the way into the unknown, vehicles for exploring it, and ways to symbolize that which is discovered. As he continues in his quest for self identity and potential, knowledge reveals what others have been and what he and others can be. As man encounters others, knowledge provides power to interpenetrate more deeply into the aloneness of each, for it provides the instruments to formulate and share personal experiences.

Knowledge serves powerfully as a summarizer of prior experience. Its many forms—science, art, philosophy—organize and summarize the experience of previous explorers and value makers; enabling the man who confronts knowledge to see the past through many eyes. The sciences enable man to summarize recurrent events, and to find similarities among events. Scientific knowledge empowers man to peer into the future and to predict what may happen, and offers him limited opportunities to control events. It provides the tools for setting goals and manipulating events to reach these goals. The arts, on the other hand, tend to summarize unique events, the life and feelings of specific people in given situations, and the imaginings of the artist. Knowledge can be beautiful to behold, and thus capable of surprising and rewarding man. As art need not always refer to objects or events, but may be a new object, created by man for its intrinsic worth, so all forms of knowledge share in this potential beauty. As creations of man, they reveal creative capabilities, a sense of rhythm, balance, and design; ingenuity and sense of organization. As some buildings are merely functional, others partake of the rich fullness of space composed into significant patterns; so some knowledge may be merely functional, while other, polished by criticism, is not only useful but is beautiful to behold. Merleau-Ponty has stated "that to know the world is to sing of it in a melody of words."[1] Math, theories of science, systems of vision and speculation, all are melodies sung by those who know the world in differing ways. The search for parsimony and elegance in the sciences and logical systems is an indication that the logician and the scientist join the artist in the search for beautiful form in addition to their search for significant, meaningful form.

THE PITFALLS OF KNOWLEDGE

Usually only the advantages of knowledge are conceded, but knowledge as a form of power, also corrupts. Knowledge has within it the power to enslave, to make one less free, rather than freer, unless the user is fully aware of the disadvantages. In many ways knowledge partakes of the "disadvantage from whatever is" and "the advantage from whatever is not" as characterized in the Tao.[2]

> Thirty spokes will converge
> On the hub of a wheel;
> But the use of the cart
> Will depend on the part
> Of the hub that is void

With a wall all around
A clay bowl is moulded;
But the use of the bowl
Will depend on the part
Of the bowl that is void.
Cut out windows and doors
In the house as you build;
But the use of the house
Will depend on the space
In the walls that is void.

So advantage is had
From whatever is there;
But usefulness rises
From whatever is not

The negative aspects of knowledge arise from the imposition of a symbolic curtain or screen between the person and reality. It is this curtain which gives man more power in his encounter with and exploration of reality, but it is the very same curtain which may blind the person to what is on the other side. As Cassirer states:

No longer can man confront reality immediately; he cannot see it, as it were, face to face. Physical reality seems to recede in proportion as man's symbolic activity advances. Instead of dealing with the things themselves man is in a sense constantly conversing with himself. He has so enveloped himself in artistic images, in mythical symbols or religious rites that he cannot see or know anything except by the interposition of this artificial medium.[3]

It is as if man were wearing a pair of shaded spectacles which colors and distorts the world beheld. The coloring and distortion may be valuable, if man is aware that spectacles are being used to behold reality, and that the spectacles may be removed and looked at, too.

The major disadvantage arises from this screening quality of knowledge. Man is apt to forget that reality is not seen "as it is," but through a man-made screen which filters out certain information and organizes the rest into patterns which exist not necessarily in the world, but in the eyes of the observer. Henri Bergson has said, "I look, and I think I see, I listen and I think I hear .... What I see and hear of the outer world is purely and simply a selection made by my senses as a light to my conduct."[4] Any form of knowledge is essentially a prejudice—molding and forming the world beheld into the patterns and organizations of the knowledge system used. The prejudice cannot be avoided—the pitfall accompanies the advantage. The disadvantage is overcome when man uses knowledge with humility and tempers it with doubt; willing and eager to entertain other ways of knowing that which is beheld, but using the existing knowledge with courage. The second disadvantage is associated with man's problem of time, or preferably, duration. The abstractive apparatus and the knowledge system which serves it, tend, in general, to take still snapshots of things. Man abstracts from the processes of life as if his only meanings were in the spatial world, not necessarily in the temporal. Knowledge tends to be a mapping in space, not in time. To recognize processes through time, man is inclined to think in terms of stages. Children go from stage to stage in their development and insects go from the egg stage to the larvae stage to the pupa stage into the adult stage. Man finds it difficult to conceptualize or know through time, to organize time as he organizes space. Henri Bergson[5] has stated the problem very cogently in his discussions of duration; although his intuitionist solution is not completely acceptable. Recognition of this problem leads to attempts to deal with duration through history,[6] the novel,[7] dramatic forms, and some process analysis in science. But the problem still exists for the ordinary man, for knowledge forms do not adequately enable him to perceive and know the durational, temporal, aspects of existence. Except for some concepts such as process, love, and faith his knowledge does not enable him to get a hold of the ongoingness and change of organisms and reality through time. Unless man is specifically aware of the spatial characteristics of knowledge, he is apt to behold and respond to the world as relatively stable in time, recognizing change as something which exists but which is hard to accept. In this day, change seems to be the one obvious characteristic of existence. Man would do well to find ways to conceptualize change as the one constant thing and constancy as that which needs explanation.

DEVELOPING THE POWER OF KNOWLEDGE

In spite of the possible difficulties and pitfalls of knowledge, it still is the most powerful instrument devised by man. The problem faced by teachers is how to teach in such a fashion that children become freer by using knowledge, rather than embedded in new cultural chains. How can the prejudices of knowledge be avoided? How can the durational stream of living be honored so life is not stopped at a given time and lived only in space. Teachers need to accept and help children accept that

> Our knowledge is a torch of smoking pine
> That lights the pathway ahead
> Across a void of mystery and dread.
> (George Santayana, from "O World")

In some way, the teacher must have an awareness, and create in the students an awareness that knowledge is but an instrument, created for use and enjoyment in living. In so doing, the teacher and the child must continue to feel more powerful as they take on the knowledge available in the society, rather than feeling less powerful because they cannot master what must be mastered. As a result of the teaching situation, the child must feel more powerful to explore, to express, to encounter others, to reveal what he and others can become, and to build a world worth life. Knowledge is plentiful. Each person should be able to find some knowledge which increases his sense of power and awareness of and sensitivity to life.

The first means of developing a feeling for the power of knowledge and a freedom from a blind acceptance to it, is to make knowledge subservient to its use. Whitehead clearly stated this when he defined education as "the art of the utilization of knowledge."[8] Knowledge need never be internalized for its own sake, for it is an instrument of man and serves him as he lives. The teacher should not need to be in the position of saying, "But you need to know this," which is an easy out, based upon superior physical and social power. More appropriately, and more difficult, perhaps, the teacher should be able to say, "If you know this, then you may do these things." For herein, is the strength and the joy of education: knowledge opens the locked doors of the world to the child and provides the child with vehicles for searching and exploring and associating with the exciting, the beautiful, the joyful and the ugly, and for building into reality that which can be dreamed. Making knowledge subservient to use does not require a pragmatic, or socially functional use, for the uses of knowledge are many. Some uses enable participation in social activities: getting along with others, earning food and shelter, assuming political responsibilities. But knowledge may also enable one to discover who he is and what he may become, as he chases idiosyncrasies down to their socially meaningless but personally satisfying ends, and as he continues to find new sights and feelings which cause a throb of excitement and wonder.

Use simply means that the user can do something with that knowledge; he is not saddled with dead weight that burdens him into despair and impotency. That doing something with, may be new exploring, more satisfying expression, deeper and more meaningful encounters with others, greater awareness of who and what he is, and more ability to build and transform the world. Each form of knowledge offers unique uses. Competency in language opens up the worlds of others and increases the power to meet others. The sciences are tools for exploration and building. The arts are vehicles for seeing and composing and expressing and imagining. Mathematics and logic are instruments for summarizing, seeking, and using relationships. And of course, all knowledge, if the teacher is sufficiently skilled, has intrinsic values. It may be used simply to please the beholder with that which has been made.

Another means of freeing the child from the enslaving possibilities of knowledge is to help the child approach the world through numerous screens or pairs of spectacles. To see the sunset only as the visual artist sees it is to know of color and hue and form and feeling. To see it only as the scientist sees it is to know of refraction and reflection and light. The sunset is all of these and more. For the child to respond to the sunset, rather than simply to color or light, he must perceive it through the eyes of the artist and scientist and poet and others. So, too, he must respond to flowers in many ways. The child may behave as the botanist and slowly take off the petals and observe carefully and perhaps sketch the pistil and stamen; or like the agronomist test out how various soils and chemicals influence the growth of the flower. But the child has not seen the flower unless he sees it through the eyes of an artist such as Van Gogh, or feels it with Tennyson:

> Flower in the crannied wall,
> I pluck you out of the crannies,
> I hold you here, root and all, in my hand,
> Little flower—but *if* I could understand
> What you are, root and all, and all in all,
> I should know what God and Man is.
> (Lord Alfred Tennyson, "Flower in the Crannied Wall")

Or with Buson:

> It falls, the peony
> and upon each other lie
> petals, two or three.[9]

Engaging in the process of making knowledge may also keep the child free from its enslaving possibilities. To make knowledge is to engage in a process which doubts the validity of existing knowledge and seeks new answers or formulations. This is the essence of the work of the scientist. Secure enough to use his knowledge, the scientist is also secure enough to doubt it. Hence, he looks for situations which will disprove his hypotheses and seeks other theories to explain phenomena. The scientist tolerates ambiguity, light is explained as both wave and particle. The child, trying to explain why the aquarium water has gone down a few inches, is not helped to make knowledge when the teacher gives the explanation: evaporation. But the child may be helped by being encouraged to find as many reasons for the disappearance as possible, to look for other places where moisture has disappeared, and to test possible answers to see which seems best. Likewise, the feelings experienced by the poet or artist are not the only feelings possible of expression. The child, too, can be encouraged to give form to unique feelings, by creating poetry and other works of art. Knowledge about man may likewise be discovered anew by the child as he sees with his own eyes, hears with his own ears, and is given opportunities to try to explain or to express feeling. To complement the child's making of his own knowledge and trusting of his question asking and answer finding, the child can also be introduced to the history of knowledge making in certain fields, e.g. the child may be led to trace the development of certain scientific theories, or concepts of number.

As the child begins to order the world, he must become aware that he is doing the ordering; that the world is not, except for the doing of other men, so ordered. The child needs to be introduced early, before the prejudice of one way of knowing becomes fixed, to a variety of ways of knowing. It is, perhaps, unwise to speak of science or social studies in the primary or intermediate grades. Rather the child is introduced to the ways of nature and the ways of people. He should be given opportunities to explore and to express in his own forms. It is not only the scientist who explores the world of nature or people, and who expresses that which he finds. So does the poet, the musician, the artist, the dancer, the philosopher. As the child begins to recognize the values and uses of scientific ways of knowing and of poetic and artistic ways of knowing, then specialization may occur and the child may take on and polish the spectacles of the scientist, the artist, and poet. The two cultures of C. P. Snow,[10] if they exist, start in the elementary school where art and poetry are considered frills rather than essential ways of knowing—necessary ways of knowing—if man is to remain free from the dogma of any one approach to the world.

To be free from the pitfalls of knowledge, and hence to be free to use knowledge effectively and powerfully, is to be aware that knowledge is made by man for his purposes. To be aware that fire was once explained by the escape of a gas called phlogiston, but today is explained by oxidation, is to help the child recognize that our patterns of explanation change. Likewise, to introduce the child to the Ptolemaic ideas as well as to those current today, is to help him build an awareness that the knowledge we have today of the solar system is not what it always was, nor always need be. Knowledge reified and revered as a picture of reality is enslaving and dangerous. The user and beholder of knowledge must be aware of its limitations as well as its power, for only in that way can one use its power. He must make it subservient to use; he must be free to use more than one form of knowledge, recognizing through participation in the making of knowledge that it is man-made. The elementary school, where the child is first introduced to knowledge as a systematic instrument of power, is the ideal place to also introduce the child to its pitfalls, and to ways to transcend these pitfalls in order that the child may become a more powerful person.

Tempered with doubt, knowledge is useful and powerful; polished by criticism it is beautiful and a symbol of man's greatness as a creator. The child must be helped to use knowledge, to make it, and to be sensitive to its beauty and limitations.

NOTES

[1]Maurice Merleau-Ponty, *Problèmes Actuels de la Phenomenologie*, (Paris, 1952), 101, quoted in Remy Kwant, *Encounter* (Pittsburgh: Duquesne University Press, 1960), 11.

[2]Lao Tzu, *The Way of Life*, the Tao Te Ching, trans. R. B. Blakney (New York: A Mentor Book, 1955), 63.

[3]Ernst Cassirer, *An Essay on Man* (Garden City: New York: Doubleday, 1953), 43.

[4]Henri Bergson, "Laughter" in *Comedy: An Essay on Comedy*, ed. Wylie Sypher (Garden City, NY : Doubleday, Anchor Books, 1956), 158.

[5]Henri Bergson, *Introduction to Metaphysics* (New York: The Liberal Arts Press, 1949).

[6]See concepts of sequence and series in George Kubler, *The Shape of Time* (New Haven, CT: Yale University Press, 1962).

[7]For a discussion of time in literature, see Georges Poulet, *Studies in Human Time*, trans. Elliot Coleman (Baltimore: The Johns Hopkins Press, 1956), and Hans Meyerhoff, *Time in Literature* (Berkeley and Los Angeles: University of California Press, 1955).

[8]Alfred N. Whitehead, *Aims of Education and Other Essays* (New York: Macmillan, 1929), 4.

[9]Buson, *An Introduction to Haiku*, trans. Harold G. Hendersons (Garden City: Doubleday Anchor Books, 1958), 109.

[10]C. P. Snow, *Two Cultures and the Scientific Revolution* (New York: Cambridge University Press, 1959), 58.

6

Knowledge
and the Curriculum

(1962)

The schools have always been concerned with knowledge. Organized bodies of knowledge, however, have not always been the basic organizing foci of a set of school experiences. Curricular specialists have proposed at least three major designs or foci for the curriculum. The possible designs are obvious and logical, stemming from an analysis of human existence which posits as fundamental categories: the individual, the society, and the culture. The individual is the basic, irreducible element of all human action. He lives and acts with others in organized and evolving patterns of habitual actions and interactions which is the society. The framework for societal actions, which also provides some cohesion among individuals, is provided by systems of perceiving, thinking, feeling, and acting. The culture or cultural heritage is thus transmitted from one person or generation to another.

CURRICULAR DESIGNS

The specialist may organize curriculum with either the individual, the society, or the culture as the central focus.[1] However, it is obvious to anyone who has taught, that no curriculum focuses only on the individual, or the society, or the culture. Teaching demands that the teacher somehow and in some way, take into consideration all three elements at one time.

The subject matter curriculum, as typified by the subject centered high school or an elementary school organized around school subjects, is based on culture or the cultural heritage. Valued knowledge is parceled into significant and teachable units which will be the major content of a class for a week, month, or semester. The knowledge can be conveniently summarized in textbook form, although few good teachers do or can depend completely on the textbook as the only or even major instructional resource. As is true of any curricular organization, subject matter teaching in the hands of a competent and skilled teacher can be an exciting and meaningful experience for children. It permits experience to be effectively compressed and channeled and provides children with opportunities for discovery and expression. In mathematics, language, the sciences or the arts, the teacher makes available to the child the systematized knowledge in some orderly fashion. At the same time, a good teacher permits and encourages each individual to grab hold of that knowledge in a meaningful way. The good teacher keeps in mind the individuality of each child and the societal context within which they live. He helps children discover the meaning of that knowledge for their own lives, that is, the relationship between that knowledge, their lives, and the society within which they live. Thus children are helped to an education which is "the acquisition of the art of the utilization of knowledge."[2]

At the opposite end of the educational ideology, is that curricular organization which starts its analysis with the individual. In caricature, the Freudian approach to this child-centered curriculum is described most hilariously, and perhaps inaccurately, in *Auntie Mame*.[3] More accurately, Hopkins'[4] proposal provides a rationale for the approach in one of its variations, and Miel and Brogan[5] provide some extremely fine examples of the approach for a part of the curriculum. The logic of the approach is that the curriculum need not be organized in advance around topics of a subject matter field. By very careful working and planning with children, their own interests, needs, and explorations can lead to appropriate curricular content. With a skilled and knowledgeable teacher, this focus can be stimulating and valuable for the children and the society. Given such a teacher and adequate resources, it is assumed that the current or immediate concerns of the children will lead into important fields of knowledge and into the significant social and economic concerns of the society. Children's appetite and need for knowledge will keep pace with their expanding interests if they constantly explore and express at their own growing edge. A teacher who begins with the children's expanding concerns, but who does not help them see the value of knowledge in their own growth, and in society, ill serves the children.

In the late twenties and early thirties a group of specialists proposed that the recurring problems or situations which all members of a society must face could be organizing foci for the curriculum. In the social studies curriculum the approach was suggested by Marshall and Goetz.[6] The most recent proponent of this focus was Stratemeyer[7] who identifies "persistent life situations" that all people face. In these proposals it is assumed that individuals face recurring problems, situations, or social processes common to all or most societies. For instance, all people must communicate, find means of transportation, build and maintain shelter, etc. Because the child is also concerned with problems of communication, food and clothing, etc., these processes or problems become the basis for organizing the curriculum. As the child's awareness extends beyond his own family and community these same processes are studied in other geographical or historical communities. Again, the effectiveness of the approach is dependent upon skilled and knowledgeable teachers, for the teacher brings into the classroom the necessary and significant knowledge which helps the child deal more powerfully with these recurring problems or situations in his own life and society.

The pros and cons of each of these approaches have been the subject of lively debates and heated feelings since World War II. The attacks of Bestor[8] on the child- and social-centered curricula and his advocacy of a subject matter or disciplined approach presaged the current interest of educators and others[9] in the disciplines as organizing foci for the curriculum. The valuable efforts of mathematicians and scientists in developing more adequate math and science programs are being followed by linguists and social scientists who also seek to establish more adequate discipline-centered, or subject-centered curricula. These current efforts do not replace, but build upon earlier efforts to improve the curriculum. However, the continuity of curricular thought can be seen only with some historical perspective.

To discuss in more detail various aspects of the elementary school curriculum, a consistent point of view is needed. The following point of view approaches a subject matter orientation. The essence of the approach, however, emerges from earlier considerations of the nature of knowledge and the nature of the child as a member of the human community. The emphasis is warranted only if the teacher recognizes that the child and teacher share the same human condition: that they are explorers, constantly striving to order their feelings and sensations; that they encounter others through speech and conversation; and that they must assume responsibility for building a world in which each may realize his potential. This means, above all, that in the classroom children need the freedom, within the limits imposed by the teaching situation, to converse and to discover, and to own the instruments of power created and conserved by others.

THE PRIMACY OF LANGUAGE

The language experiences are the most significant experiences of the school day. The basic language patterns are formed in the home, but the school program should be designed to extend the language competence of the child and to bring to his awareness the power and beauty of language. Present programs focus primarily on the development of the skills of reading, writing, speaking and listening, the importance of which is readily recognized by educators, parents, and publishers.

The significance of language, however, extends beyond the skills of reading, writing, speaking, and listening. Language is an intimate link between the various forms of knowing, and the child's thinking, perceiving, and feeling.[10] Not only do children have the potential to use language skillfully in reading, writing, speaking, and listening; they can also become aware of the increased power and freedom to act in the world so created, controlled, and enjoyed. With increased awareness, power, and language, children can become more sensitive to the development of knowledge and the channeling of imagination. Children can recognize that language is indeed "a pathway to the realization of ourselves."[11] To develop an awareness of the full potential of language as an instrument of power and beauty, the language program has to be more than the development of the basic language skills. Opportunities exist or may be found in the regular ongoing language usage in the classroom, in play with, and enjoyment of language, in experiences which develop vocabulary, and in the study of language.

LANGUAGE USAGE IN THE CLASSROOM

Prior to the development of writing skill, conversation and discussion are the primary language vehicles of children. Whereas both may get out of hand until children identify appropriate limits, they are vital language activities. Through conversation and discussion children gradually order their experiences into significant forms which can be checked against the forms of others. As children struggle to find the appropriate words to convey their thoughts to others, they discover the relationship between language and their own memory and imaginings, and begin to recognize the language wealth that each has inherited. It is through conversation and discussion that children discover that language is not simply a functional activity: the asking and answering of questions. A conversation, and some discussions, can be free and easy engagements in which flights of fancy are combined with bits of reality, leading nowhere in particular; yet always leading to closer ties between those conversing and greater realization of who each person is and can become. If children's only or predominate language activity is listening to others, then they have fewer opportunities to make new discoveries, to establish ties, or to gain control of language and consequently their thoughts. Interchange in discussion and conversation requires that children order their own ideas and to try to discover the order and meanings in the words of others; a life-long activity which profits from an early start.

To create more opportunities for conversation or discussion in the classroom, the teacher needs to further refine two sets of existing skills. The first are the teacher's habits of conversation and discussion with children. As the designated leader and control figure in the classroom, the teacher is responsible for the establishment of routines and the development of valued experiences. The teacher guides the interest and behavior of the child, frequently by speaking to the children. He also listens to the children, and the listening is crucial if the children are to engage in significant conversation and discussion. Careful listening by the teacher helps the child by providing an inter-personal situation in which the child knows that his words, and more important, his thoughts, are welcomed and wanted.[12] The child takes the chance to expose himself, trusting that the teacher respects each child, and will encourage each to be more fully present, therefore, the child dares to verbally form thoughts never uttered before. The teacher's listening habits also help the child find more adequate means to express these thoughts and feelings. As the teacher responds to the child's comments he necessarily interprets them, thus providing feedback to the child, and perhaps suggesting words or expressions that might reflect more accurately the child's intent. These listening habits can be contagious. Other children, modeling the teacher, may follow his pattern of listening with respect and responding with meaning.

The second set of skills needed by the teacher to optimize opportunities for conversation and discussion are those which control classroom procedures and routines. Certain times are usually allocated for conversation or group discussion. More opportunities can be identified by re-scrutinizing existing routines. Has the teacher reserved time to converse with individual children? What opportunities do the children have to converse among themselves? Could the beginning and closing of the school day or recess be altered to provide more time for conversation? What discussion opportunities have been created in science, social studies, art, reading, and other parts of the day's program? Could the activities be restructured somewhat to provide more opportunities for planning, evaluation, pooling information and ideas, posing and answering questions? Verbally active children can be as disconcerting as physically active ones. The solution, however, is not to silence children; this sacrifices significant language development to order. The most efficient and satisfying solution is to create activities with meaningful and legitimate opportunities for conversation and discussion among teacher and children. This requires careful planning. The teacher must compose experiences which have built-in opportunities for ordered conversation, or discussion. If these activities are carefully planned, the teacher can devote major attention to the conversation or discussion rather than to discipline. These activities must be perceived by the children as demanding meaningful speech. With sufficient opportunity for legitimate speech, the children should require fewer opportunities for mischievous speech.

Opportunities for imaginative speech, storytelling and listening, dramatic play, role playing, and other fanciful activities are as important as opportunities for conversation and discussion. Children, at times, use imaginative speech in factual situations, until they begin to realize that there is a difference between imaginings and reality. The distinction between the two is not developed by re-pressing the imaginative use of language, but by enabling the children to recognize that various forms of speech are appropriate in different situations. Imaginative speech has a place, as has functional speech. It is through the development of fanciful speech that the imagination of children is enriched and channeled, and the capacity for storytelling, poetry, drama, short stories, and novels developed. Keats' advice is appropriate:

> Then let winged Fancy wander
> Through the thought still spread beyond her:
> Open wide the mind's cage-door,
> She'll dart forth, and cloudward soar.
> Oh sweet Fancy! let her loose;
> (John Keats, from "Fancy")[13]

To wait until children can write before encouraging them to indulge their fancy is to postpone the disciplining of imaginative thought by language for three or four years. The primary or intermediate grade teacher interested in the relationship between imagination and thought needs to identify opportunities for fanciful speech. Possible opportunities are dramatic play, storytelling by teacher and children, acting out scenes from social studies, music, or reading, and story and poetry writing in the later grades.

As children develop writing competency, i.e., as their writing begins to keep time with their thoughts, some of the freer uses of language can be relegated to writing. The language contact between teacher and individual student can be via writing if the teacher reads and comments upon the written work. Written language may be more than reports of materials read. Writing should be the sincere efforts of the child to find written form for information, ideas, and imaginings which might otherwise remain diffuse. The teacher serves three functions in facilitating the development of meaningful written language. The first is to provide numerous and various writing opportunities which encourage all children, at some time, to give form to newly emerging ideas. The second function is more or less an alter-ego function: the teacher helps the child find the right word or expression and encourages him to develop his own appropriate style as he crystallizes his owns feeling and thoughts on paper.[14] The teacher's third function is that of critic. A critic is not a person who finds picayune errors and rewards accordingly, but a person sympathetic to the writer's intent who responds to the integrity of feeling, form, and technique. The continued improvement of writing skills requires that the child eventually internalize the critic role. The teacher models how criticism can contribute to good writing.

Recognizing the possibility of and the need for more written expression, the teacher needs to inspect present routines to determine how opportunities for significant writing can be increased. Are book reports simply reports, or personal reactions demanding careful reading and careful internal scrutiny of one's feeling and thoughts? Are reports in science and social studies simply factual writings and descriptions or attempts to help the child think through his encounters with new worlds of nature, people or knowledge? Are free imaginative writings encouraged frequently to help the child develop the habit of accepting, valuing and polishing his fancies? Is the teacher a supporting, encouraging alter-ego and a sympathetic critic aware of the child's intent and knowledgeable of more significant forms?

VOCABULARY DEVELOPMENT

The easy, automatic exchange of words in conversation, reading, and the mass media makes words very common. Vocabulary development is not simply the building of a store of words for future use. Seen only as letter combinations and muscular movings of air to be stored in the memory, they are nothing; counterfeit bills to be exchanged for other words. But as symbols of near infinite conceptual possibilities, they may be exchanged for new thoughts, new perceptions, and new visions. To conceive vocabulary development as an organization and refinement of the child's conceptual and perceptual powers is to recognize the function and significance of vocabulary in the life of the child. So conceived, experiences composed to develop vocabulary are experiences to extend awareness, intensify attention, sharpen discriminations, and refine abstractions.

Consequently, new words are not simply made available to the children with the instruction to use them in a sentence. The teacher, and eventually the children, must see each new word as a reshaping and sharpening of the child's perceptual-conceptual structures, not just an addition to the child's word bank. New words are not introduced in isolation; the referent and usage of the word are also introduced. Colors and hues are made visible, nuances and rhythms of sounds made audible, objects of nouns brought into the visual field, modifiers of action acted out, proper nouns brought to life by stories. Discussion is important. Children should compare well-used words with newly discovered ones to identify how they differ, how they are similar, how connotations and denotations vary, and how feelings and ideas can be altered by using various words. In the later grades the origins and history of the words can be discussed to illustrate changes in meanings and feelings.

The teacher interested in stirring up the children's interest in words is himself intrigued by words. Part of the regularly scheduled language experiences of all ages can be vocabulary-perceiving-conceiving experiences, in which the teacher either introduces new words and their consequences or inspires the children to do so. This activity need not be functional, in which the words are then put to use. Use is desirable, not mandatory; but interest and enthusiasm are desirable and mandatory. In the intermediate grades, children can be encouraged to maintain their own "new word" list or thesaurus. Each room, in all grades including the kindergarten, can have a bulletin board for new or unique words, for which teacher and children assume joint responsibility. Teacher and children can develop a second language sense with which they keep a lookout for new usages, even mis-usages, and new words in ongoing conversations, discussions, and writings. An interest in slang and its origin, in the use of words in advertising, and in the unique usages of families or ethnic groups sensitizes children to the developing and changing vocabulary resources. To help children become aware of the significance and power of words, is to help them gain control over language and knowing, thus freeing them from the confines of language prejudices.

LANGUAGE PLAY AND ENJOYMENT

Language is more than a mere tool. It is also a creation of and for great beauty, and a toy for pleasurable playfulness. Demands and requirements in some schools detract from the beauty and fun of language. Language play and enjoyment add to one's freedom from the restrictive characteristic of language used blindly or without awareness that it is a magnificent creation of human beings. Paul Valery draws a charming parallel between language and movement:

> Think of a very small child: the child we have all been bore many possibilities within him. After a few months of life he has learned, at the same or almost the same time, to speak and to walk. He has acquired two types of action. That is to say that he now possesses two kinds of potentiality from which the accidental circumstances of each moment will draw what they can, in answer to his varying needs and imaginings.
>
> Having learned to use his legs, he will discover that he cannot only walk, but run; and not only walk and run, but dance. This is a great event. He has at that moment both invented and discovered a kind of secondary use for his limbs, a generalization of his formula of movement. In fact, whereas walking is afterall a rather dull and not easily perfectible action, this new form of action, the Dance, admits of an infinite number of creations and variations or figures.
>
> But will he not find an analogous development in speech? He will explore the possibilities of his faculty of speech; he will discover that more can be done with it than to ask for jam and deny his little sins. He will grasp the power of reasoning; he will repeat to himself words that he loves for their strangeness and mystery.
>
> So, parallel with Walking and Dancing, he will acquire and distinguish the divergent types, Prose and Poetry.[15]

As T. S. Eliot points out in his introduction to *The Art of Poetry*,[16] the parallel between walking and dancing and prose and poetry may not be valid, nevertheless the distinction between the functional and playful or enjoyable aspects of movement and speech is insightful and valuable. In this age of science, when every word counts and must have an exact meaning, the enjoyable freedom of playing with language is too frequently neglected. Yet it is through the play that children feel the molding power of language, that they gain control of its fluid characteristics and make it subservient to their intentions. The sound in the ear, look in the eye, and feel in the mouth are qualities of words as enjoyable and as evocative as their impression in the mind. The power of one word to influence the meaning and feeling of another provides infinite opportunity for playful puzzling with and significant sampling from language. This play with and enjoyment of language can arouse the child's interest in and sensitivity to language. It can arouse interest in poetry, and give beauty and charm to speech. Language play can enliven the child's exploration into the greatest of wonders—language.

Again the teacher needs to scrutinize the classroom use of language to discover more opportunities to play with and enjoy language. Poetry offers innumerable opportunities to start a quest into language or game with it. The "slishy-sloshy" in the poem "Galoshes" offers a wonderful opening into the feel of words and the relationship between the words and their referents.

> Susie's galoshes
> Make splishes and sploshes
> And slooshes and sloshes,
> As Susie steps slowly
> Along in the slush.
> They stamp and they tramp
> On the ice and concrete,
> They get stuck in the muck and the mud;
> But Susie likes much best to hear
> The slippery sluch
> As it slooshes and sloshes,
> And splishes and sploshes
> All round her galoshes
> (Rhoda W. Bacmeister, "Galoshes")[17]

The word creations of Lewis Carroll start streams of word construction that mimic common usage. What could a child do after mouthing,

> 'Twas brillig, and the slithy toves
> Did gyre and gimble in the wabe:

All mimsy were the borogoves
And the mome raths outgabe.
Beware the Jabberwock, my son!
The jaws that bite, the claws that catch!
Beware the Jubjub bird, and shun
The frumious Bandersnatch![18]

Children's books, such as *A Gaggle of Geese*;[19] *Ounce, Dice, Trice*;[20] and *Sparkle and Spin*[21] may start the children down new avenues of language awareness and exploration. With a second language sense, the teacher finds and uses language during the day that sounds different, feels different, looks different, or which somehow stands out from ordinary language usage. Through activities filled with rich language, a teacher excites the children to keep their senses open for new feelings, and their minds open for new creations.

LANGUAGE STUDY

The language arts program is usually focused on the development of necessary and important language skills. The intent of the teacher, and the textbooks, is to help the child develop and refine his use of language as he reads, speaks, writes, and listens. But the phenomena of language is too wonderful to treat only as a tool. It is a vast and significant creation of man. Like all man-made things it has a history, a future, an organization, and near infinite variations. The study of grammar is frequently the only study of language made by an elementary school child, which too often becomes a study of the "shoulds" of language. But language is more than grammar. Hopefully the more that is known about all aspects of language the more competent and powerful will be the user of the language. Children's interests alight on language, as their preoccupations with codes, pig-Latin, and slang indicate. In the later grades, these interests can lead into a study of the history of language, the patterns of usage, the philosophy or science of language, and the comparative study of languages.

Perhaps little but a cursory beginning can be made of the history or comparative study, for elementary-age children lack the perspective for much historical depth. Yet the history of words or particular usages might be investigated as the children look at old books, listen to older people talk about expressions they used as children, and investigate the dictionary etymologies. Foreign language records and printed materials, and the availability of people who speak or know more than one language should make possible comparative study of words and common patterns of usage of several languages, including Asian and other languages. More practical and perhaps more valuable for the elementary school child, are studies of the nature of language and patterns of usage in their society. Grammar is one such study, dealing with hardened or fixed patterns of usage as identified by authorities.[22] In the upper elementary grades, as children start to use codes or pig-Latin and become copiers of adolescent slang, they could easily become engaged in a study of the agreements needed with respect to such codes, or the agreements which guide adolescent slang. They could make comparative studies of the language used in the family, in peer groups, or in mass media. With teachers skilled in modern linguistics or semantics children could easily move into simple, yet penetrating, study of how language actually operates: the patterning of usages, the referential characteristic of language, and the relationships between language and thought. Although there are few guides for elementary teachers to follow, this is an area laden with significant possibilities for intermediate-age children; an age when children's interest in language is frequently dampened by adults who seek conformity rather than exploration, understanding, and appreciation.

SCIENTIFIC TOOLS OF EXPLORATION AND EXPRESSION

Language is the primary symbolic medium into which man transforms his explorations, encounters, and discoveries of self and others. The transformations are of two types: scientific and aesthetic. Scientific exploration has become focused and systematic, specialized rules of usage and vocabularies have been developed, and complementary symbol systems have been introduced. For educational purposes, a simplified four-step version of a so-called scientific method has been frequently presented, adopted from Dewey.[23] Most current theorists[24] would agree that there is not a scientific method, but rather methods. To facilitate a discussion of scientific tools of exploration and expression some organization of the methods of science is necessary. The following categories are proposed as a possible organizing scheme: criteria for knowing and explanation, classification and language systems, and complementary symbol systems.

Criteria for Knowing and Explanation

One characteristic of the sciences is the acceptance of clearly established objective criteria for knowing and explaining phenomena. The authority for a claim, fact, generalization, or explanation is never simply the authority of a person, but an authority based upon sensate data, accepted trains of reasoning or inference, or clearly stated and accepted assumptions or postulates. A person stating a fact, making a claim, offering a generalization or prediction, or giving an explanation must be able to answer the question, "How do you know?" The answer must be based upon criteria acceptable to scientists, which are more than feelings, intuitions, or hunches. The latter have a place in science as means for generating potential answers, not for verifying or establishing evidence or answers. The various sciences have different criteria for knowing and explanation, or can emphasize the knowing more or less than the explaining. In history, the date of Columbus' discovery of America might be questioned, or the oft-stated fiction of Washington's cutting down the cherry tree. In both cases, "the how do you know" demands the establishment of the validity of inference from authentic primary or secondary data to the supposed statement. Can the claimant identify primary and secondary evidence and indicate his chain of reasoning? In astronomy, the question might be asked, how it is known that Venus is a planet rotating around the sun. Again, the primary data must be identified and the chain of inference established. In geology, or other taxonomic sciences, the membership of a given specimen to a class can be questioned, i.e. "How do you know that rock is limestone?" Here the answer requires identifying the criteria of inclusion to or exclusion from a given class of specimens. In the sciences which offer explanation, the claimant must be prepared to show the relationship between a series of events and certain theoretical postulates. "Why does this piece of iron attract these nails?" requires identifying the iron as a magnet, and offering the theoretical notions of magnetic attraction. A question such as "How do you know it will rain tomorrow?" requires identifying telltale signs or data, and following acceptable patterns of statistical inference.

The questions, "How do you know?" or "How do you explain?" are crucial instruments of scientific explanation and expression. They require the person stating a fact or an explanation to justify his verbal utterance, and to indicate the relationship between that utterance and some sensory data. Clear and reasonably unambiguous relationships between symbol and sense data is a mark of scientific expression. This questioning attitude, considered the basic component of scientific exploration, gives children added power as they encounter descriptions and explanations of natural or social phenomena. Consequently, a teacher interested in fostering this attitude would need to encourage the "How do you know?" question. This can be done by asking the question of children as they relate incidents or try to explain events. Any number of children's statements are fair game for this "How do you know?" question, e.g., "That is a Monarch butterfly," "The water in the aquarium must have evaporated," "This building is twenty-four years old," "The Russians want war," "It takes sunlight seven minutes to reach the earth." Reciprocally, statements by the teacher or in books are also fair game for a child's question of "How do you know?" If a teacher is really concerned with developing this questioning attitude, then the children need to be encouraged to doubt and question. Calling attention to dubious statements in books and bringing under question one's own infallibility are ways that a teacher can foster these attitudes that are basic to science.

The "How do you know?" doesn't go far enough, for children developing scientific tools of exploration and expression need to go beyond the factual, they need to reach for explanations. Teachers can help children go beyond sense data into theory by asking, "How do you explain … ? "What would happen if … ?" A child noticing that the water has gone down an inch in the aquarium can be asked to try to explain what happened to it. Likewise, children can be asked to explain why ice floats, why bees are attracted to flowers, why the moon seems to have different shapes, why it is hot in summer and cold in winter, and so on. Attempting to answer such questions encourages formulation and testing of hypotheses, and leads children into experimentation. Simple description leaves the child at the level of sense data; pushing for possible explanation forces the child to operate in the realm of the theoretical and into the unique explanatory systems of the individual sciences.

Classification and Language Systems

Each individual science contains or is made up of a specialized vocabulary and language system. As is true of all language systems each science has particular ways of abstracting significant patterns of sensory data from the flux and flow of phenomena or events; i.e. each science has a taxonomy and postulated abstractions which explain sensory data. Children can be easily introduced to the specialized vocabulary of a particular science. More important, the child needs to be able to form or identify classes of phenomena which correspond to the class terms or words. As children study trees, they should know that there are a variety of oaks. The various class names become important labels for talking about different varieties. But as, or perhaps, more important, is the ability to distinguish from among the variety of oak leaves, a skill requiring careful observation of the similarities and differences of oak leaves. The study of other plants, animals, and minerals requires the same double focus. To develop the child's awareness of the classification and language system, a teacher needs to provide two sets of experiences. The first are those experiences which help the child identify and distinguish among related phenomena. In studying birds, animals, plants, or any other class of phenomena with a major taxonomic system, the child would need many experiences to develop an awareness of the characteristics of given classes; opportunities to compare and distinguish among minerals, shells, leaves, organisms, simple machines, land regions, or cultural groups. The second set of experiences are those which provide awareness of the vocabulary which refer to these groups or classes. The grouping experiences need not consistently precede the naming experience. As the child becomes aware of the relationship between class names and groups of things, an introduction of class names can sharpen perception of the phenomena under consideration.

When children are able to use specialized language with reasonable ease new possibilities for exploration are opened. Every science has a language structure or organization which points out possible relationships among sensory data. Abstract concepts and theories bring together into logical matrices numerous sensory phenomena, making possible explanations and predictions extending beyond common sense explanation. For example, the ideas of force, friction, electrons, gravity, etc., help explain phenomena of motion, electricity, and space travel. As children become conversant with the significant concepts of the scientific languages, and engage in conversation or communication with those who use these languages, new sensory and intellectual experiences become possible.

Complementary Symbol Systems

Scientific exploration and expression is often dependent on other symbol systems for organizing and manipulating data. Mathematics and maps are examples of complementary symbol systems used in scientific exploration. Mathematics is an abstract, logical system concerned with quantities and relationships. It requires the user to be adept at identifying quantitative groups or sets in the environment and manipulating these sets in various ways. Numerals are symbols for sets of various sizes and the child must be aware of how they can refer to groups of objects. Equally important, the child must be able to engage in operations of addition, subtraction, multiplication, and division, not simply in the number system but among sets of things. To add, subtract, multiply, divide, means that someone does something to something. Adding means to bring two or more sets of something together; subtraction to take a sub-set away from a set of things and so on. Hence the child must be aware of the semantics of mathematical systems i.e., the rules of reference. The power of mathematics stems largely from the syntactical relationship in the math system, for formal relationships exist among numbers and other mathematical symbols which govern their use. A child, aware of these syntactical rules, is able to manipulate the symbols in a variety of ways, and consequently operate more powerfully in the environment.

In geography, map symbols complement language in the organization and expression of the geographer's data. Children must become familiar with the semantic rules governing the use of map symbols, i.e., to decode a map the legend must be known. Hence, the map symbols need to be internalized in much the same way as language symbols. Children need opportunities to make or encounter abstraction in their environments which are best coded into map symbols. They need to know the rules for encoding geographical information. In order to read a map, a child needs to be able to decode the symbols into their corresponding abstractions. Treated in this way, using map symbols requires some of the same skills as using other symbol systems, and the child needs the same opportunities to play with, make, and communicate using map symbols as with other symbol systems.

AESTHETIC TOOLS OF EXPLORATION AND EXPRESSION

The arts are often seen as vehicles of expression only, which is unfortunate. They are also ways of exploring the world and of encountering other people. Artists bring skills of perception and organization as well as skills of expression to their explorations and encounters. The visual artist sees more, the musician hears more, the dancer detects movements missed by others, and the dramatist is more aware of the ebb and flow of emotion and entanglements. The final expressive product is not made at the easel, or typewriter, or studio, but is composed as the artist experiences, and organizes perceptions and emotions through a chosen medium. The final product is refined as the artist struggles to bring the medium and experiences together. The artist and the scientist both engage in the creative transformation of experience into significant symbols. They differ in the media of transformation and the criteria of validity or acceptability of the final symbolic form. The sciences primarily use language and mathematical symbols. The criteria of acceptability deal with the objectivity of meaning, the predictability or power of understanding of the transformation, and the fruitfulness for future exploration. Some of the arts depend heavily, or completely, upon language as their major medium, others depend upon pigments and forms, tones and rhythms, movement, and multiple media as in opera and drama. The criteria of acceptability differ significantly from those of science, and include skillful and competent use of the media, and subjective as well as objective meanings. The acceptability of an art form is dependent upon the nature of the criticism which is operating at the time, which can change through time. The processes of aesthetic exploration and expression are a function of technical skill with the medium, heightened sensitivity to the sensory data, and craft in using the art form.

Skill with Media

As with the arts of language, the use of other art media requires skill. The painter must know the potentialities of the pigments, how to use the brushes, and how to arrange pigments on a flat surface to create awareness of shape and depth. The musician must know and have control over an instrument and the sounds it can produce. The dancer needs to know and control the muscles of the body. The orchestra conductor must know how the component parts of the orchestra can be blended. All of the arts require the artist to know the potentialities of the medium, its range of possibilities, and its limits. Furthermore, the artist must be able to use the medium to bring out its full potential, and yet do so in an almost unconscious way; for in artistic expression, the primary awareness is on intent, not on the instruments or toils of expression. Two aspects of this technical skill may be identified: the cognitive mastery of the medium and the skilled almost automatic ability to use the medium.

To gain cognitive control of a medium, children need opportunities to explore the various qualities of a medium and to discover what can be accomplished through its use. As the child uses clay, the opportunity to play with clay—to feel, pound, roll, and mold it—are not meaningless activities but the discovery of the clay's potential. Watercolors, oils, dance, musical instruments also offer opportunity for play, for testing out what can be done with the pigments or tools. To move too quickly into meaningful expression is to cut short the opportunities for cognitive control. This is not to imply that such discovery cannot and is not made as the child engages in expressive activity, for it is. Children need opportunities to explore freely, not merely incidentally, as they try to express their feelings and experiences. The response of the teacher to this exploration can help the child verbalize discoveries about the potentials of the medium. But discoveries of what a particular medium can accomplish are not simply all the result of self discovery, for the discoveries of others can also be significant. Study of the accomplishments of others support the child's movement toward more focused explorations through the confirmation and questioning of what others have already found out, and perhaps stir the child to move beyond these shared discoveries.

For expressive purposes, the child's use of the medium needs to be nearly automatic although never to the degree of being a slave to a particular set of habits. Using a medium for expressive purposes, the child can discover the technical skills that are lacking—use of graded washes, glazing, particular dance steps. Therefore, time is needed not only for exploration of media and expression, but practice time for mastery of the technical skills which require repetition as do other skills. Repetition is needed in painting and dancing as well as handwriting or basketball. Children need time to discover what a medium can do, and how they can make it serve this expressive potential.

Heightened Sensitivity to Sensory Data

The acceptance of scientific knowledge as the instrument for social transactions has encouraged the use of intellectual abstractions and theories. Consequently, the senses have become less significant in the general life of the individual. Yet, aesthetic exploration and expression require heightened sensitivity to the sensory components of experience. Awareness of colors, shapes and their interrelationships are necessary for the visual artist, as is sound and rhythm for the musical artist. Awareness of the sensory aspects is heightened by increased participation in expressive activity. By having more opportunities to paint, children more easily see the world around them in terms of the watercolors or the temperas being used. If engaged in musical composition or dance every day, the children increase their awareness of patterns and rhythms, sound and movement. This sensitivity is also increased by frequent opportunities to behold the aesthetic expressions of others. The availability of excellent art should help the children become more aware of how artists see or hear or perceive the world about them. A teacher eager to increase the child's awareness of sensory data could increase the opportunities for expression, for beholding a variety of works of art, and for discussing sensory experience.

The Craft of the Art

Heightened awareness of sensory data and skill with media are necessary requirements for aesthetic exploration and expression. With these, children may reach out into their environments to make new discoveries, encounter new phenomena and people, and compose them into new patterns of significance for themselves and others. The composing does not come easily, but demands the unification of awareness, knowledge, and skill into a craft. Effort and practice are required, as in all disciplines; but also criticism and opportunities to become aware of and immersed in the craft of others. As in scientific exploration and expression, the child need not be satisfied with the first picture, poem, or dance. First attempts can be considered hypotheses, trial runs; to be confirmed by exploring and expressing anew to see if the first attempt includes all the sensory data. At this stage, the role of criticism becomes significant. Artists internalize the role of the critic for their own purposes, but continue to depend upon the outside critic for other views and reactions. Hence, the need for sympathetic reaction to the work by others—the attempt to identify intent, the concern for appropriateness of media and form to intent, the level of skill attained, and the over-all craft of the expression.

The child becomes aware of the craft by careful, sympathetic, and critical study of those who use the same medium. As in the scientific activity, children behold and study the work of scientists, so in aesthetic exploration and discovery children need opportunities to behold and study the works of artists.

THE NATURAL AND THE SOCIAL WORLD AS FIELDS FOR EXPLORATION AND EXPRESSION

The comments above suggest a more or less typical subject-centered curriculum, with time available for language arts, mathematics, social studies, science, and art experiences. However, any division of experience is bound to be inadequate for all purposes or at all levels. Whereas this subject organization might be logical at certain levels, it does not appear logical for the primary grades or even for the intermediate grades. The early experiences of children simply are not structured into these neat compartments, as Dewey and others have indicated. If the basic motives of the child are exploration and expression, then the organization for the curriculum must be one in which this exploration and expression can find a more natural outlet, until the child's exploration and expression can be channeled by the established disciplines. As the child grows, these motives do tend to follow the disciplines as Dewey suggested in *The Child and the Curriculum*[25] although not all of a child's curiosities can be so channeled. However, in the early years, children's explorations and expressions are more diffuse. Nevertheless, in the school some ordering and structuring is necessary to increase the teacher's control and to facilitate planning ahead for necessary resources and materials. It can be assumed that whereas the child's curiosity is unstructured with respect to form, it is not unstructured with respect to content. The child's curiosity is naturally oriented toward people and the objects of the natural world. The child may be interested in flowers or plants or weather or neighborhood and family, but that interest does not take specific scientific or aesthetic form. In order to prevent the hardening of the categories of knowledge, the pitfalls and disadvantages as discussed in "Knowledge: An Instrument of Man" (see chapter five) it seems important that children have opportunities to organize their contacts with the world into a variety of forms. Primacy should not be given to one form. Children should not be led to believe that scientific ways are superior to aesthetic ways, or that scientific knowledge is true whereas aesthetic knowledge is feeling and hence dubious. As children begin to realize that both scientific and aesthetic modes can be brought to bear on the same natural or social phenomena then specialization by subject matter becomes more logical. It is convenient to think of the school day in terms of opportunities for exploration and expression into the worlds of people and nature. As children move into these new worlds they can use both scientific and aesthetic tools to aid them. The major problem becomes that of the interplay between periods of exploration and expression and periods necessary to sharpen and polish the tools and skills of inquiry and expression.

The Social World

Applying this framework to the social world, a teacher should ask what parts of the social world are available to children, and what tools of exploration do they have or are they capable of developing? Until children have the ability to read rather fluently, or to interpret other symbolic media, the social world open to them is the world of people in their immediate surroundings, or brought to them through TV, or through conversations with people close to them. How can children give form and order to these encounters? The child is not yet able to write fluently, but is able to talk and discuss. A child is able to draw and paint at one level of meaning and very able to act. Consequently, language, the visual arts, and the dramatic arts become major vehicles for guiding and organizing explorations and expressions. If these vehicles increase the child's penetration into the world, the teacher should ask, "How can I help children become more powerful in searching into the world of people? How can I help order their findings into meaningful patterns which maintain their curiosity?" The patterns could well be questions and answerings which point to specific social sciences, such as sociology, economics, and geography. However, the results of the inquiries might also be poetic in form; not the asking and answering of questions, but the composing of poetry, expressed verbally and recorded by the teacher. Other children might compose imaginary stories of the neighborhood. Dramatic play is a natural organizing vehicle for young children, as the playing of house and school indicates. Visual arts using tempera and crayon are also vehicles for the expression of social encounters. Teachers skilled in dance or music can encourage children to compose their searchings and explorations into dance or musical forms. As children attempt to organize their explorations using diverse media, the teacher can easily call attention to their need to refine their skills of asking and answering questions, composing poetry, drawing and painting, and dramatic play. Drill and practice in these skills follow naturally from their identification. Children should come away from these experiences with increased competence to explore, with greater depth and penetration the world about them; and to order the chaos that greets them.

As the children reach out beyond their own time and space through reading and other media their social world is extended almost infinitely. Exploration and expressive activities remain the same, although now children can explore through the eyes and ears of others. A variety of materials in social studies is needed if children are to have opportunities to find their own meanings, rather than being content only with the meanings of others. A wealth of materials encourage children to organize diverse stimuli into their own patterns of meaning. Children can expand their question asking capability through increased familiarization with the various social sciences, geography, sociology, economics, history, political science, and perhaps anthropology. Children's aesthetic orderings can extend beyond discussion and dramatic play into writing poetry and stories, using various visual arts; clay, music and more complex stage arts. As the children attempt to use these scientific and aesthetic tools of exploration and expression, time is required to make sharper the instruments, developing vocabularies and the various methods of search and organization, mastering the skills and craft of the arts.

A similar approach to the natural world is possible. The emphasis is not on science, per se, but on the exploration of the natural world via all of the techniques of searching and expression as developed over time. The emphasis on science as the only vehicle of exploration of nature is limiting. It denies the value of the arts in creating an awareness of the wonders of nature. As children study plants they need to look at them through more than the eye of the botanist who dissects them, but fails to put them back together. Tennyson's "Flower in the Crannied Wall" is of as much significance as the knowledge that plants have stamens and pistils, for it moves on to a new form of searching and meaning. Artists, such as Van Gogh, have also looked carefully at flowers and have recorded their observations. The study of the earth, the heavens, animals, flowers, and machines are not just scientific studies, but aesthetic studies as well. So again, children must be introduced to the possibilities of search and expression via the arts as well as the sciences. As children begin to recognize the characteristics of scientific knowledge and the characteristics of aesthetic knowledge, then they can move into a more careful study of a science or an art, becoming more skilled with the crafts of each.

Art separated from the study of man or the study of nature is not art, but technique. Likewise, science removed from the study of man or nature is also technique. Either separated from each other provides a prejudice and ignorance which is difficult to break down once formed. The elementary school is the place to create the awareness that they belong together, for it is here that they are logically connected as tools for personal growth.

RESPONSIBILITY FOR SELF AND WORLD THROUGH SOCIAL ACTION

Responsibility for one's own action or for the affairs and state of the world does not begin when a person reaches some age or position. Responsibility is a slowly evolving attitude and awareness, channeled, developed and made more powerful through cultural tools. These tools are the customs of social action, social intercourse, and political or governmental action. To know of the tools is not the same as having them internalized and part of oneself, ready for action. Hannah Arendt indicates a relationship between one's love for the world and one's responsibility for it. She has said that only those who love the world enough to assume responsibility for it should be teacher.[26] It is possible and perhaps even necessary for the teacher to create a living situation in the classroom in which children's attitudes of love and, hopefully, responsibility can be developed. This requires an openness among the people who live in the classroom so that love can develop and flourish. It requires that children assume increasing responsibility for making their classroom world, and that they have opportunities to develop the skills necessary for such responsibility. To provide the openness from which significant human relationships of conversation and care can be developed means that the teacher must be in sufficient control of the living situation in order that children be free and responsible. This is not a control by authority, but a control of significant activity: activity which has meaning and value for the children. It is activity in which the children recognize opportunities for development of their own powers to explore and express, and to interact with others with increased sensitivity, satisfaction, and responsibility. This does not mean that the children have free rein, or that their interests are followed slavishly. It does mean that the teacher design activities in which children have choice and freedom to react verbally. Furthermore it means activities in which social interaction is both possible and perhaps even necessary. It is easy for the teacher to build activities in which the children must do required amounts of work silently, and to enforce the silence by virtue of teacher's power. It is much more difficult to compose activities which demand social involvement of the children, and provide opportunities for exploration, expression and skill development. The teacher interested in providing opportunities for the development of significant relationships among the children needs to scrutinize in detail each part of the day's activities to ask, "How may I significantly involve the children in encounters with others, and gradually increase their social responsibility?"

The teacher must also search the routines of living in the classroom to identify opportunities in which children can assume responsibility for their own behavior and growth, for the conditions of living in the room and in the school community. These need not be housekeeping duties which are more effectively taken care of by the custodian, but activities which transform the room into a more significant place to live, and the activities into more significant growing opportunities for searching, exploring, expressing.

Finally, the teacher helps the children become aware of and develop responsibility for self and others. This requires helping them develop skills of conversation and discussion, of planning together, of identifying and resolving conflicts, of accepting and carrying through on responsibilities, of criticizing their own efforts and planning ahead. It requires the shaping of vision so they can look ahead and dream of that which might be, and building the means by which visions can become actualities. This requires a socially active classroom because social action is the vehicle by which they check their own meanings, become aware of who they are and can be, and help others do the same. Social action does not develop in a vacuum, but comes out of rich classroom experiences, composed initially by the teacher but with opportunities for the children to shape their own personal experiences and involvements.

NOTES

[1]See Virgil Herrick and Ralph Tyler, *Toward Improved Curriculum Theory*, Papers presented at the Conference on Curriculum Theory held at the University of Chicago, October 16-17, 1947 (Chicago: University of Chicago Press, 1950).

[2]A. N. Whitehead, *Aims of Education and Other Essays*. (New York: Macmillan, 1929, A Mentor book, 1949), 16. Page four in the 1957 Free Press edition, *Ed*.

[3]Patrick Dennis, *Auntie Mame; An Irreverent Escapade* (New York: Vanguard, 1955).

[4]Levi Thomas Hopkins, *Interaction: The Democratic Process* (Boston: Heath, 1941).

[5]Alice Miel and Peggy Brogan, *More Than Social Studies* (Englewood Cliffs, New Jersey: Prentice Hall, 1957).

[6]Leon C. Marshall and Rachel Marshall Goetz, *Curriculum-making in the Social Studies, A Social Process Approach* (New York: Scribner, 1936).

[7]Florence Stratemeyer, et. al., *Developing a Curriculum for Modern Living* (New York: Teachers College, Columbia University, Bureau of Publications, 1957).

[8]Arthur Eugene Bestor, *Educational Wastelands, the Retreat from Learning in Our Public Schools* (Urbana: University of Illinois Press, 1953).

[9]Jerome Bruner, *The Process of Education* (Cambridge: Harvard University Press, 1960).

[10]Lev Semenovich Vygotsky, *Thought and Language* (M. I. T. Press and New York: Wiley Press, 1962).

[11]Ernst Cassirer, *The Logic of the Humanities*, trans. Clarence Smith Howe (New Haven: Yale University Press, 1961), 113.

[12]Douglas Steere, *On Listening to Another* (New York: Harper and Brothers, 1955).

[13]John Keats, "Fancy" in *The Poems of John Keats*, ed. Jack Stillinger (Cambridge, MA: Belknap, The Harvard University Press, 1978), 290-293, *Ed.*

[14]See J. Middleton Murray, *The Problem of Style* (London: Oxford University Press, 1922).

[15]Paul Valery, "Poetry and Abstract Thoughts," in *The Art of Poetry.* trans. Denise Folliot (New York: Alfred A. Knopf, and Random House, 1961), 69-70.

[16]T. S. Eliot, "Introduction," *The Art of Poetry.*

[17]Rhoda W. Bacmeister, "Galoshes" from *Very Young Verses*, ed. Barbara Peck Geismer and Antoinette Brown Suter (Boston: Houghton Mifflin Company, 1914).

[18]Lewis Carroll, *Alice's Adventures in Wonderland* (New York: The Heritage Press, 1941).

[19]Eve Merriam, *A Gaggle of Geese* (New York: Knopf, 1960).

[20]Ace Reid, *Ounce, Dice, Trice* (Boston: Little, Brown and Company, 1961).

[21]Ann Rand, *Sparkle and Spin*, (New York: Harcourt, 1957).

[22]Charlton Laird, *The Wonder of Language* (New York: Fawcett World Library, 1957).

[23]John Dewey, *How We Think* (Boston: Heath, 1933).

[24]James B. Conant, *Science and Common Sense* (New Haven: Yale University Press, 1951).

[25]John Dewey, *The School and Society, The Child and the Curriculum* (Chicago: The University of Chicago Press, 1956, originally published 1902).

[26]Hannah Arendt, "Crisis in Education," *Between Past and Future* (New York: Viking Press, 1961).

7

Classroom Action

(1962)

Not all of the child's education in school stems from classroom activity. Contacts with school personnel other than the teacher may be educative, as may school experiences not connected with the classroom. Classroom action is, however, the primary means of education in the school. The social and professional responsibilities of the teacher are fulfilled through the adventures and routines in the classroom. These adventures and routines do not come into existence simply by placing children and materials together; they are generated by the teacher's ways of thinking about what does and can go on in the classroom. These ways of thinking are tools for grasping and shaping the structure of classroom action.

A way of thinking about classroom action is valuable if it helps the teacher gain better control over the design and movement of activity, there is no one way of thinking about these actions. In fact, a review of methods books or of classroom research reports would identify several ways. The teacher's search, then, should be not only for better classroom control, but for a variety of ways to think about classroom action. With this variety, a teacher has greater freedom to design and shape activities for the boys and girls. The freedom can lead to classroom adventures and routines which reflect the teacher's own sense of the meanings and values of life and provide more exciting and significant educational experiences for the children. Classroom action can be thought about in terms of four aspects: (1) the pervasive qualities in the classroom, (2) the dimensions and components of action, (3) the multiple rhythms of action, and (4) the specific behavior or skills of the teacher.

THE QUALITIES OF ACTION IN THE CLASSROOM

Students of classroom action refer frequently to the climate or atmosphere of a classroom. From the studies of Lippitt and White and others[1] have come the terms "democratic," "authoritarian," and "laissez-faire." Others have suggested that classrooms can be identified as teacher-centered, student-centered, and task-centered classrooms. The idea of a "classroom climate" or "atmosphere" suggests that a teacher can foster a tone or spirit which permeates all or most classroom activities, which in turn influences the education of the children. But equally important, if teaching is considered an expressive form, then the classroom climate is also symbolic of the teacher's own views of the meaning and significance of life. Several qualities of the classroom atmosphere could be identified, but only two are hinted at here. These are laughter and conversation. Hopefully they might be indicators of significant educational experiences in the classroom and symbolic of the teachers own meaning of life. Significantly they are also taboo in many classrooms, perhaps because they express a vitality of life uncherished by some teachers.

Laughter is prized in human affairs by Langer and Bergson. For Langer, laughter "seems to arise from a surge of vital feeling. It is a culmination of feeling— a crest of a wave of felt vitality."[2] She disagrees with Bergson who states that "We laugh every time a person gives us the impression of being a thing."[3] He argues that man laughs when behavior is rigid or mechanistic. Laughter is a way of helping one reassert the living qualities of life; of overcoming the rigid, mechanistic, thing-ness in human existence.

These two notions of laughter offer possibilities for better understanding classroom action. Accepting Langer's notion, laughter in the classroom results from "a surge of vital feeling" or "a wave of felt vitality." Laughter coming from children can be considered a sign of élan vital in the classroom. It indicates active, fully alive people, encountering the stumbling stones of experience; overcoming them with humor and joy, and thus expressing enthusiastic affirmation of life. A teacher who promotes laughter as a part of the day's routine, who accepts laughter from children, and who laughs before and with the children can be considered a teacher who enjoys living and who responds to the surge of vitality in the children.

Accepting Bergson's notion, laughter can help children and teacher overcome habits which are no longer efficient or meaningful. If Bergson is correct, laughter can be a social force which helps maintain flexibility and suppleness and fosters continual growth. It can prevent the fixation of mechanical routines and help jar teachers and children out of growth inhibiting ruts. Laughing with a mistake or error can help ease the person into searchings for more effective responses. By reducing tension which frequently accompanies rigidity, laughter helps teacher and children accept change and newness which are so important in education. A teacher who laughs and who encourages laughter is a person who sees himself and the children struggling continually to overcome binding habits, and who respects growth and development more than conformity.

Laughter with children indicates that the teacher shares the human condition with the children.

Conversation in the classroom also expresses acceptance of the basic human situation. Man uses conversation to overcome his aloneness and to check his own meanings with the meanings of others. Through conversation each shares his world with others and discovers his uniqueness. The willingness and ability to converse indicates affirmation of Macmurray's proposition that "to be a person is to be in communication with the other."[4] Conversation is not simply talking. It is talking and listening. It demands internalization of what the other says and reworking of one's own thought and being. It requires a willingness to give of one's self and to receive from the other, and an eagerness to bring the I and the Thou[5] together in a significant act of relationship and living.

Conversation in the elementary classroom is necessary. Children's ways of grasping and shaping the world cannot adequately be developed by socially isolated learning activities and individual drill. Conceptualization is closely tied to language. It is through the expansion of language that the child's conception of the world is modified and expanded. A teacher can appraise and influence children's developing conceptions of the world through conversing with them. Conversation between child and teacher is not sufficient however. Opportunities for children to converse with each other are opportunities to check their meanings and identities with the meanings and identities of others. It is through conversation among children that the individual child learns that aloneness is not the same as loneliness. Indeed, it is through the give and take of conversation that the child establishes modes of relationship which lead to the give and take of love among equals.

The uses of conversation in the classroom is also expressive of the teachers conception of and feeling toward life. The value and significance of social relationships are clearly expressed by the qualities of conversation. Are social contacts to be avoided, except for purposes of efficiency, economy, or necessity, or are they to be encouraged and cherished as invaluable and uniquely human events? Is conversation seen as cheating or as a clear intent to check one's personal meaning with that of another? Is conversation prohibited for the sake of quiet and order, or is significant social order seen as meaningful and respectful exchange among people? The control or channeling of conversation demands the utmost teaching skill. Classroom silence requires only personal or social power.

THE DIMENSIONS OF CLASSROOM ACTION

The teacher's major challenge is to develop and maintain valued action. Not all action in the classroom is appropriate educational action. Children can focus their attention on the wrong events, people or things; their responses may be unsuitable or their associations with others inappropriate. Somehow the teacher must direct classroom action with attention to multiple dimensions—to focus, kinds of responses, to who is involved, and the use of time.

The symbolic nature of much educational content means that children's attention is seldom centered on a single focus, but shifts between object or referent and symbol. In social studies the focus shifts from people and events to symbolic statements about these people and events. In arithmetic the focus shifts from symbols to quantities and relationships in the environment. Symbol and referent are seldom completely separated, for communication about a referent usually requires some symbolic form. But the focus of children's attention shifts throughout the day as the curricular content shifts. The foci are significantly different for science, reading, art and arithmetic. The teacher needs criteria for the selection of the various foci of attention. These foci determine what the children may or may not attend to during the school day.

Equally important, the teacher determines the kinds of responses which children can exhibit during action, or more exactly the teacher determines which responses are not acceptable during classroom action. The response patterns may be exploratory, in which the child seeks to locate more data about the focus of attention, or expressive, in which the child seeks to organize experience into new symbolic patterns. The responses can be primarily semantic searchings in which the child seeks clarification between symbol and data source. Response patterns required for the development of skilled behavior (e.g. computation) differ from those which seek understanding of the syntactical relationship in symbol systems (e.g. understanding the meaning of $2 + 2 = 4$).

The teacher also determines which children are to interact during any particular activity; whether action is to be total group, small group, or individual activity. If small group activity, the teacher decides the basis for grouping the children. Finally, the teacher sets time limits for any given activity. The amount of time available during the day, week, or semester for each activity or type of activity must be determined in some way. The amount of time available clearly limits the type of action which is possible.

THE RHYTHMS OF CLASSROOM ACTION

One of the unresolved and sometimes unrecognized problems in curriculum is finding more adequate ways of thinking about or discussing time in the classroom. The amount of time available for activities is probably of less importance than how the time is used. Usually a means-end format is used: certain goals are specified and a period of time is allocated to achieve them. The goals may be specified as a certain number of pages to cover, a project to complete, or behavioral changes in the students. The shape of the duration between the beginning of the period and goal achievement is usually not conceptualized. However, the shape may be as important as the amount of available time. The notion of the shape of duration seems best handled by the idea of rhythm. Several types of rhythms may be hypothesized. They are not meant to be mutually exclusive, and are suggested simply as possible lines of investigation.

Involvement-reflection-expression. Following the notions of Macmurray[6] and Ortega y Gasset[7] one rhythm might be that of involvement and withdrawal. Presumably children need to become deeply involved with events, people, things or situations. Constant involvement can lead to loss of self rather than assimilation of and accommodation to these events and situations. Time for reflection, evaluation, composition, and withdrawal time enables children to make sense of their experiences and to find order and meaning in their encounters. After periods of withdrawal children may be ready to exchange meanings with others, or to ask new questions. In social studies and science the control of time might be facilitated by thinking of the children engaged in a rhythmic series of involvement-reflection-expression-involvement-reflection-expression, etc.

Tension-resolution-relaxation. Considering the affective conditions in a class, another rhythm might be that of building up and reducing tension in a student or group. The tension can be a result of excitement, doubt, or frustration. Resolution comes as the excitement is reduced, doubt removed, or frustration relieved. Relaxation could come as children look back over the sequence of experiences to recognize how tension developed and subsided.

Physical activity and quiescence. Readily recognized in most classrooms is the physical manifestation of affective rhythms. Children engage in periods of more or less strenuous physical activity followed by periods of relative calm. The physical rhythm is an important determiner of what can be accomplished in the classroom at given times.

Individual-group. A rhythm of participation-isolation-participation-etc. might be necessary for development in any field which makes use of shared symbols or meanings. The child might engage in activities demanding essentially individual attention, which result in the necessity to check findings or conclusions with others.

Skill development-skill-use. Skill development seems most effective when the skill can be used in some way. Hence a rhythm of development-use-development-use-etc. might be a valuable way to conceptualize duration in the skill areas. Extensive use of a skill, (e.g. reading, writing, computation, batting, etc.) should show deficiencies and the need for new competencies, which then lead to practice and new uses.

Challenge-routine. This is the more commonly recognized rhythm of adventure and security. Children need times for adventure which push them out beyond their knowns, but they must also have opportunities to return to the security of their knowns. Activities can be provided in the classroom which offer challenge to the child interspersed with moments of significant routines.

The notion of classroom rhythms has several possible applications. Each unit of activity could be analyzed for existing and possible rhythms. A lesson lasting a few minutes or a unit of work lasting several days or weeks might be looked at in terms of various rhythms. Likewise a school day, week, or semester might be viewed in terms of certain individual, social, or affective rhythms. Some of the rhythms might be used to link in-school activities to out-of-school activities as skill development and skill use. Others might be used to link one activity to another activity. The idea of classroom rhythms has not been investigated, but it does provide a potential tool for dealing with the management and shaping of time.

THE TEACHER IN CLASSROOM ACTION

The teacher is the most influential actor in the classroom. The teacher's bearing and actions determine the value of the routines and adventures he dreams up. As with other aspects of classroom action, no single way of conceptualizing the teacher's action is possible or desirable. The categories selected highlight what seem to be significant competencies or skills.

Span of Control.   Each teacher is able to exert different control over various aspects of the instructional situation. The span of control over any one component necessarily influences the possible kinds of action. It is convenient to think of the teacher's span of control over subject matter, pupil characteristics, and multiple activities carried on simultaneously.

Elementary school teachers are expected to be reasonably competent in most subject matter or experience areas. Consequently, a teacher in a self-contained classroom must be somewhat proficient in language, art, mathematics, science, social studies, music, and physical education. The teacher's creativity in designing activities and spontaneity in the classroom is probably a function of proficiency in a given subject matter. The teacher's span of control over these possible curricular experiences influence what does or can go on in the classroom. A teacher with limited control in mathematics must adhere rather rigidly to someone else's plans, but with extensive control in social studies the teacher should be able to be more creative and flexible in providing social studies activity. In a given school the span of control which the teachers have over content may indicate whether there should be some form of departmentalization or specialization.

Similarly, teachers may be considered to have a span of control over pupil characteristics. Some teachers can work with children having IQ's ranging from 80–200, while others are limited to a narrower range of abilities. The same may be true of cultural differences or age ranges. Some teachers may be able to work only with children from typical "middle class" families, while others may be able to work with children from multiple backgrounds. This span of control may determine whether classrooms should be homogeneously or heterogeneously grouped.

Finally some teachers are able to oversee five, six or more activities in a class at one time, while other teachers may be limited to controlling only one or two activities at a time. Those who can control several diverse activities may more readily sub-group or individualize instruction, while others with a more limited span of control may need to work in larger groups with fewer simultaneous activities.

Modeling actions.   Some of the teacher's classroom actions serve to show the children how to do things. The teacher models social behaviors as he interacts with children and adults. But teachers also model intellectual behaviors through their ways of thinking and talking about phenomena, through the questions they ask, and the answers they give. A teacher's enthusiasms and interests, as well as mannerisms, may be contagious.

Dialogue with children.   The most important actions of teachers are those in which they engage in dialogue with children. Through the exchange of language, and other symbols, the teacher not only transmits ideas from the adult culture, but helps children give form to their own ideas. Through talking, listening and responding the teacher is able to be alter ego, stimulator, clarifier, critic, and judge, if need be. It is in dialogue that the teacher really helps the child discover meaning in the world, and in so doing, helps the child to discover who he is and might be.

The teacher also has a repertoire of professional sensitivities which guide actions in the classroom. The teacher slowly establishes a "feel" for classroom activity which sensitizes them to data at almost a subconscious level. With this feel the teacher is able to shift activity when one or two children become restless, to prevent disorder before it becomes manifest, to channel individual activity when it wanes or deviates from valued activity.

Finally, teachers also exhibit in their actions the human qualities which make life with others interesting and valuable or dull and meaningless. This is the starting point of classroom action. A teacher who is not free to be truly human in the classroom, no matter how skilled as a technician or artist, cannot provide the valued experiences nor the "surge of vital feeling" that are so needed today.

Classroom action is a multi-faceted phenomenon. It has the complexity of a work of art. For instance, one can walk around a sculpture, seeing it from many points of view. Yet its wholeness is more than can be seen from any one perspective. So it is with classroom action. Several perspectives for viewing that complexity have been suggested above. They are but leads to more careful and detailed study of that particular slice of life.

NOTES

[1] Dorwin Cartwright and Alvin Zander, ed., *Group Dynamics* (White Plains, New York: Row, Peterson, 1953), chapter 40; and H. H. Anderson, and J. E. Brower, Studies of Teachers' Classroom Personalities, *Applied Psychology Monographs*, no. 6, (1945), no. 8 (1946), no. 11 (1946b).

[2] Susanne Langer, *Feeling and Form* (New York: Charles Scribner's Sons, 1953), 340.

[3] Henri Bergson, "Laughter" in *Comedy: An Essay on Comedy*, ed. Wylie Sypher (Garden City, NY: Doubleday, Anchor Books, 1956), 97.

[4] John Macmurray, *Persons in Relation* (New York: Harper and Brothers, 1961), 77.

[5] Martin Buber, *I and Thou*, trans. R. G. Smith (New York: Charles Scribner's Sons, 1937).

[6] John Macmurray, *Persons in Relation*, chapter 7.

[7] José Ortega y Gasset, *Man and People* (New York: W. W. Norton, 1957), chapter 1.

New Modes of Man's Relationship to Man

(1963)

Relating to others cannot be a goal of life or education, for it is the sine qua non of human existence. To relate or not to relate to others is not a choice offered to the child, nor even to the adult. The problem is not to relate to others, but to find a mode of relationship, and a way of talking about that relationship, which offer the greatest meaning today.

A possible motif is offered by Martin Buber: "Hearkening to the human voice, where it sounds forth unfalsified, and replying to it—it is this which is above all needed today."[1] Man does not have a choice to encounter or not to encounter his fellow man, but he may choose to converse or not to converse with the man he encounters. Paraphrasing Buber, it is conversation which is needed today, for it is through conversation that man finds fulfillment and, perhaps, joy in his human encounters without losing his freedom.

The meanings associated with the word "conversation" could be limited by direct definition. However, the significance of conversation as a mode of human relationship is drawn more neatly by characterizing other forms of human encounter. To do so requires an arbitrary choice from among possible ways of describing man's meetings with man.

FORMS OF RELATING TO OTHERS

Free to use, and consequently to accept, the limits of modern man's knowledge, Schweitzer provides a starting point by acknowledging the "mystery in the relations of man to man." He states:

> We wander through life together in a semi-darkness in which none of us can distinguish exactly the features of his neighbor; only from time to time,

through some experience that we have of our companion, or through some remark that he passes, he stands for a moment close to us, as though illumined by a flash of lightning .... After that we again walk on together in the darkness, perhaps for a long time, and try in vain to make out our fellow-traveller's features.

To this fact, that we are each a secret to the other, we have to reconcile ourselves.[2]

The Central Question: What May Transpire?

Schweitzer describes an existential point of view, a view used by others for analytical purposes. Fromm, in developing his analysis of love, begins from man's awareness "of himself as a separate entity . . . of his aloneness and separateness."[3] The idea of man's solitude is used by both Berdyaev[4] and Ortega y Gasset[5] as a vehicle for probing man's relationship to society. Man's separateness, his aloneness, his

radical solitude ... does not ... consist in there really being nothing except himself. Quite the contrary—there is nothing less than the universe, with all that it contains. There is, then, an infinity of things but—there it is!—amid them Man in his radical reality is alone—alone with them. And since among these things there are other human beings, he is *alone with* them too.[6]

Accepting the basic mystery of man's relationship to man, and acknowledging that man wanders through life "alone with ... other human beings," then what may transpire between man and man? This seems to be the question which guides the study of all human relations. The possible answers identify the various patterns of man's encounters with his fellow man. The instrumental use of man is legitimized by the myth of functional man, supported by a goal-oriented, need-directed psychology. Man must have food, shelter, clothing, recreation; and in a modern society, specialization of economic function means that man must learn to work for and with others for the achievement of the basic and learned needs. Other men are encountered as means to an end, as "objects-of-use."[7]

This kind of transaction between man and man is functional—goods are produced, services bought. For these purposes groups of men are bought and brought together, learn to coordinate their activities and strivings for production and service, and become part of an economic process. Man cannot live without economic activity, without his fellow man's being used instrumentally. But neither does he live if his encounters with the other man are only economic or instrumental.

Four Forms of Social Encounter

Within, and transcending, the instrumental encounters are those by which man attempts to overcome his solitude and aloneness, by which he tries to break through the barriers separating him from his fellow man. These are the uniquely social encounters in which man expresses his sense of freedom. At least four forms of the social encounters can be described.

First are those in which man attempts to deny, ignore or escape from his own sense of aloneness or separateness, or that of his fellow man. To do so he immerses himself in activities with others in which his own individuality is lost. He becomes part of the crowd, the mob, and as such there is no opportunity or need to establish his own identity. Consequently, the problem of his own aloneness or solitude is never brought to conscious attention. The hustle and bustle of life with others is an escape from freedom, an opportunity to get lost in the lonely crowd.

Likewise, man may ignore or deny the existence and aloneness of those he meets. Although coming within close physical proximity to another, he may fail to acknowledge, by speech or gesture, the other. Stereotypes and prejudices function effectively as conceptual tools of denial, for by quickly categorizing another person as a thing of no significance, the first person may ignore the second. Only when the stereotyped individual breaks through the stereotype, or within the stereotype intrudes into the active life of the other, does he become a person with identity, solitude and freedom, and thus a person to reckon with.

Next are those encounters in which man may recognize his aloneness or solitude and may seek to overcome it by making himself subservient to another. Wishing to reduce his separation from others, he gives himself without question and forms a parasitical relationship with a person who accepts submissive behavior. In so doing, the dependent person not only overcomes his sense of aloneness, but forfeits his freedom.

The obverse of this is also possible, for the person who accepts domination over another is also a person who seeks to overcome his separateness. He does so by possessing the other, by keeping the submissive person within his control. In these encounters, the possessive individual denies the other's freedom and his own, for he is not open to the other but is walled off by his own self.

These encounters of denial, submission and domination may be negatively valued as unhealthy or neurotic meetings, for in them man fails to accept his solitude, or gives it up, and in so doing sacrifices his freedom or that of his fellow man. In contrast to these encounters, man transcends his solitude when he accepts his aloneness and that of the person he meets and seeks a form of transaction which maintains the maximum freedom of each. In these meetings, man freely gives to and freely receives from the person he meets, for no other reason than that each recognizes that he is alone, separate, but able to give and receive from the other. For Ortega y Gasset and Fromm, this is the essence of love; the former defining "love as nothing but the attempt to exchange true solitude,"[8] while the latter recognizes that love is the way man overcomes "his separateness ... [and] ... leave[s] the prison of his aloneness."[9]

Love is Not a New Value or Goal

But love is not a new value or goal, nor one that is easily redefined. For centuries men have thought and taught about this relationship of man to man. Motse, in the fourth century B.C., wrote:

> ... individuals have learned to love themselves and not others. Therefore they do not scruple about injuring others. . . . When nobody in the world loves any other, naturally the strong will overpower the weak, the many will oppress the few, the wealthy will mock the poor, the honored will disdain the humble, the cunning will deceive the simple. Therefore all the calamities, strife, complaints, and hatred in the world have arisen out of a lack of mutual love.[10]

And in *Leviticus*, the words which have helped shape the Hebraic-Christian tradition are found:

> You shall not hate your brother in your heart, but you shall reason with your neighbor, lest you bear sin because of him. You shall not take vengeance or bear any grudge against the sons of your own people, but you shall love your neighbor as yourself ...[11]

From almost every century other prescriptions could be found, or the same prescriptions couched in the language and style of the times.

The task is not to compete with these or other historical statements. They have an aesthetic value which makes them unique and irreplaceable. They should not be pushed into the past to be forgotten, but brought into the present, for they enable today's man to realize that today's goals were yesterday's goals and may well be tomorrow's. To attempt to redefine them in the language of today would be to foster greater estrangement from those who have shaped present values and modes of behavior.

Whereas the most highly valued form of human encounter is probably love, as defined in the great religious classics, the topic is too vast to be developed within a few pages. Furthermore, the notion of love in human relations carries with it almost a mystical, esoteric sense, an idea of softness and romance or a feeling for the young or weak. Infrequently is it discussed in the psychological and educational literature. Gordon Allport conjectures about this coy concern for love:

> Why psychologists, by and large, have sidestepped the problem of human attachment is an interesting question. Ian Suttie speaks of it as their "flight

from tenderness." He believes that in repudiating theology modern mental science overreacted, and in so doing deliberately blinded itself to the tender relationships in life so strongly emphasized by Christianity. Somehow it feels more tough-minded to study discord. The scientist fears that if he looks at affiliative sentiments he may seem sentimental; and if he studies personal attachments he may appear personal. Better leave the whole matter to poets, to saints, or to theologians.[12]

The vastness and ambiguity of the many connotations of love make it undesirable as a goal to be redefined and stressed here. Conversation, however, seems to be a form of love in action, for talk is "but a tinkling cymbal, where there is no love."[13] The requirements of love, that a person freely give, freely receive, internalize that which has been received, and give once again from the newness of one's self, are also the requirements of true conversation. In this ongoing helical process, man attempts to break through his solitude, affirm the existence of the other, and meet him as an equal—free, alone, and of infinite value.

THE NATURE OF CONVERSATION

A "real dialogue is possible only if we are willing to be influenced by others."[14] Kwant thus states the necessary requisite if conversation is to occur, for conversation is not simply communication. Communication implies only the transfer of information from one to another, whereas conversation suggests that the recipient act on this information, reshape it or himself, and continue the dialogue at a new level. This "willingness to be influenced" demands an "openness toward the world,"[15] a relative freedom to face the events and people of the world, depending only partially on the categories and habits of the known. It demands that man recognize that he is never a completed "being" but is always in the process of "becoming," and hence is willing to find the new, the unexpected, the awe and wonder in that which he repeatedly faces or which he partially knows.

He who is free to converse with others retains an element of childlike curiosity about others; a curiosity based not on a desire to verify one's normalcy and worth, but on the acceptance of and awe for the complexity and the mystery of human life. He makes "an attempt at interpenetration, at de-solitudinizing …[himself] … by tentatively showing … [himself] … to the other human being, desiring to give him … [his] … life and to receive his."[16] Furthermore, conversation demands an acceptance and acknowledgment of the reality and value of the other person; not only of his equality, but of his fraternity and solitude. Acknowledging and accepting the reality, both "are aware of their duty to discover one another, to help one another onward wherever they encounter one another and to be ready for communication, on the watch, but without importunacy."[17] Both the speaker and the listener must be disposed to speak, to listen, and to accept the responsibility and opportunity for change.

Climate for Conversation Set by Listener

The listener, perhaps, establishes the climate for conversation, for it is he who determines whether the words addressed to him are simply to be acknowledged as words, or as signs indicating the willingness of the speaker to bridge the gap separating them. He may shrug off the words, listen for information, categorize the speaker, or wait to say his piece; or he may listen to the speaker, plumbing the words for the speaker's meanings, feelings and thoughts which are only partially symbolized. He must be open to the speaker; the speaker senses this openness as an invitation to forsake his cliches, to expose his thoughts, to probe his own unformed notions, and to shape them so that he too gains new insights and satisfaction from the poetic form which they might take.

Listening, perhaps, requires a discipline, or at least a concentration, for it means full attention to the present. Steere[18] claims that "in order to listen discerningly to another, a certain maturity is required, a certain self-transcendence, a certain expectation, a patience." However, the discipline and the maturity might be necessary not because of the complexity of the listening act, but because the capacity for concentration has been lost as the child grows through a nonlistening, and frequently nonconversing, society.

Certainly the concentration and focused curiosity of the child who intently observes and listens to his new world suggests an openness which soon disappears, perhaps because being curious about and interested in people is not sanctioned. Curiosity about others, however, is not a passive, selfish act. The listener cannot listen only to satisfy his own desires. By his attitude, his interest, he listens actively; he extends himself to the other, making himself available to the other. Marcel makes a distinction between active and passive listening: "... there is a way of listening which is a way of giving, another way of listening which is a way of refusing, of refusing oneself."[19]

It is only when the listener places himself at the disposal of the speaker, that the latter finds the support to search that which is yet to be expressed. For in conversation, speaking should not be simply the utterance of the already categorized and symbolized. The socially validated and objective usages of conventional language, epitomized by mathematical and scientific language, are not vehicles for the formation and expression of the personal, the unique. They are vehicles par excellence for communication, prediction and control; but if "man were to use nothing but mathematical language he would become a robot and his brain an electronic computer."[20] Language is dependent on socially shared usages and an acceptance of common, objective categories projected into the world; but if accepted blindly, if the user reifies the concepts, then language obscures the world rather than opens it. The language of conversation is not simply a recitation of the already known but "a pathway to the realization of ourselves."[21]

Speaking as a Creative Act

Conversation permits of more than passing the time between people. The art of speaking may be, and frequently is, a creative act. Langer[22] emphasizes that language, indeed any symbol system, is essentially a symbolic transformation of experience. Man is not content to experience, he creates order and gives form to his experiences. The order and the form, and the language which symbolizes both, are not simply handed down via an educational process. All persons have the capability of creating their own form, not simply using that of others. Children use this capability. They are living examples that "to know the world means to sing of it in a melody of words."[23] Conversation provides opportunity for man to continue to sing of his world "in a melody of words," given the listener who frees the speaker and draws out his experience in new verbal forms. Free to sing of his world, in the presence of others and with others, he is free to engage in new symbolic transformations of his experience, and then, in opening himself to new insights, also to make them available to the other.

Probably few conversations attain the creative heights which are possible, but in all conversation man makes an effort to share his world, to make it known to his listener. Sharing a common language does not mean sharing the same world, for each builds his unique world out of his experience. It is this world in which man is alone, and it is this world that he tries to share with others in the social encounter. He can give to the other the world as he sees it—the people and the events and the hopes and fears which make up his own personal comedies and tragedies and explanations. It is this private world of each other that the speaker and listener try to interpenetrate, accepting their solitude, but ever ready to reach out to the other by speaking and listening. The world then becomes infinite, for man not only has the possibility of exploring the one material world within which he lives, but also of exploring the worlds which others have formed and are forming.

Speaking and listening lead to conversation only when the listening influences the speaking, and leads to new speaking, and perhaps to a new speaker and listener. Rollo May states that "the encounter with the being of another person has the power to shake one profoundly and may potentially be very anxiety-arousing. It may also be joy-creating. In either case, it has the power to grasp and to move one deeply."[24] Either the speaker or the listener may be moved or grasped by the significance of that which was revealed, the reshaping of a part of his own world, the void which now confronts him or the uniqueness or beauty of the expression. And from there the conversation continues contrapuntally, until each goes on his own way, significantly changed, with something more to his being "that has grown in him, of which he did not know before and whose origin he is not rightly able to indicate."[25]

Conversation is thus an art. Not only an art of language, by which man finds new, aesthetically satisfying language forms and symbolizes the experience of his world; but also an art which leads to the forming of oneself and the other. By speaking and by listening, man can become aware of what he is and what he may become, and may help his fellow man do the same. Within the shared confidence of conversation, man may feel free to express that which he has not been able to express before, and hence to find the next step in his pathway of self-realization and the realization of the other. It is this which man needs today—to be able to accept that in conversation as a form of human encounter reality is found, solitude transcended, and life shaped.

THE IMPORTANCE OF CONVERSATION TODAY

The opportunities for conversation increase as population continues to expand and as technical advances multiply contacts among men. Large urban centers and multiple-family housing units, public transportation and communication facilities, and the extension of economic interdependence and competition reduce the distance between men and increase the frequency of meeting. Few people share the lot of the English sportsman who could bid good morning and farewell:

> Stranger, when you appeared there on the horizon miles to the east, a speck silhouetted against the dawn, you stepped on my toes and bumped into me. Did you not feel the impact?
>
> Before you appeared this whole expanse was my body, and the light and color in it my mind. Then the collision occurred. Now look at me. My body is shrunken to a midget-trunk with four midget limbs. And my mind is in a skull.
>
> I felt the impact, Stranger. I bid you good morning—and a hearty farewell.[26]

In today's world this would be an idyllic existence, for collisions are facts of life, no longer with specks "miles to the east," and the farewells are few. Man is hemmed in by men, almost to the exclusion, for some people, of the natural, nonsocial environment. His encounters are no longer only with those who share the same language system, for he now meets those who also share significantly different value systems and language systems.

The Need For New Alternatives, New Values

If man does not learn to converse with those who surround him and impinge upon him, then he must find other ways of dealing with them; either ignoring them or turning them into objects of use or control. Ignoring, controlling or using others leads eventually to rebellion, resistance and conflict, and a realignment of the power field which supports the using, controlling or ignoring. Superior power is not overcome by conversation, but when conversation is not accepted as a significant, indeed primary, form of encounter, then the use of power may predominate. It seems imperative that man learn the value of conversation so he will seek to converse before he seeks to control or use.

Conversation does not simply function as a preventive of strife and conflict, but, as suggested earlier, has inherent values. The increasing frequency and expanding scope of man's meeting with his fellow man can be perceived as adding to his opportunities for growth, influence and aesthetically satisfying symbolic transformations of experience. Through conversation with the many men who are now available, man has more worlds to explore, more melodies of words to sing, more values from which to select, and more bonds to establish with others.

The developments which have enlarged the possibilities of man's meetings with man have also interposed a world of machine, technique and function between man and man. Friedman speaks of "the technical environment:"[27]

> These numerous techniques have transformed and daily continue to transform the living conditions of modern societies, and, consequently, the relations between individuals. Every moment of life, every aspect is more and more affected.

> This environment daily thickens, becomes more dense, more permeated, so to speak with all the techniques ... [of production, transportation, communication, and leisure] ... and envelops, on all sides, the men and women of our time."[28]

Indeed, man at times seems to be but a cog caught in the vast machinery that he has devised and frequently to have become subservient to the functional, day-by-day operation of that machine. The image created by Chaplin in *Modern Times* is no longer a comedy of man's possibility, but a comic-tragedy of his near actuality. For in the factory man is now hired to "tend" machines, to kow-tow to their needs, rather than to run them for his needs. Modern life, aimed at production, "plunges man into an atmosphere of cold metal ... [eliminating] human warmth."[29]

Even in less machine-oriented environments, man is subservient to his "role." He must become an "organization man" and fit into the functional hierarchy of the structure. Man becomes a buyer, salesman, foreman, supervisor or customer. As a consequence, his relationships with his fellow man are determined by his occupational role. The elevator operator is someone who takes people up or down, not someone to talk with unless to ask for information. A clerk is someone who sells goods to others, and the talk is limited to the buying and selling. The functional, economic contacts overshadow the social contacts epitomized by conversation. Saint Exupèry, in the simple profundity of *The Little Prince*, characterizes man's present condition as the fox asks the Little Prince to tame him:

"I want to, very much," the little prince replied. "But I have not much time. I have friends to discover, and a great many things to understand."

"One only understands the things one tames," said the fox. "Men have no more time to understand anything. They buy things already made at the shops. But there is no shop anywhere where one can buy friendship, and so men have no friends any more."[30]

The Threatened Loss of Humaneness

"No friends" is a possibility within the technical order today, for, living with machines, techniques and functions, man is likely to attribute the qualities of these machines and functions to the man he meets, thus negating his fraternity and his freedom. But it is not inherent in the technical order that man be so treated, for he is still able to exert his control over the technical order in such a way that the humaneness of man stands out.

Conversation is important as a way of asserting this control over the technical. If the functional transactions are subservient to conversation, then man meets the other first as a person to converse with, then as a functional role. During or after or even preceding the conversation, the transaction may be carried on, but the giver and receiver have given and received more than their economically assigned product or process, they have given and received of each other. The organizational structure may be not only a means for the production, transportation and trading of goods and services but may provide channels for conversational encounters with others outside of the home or immediate community. Of course, there are barriers to conversation's assuming primacy in the functional orders, but the importance of conversation within these orders must nevertheless be recognized and reckoned with.

The importance of conversation stands out clearly as the expanding population is considered, and as the influence of technique and function spreads. Equally significant, but less readily recognized, is the importance of conversation if knowledge is to retain its role as a tool in human affairs, rather than being apotheosized. Cassirer clearly states the situation:

No longer can man confront reality immediately; he cannot see it, as it were, face to face. Physical reality seems to recede in proportion as man's symbolic activity advances. Instead of dealing with the things themselves man is in a sense constantly conversing with himself. He has so enveloped himself in artistic images, in mythical symbols or religious rites, that he cannot see or know anything except by the interposition of this artificial medium.[31]

Separating man from man, and man from nature, is this symbolic curtain, frequently more powerful than the iron curtain, for man is likely to stop at the curtain rather than to go through it to deal more directly with man or nature.

Modern man has found it too easy to accept *cogito, ergo sum*, not simply as a starting point for derivation of one philosophical point of view, but as the basic premise of all life. This results in a reification of the conceptual and an interpretation of knowledge as an aerial photograph of reality rather than as a man-made policy to guide action. The power of scientific knowledge, as evidenced by medical achievement and control within the physical realm, sanctions this reification. But all too often only those who create the knowledge, who test its validity and reliability for certain purposes but always also search for new explanatory schema, are aware "that in cognition we have moved in categories which, even in their totality, are like a fine filigree with which we grasp what at the same time we conceal with it."[32]

Learning Other Forms of Knowing

Scientific knowledge is but one way of grasping and shaping the encountered world, albeit a very effective way for purposes of control and prediction. Other forms of knowing also have their criteria of effectiveness: witness the effectiveness of the poetic, dramatic or artistic statement for the one who can interpret the symbols.

The reification of knowledge, whether in the form of scientific concepts, religious concepts, or simply common sense, is a danger faced by man today. The potency of mass communication in shaping the individual's grasp of his world, the deadly efficiency of scientific thought and the consequent desire to internalize only scientific thought, and the relative impotence of art in today's culture point to a tendency to standardize man's way of making sense of his world, and hence to deny the individual the freedom to make his own sense within limits. These limits are the limits imposed by his ability to converse with his neighbors and others whom he meets. Granted that scientific knowledge permits prediction and control, this and all other forms of knowledge are also vehicles for conversation, and it is through this conversation among specialists that the limits are defined, imposed and altered.

If man is free to converse, then he is also free to set the limits which define his "sense" of the world. By being free to converse, he is also free to accept and create new symbolic transformations of his world and hence free from the hardening of the categories which plagues the prejudiced individual. By conversing with a variety of people who use somewhat different conceptual schemes, the individual is faced with the necessity of being flexible in his own conceptualization of the world. By talking with the poet, playwright, artist, theologian, and scientist, he recognizes that no single knowledge system gives adequate form to all that man faces; but that each is a tool to be used effectively at certain times. Thus he is discouraged from the reification of a particular set of concepts and freer to use all of them.

BARRIERS TO CONVERSATION

Man has the potential to converse. His basic curiosity about and openness to the world, at least in his early years, means that he can be open and receptive to those he encounters. His ability to symbolize provides him with the power to give form to his feelings and sensations and to throw these symbolic structures out before him, to be grasped by others. If he does not converse with those he meets, the probable reasons are not in the lack of potential but in the determinants that have shaped him.

Opportunities Must be Available

Conversation requires a concentration and focusing of one's powers into a skillful pattern as do all practical and theoretical acts. Opportunities must be available to permit the individual to discover the elements of the skill and to make them more or less automatic in his behavioral repertoire. If he lives his years in an environment which does not permit discovery and testing of his ability to converse and if his conversational sallies are not sanctioned and reinforced, then the skill will not be developed. Knowledge of the art of conversation and of the skills which make it possible is not generally a part of today's lore.

Furthermore, attempts to obtain more knowledge of the art are few, although frequently someone decries the disappearance of conversation from the social scene and its replacement by communal gazing at television. The study of human encounters is more apt to encompass goal oriented, problem-solving ventures, or conflict situations, than it is the study of affiliative contacts, as Allport pointed out. Lack of knowledge about conversation may prevent its development in society.

Besides lack of knowledge, there are other factors which influence individual deviation from accepted norms. The person who struggles with crippling fears or anxieties in his relationships with others will find conversation difficult or almost impossible, except with those who arouse no anxieties or with whom a therapeutic relationship has been established. Knowledge, increasing in scope and power, is available for identifying these determinants, controlling them, and reducing their influence.

Likewise, the person who is relatively incapable of symbolizing his experience, or has difficulty giving verbal form to his feelings or sensations, will be blocked from conversation. Again, some knowledge is available for rectifying these defects, and research in speech therapy and language development should increase the effectiveness of remedial techniques. These might be called idiosyncratic barriers to conversation—neurotic and physical distortions of normal competencies.

Barriers in Social Processes and Practices

Distinguishable from these idiosyncratic barriers are those operating within
the society to limit conversation among most people. Barriers at various levels
of conceptualization could be identified. For instance, by careful observation
of child-rearing and other socialization processes, the pattern of behavioral
acts which positively and negatively sanction conversation could be identified.
At the next level, an attempt could be made to identify the values which are assumed to determine the behavioral acts. Prior even to the values, however, are
the thought patterns or, preferably, the language or symbol systems which determine man's grasping and shaping of his world. The way that man explains
the world—his world hypotheses, images, conceptions or myths—are the vehicles by which he shapes values and legitimizes actions. It is at this level, the
level of man's basic thought and language patterns, that the major barriers to
conversation probably exist.

It is easy for man to fall into the conventional language or symbolic patterns
and to accept common sense definitions and explanations of man and his place
in the world or to assume that the social scientist knows best and to use his images of man without hesitation or question. But giving symbolic or linguistic
form to the world and his place in it is the prerogative of all men. He who excels
in the invention of this form is an artist. He who determines the predictive possibilities of a given form is a scientist. He who knows and uses only one form to
grasp and shape his world is a slave. But free is the man who recognizes that no
system of ideas, symbols, images or myths completely encompasses man and
his possibility in the world, and who acts accordingly. Saint Exupèry verbalizes
this well:

> When some busybody comes forward, claiming to expound man with his
> logic and neat definitions, I liken him to a child who has settled down with
> spade and bucket at the foot of Atlas and prepares to shovel up the mountain
> and install it elsewhere. Man is what he is, not that which can be expressed.
> True the aim of all awareness is to express that which is, but expression is a
> slow, elusive task, and it is a mistake to assume that anything incapable of be-
> ing stated in words does not exist. Stating is, by the same token, compre-
> hending. But small indeed is the part of man which I have learned so far to
> comprehend. Yet that which on a certain day I come to comprehend existed
> none the less the day before; and foolish indeed were I to deem that all in man
> for which I cannot find the words is unworthy of consideration![33]

The languages with the greatest acceptance today are those which are generated by or are imitations of science. Modern man, reveling in the power of scientific knowledge, considers the language of science as the superior language
for all purposes, including the shaping and legitimizing of value. Thus the prevailing educational myths depend almost completely upon psychological and
sociological interpretations of man and his place in society. In these, conversa-

tion is not valued *per se*. Man talks with other men for a purpose: for gaining information, solving problems, learning, or maybe for establishing good peer or social relationship. In schools teachers talk with students to help them learn; students talk with students to accomplish a learning task or because they have certain personal-social needs.

Limitations in Functional Language

In the broader economic life of the community, as man goes about his business, functional economic language shapes his behavior. Action is goal oriented. If public conveniences are ridden, the desired stop is the focus of attention, and man converses with man for information about how to get there, not simply because he happens to be sitting or standing next to another man; consequently the deathly silence in elevators unless friends are together or unless the operator sees his job as more than transporting people. If merchandise is purchased in a store, conversation is legitimate if it involves the business transaction; going beyond that the speaker faces negative sanctioning.

Outside the sphere of the functional, if man converses in the home or with friends, he is engaging in a "worthy use of leisure time," a time left over from his purposeful sallies into the world of business, a time for recuperation and relaxation. The reverse interpretation, of course, is also possible. His purposeful activities in the functional world could well be interpreted as providing the necessities so time would be available for the new, more important purposes of life—association and conversation with friends and foes. Leisure time implies time left over, not time sought and valued as the most significant part of the day. Whether the shrinking work day and week, resulting from increased automation, will actually change the present-day conception of the importance of leisure-time activity remains to be seen. Yet if man works three or four days a week rather than five or six, new thought patterns legitimizing his use of the non-working time will be necessary.

Modern man has become overly dependent on scientific modes of thought for shaping values and legitimizing actions. The clearest example of this is found in educational thought today. Future teachers are exposed to the psychological and developmental knowledge of the child and man to help develop knowledge of, attitudes toward, and skills for working with students. If the would-be teacher is exposed to the great religious, poetic and dramatic insights about man and his life, it is the result of an accidental encounter with an exceptional teacher rather than through the intent of an educational design. The overvaluing of scientific language has led to an undervaluing of religious and aesthetic language.

Valuing Religious and Aesthetic Language

Balancing this situation does not require undervaluing science or less critical scrutiny of the validity of religious and aesthetic insights, but it does mean assigning appropriate value to the function of all systems of language and symbols. Without question, scientific language is the language for generalization, prediction and control. But it is not the scientist who creates value—it is the artist:

> The work of the painter, the musician, the poet ... makes us see the new qualities with which the world, in cooperation with the spirit of man, can clothe itself. For art is an enterprise in which the world and man are most genuinely cooperative, and in which the working of natural materials and powers and of human techniques and vision is most clearly creative of new qualities and powers.[34]

The artist must use the predictive and controlling knowledge of the scientist to realize his vision, for it is with this knowledge that he expands his power. In the sphere of man's relationship to man, the artist might be considered the prophet or the saint. "They teach us how to see what man's life in the world is, and what it might be. They teach us how to discern what human nature can work out of its natural conditions and materials. They reveal latent powers and possibilities not previously noticed."[35]

Again the artist must use the best predictive and controlling knowledge, the knowledge of the behavioral scientist, to come closer to the actualization of man's possibilities. The message of the behavioral scientist is the message of the man who has studied man and who "knows" him. The message of the poet, novelist, dramatist or other artist may be the message of a man who has met man and conversed with him and who indicates the worth of those meetings and conversations.

Several of the social thinkers who operate within an existential framework would center the basic problems of man's relationship with man in what is known as the "dichotomy of world into subject and object,"[36] a dichotomy which has been essential for the advance of science but which is also a barrier to conversation. For man to know the world as a scientist, the phenomena of the world must be perceived as objects before him with knowable and predictable qualities, yielding in a systematic fashion to his prodding, poking and questioning. Such inquiry makes abstraction possible and hence relationship to and control of the phenomena in terms of the abstractions.

Man encountered within the framework of the subject-object attitude is potentially a predictable, controllable man; a man to be studied and known. But as Tillich states, "Man has been lost in the enterprise."[37] The existentialist would admit to the possibility of a subject-subject attitude or what Buber would call the "I-Thou" relation in contrast to the "I-It"[38] relationship. Man meeting man within the I-Thou or subject-subject mode does not encounter him as an object to be known, potentially predictable and controllable. Rather he is another subject, to be met not in terms of abstractions and concepts, but to be met face-to-face and to be spoken to and listened to.

Today, the prevailing mode of thought would seem to be the subject-object mode, whereby man's basic attitude toward the world of nature and the world of people is that it is something to be known, to be used. The language which speaks of love, of living with, of communion, whether it be uttered by the poet or theologian has its own tiny compartment in man's explanatory and shaping mythologies and does not seep readily into the main currents of man's habits and values.

THE POSSIBILITIES FOR CONVERSATION

The major barrier to conversation may be the limitation of the conventional language used to shape man's values and legitimize his actions, not a lack of knowledge about conversation. The possibilities for more adequate conversation, then, are dependent on the acceptance of a greater variety of language patterns for thinking and talking about man's relationships with man. In the creative and scholarly fields, several trends presage the movement toward greater variability in symbolizing man's encounters with his fellow man, with more scrutiny and valuing of conversation.

Sources of New Insights

In the philosophical field two current interests have possibilities for reducing the barriers. The first are the interests of those who are generally categorized as existentialist. Many of them, or at least those who are somewhat optimistic, emphasize the primacy of man's relationship to man. Berdyaev, for example, emphasizes the need for communion among people, involving "participation, reciprocal participation, interpenetration,"[39] which is more than communication. Buber uses the word "dialogue"[40] to emphasize the quality of man's relationship with man. Jaspers is perhaps most explicit. He recognizes the importance of communication as the medium for developing selfhood, as would most social psychologists. But he goes beyond this to link truth and communication and to underline the importance of these in the community:

Truth ... cannot be separated from communication. Abstracted from communication, truth hardens into unreality. The movement of communication is at one and the same time the preservation of and the search for the truth.[41]

Going beyond this he states that "for the continuity of a living community the art of conversation must be developed."[42]

Thus, the existentialist, by emphasizing the significance of man's relationship to man and the primacy of the communion, conversation, dialogue, or participation with his fellow man, makes it possible for man to value more strongly these personal encounters and provides a language to legitimize conversational acts. The language of the existentialists differs significantly from the common language of the layman and from pedagogical language. To dismiss the language because it is different, abstruse, or because it does not meet the criteria of philosophical form is to reject it for insufficient reasons.

At the other extreme of the philosophical field are the contemporary philosophical analysts, beginning with Wittgenstein. Frequently belittling each other, the linguistic analysts and the existentialists nevertheless share a common concern: communication. Whereas the existentialist is concerned with the need for and possibility of communication in its many forms, the analyst is concerned with the use of language and assumes his task to be "to get a better understanding of the language we in fact use."[43] The focus in both is on that which transpires among individuals, one being excessively concerned with the form of the communication act, the other being overly concerned without adequate attention to the form it takes.

Macmurray, in attempting to bridge the gap, claims that the analysts "discard the problem in order to maintain the method" of traditional philosophy, whereas the "existentialists relinquish the method in wrestling with the problem."[44] Nevertheless, both are significant tools for making the educator aware of his limited, and limiting, thought patterns and language systems for shaping value and legitimizing action.

In the psychological field, comparable emphases are apparent, which might eventually reduce the barriers to conversation. On the one hand, the European phenomenological and existential tradition in psychology is finding its way into American psychological circles, thus providing more ways to view man and his relationship with other men. Schachtel's notion of "activity affect" and "allo-centric"[45] perception should shake the over-dependency on need reduction and goal-oriented behavior, categories which do not necessarily legitimize conversation. Likewise the ideas developed and illustrated in May's *Existence*[46] should provide new categories for thinking about man's encounters with man and the possible values inherent in these encounters. On the other hand, the extensive studies of thinking and communication, which parallel the studies in philosophical analysis, should foster greater awareness of man's use of language to structure his universe, shape his values, and determine his interactions.

Broadened Ways of Thinking About Relationships

Slowly the languages of other fields of endeavor may also work their way into common usage and become legitimate ways to talk about man's relationship with man. Whereas modern science and philosophy helped relax the grip of older theologies, current theologians are again being listened to. Such men as Tillich, Niebuhr, Barth, Maritain, and Buber, aware of and competent to deal with modern scientific and philosophical thought, command respect in intellectual circles as they give form to religious ideas. Eventually it might be possible to encourage students in education courses to think of the significance of their own religious beliefs as a basis for interacting with pupils, along with the ideas of Freud, Sullivan,[47] and Rogers.

The compartmentalization of human thought into religious, philosophical, and scientific sections, without attempting consciously to compare and evaluate the differing language and symbol categories for the same phenomena or situations, cannot be justified. Such comparison and evaluation does not imply that one thought or language system must predominate over the others, for each has its own values. But the values can only be realized if their respective powers and limitations can be identified.

Although the evidence is less obvious today, eventually the humanistic interpretations of man, found in literature and the various arts, may also regain status as a justifiable means of shaping value and legitimizing action. The biographer, novelist, dramatist also provides models for grasping man's existence. Today the power, effectiveness and acceptance of science hinders the acceptance of the arts as an appropriate way of thinking about man and his relationship with man. Archibald Lampman states the case in a way that many other poets would willingly accept:

> Each mortal in his little span
>> Hath only lived, if he have shown
> What greatness there can be in man
>> Above the measured and the known.[48]

Freedom to converse requires an acceptance that conversation can be a meaningful and significant end in and of itself. As a mode of human encounter it needs no justification, for it is one way which man recognizes his solitude, his freedom, and his fraternity with others. In this day of egocentric and nationalistic behavior, conversation becomes more important, for it is an alternative to strife and conflict:

> War has always had an adversary who almost never comes forward as such, but does his work in the stillness. This adversary is speech-fulfilled speech, the speech of genuine conversation in which men understand one another. It

lies already in the nature of primitive war that it often begins there where speech has ceased, that is, where men are no longer able to discuss with one another the subjects under dispute or submit them to mediating talks but instead flee from speech with one another and in the speechlessness of killing one another seek a supposed decision, a judgment of God, so to speak. Soon, to be sure, war conquers speech too and enslaves it in the service of its battle cries. But where speech, be it ever so shy, again moves from camp to camp, war is already called in question. Its grapeshot easily drowns out the word; but when the word has become entirely soundless and now, here and there soundlessly bears into the hearts of men the intelligence that no human conflict can really be solved through killing, not even through mass killing, then it, the human word, has already begun to silence the grapeshot.[49]

NOTES

[1]Martin Buber, "Genuine Conversation and the Possibilities of Peace," *Cross Currents* 5 (1955): 292–96.

[2]Albert Schweitzer, *Memoirs of Childhood and Youth*, trans. C. T. Campion (New York: Macmillan, 1955), 68-69.

[3]Erich Fromm, *The Art of Loving* (New York: Harper and Brothers, 1956), 8.

[4]Nicolas Berdyaev, *Solitude and Society*, trans. George Beavy (London: Geoffrey Bles, Centenary Press, 1938).

[5]José Ortega y Gasset, *Man and People*, trans. Willard R. Trask (New York: W. W. Norton and Company, 1957), 272.

[6]Ibid., 49.

[7]Ernest G. Schachtel, *Metamorphosis* (New York: Basic Books, 1959), 173.

[8]José Ortega y Gasset, *Man and People*, 50.

[9]Erich Fromm, *The Art of Loving*, 9.

[10]Lin Yutang, *The Wisdom of China and India* (New York: Random House, 1942).

[11]Leviticus 19: 17–18, Revised Standard Version Bible, the National Council of the Churches of Christ in the United States of America (New York: Thomas Nelson & Sons, l952).

[12]Gordon Allport, "A Psychological Approach to the Study of Love and Hate," in *Explorations in Altruistic Love and Behavior*, ed. Pitirim Sorokin, (Boston, MA: Beacon Press, 1950), 145–46.

[13]Francis Bacon, "Of Friendship," in *The Essays of Francis Bacon* (New York: The Heritage Press, 1944), 83.

[14]Remy C. Kwant, *Encounter*, trans. Robert C. Adolfs (Pittsburgh, Pennsylvania: Duquesne University Press, l960), 59.

[15]Ernest G. Schachtel, *Metamorphosis*, 53.

[16]José Ortega y Gasset, *Man and People*, 93.

[17]Karl Jaspers, *Man in the Modern Age*, trans. Eden and Cedar Paul (London: Routledge and Kegan Paul, 1951), 189.

[18]Douglas V. Steere, *On Listening to Another* (New York: Harper and Row, 1955) 4.

[19]Gabriel Marcel, *The Philosophy of Existence*, trans. Manya Harari (London: Harvill Press, 1948), 26.

[20]Ernest G. Schachtel, *Metamorphosis*, 191.

[21]Ernst Cassirer, *The Logic of the Humanities*, trans. Clarence Smith Howe (New Haven, CT: Yale University Press, 1961), 113.

[22]Susanne Langer, *Philosophy in a New Key*, third edition (Cambridge, Massachusetts: Harvard University Press, 1960).

[23]Maurice Merlau-Ponty quoted in Remy Kwant, *Encounter*, 11.

[24]Rollo May, "Contributions of Existential Psychotherapy,"in *Existence*, ed. Rollo May, et al. (New York: Basic Books, 1958), 38.

[25]Martin Buber, *I and Thou*, trans. Ronald Gregor Smith (New York: Charles Scribner's Sons, 1937), 109.

[26]Virgil C. Aldrich, "Beauty and Feeling," in *Reflections on Art*, ed. Susanne K. Langer (Baltimore, MD: Johns Hopkins Press, 1958), 3.

[27]George Friedman, "Technological Change and Human Relations," *Cross Currents* 10 (1960): 29–47, 31.

[28]Ibid., 32.

[29]Nicolas Berdyaev, *Spirit and Reality*, trans. George Reavy (London: Geoffrey Bles, Centenary Press, 1939), 66-67.

[30]Antoine de Saint Exupèry, *The Little Prince*, trans. Kathleen Woods (New York: Harcourt, Brace, & World, 1943), 67.

[31]Ernest Cassirer, *An Essay on Man*. (Garden City, NY: Doubleday and Company, 1953), 43.

[32]Karl Jaspers, *Truth and Symbol*, trans. Jean T. Wilde, William Kloback and William Kimmel (New York: Twayne Publishers, 1959), 38.

[33]Antoine de Saint Exupèry, *The Wisdom of the Sands*, trans. Stuart Gilbert (New York: Harcourt, Brace & World, 1950), 107.

[34]John Herman Randall, *The Role of Knowledge in Western Religion* (Boston, MA: Beacon Press, 1958), 128.

[35]Ibid., 128–129.

[36]Ludwig Binswanger, "The Existential Analysis School of Thought," in *Existence*, ed. Rollo May, et al. (New York: Basic Books, 1958), 193.

[37]Paul Tillich, *Systematic Theology*, vol I (Chicago IL: University of Chicago Press, 1951), 99.

[38]Martin Buber, *I and Thou*.

[39]Nicolas Berdyaev, *Solitude and Society*, trans. George Reavey (London: Geoffrey Bles, The Centenary Press, 1938), 141.

[40]Martin Buber, *Between Man and Man*, trans. Ronald Gregory Smith (Boston, MA: Beacon Press, 1955).

[41]Karl Jaspers, *Reason and Existenz: Five Lectures*, trans. William Earle (New York: Noonday Press, 1955), 79–80.

[42]Ibid., 82.

[43]J. O. Urmson. *Philosophical Analysis* (Oxford: Clarendon Press, 1958), 27.

[44]John Macmurray, *The Self as Agent* (New York: Harper and Brothers; 1957), 27.

[45]Ernest Schachtel, *Metamorphosis*.

[46]Rollo May, *Existence*.

[47]See Harry Stack Sullivan, *Conceptions of Modern Psychiatry* (London: Tavistock, 1955); H. S. Sullivan, *The Psychiatric Interview*, ed. Helen Swick Perry and Mary Ladd Gawel (New York: W. W. Norton, 1954); H. S. Sullivan, *The Fusion of Psychiatry and Social Science* (New York: Norton, 1964). *Ed.*

[48]Archibald Lampman, "The Clearer Self," in *Unseen Wings: The Living Poetry of Man's Immortality*, comp. Stanton A Coblentz (New York: Beechhurst Press, 1949).

[49]Martin Buber, *Cross Currents*, 294.

9

Politics and Curriculum

(1964)

A research column should be a marshaling of facts and findings which point to new directions for study, or to new fulcrums for control of educational action. However, as the editor of this column recognizes,[1] research has two parts—the "search" and the "re." Empirical considerations should be uppermost in the REsearch phase, for only through empirical means are the instrumental values of findings identified and their power for influencing educational actions tested. Hence, the need for the curricular REsearcher to be conditioned by social science methodology. Yet other considerations must be uppermost in the reSEARCH phase—during search activity fruitfulness for educational thought becomes more important than power for educational action. The curricular reSEARCHer must consequently be conditioned by the methodologies of the imaginative enterprises—primarily poetry and speculative philosophy.

Approached from this point of view, to explore the relationship between curriculum and politics means to search for new language forms. These need not have immediate empirical validity. They are sufficient if they spark the imagination into new formulations of curricular phenomena. Dufrenne states that "the world speaks to us; it comes and lets itself be caught in the snare of words."[2] The juxtaposition of curriculum and politics does not generate new sounds in the world, but provides new snares which may catch these sounds. Imaginative searching must always be ready to doubt the efficacy of existing language, and must attempt to keep language supple, refreshed and alive. By starting from a new vantage point, old problems may disappear and new questions may emerge. The attempt in this review is to freely speculate about curricular phenomena from a political orientation. Every positive statement should be prefaced by "perhaps …" or "might it be that …," for this is not an attempt to state what is, but to suggest ways of talking about curricular events.

STRUGGLE FOR POWER

A central term in political science is "power" or, if this is too harsh on ears conditioned to the reverently intoned "democracy," then "influence." For instance, Lasswell and Kaplan define political science as "the study of the shaping and sharing of power."[3] As the educator searches for professional status and responsibility, he should not forsake the search or struggle for positions of influence or power. One of the unfortunate characteristics of the oversimplified democratic ideology, which implies that everyone should get in on the act, was a tendency to ignore this fact of social life. The leadership function, and the power qualities which go with it, were diffused among the total educational group until legitimate power figures were conceived primarily as process leaders. To be a leader with power and influence does not imply that totalitarianism is necessary, that immorality will result, or that power and influence cannot be shared. Yet the fact that power and influence exist and are necessary need not be hidden from view by oversimplified versions of democracy, nor need it be legitimized artificially by a professional ethic of responsibility.

To keep the phenomena of power, and its quest, in the open and talked about is to make these less frightening. In turn the professional curricular worker should be less defensive when he awakens one day to find that curricular decisions are being made by someone else, for this fact simply implies that the professional has lost control by default or by not recognizing that power and influence are never permanently institutionalized, but always available to the individual who has the know-how to gain it. It is tempting at this point to move into empirical investigation and to ask, "Who, in fact, does make or influence curricular decisions or actions?" Other directions may do more to illuminate curricular phenomena.

The foci of control, or of the struggle for power and influence, can be considered as the actions which occur in, or in conjunction with, the classroom and the symbol systems which identify values, provide directions and expectations, legitimize actions, and foster solidarity. The individuals or groups who can influence classroom action or curricular symbol systems, are curricular leaders—whether in the classrooms or out, professional educators or lay citizens. Traditional curricular theories, proposals or statements have done little to lay bare the network of factors which determine classroom action, or to highlight the significance and operation of symbol systems in curricular activity. Two reasons for this neglect may be postulated.

First, a curriculum has been identified as a position, course of action, or series of events or experiences which has stability, a truth value, or some more or less absolute value. Thus educators argue over the purposes of the school, the goals to be achieved, and the ideal curriculum. It seems more efficacious to conceptualize curriculum as social policy—a continual realization through classroom actions of the beliefs, values, expectations and desires of those in positions of control. As with any social policy, some commitments from the past carry over to influence present policy.[4] Yet more significant is the constant, and necessary, struggle to have that social policy serve the interests of the dominant group and thus to keep abreast of the changing social scene. So conceived, curriculum can never have a final, complete design of absolute value; it is always in the process of becoming, of change, as is society itself.

Therefore the term, curriculum making, is a misnomer; for a curriculum is never made—it is always in process. Even the term, curriculum development, leaves something to be desired, for it also carries the connotation that development can reach a stage of completion. To identify curriculum as social policy at least throws it into the seething cauldron of social and political action, and participants become policy determiners struggling with and against others who wish to establish other policies. Those who make or develop a curriculum may well feel that those who struggle against them are destroyers, or inhibitors of development, rather than participants in the quest for policy determination.

The other reason for this neglect has been the desire of the curricular writer to influence by intellectual argument only. Thus proposals are usually philosophically consistent statements about the function of the school, the characteristics of students, and the way to organize programs for goal achievement. The proposals have depended upon the force of intellectual or rational arguments to convince others of what should be done. Unfortunately, in the determination of social policy there remains some irrationality. Consequently, there is need to mobilize emotions, feelings and actions through non-discursive symbols, perhaps even emotive arguments. Furthermore, social policy in education is much too complex to be contained by the rather limited range of behavioristic language presently used in curricular writing.

Of course the curricular specialist wishes to be rational and to maximize his intellectual grasp of phenomena within his domain. Within the next 100 years educators may have more effective intellectual tools for their jobs. Presently they do not, but they must still act. Hence the irrational must be accepted and dealt with as sanely as possible, not swept under the rug of enticing but imperfect behavioristic theories. Curricular proposals and writings need to be seen within the broad functions of symbolic activity. The pervasiveness of the symbol in today's world makes the functional analysis of the symbolic sphere a complex task,[5] which can only be hinted at later.

The significance of the control of classroom action and curricular symbols for more or less traditional concerns of curriculum can be most effectively developed if the usual questions of the curricular worker are ignored and two other primary questions asked. The central problem faced by the teacher, and in turn by other curricular workers, is "What can and shall occur in the classroom tomorrow, or next week, or next year?" Related to this, but of minor significance for this analysis is the secondary question of how the activities of today are or can be related to the activities of yesterday and tomorrow—the problem of time and sequence. The second major question is, "How is value assigned to or realized through classroom action?" The usual problem of goal setting and evaluation is only one aspect of this question. It is obvious that the first question relates directly to the political control of curriculum through the influencing of classroom action. It is less obvious that the control of the symbol sphere is a political device for influencing both classroom action and the valuing mechanisms. Brief attention will be given to the first, while more detailed attention will be given to the second.

SOURCES OF POWER

Classroom activity may be influenced by controlling the input of resources—broadly conceived—into the classroom, and by controlling the sanctions applied to classroom personnel from outside the classroom. The basic determiners of classroom action are teachers with given competencies and skills, material and symbolic resources, pupils with given characteristics, and quantities of time. Classroom action may be influenced by controlling any one of these determiners. Individuals—administrators, board members, college teachers—responsible for the hiring, placement and preparation of the teachers exert control over classroom actions. Whoever controls the availability, selection and purchase of resource materials or the specification of subject matter content has power over classroom action. Here the power of board members and administrators may be shared with teachers, students, Congress through the NDEA,[6] and commercial interests. The individuals responsible for the assignment and grouping of students and the allocation of time also exert control over classroom action. Therefore, individuals seeking to control the curriculum need to identify the power they have over any resources which determine classroom action.

Equally important are the sanctions, the rewards and punishments, which may be applied to classroom personnel. Clearly, administrators and supervisors have formal and informal sanctions available. Tenure, assignments, salaries, committee loads are formal sanctions; while esteem, prestige, friendliness, and compliments are informal sanctions. Yet fellow teachers also have sanctioning power by virtue of their social contacts and signs of approval, disapproval and belonging. Custodians may bestow privileges on teachers they favor and thus influence classroom action. Parents and other community members may apply sanctions through complaints, praise, invitations, or by influencing their children to act in certain ways. The mobilization and use of sanctioning power, e.g., the ability to blow up a storm in the community, becomes a significant means of determining classroom activity. A political analysis of who controls classroom activity involves not simply identifying who has power or influence, but who has power over what resource inputs or who can apply what sanctions to classroom personnel. Because not all of these sources of power involve conscious decisions, a simple decision making paradigm does not uncover all political influence.

The control of the symbol sphere is even more elusive, hence political domination here is more subtle and analysis more difficult. It may be postulated that the symbol sphere, in this case primarily the language system used by educators and laity, serves four functions. It clarifies and shapes value, provides directives for action, legitimizes or rationalizes decisions, and serves as a visible symbol of group identification or solidarity. Writings in or about curriculum fail to discriminate among these various functions; and, consequently, the separation of propaganda from philosophies and from theories becomes difficult. Furthermore, the potential power and effectiveness of curricular writing is weakened by the failure to make these discriminations, for too many writers feel the need to be all things to all teachers.

The identification, clarification, and shaping of value is an essential task, not limited to the educators. As social policy, classroom action should maximize values of those in control. Professional educators, of course, assume responsibility for maximizing the values of the laity. Yet when they fail some segment of the population interested in education, then that segment may move in with its own value statements and do verbal battle with the entrenched educators. The educational leader must be a politician in the sense that he must balance the demands of various interested groups or lose effective control of the educational enterprise. Rapid and far reaching social changes require constant reshaping of values, and because no segment of the population can possibly see or anticipate the signification of social change, constant dialogue and intellectual differences are necessary. A monolithic structure tends to hide difference. Consequently, there is a need for many different groups, with quite different interests, to be talking and writing about education and the curriculum. Conflict is often necessary for significant value clarification.

SHAPING OF CLASSROOM ACTION

Given value statements which identify and clarify values to be maximized, the educator then needs some directives to guide the shaping of classroom action. Educational theory here is very inadequate, for the dependency upon an economic model and a learning technology has all but destroyed imaginative formulation of significant questions. The educational myth which states that goals must be identified, and then learning activities devised to reach these goals, is appropriate for the evaluation functions, but hardly an adequate model for curricular planning. The educator does need clear and valid directives, but a means-end model and a psychology of learning are not the only vehicles for identifying these directives.

As teachers and curricular workers make decisions, they need some rationale to back them up, or to legitimize their action. A clear statement of value and of directives may serve this end. However, these are not always possible or desirable. Parents may not understand the technical rationale, or the language which shapes the values. Yet they may understand that a professional organization recommends this course of action, or that research proves it to be effective. Rationalization and legitimation are necessary if new actions of teacher or educator are to be readily accepted.

Finally, the symbol systems provide a basis for collective security, reinforcement and solidarity. To realize that one shares the same beliefs and secrets or knowledge as another may create a bond which facilitates group cohesiveness and consequently increases the effectiveness of political action. The slogan systems of the progressive era, and indeed today some of the expressions from Bruner's *The Process of Education*[7] serve this unifying function. At one time the statements of philosophy of individual schools served this purpose for the faculty.

The symbol systems, and hence the four functions outlined above, are generally controlled by the intellectuals, the journalists, and the propagandists. By making available coherent and seemingly meaningful philosophies, theories, impassioned appeals, and criticism, those who control the symbol systems influence the thought and eventually the action of teachers, other educational workers, parents, and lay citizens. The symbol systems enable teachers to structure classroom action and provide value frameworks against which people outside the classroom can assess information originating in the schools. On the basis of these assessments they act to sanction classroom personnel or to tolerate and accept what seems to be going on.

This system of ideas, generated by a political orientation, could be and should be developed further. The concept of power suggests that because teachers, administrators, college teachers, and non-professionals have different control points or different types of decisions and sanctions, they might also need quite different ideologies. The educational search for an acceptable curricular theory or philosophy might actually be hiding the need for quite different curricular points of view for various groups of educational workers. In other words, current curricular theories or proposals are simply not adequate for grasping and shaping today's curricular problems and possibilities as these emerge within a political framework.

NOTES

[1]This essay was originally published in "Research in Review," a column edited by James B. Macdonald, see *Educational Leadership* 22, no. 2, (1964): 115–129, *Ed.*

[2]Mikel Dufrenne, *Language and Philosophy*, trans. Henry B. Veatch (Bloomington: Indiana University Press, 1963), 95.

[3]Harold Lasswell and Abraham Kaplan, *Power and Society* (New Haven: Yale University Press, 1950).

[4]Paul Diesing, *Reason in Society* (Urbana: University of Illinois Press, 1962), 172.

[5]Lasswell and Kaplan, *Power and Society.*

[6]National Defense Education Act of 1958. *Ed.*

[7]Jerome Bruner, *The Process of Education* (Cambridge, MA: Harvard University Press, 1960).

BIBLIOGRAPHY

Dahl, Robert A. *Modern Political Analysis* (Englewood Cliffs, New Jersey: Prentice-Hall, 1963).

Froman, Lewis A. *People and Politics* (Englewood Cliffs, New Jersey: Prentice-Hall, 1962).

Huebner, Dwayne E. "Politics and the Curriculum" In: *Curriculum Crossroads*, ed. Harry Passow, 87–95 (New York: Bureau of Publications, Teachers College, Columbia University, 1962).

Lasswell, Harold. *Politics: Who Gets What, When, How* (New York: McGraw-Hill, 1958).

Mannheim, Karl. *Ideology and Utopia* (New York: Harcourt, Brace, first published 1936).

Mackenzie, Gordon. "Politics of Curriculum Change." In *Curriculum Crossroads*, ed., Harry Passow (New York: Bureau of Publications, Teachers College, Columbia University, 1962), 76–86.

—. "Curricular Change: Participants, Power and Processes." In *Innovation in Education*, ed. Matthew Miles (New York: Bureau of Publications, Teachers College, Columbia University, 1964), 399–424.

10

Curricular Language and Classroom Meanings

(1966)

The educator participates in the paradoxical structure of the universe. He wishes to talk about language, but must use language for his talk. He infers that meanings exist, but has only language, or other symbol systems, as a vehicle for his inference. Hemmed in by his language, he nevertheless has audacity to tackle problems on the edge of his awareness. The educator would talk of the language of children? With what language would he do this? Would he identify the meanings significant for young people? What meanings, shaped by what language, give him the power to do so? It is as if he detected a speck in his student's eye, but failed to notice the log in his own.

Release from the confinement of existing language, or more appropriately, transcendence of existing patterns of speech is available through several channels. The theologian would argue that the vicious circle is broken or transcended only by grace, mediated through the openness and receptivity available through prayer. The esthetician would argue that literature, specifically poetry, enables lowly man to break out of his verbal prison and to achieve "a victory over language."[1] The scientist would point to his success with observation, classification, hypothesis formation, and experimentation as a way of breaking through language barriers. The critic of social ideologies would argue that "conventional wisdom" is destroyed and reformed only by the "massive onslaught of circumstance with which they cannot contend."[2]

If grace operates in the educational realm, it does so through other channels. Likewise, curricular language is, again unfortunately, not within the realm of literature. The formulator and writer of curricular language is seldom an artist. The penetrating image or significant metaphor is infrequently found in pedagogical materials. This misfortune is intensified by the nearsightedness of the educator who tries to be scientific by throwing out subjective formulations, yet who never quite produces a language system which can be made, shattered and reconstituted through the creative methodologies of science.

The curricular worker is stuck, so to speak, with conventional wisdom, which yields only to the "onslaught of circumstance." The onslaught of educational circumstances is felt differently by various educators. The individual educator's professional sensory and cognitive system is a delicate instrument for detecting shifts in his educational world. His responsiveness takes the form of new actions and new speech. Fortunately, all educators have not been shaped by the same conditioning agents, their sensory and cognitive systems detect different shifts, and their responsiveness takes different forms. Who knows, from such chaos a science might emerge! Given sufficient grace, the educator might even be blessed with the highest possible form of human creation—poetic wisdom.

Today's curricular language seems filled with dangerous, nonrecognized myths; dangerous not because they are myths, but because they remain nonrecognized and unchallenged. The educator accepts as given the language which has been passed down to him by his historical colleagues. He forgets that language was formed by man, for his purposes, out of his experiences—not by God with ultimate truth value. As a product of the educator's past and as a tool for his present, current curricular language must be put to the test of explaining existing phenomena and predicting or controlling future phenomena. Such curricular language must be continually questioned, its effectiveness challenged, its inconsistencies pointed out, its flaws exposed, and its presumed beauty denied. It must be doubted constantly, yet used humbly, with the recognition that that is all he has today. Perhaps tomorrow the educator will have better language, if he stays open to the world which speaks to him, and responds with the leap of the scientist, or the vision of the poet.

Myths In Curricular Language

Two tyrannical myths are embedded deeply in curricular language. One is that of learning—the other that of purpose. These have become almost magical elements within curricular language. The curricular worker is afraid to ignore them, let alone question them, for fear of the wrath of the gods. Fortunately, curricular language is not basically a ritualistic form, although incantations are frequently offered in the educational temples identified as college classrooms and in sacramental gatherings called faculty meetings. The roof will not fall in if these elements are deprecated and partially ignored. A talisman need not be rubbed if one acknowledges that learning is merely a postulated concept, not a reality; and that goals and objectives are not always needed for educational planning.

Indeed, curricular language seems rather ludicrous when the complexity and the mystery of a fellow human being is encompassed in that technical term of

control—the "learner." Think of it—there standing before the educator is a being partially hidden in the cloud of unknowing. For centuries the poet has sung
of his near infinitudes; the theologian has preached of his depravity and hinted
of his participation in the divine; the philosopher has struggled to encompass
him in his systems, only to have him repeatedly escape; the novelist and dramatist have captured his fleeting moments of pain and purity in
never-to-be-forgotten esthetic forms; and the man engaged in curriculum has
the temerity to reduce this being to a single term—"learner." E. E. Cummings
speaks with greater force to the same point.[3]

O sweet spontaneous
earth how often have
the
doting

        fingers of
prurient philosophers pinched
and
poked

thee
,has the naughty thumb
of science prodded
thy

    beauty   .how
often have religions taken
thee upon their scraggy knees
squeezing and

buffeting thee that thou mightest conceive
gods
        (but
true

to the incomparable
couch of death thy
rhythmic
lover

        thou answerest

them only with

                spring)

The educator confronts the human being and no language will ever do him in or do him justice. Yet the curricular worker seems unwilling to deal with mystery or doubt or unknowables. Mysteries are reduced to problems, doubts to error, and unknowables to yet-to-be-discoverables. The curriculum worker cannot deal with these because his language is selected from the symbol systems of the social scientists and psychologists—whereas mysteries, doubts, and unknowns are better handled by poetry, philosophy, and religion. His language, his pedaguese, hides the mysteries, doubts, and unknowns from him. Likewise, he assumes that all human behavior is caused or has purpose, and that consequently his educational activities must be goal oriented. This leads, at times, to ignoring the fullness of the eternal present for the sterility of the known future. This has also led to the continual discussion of educational purpose as if such discussion is the only valid entrance into the curricular domain.

As with any myth, there is sufficient truth or value in these concepts of learning and goals or purpose, and the language which supports them, to warrant their continual use in curriculum. However, to the extent that these notions are tyrannical and prevent the development of other forms of curricular thought, they serve demonic forces. No language system is so good or significant that other language systems cannot eventually take its place—unless it is an esthetic form. But an esthetic form has no instrumental value. Other conceptual models are possible for curricular problems and phenomena, and concepts which inhibit their development must sometimes be violently uprooted in order that the phenomena of concern can be more clearly seen.

Traditional Curricular Tasks

More or less traditional curricular thought, at least since Tyler,[4] has operated with four basic problems or tasks: the formulation of educational "objectives," the selection of "learning" experiences, the organization of those learning experiences, and their evaluation. Other curricular writers expand or add to these four, but the basic framework does not change. Here tyrannical mythology is freely displayed. The title is "The Organization of Learning Experiences." Why not the organization of educational experiences? The formulation of objectives is the first step; necessary, incidentally, because evaluation is the final step. With these objectives, experiences can be selected, organized, and evaluated. By framing curricular tasks in this language, the curricular worker is immediately locked into a language system which determines his questions as well as his answers.

To break from this framework, the language of learning and purpose must be cast aside and new questions asked. To do this the curricular worker must confront his reality directly, not through the cognitive spectacles of a particular language system. As he does this, he is then forced to ask, "What language or language system can be used to talk about these phenomena?" His reality must be accepted, not his language; for many language systems may be used for a given reality.

The two major realities which confront the curricular worker are the activities within a classroom, or activities designated in other ways as educational, and the existential situation of choice among differing classroom activities. This is an oversimplification, of course, for the educator's primary dimension of existence is time, rather than space, and the temporal nature of these realities is ignored for this analysis.

Educational Realities

The first reality is that of educational activity. What is and what is not educational activity becomes, at the extremes, a category problem, but generally educators can walk from one classroom or school to another and point out to a non-educator what they consider to be educational activity. Furthermore, they can dream about the future and envisage educational activity in certain places or among certain people. The language problem which emerges when the educator confronts this educational activity, his first reality, is how to talk about it or how to describe it. How does the teacher talk about his instruction as he plans it or as he describes it to another? How does the supervisor describe the classroom situation as he seeks to help the teacher? How does the curriculum planner talk about events which he wants to happen in classrooms? How does the teacher educator discuss classroom phenomena with his students? How does the researcher describe the classroom events that he studies?

The power of curricular mythologies becomes visible when the problem is posed this way, for the educator is apt to describe the student as a learner, the teacher becomes a goal setter, or a reinforcing agent. Classroom activity is seen as a learning process in action, and indeed teaching is often seen as the mirror image of learning. This problem of description of educational activity has been solved in many ways. Most methods books have some kind of solution. The studies of teaching by Hughes, Smith, Aschner, Bellack, and many others are all efforts to develop a language which can be used to describe classroom action.[5] Teachers have their own way of talking and thinking about what they are doing in the classroom. Many of the studies of newer curricula are descriptions of what teachers can do in the classroom with students. This descriptive problem is both a scientific problem and an esthetic one,[6] for it is at the level of description that science and poetry can merge.

The first reality is also related to a second problem—that of choice among viable alternatives. Selection among alternatives requires some form of valuing, or at least some hierarchy of values. The second language problem becomes that of making conscious or explicit the value framework. When values are explicated a rationality is produced which enables the maximizing of that value. In turn, this rationality contains descriptive terminology which may be used to solve the first problem. The valuing problem and the description problem are consequently intertwined, thus complicating curricular language.

The key curricular questions, rather neutral from most descriptive and value points of view, are "What can go on in the classroom?" and "How can this activity be valued?" The central notion of curricular thought can be that of "valued activity." All curricular workers attempt to identify and/or develop "valued educational activity." The most effective move from this central notion is the clarification of the value frameworks or systems which may be used to value educational activity.

VALUE SYSTEMS

Five value frameworks or systems may be identified. The terms which identify them are not as precise as they might be, but discussion and criticism should aid in sharpening them. For purposes of discussion, and eventually criticism, they may be labeled *technical, political, scientific, esthetic* and *ethical* values.

Technical

Current curricular ideology reflects, almost completely, a technical value system. It has a means-ends rationality that approaches an economic model. End states, end products, or objectives are specified as carefully and as accurately as possible, hopefully in behavioral terms. Activities are then designed which become the means to these ends or objectives. The primary language systems of legitimation and control are psychological and sociological languages. Ends or objectives are identified by a sociological analysis of the individual in the present or future social order, and these ends or objectives are then translated into psychological language—usually in terms of concepts, skills, attitudes or other behavioral terms. With these ends clearly in mind the language of psychology, primarily of learning, is used to generate, or at least sanction, certain activities which can produce these defined ends.

Major concerns of the curricular worker are the mobilization of material and human resources to produce these ends. Books and audiovisual or other sensory aids are brought to the students, or students are taken to actual phenomena. Teachers are trained, hired, or placed to produce the right mixture of human and material resources. Organization and, to an extent not readily recognized in curricular thought, costs are carefully scrutinized, and some effort at efficiency is made. The control of the input of materials and human resources is a major source of control of this means-ends system. Evaluation, from the point of view of the technical value system, may be considered a type of quality control. The end product is scrutinized to see if it can go on the market with the stamp of approval, or if not yet at the end of the production line, the inadequate products-in-process are shunted aside to be reworked by remedial efforts until they can return to the normal production line. Evaluation, or inspection, also serves to check the quality of activities in the producing sequence. These activities may be improved or altered if the end states are not what they should be.

Technical valuing and economic rationality are valid and necessary modes of thought in curriculum. The school does serve a technical function in society by conserving, developing, and increasing human resources which are essential for the maintenance and improvement of the society. This technical function is obvious during wartime, when schools and universities are taken over to serve national purposes. During peacetime, the same social needs exist, but the technical values and economic rationality are apt to be hidden behind the verbal cloaks which a democratic society wraps around itself. So the educator talks of the need for individuals to read, to write, to compute, to think in certain ways, and to make a living in order to exist productively in his society. Technical valuing and economic rationality are necessary in curricular thought, for problems of scarcity and of institutional purpose do exist. However, this is but one value system among five, and to reduce all curricular thought to this one is to weaken the educator's power and to pull him out of the mysteriously complex phenomena of human life.

Political

The second category, political valuing, also exists in curricular thought; more often covertly than overtly. This value category exists because the teacher, or other educator, has a position of power and control. He influences others directly or through the manipulation of resources. To remain in a position of effective power, he must seek the support of those in positions to reward him or influence his behavior in some way. His work, his teaching or educational leadership, becomes the vehicle by which people judge the worth of his influence and hence decide whether he is worthy of their support, respect, or positive sanctions. Educational activity is consequently valued by the teacher, or other curricular leader, for the support or respect that it brings him.

The teacher acts in ways that bring positive support from the principal, superintendent, parents, colleagues, or college professors. Merit ratings, promotions, positions of responsibility, respect in the community, informal leadership among staff members are all fruits of acceptable and enviable efforts. The teacher may produce classroom activity which pleases the custodian, thus assuring him of a quick response when the room needs special attention or when supplies are needed. The superintendent may act to create classroom activity which brings forth rave notices from critical reporters, or accolades from university professors, thus gaining him more prestige in the community. He may need to act in certain ways, to influence classroom activities, in order to gain maximum support for the next bond issue.

The search for increased recognition or power is not inherently bad. A teacher or educational leader must have minimal power to influence others. His efforts are apt to be more successful if he has this power, or at least the trust and respect of those who count. The rationality that accompanies this form of valuing is a political rationality, in which the curricular worker seeks to maximize his power or prestige in order that he may accomplish his work as effectively as possible.

All educational activity is valued politically. The teacher who claims to be immune is so only because he is in equilibrium with his educational community. But given a change of situation, administrators, lay attitudes, or colleagues, that one-time nonpolitically oriented teacher must again rethink how his educational activity reflects upon his standing in the local educational community. There is nothing evil or immoral about political rationality and valuing. Indeed it is necessary if personal influence and responsibility are to be maximized. Of course, if power and prestige are sought as ends, rather than as means for responsible and creative influence, evil and immorality may be produced. Yet dreams and visions are not realized without personal or professional power. Hannah Arendt, in her *Human Condition*,[7] identifies politics as one of the great arts of man, a fact too often forgotten in this day of self-aggrandizement and materialism.

Scientific

Scientific activity may be broadly designated as that activity which produces new knowledge with an empirical basis. Hence educational activity may be valued for the knowledge that it produces about that activity. The teacher, the curricular worker, the educational researcher are always in need of more and better warranted assertions about educational activity. They can construct and manipulate teaching situations to test new hypotheses, or to produce new facts as new technologies and techniques are introduced. Whereas technical valuing seeks to maximize change in students, scientific valuing seeks to maximize the attainment of information or knowledge for the teacher or educator.

The rationality by which scientific values are heightened is some form of scientific methodology. This methodology may take the form of action research or of controlled experimental design. It may be nothing more than exposing students to new situations and ordering the forthcoming responses. Teachers may seek to create unique classroom situations which will give them more information about individual students. Researchers may expose children to new teaching strategies in order to discover necessary conditions for the use of given materials or the accomplishment of certain ends. A total packaged curriculum may be tested to produce information about how teachers and students respond to a given curriculum.

Scientific valuing is a necessary form of curricular valuing. Only as new facts are produced and as new assertions are warranted can the educational enterprise keep pace with the world of which it is a part. Only as individual teachers seek more precise knowledge about their students and about their teaching procedures can they stay abreast of the "onslaught of circumstance." Educational activity valued only for the change produced in students or for the support it brings to teachers is narrowly conceived, for it may also produce significant changes in the educator if he undertakes it with the sensitivities of the scientist.

Esthetic

The esthetic valuing of educational activity is often completely ignored, perhaps because the educator is not sufficiently concerned with or knowledgeable about esthetic values or perhaps because esthetic activities are not highly prized today in society. Scientific and technical values are more highly prized consciously, and political values are more highly prized unconsciously or covertly. Valued esthetically, educational activity would be viewed as having symbolic and esthetic meanings. At least three dimensions of this value category may be identified.

First is what Bullough calls the element of psychical distance.[8] The esthetic object, in this case educational activity, is removed from the world of use. It is a conditioned object which does not partake of the conditioned world; that is, it has no use, no functional or instrumental significance, and consequently may partake of or be symbolic of the unconditional. It is possibility realized, ordinarily impossible in the functional world. It is spontaneity captured, normally lost in the ongoing world. Because of esthetic distance, the art object, in this case educational activity, is the possibility of life, captured and heightened and standing apart from the world of production, consumption and intent. The art object has beauty. Educational activity can have beauty.

The second dimension of the esthetic category is that of wholeness and design. Because the esthetic object stands outside of the functional world it has a totality and unity which can be judged or criticized. The art critic speaks of balance, of harmony, of composition, of design, of integration and of closure. The art object may be a source of contentment and peace, of a unity to be found only in the realm of perfection, the land of dreaming innocence. Educational activity may thus be valued in terms of its sense of wholeness, of balance, of design and of integrity, and its sense of peace or contentment.

The third dimension of esthetic value is that of symbolic meaning. Any esthetic object is symbolic of man's meanings. It reflects the meanings of the artist as an individual; it also reflects the meaning existing in and emerging from man as a life form. The esthetic object, indeed educational activity, may be valued for the meanings that it reveals, and may be valued for its truth. Educational activity is symbolic of the meanings of the educator, as an individual and as a spokesman for man. The teaching of educators who are spiteful, unrealized human beings reflects these inner meanings. The meaninglessness and routine of much educational activity today reflects the meaninglessness and routine of a mechanistic world order. In the rare classroom is the possible vitality and significance of life symbolized by the excitement, fervor, and community of educational activity. Educational activity can symbolize the meanings felt and lived by educators.

Ethical

Finally, educational activity may be valued for its ethical values. Here the educational activity is viewed primarily as an encounter between man and man, and as ethical categories for valuing this encounter come into being, metaphysical and perhaps religious language become the primary vehicle for the legitimation and thinking through of educational activity. The concern in this value category is not on the significance of the educational act for other ends, or the realization of other values, but the value of the educational act per se.

For some, the encounter of man with man is seen as the essence of life, and the form that this encounter takes is the meaning of life. The encounter is not *used* to produce change, to enhance prestige, to identify new knowledge, or to be symbolic of something else. The encounter *is*. In it is the essence of life. In it life is revealed and lived. The student is not viewed as an object, an *it*; but as a fellow human being, another subject, a *thou*, who is to be lived with in the fullness of the present moment or the eternal present. From the ethical stance the educator meets the student, not as an embodied role, as a lesser category, but as a fellow human being who demands to be accepted on the basis of fraternity not simply on the basis of equality. No thing, no conceptual barrier, no purpose intrudes between educator and student when educational activity is valued ethically. The fullness of the educational activity, as students encounter each other, the world around them, and the teacher, is all there is. The educational activity is life—and life's meanings are witnessed and lived in the classroom.

Educational activity is seldom, if ever, valued from within only one of the value categories. Rather all five are, or may be, brought to bear in the valuing process. Today, classroom activity is viewed primarily from the technological value category, but political considerations are also brought to bear; and scientific, esthetic, and ethical values may be brought to bear. The proposition may be put forth that educational activity in classrooms will be richer and more meaningful if all five categories are brought to bear. Indeed, the insignificance and inferior quality of much teaching today may be a result of attempts to maximize only the technical and political and perhaps scientific values without adequate attention to the esthetic and ethical values. Classroom activity which is socially significant because of heightened technical efficiency might have greater personal significance for students and teacher if the esthetic and ethical categories were also used to value the activity. But these notions become possibilities for further search and eventually research.

SYSTEMS OF RATIONALITY

Curricular language is not simple. Many ways can be found or utilized to identify and choose "valued educational activity." The five value categories which have been proposed carry with them forms of rationality which may be used to talk about classroom activity. These forms of rationality are not adequately developed here, and require much more effort before they can be used to analyze, describe, or create educational activity. However, the general aspects are perhaps sufficiently developed to explore the dimensions of classroom meanings which may exist. Attention will be given to ethical and esthetic valuing and possible forms of rationality which may accompany them. The technical is well represented in current curricular literature. The scientific and political are hinted at in a few places, although specific curricular implications need to be developed.

Ethical Rationality

Ethical valuing demands that the human situation existing between student and teacher must be uppermost, and that content must be seen as an arena of that human confrontation. This human situation must be picked away at until the layers of the known are peeled back and the unknown in all of its mystery and awe strikes the educator in the face and heart, and he is left with the brute fact that he is but a man trying to influence another man. A man is being influenced, even if in the form of a child. And it is another man who is influencing, somehow daring to make judgments, to direct attention, to impose demands, and to recommend action and thoughts. How dare he so dare? Probably because he is aware that he has, as have all beings, the power to influence.

Awareness of the power to influence may lead to hubris, the demonic state of false pride in the educator's own omnipotence, or to the humbling recognition that with the power to influence comes the lifegiving possibility of being influenced. The humble acceptance of his power to influence and to be influenced makes possible his freedom to promise and forgive and his willingness to do so.

An act of education is an act of influence: one man trying to influence another man. Educational activity is ethical when the educator recognizes that he participates in his human situation of mutual influence, and when he accepts his ability to promise and to forgive.

The educational activity differs from other human encounters by this emphasis on influence, for clearly the educator is seen, and accepted, as a person who legitimately attempts to influence. However, he operates within the uniquely human endeavor of conversation, the giving and receiving of the word at the frontiers of each other's being. It is in conversation that the newness of each participant can come forth and the unconditioned can be revealed in new forms of gesture and language. The receptive listener frees the speaker to let the unformed emerge into new awarenesses, and the interchange which follows has the possibility of moving both speaker and listener to new heights of being.

Educational activity is activity not only between man and man, however. It also involves activity between the student and other beings in the world. The student encounters other people and natural and man-made phenomena. To these he has the ability to respond. Indeed, education may be conceived to be the influencing of the student's response-ability. The student is introduced to the wealth and beauty of the phenomenal world, and is provided with the encouragement to test out his response-abilities until they call forth the meaning of what it is to be thrown into a world as a human being.

Here, then, are concepts which might possibly be used in an ethical rationality of educational activity: response-ability, conversation, influence, promise, and forgiveness. How can these concepts be used to explore the meanings of classroom activity?

First, the sanctity of response-ability and speech must be recognized. The human being with his finite freedom and his potential participation in the creation of the world, introduces newness and uniqueness into the world, and contributes to the unveiling of the unconditioned by the integrity of his personal, spontaneous responsiveness. His responses to the world in which he finds himself are tokens of his participation in this creative process, and must be accepted as such. Forcing responses into preconceived, conditioned patterns inhibits this participation in the world's creation. Limiting response-ability to existing forms of responsiveness denies others of their possibility of evolving new ways of existing.

Speech may be considered a basic form of man's response-in-the-world. Indeed, Heidegger[9] equates speech with man's reply as he listens to the world. New speech, poetic nonritualistic or nonconditioned speech, is part of this creative unfolding of the world, and demands from the other a response in kind. The expressions of young children may be pure poetry, in that they can reveal to the adult previously unnoticed newness and possibility. The new theories of the scientist are likewise poetic statements which partake of this joy of creation.

Unfortunately, the expressive statements of young children are too frequently ignored or pushed into the venerable coin of the realm by tired adult questions or conditioned responses, and science is taught as a body of knowns and sure things rather than as an activity of man which illuminates the unknown and man's poetic character. To accept the nonconditioned speech and response of the student is to accept him, and in so doing to accept the emergence of the unformed and to-be-formed in the world.

Next, knowledge and other cultural forms must be seen as vehicles for responsibility, conversation, and promise. The various disciplines—mathematics, biology, physics, history, sociology, visual arts, drama, and others—are not only bodies of principles, concepts, generalizations, and syntax to be learned. They are patterned forms of response-in-the-world, which carry with them the possibilities of the emergence of novelty and newness. Introducing the child to the language or symbols and methods of geography or chemistry or music or sculpture is not to introduce him to already existing forms of human existence which he must know in order to exist. Rather these disciplines increase his ability to respond to the world, they increase his response-ability in the world and thus aid in the creation and re-creation of the world. Through them he finds new ways to partake of the world, and he becomes more aware of what he can become and what man can become.

Furthermore, the existing disciplines are language systems linking men to each other via a vocabulary, a syntax, a semantic, and a way of making new language. The botanist is not simply a man who is interested in plants; he is a man who talks botany with other men. Disciplines define language communities with their own symbolic rules, and knowledge facilitates the conversations which may emerge. Knowledge becomes a way of conversing between educator and student about some phenomenon in the world. The educator, as a more experienced member of the language community, responds to the student's speech critically yet supportively. Knowledge, used in the process of educational influence between educator and student, becomes an instrument of promise.

The educator does try to influence, but with the optimism and faith in knowledge as a vehicle to new response-abilities and to new conversational possibilities. In essence, he says to the student "Look, with this knowledge I can promise you that you can find new wonders in the world; you can find new people who can interest you; and in so finding you can discover what you are and what you can become. In so doing you can help discover what man is, has been, and can be. With this knowledge I promise you, not enslavement, not a reduction of your power, but fulfillment and possibility and response-ability." The real teacher feels this promise. He knows the tinge of excitement as the student finds new joys, new mysteries, new power, and new awareness that a full present leads to a future. Too often today, promise is replaced by demand, responsibility by expectations, and conversation by telling, asking, and answering.

Finally, ethical rationality for thinking about educational activity provides the concept of forgiveness. This comes from the educator's awareness that with the power to influence is the power to be influenced. To avoid hubris, the educator must accept the possibility of error—error as he influences and as he has been influenced. Hence forgiveness becomes necessary as a way of freeing one's self and the other from the errors of the past. Forgiveness unties man from the past that he may be free to contribute to new creation. With the power to forgive and to be forgiven, the educator dares to influence and to be influenced in the present. With the possibility of forgiveness the student dares to express himself, to leap into the unknown, and to respond with the totality of his being. As long as man is finite, promise must be accompanied by the possibility of forgiveness, otherwise only the old, the known, the tried and tested will be evoked. Because the educator dares to influence, he must have the courage to permeate classroom activity with the ever present possibility of forgiveness; for if he does not, his influence carries with it seeds of destruction through omniscience which can be only demonic.

Esthetic Rationality

When classroom activity is viewed from the point of view of an esthetic rationality, quite different categories of meaning are derived. As with the ethical, a variety of esthetic viewpoints is possible, but Paul Valery's view will be used here.[10] The general scheme is that the teacher creates an esthetic object to which the students respond. Their responses may also be considered esthetic objects to which the teacher responds as a critic. The intent throughout classroom activity is not a search for preconceived ends but a search for beauty, for integrity and form and the peace which accompanies them, and for truth as life is unveiled through the acting and speaking of the participants.

Valery defines the execution of a work of art as a "transition from disorder to order, from the formless to form, or from impurity to purity, accident to necessity, confusion to clarity."[11] André Maurois expands this by stating that esthetic

> order must dominate an actual disorder ... the violent universe of the passions, the chaos of color and sound, dominated by a human intelligence ....
> In great music, the torrent of sound seems always on the point of turning into hurricane and chaos, and always the composer, . . . soars over the tempest, reins in the chaos. But it is because the chaos has overwhelmed us that we are moved when it is checked.[12]

The teacher, then, in classroom activity can tame the incipient chaos and dominate it with human intelligence. Classroom activity can seem ready to disintegrate but for the esthetic order imposed by the teacher. The influence of this ordered disorder upon the student, if it is an object or event of beauty, is to make him mute. But the response is not dead silence, nor a response of admiration, but of "sustained attention." The artist's intent is "to conjure up developments that arouse perpetual desire," "to exact of his audience an effort of the same quality as his own," and "to provoke infinite developments in someone."[13]

> The students, awed by the teacher's art, can be moved, then, to the enchanted forest of language ... with the express purpose of getting lost; far gone in bewilderment, they seek crossroads of meaning, unexpected echoes, strange encounters; they fear neither detours, surprises, nor darkness; but the huntsman who ventures into this forest in hot pursuit of the 'truth,' who sticks to a single continuous path, from which he cannot deviate for a moment on pain of losing the scent or imperiling the progress he has already made, runs the risk of capturing nothing but his shadow.[14]

So the student seeks to dominate his newfound chaos by his own intelligence, and as a critic the teacher responds with critical concern but sympathetic intent. Classroom activity unfolds in a rhythmic series of events, which symbolizes the meanings of man's temporal existence.

Here, then, are concepts which could serve in an esthetic rationality of educational activity: the continual caging of chaos, Psychical distance or non-instrumentality, beauty or harmony and form, truth as unveiled meaning, and criticism. How can these concepts be used to explore the meanings of classroom activity? It would be possible to use these notions to discuss the dynamics of teacher-student interaction. Yet more fruitful in this day of knowledge and intellectual concerns is to hint at the place of knowledge in educational activity from the point of view of esthetic rationality.

First, knowledge can be viewed as the ordering of particular bits of chaos. The irrational or unconditioned constantly creeps out of all forms of knowledge. As Jaspers states:

> We become aware of the fact that in cognition we have moved in categories which, even in their totality, are like a fine filigree with which we grasp what at the same time we conceal with it . . . pushing ahead restlessly into the ocean of Being, we find ourselves always again and again at the beach of categorically secure, definite, particular knowledge.[15]

In science it creeps out through the continual destruction and construction of existing concepts and theories through the methodologies of science. In social ideologies it creeps out through the onslaught of circumstance. Thus in teaching, educational activity must order, but the unbridled chaos should not be hidden from the student. To do so is to deprive him of the element which calls forth the mute response, the "sustained attention" and the "perpetual desire."

The psychical distance or non-instrumentality of valued educational activity means that the playful involvement with the tools and products of knowledge need not be subjugated to the demands of social or biological necessity. The teacher and the students can be freed from the demands of utilitarianism, and the classroom can become a place where the purity and beauty of knowledge may be enjoyed for itself. The student can be freed to use knowledge to heighten his own significance, to enlarge his own sensitivities to the world, and to realize what he could be. The near infinite possibilities of knowledge and knowing can be hinted at, and the mysteries of the world can be pointed to without the need to reduce them to problems to be solved.

Esthetically valued, knowledge has more than power; it has beauty. As a man-made form its balance and harmony, its composition, its integrity and wholeness, point to the peaceful possibilities inherent in human existence. The scientist, the engineer, as well as the artist, are creative artists who engage in the creative evolution of new forms and who bring harmony to a discordant world. Participating in the making of his own knowledge, the student can recognize his inherent potential to add to, and conversely to subtract from, the possibility of man-made beauty. Intellectual disciplines as well as esthetic crafts are vehicles for this continuing creation.

As an esthetic form, knowledge in educational activity becomes symbolic of man's meanings and of his discovered truths. Knowledge as an esthetic form is a token of man's responsiveness to his own feelings and inner life and to his being a part of its world. Scientific forms of knowledge point to man's willingness to listen to and observe the world around him and to be conditioned by the unknown world. Technical forms of knowledge are symbolic of man's power over the world, and of his desire to shape the world into his own image. Knowledge treated as having an existence beyond the individual or separated from man may be symbolic of man's unwillingness to assume responsibility for his own condition. Knowledge being made and remade in educational activity may symbolize that the educator recognizes that his knowledge is but one of the flowers of his life, which blooms and dies, and yet is the seed of new life.

Finally, the act of criticism becomes a part of the esthetic process. All esthetic events and forms must be able to withstand the criticism of knowledgeable and responsible critics. The utterances and acts of teacher and student are proper targets of sympathetic but critical concern. Scientific criteria of empirical validity, parsimony, and logical structure are instruments for the criticism of scientific knowledge. Pragmatic considerations can be a form of criticism of social ideologies. Teacher and students, through their conversations, engage in the mutual criticism of each other's orderings, and thus contribute to the continued transcendence of form over chaos.

In conclusion, present curricular language is much too limited to come to grips with the problems, or rather the mysteries, of language and meaning of the classroom. The educator must free himself from his self-confining schemas, in order that he may listen anew to the world pounding against his intellectual barriers. The present methodologies which govern curricular thought must eventually give away.

Identifying and proposing a solution to the twofold problem of describing and valuing educational activity identified in this paper is but one attempt, among many that should be made, to reformulate aspects of curricular language. With it other meanings of classroom activity might be identified. As Conant points out, the significance of scientific theory is not its validity, but its fruitfulness. The scientific value of these roughly sketched ideas will be their fruitfulness. Their technical and political value are of no significance. Their ethical and esthetic meanings may be pondered.

NOTES

[1] John Middleton Murray, *The Problem of Style* (London: Oxford University Press, 1922), 101.

[2] John Kenneth Galbraith, *The Affluent Society* (Boston: Houghton Mifflin, 1958), 9, 20.

[3] Copyright 1923, 1951, by e.e. cummings, 1963, 1965 by Marion Morehouse Cummings. See "La Guerre II," in E.E. Cummngs *a selection of poems* with an introduction by Horace Gregory (New York: Harcourt Brace and World, 1965), 32–33.

[4] Ralph W. Tyler, "The Organization of Learning Experiences," in *Toward Improved Curriculum Theory*, ed. Virgil Herrick and Ralph Tyler (Chicago: University of Chicago Press, 1950), 59–67.

[5] Arno Bellack, *Theory and Research in Teaching* (New York: Bureau of Publications, Teachers College, Columbia University, 1963); Arno Bellack, *The Language of the Classroom* (New York: Institute of Psychological Research, Teachers College, Columbia University, 1963).

[6] F. S. C. Northrup, *The Logic Of the Sciences and the Humanities* (New York: Macmillan, 1947), 169–90.

[7] Hannah Arendt, *The Human Condition* (Chicago: University of Chicago Press).

[8] Edward Bullough, "Psychical Distance as a Factor in Art and an Esthetic Principle," in *A Modern Book of Aesthetics*, ed. Melvin Rader (New York: Henry Holt, 1952).

[9] Martin Heidegger, *Being and Time*, trans. John MacQuarrie and Edward Robinson (New York: Harper & Row, 1962).

[10] Paul Valery, *Aesthetics*, trans. Ralph Mannheim (New York: Bollingen Foundation, 1964).

[11] Ibid., 158.

[12] Ibid., 163.

[13] Ibid., 58, 161, 193, 161, 151.

[14] Ibid., 48–49.

[15] Karl Jaspers, *Truth and Symbol*, trans. Jean T. Wilde, William Kluback, and William Kimmel (New York: Twayne Publishers, 1959), 38, 79.

11

Facilitating Change
as the Responsibility
of the Supervisor

(1966)

There is something about the terms "change" and "innovation" that produces a feeling of discomfort in me or at least a sense of inappropriateness. This feeling on my part is not a result of a complacency about the present effectiveness or quality of education in the United States, for I have been reasonably dissatisfied with most public education as long as I have been a professional within the field of education. This feeling is not a result of hostility toward present change agents within the American educational scene, for I recognize that the quality of education within the schools is the responsibility of all members of our society, not just old-line professional educators.

I have the hunch that this feeling springs from a style or mode of thought which accompanies recent efforts to modify education. This style or mode of thought is centered around the words "change" and "innovation." Most people agree, including the proponents of new developments in curriculum, that change for its own sake is not valuable; that, indeed it is not wanted. It isn't simply change that is wanted, it's something else. Look at this problem from the other end. The antonym of change is sometimes given as "permanence." It is just as obvious that educators are not interested in permanence for its sake either. Assuming that there is a continuum from permanence to change we can postulate that the educator is interested in something in between the two extremes. He is interested in a balance between change and permanence; neither for their own sake, and yet perhaps for the sake of each. An ambiguity? Yes. We might say that the educator is interested in change for the sake of a given type of permanence; and on the other hand that he is interested in permanence because it provides for a certain kind of change.

118

The same problem exists for me with the term "innovation." It implies that something is to be introduced; that there is a plan or a procedure or something that can be introduced in its totality, or perhaps with minor modification. In connection with this word, the dictionary mentions the act of renewing or of introducing something new. I have no problem with either of these meanings—renewal, or introducing something new. Connected with these meanings, however, is the notion of novelty, and this may be a source of my discomfort. Another potential source of discomfort is that innovation is somewhat distinct from evolution and from history. To what extent should innovations be retained, made a part of an ongoing evolving situation? It is this sense of a lack of historical continuity that I think grates against me. By all means schools should have innovations and a climate should be fostered in which innovations can come to the surface; for these are the sources of renewal. But evolution takes place not by simply introducing something new, but also through respect for the historicity of a given situation. Newness must be internalized and made a part of the old and the old a part of the new. This concern for newness itself, something that stands outside of the historical context, is a source of my discomfort. Newness can be introduced, or an old situation brought up to date, but the new in a short time can become the old. It is the continuous process of keeping something alive and viable that should concern educators.

Educators must conceive of the school as a viable, growing, living organism within the society. As an institution, a school and its program can become dated, a reflection of the past. But the social organism and the world that supports it keep changing, growing, and evolving. Somehow the mechanisms that make the society grow and evolve must also be operative in the school. It, too, must grow and evolve.

Perhaps a more adequate term to describe that which is needed in schools today is neither "change" nor "innovation," but "responsiveness." What we need are responsive schools, schools that respond or answer to the forces in the world that are changing other social structures. Somehow or another, those individuals who obligate themselves to run our schools must be sensitive to the many faceted world about them; they must observe and listen with care, and they must enable the schools to respond to the goings on which they see and hear and feel. But responsiveness, too, can be a flighty sort of action; a neurotic response to every minor modification that comes into being in this complex world. On the other hand, responsiveness also refers to the permanence side of the change–permanence continuum. The conservative, too, must be certain that his proposals are really a response to something that was, but is no more; and by all means not just a hanging on for empty symbolic reasons.

This notion of a "responsive" school needs a qualifier in order to avoid the idea of neurotic or flighty response. I would suggest that we qualify responsiveness with the word "responsibly." What we need are "responsibly responsive" schools. The word "responsibly" is used in the sense of being aware of one's obligations as an historical being for the continual creation of the world and in the sense of being accountable for one's acts. The educator makes decisions in a particular time and place. Those who share that time and place rightfully hold him responsible for the consequences of his decisions. However, his decision is a factor in the continual emergence or evolution of that situation as it exists through time, thus his accountability extends into the past and into the future. To be responsibly responsive, then, is to be aware of the history and destiny of the given situation and to be answerable for the consequences of any responses made. A responsibly responsive school is one that serves as a bridge between the past and the future, yet which answers or responds to the world of today.

The educator's problem is not change or innovation, but the maintenance of an institution that remains responsive to the world around it, responsibly responsive to that world. The function of the supervisor, then, is maintaining or facilitating the responsible responsiveness of the school. Or perhaps—helping the school be a bridge between yesterday and tomorrow, yet responsive to today.

Four aspects or ingredients can be postulated as necessary if schools are to be responsibly responsive. The first is the listening to or perception of the events that are taking place outside, and perhaps even within schools. This could be called the scanning or sensitivity function. The second is the ability to create visions of what might be—the envisioning or imagining function. The third is the valuing function—the ability to assign value to that which is envisioned. And the fourth is the power to bring into reality the vision that is valued—the power function. The remainder of the paper will be devoted to the four characteristics, for they are valuable handles by which the supervisor can grab hold of his job in this very complex educational world.

The Scanning or Sensitivity Function

The school is part of a much larger world, and if it is to be responsive to this larger world, someone must know what is going on in it. This certainly must be one function of the supervisor. It is extremely easy to get involved in maintenance functions in connection with a given school; making sure that schedules are kept, plans are fulfilled, teachers are hired, materials are on hand, and students in classes. But these are all internal problems connected with the upkeep of a given situation. To be responsive, the school must detect events and developments in the outside world which can, will, or should impinge upon it. Thus the supervisor must stay tuned in on the world; he must listen, observe and read with care. He must remain open to what is happening about him and distinct from him.

There are several ways of cutting or slicing this world so he knows what sections to monitor. Certainly the social sector is one of the most important sections to monitor no matter how the world is sliced. What is going on in the various societies around the world to which the school should respond? What changes are taking place within our social order to which the school should respond? The revolutions and potential revolutions in Asia, Africa, and South America are sources of major rumblings and the sensitive supervisor is aware that the world is about to be different because of these revolutions and potential revolutions. Within our own country the shift in racial relationships, and the problems of the metropolitan areas are factors to which the schools should respond. Today the curriculum certainly is not responsibly responsive to many of these social developments, although at times someone gets on his high horse to plead for action which seldom finds its way into the curriculum.

At another level, the person who seeks to keep the schools responsibly responsive must also be aware of the changes that are taking place in our "thing" world. He must be aware of the consequences of technology. The development of the whole information handling field is becoming a major source of great changes within our society. It is not simply the introduction of TV, communication satellites, and xerography. It is the extensive insertion of the computer and miniature information storing, processing, and retrieval units into all spheres of human activity. For instance, new microfilming techniques have made it possible to record the content of the Bible on a 2 x 2 inch sheet of film. It is comfortable to think that such electronic and technical marvels will simply permit us do what we have been accustomed to do with greater efficiency and power. However, this is only part of the truth. The popularity of McLuhan and his slogan that "the media is the message" is a case in point. He raises very serious questions about the limits of a book mentality in an electronic age. Yet most of the developments in the schools accept the sacredness of the book and do not reflect the revolutionary and revealing character of newer media. In the schools these changes in electronic technology are much too scantily previewed by computer programming of instructional materials, and the use of computers in administrative problems within the schools. But too few supervisors are concerning themselves with the deeper meanings of this revolution.

At still another level, the supervisor must be alert to the changes and developments in the intellectual fields. Awareness of the knowledge explosion which is assumed to have occurred recently is common. This phenomena is related most often to the sciences. Equally significant are the changes taking place in philosophy and theology; changes which have been somewhat previewed in fiction, drama, modern art, and to some extent popularized in the mass media. The ecumenical movement has influenced many people and the Death of God movement has stirred up controversy; but more significantly the modern theologians are making important contributions to the world of ideas.

Educators who are obliged to help shape responsibly responsive schools must have their antennae tuned for developments in the world outside of the school, otherwise they cannot help the school respond to these phenomena which are shaping human life today. Educators obviously cannot keep abreast of everything, but they certainly must have some kind of system that alerts them to almost all of the everything even if in abbreviated form.

There are, of course, also changes within the school and education to which the supervisor must keep tuned. He must be aware of the changing characteristics of the students in his charge. These young people are different than we were when we were at their age. For one thing television has enlarged their real world and their imaginary world. For another, the ease of transportation has increased their mobility and broadened their reference groups. The easy access of information and images has changed their hopes, fears, and values. Certainly everyone agrees that schools should remain responsive to the students who come to them. Unfortunately the history of the school as an institution does not support this expectation.

Another level of sensitivity to educational phenomena is to the materials that are available for educational purposes. At one time the supervisor might have thought that he was doing his job if the textbook or map salesman stopped by his office every year or so to keep him abreast of his wares. Today this is no longer sufficient, for materials are changing fast and the regular textbook route sometimes takes us over well traveled ground rather than into exciting new territory. Films, programmed materials, telephone conference-calls which tie students to people all around the world, TV, the newer science materials and kits, and increasingly the social studies games and data banks mean that the supervisor must be abreast of what is happening in the educational material world. Furthermore, he must have some criteria for knowing what is new and good and what is simply new, or even old but in new bottles.

At another level of sensitivity the supervisor must be aware of the kinds of changes that are taking place in colleges and in teacher education programs, for the nature of beginning teachers is also changing. Schools should be responding to these changes, too. Again, the person accountable for schools must be able to make his own decisions about teachers, and not be sold a bill of goods by propagandists in the teacher education industry any more than he is by the material producing industry. Nor should he be permitted to use outdated criteria for evaluating the new college students who are coming into the teaching profession.

Thus the first function of the supervisor who seeks to maintain a responsibly responsive school is that of keeping an ear to the ground so the swells of changes vibrate in his nervous system. He must serve as the radar system of the school, the early warning system, for if he responds with awareness and sensitivity then the rest of the school might respond—with awareness and sensitivity.

The Envisioning Function

The scanning and sensitivity function is an intelligence function, entailing reconnaissance and data gathering. The next function is more difficult, for the supervisor must take these rumblings of a world that is becoming and, with the aid of the imagination, transform them into images of what might take place within the school. He must become a visionary. Here the educator has difficulties, for the conventional wisdom of curriculum follows a technical or manufacturing paradigm. It assumes that the first question to be answered is that of the role of the school or the purposes to be achieved, or if you wish, the objectives. Given these objectives, and a reasonably valid psychology of learning, he assumes that he can somehow generate, much as an engineer does, the activities and experiences that students must have if they are to reach these objectives. This postulated procedure is much too rational, in a logical discursive way, for the design of educational programs follows more aptly the rationality used by the artist or the politician than that used by the technician or engineer. The educator who is sympathetically vibrating to the world about him must convert these vibrations and the situational givens into visions of what schools and classrooms and educational activity might be. Not visions of what is possible, or even of what is needed, but visions of what might be if he had all of the needed power and resources. This envisioning function is not simply a result of technical know-how or even of educational knowledge. It is a function of the richness of personal, professional imagination. Here, too, the profession of education is frequently deficient. Educators have been too content to accept canned visions. They have been too willing to limit their visions to what is simply possible, thus constricting the emergence of new possibilities. They have been too eager to please others rather than to venture out into the unknown world of the future and to dream their dreams. Because of these tendencies educators have restricted the development of their imaginations. They have been so busy trying to perfect the technical control of the world through scientific knowledge, (hence the emphasis upon statistics, psychology, sociology) that they have failed to perfect their visions, which requires emphasis upon the arts and the humanities. The educators bookshelves must be lined not only with scientific books, but with poetry, novels, and drama. His walls should be lined with art objects and his spare time occupied as much with visiting new avant-garde films, dramas and art exhibits as pouring through educational journals. The imagining or envisioning function must be used and developed and perfected as must the reconnaissance functions.

What kinds of visions? Visions of the kinds of experiences which educate young people not those which simply help them learn. Visions of the kinds of relationships among students and teacher which can be truly educative not simply routine. Visions of ways in which schools and classrooms can be organized. Images of how new media can be used for educational purposes. Visions of how students and the world can be brought together, of how walls of schools can become permeable membranes which permit the passage back and forth between the students and the world. Visions of how teachers can be made to feel that their teaching is indeed a part of the continual creation of the world and that they are artists who participate in the struggle to give form to a new and seemingly chaotic world.

Some educators seem to have lost confidence in their individual ability to create visions of what might be in their schools or school systems. Some have left the visionary function to so-called professional visionaries, who frequently do not come up to the needs of today and tomorrow because they cannot know and feel the world in a specific community. Hence the canned visions, which unfortunately are not seen simply as visions, but as prescriptions for action. Of course these canned visions can become stimulants to an educator's imagining process, if he would but use them as goods. The proposals on organization, team-teaching, content organization, and teaching styles are not, or at least should not, be meant to be taken over in toto. They are examples of the kind of visions that are possible. But only an individual educator, working within his own home community, can envision what could be in that community if provided with all that is needed.

The Valuing Function

Of course, an educator never has all necessary resources or power. Furthermore, it is possible to create many visions. The educational imagination can go wild sometimes and dream up all sorts of things, and such wild-eye dreaming should not be discouraged. Not all visions, however, are valuable in or for a given situation. Hence the third function of the supervisor who seeks to keep his schools responsibly responsive—his valuing function. He must be able to assign value to his visions or those of others. He must be able to determine if these visions are of worth at the present time and in the present situation. There are many criteria for getting at the worth of an educational vision or of an educational situation. The focus upon responsible responsiveness leads to at least three criteria. Two stem from the accountability mentioned earlier. The third concerns the values which are wrapped around educators as human beings, not simply as educators.

Value is always related to the immediate situation within which the vision is to be realized. The person who seeks to transform dream into reality must necessarily face up to the possible reactions to his actions by those who share that situation. There is consequently, a kind of social or political value criterion which can be used to evaluate any dream. How will teachers accept the idea? The board? The members of the community? The students? This social or political form of valuing means that the supervisor who entertains visions must play those visions against the individuals and groups with potential sanctioning power, people who can hold him accountable. This is something that need not be done overtly, in the sense of exposing his vision to them. It is more a matter of taking their role and trying to anticipate how they will react to the vision. If it is too far out for them, perhaps the vision lacks value in that situation. If the anticipated consequences will disrupt the whole educational situation so severely that other values are lost, then perhaps the vision should be pushed into the background for the present time. This social-political valuing is a concern for the immediate.

But the educator's responsibility as historical agent means that he cannot use the social-political criterion as the only or even as the most significant valuing base; for his chief concern is not the immediate. A responsibly responsive school is one that serves as a bridge between the past and the future. The value of a vision cannot be determined solely by the present, it must also be determined by the past and the future. A vision must be valued historically, with one eye on the past, and one on the future. Here, too, is a sadly neglected realm of competency in the educational profession. The educator is too often a missionary who has forgotten his historical roots and his destiny. He no longer thinks historically, if he ever did. Nor does he think of the continuing, evolving future which extends beyond him, and this is sad. To try to live outside of one's temporality, one's historicity is to forget that laughter is sometimes a sign of a rootedness to a past; that tears are frequently a sign of inability to control the future; and that promise and forgiveness make the present bearable even if filled with ignorance and error. Visions must be screened from the perspective of the past and from the perspective of the future. Does the educational vision show respect for the efforts and contributions of the past? Does it conserve the qualities of that community and those people which are indeed unique contributions to human life? Does it bring into the present and into the future the best that man had found in his hard struggles to give meaning to life in that community? On the other hand, does the vision make it more likely that school and community can make the very difficult transition into a future which to a large degree remains unknown, or does it lock the situation into a form which will not lend itself readily to evolution and development? Is it a fly-by-night vision, that seems like a novel idea with no significance for the conservation of the past or the emergence into the future? Questions of this kind can be asked and answered only by people who have a sense of the value of the past, who respect its contributions to the whole stream of human life. They can not be asked, or at least answered, by those who hang on rigidly to the past because it is the easiest thing to do. They can be asked only by people who have a sense of destiny: people who do not see the future clearly, but who catch glimmers of an emerging future; people who welcome these evolutions with joy because they reflect the continuing creation of the world. These visions, then, must be scrutinized by the wisdom of one who brings to the present both the virtues of the past and the promises of the future; one who is ready to forgive and forget the errors of the past but who can at the same time hope and perhaps promise that the future will be better. Self complacency or a mechanistic concern for the present destroys such wisdom or prevents it from developing.

Finally, any educational vision must also be projected against the human and ethical values that one holds as an individual, as a human being living in a moral universe. The educator must ask questions about the significance of his visions and the visions of others for the individual students and teachers who live this school life with him. Will the vision if realized, make it more possible for these individuals to be themselves, to control their own destiny, to meet courageously their own tragedies, to feel the awe-some responsibility of freedom, to face up to the possibility of error without self condemnation? Will the vision, if it is realized, help these young people and teachers feel that they too are participating in the projection of meaning into an ambiguous world? Will the children in the first grade feel that the world brought into the classroom is indeed a joyful place, filled with a number of things? Will the early adolescent be helped to realize that those stirrings in his body and mind with which he can barely deal are harbingers of new powers and new satisfactions that can remake him and his world? Will the senior be able to see that the transition from the protected school society to the open society is but another step in the many that he will be taking in the future—steps to be anticipated, not feared, because the school has had some significance in shaping these steps? Will teachers feel that the new vision does not decrease their potency, but gives them increased power to realize their visions as they work with students? Will they feel that they will not be decreased but will be increased with more power to do, to dream, to think, and to feel? Will the vision, if realized, help all of the people in that school be more human, or will it contribute to the tendency toward dehumanization which seems rampant today?

Such ethical valuing is not simply a checking against old feelings of do good and morality. The criteria used to make decisions of ethical value must also be educated and disciplined. For instance, new technologies—computers in classrooms, talking typewriters,[1] programmed texts—do not in and of themselves lead to a dehumanization. It is the use of them which can be moral or immoral. They can very well increase the moral dimensions of education by providing forms for human life in the schools which were not possible before. To identify these potential human values the educator must continue to grow as a human being.

The Power Function

To be sensitive or aware, to be able to dream, and to be able to identify potential value are but the beginning aspects of the supervisors role. The educator is then faced with the problem of bringing into being his valued visions. To bring vision into being, to help the past and the future coalesce into a present filled with value requires power: political power to influence others, financial power to mobilize scant resources, technical power to organize everything into effective designs, and artistic power to build beautiful and truthful designs.

Again, educational conventional wisdom has reduced the educators ability to see and feel the complexity of the world building task which is his. He has been put on a one-dimensional track, for he assumes that the best will come about through group discussion, rational arguments, existing financial and social structures, and the knowledge which exists within the scientific camp. This is not so. For one thing, to bring valued visions into reality can produce conflict, human inertia, differences of opinion, and what sometimes seems like dogged cussedness. Power is needed to work in this morass of human passion and belief—not the powers of the authoritarian dictator, but of the wise and astute statesman who is a consummate politician. For another, to realize valued visions requires the mobilization and allocation of very limited resources. Difficult choices must be made between money for the teacher's salaries, new materials, organizational structure, or new buildings, and at other levels money for education, for roads, for wars, for the aged. These choices require the power of the economist to see through the maze of limited resources and to deal with obsolescence and capital investment. The realization of vision also requires technical know-how. How can teachers be helped to develop new teaching behaviors? How can materials be built which will be effective for developing new skills in students? How can the complex organizational problems of the high school be seen so all of the parts fit together into a smoothly working whole. But even these powers do not complete our task. For the curriculum does not simply do something for or to students through the content. It speaks to them about the educator, who he is, what he believes and feels, the kinds of meanings that he finds and projects into the world. The curriculum becomes the symbol of his life; to make this symbol stand out with beauty and truths requires artistic power. Somehow, the educator must not simply solve educational problems. He makes his mark on the world through his artistry, by projecting himself out into the world so he can say: "This is what I am, what I believe. Here is my contribution to the truth and beauty in the world."

Educators have shied away from the idea of power and politics. Somehow they think that politics is a dirty word and that power is immoral. Quite the contrary. Politics is the noblest art of man, although it has frequently been debased by men who use it selfishly. But it has been debased as much by the failure of others to get involved in the great human struggles which shape mankind. Thus power is given to those who seek it for its own sake, rather than given to those who seek it for the sake of world building. Conflict has also been rejected as a legitimate form of social evolution, and thus educators seek to reduce conflict within the staff. But conflict can be constructive, for it permits differences to come to the surface and compromises to emerge. Conflict permits the way-outers to suggest new ways, while the hanging on by traditionalists means that older valued ways are not lost. Compromise can unite both. To seek consensus, blurs the image of the battle between the future and the past; and indeed it must be a battle. But conflict does not imply lack of conversation and communication. Conflict can be constructive. Why should conflict not be fomented within staffs if it will help clarify the value struggles that are going on?

The use of political power is seen in the uses of personal power to influence others. To influence others is not evil, but to do so without the willingness to be influenced might be. Political power to realize valued visions requires one to use personal relationships effectively, to be skilled in the rhetorical uses of language, to be able to use sanctions and decision making powers skillfully. But the use of personal power and institutional power does not sanction immorality, self-righteousness, nor the failure to listen and respect others. Hubris can destroy, and the failure to listen to or to be receptive of others can lead to the missing of very significant cues, visions, and values that others might have.

Curriculum people have also shied away from the economic realities that go with responsible responsiveness. It is too much to expect teachers to evolve new teaching procedures and to internalize new instructional materials and technologies out of their own hide. It costs money to develop new skills, to learn to handle new materials and to work with different kinds of students. To expect teachers to develop these new skills on their own time after school is to ignore the fact that plain good teaching is in and of itself a full time job. After a day of teaching very few have energies left to try to remake themselves. It costs money to work up new materials, new units; and this money buys time. Time is a commodity, and good teachers have little of it after working with students. The problem becomes one of finding new resources so more teacher time can be purchased, so teachers can indeed contribute to the evolution of new educational forms. Summer workshops in connection with some of the new science and math curricula have been reasonably successful for this reason; the time buying idea was accepted as necessary. Probably there is no alternative, eventually, but to have a twelve month school year for teachers, during which part of that time is used by the teachers to update their skills and materials and to share in the continual creation of school.

Materials also cost money. Some of the arguments over individualized reading versus textbook reading are really controversies over how much to spend on reading materials for the elementary school, for a good individualized reading program requires a good elementary school library, indeed, is impossible without it. Materials also wear out, and an investment in a new set of materials is something that must be justified over a period of years. These problems of obsolescence and capital investment are seldom mentioned as problems inherent in supervision, but are nevertheless there, even if ignored. To facilitate a responsibly responsive school requires the economic power to deal with these financial matters wisely and astutely.

Much discussion among supervisors deals with the aspects of technical power. They must know how to mobilize teachers, how to organize materials, how to group students, what kinds of materials will be effective for what purposes, how to be a sympathetic critic of teaching style. Knowledge of this kind—technical power—is contained within the lore and esoteric knowledge of supervisors. Supervisors have perhaps over-stressed the technical power which is required, to the neglect of the political, economic and artistic power which must also be there if they are to help school be responsive. Supervisors have hoped that scientific research might eventually produce enough know-how so that our technical power would be great enough to compensate for their other power lacks. This is impossible, but nevertheless, political, economic and artistic powers are useless unless supervisors also have some power based upon technical-scientific knowledge about the supervisory process.

Perhaps it is strange to write of artistic power when supervision is discussed. However this is a power exerted by the very need to form and design actions and programs. Because the educator lacks artistic awareness and power, much of his designing and many of his programs and procedures end up as ugly affairs rather than as beautiful affairs. A curriculum too frequently is symbolic of untruth rather than truth. As a result the educator's wish to dissociate himself from his work. But he is his work. The programs that he establishes, the forms of relationships that he evolves, the visions that he makes manifest are really him. Yes, it is a "him" that has been shaped by conflict, and the realities and limitations of the situation in which he lives. But how does he look when he sees himself out there in the flesh of the world. Are his tensions displayed, his doubts expressed with acceptance, his sureness with humility? Are the compromises there for everyone to see so they can also see how he has been buffeted by others? Does the program that he has helped design reflect what he believes about man—his goodness, yet his tendency to fall. Has he incorporated enough humor or possibilities for humor into his design that his rigidities and tom-fooleries can be revealed. Does his responsibly responsive school incorporate enough of his real hopes so genuine tears fall when his failure to see clearly enough breaks through. The school, the social and technical world of education, is his creation. Is it a significant contribution to the continuing creation of the world, or have the magic oils been poured on that reduce the swells of the wave but do not really bring to fruition the teeming forces at work in and around him? This school which is his, which he makes through his personal-professional efforts, they speak of him. They reveal who he is as an adult. What do these schools tell the young people about what he values, how he feels, the truths he holds? Why doesn't he have more power, more artistic power to turn these schools into symbols of what he is and believes. Yet they are, they really are, symbols. Political power is not necessary for honesty, money is not necessary for beauty, technical power is not needed for truth. These require only the artistic power to create, to project meaning, and the courage to reveal himself in his work.

What is the function of the supervisor in maintaining a responsibly responsive school? To be alert and sensitive to a darkened world. To be bold and imaginative in the dreaming of visions. To be courageous and steady in the valuing of visions. To be powerful in the projection of visions that might brighten the world.

And to realize that he is not alone in this process of responding, envisioning, valuing and creating—that he must have the humility and the strength to enable others to do the same—the principals and teachers and students who live with him. For it might just be that some of them are more in tune with this world which he shares. It could very well be that others have more profound visions. It is very possible that others may have a greater sense of history or a more significant feeling of destiny. And it is true that one person has limited power. To build greater edifices requires the power of many—the political power of some, the economic power of others, the technical power of a few, and the artistic power of the real artists. A responsibly responsive school can only be aided by a supervisor—it cannot be produced by him.

NOTES

[1] The "talking typewriter," was one of the early, and at the time exciting, computerized technological developments in education. Developed during the 1960s by Omar Khayam Moore (Learning Research and Development Center at the University of Pittsburgh), the "talking typewriter" was used to teach very young children to read, spell and compose stories. The following description is given in Don D. Bushnell and Dwight W. Allen, ed. *The Computer in American Education* (New York: Wiley, 1967), "The Edison Responsive Environment Instrument (ERE) is a computerized typewriter with capabilities intended to reproduce several of the response actions of a … teacher. When a pupil depresses a key on the typewriter keyboard, the key symbol is typed in large type on the typewriter paper and is pronounced at the same time. On a rear projection screen, letters, words, and sentences can be displayed automatically with accompanying audio explanations and pointer designations. The keyboard can be locked except for the key the child is expected to press. As well as playing the model soundtrack, the device can record and play back the child's voice for comparison purposes." Quoted in George B. Leonard, *Education and Ecstasy* (New York: Dell, A Delta Book, 1968), 188-189. *Ed.*

12

Curriculum as Concern for Man's Temporality

(1967)

If a science is to come into existence at all, it will do so as more and more powerful concepts are introduced. Their formulation is often the work of empirical investigators, but it is philosophical, nonetheless, because it is concerned with meanings rather than facts, and the systematic construction of meanings is philosophy. Wherever a new way of thinking may originate, its effect is apt to be revolutionary because it transforms questions and criteria, and therewith the appearance and value of facts.

The state of having turbulent notions about things that seem to belong together, although in some unknown way, is a prescientific state, a sort of intellectual gestation period. This state the "behavioral sciences" have sought to skip, hoping to learn its lessons by the way, from their elders.

> The result is that they have modeled themselves on physics, which is not a suitable model. Any science is likely to emerge ultimately with physics, as chemistry has done, but only in a mature stage, its early phases have to be its own, and the earliest is that of philosophical imagination and adventure.[1]

Langer is not quoted to legitimize this essay as philosophical, but, rather to indicate that my notions are turbulent, that I am in "a prescientific state— a sort of gestation period" and want to share my sense of adventure. It might very well be a wild goose chase, but, as a long-time curriculum specialist, I am inclined to believe that my unrest is a result of unrest in this endeavor called "curriculum." Many gathering together under this label have sought the legitimacy of the "behavioral sciences" and have moved directly to worship what Langer terms the "idols of the laboratory." They have ignored the hard and frustrating work of disciplining the imagination. I, myself, claim no special competency in this realm. My only discipline has been the frustration of trying to live with and use modes of thought presumed effective for generating educational programs. However, this has been with the increasing uneasiness that our questions and answers and the concepts which frame them are indeed inadequate.

This growing uneasiness centers upon two central categories in curricular language: learning and objectives. It seems to me that the unquestioning acceptance of these is one of the reasons that the curriculum person has failed to generate the ideas necessary to keep educational institutions and language abreast of the times. If these categories were not used as symbols of assumed educational realities, they might more readily become pointers in the search for other ways to look at and act upon educational phenomena. For me, they point to man's temporality and the concern for it as the focus of curricular action.

Goals, Purposes, and Objectives

For the purpose of this paper there is no need to make distinctions among the various uses of the words "goals," "purposes," or "objectives." These are terms that indicate the orientation of educational activity to the future. The educator looks ahead to expected outcomes, plans for tomorrow, and attempts to specify the future behavior of the student. Inherent in these terms is the notion of value, and the pseudoconflict between tradition and evolution or reconstruction. The process of arriving at these objectives, goals, or purposes (call them what you wish) involves inspection of the past (or the present as the already-past); identification of forms of existence or aspects of life considered worthy of maintenance, transmission, or necessary for evolution; and the projection of these valued forms into the future. Basically, the determination of objectives is the search for the bridge between the past and the future; it is argument over the degree of continuity necessary for change, or the amount of change that is necessary for continuity; it is concern for the balance between succession and duration. All of these categories are concerned with society's existence "in time" and refer to man's concern for the historical continuity which gives his social forms and institutions some kind of stability, yet vitality, as they emerge from yesterday into tomorrow. Unfortunately, the educator's too easy acceptance of the function of or the necessity for purposes or objectives has replaced the need for a basic awareness of his historicity.

This search for clear and unambiguous goals is a fanciful and, to a large extent, idle search. It serves almost the same function to those over twenty-six that drugs serve for the younger—tune in, turn on, drop out. To find the purpose of the schools is thought to restore the calm and enable educators to drop out of the troublesome political process of living historically. It has almost been assumed that if the educator can clearly specify his goals, then he has fulfilled his responsibilities as an historical being. But historical responsibility is much too complex to be so easily dismissed. It is too easy to forget that debate about educational objectives is part of the continuous struggle of rival political ideologies, which has its consequences in who controls the educational environment. The problem of living historically, or at least of living as an historically aware person, is not resolved by pronouncements of goals or purposes, but by engaging in political action.

History, not sociology, is the discipline which seems the most akin to the social study of education. The historian can be interpreted as looking back to where a society has been to determine how it arrived at a given point. In so doing, he identifies certain threads of continuity to unite diverse moments in time. In contrast, the educator looks forward. He, too, seeks to identify threads of continuity to unite diverse moments in time, but these are moments of yesterday and tomorrow, not of two yesterdays. It might be said that an educator is an historian in reverse. The curriculum person deserves to be chided for his ahistoricalism—not only is he ignorant of where his own field has been or is going, but he may also be missing a possibility that historical modes of thought might lead to more powerful tools for use in curriculum design.

The present does not easily find its way into the category of goals, objectives, or purposes. To identify these values requires withdrawing from the present moment and looking down upon it as if it were past. There is always a process of inspecting something which was. By their very nature, goals, objectives, and purposes become statements of a desired future—a tomorrow. The present creeps in in the teaching. It is when the educator must deal with the student that he seemingly drops the concern for the past or for the future and focuses upon the present. If he remains focused upon the past or upon the future, he loses contact with the student, and the educational process may suffer. It is by criticizing the category "learning" that the significance of the present is brought into perspective with the past and the future.

Learning

As with the categories of purposes, goals, or objectives, learning also points to the temporality of man, to the temporality of the individual man. Learning has been associated with a change in behavior of an organism. An observer concerned with the process of learning certain specified aspects of behavior at a given time, for example at t_1, and later at t_2, seeks to identify the changed status. If change is detected and it is assumed to be related to interaction with the environment, it can be said that learning occurs. It must be emphasized that "learning" is a postulated concept. There is no such "thing" as "learning." Learning theory is postulated as an explanation of how certain aspects of behavior are changed.

The category "learning" points to those aspects of a person's existence concerned with change and continuity, change and permanence, or succession and duration. That is, this postulated category points to the fact that man is a temporal being, whose existence is not given by his occupation of space, but by his participation in an emerging universe, the meaning of which is shown by the relationship between duration and succession. In the individual, this temporal existence is given by or identified with the relationship between those aspects of his being which appear to be continuous and those which appear to change. This pointing aspect of "learning" is most clearly suggested by two phenomena.

The first has led to the quaint expression "learning how to learn." Two questions emerge from this quaint phrase. The first is whether an infant has had to "learn how to learn" and, if so, how did he do it? "Learning how to learn" is an expression usually reserved for older children or people who have gone through some beginning "learning" experiences. The other is more facetious. Will a time come when the world is so complex and changing so rapidly that we will have to "learn how to learn how to learn?" An infinite series is possible as we step further and further back to understand and resort to more regressive nonexplanatory explanations. Would it not be better if the educator would try to reconceptualize this phenomena of human change, rather than resort to such redundancies?

The second phenomena, "creativity," forces the educator, by the logic or illogic of his own language, to ask how a person learns to be creative? The very question itself demands a definition of the word "creative." I am always struck by the mythical explanation of man's creativity found in Genesis: "So God created man in his own image." Could it be that creativity is not learned, but an aspect of man's nature? Certainly, much theological thought would support this, for theology concerns itself with the transcending possibilities of man. Perhaps it would be more appropriate to ask what prevents creativity than to ask how one learns to be creative.

Is the "learning how to learn" question a real question or does it stem from inadequate explanations of human characteristics or from explanatory systems that force us to ask misleading questions? For me, these questions stem from an explanatory system which is either being misused or misinterpreted. It seems to me that the appropriate question is not how to explain behavior change but how to explain behavior patterning or fixation.

One significant characteristic of this rapidly changing age is that it forces a relook at the nature of man. When individual and social change was a gradual process and the forces of change were limited, the problem of facilitating human change seemed real. Today, however, the same problem seems poorly defined, for the world reveals man as a being having the capacity for almost infinite change. The problem is no longer one of explaining change, but of explaining nonchange. Man is a transcendent being, i.e., he has the capacity to transcend what he is to become something that he is not. In religious languages this is his nature, for he is a creator. A common theological description of man's nature is that he participates in both the conditioned and unconditioned, or in necessity and freedom. Man is conditioned to the world; he participates in the world's structures of necessity. But given this patterning, fixation, and conditioning, he also participates in the unconditioned—in freedom, or (if you wish) in the continual creation of the world. The explanatory problem is not to explain the unconditioned, or freedom, but to explain those conditions which make man a part of the world of necessity. This, I believe, is the function of the "learning" category. It attempts to explain man's conditionedness, the patterning of his behavior. By raising questions about learning how to learn or be creative, man is probing the very nature of what it means to be a human being and hence delving into metaphysics and theology.

This meaning is tied to the meaning of time. In fact, man can be defined by his temporality. The problems of change and continuity, conditioned and unconditioned, necessity and freedom, or of fixation and creativity are essentially problems of man's temporality. He is not a fixed being. His existence is not simply given by his being in a given place, but by a present determined by a past and a future; thus offering possibilities for new ways of being in the anticipated future. A man's life cannot be described by what he is or what he does at a given time. His life is a complete something, capable of description only when the moments from beginning to end are unified by death. Retrospection about the threads of continuity and change composing an individual is the discipline of biography. These same threads projected into the future become the concern of the educator. Might it not be possible, then, that insights into curriculum planning for the individual are to be sought in the discipline of biography, as well as within the discipline of psychology? Whether or not this is true, it does seem obvious that education must be concerned with man as a temporal being. The focus upon learning (as simply the change of behavior) has detracted the educator from this larger and more complicated phenomenon of man's temporality.

Dependency upon "learning" as the major concept in curriculum thought leads to one other problem. The very nature of such "learning" suggests abstraction and generalization. In so-called cognitive learning, certain patterns, assumed to exist with the object world, are abstracted by the individual and carried into new situations. In psychomotor learning, certain patterns within the individual are abstracted and carried into new situations. The learning process implies the possibility of abstracting certain patterns of events from a specific situation or a series of like situations and transferring them to new situations. Thus, learning is assumed to be something that happens within the individual. Education is consequently conceived as doing something to an individual. This leads to the proposition that there is the individual and there is the world, and that the individual develops in such a way that he has power over the world or to act upon the world. Such thinking leads to consideration of the individual as something distinct. Obviously, this is not the case. The individual is not separated from the world, or apart from it—he is a part of it. The unit of study, as Heidegger, among others, points out, is a "being-in-the-world." Any system of thought dealing with human change as something that happens within the individual is likely to lead the educator astray. However, if a curricular language can be developed so that the educator looks at the individual or the situation together, not separately, then his powers of curricular design and educational responsibility might be increased.

"Learning" seems inadequate as the key concept for curriculum and points to what must concern the educator, viz, the fact that man is above all else a being caught in succession and duration, or change and continuity. "Learning," however, concerns itself with only a part of this total phenomena. It explains how patterning or conditioning occurs, and focuses upon abstraction and generalization. It yanks man out of his world and freezes him at a stage in his own biographical evolution. The problem for educators is to conceptualize man's temporality and to find means to express his concern for man's temporality.

Temporality

> What then is time? If no one asks, I know: if I want to explain it to a questioner, I do not know. But at any rate this much I dare affirm I know: that if nothing passed there would be no past time; if nothing were approaching, there would be no future time; if nothing were, there would be no present time.

> But the two times, past and future, how can they be, since the past is no more and the future is not yet? On the other hand, if the present were always present and never flowed away into the past, it would not be time at all but eternity. But if the present is only time, because it flows away into the past, how can we say that it is? For it is only because it will cease to be.[2]

Thus is the complexity, or perhaps the mystery, of time. Among the rather extensive literature, I have found Heidegger's *Being and Time*[3] the most fruitful, although his complexity almost equals the complexity of the phenomena of time. I do not intend or presume to provide either a presentation or an interpretation of this phenomenological ontology as he develops Dasein's temporality. A similar treatment of temporality may be found in an article by Friedrich Kummel.[4] For the purposes of this paper, Heidegger's crucial idea is that "Dasein's totality of being as care means: ahead-of-itself-already-being-in (a world) as being-alongside (entities encountered within-the-world) .... The 'ahead-of-itself' is grounded in the future. In the 'Being-already-in ...' the character of 'having been' is made known. 'Being-alongside ...' becomes possible in making present."[5] Kummel's statement further clarifies this idea:

No act of man is possible with reference solely to the past or solely to the future, but is always dependent on their interaction. Thus, for example, the future may be considered as the horizon against which plans are made, the past provides the means for their realization, while the present mediates and actualizes both. Generally, the future represents the possibility, and the past the basis, of a free life in the present. Both are always found intertwined with the present: in the open circle of future and past there exists no possibility which is not made concrete by real conditions, nor any realization which does not bring with it new possibilities. This interrelation of reciprocal conditions is a historical process in which the past never assumes a final shape nor the future ever shuts its doors. Their essential interdependence also means, however, that there can be no progress without a retreat into the past in search of a deeper foundation.[6]

Time is not a dimension in which we live—a series of "nows," some past and some in the future. Man does not have so many "nows" allotted. He does not simply await a future and look back upon a past. The very notion of time arises out of man's existence, which is an emergent. The future is man facing himself in anticipation of his own potentiality for being. The past is finding himself already thrown into a world. It is the having-been which makes possible the projection of his potentiality. The present is the moment of vision when Dasein, finding itself thrown into a situation (the past), projects its own potentiality for being. Human life is not futural; nor is it past, but, rather, a present made up of a past and future brought into the moment. From his finite temporality, man has constructed his scientific view of time as something objective and beyond himself, in which he lives. The point is that man is temporal; or if you wish, historical. There is no such "thing" as a past or a future. They exist only through man's existence as a temporal being. This means that human life is never fixed but is always emergent as the past and future become horizons of a present.

Education recognizes, assumes responsibility for, and maximizes the consequences of this awareness of man's temporality. The categories of learning, goal, purpose, or objective point to this awareness. Their present inadequacy is not a consequence of their inherent limitations; but, rather, the educator's failure to recognize these limitations. He expects them to perform work for which they are not designed. The challenge to the educator, and particularly to the curriculum specialist, is to find a way to talk about man's temporality which will increase his professional power in the world.

The Individual-World Dialectic

Temporality, or historicity, is not a characteristic of isolated man, but a characteristic of being-in-the-world. A young child emerges as he encounters different aspects of the physical world. A man who has neither participated nor lived with others is ahistorical. The springs or sources of temporality do not reside in the individual, but in confrontation between the individual and other individuals, other material objects, and other ways of thinking as they are objectified in symbol and operation. Furthermore, these springs or sources, although again not residing in society, are nevertheless unveiled, maintained, and protected by society. Thus man shapes the world, but the world also shapes man.[7] This is a dialectical process in which cause is effect, and effect is cause. The world calls forth new responses from the individual, who in turn calls forth new responses from the world.

One of man's characteristics is his ability to respond. Heschel, in answering the question, "Who Is Man?" defines him as the being who answers to the world. Heidegger states that speech is man's answer as he listens to the world. Niebuhr builds a moral philosophy around the image of "man-the-listener."[8] These responses take the form of speech, or other symbolic expressions and of action upon or in the world. One form of man's response is his understanding of himself in the moment of vision, as he projects his own possibility for being in terms of the "having been." Man's world responds by withholding or giving, yielding or resisting, punishing or criticizing, and supporting or negating. This is the dialectic, greatly oversimplified, leading to the continual creation and re-creation of man-in-the-world.

The scientific enterprise can be interpreted as an institutionalized form of the dialectic—a three way exchange between an individual, the natural world, and a social group. The scientist questions the world via his theories and hypotheses. Through his experimental and observational procedures the world speaks back. Other scientists, however, also answer him by offering criticism—logical, aesthetic, or even political. The scientific methods are ways in which men have institutionalized their temporality and potentiality for transcendence and emergence.[9] This process is well exemplified by the interrelationships between science, technology, and politics. New scientific explanations and theories build new material conditions through various technologies. As technology changes the world and new scientific possibilities emerge, social problems arise which demand both political and scientific endeavors. Air pollution, mass transportation, mass communication, atomic power, and space exploration are all creators of such problems.

Language, particularly poetry, as pointed out by Heidegger, is also an aspect of man's temporality and his transcending possibilities.[10] Social conflict of any type becomes another form making man's historical nature manifest. Interpersonal encounter, through conversation or other modes of meeting, including the use of types of power, also carries the possibility of change within continuity.

The responsibility of the curriculum person, then, is to design and criticize specialized environments which embody the dialectical relationships valued in a given society. These are environments expressing concern for the temporality or historicity of man and society. These environments must encourage the moment of vision, when the past and future are the horizons of the individual's present so that his own potentiality for being is grasped.[11] Education is a manifestation of the historical process, meshing the unfolding biography of the individual with the unfolding history of his society. The past becomes the means by which the individual can project his own potentiality for being. The educational environment must be so constructed that the past is in the present as the basis for projection.

Curriculum as Environmental Design

An environment which would embody the dialectical forms valued by society would require three aspects or components. The first two could as easily be identified by most learning paradigms, although this analysis suggests different categories for conceptualizing them. The environments must include components which will call forth responses from the students. The individual is thrown into a world, not necessarily of his own making, but an embodiment of the past. What aspects of the past are so valued by those controlling educational environments that they should be used to call forth such responses? What aspects of the past can become a horizon of the student's present so that his future becomes his own potential for being? Next, the environment must be reactive, or else the student must question it so that it responds to him. This aspect is also part of the valued past brought into the present of the student. Valued forms of responsiveness are maintained in speech patterns and forms of dialogue, the structural forms of the various disciplines, the social customs shaping interaction patterns, and the man-made things (e.g., automobiles, talking typewriters),[12] which make up much of man's world. This shaping component of the world channels man's transcendence into accepted patterns of social transcendence.

Finally, the environment expressing concern for man's temporality must make possible those moments of vision when the student, and/or those responsible for him, project his potentiality for being into the present, thus tying together the future and the past into the present. Somehow, the environment must provide opportunities for the student to become aware of his temporality, to participate in a history which is one horizon of his present. Only in this way can he contribute to the continual creation of the world and recognize his own active participation as an ingredient in the transcendency of the world.

This framework provides the possible reinterpretation of the significance of the categories of purpose and learning in the educational process. Given man's temporality, the future makes sense only as the horizon of his present. Heidegger's "ahead-of-itself" is not a future "now" that can be prescribed. Rather, it is Dasein coming toward itself in its own potential for being. It is the projection of a "having-been" onto a present to create the "moment-of-vision." Hence, the so-called purpose or objective is not a specification of a determined

future; it is a value category used in selecting the ready-at-hand and present-at-hand in the educational environment. This is in accord with Peters' claim
that the function of this purpose category is to determine the content of the educational environment.[13] Thus, the objective is a value category to select the educational environment. In effect, the function of this value category is to screen
the past and the present-as-already-past to determine which components can
serve man's temporality and society's evolving history. As indicated above,
these components serve to call out the environmental responses from the students which are part of the being-in-the-world dialectic.

School people are concerned not only with the temporality of the individual,
but also with the temporality of the society. In their concern for dura-
tion-succession, or continuity-change, they must consider the different
rhythms of continuity-change between society as a whole, and the individuals
who compose it. Society shapes man, but man, in turn, shapes society. However, the man who tries to shape society beyond its limits of tolerance is out of
tune with his society and must be held in check. Hence, educational institutions
must concern themselves with the individual's temporality within the historical
rhythm of the society.

The selection of the content of the educational environment is consequently
related to the forces controlling the continuity-change rhythms. Shifting educational purposes indicate shifts in society's evolution. Arguments over school
purposes are not simply academic arguments, but efforts to shift the values determining the educational environment and, hence, influencing the continuity-change tempos or rhythms of individuals and society.

Today, for instance, the components making scientific dialectic possible
(materials and language systems) are readily accepted as environmental conditions, for the continuity-change rhythm produced by science and technology is
almost universally accepted as good. The emphasis is not simply upon abstract
theoretical science, but upon the relationship between science and its
uses—technology.

However, the social sciences have done less well in the schools. Part of this
is, of course, because of the adolescent state of the social sciences. However,
part of it is also because the technology appropriate to the social sciences takes
the form of political action, and people responsible for schools aren't about to
have youngsters use these tools to poke around in certain sectors of the society.
The transcendences which could emerge might, indeed, increase the tempo of
social change and continuity.

Of course, certain components of the world are more continuous than changing, more durable than succeeding. In these cases, it might be possible to speak
of objectives as future. These components require complete submission. Their
transcending possibilities lie not in the component's relationship with the individual, but in the individual's use of the component. In Heidegger's terms, they

are the ready-to-hand: equipment. The typewriter is an example for, indeed, the person is conditioned to it. A future can be identified because the typewriter is fixed, and conditioning is possible and necessary. However, in such case, the individual uses the typewriter as an extension of himself, incorporates the equipment into his being, and makes it an instrument of his own temporality. The moment of vision is equally significant. Given this ready-to-hand, this along-side-of, this past, what is the individual's potentiality for being? How can he, with the typewriter a part of him, project his new potentialities in that moment?

Thus "purpose" is really a value category used to select the educational environment. However, because of its involvement in shaping the environment, therefore, participating not only in the dialectic between individuals and society but in the rhythms of continuity and change, it falls into the political domain. Conflict and argument over educational purpose is hence a part of the political ideological struggle existing in any evolving society.

"Learning" is likewise a category for building the educational environment.[14] The study of learning in psychology is a science, evolving theories or explanations of certain aspects of change. In education, learning theories serve as technological tools to help shape the sequence of educational experiences. They enable the educator to program environments and the forms and rhythms of their responsiveness. The talking typewriter is perhaps the best example of this embodiment of learning theory into environmental form. Learning theory makes possible the determination of conditions of the environment facilitating the dialectic between the individual and his world: conditions of the material components and of the human skills which are also, then, environmental conditions.

Neither of the categories objectives nor learning provide guidelines for the third essential ingredient of the education environment: the moment of vision. The student, either by his own understanding or that of others, must be able to envision his own projected potentiality for being as it exists in the past-present-future. This is the uniquely human quality of the environment and requires the presence of human wisdom. This is the unique function of the teacher, the human aspect of that specific educational environment, who shares the rhythms of continuity and change, of necessity and freedom, with his students.

NOTES

[1] Susanne K. Langer, *Mind: An Essay on Human Feeling*, vol. 1 (Baltimore, MD: Johns Hopkins Press, 1967), 52.

[2] *The Confessions of St. Augustine*, trans. F.J. Sheed (New York: Sheed & Ward, 1943), 271.

[3] Martin Heidegger, *Being and Time*, trans. John MacQuarrie and Edward Robinson (New York: Harper & Row, 1962).

[4] Friedrich Kummel, "Time as Succession and the Problem of Duration," in *The Voices of Time,* ed. J. T. Fraser (New York: George Braziller, 1965), 31–55.

[5] Heidegger, *Being and Time,* 375.

[6] Kummel, "Time as Succession," 50.

[7] See Peter Berger and Thomas Luckmann, *The Social Construction of Reality* (Garden City, NY: Doubleday, 1966).

[8] Abraham Heschel, *Who Is Man?* (Stanford, CA: Stanford University Press, 1965); Martin Heidegger quoted in "New Frontiers in Theology," *The Later Heidegger and Theology,* vol. 1, ed. James M. Robinson and John Cobbs, Jr. (New York: Harper & Row, 1963); H. Richard Niebuhr, *The Responsible Self* (New York: Harper & Row, 1963).

[9] See John MacMurray, *Reason and Emotion* (New York: D. Appleton-Century, 1938); Michael Polanyi, *The Tacit Dimension* (Garden City, NY: Doubleday, 1966); Thomas S. Kuhn, *The Structure of Scientific Revolutions* (Chicago: University of Chicago Press, 1962).

[10] Martin Heidegger, "Holderlin and the Essence of Poetry," in *Existence and Being,* trans. Douglas Scott (Chicago: Henry Regnery, 1949), 293–315; Georges Gusdorf, *Speaking,* trans. Paul Brockelman (Evanston, IL: Northwestern University Press, 1965).

[11] This analysis has been shaped to a large degree by my understanding of Heidegger. Unfortunately, Heidegger has not attempted a developmental ontology, and attention should be focused upon those concerned with human development who have been influenced by Heidegger's ontology.

[12] For a description of the "talking typewriter" see note one, Chapter Eleven. *Ed.*

[13] Richard S. Peters, *Authority, Responsibility, and Education* (New York: Paul S. Eriksson, 1960).

[14] See Philip Phenix, "Curriculum as Transcendence," in *Curriculum Theorizing: The Reconceptualists,* ed. W. Pinar (Berkeley, CA: McCutchan, 1975), 321–340.

13

Language and Teaching: Reflections on Teaching in the Light of Heidegger's Writings About Language

(1968)

Many of us are teachers. How do we ask the questions about our being-in-the-world as teachers?

Do we ask "What is Teaching?" If so, are we asking if there is a formal operation or an institutionalized role to which our behavior should conform as an ideal? Are we projecting a scientific study to guide interaction between theoretical and empirical activity, and to produce assertions or prescriptions to guide teachers?

Do we ask "What does it mean to teach?" If so, are we asking about the meaning of our life with students in those activities in which we assume teaching responsibility? Are we asking about the influence we have or perhaps should have on those who share those times and places in which we teach? Are we asking about that "content" within which we engage students while we teach?

Do we ask "Who are we as teachers?" If so, are we asking about our own identity as a human being with another human being in those "teaching" times and places? Are we asking about our identity as teachers in contrast to the identity of others as researchers, policemen, administrators, or parents?

Do we ask, "How do we teach?" If so, are we asking for rules to guide our actions with others in those situations identified as teaching situations? Are we asking how to organize that in which we are to engage students? Are we asking what other people do or have done when they engage in the same type of activity?

How do we ask the questions about our being-in-the-world as teachers? Surely we need answers to these and other questions if we are to teach ... what shall I say: effectively, honestly, truthfully, sincerely, with satisfaction, successfully? But are the answers crucial? Is it not equally important that we ask questions which tear away the language now used to frame and interpret our being-in-the-world-as-teachers so we can confront ourselves and students more openly and resolutely as we teach—questions which disclose what relates us as teacher and student.

LANGUAGE IN TEACHING

We could ask, simply, "What do we do as teachers?" or "How are we, as teachers, in the world?" If someone looks at us as we teach, or if we look back upon our teaching, how is it that we are together with others. In most of those moments, we are as speakers. We lecture, answer or ask questions, or engage in discourse with others. We can be doing other things, depending upon the world in which we are at the moment; but most of us speak with or speak to students. How can we articulate or talk about our being with others in a speaking way when we teach? Are there differences between the way we speak when we are in the world with others as teachers and the way we speak when we are with others in some other way?

For the most part, when we teach we are in the world with others by way of language. Surely this is nothing new. Those who study teaching as a phenomena have long recognized that language is crucial in teaching. How have they talked about this language and the people who are caught in it as teachers and students?

Language is a tool of communication, and there are educators who talk about teaching as communication. But as I am with others in a teaching way, my language is not always a communicating language. In fact, if I want to communicate something to others, there are often better means than language for doing so. The permanency of the printed page, the vividness of the visual image, the simultaneity of the TV image, or the accessibility of electronically stored information offer possibilities for effective communication not matched by speech.

Language is a vehicle for facilitating learning; and many educators, most in fact, have talked about language as a way to develop concepts, generalizations, facts, and attitudes. But are not concepts, generalizations, facts, and perhaps attitudes primarily ways of using language. To say that language is a tool for developing language provides no new information. To focus upon what is learned, hides the significance of language as a way of being with students and focuses upon something which is beyond, indeed, removed from our being with students.

Language is a logical form with rules for organizing data, making inferences, deducing consequences and performing other operations. There are educators who have studied language in teaching as a logical form.[1] Yet logical form is secondary in language.[2] Speech in teaching is often spontaneous, disorganized, contradictory. Logic is most applicable when that which has been spoken in an original way is to be organized for further use; when intonation, mood, and other symptoms of the autobiographical are secondary to the formal aspect.

Language provides procedures, customs and/or rules for the structuring of interactions among people throughout a period of time. Educators have studied language in classrooms as rules to a teaching game.[3] But language is not only a relationship among people; it is also a relationship between the person and his world. When a teacher speaks, he not only speaks to students, he speaks about something or that something speaks through him. When a teacher listens, he listens not only to the student who asks the question, but to the world that is the source of the answer.

The teacher, in speaking, is using language not only as an instrument; although language can be used as a tool. He is not always engaging in rule based behavior or establishing rule governed communities; although rules provide some platform for being with others. In speaking, the teacher is being-in-the-world with others; he is there among and with others as only man can be[4]—in language. Language is the medium within which he lives, grows, and projects his possibilities for being. Language is his culture, as agar medium is the culture of microorganisms. Language sustains man, opens up possibilities for being-in-the-world, comforts him, preserves truth, and provides the platform to jump momentarily beyond himself. Language also hides man from his world and from himself. As it opens up some possibilities it covers others. The veil torn from some aspects of the world conceals others. Considering language a "thing" within the world, man turns language into a business; into the busy-ness of a science, the business of propaganda, the industry of tool making. In his busy business of making, he forgets that he is living within that "thing," that language. By forgetting that language opens these possibilities, he proceeds thanklessly and thus unthinkingly, down the paths laid out by others. He remains unaware of the source of these paths, and thus is unable to return to the freedom of the original decision points.

It is in language, "the most dangerous of possessions"[5] that the teacher lives with students. How does he live? Can we articulate our speaking with students to open up new possibilities for being with them, and indeed new possibilities for our being in the world? Let us stay on that path cleared by Heidegger a little longer. It is not *THE* path, but a path down which we can tarry. On it, we can journey with someone else, listening to his speech, tuning our eyes to our ears that we might detect the clearings hidden by our common language. Standing momentarily in those clearings we can see if new openings and new possibilities appear in our teaching world.

LANGUAGE AND BEING

Heidegger refers to language in many contexts. Language as already in the world wherein one finds himself is part of the totality of instruments available for use. It is ready-to-hand in one's dealings with the world.[6] One can also come across language as present-at-hand, a part of the world discovered in its own right. The foundation of language is discourse or talk, by which a person articulates the intelligibility of his being in a situation.[7] But language is not simply a tool, not simply discourse, it is a gift to man that "has the task of making manifest in its work the existent, and of preserving it as such."[8] It is poetry, "the inaugural naming of being and of the essence of all things."[9] Language grounds man in his history, in the past which is present. To forget this past is to use language as that which is commonplace, and thus to project our possibilities for being without thinking and without thanking.[10]

> Words are not terms, and thus are not like buckets and kegs from which we scoop a content that is there. Words are wellsprings that are found and dug up in the telling, wellsprings that must be found and dug up again, and again, that easily cave in, but that at times also well up when least expected. If we do not go to the spring again and again, the buckets and kegs stay empty, or their content stays stale.

These ways in which Heidegger writes of language must be more adequately identified before teaching, as a way of being in language, can be, articulated.

Language in the World

Language as a totality of words and expressions partially constitutes the world wherein man has his place. It is there in the spoken word of the other and in the printed word of the page. Man uses that language in his dealings with the world, i.e., it is part of the totality of equipment which empowers man to act in the world. It is ready to be used, and in its serviceability and manipulability it does not show itself as something, but points toward that for which it is to be used. To use an expression of Polanyi,[11] language becomes subsidiary to that which occupies man's focal attention. It is as if the language used as an instrument were absorbed by the task. As equipment, language often functions as a sign;[12] it indicates a complex or totality of instruments, language and artifact, available to man as he projects his possibilities upon the world. It indicates the involvement he can have with the instruments and entities of the world.

When language becomes conspicuous as unusable in a given situation, when it becomes obtrusive and gets in the way, or when the "right" words or language forms are not available to be used, then language shows itself as language—as words, expressions, and rules for usage. At these points, language is not ready-to-hand to be used, but is present-at-hand as something within the world, and can itself become the object of focal attention. Language as present-at-hand, as that which is not being used, stands out as something; it becomes an entity with form and history, and can be taken apart and analyzed. It can become an entity for theoretical inspection and be freed from its situation and the totality of instruments within which it is involved.

It is as present-at-hand that language is the content for teaching. In books and in the speech of the teacher language shows itself as something. It is not hidden or absorbed in its use, but is visible as an entity. One of the tasks of the teacher is to make the present-at-hand usable for the student; to help him absorb it within the totality of instruments for his use—to turn the present-at-hand into the ready-to-hand. It must become an instrument to be used by the student in his dealings with the world.

Being-In-The-World As Discourse[13]

Language is not simply an entity within the world. It is grounded in a basic characteristic of man, his capacity for speech or discourse.[14] In discourse man discloses his being there in a given situation; through his mood, his state of mind, man discloses his throwness into a world. It makes manifest "how one is, and how one is faring."[15] Through his understanding he projects his own potentiality for being, the possibilities which are his.[16] Through discourse man articulates his being-in-the-world as thrown and as possibility. Discourse puts into words the totality of significations, the related instruments and entities which man can use for his own sake. In all talk, man talks about something. At the same time, his being is expressed and "explicitly shared" with others.[17] Discourse involves hearing and keeping silent. Listening to another is a way of being open to another. In being with others, however, there is the possibility that talk will become "idle talk"[18] in which man's own possibilities are passed over and discourse becomes groundless and gossipy. As idle talk, discourse no longer discloses man's being in the world, but covers up entities and closes off possibilities.

Talk in teaching can be teacher and student being-with-others in communication. In the hurry to "cover" the content, however, the talk of teaching borders on idle talk; listening and keeping silent are not considered constitutive for discourse. Talk in teaching, as the passing along of common language, provides no opportunity for students or teachers to articulate their potentialities and their states of mind and understandings are apt to be hidden. As a consequence, the talk of teaching can be groundless. It can fail to root the teacher and student in a world of entities, others, and possibilities.

Being in Language as Poetry

Language as an instrument and in discourse serves man, and thus empowers him for his own possibility. But Heidegger assigns to language overpowering possibilities, as well as, empowering ones. Man does not simply live in language; language also lives in him and speaks through him. In referring to thought and poetry, for instance, Heidegger states that they do not "use language to express themselves with its help; rather thought and poetry are in themselves the originary, the essential, and therefore also the final speech that language speaks through the mouth of man."[19] It is in poetry, "the inaugural naming of being,"[20] that truth establishes itself. Truth is the bringing forth of what is into unconcealment, into the open. Language does this by "bringing what is ... into the open for the first time."[21] Poetry, as a work of art, sets up a world, "the ever un-objective realm that shelters us as long as the paths of birth and death, blessing and curse keep us exposed to being."[22] Man listens to that wherein he moves and has his being in order that language can speak through him, name that which is, and open up a world. It is in the openness of the world that man projects his own possibilities for being. In being in language poetically, man does not force language to do his bidding, nor to disclose his potentialities, rather he waitingly listens that he may name that which is and establish it as such.

Language as Being-In-The-World Historically

Heidegger does not thematically concern himself with language as historical being-in-the-world; but his concern is manifest in many ways and places. In "The Origin of the Work of Art," he states that "Art is historical, and as historical it is the creative preservation of truth in the work."[23]

> Whenever art happens, i.e., whenever there is a beginning—a thrust enters history, history begins for the first time or over again. History means here not a sequence of events of any sort, however important they may be, in time. History is the transporting of a people into its appointed task as entrance into what has been given along with the people.[24]

The preservation of the work of art, of poetry, is a way of being in the world of language. Heidegger demonstrates this preservation which is also a repetition, a "going back into the possibilities of the Dasein that has-been-there,"[25] in much of his later work. His "destruction of metaphysics" is a return to the language of other philosophers to find that which is unthought in it.

People still hold the view that what is handed down to us by tradition is what in reality lies behind us—while in fact it comes toward us because we are its captives and destined to it ... That [view] ... prevents us from hearing the language of thinkers. We do not hear it rightly, because we take that language to be mere expression, setting forth philosopher's views. But the thinkers' language tells us what is. To hear it is in no case easy. Hearing it presupposes that we meet a certain requirement ... We must acknowledge and respect it. To acknowledge and respect consists of letting every thinkers' thought come to us as something in each case unique, never to be repeated, inexhaustible—and being shaken to the depths by what is unthought in his thought. The unthought is the greatest gift that thinking can bestow ... For acknowledgment and respect call for a readiness to let our own attempts at thinking be overturned, again and again, by what is unthought in the thinkers' thought.[26]

Language as thought, language as poetry, language as present-at-hand and as ready-to-hand are historical in that they are preserved and thus available for the repetition which is a going back and a retrieving possibility.

THE TEACHER AS GUARDIAN
AND SERVANT OF LANGUAGE

The teacher, for the most part, is with students in language. But dwelling alongside of and in language with others does not differentiate teachers from non-teachers. A teacher presumably has concern for the potentialities of students, for their possibilities as these are projected upon the world. Possibility is disclosed in understanding which is articulated in discourse. Therefore, a teacher must be alongside of and in language with others in such a way that the language used in discourse discloses and projects the students' possibilities. A teacher must guard speech against idle talk; using language with care and respect, articulating his own understanding of the world, and conversing openly with others. He is a servant of language, using it in such a way that the student can project his own possibilities upon it and by means of it.

A teacher also has concern for the institutions and traditions within which he lives and for which he is an agent as teacher. He seeks to preserve these institutions and traditions. In part, these institutions and traditions are preserved in and through language—in the poetry of the people and the thought of the thinkers. To be alongside of and in language in such a way that poetry and thought are preserved is to guard openings in the world, happenings and truth, which are the works of art; and to respect and acknowledge the thought of thinkers.

A teacher's concern for the institutions and traditions within which he lives is not made manifest by guarding the language as if it were a museum piece, beyond the touch and use of the student. His concern is a temporal concern, a concern for the evolution and development of those traditions and institutions, for their history and their destiny. His concern is with the future as well as the past. The past and future come together as the teacher serves language in the present moment. The teacher serves language by listening to the world and silently waiting for speech to speak through him. He serves language by welcoming the origins and the beginnings disclosed by language in the speech of students. Serving language by bringing the past and the future into the present, he serves the student by leaping ahead of him in solicitude that the student might live authentically in language.

Teachers can be differentiated from non-teachers by the care they have for the language within which they dwell with students. This "most dangerous of possessions" must be guarded with care, ere it erode, conceal, or is misused idly or idolatrously. As an entity that empowers and overpowers, language cannot be taken for granted; neither can it be worshiped. The teacher must live alongside it and in it with great concern—vigorously guarding it that its power not be weakened, gingerly serving it that its power not corrupt. The teacher is the guardian of language, but he guards it that he might serve both it and the student. Language is entrusted to the teacher until the student can receive it as his trust, and thus assume guardianship of it. Teachers guard and serve language by being alongside of it concernfully, by being with others in it conversationally and by dwelling in it thoughtfully and poetically.

Teaching as Being Alongside Language Concernfully

To guard and serve language the teacher must disentangle himself from the language within which he teaches. When teaching, the teacher, for the most part, is absorbed in the language or it is absorbed by him as an instrument; hence, he is not aware of it as it is. To be alongside language he must step out of it (and necessarily into another), free language from the many involvements it has in his life, and turn it into something for theoretical concern. Stepping out of the language within which he teaches, he can project his own possibilities for being with others as a teacher. This is what the educator does when he talks about the "structure of the disciplines;" about the concepts, understandings, principles, or theories of a subject; or about the rules and logic of the subject. The difficulty of articulating the language problem in these ways is that the teacher "sees" something to be "learned." "Learning," if one grants the validity of the concept, is a *consequence* of being with students, not a *way* of being with them. How can the teacher articulate his understanding of language to project his possibilities for being with students in language?

If a teacher steps out of the language within which he teaches, and theoretically concerns himself with it as something alongside of himself, he discovers something present-at-hand. Language as present-at-hand can be articulated as an instrument, as a happening of truth (a work of art) or as the thought of thinkers. By stepping out of the language within which he teaches to look at and talk about it as an instrument, as a happening of truth, or as the thought of thinkers, the teacher can project more clearly the language situation within which he teaches.

Language As Ready-To-Hand

As an instrument, a present-at-hand which can be a ready-to-hand, language must be in the teaching situations as accessible, serviceable, and reliable. As an instrument, language is to be used in the student's dealings in a world. It is a tool to form his intentions and projects. It can be a sign, pointing out a totality of instruments and involvements for the sake of his potentialities. It can be a vehicle for his being with others intentionally, e.g., shaping their projects and moods, making demands or asking questions of them, guiding cooperative action. Among other artifacts, such as scientific equipment, it can guide the use of equipment and organize events and data associated with the use of that equipment. As part of a totality of equipment, the language must be readily accessible to the student. Somehow or another it must be laid out before him. As ready-to-hand, the student must be as at ease with the language as with a hammer when driving nails, or a typewriter when writing letters.

As ready-to-hand, language must have serviceability as well as accessibility. Language which is ready-to-hand but unusable gets in the way and intrudes on other projects. Obtrusive and obstinate language stands in the way of the student's possibilities and befuddles his being in the world; it erodes the power of language. The teacher who permits such erosion inadequately guards language.

But serviceability is of no consequence unless language as ready-to-hand is also reliable,[27] unless it adheres to the world opened to the student and permits him to project possibility into the opening. The student can be certain of his world and secure in it if language as ready-to-hand is reliable. The reliability of the ready-to-hand can wear away, be dissipated or atrophy; and the teacher as guardian of language should guarantee its continued reliability. In an age of rapid change and generation gaps, such guarding requires great effort for language as ready-to-hand can become obsolescent.

A variety of problems or questions are raised if a teacher steps out of language within which he is with others and talks about it as ready-to-hand with accessibility, serviceability and reliability. How can language, that most intangible of entities, be accessible as ready-to-hand? How can a teacher "lay out" the language within which he and the student are to dwell in order that the student might come across it as present-at-hand, and circumspectively discover it as ready-to-hand. Lacking the substance of a hammer, a typewriter, or a "thing" which can be seen and manipulated by the student's arms or legs, language is assumed to be something which cannot be ready-to-hand. But language can be incorporated into the psychomotor and perceptual structures of the student as can a hammer or a pencil. The problem is confounded by talking of language in terms of "knowledge" or "learning," thus hiding the task of "laying out" language as ready-to-hand. Often, lectures or discussions inefficiently "lay out" language as ready-to-hand. Perhaps computers and other programmed forms offer more access to language as ready-to-hand. The visual storage of language in forms other than books, such as video images of language in use in selected situations, might make language more readily accessible for the student. With opportunities to see and hear language in use, to discover language as instrumentality, and to play with the language in the manner that a child plays with a hammer or typewriter, to incorporate it into his physiological and perceptual structures, students would have more choice among available language tools. Modern electronic technology provides the technological tools for such imaginative "laying out" of language. Perhaps modern philosophy provides some of the conceptual tools necessary for the imaginative "laying out" of language as ready-to-hand.

How can language, as being alongside the teacher, be articulated as ready-to-hand with serviceability? This question asks how language can be useful in the student's dealings in his world. In what situations can language be used? What is the serviceability structure of the language as ready-to-hand, i.e., how does it fit together as part of a totality of instruments? Both of these questions have been the concern of the linguistic philosophers. Wittgenstein and other analytic philosophers associate meaning with use, and differentiate among the ways language is used in various situations. Language functions differently when used by the scientist and when used in common everydayness; the preacher uses it differently than the scholar. Serviceability depends upon the world that is opened up to the student; therefore the serviceability structure is, in part, a function of the situation within which it is to be used. But serviceability also depends upon the person who is using it, e.g., a left-handed golfer needs a left handed iron. This does not imply that language as ready-to-hand is different for different people, but that its serviceability structure, its way of being entered or controlled and used might be different for different people. Research on learning styles suggests that this is the case. The problem the teacher faces is to look at and talk about language as fitting particular situations and different types of students. If he solves this problem he can permit students to enter or control language and use it in ways appropriate to their situation. Recently, the educator has been most concerned with the use of language in knowledge production situations. The spate of studies focusing on the structure of the disciplines and the discovery process points to language usage modeled after its use by research scholars and academicians. However, there is no necessary reason to believe that the structure of language for use in one's everydayness is the same as the structure for use in knowledge production.

How can language as alongside the teacher be looked at and talked about as having reliability? This question asks how language helps the student adhere to the world opened to him. Reliability of language makes certain his world. Language provides hand holds for the student to grasp his world and project his own possibilities for being in that world. The reliability of the language as ready-to-hand can be worn away or eroded by changes in the world itself. As the social and technical world changes, the language by which one functions effectively in that world no longer "holds." The reliability can also be worn away by the misuse of language, as in idle talk. By failing to keep his language instruments sharp and precise, the student loses his "grip" on the world and is no longer where the action is. Reliability is a relative quality; as new instruments are produced, old ones lose their purchase. Thus, maintaining reliability requires comparing new languages with older ones, and discarding those which are no longer maximally reliable.

Alongside language as ready-to-hand, the teacher must look at and discover how language can be accessible to the student, how its serviceability can be arranged, and how its reliability can be assured and protected. A teacher does not guard language for ready-to-hand by letting language be as he steps outside of it, but by organizing it for display, for use, and for continued reliability.

Language as Happening of Truth

As the teacher steps outside of language to confront it as present-at-hand, he might discover it as a happening of truth: poetry, a work of art.[29] Heidegger makes frequent references to poetry as the naming of that which is. By poetry, however, he means language in the broadest sense of the word. "Language itself is poetry in the essential sense." "Projective speech is poetry: the saga of world and earth ... Poetry is the saga of the unconcealment of what *is*. Actual language at any given moment is the happening of this speech, in which for a folk its world historically arises and the earth is preserved as that which is closed up."[30] Poetry functions to open up the world, and to hold it open: " ... language brings what *is* as something that *is* into the Open for the first time. Where there is no language there is also no openness of what *is* ... "[31] The work of art sets up the world.

As a teacher steps outside of language within which he teaches to let it be as it is, the "workly" character of the language can show itself. The language within which he teaches opens up a world; it points to that which is; it establishes a clearing within which that which is can shine forth. Within this clearing, in the open, which is held open by language as poetry, the student can project his being as potentiality.

The teacher surveying language as present-at-hand, searches for those happenings of truth, the poetic occurrences in language, whereby the curtain of everydayness is rent and that which is, is named and stands forth. The guarding here is a guarding against the idle talk and scribbling of everydayness which covers that which is. The problem for the teacher is to preserve the truth which is instituted in language as poetry; to preserve it in such a way that the student is taken aback by the unconcealment of the opening to reconsider his own being in the world. Being alongside of the language of science, the teacher looks for those poetic occurrences wherein a beginning is instituted and that which is, is named for the first time. Within the openings so established, the serviceability of language as ready-to-hand takes hold so the student can dwell in the clearing in a research and technological way. Being alongside of language as narration, the teacher looks for those poetic occurrences wherein the truth established through deed or sacrifice in the lives or imagination of historical people is grounded and preserved.

The "laying out" of language as poetry and the happening of truth is quite different from the "laying out" of language as having serviceability and accessibility. As preservation of a happening of truth, the "laying out" takes on the aspects of artistry. The teacher must establish the language situation to set up a world for the student.

Language as Thought of Thinkers

As the teacher steps outside language to come upon it as present-at-hand, the thought of thinkers can come forth more noticeably. It comes forth "as something to be repeated, inexhaustible,"[32] and as a "multiplicity of meanings." [33] It is the thinkers response to the call of the most thought provoking of an age. Gathered in the world and language of the thinker is "all that concerns us, all that we care for, all that touches us insofar as we are, as human beings."[34] In giving "thought to what is most thought-provoking, we give thanks."[35] To hear the thought, we must attend to the language with respect and acknowledgment. Heidegger's use of language demonstrates the meaning of respecting and acknowledging the unique and inexhaustible thought of thinkers. His careful exegesis of words, tracing their meanings back to root meanings and searching for the forgotten or ignored meanings, discloses the "unthought," as well as, the "passed along" thought. The historical ground of the language is re-established, and that which called forth the language is identified.

The teacher, inspecting language for the thought of thinkers, searches for "that which is unique, never to be repeated;" lays it out that that which called forth the thought can be recognized and that the memory gathered in the words of the thinker can be recalled. The thought of thinkers must be guarded against easy interpretation which casts the words of the thinker into everyday language and thus covers his thought with "worn-out language" with which "everybody can talk about everything."[36]

The teacher serves the thought of thinkers by laying out language to prevent erosion of the uniqueness by idle talk, the concealment of that which called forth the thought and the wiping away of memory. The thought of thinkers points to the past which is a horizon of today. The teacher who serves and guards this language makes visible the horizon of today that it can be re-entered thankfully. The teacher must lay out the language of the thinker to make possible an exegesis which unearths the thinker's world and which encourages the rethinking and regathering of all that is cared for by man today. The laying out must be with great clarity and purity. Interpretations and re-interpretations must be used cautiously that the unique thought is not covered with language which hides the multiplicity of meanings, blocks or discourages respect or denies the past which offers possibilities for the future.

Disentangling himself from the language within which he teaches, the teacher can step back to inspect that language as present-at-hand. Understanding the language in some such fashion, the teacher can project the lay-out of the language situation within which he will be with the student. Language can be laid out to show its being as instrument, work, or thought. It must be laid out to be accessible and serviceable as an instrument, to be an opening into a world, or to be an invitation to rethink that which calls forth thought. As the teacher lays out the language in these ways, he projects a situation within which he can again be with students. In the teaching situation, he steps back into this language with potentially greater understanding of his possibilities for being with his students.

TEACHING AS BEING WITH OTHERS CONVERSATIONALLY

In the newly understood situation, the teacher can be with others in language conversationally. Teacher and student, being together in the situation can articulate their understanding and their moods through discourse, and in so doing project their possibilities for being. The teacher functions conversationally by being open to the student through listening. His solicitude for the student is manifest by jumping ahead of the student to disclose the student's possibility for being in such a way that the student can assume care for it. Through listening and speaking, the teacher helps the student see the present as a moment of vision, a moment when the past and the future come together to disclose the present as possibility.

The danger of idle talk must be guarded against. Too easily can the teacher simply pass "the word along"[37] so what is said does not get understood in the sense of disclosing possibility for the student, but covers up possibility and the present moment. Idle talk makes possible talk about the world without it being grounded in the student's life or understanding.

The teacher, in establishing situations in which language, as present-at-hand, is laid out differently, provides diverse possibilities for discourse and for understanding. Language as ready-to-hand, as opening into or setting up of a world, as thought, provide different possibilities for the student's being in that situation. His understandings of these possibilities would be articulated differently in each situation, and as a consequence the form of the conversation in each situation would be different.

TEACHING AS BEING IN LANGUAGE POETICALLY AND THOUGHTFULLY

In teaching, both student and teacher are in language. They dwell in it. They "use" language to speak together, but language also speaks through them. The teaching situation must be interpreted not only as the laying out of language and as conversation among teacher and student, but as both teacher and student letting himself be in, and perhaps taken over by language. The teacher guards language by establishing a situation within which both he and the student can serve language by hearkening to the world and to language. The situation must be so established that both teacher and student are absorbed in that which is most "thought provoking" and caringly attentive to the world. Absorbed and attentive, they silently wait for language to speak through them as originative speaking—naming that which is; or rethinking that which calls for thought. The teacher, functioning as a lecturer, would seem to be one who dwells in language so thoroughly that speech speaks through him. To repeat what has been uttered before is not guarding language. It is returning to the past to repeat what has been said, not to rethink what has been thought. In lecturing the teacher guards and serves language by respectfully acknowledging the thought of others, by being open that that which is can be named through him, and by disclosing his own possibilities in the language situation within which he lives. In seminars and discussions, the teacher serves language by listening for and welcoming the poetic and thoughtful speech of students. Their speech might disclose that which is hidden from the teacher, or might gather that which remains unthought in the teacher's own thought.

How are we in the world as teachers? For the most part, we are with others in language. As teachers, we differ from others by the care with which we dwell in that language. Language must be guarded if we are not to fall into the idle speech which covers the earth. Language must be served if a world is to be set up. The teacher is a guardian and servant of language. He must impart this trust to his students. He does so by the way in which he dwells with them in language.

NOTES

[1]B. Othanel Smith, "A Study of the Logic of Teaching," *Teaching: Vantage Points for Study*, ed. Ronald Hyman (New York: J. B. Lippincott, 1968), 101–117.

[2]"What we usually mean by language, namely, a stock of words and syntactical rules, is only a threshold of language." Martin Heidegger, "Holderlin and the Essence of Poetry," in *Existence and Being*, trans. Douglas Scott (Chicago: Henry Regnery, 1949), 301.

[3]Arno Bellack, et al, *The Language of the Classroom* (New York: Teachers College Press, 1966). See also Heidegger:

"If we may talk here of playing games at all, it is not we who play with words, but the nature of language plays with us …. For language plays with our speech—it likes to let our speech drift away into the more obvious meanings of words. It is as though man had to make an effort to live properly with language. It is as though such a dwelling were especially prone to succumb to the danger of the common place …. Is it playing words when we attempt to give heed to this game of language and to hear what language really says when it speaks?" From, Martin Heidegger, *What is Called Thinking*, trans. Fred D. Wiek and J. Glenn Gray (New York: Harper and Row, Publishers 1969), 110–119.

[4]Martin Heidegger, *An Introduction to Metaphysics*, trans. Ralph Manheim (Garden City, N.Y.: Doubleday, Archer Books, 1961), 69.

[5]From a letter by Holderlin, quoted by Martin Heidegger in "Holderlin and the Essence of Poetry," *Existence and Being*, 297.

[6]Martin Heidegger, *Being and Time*, trans. John Macquarrie and Edward Robinson (New York: Harper and Row, 1962), 204, 121.

[7]Ibid., 203–210.

[8]Heidegger, "Holderlin and the Essence of Poetry," 298.

[9]Ibid., 307.

[10]Martin Heidegger, *What is Called Thinking*, 130.

[11]Michael Polanyi, *The Tacit Dimension* (Garden City, N.Y.: Doubleday, 1966).

[12]Heidegger, *Being and Time*, 107–121.

[13]Ibid., 203-210.

[14]"The existential-ontological foundation of language is discourse or talk." Ibid., 203.

[15]Ibid., 173.

[16]Ibid., 184.

[17]Ibid., 205.

[18]Ibid., 211-214.

[19]*What is Called Thinking*, 128.

[20]"Holderlin and the Essence of Poetry," 307.

[21]Martin Heidegger, "The Origin of the Work of Art," trans. Albert Hofstadter, *Philosophies of Art and Beauty*, ed. Albert Hofstadter and Richard Kuhns (New York: The Modern Library, 1964), 694.

[22]Ibid., 671.

[23]Ibid., 698.

[24]Ibid., 697.

[25]*Being and Time*, 437.

[26]*What is Called Thinking*, 76-77.

[27]"The Origin of the Work of Art," 663.

[28]Maurice Merleau Ponty, *The Structure of Behavior*, trans. Alden L. Fisher (Boston: Beacon Press, 1963).

[29]*The Origin of the Work of Art*, 685.

[30]Ibid., 695.

[31]Ibid., 694.

[32]*What is Called Thinking*, 76.

[33]Ibid., 71.
[34]Ibid., 144.
[35]Ibid., 146.
[36]Ibid., 127.
[37]*Being and Time*, 212.

14

The Leadership Role in Curriculum Change

(1966)

In one of his many unfortunately ignored statements, John Dewey remarked "that the only way in which adults consciously control the kind of education which the immature get is by controlling the environment in which they act.... We never educate directly, but indirectly by means of the environment."[1]

The developments in education since Dewey wrote *Democracy and Education* support his contention. Attempts to change the curriculum by simply rewriting courses of study or curriculum guides have seldom, if ever, worked. Courses of study do not control the environment. In the thirties and forties this fact was generally recognized, and attempts to change the educational environment were made by changing the teacher, who, after all, is one of the major characteristics of the educational environment. This effort was best formulated in the now classic statement by Alice Miel, *Changing the Curriculum*.[2] Since then similar efforts have focused upon developing further the techniques and philosophy of teacher change.

The curriculum efforts of the fifties and sixties can be seen as other attempts to change the educational environments. The integration struggles of this period, sanctioned by the decision of the Supreme Court, drew attention to the fact that a segregated classroom is a different kind of educational environment. The type of student within the classroom is one of the conditions in the educational environment and must be consciously considered by the educator. The major curriculum efforts of today [1966] are effective because they seek to introduce into the schools new materials of education which call forth new responses from students and teachers. These new materials are a reflection of the concern of the academician and of the scientist-technician for the quality of educational material within the classroom. Both see the classroom as a part of the modern world, and as such they believe it should reflect some of the intellectual and

159

technological advances of this civilization. In other words, the last thirty years of educational change would support Dewey's contention that to control the environment is to control education.

Dewey further states that "the environment consists of those conditions that promote or hinder, stimulate or inhibit, the characteristic activities of a human being."[3] His use of the word *condition* is a felicitous choice, for it encourages the kind of probing which seems to be needed today. The word *environment* is too amorphous to be of much help in identifying crucial characteristics within schools. It lends itself rather readily to the interpretations which clustered around the word *climate* or *atmosphere* in the forties and fifties, e.g., democratic, teacher centered, integrative, etc. These climate studies led to value laden research which hid or ignored some of the controllable factors within classrooms and substituted, instead, concern for feelings, attitudes, and styles of teaching which are very hard to grasp operationally. The term conditions suggests that the classroom or school environment is composed of a variety of things, states, or acts; and that these entities may be identified as they "promote or hinder, stimulate or inhibit" educational activity, which is, after all, a "characteristic activity of a human being." Thus the school or classroom environment may be conceived as an aggregate of conditions which educate. The curriculum person is concerned with the nature of these conditions and their integration into an environment which reflects the values of those controlling education.

To explore the various dimensions of "conditions which educate" is an undertaking too vast for this paper, which must focus upon the dimension of change. However, the relationship between "conditions which educate" and the idea of conditioned behavior should be noted. Patterned or learned behavior is frequently identified as conditioned behavior, i.e., behavior which has been formed by the conditions within the individual's environment. Furthermore, within certain philosophical and theological circles, the dichotomy "conditioned and unconditioned" is used; this dichotomy points to the determinateness of man versus his creative freedom or, in other terms, the relationship between necessity and freedom. Thus, the notion of "conditions" makes possible the entrance of the discussion into psychological and philosophical idioms.

For the purposes of identifying aspects of curriculum change, two major categories of conditions can be postulated. On the one hand are the artifacts or "things" which are made, produced, or used for educational purposes: the educational materiel. These are conditions which can be compared with other possible artifacts purchased, which sometimes wear out and frequently become obsolescent. Many of the newer curricula are basically collections of artifacts, including books, experimental materials, and newer media packages. On the other hand are the ways of working with these artifacts and with students. Just as most textbooks at the primary level specify clearly ordained ways for teachers to use them, so newer materials also specify the teacher behaviors, including teacher language. These more or less determined "ways of working" are the other type of conditions which can be identified. They are the patterned behaviors of the teacher—his conditioned behaviors. In Ortega y Gasset's[4] terms, they are the usages which can be identified; that is, the customs and habits which have been more or less institutionalized. Perhaps Wittgenstein's word *rules* would be more appropriate, for the following of a rule is a custom, use, or institution.[5] Not all teacher behavior is free and creative; much of it is carefully patterned behavior, the result of prior education and training or experience. This training or education has resulted in more or less durable and recognizable patterns of using artifacts and language, and of relating to the students. In other words, aspects of the teacher's behavior have been conditioned, and they become, then, part of the conditions of the environment which educate. The existence of conditions which are more or less durable within a supposedly free human being points to many philosophical problems and also to some very difficult, practical ones. This is one reason for the many efforts which explore the problem of changing teacher behavior. Nevertheless, the conditions which are supplied by or in teachers may also be compared with conditions in or of other teachers. They may be purchased (that is, teachers can be hired or employed), and they can become obsolescent. In other words, there are certain aspects of teacher behavior or skill which warrant discussing them as part of the conditions of the educational environment and which also justify the application of the term technician to the work of the teacher. Only when the educational enterprise is seen within different categories, e.g., as a humane and moral activity, does this notion of "teacher as conditions" get in the way. This problem will be the focus of attention later. Certain consequences follow from this consideration of curriculum as an aggregate of environmental conditions which educate.

THE REALITIES OF EDUCATIONAL CONDITIONS

Considered as an aggregate of conditions, the curriculum is not simply an ideological phenomenon, but a reality which has substance and durability. This reality, of course, is related to the various ideological structures which shape man's values, determine, to some extent, his environment, and suggest directions for the future; but the relationship is complex and is yet to be made sufficiently transparent in the curriculum literature.

Economic Realities

The aggregate of conditions within the school costs money. The purchase of materials and the hiring of personnel involve an initial investment. Their functional upkeep requires inventories, repairs, and, on the part of teachers, something like reconditioning or perhaps recreation or the infusion of new spirit.

Materiel becomes obsolescent and needs to be replaced or updated as the characteristics of the surrounding social environment alter and as the student population changes. For instance, mathematics programs become dated and teacher skills and language become anachronisms. New math materials must be purchased, and teachers must be reconditioned to those materials in order that their languages and teaching skills are coordinated with the new materials.

In other words, considered as an aggregate of conditions, the curriculum is a capital investment, and an economic rationality is necessary for thinking about these conditions over a period of time. Curriculum change is not simply a matter of theory or value or ideology. It is a matter of hard cash, of old materials being thrown out and of dysfunctional skills and language of teachers being replaced by functional ones. One of the planning models necessary for thinking about curriculum change is an economic model. The curriculum specialist has failed to give adequate attention to these financial or economic considerations. No curriculum textbook considers the problem of curriculum change from an economic viewpoint. Nowhere are discussions of the obsolescence and renewal of educational materiel considered as curriculum problems. Long range planning for educational environments and conditions requires consideration of the expectant longevity of new conditions, of their estimated life in terms of changes in the social environments which have helped determine them and make them of value, and of the phasing in and out of new systems of materiel.

The problems concerned with the cost of teacher conditions are primarily extensions of the above considerations. It costs money to help experienced teachers develop new teaching and language skills. The need for summer workshops to help teachers develop the skills to be used with new programs and hardware is a case in point. Given the rapidity of change in the educational technology, how is teacher reconditioning to be financed? It seems completely unreasonable to expect teachers to remake themselves when they already have a full, emotion draining job each day. Given the change which is now evident in educational materials and programs, the changes which are yet to come as the technologists really start developing new hardware, and the drastic changes society will have to undergo in response to the world's developments, it may be necessary to consider teaching, a twelve month occupation, with two or three months devoted to reconditioning and mastering the skills necessary for the new educational conditions which will be required. Public school systems probably will not be able to escape this responsibility much longer by simply sending teachers to universities during the summer and encouraging higher degrees. As with industries and other agencies within this society, they will have to assume responsibility for their own fights against obsolescence.

Some of the innovations in school organization, such as team-teaching and dual-progress plans, could be conceptualized as attempts to deal with the economic realities of the reconditioning of teacher skills and languages. Given the rapid changes in educational expectations, many teachers cannot be expected to develop competencies in all of the new fields of education. In this transitional stage, it is perhaps cheaper and more effective to ask teachers to specialize as a way of developing new competencies, or to team up with other teachers who have other valued educational conditions and hope that some of them might rub off. The organizational schemes which seem viable today might be extremely out of place in a few years when different kinds of teacher conditions are being developed in universities.

Historical Realties

Only in the establishment of a brand new educational environment can a curriculum change agent start from scratch. In most situations, the responsible person is confronted by a situation which has a past and a future. His actions are limited and partially prescribed by that past and those factors which seem to be shaping the future. In other words, the actions of the curriculum person are historically determined. This is not an historical determination in a general social sense; although to some extent all educators share common problems and determining factors. Rather, he is a participant in the evolution of a particular situation, and this particularness must be emphasized. Curriculum literature, by its very nature, must deal in abstractions and generalizations. The responsible curriculum leader, on the other hand, is confronted by human beings in specific situations. Whereas generalizations may be used to explore these specific situations and to disclose aspects which might otherwise remain hidden, they cannot be used as the sole base for making decisions. In fact, to the extent that a curriculum leader attempts to respond to a given historical situation only in terms of certain abstractions, he may be said to be irresponsive and perhaps irresponsible to the situation and the people in it. The curriculum leader needs an historical sense, for he is an event-maker who attempts to modify the direction of social evolution within a given situation. Thus, his primary mode of analysis or, at least, sensitivity, is an historical one. He must take what has been given to him. He seeks to direct the flow of future events in such a way that those individuals interested in the situation accept the change or, at least, do not seek to overthrow him and his directions.

The difficulty with much curriculum literature is that it does not suggest even the need for such an historical awareness or sensitivity, let alone provide those cognitive tools which would enable the leader to analyze the basic social-historical structure of the specific situation within which he operates. Consequently, innovations or pseudo-innovations are frequently imposed on specific situations in which they have no chance of ever catching on because they are inappropriate to the conditions that exist within that situation. They are eventually rejected as a foreign graft is rejected by the human body. Much money and effort are being wasted for lack of a sense of historical responsibility.

Political Realities

Given the vast number of educational conditions available within the broader society, the leader in a specific situation is faced with the task of choice and selection. Which educational conditions should be brought into the schools? What kinds of teachers? What types of materials? Priorities should be given to which programs? Decision-makers would like a foolproof system for helping them. This is impossible except within very narrow technological fields which are built and guided totally by scientific fields of knowledge. The curriculum leader basically is making policy decisions. In fact, in most schools he is making policy decisions within the public realm. The educator likes to cry out that he is a professional and that he has professional responsibility and professional prerogatives; but even tenure doesn't protect him from the blasts of the public, nor guarantee status. A decision about educational conditions is essentially a political decision which involves personal-professional risk; for the leader must weigh and balance all of the conflicting demands which exist within the situations and come up with a solution which is acceptable to all or most. To risk himself in a decision does not imply that professional knowledge is not used or that his decision is not informed by the many fields of knowledge applicable in that specific situation. But no field of knowledge and no professional associations can be held responsible for his decision. He can utter the cry "But research says ..." until blue in the face but it won't take the burden of responsibility off his shoulders. In fact, research has said some rather unfortunate things in the past as well as some good ones.

Caught in the midst of this specific human situation which demands an historical sensitivity, the educator is confronted by conflicting demands and conflicting possibilities. The resolution of such conflicts among individuals and groups of people requires a political sensitivity and a political rationality. He must be able to determine where pressures are building up, where hidden possibilities exist, and why certain possibilities are in the forefront in spite of their seeming lack of educational value. For example, the availability of federal funds today becomes a strong attraction for making certain kinds of decisions which might be completely unfunctional in a given situation. On the other hand, the availability of federal funds might also arouse certain pressure blocks in the situation which should be overcome if the school system is to move ahead. Their availability might point out and delimit the professional-political struggles which he could easily avoid or daringly accept.

Current educational debates and their respective ideologies—such as the debates about the role of the school, the place of subject matter, or the organizational structure of the schools—prepare the way for certain changes of educational conditions. These debates and their supporting ideologies serve to alert public opinion, to marshal social forces which might support change, and to legitimize action once decisions are made. Again, the ideologies do not prescribe action; they are not predefined answers to slowly emerging questions or problems. They are simply part of the value clarification process that goes on constantly within a partially open society, and they reflect the tides of change. New educational ideologies cannot replace all prior educational values; they simply move the value clarification process ahead and must, consequently, be seen in historical perspective. However, they do engage the other members of the community in emerging value problems and prepare the way for changes in the educational conditions within a given situation. The educational leader must be aware of the prevailing ideologies and educational debates, and indeed must be prepared to use them as a vehicle in his policy-making. This is most clearly seen today as educators and others interested in education have moved upon the cognitive development bandwagon as a way to introduce new content into the schools. Without the softening up process begun by Bestor[6] and others in the early fifties this change might not have come about; for it must be acknowledged that Dewey forcefully and clearly pointed out the need for intellectual content in the first twenty years of this century and certainly Florence Stratemeyer's[7] "Persistent Life Situations" approach was not devoid of rigorous intellectual content, although its organizational form differed from the form that intellectual content is taking today.

The Fabrication of Educational Conditions

Neither the teacher nor the curriculum leader starts from scratch in designing educational environments. Many of the conditions which are to be a part of the educational environment are fabricated outside of the specific school situation. This has been true since the textbook industry got its foot in the educational door and is bound to continue to be so as the various communication and technological industries see the educational enterprise as a potential source of income and a field of service. The academic community also has expressed an interest in educational conditions used within schools. The academicians have more often than not been the writers of text materials; but even more potently, they have sought to determine or at least influence the language patterns and skills of the teachers through their university courses. In other words, most of the educational conditions used in the schools are produced outside of the schools. In some situations teachers may construct their own materials or evolve their own teaching styles; and a few communities prepare some of their own resource materials. However, the complexity of educational materiel and the amount of time required to produce effective conditions probably suggest that they will continue to be fabricated outside of the immediate situation, except as a few teachers try to evolve their own specialized materials and ways of working. Even in such cases, however, teachers are more apt to resort to using prefabricated material in unique ways rather than to start from scratch.

The production of these materials is a crucial aspect of education, and prior conceptions of their nature do a disservice to them and their function. Perhaps they are best viewed as communication vehicles between people with special interests and concerns and neophytes who might be expected to have some reason for being involved in those interests and concerns. Science texts and other scientific materials can be interpreted as vehicles to so-called scientific understandings. More advantageously, they can be interpreted as a communication vehicle between the student and those scientists who produced them. The same is true of math, social studies, language, and, indeed, all aspects of the curriculum. The teacher, likewise, is a mediator between the student and those specialists who have certain defined interests. His language skills, his ways of asking questions and posing problems, of responding to the students, his ways of selecting, using and interpreting various materials reflect this communicating function. In effect he serves as a vehicle of communication between the student and the specialist. This communication need not be interpreted as a passing on of information or viewpoints, but as initiating the student into the language and concerns of the specialists.[8]

Educational conditions may be interpreted, then, as messages formed or fabricated by others for students and as rules for decoding, interpreting, and using those messages. The forming, fabricating, or shaping of these messages requires knowledge of the communication process and hence inherently involves craftsmanship and certain artistic skills. It is in this area that education is making the greatest progress today, for the communication and information processing industries have moved with great enthusiasm into this task. Furthermore, the academic groups which are bringing about change within certain content fields are working cooperatively with learning theorists, teachers, and these industries to build systems of materials for educational purposes. Indeed, learning theory finds its fruition as the scientific theory used to fabricate these conditions. That is, learning theory today is less helpful for thinking about the student and his actions and more helpful for producing conditions to be used in the educational process. This is most clearly seen in the production of programmed materials, but it holds true for most of the new materials which are becoming available. At the present time the technology of fabricating these educational materials is far advanced over the artistic aspects of the fabrication; a situation which will hopefully be rectified as the technology becomes more second nature and as the aesthetic problems or dimensions loom larger.

Designing the Educational Environment

Given the availability of educational conditions, the educator must then put them together. They are not simply plunked into a school or a classroom in random order. The teacher conditions and the material conditions must be integrated into significant patterns, which reflect the dominant educational values. This is essentially a design problem which is best considered with an aesthetic rationality. The problem of design is frequently pushed aside with the assumption that curriculum is basically a technological operation and that there is a linear relationship between objectives, experiences within the schools, and outcomes; that is, that the specification of objectives leads directly to the selection of experiences which then produce the desired outcomes. This over-simplified rationality legitimizes the selection of a given textbook series as the vehicle to given ends or the use of stereotyped experiences in any and every educational situation.

The difficulty with the technological resolution of the design problem is that educational experiences are more than means to ends. They are a slice of life itself; expressions of the values of people in control. Consequently, they are the meanings that these people impose upon existence. The patterning or design of the educational environment reflects the following types of values:

1. The nature of human experience as it is seen, viewed, or felt by those in charge,
2. The meaning of the adult-student-thing-relationships: the significance of one person for another and the value of things in that relationship,
3. The types of orderliness exposed in the world: how the human and man-made world is ordered spatially and through time.

These values are given by the way that conditions pertaining to similar phenomena are brought together, the way that conditions pertaining to non-similar phenomena are brought into some kind of relationship, and the manner in which the sequence of events throughout the school day and year unfold. The first is illustrated by the way in which various resource material, teacher skills, and student backgrounds are brought together and organized within a given content area, such as social studies or math. The second is illustrated by the relationships manifest among given content areas, such as the relationships which exist or do not exist between science and art, or music, social sciences and social problems. The third is illustrated by the way in which a total school day is organized or the way in which a teacher designs the sequence of a course or a unit of study.

As pointed out earlier, these are basically aesthetic problems of design or organization. They are problems of the organization of space and time, of the composition of materials into meaningful patterns, and of the rhythm and dramatic flow of events. It should be pointed out that the developments of modern art—visual, musical, dramatic, and language—probably offer significant clues about the possible design of experiences. The iconic structure of TV as an art form,[9] the so-called theater of the absurd in which plot and structure differ significantly from traditional drama, and modern visual and spatial art with different, nonrepresentational forms of composition or structure may all offer new visions of the form that educational experiences might take. The availability of a variety of new media, e.g., the 8mm film projector and loop and telephonic hookups, offers brand new tools for reconceptualizing the patterning of the educational environment, perhaps based upon the structures and designs of modern art.

The Reality of the Human Situation

The conditions and the design of the educational environment can never be brought completely under the control of any one individual or group of individuals, for the educational environment is a human environment. It contains the unconditioned as well as the conditioned; and the unconditioned breaks into the settled environment as disruptive novelty. It is the source of the creative evolution which is possible in human affairs and structures. It is also the source of those destructive events, which suggest that an era is at end or that previous structures or courses of action are no longer functional. One does not channel the human qualities within a situation—he lives with them and responds to them. This fact is perhaps the major stumbling stone of educational thought and action, for there is always the lingering hope that educational change can become completely rational and predictable. It cannot, for educational events and processes are infused with the mystery of man: the major and controlling reality of the educational situation. Hence any form of thought about educational change and practice must make room for that mystery. The educator needs what Keats called the quality of " ... negative capability, that is, when a man is capable of being in uncertainties, mysteries, doubts, without any irritable reaching after fact and reason."[10] Educational action must consequently be informed by philosophy, the arts, and theology, for these fields of human endeavor attempt to come to grips with the mystery of man without the "irritable reaching after fact and reason" which is the necessary quality of the behavioral sciences. This is one of the major reasons that teachers and other personnel involved in educational change must have some role in determining the nature of that change; not because involvement is more effective, but because of the sanctity of the person and the need for the emergence of the novelty which is both disruptive and creative, but which can come only from free man.

Teacher conditions can never be simply fabricated, purchased, reconditioned, or integrated with other conditions. An ethical response to the human reality demands that the person within whom the conditions exist must also assume responsibility for the fabrication, the hiring out, the reconditioning, or the integration of these conditions. In other words, Western morality accepts the right of self-determination. A person is never a thing or set of conditions. He has always the possibility of becoming other than he is. The change of human conditions is always a joint venture then. It can never be one person influencing another—but two or more people—engaging in mutual influence through conversation, power, and love. The building and renewing of the educational environment is not only a technological and economic task, taking place within a political, historical, and aesthetic framework; it is also an ethical task, taking place within the mystery of the social world.

RESPONSIBILITY FOR CURRICULUM CHANGE

Given these realities of educational environments, how can the curriculum leader conceive of his leadership role? He is situated within a particular historical situation, which, to a very large extent, determines his personal and his professional responses. However, this situation is bounded on all sides by the events, values, and resources which circulate about him and impinge upon him from the world at large. To be responsible he must first of all be responsive; that is, he must be sensitive and aware of all that goes on about him, within the historical community but also within the broader social, intellectual, technological situation. His first responsibility, then, is that of reconnaissance.

The Responsibility For Awareness

As a decision-maker, the curriculum leader must have all necessary information at his finger tips. Like any executive he must be aware of all available conditions and values which might influence his own field of action; hence the need to have an aspect of his role or his office devoted to intelligence—to sizing up what is going on in the world. Because the educational environment is an aggregate of educational conditions patterned to maximize value, he must be aware of existing educational conditions and existing values which determine the selection and arrangement of these conditions. Awareness of educational conditions implies awareness of what is transpiring within the technology of communication, particularly educational technology. Thus he must be sensitive to the commercial market. However, awareness of the commercial market is not sufficient because of the tie between production and advertisement and the building of pseudo-educational need through propaganda and advertising media. The educator is as prone to gimmicks as the householder, and the only adequate counter is basic familiarity with significant educational conditions and communication media. For example, television offers extremely significant possibilities for educational communication. However, most present uses of educational TV are pitifully inadequate. Infrequently do educational TV programs realize their possibility as a significant art form which can present new kinds of messages to students. The same is true, although to a lesser degree, of film. The development of auto-instructional techniques will also result in some pretty shoddy material until the technological and artistic phases catch up with each other and the auto-instructional materials really become a new communication art form. It is not sufficient that the intelligence function search out what is new—someone must be a shrewd critic of what is and what might be within a given media or type of conditions. This requires more than educational know-how; it requires an aesthetic snsitivity to various communication art forms and their possibilities.

There is a similar need to gather intelligence about the conditions which teachers might have. Here, too, a kind of independence and some critical acumen are necessary. There are propaganda and advertisement within the teacher preparation realm, too, and attempts to define standards by state departments or universities which might be quite out of line with other existing conditions. The only saving grace is to know what is going on in the intellectual world at the forefront of the world's problems and promises and to judge teacher conditions in terms of their potential for conveying messages and systems of interpretation between the front runners in the world's evolution and the students within the classrooms. This means having some awareness of what the various intellectual fields and social problems offer for the future, which ones have outlived their usefulness, and the kinds of teachers who can communicate the viable possibilities.

Because the curriculum leader operates within a field of mixed and sometimes ambiguous or even emergent values, his intelligence system must keep him aware of and sensitive to these value orientations which shape the political side of his decisions. This means being attuned to educational and social controversy, sensitive to the educational and social values which have historical significance within his educational community, and aware of the shifts in these values. With these sensitivities he can think ahead and plan for a future which is not yet. In short, the responsible curriculum leader must be responsive to this mixed up, troubled and changing world around him. He must know what is going on not simply within the schools and the educational world, but within the world working its way into the life of the students.

Finally, to design the most effective educational environment, he must be cognizant of all the streams of thought which might influence his designing. Because the designing is a political-aesthetic act, it cannot follow from any single body of theory. Psychology and the behavioral sciences have been proclaimed as the major imprinting tool. However, the sciences disclose only certain aspects of the human situation, and their insights must be thrown against those from the fields of art, philosophy, and theology. Any single source of knowledge is not a carrier of wisdom, but only of power and penetration. Only when multiple sources of knowledge are used and consequently various types of power are available, can decisions be wise and the educational environment viable and responsive. The curriculum leader's intelligence system must be attuned to many fields of human endeavor and cannot depend simply upon one—whether a behavioral science, a philosophy, or a theology.

Political Responsibility

The curriculum leader is a leader. That is, he is an event-maker and a shaper of an environment. He is an actor in the world's history, helping to give form to a specific emergent situation. This means that he is, by vocation, a politician. The notion of professionalism has destroyed this basic awareness, for it tries to remove the educator from the historical world into a privileged sanctuary of professional associations and responsibility. The educational leader has consciously chosen to use his working time to shape a human institution. Consequently, he must operate not simply within the realm of differences of opinion, but within conflicts of opinion. Indeed, he must use conflict as one of the wellsprings of human action. He is caught in an existing historical situation, which will pull him into the oblivion of the past unless he seeks to renew it by creating new events and building new environments. He lives among different values, yet must steer a positive course through these different values and use them for forward movement. Some of the value differences and limitations are in the economic realm. With limited resources and conflicting demands for their use, he must make decisions which reflect economic awareness. Economy and efficiency are criteria that must be considered, for political responsibility requires sensitivity to economic values. If they are ignored, he risks the displeasure of those who treasure economic values, and he squanders limited resources.

To work his way through differences of value and conflicts of opinion and to renew the environment require the use of power. He must influence others. He must build new organizational structures. To do so, he must destroy old institutional structures. He must weed out obsolescence, whether in materials or in teachers, and he must introduce the community to the new which is the harbinger of today and tomorrow. But he cannot do these things if he destroys wantonly. He must conserve that which is still valued and treasured within the community; and he must operate within the streams of change which exist within that community. He must operate within the historical givens of that situation. Educational ideologies, curriculum proposals, and organizational patterns are not blueprints to follow; for the givenness of the historical situation prevents the imprinting of a general pattern upon it. They are but guides—to be used, to be doubted, to disclose possibility—but never to be used in their totality. They are but one source of value, one potential organizational possibility; and they must be checked against the historical determiners within the given situation.

The person who builds environments and makes events is always held accountable for his actions. He cannot escape. Accountability means being open and receptive to social criticism, indeed welcoming it as one of the social techniques whereby values are unearthed. Accountability means being willing to face the consequences of one's acts, legitimizing them with as many forms of rationality as possible, but recognizing that rationalities are vehicles for decision-making, not excuses. Only a man can be held accountable. But only a man dares to act boldly and courageously within an historical situation. Only a man can be political and shape his world.

Aesthetic Responsibility

Political responsibility requires a responsiveness to the values and interests of people who influence the educational environment. Judged politically, the significant educational environment is just, for it reflects or speaks to these varied values and demands. Aesthetic responsibility requires a responsiveness to the conditions of the environment—to the givens which determine the educational possibilities. Judged aesthetically, the significant educational environment has meaning, beauty, and truth, and reflects vitality and promise.

The curriculum leader is confronted by a wide range of materials, teacher competencies and skills, and limited space and time. Some of these givens seem opposed to others—as two teachers who differ in their use of language or work with students, or as viable materials which seem out of place with certain teachers. Given this mass of potential he must somehow compose it into meaningful structures, and let it be shaped by the limitations of space and time. Given raw space, he uses the given conditions to turn it into beautiful architectural and physical structures. Given unstructured time, he uses the conditions to turn it into rhythm, melody, and dramatic event. He makes this transformation from givens and limitations through the quality of his educational vision. Educational conditions are incarnate educational possibilities, sometimes hidden from view, but awaiting the creative touch of the visionary who can imagine these possibilities coming to life in appropriate contexts. The designed educational environment is a fusion of given conditions and vision—it is the creation of meaning.

Meaning isn't something which simply exists within the world. It is man-made. It reflects what man is or what man makes himself to be. To ignore the creation of meaning is not simply to let natural meanings come to the fore; but to let meaning emerge out of the careless and routine activity of man. The educational environment has meaning; it is the meaning of those people who have responsibility for it. Monotony can rule supreme. Things and schedules can be more important than students and teachers. Plant can be of greater concern than the creative outbursts of students. Joyful discovery can be the meaning. Enthusiastic responsibility of young people can be manifest. Knowledge as truth and possibility rather than as grades and promotion can be the meaning.

Community rather than isolation and division can be reflected in the design. What would the curriculum leader have man be? The school is that place where man is that which he would be.

Aesthetic responsibility for the design of meaningful educational environments requires a sensitivity to truth and beauty. That which is created reflects man; and it must be a truthful reflection of what man is. The way that students and teachers use materials and language exposes how man is related to the world of things. It signifies the importance of language as man's most important instrument of growth and possibility. But the environment not only reflects man as he is, but as he might be—as possibility. Beauty can be considered the disclosure of possibility, the bringing into awareness of the perfectibility of man, and perhaps even the exposing of his potentiality for tragedy and comedy. Today for instance, the schools are perhaps the best symbol of man's tragic vision; for the possible can be envisioned, but only infrequently, if ever, realized.

As a designer of a more or less durable environment, the educational leader is also responsible for the qualities of vitality and promise. The designed environment is the answer of the curriculum leader to the available conditions. The conditions change as changes take place in the broader social-technological order. If the designed environment is to stay viable, then it must grow and change with the changing conditions. That is, it must remain vital—almost alive as it reflects the growth of man and his environment. There can never be *the* curriculum or the unchanging educational environment. The curriculum must always be in process. To conceive of it as a static entity, which must be changed occasionally, is to misconceive and hence to interfere with its continuing evolution. The designing is never a one shot job with a state of completion; it is always in process. It must reflect the life of the people responsible for it and the life in the surrounding communities of knowledge, social action, and technology.

The designed environment is not something which stands as a symbol, as something to be admired. It is an agency of man and is designed to serve. It serves the community in a variety of ways, but more significantly it must serve the students who live in it. Aesthetically, it must offer promise. The student must be able to see in the structures of the design promises of what he might become and of what he is. It must reveal to him a future which will be new and significant. It must promise the potential that he can become what only he can become, not what his neighbor can become or what some adult might want him to become. Aesthetically, a design without promise to the individual is meaningless or, at the most, symbolic of chains and confinement. A design without promise can easily be ignored.

Professionally, the curriculum leader is responsible for an adequate intelligence function; for balancing and using the political forces influencing the situations and for creating a meaningful educational environment. But throughout all of his activities he is called upon to be a man. His life is an answer to the world. He must be responsive to that which is without and that which is within. By his responses to the things in this world, the events within his world, and the people who share his life, he acknowledges what man is. He defines man by the life that he leads. This is not an idle responsibility today. The educator finds it too easy to ignore this question of "Who is Man?" Hence the efficient administrator, the smart dean. Hence also the scarcity of wise and humble people who are witness to the complexity of today's world; people who have the courage to listen to other people with sincerity and interest because they realize that in the words of others may be a bit of the newness which moves the world forward. The school can easily become another vast technology in which man is lost—encapsulated within his own means. But technology is not the villain, for as an expression of man it offers new possibilities. The school, like all other complex organizations of man, is a battleground. Man may live or die fighting himself and his products. But each person who aspires to add to this world must first do it through his responsiveness and responsibility as man. He must help man be through the answerability of his own life. Fulfilling this responsibility, he then has the vitality and promise to contribute to the education of others.

NOTES

[1] John Dewey, *Democracy and Education* (New York: The Macmillan Company, 1961; first published in 1916), 19.

[2] Alice Miel, *Changing the Curriculum, A Social Process* (New York: D. Appleton-Century, 1946).

[3] *Democracy and Education*, 11.

[4] José Ortega y Gasset, *Man and People* (New York: W. W. Norton).

[5] Ludwig Wittgenstein, *Philosophical Investigations*, trans. G.E.M. Anscombe (New York: Macmillan, 1953), section 199.

[6] Arthur R. King and John A. Brownell, *The Curriculum and the Disciplines of Knowledge* (New York: John Wiley and Sons, 1966).

[7] See Arthur E. Bestor, *The Educational Wastelands; The Retreat from Learning in Our Public Schools* (Urbana: University of Illinois Press, 1953), *Ed.*

[8] See Florence Stratemeyer, et al., *Developing a Curriculum for Modern Living* (New York: Teachers College, 1947); for a brief overview see Florence Stratemeyer, "Developing a Curriculum for Modern Living," in *Approaches in Curriculum*, ed Ronald T. Hyman (Englewood Cliffs, NJ: Prentice-Hall, 1973), 53–72. *Ed.*

[9] Marshall McLuhan, *Understanding Media: The Extensions of Man* (New York:McGraw-Hill, 1965).

[10] John Keats, letter to the brothers George and Thomas Keats, dated 21 December, 1817, Hanstead, England. Published in *The Selected Letters of John Keats*, selected and edited by Lionel Trilling (Garden City, New York: Doubleday, 1956), 103.

15

Education in the Church

(1972)

When church people were engaged in the Honest to God and God is Dead debates a few years ago I thought they were lucky compared to school people. The questioning of their institutions provided a significant opportunity to rethink what they are about, whereas school people were inhibited from such fundamental rethinking by the sheer inertia and magnitude of the school enterprise. The unquestioned acceptance of schools as social institutions, if not as educational institutions, meant that school people would always have teachers to prepare and school problems to solve. School people had not been forced to do the fundamental rethinking required by church people. But this is changing. With the move toward free schools and the call by an ex-religious to DeSchool Society,[1] school people may yet be forced into the uncomfortable but very necessary practice of rethinking what they are about.

The mutual failure to rethink what we are about makes the linking of education and religion a tragic activity. We continue to depend upon our own short unreflective institutional pasts, or we continue to depend upon external enterprises such as psychology, to provide clarity or insight about our goings on. The complexity of education and religion makes the linking a risky activity. With religious and educational institutions undergoing or about to undergo significant change, identifying points of contact is difficult. Furthermore staying informed of developments in each enterprise is extremely difficult, in spite of Martin Marty's[2] annual efforts, unparalleled in education.

In education the necessity to rethink what we are about is hidden not only by the assumed value of schools but also by accouterments that go with schools. Schools are accepted as if they were the primary educational vehicle and minor modifications of organization, curriculum, or teaching methods reduce the pressure for radical change. Rhetorical systems are built which identify the problems of education as if they were problems of students, thus denying students the respect due another person. Discourse systems are used which hide

175

our need to control others; consequently, control over others is labeled motivation, discipline, or the need for credential. Our proclivity for prejudging and stereotyping others is legitimated by reference to IQ, grade levels, years of schooling, or standardized test scores.

The necessity to rethink education is also hidden by developments in behavioral sciences. These developments are the source of a false optimism. The assumption is made that as more is known about people and education, educators will be more effective with the educational arrangements now formalized in schools. If development and learning can be more precisely explained, then learning experiences can be more effectively designed; a fine excuse for not attending to how we live with your people. If the stages of thinking through which children go can be identified, then better materials and teaching techniques can be designed; a splendid excuse for not listening and conversing more carefully with children. If the social structure of a school can be described more accurately, people can be prepared more effectively to live in them, thus escaping the responsibility to rethink and re-shape institutions within which people dwell together. If the goals of education can be more clearly specified, the content of schools can be organized more efficiently, thus hiding the political control of knowledge and education. If the structure of a discipline can be identified, teaching can be easier, thus hiding the responsibility for the way language is used with others.

The necessity to rethink education is hidden by accepting the established as real. Origins and choice points are forgotten. The times and places of origin are not recollected; to rethink what might have been or what might be. This is the danger of positive thinking.

Education in the church suffers in similar ways. Many religious concerned with the young and their education are not rethinking their foundations and their historical turning points. Even as the religious rethink their institutional arrangements and community meanings, they are blinded to the need to rethink the linkage between religion and education by rays of worldly hope originating in secular education. They have compounded their problems by accepting uncritically an assumed relation between education and religion. The religious who cares educationally for others is doubly handicapped, for he falsely assumes the secular educator's problematics, mimics his errors and takes on his false optimism. The religious educator, in doubting what he is about, turns for assurance to the secular educator who suffers not from doubt, but from hubris. In so doing, the religious educator infrequently penetrates into his own foundations and uniqueness. He does not live within his doubts, which if I interpret Paul Tillich appropriately, is necessary for faith. He escapes into the pseudo-assurance of the secular educator, and does not call into question the practices and rhetoric of secular education.

This is disclosed most clearly to me as I work with teachers in seminaries. When asked to reflect about their teaching, their mode of reflection follows that used by teachers in secular educational institutions. When faced with problems of curriculum organization or teaching, they hope that a technology of education, based upon behavioral sciences and empirical methods, will provide solutions. This misplaced hope is often accompanied by a hesitancy to change their own ways of being with others, or to modify the discourse system within which they teach. Technology appears as an external salvation mechanism requiring no personal conversion. When faced with non-responsive students their uncritical tendency is to turn to psychology as a way to understand students which short circuits reflection about the meanings of two people in relationship, even a teaching relationship. When faced with problems of class morale or seminar discussion, some turn to social psychology and group dynamics, rather than rethink the meaning of community. Does "church" as "community" apply to groups of students with teachers? When faced with the possibility or desirability of creating new educational procedures, the models of academic respectability of graduate study loom as absolute standards. The lecture method, the graduate seminar, or clinical procedures used in medical schools are the appropriate forms of relationship between he who knows and he who doesn't yet know.

The failure to rethink is also disclosed by those who plan curriculum, prepare educational workers for church schools, or write books about church education. In most cases, the ideas and approaches follow, with sufficient lag, the developments in secular school education. Child centered approaches and the needs of students were visible at one time. The structure of religion or moral development à la Bruner, Kohlberg and their colleagues is now a concern. Is there not a uniqueness about education in religious communities which governs the asking, critiquing, and answering of questions? Should secular educational systems and ideas be normative for education in religious communities?

Drawing upon the disciplines associated with secular education for informing and critiquing educational thought and practice is most necessary. Dependency is not. It is appropriate for the religious to use the reflective devices of secular education as disclosure models, but not as analogue models. Most necessary is critical reflection about what it means to be an educator. Those who reflect, however, must be aware that truth does not reside in any one mode of reflection but in between differing modes.

My own reflections about the relationship between education and religion, church and school, take strange and divergent paths. The paths are not mapped with assurance, but hesitantly with caution signs all about. My reflection paths are intended as an aid to your own reflection not as a model for it.

First, I am intrigued that the terms "religious education" and "church school" have been around so long. They appear to remain unquestioned, although without uniformity of interpretation. To speak of "religious education" is to place that activity in the same category as driver education, math education, sex education, nursing education and so on. Education is the ground for each of these, the source of a human activity. Is this not strange? My familiarity with theological thought, and indeed my awareness of my own life, points not to an educational but to a religious ground. Do you not find it strange that the religious should postulate an educational ground for religion? Is it not rather that religion is the ground for education? Is education possible without assuming, tacitly, a religious ground?

Perhaps I use the term education and religion idiosyncratically. I find it convenient to use language more appropriate to your traditions than mine; to speak of man as caught between freedom and necessity, as the conditioned being who also participates in the unconditioned, or the created being who participates in creating. The source of education resides in this paradoxical structure. The new, the novel, the creative, the unconditioned breaks the world asunder, to permit new creation, new conditions, new structures of necessity. Without transcendent possibility, man would be caught and incapable of the continuous education which seems to be his. Radical thought, the untamed, the power to negate, the inbreaking of the word—are not these the sources of education, not vice versa? Why then do we have an expression "religious education" which makes of religion a phenomena like driving, math, housing, business—activities for which education is the source? Is this not an expression which requires rethinking? Are we in religion in an educational way, or are we in education in a religious way? Education which assumes the possibility of finite transcendence is based upon man's participation in the infinite. Education which brings about the formation of men draws upon his unformed—the infinite possibility of all forms.

What are we about, then, when we speak of "religious education." Are we claiming that education is the ground of religion? Probably not. Are we not, rather, claiming that education is a process by which we introduce the young, the neophyte, into the man-made traditions which protect and illuminate the religious. It is at this point that caution is required, and where rethinking is most critical

In *The Big Little School*,[3] Lynn points to the evangelical origin of the church school. This origin is a starting point for the rethinking of the relationship of education and religion. Robert Raikes, 200 years ago, was concerned with reforming the "morals of the lower class."[4] Lyman Beecher, 150 years ago, saw the Sunday schools as the promoter of the "intellectual and moral culture of the nation."[5] The Sunday School Union wanted to bring "every child and youth under the influence of the gospel," and at the same time to avoid sectarian or social controversies or disputes.[6] Little Henry, a model youngster, at the age of 8 ½ was "conducting arguments about faith and assisting others toward conversion." Why did the religious at that time choose to be with children in an educational way? Why did they establish schools?

By this question I mean why did Raikes choose to be with the poor to reform their morals? Why did Beecher choose to be with children to promote the intellectual and moral culture of the nation? Why was the adult image of the child that of the adult writ small? I sense here the use of education to control the life of the children, to shape the child in the image of the adult, to impose the mores of the adults. Education seemed intended to project and protect social institutions and the adult behavior which these institutions sheltered. Can not the concern for the moral development of the child be one way to express the unquestioned acceptance of adult mores?

Were there then, or are there now, other ways to be with children or youth—with those who are not yet full members of the community? Why should the powerful and powerless be together in educational ways? Why should the norms of the adult community be used to judge the behavior of the neophyte? Why must the adult reflection of the adult community be the mode of reflection in the youth community?

Friedenberg, a romantic critic of secular education, refers to students in schools as colonial people subjected to the will and dictates of the controlling powers—the adults. That we tend to be with children or young people in educational ways speaks to our desires to accept, uncritically, our power over children, and to accept, equally uncritically, our ways of being in and about our world, including our projection of the future. Can we not be content to be with the neophyte in song, worship, prayer, storytelling, service, reflection, or other activities more clearly identified as religious activities?

These concerns point, for me, at the relationship between education and religion. Education is, for me, care for the finite transcendence of men, for the forms a life takes between birth and death, for the emerging biography of others. Religion is, for me, responsiveness before infinite transcendence; attention to the norm of absolute otherness which raises into question all finite condition, all life styles. The man who would educate another, using finite norms i.e., already established ways of being, can without a second thought, control the formation of another's life; he can unreflectively and uncritically accept his own ways of being in and about the world.

Education, not grounded in religion, permits or encourages this thoughtless control of another. Education grounded in religion, however, requires attention to the norm of absolute otherness, infinite transcendence, as the basis for reflection about the significance of being together. Education grounded in religion, then, cannot be a vehicle of control; it can only be an opportunity for reflection about the meaning and significance of the life styles of educator and educatee. This can be so even with children. The norms which adults seek to impose upon youngsters are necessarily brought under judgment by the unformed or unconditioned responses, i.e. the negations, the doubts, the creations, the words, the actions, of the child or neophyte.

Is it possible that at the historical choice points the established members of the community discovered that it was easier to be with the neophyte in an educational way, modeled after secular education, because they did not know how to be with him in religious ways? Was it easier to impose than to reflect with others? Was it easier to tell children, to "teach" them, than to reflect with them, or to be with them in other ways? By reflection I mean mutual reflection, reflecting about the meanings and actions of the adults as well as the meanings and actions of the child or neophyte. Was it easier to accept, uncritically, the forms and styles of their religious community life, than to use the unformed responses and probings of neophytes as protests against form, and consequently as protections against the dangers of idolatry? Is the mote in the adult's eye the idolatrous life form which he imposes upon the powerless child, the newcomer to the established community?

We are at a time of theological and educational awareness and development when we need not be with the young in educational ways, in school ways; we can be with them in religious ways. To do this, however, requires that we shift the burden from the neophyte to the adult. To be with the young reflectively requires more self control, not control of the child. To be with the young in religious ways demands that the adult be able to tell his story with joy and listen into form the emerging story of the child; that he be disciplined to recognize valid protest and new creation.

By this I intend that established ways of thinking, of doing, of being with others are always, and must always remain, questionable. To engage in questioning and reflection about origins and alternatives without destroying or inhibiting the capability to act requires discipline. The use of biblical tradition is strengthened by exegetical and hermeneutical skills. The freedom to live in and use church traditions requires knowledge of church history. The ability to trust one's own feelings and ways of thinking requires the confidence which goes with biographical awareness, which can be developed therapeutically, or by being with others who facilitate recollection and celebration of major formative events and relationships. Confidence in social forms requires the discipline developed in political action. To live and act faithfully requires doubt, which, if accompanied by disciplined reflection, does not close off possibilities, but opens up new ones.

If I am appropriately informed and correctly interpret this information, those now concerned with religious communities are subjecting all established traditions to critical reflection, through a variety of intellectual and social disciplines: the narrative and story traditions by various hermeneutics, the dogmas and world views by philosophy and sciences, the social and interpersonal structures by the behavioral sciences and the political movements of the disenfranchised. Do not these reflections add to the continuous story of the church as a people governed by the norms of absolute otherness?

Gradually these disciplines of reflection, centered or developed in the avant-garde, filter throughout and permeate the actions and consciousness of the total community. Is adult education in the church this process of developing the reflective consciousness of the total community? Is this what a religious community is about; a community of people responsive to the norm of absolute otherness, historically aware of its origins, its present, its possible futures, and always open to the word? Is a religious community possible without this awareness, without reflection? Is the concern for the images of the future a vehicle for reflective consciousness?

If this is the case, is education in a religious community necessary or is living religiously with others inherently educational? If we focus upon being religious with others, need we attend to education? By attending consciously to education, do we not endanger the religious? By focusing upon dogmas, fixed rituals, accepted beliefs, established ways of thinking, i.e. the finite and the need for control which goes with it, do we give up the focus upon the infinite? Do we forget the story making of a people constantly under the judgment of the absolute norm of otherness, a people reflecting upon and recollecting the judgments and reconciliations disclosed in community life?

Being with those who have not yet accepted our established traditions, whether the young or the newcomer, is an opportunity to engage in reflection about what we hold of value; to question whether our values, our activities, and our images are idolatrous or transparent and numinous. The burden is on he who would educate, not on he who is to be educated. Established forms of life should be questioned as they come up against the novelty and the unformed, or otherness, of the young. Unfortunately, doubt often increases our tendency to control others; it does not encourage reflection and penetration into our sources, our ground.

Am I pointing to impossible modes of being with others—the young, the neophyte? Can we expect such reflective behavior, such discipline, on the part of the adult or committed community?

But here too we must point to the origins, and ask what are schools. Schools are places where people gather together. We have elementary schools, medical schools, prison schools, nursery schools. But are not churches already the gathering of people, i.e. communities? To build schools, or to have schools is to wall in or wall off some of those who gather from others. By establishing schools, educational institutions, storytelling is separated from the judgments, the reflections, and the reconciliations which keep the story alive and evolving. By making the school a place and time where history is taught, the historical awareness is disassociated from community activity and reflection about that activity.

The investment in building schools, preparing materials, and training teachers could be mis-spent. The willingness to invest points to the willingness to build futures, not simply talk about them. It is this intent to invest which can be informed by the previous discussion.

Should adults be with the neophyte, the young, in educational ways? Should the bridge between the adult community and the young be the teacher and prepared curriculum material? Should the stance between the young and the adult be that of "learner" and "teacher"? As the unformed and evolving ways of the young come in contact with the preformed ways of the adult, must the attitude of the adult be "to teach"? Is the teacher the one who seeks to ward off the critical thrust of the young, by socializing him into accepted and preformed ways? The teacher is, frequently, the protector of the idol. But who is charged with listening to the neophyte, interpreting his actions and speech as protest and possibility? Where, in the church, does reflection occur about the meaning of the preformed as it comes up against the unformed of the child?

Should adults build schools and materials which partition off the children from the adults, and divide the gathering which is the "church?" Should there be places and times of separation? If so, should the separate times and places for the young be under the control of the preformed adult community? Should the emerging story of the "church" as historical community be protected by classrooms from the intrusions of the young or are the intrusions of the young what the story is about? Are classroom walls and "religious education" materials barricades? Are they symbols of a finished story?

What does it mean to be with the neophyte in religious ways? I am but the bearer of the question, not of the answer. Do you have the discipline, as adults, to forge the answer? Probably our conception of religion and of "being together" religiously is adult and tradition bound, based upon adult experience and historical continuity. Ritual, celebration, prayer, service, storytelling, reflection—we tend to think of these as adult activities; we do not think of them as developmental and incipient with the child. Or if we do, we see these through adult eyes. One of the consequences of the work of Piaget for the secular educator has been a new look at the child and the significance of his activity. Piaget has developed his discipline of genetic epistemology as a vehicle for understanding the nature of adult knowledge. Does the adult religious community have the wherewithal to develop a discipline of genetic religion; not as a science but as a theological study? If it has, then perhaps it can identify ways to be with children in ways which have religious significance for the child, not for the adult. If we have some grasp of the form and meaning of ritual, celebration, prayer, service, storytelling, and reflection of the two year old, the five year old, and so on up the age continuum, then we can invest in times and places to be with them religiously. As a consequence, we would not feel the need to impose our ways of being upon them, but more able to reflect with them about the meaning and significance of their ways and our ways.

It seems to me that the focus upon religious education and church schools mandates the way you are with members of your religious community. Is not this what you must rethink and re-establish? Don't let the language of secular education and the form of school intrude upon your rethinking. To be with the young person does not imply a responsibility to educate him, but a responsibility for mutual judgment and reconciliation. His speech, his actions, his concerns are as much a judgment of your dogmas and ways as your dogmas and ways are a judgment of him. In the spirit of mutual judgment, the future emerges through reconciliation. Are you investing in times and places where the judgment and reconciliation occur across age lines as well as across community lines?

NOTES

[1] Ivan Illich, *Deschooling Society* (New York: Harper and Row, 1970).

[2] Martin Marty is Fairfax M. Cone Distinguished Service Professor of the History of Modern Christianity, University of Chicago Divinity School. His scholarly work, public lectures and numerous publications, have focused on religion and ethics in America. Most recently he has published *The One and the Many: America's Search for the Common Good* (Boston, MA: Harvard University Press, 1997); see also Martin Marty and R. Scott Appleby, *The Glory and the Power: The Fundamentalist Challenge to the Modern World* (Boston, MA: Beacon Press, 1992); and Martin Marty, *Modern American Religion*, vol. 1, *The Irony of it All* (1986), vol. 2, *The Noise of Conflict, 1919–1941* (1991), vol. 3 *Under God, Indivisible, 1941–1960* (Chicago, IL: University of Chicago Press, 1992), *Ed.*

[3] Robert W. Lynn and Elliot Wright, *The Big Little School* (New York: Harper and Row, 1971).

[4] Ibid., 5.

[5] Ibid., 16.

[6] Ibid., 20.

16

Toward a Remaking of Curricular Language

(1974)

The institutions of education are so pervasive and the problems raised by these institutions are so pressing that to escape from their everydayness is nearly impossible. The danger to an educator, or a would-be educator, is that he will be socialized into the existing institutions or into the language generated by them. One cannot be socially critical as a positivist. That which is, a consequence of historical conditions that may not exist today, is not necessarily what should or could be. To answer questions derived from dated institutions or framed by limited ways of speaking is to limit the imagination and the future. To honor a question does not entail answering the question, but responding to the situation that is the source of the question. To honor an institution or the people associated with an institution does not require maintaining the institution or the behavior of the people; instead, it is an articulation of the time and place of their origin, the time and place of today, and the discrepancies or contradictions that prevail between the two times and the two places. We do not honor educators, their language, and their institutions by accepting at face value the concerns and problems that they generate. We honor them by indicating how these concerns derive from historical commitments and how these problems are a consequence of new technical and political conditions. In the everyday talk of educators, the phenomena of education have been too closely associated with the institutions of schooling and the language of learning. Schools are a necessary social construction, and learning is a necessary intellectual construct. In discussing education, we should not be limited to these two constructs; nor should our discussion ignore them.

My previous work has been an effort to attend to the phenomena of education without being unduly and perhaps unconsciously socialized to the language, the institutions, and the norms of everyday educators. I think that I can now penetrate the realities that the everyday educator takes for granted, and I can illuminate what he is about in such a way that his own concerns and the complexities of the age can be more clearly seen and acted upon. I intend to articulate the phenomena of education in such a way that school people can see what they are about and nonschool people can envision other possibilities. In so doing I intend, eventually, to provide a language that can reveal how the educator has decided to live in the world and what he sees as possible futures.

In "Curriculum as Concern for Man's Temporality," I pointed to education as concern for the evolving biography of the person and the evolving history of societies or communities, and I stated that the task of the curriculum person was to think through the dialectical relationships between the individual and the society or community in such a way that both maintained some kind of rhythmic continuity and change. Since the writing of that paper, I have become aware of three facets of man's temporality that facilitate the discussion of intentional education. The first is the phenomena of memory and traditions as these store and make accessible the past. The second is the activity of interpretation, the hermeneutical art, which is the bridge between self and other; a linkage among past, present, and future; the vehicle by which individuals, in community, arrive at mutual understanding in the conduct of their public affairs. The third is the phenomenon of community as a caring collectivity in which individuals share memories and intentions.

Everyday usage of the word *education* tends to emphasize the individual. We tend to talk about educating a person. This everyday usage, however, does not correspond to some of the concerns of the educator, who also acts to maintain aspects of the society. The educator too easily speaks of what a child "must learn." He does so, not necessarily because he cares for the child, but because he is concerned that certain aspects of our society be upheld or maintained. The conflict between the "needs" of society and the "needs" of children creates tensions that are manifest in problems of control, in guilt over the educator's use of power, and sometimes in a neurotic incapacity to act. The perceptions that are the source of the tension, the guilt, and the inability to act can be modified if the word *education* is used to refer to the futuring of the person and the futuring of a society. If education is talked about as concern for the evolving biography of the person and the evolving history of a community or society, then the phenomenon of power can more easily be lived within. The conflict between the individual and the community becomes a fact of human existence that need not cause neurotic inaction but could create, instead, an awareness of one's freedom to participate in public life. Conflict can free a person to be political, to use power, and to struggle with others over the various manifestations of power. The language of learning and of socialization hides the conflicts, the freedom for political action, the significance of power, and, indeed, the whole temporal nature of man. The languages of human development, political socialization, objectives of education, and therapy tend to hide the problems of community, power, tradition, and temporality and the hermeneutical arts. If the educator is to be conscious of what he is about and how he is to act, then his everyday languages must be rethought and reconstructed.

At birth a child is pushed out, not thrown, into an already established world. The reception he receives in the delivery room and in the maternity ward of the hospital speaks of the world today in the United States in contrast to the world elsewhere. The child is pushed out among people with specific traditions or memories and intentions. Some of these traditions and memories are sedimented in the various institutions and instruments that make up the public world. But they are also sedimented in the way that people, preconsciously, are with others and speak with others. To speak of a child's inheritance at this age can be verbal self-justification of the adult. We want the child to maintain the life style into which he is pushed. To soften that demand, we claim that the child inherits.

We can easily teach the new being to accept our standards, concealing from ourselves the power that we exercise over another in the act of teaching. In the early months this is not as obvious. Care for the new being is easy, and his intrusions into the already established are not too demanding. They may, indeed, be a part of our expectations. But, as the child becomes more demanding, our care for him conflicts with our care for ourselves. We hide the conflict under the language of social necessity.

From the moment of someone else's birth we must scrutinize the language we use to describe what happens to the new being in our midst. We must become aware that our language is reflexive, at least to a knowledgeable observer. It expresses something about us as well as something about the world. In talking about something outside ourself, we also talk about ourself, even if we have not been trained to recognize it. As we talk about the new being among us, we forgetfully take ourselves and our ways for granted, thus unthinkingly shaping the new being into these ways. The language of socialization encourages us to assume that the new being must be brought into near conformity with what we take for granted to be our world. Our language does not encourage us to see him or her as a living question about that which we take for granted. As we condition the new being to our taken-for-granted ways, we hide from our awareness that living together is the sharing of memories and intentions and the building of public, or shared, worlds.

By making these comments about the child as a new being, I do not intend to take a romantic view of the child, nor to make a statement about the goodness of man versus the evil of society. I do intend to call attention to the language for talking about the infant and child that tends to mask the life style of the parent or educator: traditions, memories, and intentions. This language is unconsciously furthered and developed by the scientific study of the child, a study that has ignored the place of the adult in the child's world, the politics of adult-child relationships, the child's participation in the building of public worlds, and the art of interpretation about the meaning of life as people, children, and adults live it together.

The presence of the new being gives rise to one of our concerns in education. That is the concern for transcendence, liberation, emancipation, or however you might wish to speak about temporality of the person. It is the question of how a new being is sheltered in this world, how he is cared for and honored, how he is respected and responded to as creator. It is the question answered by the language of human growth and development, but the uncritical acceptance of this terminology must be questioned.

The presence of the new being is not the only presence which gives rise to educational concern. The public world into which a new being is pushed is already established. Aspects of the natural world have been converted into social goods. The ways in which people have lived together have been converted into certain services. The new being is thrown into the midst of a complexity of goods and services, traditions and embodied memories, and the intentions of those who have lived in this place at another time. These goods and services are manifest in our technologies, and in the economic and political institutions sedimented out over the years. The traditions, memories, and intentions of our predecessors are embodied in the public world and taken for granted. Our collective wealth as a species consists of the embodied traditions, the technologies, and the institutions that now make up the diverse public worlds. Two educational concerns are brought forth by the presence of the past. First, who should have access to what segments of this collective wealth? Second, how should the collective wealth, the memories, and the traditions be maintained and protected from loss or forgetfulness?

The presence of the new being and the presence of the past create tensions where they are together. Without the loving care of people, the traditions embodied in technologies and institutions would decay and return to the earth, no longer a part of the social world but of the natural world. Without the loving care of people, the new being would die and also become part of the natural organic world. Care for the new being, the child, can be inhibited or even prevented by the way in which care for the public world is manifest. If the collective wealth is distributed in certain patterns, for example, if nutrients are not equitably distributed by our technologies, by our economic delivery systems, and by our patterns of political justice, then some children will never be able to participate in the public world. Care for the past can be inhibited by the way in which we care for the new being, for memories, traditions, and collective wealth can be forgotten and disappear from human memory.

The tension between care for the new being and care for collective wealth is lived out in the community and in the struggles among diverse communities. If a community is a group of people with common or shared memories and intentions, then the new being is pushed out, not only into a public world but into an ongoing community with traditions of care for people and traditions of care for collective or public wealth. The Biblical image of people in pilgrimage is what I have in mind. The wayfaring communities carry with them their care for each other and care for their possessions and their memories stored in their poetry, their songs and rituals, their tools, and their other traditions. The presence of a community with traditions of care for people and for collective wealth, a community that honors and develops individual and collective memory, that articulates and acts out intentions is the third fact that gives rise to educational concern. Without education the community could not maintain its pilgrimage beyond a single generation. It would die out along the way and foreclose the rest of the journey. Without education, traditions and memories would be forgotten, hope would be ignored, and futures would remain unclaimed. Without education the new being would be lost and transcendence would be unknown.

I am right where every other educator has been. Nothing is new here, except perhaps some of the terminology used to articulate the place. An educator cannot intentionally educate without thinking about the individual, the society, and the culture or tradition. It is in talk about these three presences and their being together in a place that we clarify our memories, share our intentions, and feel our powers in conflict. It is in talk about these three presences that we find the stuff for our hermeneutical and world-building arts. It is in asking how these three presences have been together in the past that we give direction to historical inquiry. It is in thinking about the togetherness of these three presences that we articulate educational organization and educational method.

Most recently our thinking about these three presences has been governed by talk about the individual. This is not to say that our priority is the individual and that his concerns and feelings, his memories and intentions are uppermost. Rather, it is to say that our language starts with the individual. We ask how he learns, what he should learn, and what materials are necessary if he is to learn. This starting point in our thinking has pushed individual psychology to a position of primacy in educational talk. It has also placed concern for educational material and the quality of school life into a secondary position. I do not wish to displace the individual from a position of primacy in our thinking. I do wish to claim an equal place for the past and for the community. In thinking about education we cannot effectively start our thinking with the individual and then make the past and the community secondary. Rather, our thinking must start with all three: the individual, the past, and the community. Then we can ask how the three are interrelated. We need not relate them by the language of teaching and learning, or by goals and objectives. I suggest that they can be interrelated by hermeneutical or interpretive activity, by political activity, and by work activity.

It seems to me, then, that our curriculum questions should be phrased something like this: What past, that is, what collective memories, traditions, and artifacts can be made present for what child in the presence of what community? What kinds of activity occur among those three presences? By these questions I intend, ultimately, to bring into focal attention the phenomena of subjectivity and intersubjectivity, freedom as participation in a public world, and power. By asking the questions this way, I wish to make explicit the tensions which exist for the would-be educator. He must care for the new being, for the child. What is intended by the expression "care for the new being" will require more elaboration than is possible here, although I will refer to aspects of this care. The educator must also care for the past, conserve it so it will not be forgotten or lost for use and reference. It is this aspect of the educator's task that receives most attention here, but he must also care for the community of which he is a part. This means attending to the memories, intentions, and power of those with whom he dwells; in other words, the educator must seek to be part of a pilgrimage. This concern for community will be alluded to, but not developed directly.

I shall begin with the presence of the past: traditions, memories, and artifacts. Normal educational talk goes like this: We are trying to achieve certain objectives, or to maximize certain values in the behavior of the student. To learn these behaviors, certain materials and adults or teachers with certain skills are needed. How or where can we get them?

What I wish to do is to bracket and remove the steps leading to the selection of the materials and teacher skills and to consider those materials and skills a primary educational good, a manifestation of certain memories, traditions, or artifacts that are to be conserved. Education for reading will provide an example.

Reading is spoken of as a skill—a very complex one made up of many subskills. Our strategy for thinking about education for reading has been something like this: We have identified the components and subcomponents of the reading skills. We have asked ourselves how these various subcomponents are learned and the order in which they should be learned. This has led, in turn, to the production of readers, and, gradually, to the production of workbooks, and, recently, to other diverse material such as kits of self-diagnostic and learning materials, talking typewriters,[1] and other computer-based technologies. Some of these materials are a consequence of psychological theories such as reinforcement theories. During the same period the quantity and quality of literature for young children has increased, by way of paperbacks and the increased number of elementary school libraries. Until about ten years ago the talk about individualizing instruction in reading was primarily that—just talk. The places where such individual instruction was carried out required unusually hard-working teachers who laboriously collected materials, cut up workbooks or developed their own dittoed materials and games. Today the individualization of reading instruction is within the possibility of almost every school, for the marketplace makes available a variety of reading materials. We now have a plurality of methods, a variety of materials, and the lockstep induced by text material has been broken. These developments, except the increase in literature for children, have been brought about by the educator's concern for helping children learn to read and the psychological study of reading processes. It is necessary that we continue to increase our scientific study of the processes of reading, but our concern that young people actually read should not be consumed by scientific methods.

When reading materials did not fit the characteristics of the student population, the educator resorted to three games, predominantly language games: readiness, motivation, and discipline or control. If a child was not "ready" to use the primers or other materials, we talked about readiness and how one developed readiness in the child. If the child was not interested in the materials or the methodology accompanying the materials, we talked about motivation. In fact, when teachers were bound to a single set of readers, a significant segment of the manual for teachers was devoted to motivational exercises, or ways to prepare the children to "receive" the materials. If, after readiness and motivational activity, the materials still did not fit the child, then we had a control problem. Questions of discipline were raised by the teacher. For many, if not most, teachers the problems of teaching reading were primarily discipline or control problems: How do I keep some kids quiet while I work with others, and what do I do with the "slow readers?"

By these comments I intend to call attention to the fact that, when the materials and traditions did not match the child and when the memories and intentions of the educators did not coincide or fit the memories and intentions of the students, power came into play in the guise of manipulative activity. I prefer to call it political activity. The teacher asked how he could impose his subjectivities, memories, intentions, and behaviors on the child. How could the child be brought into the white, middle-class community of the teacher? The use of power, political activity, was necessary because creating a match between child and material was seen as a problem of doing something to the child, not doing something to the public world, not changing the goods or services. In other words, the child was oppressed by the educator because of limited or restricted material and skills, or, in other terms, limited goods and services. The teacher did not serve as the agent of a free individual—the child—but of repressive communities, repressive in part because of limited goods and services. The teacher did not serve as an agent of the child, helping him participate in the continuous reconstruction of the public world, in this case in the continuous reconstruction of the traditions and artifacts of reading. This unconscious choice of agency, the unquestioned use of power, and the denial of the subjectivity of the child for the reaffirmation of the teacher and of those associated with available reading goods and services was the result. It is true, of course, that limited monies and perhaps limited technologies prevented, or presumably prevented, the development of more adequate reading goods and services for a variety of children, including those of different economic classes or communities or with different physiological characteristics. But the influence of the inequitable distribution of public and private wealth was hidden from the educator and the student by the language games of readiness, motivation, and discipline, reinforced by rituals of schooling such as grading, promotion, and the credentials that go with graduation.

In the actions of the student, either as he conforms to or opposes the expectations manifest in the materials and the skills of the educator, and in the actions of the educator as he attempts to overpower the student via readiness, motivational, or disciplining games, we probably find clues to the incipient or actual community to which each belongs. These actions of submission, rebellion, or consent on the part of the student, and love, work, or control on the part of the teacher, are manifestations of the memories and intentions of the communities of which they are a part. More commonly, we would term these values, but that term hides the historical community which is their source. I do not point to this phenomenon with any degree of assurance, but with the suspicion that in the behavior of each we have empirical data to illuminate the nebulous idea of community as it now appears in the educational literature. This idea has increased in importance with the advent of community control.

How else can we articulate what has been happening in this sphere of education known as the teaching of reading? Can we speak of education for reading more directly, using the notion of presences of past, child, and community?

When we speak of reading, we normally speak of what a person does: he reads something to some end. From the perspective of the past, print is a technology in which individual and collective memory, imagery, and intention are made a part of the public world and conserved for others. My use of the word memory is intended to cover theories, stories, and rules or procedures, but the development to that usage would be a long aside. For whom is this past conserved? This question points to those who control print: not simply the writer, but the whole publishing and translating industry, the print distribution systems in the world, and the community traditions of being together and talking together about print. The history of the Bible from manuscript to printed book in Hebrew and Greek, to the Vulgate edition and then into the language idiom of the people via the King James Version and the Revised Standard Version illustrates my intent. The presence of the Bible is often accompanied by other printed materials, such as commentaries or other works of exegetical and hermeneutical arts, along with the oral traditions that accompany the book in diverse communities. At one time access to the printed Bible required command of Hebrew and Greek. Today that no longer applies unless the word Bible is restricted to the earliest Hebrew or Greek texts.

Behind these conserved phenomena of print and print traditions is the educational question: To what extent are they accessible to children three years old, six years old, twelve years old, fifteen years old? To extend the image, what traditions conserved in print are available to the six-year-old child in Appalachia, the Spanish-speaking six-year-old child in Manhattan, the deaf six-year-old child in a school for the handicapped, the six-year-old child in the bush of Uganda? What community traditions accompany the use of these print materials? In our home, my children grow up with books scattered all over the house. They sit next to us while we read silently. We purchase and borrow printed goods for them. We point to the pictures and elaborate in speech, even for the youngest who cannot yet speak. The children sit next to us as we read and reread stories and interpret them; we point to words as we say them; we read and act out *Where the Wild Things Are*. Print is not just something that we come across; print is something that we put into the world via an electric typewriter. Even the fifteen-month-old child sits at the typewriter to see what happens to a sheet of paper as she presses keys. These are communal traditions accompanying print. What communal traditions are present when the only print present to the child is that of one textbook in the presence of thirty other like-age children? What oral reading traditions accompany the textbook in school? What kind of individual or collective memory, image, or intention is found in a textbook? How significant are school-bound traditions when a home embodies no print traditions? How much of the overwhelming richness of the world is present to the child in the print available to him?

The question school people ask is: How effectively or efficiently is reading being taught? I would come back and say that this is a schooling question, not an educational one. The educational question is: How is the wealth of, or in, the public world made available to the child who is six years old, or any other age, and how effective are the embodied past and its traditions for the same child?

The capability of our society to conserve the stories, images, and intentions from diverse communities in forms accessible to the young child has increased significantly. The number of children's writers and publishers devoted to children's books has increased. Over the past twenty years, the capability of this economic sector has expanded greatly, and the improvement of reading methodologies in the schools is but a related effect. Today, the reading textbook is a severely limited manifestation of this public wealth, and a child who has access only to a commercial school text is indeed a deprived child, an economically and technically deprived child. The question, then, is: How is the print wealth of the world distributed to people of all ages and all characteristics? What are the vehicles of print production, translation, distribution? How is private and public wealth distributed to bring print to the six-year-old child in Appalachia, to the six-year-old deaf child? How are community traditions that accompany print communicated? Who controls the production and distribution of print and the communication of traditions that accompany print? How much does it cost to initiate an adult into the traditions of oral reading? Into the traditions of caring for print and simultaneously caring for children? How does a society organize politically to adjudicate among those sectors of its technology and economy that produce and distribute pornography for adolescents, delivery systems of word and visual print images for five-year-old children, or napalm delivery systems for Asian children? These questions, which deal with the politics and economics of education, as well as with curriculum, indicate something about the control of schools. They indicate how the narrow concerns for effectiveness, behavioral objectives, and principles of learning have hidden much broader problems of economic and technical policies pertaining to education.

One part of the question of a reading curriculum asks about print and traditions accompanying that print which are available to particular children in particular communities. We can now turn to the other part of the question governing curriculum, namely that of method. When the presence of print and print traditions are brought together with the presence of children and in the presence of particular communities, what activity is possible? Earlier I suggested three forms of activity: hermeneutical, political, and work. By hermeneutical, I intend interpretation; by political, I mean the arriving at agreed upon collective memory and intention or action; by work, I mean the maintaining and building of a public space, a technological consequence of political activity.

I have already alluded to the political activity, which is a consequence of limited material and human skill: control by the educator and the imposition of actions and perhaps intentions and memories. I hope to return to this later. I wish now to attend to what I have called hermeneutical activity, for therein I see a way of getting at pedagogical method and interpreting what goes on in the classroom or other educational places. My source is Palmer's book *Hermeneutics*,[2] although my own introduction to hermeneutics is by way of Heidegger in his many writings, Ricoeur in his work on Freud,[3] and Habermas' *Knowledge and Human Interests*.[4] Palmer traces the word hermeneutics back to its Greek source and claims that it "points back to the wingfooted messenger-god Hermes ... Hermes is associated with the function of transmuting what is beyond human understanding into a form that human intelligence can grasp. The various forms of the word suggest the process of bringing a thing or situation from unintelligibility to understanding."[5] He states that the "Hermes process" is at work when "something foreign, strange, separated in time, space, or experience is made familiar, present, comprehensible: something requiring representation, explanation, or translation is somehow 'brought to understanding'—is interpreted."[6]

It seems to me that the "Hermes Process" as described by Palmer is the pedagogical process, is educational method, at least with respect to education for reading. Thus, in the presence of print, the child is faced with "something foreign, strange, separated in time, space, or experience," and the problem of method is to make it "familiar, present, comprehensible." In this sense, phonetic methods are a form of hermeneutic, of taking the strange symbols in print and making them comprehensible by translating them into sound. I do not wish to pursue this relationship too far for this has the danger of simply substituting the word *hermeneutic* for the words *teaching method*. The significance of the association is that it opens up educational method to new forms of inquiry. Hermeneutics, the art of interpretation, has a long tradition in Western thought. The use of hermeneutics in educational thought could reduce the strain on learning and psychology, thus reserving that body of knowledge and the technology it spawns for more specific and clearly relevant tasks.

Hermeneutical activity is also a tradition carried by communities. The teacher in engaging in instruction, whether by asking questions, establishing written assignments, reading to the child, or pronouncing words for him, is introducing him to traditions of interpretation. The question to be asked is not how the child learns the traditions of interpretation, but how he can dwell in the midst of living traditions and affirm them. I suggest that the various exercises in workbooks and independent skill development activities are forms of interpretational activity, hermeneutical forms, that have been embodied in software rather than in the social relationships between students and teachers. This notion of educational method as a form of hermeneutical activity has been recently opened up to me, and the exploration of its consequences, not only in the education for reading but in education with respect to the past embodied in other forms, is yet to be done.

The scientific study of reading and the technologies that it spawns contribute to the establishment of new traditions and new artifacts. That is, work activity is associated with education for reading. By establishing new instructional materials and methods, this work activity makes a potential contribution to the public wealth and its conservation in new artifacts and traditions. Since 1920 or so significantly new materials have been brought to children, and new interpretational activities have been initiated between children and adults. Some of these work products are worth conserving and should become part of tradition. This is not true of all of the reading apparatus that has been produced in the past fifty years. Some of the material and methods have been designed as extensions of schools. If schools are seen as manifestations of educational concerns at particular times and places, now possibly obsolete, then we must be critical of innovations that simply add to the stuff of schools and encourage us to continue to take the schools for granted. By that I do not intend that we should seek to overthrow the school, but, rather, that we should be somewhat certain that new materials and methods have educational meaning, not simply school meaning.

In this concern for conserving the past the question of value is exposed: Is this innovation worthy of becoming part of the collective memory and wealth of a community, of being conserved? If so, is it worthy of being conserved simply as part of the story, an event that did not change the nature of our pilgrimage; or is it a new image, a new instrument that changes significantly the nature of the pilgrimage? The question of value that should be asked in education, then, is not what is valuable and hence should be learned by the young, but what is valuable enough to be conserved as part of the past and made present to the young? By that question I wish to draw attention to the way the educator too frequently talks about learning as a form of normative control rather than as a possibility for the future.

The child, in coming into the presence of print and the communal traditions surrounding or accompanying print, comes up against the public world of others. It is a public world established and maintained through the work and power of writers, editors, publishers, and distributors. It is a world maintained by the work of the child and the teacher within the school. The child must too frequently take that public world for granted, accepting its ready-madeness, perhaps conforming to its demands and requirements. If that ready-made world of print and the communal traditions that accompany it do not fit him, that is, if they do not mesh with his memories and intentions and the Hermes process does not work, then either he is alienated from his own memories and intentions by the power of the teacher or he must withdraw in one way or another from the presence of that formed world. Now, of course, the other option is that he participate in the criticism of that world and seek to establish a better-fitting public world, a world of print and communal traditions surrounding that print that make interpretation possible. This may be in the establishment or development of new forms of interpretational activity via the development of new skills on the part of the teacher, the redevelopment of new skill development software, or the establishment of new stories in print. It may be in the development of other print materials. The young child, however, has too frequently been overpowered by the already existing world and the power of the adult. He has had the incipient political activity of negation and negotiation associated with two- and four-year-old children knocked out of him by adults who see negation as bad. They do not see these negative periods as the establishment of political schemas at a sensory-motor and pre-operational level. Hence, the child does not see a misfit as an invitation to rework the public world. He is left with the awareness that the public world is made and that he is a misfit, rather than with the awarenss that the public world is always in the process of being reworked and that he has a right to rework it. He does not perceive himself as engaged in work activity or political activity. Hence, he picks up—and becomes a manifestation of and takes on the characteristics of—labels and stereotypes directed at those for whom the public world is a bad fit. However, the slow learner and the handicapped are merely those who do not have the appropriate educational goods and services in their presence. The monies and technologies directed at building the public world of educational goods and services have not been used to build a public world big enough for the educationally disadvantaged—the handicapped, the slow learner. Of course, if monies and technologies are scarce, then it is a problem of economic and political value, a consequence of the distribution of wealth. The production, distribution, and consumption of economic goods influences social relationships in educational places. Given the present distribution of wealth, of money, of technologies, of other values, who indeed is to be disadvantaged, slow, handicapped?

The child is able to participate in work, or at least to see people working to reform the world, in the efforts being made to restructure the public world to better fit those who are in it. To see the teacher actually form her behaviors through videotaping and experimentation and perhaps to participate with her in the study of her own teaching is one example. Another is student participation in the creation of their own software, the writing of their own stories which are then bound into book form and deposited in the school library. Another is serving as an agent of interpretation for a child for whom no present interpretive activity seems to fit. Most desirable, and least accessible presently, is to be tied into the commercial production of print forms via two-way communication channels between schools and publishers. At the present time these are but one-way channels, and teachers and children have only the option to buy and to use or not to use, not the option of participating in the construction of the new forms. Of course, the channel from child to publisher does exist, but indirectly as the publishing industry recognizes new market demands and creates materials to meet these new demands. However, this process could be much more visible and transparent. The existence of a media center in each educational place, which would be responsible for producing educational goods and services or for negotiating with other producers for such production, would be a way of institutionalizing this two-way process.

The school has been seen primarily as a place where the adult community imposes its demands or life styles on the young, or at least as a place where the memories, traditions, and intentions of the adult community are placed in the presence of the young. Everyday usage of school talk, as well as everyday usage of school institutions and instruments, suggests that the learning, the molding, and the forming is of the young by adults. In effect, this means that the child is walled off from public life and participation in that public life as a free agent. By seeing the school as a one-way educational process, from adult to child, and by talking about it as such, the other direction of the process is not seen, the impact of the young on the so-called adult world. In effect, the school serves as a barrier to protect the adult community from the probes, critiques, questions, and doubts of the young. The language of socialization, of course, justifies this barrier, and we proclaim that the young have few rights of participation until socialized. That claim should not stand uncriticized. The school serves as a barrier whereby the world is protected from innocence, from embarrassment by the unsocialized, from shock by the untutored question of the young which shatters the adult conception. The school removes children from everydayness, so that, when adults ride by in the new clothes of the emperor, they are not embarrassed by the children who might see their nakedness if they were not in school. The school, by being a separate place, separates the young from the publicness of interpretation, work, and political activity. In a sense, the rights of the child to participate in public life, to be free and to face the consequences of being free, have been abridged or perhaps never realized. Although we justify this abridgment of the rights of the young by the talk of protecting them, we are perhaps more likely to do it because we want to take our adult world for granted and not have it brought into question by the young. As a consequence, the young seldom feel that they participate in a public world, that they have rights to criticize it, to articulate their intentions and memories in response to it, or to reform it.

The idea of political and work activity as a form of activity interrelating the new being, the past, and community calls attention to the closed nature of the school and the need for open structures of education. But open must not be seen as simply a destruction of the walls that separate the school from other segments of society, or one segment of the school from another. Rather, an open place of education must be interpreted as a place where adults seek to influence the young, where the young seek to influence the adults; a place where the past as present may be used, interpreted, rethought, and reworked; a place not of submitting to someone else's power and accepted ways but of negotiating for power in the maintaining and reforming of the public world. Open education points to the search for communities by groups of people on pilgrimage, working the land with their tools, building the structures that house them from the elements, caring for those who are pushed into their presence, reshaping their life together, and telling and retelling the stories of where they have been and where they seem to be going.

NOTES

[1] For a description of the "talking typewriter" see note one, Chapter Eleven, *Ed.*
[2] Richard E. Palmer, *Hermeneutics* (Evanston, Illinois: Northwestern University Press, 1969).
[3] Paul Ricoeur, *Freud and Philosophy* (New Haven, Connecticut: Yale University Press, 1970).
[4] Jürgen Habermas, *Knowledge and Human Interests,* trans. Jeremy J. Shapiro (Boston: Beacon Press, 1971).
[5] Palmer, *Hermeneutics*, 13.
[6] Ibid., 14.

17

The Thingness
of Educational Content

(1974)

The educator does not often look directly at educational content—at it: as a thing. His looking is directed by language which calls attention to the "learner" and his "learning." Content is usually seen only as it comes up against the educatee or as it is presumably integrated into his "understandings" or behavioral structures. This directing of attention to learning has paid off in the past. We are presumably much more informed about the processes of learning than we have been at any time in our collective past.

But permitting the language of learning to direct his attention also has dysfunctional value for the educator. Heidegger states that language serves to cover as well as uncover phenomena. We must always ask what a language habit hides as well as what it exposes. And in this case, I believe that the thingness of educational content has been hidden by the language of learning. With the expression, "thingness," I intend to call attention to the object quality of educational content. If we sharpen our looking we can see it directly in contrast to "learning" which we can only infer. Seeing content has untold advantages for the educator. One advantage is that he can build an educative environment more effectively if he can see, hence control and manipulate, the objects which make up the educational content. Another advantage is that attention to making, controlling, and manipulating content permits or encourages the educator to be with the educatee in non-controlling ways.

In this paper, I wish to describe the patterns of language usage which have brought me to this point, and to describe some consequences of this way of speaking about educational content.

FROM "LEARNING"
TO "THINGNESS OF CONTENT"

As I try to recollect my past, I can identify three types of concern which seem to have influenced the position that I am advocating now. The first centers around an expression of Steve Mann's[1]—the student rights strategy. I attribute this to Mann because of his overwhelming impact on me, the near speechless position I find myself in when I listen to him. However, he is but a symbol of a wider variety of influences which I associate with the diverse liberation movements and the dialectical relationships between the powerful and the powerless as these are articulated, for instance, by Freire.[2]

The second centers around critical theory,[3] as it is found in the works of Habermas,[4] Horkheimer and Adorno,[5] Marcuse,[6] Schroyer,[7] and Gouldner,[8] and as it is used to criticize the social and behavioral sciences. Although not directly related to this school of critical theory, deMause's[9] *Evolution of Childhood* is paradigmatic of what I intend here; for by placing conceptions of childhood in historical perspective he calls attention to the changing relationship between the adult and the young over time.

The third influence I associate with Paul Ricoeur,[10] who in his "Model of the Text: Meaningful Action Considered as a Text" nicely pulls together tendencies which I sensed in Schutz's[11] expression "stock of knowledge" and Heidegger's[12] concern for "instruments." Ricoeur's[13] use of hermeneutics calls attention to the aspects of story as found in Novak[14] and Cox,[15] and makes me rethink what I mean when I use the word "tradition." This word, "tradition," has only recently taken on significant meaning for me, and I am certain that I will have to attend to other usages of the word.

Student rights—The various liberation movements have or are beginning to make a reasonable impact on educational thought. Certainly the black power movement of the 60s had its impact. Women's lib is leading to a reconsideration of sex stereotyping in text materials for young people, has the possibility of refocusing the role of the teacher, and is calling attention to the need for equal and non-stereotypical education for boys and girls with respect to sports, vocations and sex. The liberation movements of the oppressed groups in the United States and the writings about the imperialistic nature of educational development in other countries as reflected in the works of Illich[16] and Carnoy[17] have added significantly to our awareness of some of the oppressive aspects of our education system. Finally, the revisionist historians such as Karrier,[18] Katz[19] and Spring[20] have enabled us to see the controlling mechanisms, some of them economic and class related, built into our educational system. All of these efforts point to the rights of students and children discussed most recently in the Harvard Educational Review.[21]

For me, the significance of these liberation movements lies in calling attention to the constitutional rights of the young person in our society, and to the inherent rights of young people everywhere as they come up against the already established societies of adults. This concern points to two questions. First, under what conditions do adults have the right to impose controls or specific "learnings" on the young, if they have this right at all? Specifying curriculum content in terms of educational objectives and purposes can be a rationale for adults who put their thing upon the young, under the aegis of citizenship, social need, social adjustment, vocational training or what have you. Insisting that each child should learn to read can be interpreted as an imposition, albeit justified under many circumstances. The second question asks about the availability of child advocates in our society and specifically in our schools. The gradual establishment of educational ombudsmans is a reflection of this need, as is the increasing attention to student advocates and child advocates in civil proceedings.

The talk and writing about the rights of youth can be compared with the rhetoric of the curriculum person. Talk of the emerging curriculum is a reflection of this concern at one level. A major problem in the rhetoric, however, has been the un-adulterated presumption of the educator. Our literature too frequently expresses concern for the present and future welfare of the young, as if we educators were indeed able to subordinate our own interests for the interests and future of the child and youth. The student rights movement points to the potential and actual conflict of interests between the educator and the educatee. Can school people and other educators really presume to speak for the educatee? It seems to me that the liberation and rights literature brings into serious doubt that presumption, and tells us to look inward for our oppressive qualities, hidden behind our educational rhetoric and practice. Can the school or other educator presume to be about the rights and future of individuals other than himself? What are the consequences if we back off this presumption, if we recognize that we may indeed be acting in our own interests and oppressively in our relationships with students? One consequence is to reduce our concern for behavior whether we speak of it in terms of Tyler, Popham and other positivistically oriented educators who specify behavioral objectives—future states of being—or whether we speak of it in terms of Skinner and psychologists concerned with behavior modification. Do we have a moral or civil right to define objectives, future states of being, and impose them on children and young people? If we accept the student rights and child advocate thrusts of today, the consequences are to attend more carefully and attentively to the nature of the environment which we build for and with young people. That which must be brought to focal attention is not the future behavior of the child, but the present behavior and offerings of the adult community. Content can be identified as that which we make present to the educatee, not that which happens to the educatee as a consequence of our offerings. The consequences of this line of talk lead to a different domain, and for elucidation of that I must now turn to some insights which I attribute to the critical theorists and deMause[22]

Critical theory—Critical theorists seek to unearth or lay bare the relationship of one person to another person in any social, economic, technical, or intellectual form or structure. As Habermas has pointed out, we should seek out the human interest behind any kind of knowledge, which means that in our patterned speech we should seek to uncover the relationships of people to people, of the powerful to the powerless. Similar concern is reflected in the statements of students advocates and those of the critical theorists, although I wish to take us in a slightly different direction right now with potentially greater consequences. DeMause can hardly be considered a critical theorist, but his concern for the history of childhood and his reconceptualization of social evolution as a consequence of the pattern of child-adult relationships witness to similar concerns—tracing the historical relationship among two classes of people with unequal power.

DeMause offers a "psychogenic theory of history," which if pushed too far becomes as reductive as any other single theory for explaining social evolution. I believe his most important contribution is not the psychogenic theory, but rather his psychological principles of childhood history. He states that

> In studying childhood over many generations, it is most important to concentrate on those moments which most affect the psyche of the next generation: primarily this means what happens when an adult is face to face with a child who needs something. The adult has, I believe, three major reactions available: (1) He can use the child as a vehicle for the projection of the contents of his own unconscious (projective reaction); (2) he can use the child as a substitute for an adult figure important in his own childhood (reversal reaction); (3) or he can empathize with the child's own needs and act to satisfy them (empathic reaction).[23]

DeMause's work points to the historical nature of the relationship between the young and the old, and to the way that this relationship changes as the adult comes to terms with his own characteristics. Today, then, we must recognize that the particular relationships which exist between the young and the adult are not fixed, but may be further modified as adults develop other ways of seeing and being themselves. DeMause does not take his point far enough for me and hence the importance of critical theory for the study of the child. If critical theory is brought to the study of the child-adult relationship, two dimensions show themselves. First, there is the actual relationship that exists, can exist and has existed in various social and interpersonal situations between the young and the adult. Second, there is the language which the adult uses to give form to this relationship. Both the relationship and the language which give form to it must be seen in historical and critical perspective. DeMause describes the relationship only in terms of the psychic needs of the adult and young. He does not attend to the broader social, economic, political, and intellectual dimensions of that relationship. Why is it that adults have seen fit to be with the young in schooling ways for fourteen of the first eighteen years of the young person's life?[24] Why has the adult seen this relationship in terms of an educating or schooling relationship rather than in some other way? As it has turned out, schooling, and indeed most of education, is a process of domination legitimated by the language of socialization, which suggests that education is the process by which the young become socialized adults.

It is the concept "socialization" which must now come under critical scrutiny, as should the term "learning." I lack the historical skills to place these terms in historical perspective, which will be needed if we are to understand the interest structures that underlie them. However, I am aware that the literature of "socialization" is primarily associated with the positivistic social sciences and seeks to describe the growing relationship between the young and the adult from the perspective of the adult. The term "acculturation" serves the same function in positivistic anthropology. In over-simplified language, members of the adult community have taken as determined and relatively fixed the adult society, and have asked how the young "adjusts" or "adapts" to it. The norms of the adult world are interpreted as the norms for the young. Sociologists, anthropologists, or educators are adults who have a vested interest in adult structures and necessarily seek to understand or interpret how the youth "learn" to fit into those structures. "Socialization" is consequently a term which comes out of a dominating relationship between the adult and the child, perhaps an oppressive one, clearly one of the powerful over the powerless. The very use of the term "socialization" prevents the easy imagination of alternatives, or even its own negation. We are somewhat taken aback, then, when Margaret Mead[25] suggests that this age differs from others by the fact that the adults might have to learn from the youth who are more in tune with the times. Is this insight a description of the changing times, or simply a recognition that the changing times makes it easier for adults to see other relationships with the young besides those of socialization, schooling, and perhaps even education?

The concern for the rights of the young, and the possibility that studies of childhood and youth deny or hide the fact that these very studies grow out of situations of domination of one group (the young) by another (adults) suggests that the relationships between the young and the adult are currently oppressive. What does this awareness suggest for the educator? The language usages which express this awareness call attention, each in a different way, to the sanctity of the young and suggest the need for negation of actual relationships that we might better imagine possible relationships between a young person and an adult. The predominate language of the adult seems almost defensive and self-righteous at this point, proclaiming the "needs" of the young, and making claims about his future. The reflexive dimension of this rhetoric speaks about the fear or anxiety of the adult as he contemplates a change in his relationship to the young from power over to mutuality of power, as he vaguely intuits changes in his lifestyle, or as he questions his well-being in the present or the future which listening to youth can bring about. Are we as adults concerned about the child's future, or about maintaining our own?

It is this line of questioning which brings into doubt and uncertainty, under suspicion, our taken-for-granted ways as educators based upon our taken-for-granted attitudes or relationships with the young. If we bracket out our own self-interests and bring under suspicion our use of power in our relationships with the young, then what do we have before us? We have the environment that we create, fabricate or maintain, with or without the participation of the young. We have the young who dwell in that environment. We have ourselves. We have our relationships with the young which now can be rethought in terms of our awareness of the inequality of power and possible oppression.

What is this environment that we create as educators? It is, it seems to me, our educational content. Somehow or another we place in the environment this content which is presumed to be educative, whatever that might mean. It is at this point that Ricoeur has been helpful in shaping my language and hence my attention.

Tradition—Ricoeur has developed the thesis that the human sciences are hermeneutical, "inasmuch as their object displays some of the features constitutive of a text as a text and ... inasmuch as their methodology develops the same kind of procedures as those of Auslegung or text-interpretation."[26] To develop this thesis, Ricoeur speaks of the objectification of action, its fixation, and implies that it has a structure. Actions leave "marks" or tracings which can be interpreted. He quotes Winch[27] that the object of social science is a "rule governed behavior." Perhaps I did not need to bring in Ricoeur, for certainly that to which I call attention is merely that adults, as they live in, maintain, and add to the sedimentation of others, necessarily live in an object world. This object world consists of material objects, and objectifications in the form of rule-governed behaviors of diverse sorts. The adult, in creating an environment in which he dwells with the young, has created an environment which is made up of material objects and complex action patterns which follow certain rules of procedure. The adult dwells in traditions, remakes them, establishes new ones, and constantly interprets and reinterprets them. The young obviously share this manner of living.

The educator, in fabricating specialized environments for the young, merely selects, organizes, and perhaps remakes or re-presents these traditions for the young. Content consists of these traditions. Inasmuch as it is the traditions that we make present for the young, it behooves us to see these traditions for what they are—and to see how our educational concern or interest leads to the re-presentation of these traditions to diverse classes of individuals. The long and involved import of this section of the paper is this: If we bring under suspicion our motives with respect to the young, if we recognize that our practices and our language maintain the superior power of the adult over the young, if we seek to redress this power balance and seek to overcome our oppression of the young, then we must recognize with Freire that both the young and the adults are oppressed as well as oppressors. If we at the same time recognize that as adults we make present certain traditions and that we live with the young, educationally, in these traditions, then it seems to me that we must seek clarity about that which we make present—the traditions that we re-present for the young—and greater clarity about our interaction with the young and their action on the environment with or against us.

The conventional language for discussing curriculum matters hides most of these concerns. Using Tyler's[28] questions as an exemplar, they call attention to the following activities:

1. The identification of educational objectives and purposes
2. The selection of learning experiences
3. The organization of learning experiences
4. The evaluation of learning experiences

These questions suggest or point to operations of the curriculum person, but the phenomena to which they call attention are hypothetical, inferred, or intellectual phenomena. Objectives are statements. They do indeed express values, and in that sense are significant as potentially reflective and mindful acts. The other three questions call attention to "learning experience" and hence require focus upon activity and the inferred impact of these activities for behavioral change. The educators attention to adult skills and material is a secondary and derivative concern, hence seen as resources for learning. It is the secondary and derivative nature of this concern that I intend to bring under suspicion. I intend to make material and skill a primary concern, the question of organization a derived and secondary concern, and the concern for value a consequence of the dialectical relationship between material substructure and the intellectual, indeed historical political ideas, which legitimate or articulate them. In the first part of the paper I have tried to bring under suspicion the concern for behavioral change—which is not to say that I do not see learning theory as an important tool of curriculum construction. I have also suggested that a concern for content is indeed a concern for material and skill.

I shall attempt to elaborate on these intimations by stating what I consider to be a more powerful question for a curriculum maker. I intend the question to keep us conscious of our rootedness in tradition and of our political concern to maintain or surpass these traditions, our ever present activities of interpretation, the rights of the young to participate in our mutual work, and the potential for misuse of our power as adults. In a sense, I hope the questions will focus more attention to a kind of historical dialectics of curriculum, by means of which the relationship between objects and ideas and ideals can be more readily seen.

I propose that the activities and concerns of curriculum makers are responses to the following question:

1. What educative content
2. can be made present
3. to what educatees
4. within what social-political arrangement to govern and adjudicate the distribution of power between educator and educatee?

By "what educative content," I intend two consequences. First, I intend that we make articulate and conscious our use of the words "educate" and "educative." Personally, I intend the word "educative" to refer to those conditions which either project possible futures for the educatee or reclaim his past. Secondly, I intend that we make articulate and conscious our use of the word "content." By content I intend to refer to tradition as it is established in material goods and services—diverse patterns of social and intellectual usages which are rule-governed, even though we may not be conscious of the rule-governedness of such usages. By calling attention to such rule-governedness, I hope to encourage educators to make conscious many of their taken-for-granted realities.

By asking how content "can be made present" I intend to focus attention on the materiality or object nature of content if it is to have educative value. To make present entails, for me, that the adult consciously construct the environment by means of his diverse technologies (of which learning theory is one of the major technical tools). To construct the environment is to embody the content (the traditions) which he deems valuable and educative into things and skills. To tie the educational enterprise to other social-political-economic enterprises, I would prefer that our talk of "making present" take the form of making present educative "goods and services." That is, tradition, in the form of educational content, consists of those goods and those services which on the one hand re-present the traditions—the materials and rule-governed social-intellectual usages considered worth maintaining and assumed to make possible the projection of futures or the reclamation of pasts. Shortly I shall attempt to elaborate this theme and to indicate how it seems to articulate the concerns of other curriculum makers.

By asking what content can be made present "to what educatee" I intend to question the domination of the language of learning and the language of schooling by negating the word "learner" and "student" and by suggesting a word which is the functional opposite of educator. I also intend to call to attention that "goods and services," whether in education or elsewhere, do not have educative value for everyone and that our responsibility as educators is to build environments, fabricate "goods and services," which enable specific individual or classes of individuals to future or reclaim their pasts. Our evaluation, grading, and other judgmental processes take as given the existing goods and services and the educator passes judgment upon the educatee. By speaking of content made present to specific educatees I intend that we take as given individual or classes of educatees and that we pass judgment upon the adequacy of the goods and services, or at least to recognize the material, e.g., the economic, technical and political, aspects of our judgments.

With the expression "within what social-political arrangements which govern and adjudicate the distribution of power," I intend to call attention to the fact that we have no choice but to build environments which potentially future and reclaim pasts for individuals, but that we do have choices as to the exercise of power. Within environments great diversity of activity is possible. The effort to control the direction or shape of any one person's activity is necessarily an act of power. Whereas manifestation of power cannot be avoided, the educator can make conscious and intentional the governance and adjudicating structures which guide and legitimate his diverse uses of power. The diverse manipulating and controlling acts of the educator—disciplinary acts sometimes motivating and focusing acts, acts of judgments—must be interpreted as power over the young. Likewise acts of resistance, defiance, independence, copping out on the part of the educatee must be interpreted as power over the educator or at least up against the educator. It is these acts, frequently associated with the hidden curriculum, which must be articulated as manifestation of the governance and adjudicating structures within which education presumably occurs. I cannot possibly go into all of the entailments of this way of speaking. In the Rochester paper[29] I pointed to the hermeneutical, work, and political aspects of activity and those lines of thought could be extended here. However, I believe it is more fruitful at this time to use this schema as a vehicle for reclaiming some of our past as curriculum people and hence to indicate what I intend when I use the expression the "thingness of content."

The Thingness of Content and Traditional Conceptions of Curriculum Content

Turning once again to more or less traditional—or mainline—curriculum language most of us would recognize three different sources of content. Sometimes these sources of content are articulated in terms of the function or purpose of education. Tyler is again helpful in a pointing way, but not in an understanding way. As he directs the educator to state objectives he identifies three possible sources for these objectives—the subject matter specialist or academician, the society or social problems, and the students. A far richer historical source for pointing out these three dimensions is the 26th yearbook of the National Society for the Study of Education[30] wherein the classicist or essentialist, the child-centered educator, and the socially-centered educators take their stands. In that yearbook the differences in approach are seen as different viewpoints about the function of education—and the differences stand. Tyler collapses the differences, hides the conflict and tension within his technical management system, and assumes that these differences are merely different objectives which can be synthesized by educators working within specific situations.

I believe the editors of the 26th yearbook were wrong in that the differences were not philosophical or social differences with a political-philosophical base. I believe Tyler erred in treating these differences as differing sources of objectives which could be synthesized technically and situationally. However, neither Tyler nor the writers of the 26th yearbook can be faulted for error, for the necessary insights to reconceptualize this conflict come from the Husserlian and critical behavior sciences—such as Alfred Schutz's *Phenomenology of the Social World*,[31] the work of such thinkers as Paul Ricoeur, and the efforts of the analytic philosophers who call attention to language games and rules of usages. I also believe that the work of Piaget[32] and Polanyi[33] help us in the reconceptualization.

The claim that I would like to make is that these three different sources are not in conflict nor even different ways of organizing schools or curriculum. They are rather three quite distinct types of educational content. Unless we make this "thingness of content" stand out, we cannot recognize them as distinct types of content. If we use language which focuses on learning or student behavior or other intellectual schemas we cannot see the differences in content as having any validity. Briefly I will attempt to elaborate some entailments of this way of talking, although much more time would be required to do an adequate job.

The subject matter position I see best represented today is described in the first half of King and Brownell[34] who use Polanyi to get at the notion of disciplined knowledge. They allude to the symbolic and syntactical nature of disciplined knowledge, and also point out that the curriculum worker must attend to the community of discourse which support it, the tradition of which it is a part, and the imaginative or what I would call poetic part of the domain. In these pages are the accumulation of about fifty years of thinking about content. If they had also used Piaget, they would have recognized the operational base of most disciplines.

I see this type of content primarily as the use of symbol systems—with all that the expression "symbol systems" entails—knowledge as it is understood by "everyman." It would be possible to show linkages to the structure of the disciplines movement of the 1960s,[35] Bestor[36] of the 1950s, Hutchins[37] of the 1940s, Bagley[38] of the 1920s and 1930s, and so on back.

King and Brownell break down in their application of these ideas, because indeed they see the problem as one of application. However, the problem must be seen as one of embodying these diverse components or dimensions of symbolic knowledge in goods and services which serve to future the educatee. We have attended, in part, as curriculum makers to the equipment side of these goods, but we have hidden the services side behind method of teaching. Briefly and to use Heidegger, Polanyi, Piaget, and Wittgenstein[39]—we need to identify the poetic and instrumental aspects of the symbolic knowledge, and ask how these are displayed and made accessible to the educatee. Displaying such content enables the educatee to recognize his own possibilities. We need to identify the environmental goods which can display and make accessible this poetry and these instruments. We need to identify the operations which link environmental goods with the educatee— and set up the environment so these operations stand before the educatee as one of his possibilities. We need to embody re-presentations of the communities of discourse, which means the rules governing operations and discourse must also be constructed into the environment via the services offered. Finally, the discourse rules, the poetry and instruments, the operations, the communities must be displayed in such a way that the historical dimension is on the surface—immediately accessible for interpretation.

This presentness or presentation is now done primarily through texts and teacher behavior, presenting severely limited environments to educatees. Their limited response is indeed a consequence of the economic, technical, and political limitations—hence the linkage of curriculum to Marx.

Notice, however, I have been talking about the content or environment—not about the behavior of the educatee. Objectives must be seen as attempts to describe the structured dimensions of the content—not to pre- and pro- scribe the behavior of the educatee. Whether educatees should be coerced by tests, grades, credits or other controlling, manipulating devices is a question of the structures which govern and adjudicate the distribution of power. Obviously, also, the educatee has a perfect right to remake any of these component parts—contribute to the emerging tradition of this content—within the governing and adjudicating structures.

The same analysis is possible of socially-centered content. I associate this type of content with Bobbitt,[40] Stratemeyer,[41] vocational education, and the coping skills orientation of such as Winn Adkins.[42] The work of Freire[43] who re-presents boundary situations for literacy and liberation is of the same genre. For orientation of this content we must draw from those who describe the social world—the lived world of everydayness. Alfred Schutz is an outstanding source, although today we would also have to attend to the work of Habermas and the philosophers of action, including Austin and his *How to Do Things with Words*.[44]

The analytical-technical problem is to identify the rule-governed social, technical interactions—and make these present for educatees. In vocational education this is easy. Simulation techniques also make present other rule-governedness traditions. Video-taping modernizes the technology used by Freire. The analytical technical capabilities of the 70s are clearly superior to those capabilities in the days of Bobbitt or Charters.

In this type of content, the governing-adjudicating structures are even more crucial, for power can easily be used to bring about social conformity. But with the appropriate displays of this content and accompanying hermeneutical skills, these presentations of social-economic regularities can be liberating à la Freire—not constraining à la Bobbitt.

Finally we come to the third type of content which can be made present. Again, we must speak of environmental goods and services, not behaviors of educatees. This third is associated with student-centeredness. Historically, I associated this with the Freudian movements of the 20s,[45] Hopkins[46] in the 40s, Rogers[47] in the 50s, the gestaltists of the 60s, and the Pinar's[48] of the 70s. I find Ricoeur's notion of archaeology, teleology, particularly helpful. That which these educators are about is derived from the traditions concerned with biographical integration—or in the words of Cox[49] and Novak,[50]—personal storytelling. The educator must make present the possibility of intentional personal reclamation and projection through appropriate goods and services. Therapy becomes one model— but not the only one. We are now in the process of identifying those goods and services which make this a real possibility for the educatee. Much work is yet to be done in placing these educational goods and services in the environment. I have tried to call attention to what the educational environment is if we bracket out the concern for learning and social control. Content can stand out as a "thing," but to do so we must indeed consciously rework our language so our new language particulars can become tacit and point out these needed environmental goods and services.

NOTES

[1]John S. Mann, "Student Rights Strategy," *Theory into Practice* 10 (December 1971): 353–66.

[2]Paulo Freire, *Pedagogy of the Oppressed*, trans. Myra Bergman Ramos (New York: Herder and Herder, 1968).

[3]For a history of the recent origins of critical theory see Martin Jay, The *Dialectical Imagination: History of the Frankfurt School and the Institute of Social Research, 1923–1950* (Boston: Little, Brown, 1973).

[4]Jürgen Habermas, *Knowledge and Human Interests*, trans. Jeremy J. Shapiro (Boston: Beacon Press, 1971).

[5]Max Horkheimer and Theodor Adorno, *Dialectic of Enlightenment*, trans. John Cumming (New York: Herder & Herder, 1972).

[6]Herbert Marcuse, *Reason and Revolution* (New York: Oxford University Press, 1941).

[7]Trent Schroyer, *The Critique of Domination* (New York: George Broziller, 1973).

[8]Alvin Gouldner, "Marxism and Social Theory," *Theory and Society* 1, no. 1 (1974): 17–36.

[9]Lloyd deMause, "The Evolution of Childhood," *The History of Childhood* (New York: The Psychohistory Press, 1974), 1–74.

[10]Paul Ricoeur, "Model of the Text: Meaningful Action Considered as a Text," *Social Research* 38, no. 3 (Autumn 1971): 529–562.

[11]Alfred Schutz, *The Phenomenology of the Social World* (Evanston, IL: Northwestern University Press, 1967).

[12]Martin Heidegger, *Being and Time,* trans. John MacQuarrie and Edward Robinson (New York: Harper & Row, 1962).

[13]Paul Ricoeur, *Freud and Philosophy*, trans. Denis Savage (New Haven: Yale University Press, 1970).

[14]Michael Novak, *Ascent of the Mountain, Flight of the Dove* (New York: Harper & Row, 1970).

[15]Harvey Cox, *The Seduction of the Spirit* (New York: Simon & Schuster, 1973).

[16]Ivan Illich, *De-Schooling Society* (New York: Harper & Row, 1971).

[17]Martin Carnoy, *Education as Cultural Imperialism* (New York: David McKay, 1974).

[18]Clarence Karrier, Paul Violas and Joel Spring, *Roots of Crisis* (Chicago: Rand McNally, 1973).

[19]Michael Katz, *Class, Bureaucracy, and the Schools:The Illusion of Educational Change in America* (Praeger Press, 1971).

[20]Joel Spring, *Education and the Rise of the Corporate State* (Boston: Beacon Press, 1971).

[21]*Harvard Educational Review*, "The Rights of Children," Reprint No. 9, 1974.

[22]Lloyd deMause, "The Evolution of Childhood."

[23]Ibid., 508.

[24]Dwayne Huebner, "Education in the Church," *Andover Newton Quarterly* 12, no. 3 (January 1972): 122–129. See Chapter 15.

[25]Margaret Mead, *Culture and Commitment* (New York: Natural History Press, 1979).

[26]Paul Ricoeur, "The Model of the Text: Meaningful Action Considered as Text."

[27]Peter Winch, *The Idea of Social Science* (London: Routledge, Kegan Paul, 1958).

[28]Ralph Tyler, *Basic Principles of Curriculum and Instruction* (Chicago: University of Chicago Press, 1949).

[29]Dwayne Huebner, "Toward a Remaking of Curricular Language," in *Heightened Consciousness, Cultural Revolution and Curriculum Theory*, ed. William F. Pinar (Berkeley, California: McCutchan, 1974), 36–53. See Chapter 16.

[30]National Society for the Study of Education, 26th Yearbook, Part II, *Curriculum Making: The Foundations of Curriculum Making* (Bloomington, Illinois Public School Publishing Co, 1927).

[31]Alfred Schutz, *Phenomenology of the Social World.*

[32]Jean Piaget, *Genetic Epistemology*, trans. Eleanor Duckworth (New York: Columbia University Press, 1970).

[33]Michael Polanyi, *Personal Knowledge* (Chicago: University of Chicago Press, 1958).

[34]Arthur R. King and John A. Brownell, *The Curriculum and the Disciplines of Knowledge* (New York: John Wiley, 1968).

[35]For example, see *Education and the Structure of Knowledge*, ed., Stanley Elam, (Chicago: Rand McNally, 1964).

[36]Arthur E. Bestor, *The Educational Wastelands; The Retreat from Learning in Our Public Schools* (Urbana: University of Illinois Press, 1953).

[37]Robert Hutchins, *Education for Freedom* (Baton Rouge: Louisiana State University Press, 1947).

[38]William C. Bagley, *Education and Emergent Man* (New York: Thomas Nelson and Sons, 1934).

[39]Ludwig Wittgenstein, *Philosophical Investigations* (New York: Macmillan, 1953).

[40]Franklin Bobbitt, *The Curriculum* (New York: Houghton Mifflin Co., 1918).

[41]Florence Stratemeyer, et al., *Developing a Curriculum for Modern Living* (New York: Bureau of Publications, Teacher's College, Columbia University, 1947).

[42]Winthrop Adkins, "Life Coping Skills: A Fifth Curriculum," Teachers College Record 75, no. 4 (May 1974): 507–526.

[43]Paulo Freire, *Pedagogy of the Oppressed*, trans. Myra Bergman Ramos (New York: Herder and Herder, 1968).

[44]J. L. Austin, *How to Do Things with Words* (London: Oxford University Press, 1962).

[45]Margaret Naumburg, *The Child and the World* (New York: Harcourt Brace, 1928).

[46]Thomas Hopkins, *Interaction* (Boston: D.C. Heath, 1941).

[47]Carl Rogers, *Client-centered Therapy* (Boston: Houghton Mifflin, 1951); for his own recent educational recommendations, see *Freedom to Learn* (Columbus, Ohio: C.E. Merrill, 1969).

[48]William F. Pinar, ed. *Curriculum Theorizing: The Reconceptualists* (Berkeley,CA: McCutchan, 1975). In press at the time this essay was written, *Ed.*

[49]Harvey Cox, *The Seduction of the Spirit*.

[50]Michael Novak, *Ascent of the Mountain*.

18

The Tasks
of the Curricular Theorist

(1975)

Obtaining a perspective of the curriculum theory movement, if one exists, is somewhat difficult. It is hard to tell whether the search for something called theory is the curricularist's attempt to establish prestige in academic circles, whether he has simply been caught up in the behavioral science web and its increased concern for theory, or whether the search really indicates a maturing search for greater rationality. The quest for perspective is further complicated by the educator's failure to discriminate among the various phenomena with which he is concerned. Within the past several years, several books and writings concerned with educational theory have become available.[1] Might these efforts also be categorized as curriculum theorizing or necessary for curriculum theorizing? With the publication of the report of the Committee on the Criteria of Teacher Effectiveness in 1952 and 1953, and the subsequent *Handbook of Research on Teaching*, there has been increased concern for and systematization of research on teaching.[2] Might these also be considered curricular from any one point of view? If they are, they have not been well integrated into the curricular theory literature. This divorce probably implies nothing more than the failure of incipient curricular theorists to get control of relevant data and resources.

This is to be expected, for attempts to theorize about curricula are recent. Determination of how recent, of course, is a function of the definition of curriculum and theory. My own preference is to date the beginning of the current interest to the 1947 Conference on Curriculum Theory held at the University of Chicago.[3] However, as Herrick and Tyler describe their efforts they would evidently date the origin much earlier, for they state "that very little progress has been made in the realm of curriculum theory in the past twenty years."[4] Today, twenty years later, the same comment could be made, that little progress has been made in the last twenty years.

The current state of the curricularist's interest in theory is illustrated by three recent documents.[5] All three documents point to the lack of organization of the ideas and efforts related to theorizing about curriculum and to the problem curricularists have with their own history of theorizing. The bibliographies in each of the three documents serve as a good starting point for a beginning awareness of this history.

There are those educators who would seek clarity about the incipient field and its potential direction by attempting definitions of *theory* or of *curriculum*. I believe, however, that definition is a stage along the way, not necessarily a beginning point. In fact, if the notion of theory is taken as a starting point, the possibilities of being led astray are increased. Certainly the intellectual community that has made the most laudable theoretical progress has been the scientific community. It seems, therefore, that if curricularists wish to increase their theoretical sophistication they should model the efforts of the scientists. The appropriate literature is vast and very informative.[6] In fact, out brethren in educational administration have made good use of such theory.[7] Yet curriculum is a somewhat different phenomenon, and theorizing about it has brought out the fact that the curricularist must be concerned not only with descriptive or scientific theory, but also with prescriptive or normative theory. That is, he who would talk about curriculum must do more than describe what goes on; many people want him to issue imperatives about what should be done. This mix up between descriptive and prescriptive theory compounds our problems and leads to a continuation of the old theory-practice distinction, thus sanctioning old saws such as "that won't work, it's just theory" or "he is no good in the classroom, for he is just a theoretician." It seems more promising to start with the interrelationships among three different activities engaged in by curricularists.

There are those who engage in educational practice: teachers, curriculum consultants, and supervisors. There are those who conduct empirical research about curricular matters. These can be professional researchers, teachers, college professors, or advanced students. There are those who talk and write about curriculum. They can be creators of new ways of talking about curricular matters, or people simply using the language of others. Practice, research, and talking (or writing) are not three distinct occupations. Indeed, the same individual could engage in all three occupations. In fact, a person who is somehow involved in matters of curriculum usually talks and practices, or talks and does research, or he may simply practice and do research without talking. The truism that there is practice, research, and talk in curriculum is not the point. The point is to untangle the relationship among these three activities, which is not an easy task or at least not an obvious task. The untangling becomes more difficult and at the same time more illuminating if we recognize that these relationships are historical and cannot be disentangled once and for all. That is, it is well to make the working assumption that there are evolving dialectical relationships among practice, empirical research, and language. How can the curricularist articulate the relationship between his practice and his language, or between his empirical research and his language, or between his practical actions and responsibilities and his research?

LANGUAGE

What is theory? What ever it is, it seems to be rooted in the language that we use to talk about what we do, and it is this language web that must be our starting point. Like a spider web, it is sticky, useful, beautiful if we are not caught in it, and all of a piece, for if one corner is touched, the whole quivers. Many curricularists are flies caught in the web of someone else's language. Some are spiders, weaving webs as a consequence of their inherited ability. But the unique characteristic of the curricularist is that he is a human being: able to be caught in someone else's web, able to make his own, but more significantly, able to stand back and behold its beauty and form, to study its structure and function, and to generate new weblike patterns. Man and his language form a paradoxical relationship. He is inevitably caught in it, yet as its creator he can seek to transcend its confines, but in so doing he builds new snares which are equally confining.

The curricularist uses language. Some of us just talk, and the talk is not related to anything other than someone else's talk. Some use language in a variety of ways as they engage in their practical thing, whether it be teaching or supervision, or any number of other activities associated with curriculum. Some use language as they engage in research about curricular phenomena. It seems to me that one of the tasks of the theorist is to identify the various situations in which we use language, and to find categories that describe the various functions our language serves in those situations. Having done this, it might be possible to tease out the relationship between language, practice, and research. Then perhaps we can undertake some historical studies that will provide the kind of historical awareness necessary for men who would be free in their world building. Without historical awareness we are apt to remain caught in a language web of our own or someone else's making.

The Use of Language by Curricularists

The search to identify the various curricular situations in which language is used and the categories to describe this language is necessary because the curricularist has too frequently assumed that his language is all of a piece. The many books written about curriculum contain a wide range of language forms.

Criticism has not led to cumulative refinement because the critics fail to recognize the diversity of language usage. The failure to recognize the unique contribution of a Smith, Stanley and Shores, of a Stratemeyer, or of a King and Brownell, is partially because curricular critics have not separated out the various types of language in such proposal type books.[8] Furthermore, the curricularist's search for *the* curriculum theory, or a one-dimensional way of talking and writing about curricular phenomena, hides the fact that different educators—say teachers and principals, or teachers and textbook writers, or supervisors and the mass media romantic critics—use language quite differently because their intentions and systems of relevancies differ. Unless we can begin to differentiate among the various uses and categories of curricular language, we will not be able to refine and polish any of it. What follows then is but one attempt to identify a series of categories for distinguishing among the contexts and uses of curricular language. The categories are meant to be suggestive for further inquiry; hence their values and limitations will not be pressed at this time. The categories are not new or original but are common distinctions to be found in a variety of literature.

Curricularists, whether practitioners, researchers, or simply talkers, use language to describe curricular events or phenomena. We need not at this point get involved in attempts to identify or define curricular events or phenomena, for these attempts would push us to a kind of rigor inappropriate for this stage of inquiry. Teachers, for instance, talk in a descriptive way about what they do in classrooms. Some of the research on teaching is an attempt to build a *descriptive language* for talking about what goes on in classrooms.[9] Some of the language used by Ashton-Warner in *Spinster* is descriptive of what went on in her classroom. But there are other phenomena or events that are also considered curricular and are described in one way or another. Description, however, need not be of events and phenomena in a given place or time. Imaginary events or phenomena—those wished or those dreamed—can also be described. In other words, *descriptive language* can be a link between a reality and an image or a dream; between a present and a future, or a future and a past. The language used to describe what could be is also or can be the language used to describe what is, and vice versa. The limitations of the educational imagination could very well be a consequence of the limitations of the language used to describe present events or phenomena.

Another form of talk used by curricularists is *explanatory language*. We try to give reasons for what occurs, to establish causes. Descriptive language permits one to skate linguistically over the surface of events and phenomena, whereas *explanatory talk* digs below the surface. *Explanatory language* seeks to explain why something occurs or how it occurs. It is usually concerned with postulated concepts and inferred relationships. For instance, the term "learning" cannot be used to describe anything; it is a postulated concept to explain a presumed relationship between two events at different times: a change in behavior. Much of the language used by curricularists, particularly that coming from psychology and the behavioral sciences, is explanatory language. To describe with explanatory language is impossible, which is probably why curricularists have a rough time talking about practice with the language of learning, and why they have been preoccupied with a pseudo argument about whether to use behavioral definitions of outcomes. It would be fascinating to establish how frequently the curricularist attempts to use explanatory language to describe what goes on or what might go on.

Very close to and perhaps even similar to the use of explanatory language is the use of *controlling language*. We use language to construct and manipulate things, events, phenomena, and people; we use it to predict what might happen and thus to determine events that become part of a cause and effect chain. The *language of control, manipulation*, or *prediction* is essentially the bringing together of descriptive and explanatory language. We talk about how to get from what is to what might be. To do this language is needed to describe what is and what will be and to articulate the inferred causal linkages between the two. The language of learning is an auxiliary symbol system to serve this in-between function, and if tied to a good descriptive language it enables us to control events or phenomena in such a way that we can predict, within statistical limits, what might happen.[10] In the *controlling language* of curriculum, however, little attention is paid to the differences between descriptive language and explanatory language, much to our loss of vision and power.

If the language used by curricularists was totally language of description; explanation; or control, prediction, and manipulation, our analysis would be relatively easy, for these are forms of language common to scientific and technological endeavors. Fortunately, or unfortunately, depending on the friends you keep, the person engaged in occupations associated with curricular phenomena also uses language in other ways. He uses it *to rationalize* or *legitimize* his actions. As he acts in a certain way or creates a given situation, he frequently needs to reassure someone, perhaps himself, that he knows what he is doing and that he has a right to do it. He uses a *legitimating language,* which serves to establish his claim that he knows what he is doing or that he has the right, responsibility, authority, or legitimacy to do it. *Legitimating language,* or the language used to rationalize action, can be interpreted as an appeal to some social group for acceptance of the rightness or appropriateness of the action undertaken. Language used to legitimate is addressed to someone else who is in a position to judge professional adequacy and competency. Explanatory language can be used to legitimate action. However, explanation of the possible causes of or consequences of action might not be accepted by the judging group as sufficient or even necessary rationalizations. Language appropriate for the legitimating action ties the reasons for the action into the functional value system of the community to which the claim is addressed. Statements of educational objectives or goals are frequently uttered as claims for legitimation. The attempt to translate goals and objectives into behavioral objectives is an attempt to shift from legitimating language to descriptive language, so goals and objectives can be tied into the language of control and manipulation. However, other forms of legitimating or rationalizing language could be identified easily in educational discourse.

The curricularist not only seeks to legitimate or rationalize his actions, he also seeks to convince or influence others to undertake similar actions. That is, he uses language to prescribe a course of action or to influence others to undertake similar actions. Such *prescriptive language* is not simply descriptive of a future course of action; it carries with it an imperative, a command, or an attempt to impose a course of action. *Prescriptive language,* while often couched in the language of ethics and morality, is, nevertheless, primarily political language inasmuch as it seeks to influence and to involve others in desired or valued action.[11] Hence, prescriptive language requires attention to the rhetorical uses of language, and to the characteristics of the recipients or listeners.

Finally, language used by curricularists frequently serves as a symbol of cohesiveness or of belonging to a particular community. It becomes, in some instances, the *language of affiliation*, which serves as a vehicle and token of cohesion. Mastering the language is frequently part of the initiation into the community, and proficiency with the language indicates one's belonging to the community. For instance, the increased use of behavioral science language in curriculum can be interpreted as an attempt by curricularists to belong to the social scientific community. The use of slogans in education also symbolizes solidarity and membership in a given community. A look at the language formerly used by curricularists could produce an awareness of the communities and subcommunities that have existed in the overall field. The language centered around the slogans "the whole child," "democratic teaching," or "structure of the disciplines" points to collegial relationships that exist or that someone wishes to establish. The language associated with Bruner's *The Process of Education*[12] might be interpreted as a significant effort to find a way of talking about education that brings the academician, the psychologist, and the educator into a single community of concern and language.

These six suggested categories of language usage in curriculum—descriptive, explanatory, controlling, legitimating, prescriptive, and affiliative—are not meant to be discrete. They are offered as pointers to various ways in which curricularists use language in a variety of situations. The categories do not necessarily depend on the structure or form of the language; rather they depend on the use of language in a particular time and place. To explore the interrelationships among these six categories would pull me away from my intention, which is to explore the tasks for the curricular theorist. My point so far is to suggest that the language used by the curricularist in his talking and writing takes many shapes or at least serves various functions. It seems to me that one of the tasks of the curricular theorist is to articulate the uses of language within the curricular domain, and to identify the various modes of language used. When this is done, the curricular theorist can more readily critique the language forms used in curricular discourse.

The Sources and History of Curricular Language

Language is never found ready-made in the world of nature. It is a man-made phenomenon, and its source is the creative efforts of people . Furthermore, it is never a complete or finished system or tool of man; it is always in the process of being recreated, which means that it is criticized and scrutinized in a variety of ways, parts of it are dropped from usage, and new usages and terminologies are introduced. It is an evolving form, and thus has a history or past that can be articulated. Individual men are the source of its vitality and its growth, and new ways of speaking by an individual can enliven a system of discourse and open up new possibilities. To recognize language as an emerging form is to accept its limitations and to be alert and receptive to new ways of talking. To be aware of the history of this emerging form and its various sources of novelty and emergence is to increase one's ability to contribute to its vitality.

Curricularists have tended to be ahistorical in the awareness of the various forms and institutions that make up their professional gear. Too frequently our tendency has been messianic. The search is often for the new and permanent vehicles of salvation, and thus we fall prey to bandwagons and the bandwagon mentality. We have a tendency to search for the final solution, and to think that we can discover the one and only best way to talk about curricular phenomena. In so doing, we fail to operate as historical beings and shirk our responsibility for the continual criticism and creation of new language forms and new ways of speaking. To be aware of our historical nature is to be on top of our past, so we can use it as a base for projection into the future. Another primary task of the curricular theorist, then, is to articulate the history of the various language uses that he has and to search for the origins or sources of his expressions and ways of talking. This is essentially a task of intellectual history, and it requires tracing the evolution of our various ways of talking and writing about curricular phenomena.

Even a cursory glance over the language referring to curricular phenomena throughout the years indicates the multiple sources of our language. At various times curricularists have drawn freely from philosophy, theology, psychology and other behavioral sciences, sometimes various humanities and technologies, and often the commonsense language of nondisciplined people. This will probably always be the case; for except for a very few words or expressions, such as *scope and sequence*, we do not seem to have a vocabulary or language that is primarily our own. Whether we will ever arrive at a unique symbol system that refers to curricular phenomena remains to be seen. This uniqueness is one of the fruits of scientific inquiry.

The curricularist's dependence on a variety of other disciplines and enterprises as the sources of his language creates no insurmountable problem. Indeed, it can be a strength of the field for without built-in structures of criticism and creation, as in an established scientific community, curricular language could stagnate. Our responsiveness to a variety of other fields means that we do indeed have sources of language renewal. The only danger arises from the lack of awareness of our own actions, the recurring failure to achieve historical perspective of the shifts in ways of talking, and the potential entrapment in a given way of speaking. Somehow we must become aware of the sources of our language, and the ways we have generated productive shifts in our ways of speaking. If an historical awareness can be developed, then the dangers of entrapment and obsolescence are less menacing.

At this point the distinctions among the descriptive, explanatory, controlling, legitimating, prescriptive, and affiliative language uses may be helpful. Failure to identify multiple uses of language in curriculum has clouded the relationships between curricular language and the language used in other domains. The untangling of these complex relationships could be approached in a variety of ways. A start might be to articulate the history of one language use, such as the explanatory or the prescriptive, in an attempt to identify its sources at various times. Another start might be to turn directly to the language of a particular noneducational domain, such as psychology, and identify how psychological language has been used or misused to describe, explain, legitimate, or prescribe. For instance, the language of learning is probably not very good descriptive language, but it is handy for certain kinds of explanation and perhaps for certain kinds of control and manipulation. Philosophical language has often been used for legitimating and prescription, but is probably rather ineffectual for explanation. Literary language, such as poetry, might be good for description but inadequate for explanatory or affiliative functions. Historically, dependence on a particular language use is apt to be a function of many different variables. The reason for appropriating the languages of the behavioral sciences today is not simply that these languages offer the possibility of increased power of control, but that they are also major vehicles of legitimation and affiliation; scientific-technological language has more cash value in today's economic and political spheres. Disregard for the language of theology is only in part a consequence of the circumscribed usefulness of theological language in education; it can also be explained as a subconscious attempt to deaffiliate from religious communities. The deaffiliation from theological language communities illustrates, incidentally, the need for historical awareness. The rupture between theology and curriculum was valid at one point in the history of both curriculum and theological thought. To ignore theological language today, however, is to ignore one of the more exciting and vital language communities. Of course, theological language would not carry much weight as an explanatory language in most circles, and would prove quite ineffectual as controlling language. However, it might serve as descriptive and legitimating language.

Another value of the historical search for our language sources is that language pulled from its primary domain is disengaged from established forms of self-correcting criticisms. In psychology, for example, expressions and terms are constantly scrutinized, empirically and logically, for their validity. Meanings shift and the use of given words or expressions are altered or dropped as new experimental data accumulates and as explanatory paradigms change. However, when a term, such as *learning*, is pulled out of psychological discourse and used in another realm, such as curriculum, the scientific checks are not brought with it. A word or expression current in curricular discourse might be no longer viable in the parent discourse system. This is also true of philosophical language, and perhaps is also illustrated by the relationships between theological language and curricular language. If curricularists can become historically aware of these patterns of shifting meanings, they can more freely draw on and reject language of other domains.

It seems to me, then, that another task of the curricular theorist is to articulate the history of the languages used by curricularists. Articulating this history would require charting the changes in the various language usages and the relationship of curricular language to language of other domains. Articulation of these relationships would require attention to established relationships and relationships that were not established for a variety of social or intellectual reasons. To articulate the patterns of relationships between curricular language and the language in other domains might increase the awareness of our connections to a host of other existing and emerging language communities.

PRACTICE

Within the so-called curriculum field there are people concerned primarily with practice rather than with the language used to think and discourse about practice. The very close relationship between language and practice (an old and significant dichotomy usually formulated as a theory-practice distinction)[13] makes it extremely difficult to conceptualize something known as "pure practice."

What is practice? Whatever it is, it is grounded in an environment constructed by man, and it is a human event occurring within that constructed environment. Dewey provides the support for the focus on environment. In 1902 he stated that the function of the educator is "to determine the environment of the child."[14] He developed this more fully in *Democracy and Education,* in which there is a special section entitled, "The School as a Special Environment." There he states that "We never educate directly, but indirectly by means of the environment."[15] Analysis seems more generative if the practice dimensions of curriculum are viewed initially as concern for the characteristics of the educative environment. As with the analysis of language, the task is to establish categories for discriminating among the various components of the environments, to identify the actual or potential sources of these components, and to articulate the history of educational environments.

Practice as Educative Environment

Definitions are again a stage along the way, not beginning points. To attempt to define *educative environment* would immediately draw forth old solutions and arguments rather than push us to new levels of awareness. Arguments over the meaning of education have their value, but they can also serve will-o'-the-wisp functions. If the analysis begins with schooling, we need not get involved with definitions of the meaning of education or educative environments, for the schools can be looked at historically as a set of environmental components or conditions that shift and change through time.

Obviously, schools are made up of and contain things: material. "Material" consists of books, laboratory equipment, educational media, and programs stored either in print or electronically; but the buildings as well as the furniture are also part of the "thing" environment. In one sense, the curriculum consists partly of the buildup of capital investment in the educative material. For instance, development of the reading curriculum in an elementary school can be construed as the buildup of texts and other reading materials such as paperbacks, diagnostic and remedial skill materials, and films or audio resources. The development of science curricula in the elementary school can be traced by the shift from science texts to other types of science equipment, e.g., laboratories, and other materials such as film loops. The history of secondary school curricula can be identified, again in part, by the shift from wood-working, metal, and print shops to the capital investment in science laboratories, a greater diversity of library facilities and materials, and the movement from classrooms or groups for thirty students to flexible spaces. One of the significant aspects of today's curricular changes is the increase in the range, novelty, and complexity of educative material.

Another aspect of the educative environment is the language and symbol systems used for discourse among students and teachers within that environment. Discourse systems are major focal points of research and development today. Much of the concern for the structure of the disciplines can be subsumed under the topic of how a language or another symbol system is to be used within the classroom. King and Brownell use Polanyi's notion of a "community of discourse" as a way to specify the disciplined content of the classroom.[16] Phenix's *Realms of Meaning*[17] can be interpreted as a concern for the systems of discourse used to talk about the experiences of people in the world. Smith's work focuses upon the logical dimensions of the language used within the classroom. The material environment—the books, other media, and the architectural structure of the building—determine, again in part, the forms of language or symbol systems used. An arithmetic book specifies how the young person is to use certain symbols in interaction with people in action on, or with, the environment. Science and social studies materials also specify, in part, the way the student might use language forms to articulate aspects of the world.

A third aspect of the educative environment consists of the patterned or conditioned behaviors of the individuals who live in that environment: teachers, students, and other personnel. The intent here is to point to the stable skills and habits normally associated with roles and institutions rather than individuals. Again, the educative environment can be articulated, in part, as a capital investment in human resources, manifest in the conditioned and interchangeable behaviors of school personnel. This does not imply that the uniqueness of the individual teacher has no significant educative value in the classroom or school; it simply means that it is possible to talk about the input and maintenance of given levels and qualities of human skill and habit. The conditioned patterns consist of symbolic skills, skills of coordinating human action and speech with material, and the habits and skills necessary for social interaction. Administrators can legitimately speak of the need of their system for skilled manpower, and the possibility of building these resources through education of the staff or by bringing in personnel with new or different skills.

Material, symbolic systems, and human resources are organized into identifiable organizational structures. That is, the patterns of relationships among people, things, and discourse or symbol systems are relatively stable through given periods of time and can be identified as particular organizational forms. The various schemes of curricular content are cases in point. The subject matter curriculum can be conceptualized as one pattern of material, symbol systems, and teacher skills, whereas the core curriculum involves different patterns of symbols, things, and human skills. Grouping patterns, such as homogeneous and heterogeneous groups, team teaching, tutorial, and other organizational schema can be described by the different patterns among discourse systems, materials, and human skills.

It seems to me that one of the tasks of the curricular theorist is to focus his attention on the characteristics of the educative environment. This involves primarily the development of a descriptive language that will enable him and other curricularists to catalog and chart the environmental dimensions of practice. It might be said, as indeed Dewey in effect did say, that the curricularist's responsibility is to fabricate an environment that educates. Focusing attention on the components of the environment as distinct from the language used to explain, prescribe, or legitimize them could increase the power of the curricularist to design more effective environments and to see them in historical perspective.

The History of Educative Environments

To see these educative environments in historical perspective and to articulate this history becomes another possible task of the curricular theorist. There are two aspects of this task. The first is to trace the development of the environmental components within specific arenas of educational activity. For instance, the history of the "teaching" of reading is in part the development of resources for "teaching" reading. The shift in the kinds of books, programmed materials, and teacher skills must be traced, for the history is not simply a shift in ideology. Individualized reading programs, for example, are functional only when there is a wealth of trade books, a range of skill development materials, and teacher skills of diagnosis and remediation. The designers and distributors of reading materials are as much a part of the history of the teaching of reading as the theorists or researchers. O. K. Moore's talking typewriter[18] is also a part of the history of the teaching of reading. The history of science teaching can also be traced, in part, by the changes in scientific equipment, and the coordination of this equipment with the development of teacher skills and new science language patterns.

Perhaps a more important historical task is to articulate the development of the environmental components within a specific educational situation. I am suggesting partial acceptance of a form of materialistic determinism. Educators have been deficient in ignoring the social theory derived from Marx's work. Environmental conditions are as important determiners of action and history as ideas. Curricularists have traditionally shown their idealistic bias by paying more attention to rhetoric than to things and environmental conditions. Curricularists responsible for given educational situations are often alienated from their own roots because of this concern for ideas to the exclusion of concern for environment. The professional language of the curricularist often pulls him away from his own feelings and his own language, thus alienating him from his own biography. On the other hand, the language used in professional circles and meetings is often not appropriate to the conditions within the local school system and consequently alienates the individual from the history of the situation in which he assumes professional responsibility. To focus on the environmental conditions within a specific political and historical situation is to help the curricular practitioner recognize his responsibility for emerging environmental form. To be aware of the possible evolution of existing conditions within a given historical situation is to be aware that curricular change, as environmental criticism and renewal, is a function of capital investments. Historical awareness brings to the fore the problems of environmental obsolescence, including the obsolescence of human skills and habits, and the problems of environmental inertia. With an eye on the evolution of environmental form, the curricularist can more readily accept that one of his responsibilities is the renewal and creation of environmental conditions, such as material, teacher habits and skills, and discourse systems, and their organizational interrelationships.

The Sources of Environmental Components

The search for the sources of the conditioned components of the educative environment points to one of the uses of curricular language. However, the relationship between language and environmental conditions is not simply a one-way street; it is sufficiently important to be pulled out for separate discussion. The concern here is with the nonlanguage sources of environmental conditions, granted that this is an arbitrary, and in part, superficial distinction. Creating an awareness of the sources of educational conditions and how they are brought into specific situations seems to me to be one of the tasks of the theorists. Not all components of the educative environment are a consequence of educational intention or rationality. The intrusion of newer instructional media into schools, such as television, computers, talking typewriters, and architectural forms, are all a consequence of creative actions outside of the educational domain and force the educator to ask how they can be used educationally. Some of the conditioned and relatively fixed patterns of behavior of teachers are also a consequence of forces operating outside educational practice or rationality but nevertheless crucial as components of the educational environment. The same can be said of the existence of various patterns of symbol usage within classrooms and schools. Again, the search to articulate the relationship between environmental components and their sources might be accomplished in two ways. The first is detailing the existence of the various components within a given situation and then searching for the source or determiners of those conditions. The second involves scanning the society within which schools exist, and asking how various materials, symbol systems, or human skills have been or can be related to conditions within the school.

Relationships Between Language and Environment

The descriptive and controlling functions of language are significant vehicles for developing and introducing new conditions into the environment. The descriptive functions of language facilitate the envisioning of new possibilities by permitting description of conditions that might exist in the future. The predictive and manipulating functions of language permit the construction or fabrication of new environmental conditions by facilitating the specification of environmental variables and their interrelationships. Writers, using story, novel, or hypothetical form, can describe students and teachers in new and strange environments, in the manner of good science fiction. The language of psychology permits the construction of new environmental conditions, such as the electronic responsive environment and other computer-based devices.[19] Psychological language also enables the conditioning of teacher skills and permits teachers to increase their behavioral repertoire in new and perhaps undreamed of ways. In fact, all of the behavioral sciences increase the curricularist's ability to fabricate new environmental conditions; as do many of the technologies used in communication and other industries.

The reverse relationship also exists. The availability of new conditions can also call forth new language responses. Developing technologies create new environmental conditions that can foster the creation of new descriptive language, increase the need for new explanatory language, and suggest the necessity or possibility of new legitimating and prescriptive language.

A reciprocal relationship exists between language and environment. Language can be used to create new environmental conditions, and new environmental conditions can lead to the emergence of new language patterns. However, these are not dependent relationships, for both language and the various environmental conditions can evolve independently. It seems appropriate that the curriculum theorist should explicate this reciprocity between language and environment.

Practice as Human Event

Curricular practice is not simply concern for the construction of the educative environment; it is also concern for the human events that occur within that environment. The theoretical problem is one of finding, creating, or borrowing a language that can be used to describe and explain human events in educative situations. Within the past several decades the curricularists have been satisfied with psychological language to describe such events, and the language of learning has been the major tool. This dependence on psychological language or the language of other behavioral scientists is almost a direct consequence of the unconscious bias of curricularists for positivistic thought.[20] The problem of talking about human action and events, however, is one that is faced by most disciplined traditions. Other philosophical traditions, including phenomenology and existentialism, and certain theological traditions have been ignored by curricularists. Heideggerian thought seems particularly valuable, as does the language of recent French phenomenologically oriented philosophers such as Merleau-Ponty and Paul Ricoeur.[21]

Practice as human event suggests the essentially temporal nature of man and points to the linkage of biography to history as a major educational concern.[22] Curricularists have ignored such questions as destiny, finitude, and the meaning and morality of the influence of one human being on another. We have tended to lump these questions under the problems of learning and objectives and have been inclined to conceptualize the phenomena of interpersonal influence as a technological problem.

But the focus on practice as human event also increases awareness of the event structure of the educator's life. Practice as human event implies that the curricularist is also a human being with a biography in conflict and harmony with other emerging biographies being played out in historically evolving institutions. A concern for the history of practice as human event calls attention to the biographical structure of people involved in educational environments. The life history of the individuals involved in educative situations becomes a potential focal point of the concern and suggests the need for conceptual systems that articulate the phenomenon of human power and the dramatic shape of human events. This, it seems to me, is another task of the curricular theorist.

Practice as Design

The practitioner can be considered a designer of educational environments for human events. This is a two-fold design problem. The first is an esthetic problem of composing the environment in such a way that events flow in valued ways. The solution to this problem requires attention to the many qualities of the environment and their interrelationships, and to the durational aspects of the interaction among the individuals within the environment. The second is a political design problem. Fabrication of educational environments is essentially social policy, involving people with different values and intentions. Reaching agreement about the characteristics of a particular environment requires a potential conflict among those concerned and the use of power to shape the environment. The resolution of conflict and the organization of power is essentially a problem of political design.

Curriculum as a form of human praxis, a shaping of a world, means that the responsible individuals are engaged in art and politics. The curricularist has tried to ignore the artistic and political dimensions of his environment building by speaking as if the design problems were essentially problems of technology and authority.[23] Hence the ready acceptance of science and technology as educational tools and the frequent coronation of new educational authorities. The task for the theorist is to develop conceptual tools for grouping this two-fold design problem. Hence the need for the curriculum theorist to be associated with the artistic and political enterprises and their literatures.

RESEARCH

Within the curriculum field there is also research, a term covering a multitude of activities. It is frequently associated with scientific activity and presumed to be related to scientific theory. However, this is not always the case. In fact the word *research* has a legitimating function, for research is "in," and the researcher's "thing" is valued, even if the research itself is not. This legitimating function has even carried to the elementary school level, where even children carry out "research" projects. The word *research* has not been adequately distinguished from the word *search* and the meaning of *re-* has been ignored.

What is research? I prefer to identify it as the use of the unformed to create form; as a focusing on the unconditioned in order to develop new conditions; as attention to human events in order that human institutions can be created or evolve; as the dialectical relationship between criticism and creation. In scientific fields it involves creating symbolic statements that point to a presumed reality, withstand empirical criticism in the sense of predicting or explaining the phenomena of that reality, and withstand the logical criticism of the scientific community. Research is not simply the gathering of "facts," but the development of a form to "fit" those facts. The data that fit the form consequently can be explained or manipulated by the use of that form. Thus the form is a man-made institution that contains, and enables one to work with, empirical data or unstructured givens. Scientists work with them to uncover new phenomena or empirical givens and to create new symbolic forms. Scientific research in curriculum can be considered, then, as the disciplined attentiveness to phenomena related to curriculum in order to create language forms. These forms enable the curricularist to contain and work with those phenomena for the purpose of uncovering new phenomena and creating new language statements.

Research is not related simply to symbolic statements. Within a much broader context, research is a vehicle by which man keeps all of his institutions viable and vital. Human institutions are intentional. They have been created to contain certain phenomena and to enable people to work with or use them for human purposes. Through research, people responsible for these institutions criticize them to determine if they reflect the givens to be held and whether they need to be revised or completely destroyed and recreated. The empirical critique determines the adequacy of the form for the facts. The social critique determines the adequacy of the form in terms of the logical, esthetic, economic, and political values of the users.

For curricular language, then, research is a vehicle by which the curricularists criticize existing language and create new language. Existing empirical research methods are appropriate forms of critique for the descriptive, explanatory and controlling language usage. Other research methods are probably necessary for the criticism and creation of prescriptive, legitimating, and affiliative language usages. At this time, I cannot specify the nature of these research methods. I have no doubt, however, that prescriptive language has no longer life or greater permanency than explanatory language. It too must be recreated to fit the givens for which it is to be used. The same is obviously true for legitimating language, for the values it seeks to align and coordinate also shift and must be reassessed.

The conditioned aspects of the environment—materials, symbolic systems, and human skills—can also be conceptualized as institutional forms that "fit" appropriate givens. As institutional forms, they too must retain their vitality and viability. Research can be interpreted as a vehicle by which these forms are criticized and recreated that they might continue to be appropriate to empirical givens and social values. Research is necessary to determine whether materials do indeed serve their intentional function; a form of empirical criticism that need not be mediated by language. Teacher skills are also conditioned forms that embody human intention, and must be amenable to empirical criticism and recreation. Symbolic forms used in curriculum are also intentional forms subject to empirical criticism and social judgment.

Research is the human activity that maintains the vitality and viability of man-made form by subjecting it to empirical and social criticism appropriate to given historical communities. According to Tillich, man must continually protest against existing form lest it become an idol, that new form might emerge.[24] Research is a vehicle of empirical criticism directed at man-made form, so new forms can emerge. In curriculum, language is not the only man-made form; educative environments and their components are also man-made forms that must be protested against that new forms can emerge.

CONCLUSION

What are the tasks of the curriculum theorist? As is true of all theorists his task is to lay bare the structure of his being-in-the-world and to articulate this structure through the language and the environmental forms that he creates. His responsibility is for the forms that he creates and uses, that they might be controlled by him rather than controlling him. It is necessary that he be conscious of his man-made equipment, his languages, his environmental forms. To be aware of these man-made forms is to be aware of their history, of their sources in human activity and intention, and continually to subject them to empirical and social criticism that they be not idols but evolving tools. All educators attempt to shape the world; theorists should call attention to the tools used for the shaping in order that the world being shaped can be more beautiful and just.

NOTES

[1]Marc Belth, *Education as a Discipline* (Boston: Allyn & Bacon, 1965); Charles Brauner, *American Educational Theory* (Englewood Cliffs, NJ: Prentice-Hall, 1964); John Walton, *Discipline of Education* (Madison: University of Wisconsin, 1963).

[2]"Report of the Committee on the Criteria of Teacher Effectiveness," *Review of Educational Research 22*, no. 3 (June 1952): 238–63; "Second Report of the Committee on Criteria of Teacher Effectiveness," *Journal of Educational Research 46*, no. 9 (May 1953): 641–58; N. L. Gage, ed., *Handbook of Research on Teaching* (New York: Rand McNally, 1963).

[3]Virgil E. Herrick and Ralph W. Tyler, eds., *Toward Improved Curriculum Theory*, Supplementary Educational Monographs, No. 71 (Chicago: University of Chicago Press, 1950).

[4]Ibid., iii.

[5]*Theory Into Practice* (October 1967); Mauritz Johnson, "The Translation of Curriculum Into Instruction" (Prepared for an invitational pre-session on curriculum theory at AERA in February 1968); John S. Mann, "Toward a Discipline of Curriculum Theory," mimeographed (Baltimore, MD: Johns Hopkins University, Center for the Study of Social Organization of Schools, January 1968).

[6]James B. Conant, *On Understanding Science* (New Haven, CT: Yale University Press, 1947); Thomas S. Kuhn, *The Structure of Scientific Revolutions* (Chicago: University of Chicago Press, 1962); Ernest Nagel, *The Structure of Science: Problems in the Logic of Scientific Explanation* (New York: Harcourt, Brace & World, 1961); Michael Polanyi, *The Tacit Dimension* (Garden City, NY: Doubleday, 1966); Ralph G. Siu, *The Tao of Science* (Cambridge, Mass: MIT Press, 1957); Stephen E. Toulmin, *Foresight and Understanding* (Bloomington: Indiana University Press, 1961).

[7]Arthur P. Coladarci and Jacob W. Getzels, *The Use of Theory in Education Administration* (Stanford, CA: Stanford University Press, 1955); Daniel E. Griffiths, *Administrative Theory* (New York: Appleton-Century Crofts, 1959); Andrew W. Halpin, *Theory and Research in Administration* (New York: Macmillan, 1966).

[8]B. Othanel Smith, William O. Stanley, and J. Harlan Shores, *Fundamentals of Curriculum Development* (New York: Harcourt, Brace & World, 1957); Florence B. Stratemeyer et al., *Developing a Curriculum for Modern Living* (New York: Teachers College Press, Columbia University, 1957); Arthur R. King and John A. Brownell, *The Curriculum and the Disciplines of Knowledge* (New York: John Wiley & Sons, 1966).

[9]Arno Bellack, *The Language of the Classroom* (New York: Teachers College Press, Columbia University, 1966).

[10]Ernest Nagel, "Symbolism and Science," in *Symbols and Values: An Initial Study*, ed. Lyman Bryson et al. (New York: Harper& Bros., 1954).

[11]This is a moot point. Cf. Hans Reichenback, *The Rise of Scientific Philosophy* (Berkeley: University of California Press, 1951); Richard Hare, *The Language of Morals* (Oxford, England: Clarendon Press, 1952); Patrick Corbett, *Ideologies* (New York: Harcourt, Brace & World, 1965).

[12]Jerome Bruner, *The Process of Education*, (Cambridge: Harvard University Press, 1960).

[13]Nicholas Lobkowicz, *Theory and Practice* (Notre Dame, IN: University of Notre Dame Press, 1967).

[14]John Dewey, *The Child and the Curriculum* (Chicago: University of Chicago Press, 1902).

[15]John Dewey, *Democracy and Education* (New York: Macmillan, 1961), 19.

[16]King and Brownell, *Curriculum and Disciplines*.

[17]Philip Phenix, *Realms of Meaning* (New York: McGraw-Hill, 1964).

[18]For a description of the "Talking Typewriter," see note one, Chapter Eleven. *Ed.*

[19]Dwayne Huebner, "The Implications of Psychological Thought for the Curriculum," in *Influences in Curriculum Change* (Washington, DC: ASCD, 1968). See also Maxine Greene "Curriculum Consciousness," in *Curriculum Theorizing: The Reconceptualists*, ed. William Pinar, 299–320 (Berkeley, CA: McCutchan, 1975).

[20]Herbert Marcuse, *Reason and Revolution* (New York: Oxford University Press, 1941).

[21]See James B. Macdonald, "Curriculum and Human Interest," in *Curriculum Theorizing: The Reconceptualists*, ed. William Pinar, 283–298 (Berkeley, CA: McCtchan, 1975).; Maurice Merleau-Ponty, *The Primacy of Perception* (Evanston, IL: Northwestern University Press,

1964); Paul Ricoeur, *Freedom and Nature: The Voluntary and the Involuntary*, trans. V. Kohak (Evanston, IL: Northwestern University Press, 1966).

[22]See James B. Macdonald, "Curriculum and Human Interest."

[23]Dwayne Huebner, "Poetry and Power: The Politics of Curricular Development." See Chapter Nineteen

[24]Paul Tillich, *The Protestant Era* (Chicago: University of Chicago Press, 1948).

19

Poetry and Power: The Politics of Curricular Development

(1975)

Fellow educators—are we not lost? Do we know where we are, remember where we have been, or foresee where we are going? We've talked about education for individuals since Rousseau, Kilpatrick, and Harold Benjamin. In our lostness, are we not jumping on bandwagons—yesterday core, group process, team teaching; today open classrooms and alternative schools—and assuming that at least these bandwagon experts know where they are? In our lostness are we not imbibing the snake oils and patent medicines—programmed individual computers, TV, structure and disciplines, sensitivity training—hoping that we can cure our maladies? But we find that our pain has been relieved only temporarily and that we may indeed have been taken in by a new breed of pusher. In our lostness, we recite the familiar litanies of humanism and individuality, hoping that the gods of our past will recognize our goodwill, forgive us our sins of omission and commission, and restore our sight and vitality.

Why do we move around so frantically—tugging at the coattails of our also lost neighbor and sampling his diverse wares? Why do we not comport ourselves in such a manner that our center—our sense of who we are and what we are about—can be restored and reformed? Why do we not pause to feel the painful tensions and pulls in us, which are reflections of the tensions and pulls of our society? Why do we not notice more carefully the direction of technical changes, social changes, and political changes? Why do we not listen more thoughtfully to the songs of the young, the anger of the oppressed, the labored breathing of those dying of overdoses of heroin or methadone, the painful cry of those bombed at Christmas time, the prideful platitudes of those in power? Why do we not act with courage—with the awareness that creation requires risk taking as well as statistical evidence? Why do we not reflect more critically on what we and others do—to discover in our institutions our bondage to others, and the bondages we impose?

Is it because we are afraid to acknowledge that power makes up our center—a power that necessarily comes up against the power of others: principals, parents, kids, board members, text writers. We are afraid, maybe even ashamed, to acknowledge that that which we are about as educators is politics: a struggle to maintain, maybe even change through destruction and reconstruction, the world we make with others. If we acknowledge that we are political we necessarily risk defeat, or maybe the awareness that we are indeed doing someone else's thing and are alienated from ourselves. If we acknowledge that we are political we risk recognizing our importance and hearing ourselves as braying asses or clanking symbols. It is far easier or safer to proclaim the individual and to then fit ourselves into a prepared slot: buy someone else's package of objectives, materials, and bets; or put on someone else's alternative school. Then if we fail, it is their fault, not ours.

Why are we lost? I think it is because we have let the school become our center and we have become an appendage, nothing but a role or functionary in someone else's institution. Institutions do not have memories, they cannot recall their past; who established them, under what circumstances, for what purposes. The people who started them disappear in the mindless routines. Only men and women have memories, an historical consciousness, and can recall how things got started, why and by whom. If we forget or never knew that schools are a product of men and women who used their power to build or maintain a certain kind of public world, then we easily become bondsmen of those who live only in the routines. We do their things, maintain their world, distribute their awards. And they reward us by a humdrum comfortable life style, perhaps with tenure and retirement, access to the more common goods of our production lines, and permit us the privacy of sex and family life, but deprive us of public vitality and joy, clean air and water, safe, comfortable, exciting urban areas that support our well-being and sociality.

If we remember that education is a political activity in which some people influence others, and that the school is one way to organize that power and influence, then perhaps we can try to share the control of the school and use it for our political purposes. Instead of our being an extension of the school, of someone else's will and power, the school can be, in part, an extension of our will and power—a vehicle for our political concerns. If we remember this, then we can recognize that the struggle to remake the school is a struggle to make a more just public world. If the school is a vehicle of political activity, then our lack of clarity, our lack of vision about the school is a function of our lack of clarity and vision about our public world—a breakdown in our talk, our poetry, about the world we make.

We do not talk about a more just public world; we talk about school, we think about school, and we see the world through the windows and doors of the school. The school has become our place. We have become school people, our language of learning, discipline, motivation, stimulus, individualization, is school language. Our images for generating new educational possibilities are school images. So we seek more diversified and smaller packages of instructional materials, not greater public access to information without federal control, or better development of cable television for neighborhood use. We seek open classrooms, not open societies. We seek alternative schools, not alternative public worlds. And because we are school people our public statements affirm the school, defend the present public school, and hide social injustice. Our propaganda of individualism is liberal cant that hides the basic conservatism of school people and permits those who control our public world to continue to control it. Our public statements are not socially or personally liberating. They do not excite us to imagine more just public worlds. They do not harness the power of people in the political struggle to reform our present inequitable institutions. They do not enable men or women to recognize and grasp their political right to share in the maintenance and reforming of our public world.

For instance, how much individuality can school people tolerate in an institution that is compulsory? The expression "curriculum for individuals" hides from our awareness that the school is a place of control; of socialization if you prefer this pseudo-scientific term that hides political domination. We maintain that control by our power. Of course, with our goodwill and out of our good graces we grant reasonable power to students to be individuals, providing they are not too individualistic in their speech, their actions, their commitments. Do we prefer the individualism of Thomas Paine, the Berrigan brothers, Ellsberg, Cleaver, Angela Davis, and the young men who went to Canada or Scandinavia rather than die in a tragic imperialistic war or the individualism of the Watergate caper boys, the I. T. T. executives, and perhaps those in the executive offices of the federal government?

Why have the court cases for racial equality, to permit long hair and dress options in schools, freedom of high school people to print politically oriented papers sometimes critical of the schools, the rights of pregnant girls to be in school, and the rights of Amish kids to stay out of public school been pushed by a few parents and civil libertarians rather than ASCDers? Can we honestly read those three words, *curriculum for individuality*, as other than propaganda to hide from our awareness our commitments as school people, and to put a verbal gloss on our intentions, which do not coincide with our practices. If we really believed those three words, we would not only be waiting for better materials, we would also be looking for court cases to restrain the power of school people and extend the constitutional rights of children and young people in the school. We would be training educators in workshops here at ASCD to attend to the legal implications of their control of and talk to the young, as Thomas[1] is doing for kids in Dayton. We would be building up a body of civil law about the rights of children that would be as much a part of our curricular knowledge as is child development. If we really believed those words, should not ASCD initiate movement among professional educators to modify or revoke compulsory attendance laws, to urge the U.S. postal service to stop subsidizing junk mail and advertisements and subsidize the publication of journals of opinion and fact which are dwindling in number. If we really believed these words would we not be working with nonschool people who are trying to increase the educational possibilities that exist outside the school?

By saying these things, I do not intend to come down on the side of Reimer[2] or Illich[3] who tell us that school is dead and urge us to deschool society (although I grant the value of contemplating death as a way of identifying the choices we have and have not made). Those proposals are also nonhistorical for us in the United States. It is necessary, rather, to see our schools, the materials and resources within them, and the social organizational patterns that result in historical perspective. The ways that we have thought about these during the first half of this century are not the ways we should think about them during the last quarter. Since the Second World War we have assumed that more of the same with better research for better living would do it, but Jencks,[4] among others, warns us that this is not so. Because we lack an educational poetry which stirs the imagination and harnesses our power we are forced to push our school images, our present school materials and organization to the breaking point, without conviction or results, but with a naive faith in our past ways. But the past must be rethought, not reused.

What then are we about as educators? We are not about maintaining schools, for that is the self-serving concern of school people who see their livelihood in the maintenance of that institution. We are about the conscious shaping of the future by helping the young work out, work through, or work into their futures and into our future. We have the utter gall to be concerned with the mundane destiny of individuals, ours and our students. Ours is not a power over individuals, but a power for individuals. And a power for the future of our public world. But which individuals, and what kind of future?

Oh yes, we are for the urban black, if he is not angry and will speak in moderate tones, accept our middle-class behavior, and affirm our future, thus perhaps giving up his. Oh yes, we are for the American Indian if he will give up his past and accept our future and our last forty-five years of public policy. Oh yes, we are for the homosexual if he will stay in the closet and not let his peculiarities stain our image of the future. Oh yes, we are for women, if they will accept their female role in our male future. Oh yes, we are for the Asian Marxist or Maoist if they will recognize that the way to the future is by maintaining present power balances. We are for those individuals who will protect and maintain our image of the future, but what of their imagined futures? If their tomorrow requires that we give up some of our privileges, will we still be for those individuals?

Those are the tensions we live in, are they not? The ambivalences of our commitments become obvious, do they not? For if we use our power for the future of all young we may indeed be in political conflict with our own self-interests. We are in that conflict, which is one reason that school people, although speaking a liberal political rhetoric, are essentially conservative in the political spectrum. Our individualism is a nineteenth-century individualism, aimed at the freedom of those who partake of the prevalent means of production and consumption. But with the 1972 election, it seems that liberalism is dead. We must now acknowledge that we are rightist or leftist and that there is no middle. But the school, make no mistake about it, is in the hands of the silent majority or conservative right, which might be an explanation of why the young radical leftist teacher either becomes socialized to the school and gives up his images of the future, or finds other ways to educate the young.

So our center of power as educators, a power for the future of the individual, comes in conflict with our own future, which is frequently an extension of the present. In this conflict we shift from power for to power over and thus to the conservative inertia of school people. Let us keep looking for other reasons, but if we turn to our center of power we easily recognize that a dedicated educator risks his imaged future as he works with the young. The educator working in schools can use the rules and rewards of the school to reduce or even remove that risk. He is thus tempted to control, not to liberate, and to justify the control by the political ideology of the free individual, which was rampant when some of us in this country had slaves and when many of us were in bondage to those in political and economic control.

Don't talk psychological individualism to me. Don't preach Kant's moral imperatives tinged with a religious doctrine of salvation. That is put-down language. Given the history of American education, the talk of school people about individuals is to be taken at face value—the clean face of middle-class America, the faces of blacks and Asians and Spanish and Native Americans and the poor and the handicapped.

Talk, rather, about the political tasks of making a more just public world. Talk about it in such a way that the political and economic nature of education can be clearly seen. Then talk about schools as our small share in the making of a more just public world.

What are the ingredients of this talk? There are three, three rights, if you wish, to which we must attend and which must govern our talk about the public world and then the school.

First, the unconditional respect for the political, civil, and legal rights of the young as free people participating in a public world. This is what Frymier[5] is urging. But for thousands of years we have been talking this way, and only within the past hundred—nay the past ten or fifteen have we grounded this right in law. Discrimination by race, sex, or religion has only recently come under legal attack, and gradually the rights of individuals are being publicly recognized. Now we are about to struggle to end discrimination by age—and the power over the young by adults must be brought into question. Thus Thomas, in his Student Rights Center in Dayton is teaching kids to sit back when teachers verbally accost them or manhandle them and then to say quietly: "You know, ma'am, I can sue you for that—and I will with the support of adults who really believe in the individuality—the civil rights of kids."

The second right is the right of access to the wealth in the public domain—I mean primarily the knowledge, traditions, skills that shape and increase a person's power in the public world.

This is what we are about today, although we are not consciously aware of it. The exciting development of the past ten to fifteen years has indeed been the increase in scope, quality, and quantity of instructional materials. But expressing these developments as developments in instructional materials hides more important considerations. Instructional materials are a way—almost the way—that adult society makes the public wealth available to the young. The skills of teachers are the other major way. We tend to talk of these resources as means to learning, and indeed this is an appropriate way to speak—but no longer a powerful way. For instance, reading is not just a skill that must be learned, it is a tradition of using printed materials. Now children of two and three and four have access to that tradition in trade books, in *The Electric Company*,[6] in story reading in preschools. It is an expensive business, but publishing paperback and hardcover books is now a money-making activity, so our commercial world now seeks to make this tradition available to young children. If the tradition, the wealth of print, is not being brought to certain kids, the question is not how can they learn to read, but how can the tradition be reworked, embodied in new materials and skills. This is a technical problem—of print technology, of the art of book writing and making, of teacher education. It is an economic problem, for it costs money to design materials for new populations. It costs money to give teachers the skills to bring the wealth of print to children who have not shared in that wealth for the first four or five years of their life. It is also a political problem, for two reasons. If private industry cannot make money distributing the public wealth, then will public funds be used to design new delivery systems for our print wealth; or will we use public monies to design delivery systems for our new traditions of death, killing innocent populations of Third World children? In addition, not all of our collective wealth in print is seen as valuable by all people. Those who want to maintain a certain kind of public world will see that some traditions are available to the young and others are not. Thus for years the language of sexual development and sexual relations was distributed via the peer group; only within recent years has it been deemed valuable enough to distribute it in print for children. Community fights over library books, books assigned to certain courses in high school, and the censorship and bias of text materials demonstrate lucidly the political control over the distribution of our print traditions. This reinterpretation of instructional materials has other explanatory power, best illustrated by the changes in the teaching of reading over the past fifteen years which now makes possible today the open primary classroom.

Remember that twenty years ago Olson[7] at Michigan was talking about individualized reading. Then we had reading textbooks, reading workbooks, and a few elementary school libraries. We had no paperback books, few language games, and no talking typewriters.[8] Even ten years ago Alice Miel[9] and Leland Jacobs[10] of Columbia were talking about individualized reading— but the practice demanded that teachers spend hours of their time cutting apart workbooks, gathering reading materials, making language games. Today the picture is different. Reading texts and workbooks are becoming passé. Almost every publisher is now working on self-diagnostic and self-prescriptive materials keyed to collections of paperback books. The group reading instruction is almost over, and the day of the bluebirds, the cardinals, and the chickadees is over or can be over. As Frymier[11] pointed out, an increased variety of materials can change the organization of the school.

What Frymier did not point out is that we have here an example of an old Marxian insight. The means of production and consumption determine (or at least influence) the relationship of one person with another. The quality of the relationship of kids to kids and kids to teacher depends on the goods in the school. Authoritarianism and dictatorships are frequently necessary when we have scarce goods. Furthermore, human skills are developed to be compatible with the goods. Teachers who develop authoritarian skills to match textbooks can easily transform diverse reading goods into textual type materials. Thus, we have an inherent tension between the rights of an individual as an individual, and the demands placed on him by the inequitable distribution of public wealth.

How do we make the public wealth of this world—the traditions, knowledge, information— accessible to children? We do so through our economy and through the political process of allocating scarce funds. We do it by training artists and technicians to redesign this wealth for children of a variety of ages. We are doing it with print—it remains to be done for the traditions of math, knowledge of humankind and society, the knowledge of the natural or physical world, the traditions of music, art, dance. But the problem is not a school problem. It is a problem about the shape of our public world. It is related to the debates over xerography and copyrights, the use of cable television, the rights of reporters to the privacy of their sources, the censorship of the "Pentagon Papers" and "Deep Throat," the pressures of this administration on the press and the national television networks, and presidential control of information.

What we should keep in focus is the right of access to public wealth; the traditions, knowledge, and information that should be in the public realm. This is a problem of technology, of economics, and of politics. As educators we cannot simply await the development of new technologies, we must be politically active to create a public world where this access is increased. As this public world becomes more accessible to the young in a variety of materials, media, and skills, then the shape of the school will change. We should not concern ourselves primarily with the shape of the school—but with the accessibility to public wealth from which new alternatives to school will become obvious.

The last right with which we must be concerned as educators is the right of each individual, regardless of age, to participate in the shaping and reshaping of the institutions within which he lives. This right carries with it the possibility of the destruction of existing institutions and the formation of new ones. This is what community control and teacher unions and negotiation are all about. It was what teacher-pupil planning was about fifteen to twenty years ago. It is *not* what competency-based teacher education, PPBS,[12] and performance contracting are about.

For years teachers suffered under the nearly-absolute power of boards and administrators. Teacher unions corrected this. Strong community pressure groups have now come up against strong boards and teacher unions. Left unorganized is the student group, although this is being done slowly. The student rights and student advocacy movement is to this end. But the movement in education is slow because of our technical mentality of means-ends and our political conservative mentality. If we are concerned about the individual, then we must be concerned with his right to participate in governing the structures that determine his public and private life, including the school.

ASCD has backed off from this right of individuals. When first formed in the late forties, ASCD had as its major concern the development of process skills for the democratic running of schools, helping administrators and supervisors work with teachers in supportive ways to improve the schools. As the fifties and sixties unfolded and it became obvious that curricular development was a function not only of staff development, but also of planning with academicians, material specialists, laity, and kids, ASCD lost hold of its role in the development of the skills of institution building. Working with teachers and administrators was one kind of political task, working with blacks, with parents, with kids, and with interest groups was another kind of political task.

So ASCD gave up its concern for developing political competencies and leaned back in the characteristic style of liberal individualism. It said people need to know what is happening, what is new, and then in the good old spirit of American individualism they will make changes in the school.

The school is but a manifestation of public life. As educators we must be political activists who seek a more just public world. The alternative, of course, is to be school people—satisfied with the existing social order—the silent majority who embrace conservatism.

If the members of ASCD remain school people, I predict the death of ASCD as a professional organization.

Harold Shane is wrong when he said we can have a big enough umbrella to embrace all school people. To me that evokes an image of a group of people under a wind-blown umbrella, heads dry, feet in the mud, the rivers rising. We should leave the umbrella. Some of us should be building the dikes of civil rights legislation for children. Some of us should be building organizations for better governance of institutions. Some of us should be preserving and making accessible the storehouse of knowledge and traditions and information for our young and old.

Another image: this conference and those of the past few years strike me as a smorgasbord. Take your pick, please your palate, take home a memory or two—all in the spirit of free enterprise and rampant individualism. Contrast that image to the Last Supper—a few people, sharing something in common, breaking bread and drinking wine, and then changing the shape of the public world.

ASCD will surely die if the smorgasbord continues as its metaphor. It might live—smaller, more powerful—if the metaphor shifts.

NOTES

[1]Arthur E. Thomas, was the director of The Center for the Study of Student Citizenship, Rights and Responsibilities in Dayton, Ohio. A former elementary school teacher and assistant principal, Thomas founded the center following his dismissal by the Dayton Board of Education for his involvement in protecting black students during the first violent days of school integration in Dayton. The Center's work focused on the advocacy and protection of student rights through legal assistance, parent and community information, and the organization of student groups. The Center's publications include A. E. Thomas, "Can They Do These Things to Us?," *Rap Magazine*, November, 1971; Ralph Faust and A. E. Thomas, *Student Rights Handbook for Dayton Ohio*, (Dayton, Ohio, Center for the Study of Student Citizenship, Sept. 1971). See also "Community Power and Student Rights: An Interview with Arthur E. Thomas" *Harvard Educational Review* 42, no. 2 (May 1972): 173–216. *Ed.*

[2]See Everett W. Reimer, *School is Dead: Alternatives in Education* (Garden City, NY: Doubleday, 1971). *Ed.*

[3]See Ivan Illich, *Deschooling Society* (New York: Harper and Row, 1970), also Ivan Illich, *After Deschooling, What?* ed. Alan Gartner et al. (New York: Harper and Row, 1973). *Ed.*

[4]See Christopher Jencks, *Inequality; A Reassessment of the Effect of Family and Schooling in America* (New York: Basic Books, 1972); C. Jencks and Susan Bartlett et al., *Who Gets Ahead?: The Determinants of Economic Success in America* (New York: Basic Books, 1979); C. Jencks, *Rethinking Social Policy: Race, Poverty, and the Underclass* (Cambridge, MA: Harvard University Press, 1992). *Ed.*

[5]See Jack R. Frymier *The Nature of Educational Method* (Columbus, Ohio: Charles E. Merrill, 1965): Jack R. Frymier, *A School for Tomorrow* (Berkeley, CA: McCutcheon, 1973). *Ed.*

[6]"The Electric Company," was a production of the Children's Television Workshop, creators of "Sesame Street." The programming sought specifically to teach second graders to read.

Through music, skits, comedy, acting (Bill Cosby and Rita Morena), and diverse electronic media, the sights and sounds of the alphabet were brought to life for half hour segments. In 1972, according to Martin Mayer, the show had gained such wide acceptance in the schools that fifty percent of the nation's elementary schools with televisions in the classroom were viewing the show, twenty-three percent overall. See Mayer, "The Electric Company: Easy Reader and a Lot of Other Hip Teachers," *New York Times Magazine* (January 1973), 15–26. *Ed.*

[7]Willard C. Olson, *Child Development* (Boston: Heath, 1949); see also Willard C. Olson, *How Children Grow and Develop* (Chicago: Science Research Associates, 1953). *Ed.*

[8]For a description of the "talking typewriter" see note one, Chapter Eleven. *Ed.*

[9]Alice Miel et al., *Individualized Reading Practices* (New York: Teachers College, Columbia University, 1958). *Ed.*

[10]Leland Jacobs, ed., *Using Literature with Young Children* (New York: Teachers College Press, 1965); see also Virgil E. Herrick and Leland Jacobs *Children and the Language Arts*, (Englewood cliffs, NJ: Prentice-Hall, 1955). *Ed.*

[11]See note five.

[12]PPBS refers to "Planning, Programming, and Budgeting System." Variously it was employed during the 1970s by the Department of Defense, library information managers and in educational administration and policy. For a discussion and critique of this approach to edcuational planning see R. A. Smith, ed., *Regaining Educational Leadership: Critical Essays on PBTE/CBTE, Behavioral Objectives and Accountability* (New York: Wiley, 1975). See also Melvin R. Levin, et. al., ed., *Educational Investment in an Urban Society: Costs, Benefits, and Public Policy* (New York: Teachers College, 1970). *Ed.*

20

Curriculum Field: Its Wake and Our Work

(1976)

The field of curriculum has been diagnosed as moribund by Joseph J. Schwab.[1] The symptoms he noted were the incoherence of the curriculum, the failures and discontinuities within schooling, and various flights from the proper subject of the field. The cause of the malady was identified as the "inveterate, unexamined, and mistaken reliance on *theory*"[2]—theories adopted by and constructed within the field. Professor Schwab predicted that a "renascence" of the field would occur only if curriculum energies were "diverted from theoretic pursuits" to "modes of operation" that were "practical, ... quasi-practical, and ... eclectic."[3] In an intellectual tour de force, he then developed his theories of the arts of the practical and of the eclectic. His theory of the nature of deliberation, one of the arts of the practical, is a significant contribution to those aspects of educational practice concerned with decision-making and institutional governance. Even more significant is his theory of the eclectic procedures by which the diverse theories can be used in and for educational practice, while maintaining both the integrity of the theories and the practical contexts of education.[4]

Obviously, the soundness of a diagnosis is a function of the available evidence and the visibility of the symptoms. In a field such as curriculum, traditionally ambiguous and replete with ideological stands, such evidence and symptoms are themselves apt to be a function of the observer's interest. Schwab grants that his evidence is only suggested, not cited. Indeed, it is too sketchy to warrant consensual validation. The opposite claim is asserted by B. O. Smith—that the curriculum movement has been and continues to be a powerful force in educational progress. Professor Smith claims that from the "nebulous concepts" of "freedom, openness, activity, self-expression, and creativity" have sprung a succession of innovations; and that the very "vagueness and am-

241

biguity" of the concepts "is their fertility."[5] He acknowledges the ideological and slogan function of curricular discourse.

For me, Professor Smith's claim is warranted historically. But the fact that the curriculum field has always attracted individuals with strong convictions certainly militates against my agreeing generally with this diagnosis. From where I stand, Schwab's diagnosis carries more weight today. The poor health of the field is shown by the lack of vitality in its publications and national conferences, by the failure of so-called curriculum specialists or leaders to make an impact on national debate about educational programs, and by the general state of the schools, at least those within my ken.

Professor Schwab is not alone in identifying the cause of the field's difficulty as the use of "theory." Decker Walker takes a similar stand in his fine critical review of the twenty-sixth yearbook of the NSSE.[6] He claims that the foundations of the field, laid in the 1920s and 1930s, were inadequate or unsound, in part because the members of the NSSE committee "attempted to resolve practical disputes—disputes over what should be done about the curriculum—as if they were theoretical disputes."[7] Walker, like Schwab, makes valid prescriptions, one of which is that curriculum discourse should be disciplined by actual policy debates in concrete educational situations; without such focusing, "curricular discourse lacks point."[8] Professor Walker grants the potential oversimplification of his claim, yet argues, correctly I believe, that greater attention to the mechanisms and procedures of curriculum policy-making would be an expedient corrective.

Neither Schwab nor Walker has convincingly established that theory is the cause of the problem. Both state that theoretic discourse seeks to establish truth, whereas practical discourse seeks to establish right or appropriate action. I believe they would not find support for the distinction between theoretic and practical discourse from the positions of Heidegger, the later Wittgenstein, the Critical Theorists, or Alan Blum. Although I, too, find much ineffective discourse within the curriculum field, that is not because it is theoretical but because it accomplishes little in the social world and has little use value. The problem is that the language and the practice of education are nearly independent. Educational practice too often is inarticulate, unconnected to the legitimating and descriptive powers of language; and educational discourse is too often unconditioned by educational practice, except by the practice of college classrooms and educational conventions.

I am less sanguine than Schwab and see no reason to hope for a renascence, although I wish for a reincarnation in a simpler and more original form. If the publication of Bobbitt's *The Curriculum*[9] marked the early maturity of the curriculum field, then the past ten to fifteen years were its golden years. Now the end is here. Many individuals and groups with various intentions have gathered together around this now aged enterprise, "curriculum." Let us acknowledge its demise gather at the wake, celebrate joyously what our forebears made possible—and then disperse to do our work, because we are no longer members of one household. The term *curriculum* no longer serves to unify us. The dispersing forces are too great, the attraction of new associations and the possibilities of new households too compelling. The people need our diverse capabilities; but if our energies continue to be applied to holding ourselves together, we will have no energies left to serve them. If the diverse interests and collectivities that have been gathering over the past seventy years were cleared away, we might be able to see the original conception of curriculum and to do and describe our work more effectively.

The historical groundwork for such a reassessment is lacking, as writer after writer has observed. The few historical studies available have helped us with our general orientation in time, but we still do not have the historical critiques needed to reinterpret our task and suggest the work before us. To be sure, Walker has attempted such a reassessment in his review of the twenty-sixth yearbook of the NSSE.[10] Seguel's *The Curriculum Field: Its Formative Years*[11] helps us understand the basic literature and early workers in the field. Kliebard[12] has helped us to see the relationship between the work of Bobbitt, Charters, and Tyler, and the efficiency movement associated with Taylor in the first decades of this century. Cremin[13] has called our attention to the significance of William Torrey Harris as a precursor usually ignored by the curriculum specialist. Barry Franklin[14] is working on the relationship between curriculum study and the interest in social control in the twenties. But the crucial period, it seems to me, is not the past sixty years; I think that Cremin is correct in claiming that the basic paradigm was established in the post-Civil War period, the work of Harris being extremely significant. Cremin says:

> Education, Harris once explained in a brief statement of his pedagogical creed, is a process "by which the individual is elevated into the species" or alternatively, a process by which a self-active being is enabled to become privy to the accumulated wisdom of the race. And it is the task of the curriculum to make that accumulated wisdom economically and systematically available. "The question of the course of study—involving as it does the selection of such branches as shall in the most effective manner develop the substantial activity as well as the formal activity of the child—is the most important question which the educator has before him...." The instrument of the process would be the textbook, which Harris saw as the pedagogical tool par excellence in a newspaper civilization where public opinion ruled and where the entire community needed access to similar facts and arguments if harmony was to be achieved. The energizer of the process would be the teacher, who would use the recitation to get the pupil to deliberate over what he has read and to relate it to his own life. And the monitor of the process would be the examination, whereby pupils could be frequently classified and then moved individually through a carefully graded system.... All the pieces were present for the game of curriculum-making that would be played over the next

half-century; only the particular combinations and the players would change.[15]

But identifying the paradigm as originating with Harris does not reveal the current problem, which is to distinguish those interests essential to the curriculum from others that can stand on their own or might more profitably be associated with other facets of education. It is helpful to begin with the meaning of "curriculum." The word points to the diverse, perhaps even paradoxical, intentions of educators, it is loaded with ambiguity; it lacks precision, generally referring only to educational programs within schools. The political significance of educational programs and the ambiguity of the word encourage programmatic definitions of "curriculum"[16] and its frequent use in educational slogans.[17] These usages have brought together educators or individuals with diverse educational interests wishing to legitimate their programmatic interests in the content of the school. Since the 1900s the curriculum family has included those interested in content, method, teacher education, human development and freedom, social progressivism or conservatism, educational technology, evaluation, and educational objectives or purposes. These diverse interest groups have made their impact, in one way or another, on our ways of practicing and talking about curriculum. However, the word can no longer contain such diversity. Meetings of curricular specialists and departments of curriculum lack focus, and "curricular" discourse is losing or has lost its effectiveness. Our solution to this problem is not to abuse our discourse by labeling it theoretical, but to sort out the different interests it expresses.

Some of these interests, such as curriculum development have served their function and now require relocation within other practices of education. Others, such as "child-centered curriculum," have distorted the way our work is understood and confused our intentions by covering inherent tensions or contradictions; these contradictions must now be faced. Yet other interests, such as social content, have fundamentally altered our work, but our language is inadequate to describe the new task.

My central thesis is that we accept, as the core of our work, the root meaning of "curriculum"[18]— that we attend to the course of study. We must, of course, be careful not to become entangled in the historically limited meanings of that term, not to refer only to a syllabus, for what is studied is much more than that. Dewey warns us of this limitation when he reminds us, in *Democracy and Education*, that "we never educate directly, but indirectly by means of the environment."[19] Our problem is to explore the nature of the course of study—the content—and to eliminate the interests which do not bear directly upon this content. A return to Harris and Dewey will help focus our problem and place in perspective the interests peripheral to it.

In 1870, before the National Teachers' Associations in Cleveland, Harris said:

> The state of human nature only exists as a product of culture.... To achieve his destiny, to become aught that is distinctively human, he must be able to combine with his fellowman and sum up the results of the race in each individual.... It is not necessary for each member of the human family to repeat in detail the experience of all his predecessors, for their results descend to him by the system of combination in which he lives, and by education he acquires them. With these he may stand on top of the ladder of human culture, and build a new round to it so that his children after him may climb higher and do the like.[20]

Harris moved very quickly from this concern for "culture" or the "wisdom of the race" to its embodiment in books, especially textbooks, which made specific the course of study. In a later essay, delivered at the 1896 National Educational Association meeting in Buffalo, he concisely summed up his view:

> The proper use of the printed page is the greatest of all arts taught in the school. How to get out of printed words and sentences the original thought and observation recorded there—how to verify these and critically go over the steps of the author's mind is the method of discovery and leads to the only real progress. For real progress comes from availing one's self of the wisdom of the race and using it as an instrument of new discovery. That other method, sometimes commended, of original investigation without aid from books forgets that mankind have toiled for long thousands of years to construct a ladder of achievement and that civilization is on the highest round of this ladder. It has invented school education in order that youth may climb quickly to the top on the rounds which have been gilded one by one slowly in the lapse of the ages. The youth shall profit vicariously by the thought and experience of those who have gone before.[21]

Harris associated the origins of Western schooling with the establishment of the printing press, and seemed to claim that "culture," the "wisdom of the race," is stored or made accessible in books. He opposed rote memorizing of the contents of books and made a case for students' interpreting textual material. Today it could be said that he argued for a hermeneutical approach to the text. Harris distrusted the teacher's ability to make available the "wisdom of the race" orally, a method he associated with Pestalozzi and Rousseau. We cannot easily dismiss Harris, because he played an extremely important part in the formation of village and city graded schools as superintendent of St. Louis from 1868 to 1880, and U.S. Commissioner of Education from 1889 to 1906.

The course of study, embodied in the text, is a selection from the culture or the "wisdom of the race," preserved and presented to the student for his interpretation and use. Underlying Harris's orientation was the technology of the book, which shaped his conception of education and indeed his educational

method and school organization. Print technology was part of the substructure—the economic system—that made possible his curriculum paradigm, his
educational method, and the graded school organization. Harris associated culture and the wisdom of the race with the printed word. Interestingly enough, in
his defense of the kindergarten methods established in St. Louis, he acknowledged the significance of language as it is learned in the home and the significance of play for children aged four through seven, particularly when shaped by
Froebel's methods. For Harris, play stopped and work started at the age of
seven, when confrontation with text began.

> By language the child rises from an animal individuality to a human individu-
> ality. By realizing his membership in society, and conforming his deeds to the
> general standard, he develops a higher spiritual individuality. This ... is the
> object of the kindergarten plays and games. When it is achieved, the method
> of play gives place to the method of work; the symbolic yields to the conven-
> tional; the kindergarten methods to the methods of the primary schools.[22]

Two themes in the work of Harris are central to our work. The first is that
concern for the course of study in educational institutions is a concern for content, which is in turn derived from conceptions of "culture" or the "wisdom of
the race." Harris, as he wrote about and shaped primary and postprimary education, seemed to define culture as that which was available in books ("knowledge," as it was known before Piaget and Wittgenstein).

From culture to content to course of study is the direction of our work as seen
by Harris. Although he thought that the wisdom of the race was primarily to be
found in books, his attention to the language of young children, and to play and
games as appropriate content of the kindergarten, seems to anticipate the difficulty that curriculum people have always experienced with the word "culture."
I shall argue that discourse about educational content is discourse about culture,
and that different interpretations of content since the turn of the century are, in
part, contributions to the discourse about culture. The curriculum specialist
seems to have gotten caught in a distinction between culture and society, a distinction that became reasonably well fixed through the influence of Parsons[23]
and other positivistically inclined social scientists; it has contributed to our recent malaise. Differing conceptions of culture have confused our sense of direction and our discourse, because they have been framed, not as problems
concerning a course of study, but as problems concerning the purpose of
schools. We have confused possible content with purpose. Of course, we must
consider purpose when we concern ourselves with the form and potential educational value of curricular content. Only when we do can we consider whether
we want some particular content in a particular school. But we have tended to
subsume questions about content under questions of purpose. By doing so we
have seldom thrown much light on the form and the educational value of what

we plan to teach. We have instead become trapped in debates about what is good for society, trapped in ideological or political discourse.

The second theme in Harris, and one that seems to me to be central to our work, concerns *the way* in which this culture is made accessible or made present for specific students.[24] This educational technology thread is commonly thought to have followed from the scientific developments of this century (or late in the last century) as they were applied to education and schooling. However, I am inclined to believe the opposite, that the scientific interests follow from the technical interest of educators.[25] The development of the so-called scientific movement in education may have been an extension of the technologies or techniques of education. The development of a science, or indeed of any body of knowledge, illuminates the human condition, if technical knowledge is used reflexively to interpret one's actions and history rather than as an instrument of control.

The other components of Harris's curriculum, as identified by Cremin—the nature of the student and the function of the teacher, examinations, and school organizations—are not, in my view, part of the work of the curriculum person, although they necessarily impinge upon his work in school settings. Rather, they deal with the interest of all educators in the rights and freedom of the individual, in the nature of educational relationships and social control, and in the management and evolution of social institutions.

Dewey addressed the problem of the course of study in a variety of places.[26] His short essay on the theory of the course of study in Paul Munroe's 1915 edition of the *Cyclopedia of Education* neatly summarizes his views. Writing during a transitional period, Dewey says that the "subjects" of the school are not set and fixed, that new ones have been and should be introduced. He recognizes, as does Harris, that "*the studies represent selections* and formulations of what is regarded as most important in the experience of the race, and hence most necessary to transmit for the sake of the future of society."[27] He regards studies from the external or social perspective, as well as from the perspective of the student. Dewey did not suggest that we select content by studying the child; rather, he showed how content, selected from culture, could be formed so as to be useful to the child. He states, for example, that "the child's present experience and the subject matter of instruction, instead of existing as two separate worlds, one wholly psychological and the other wholly logical, *represent two changing or dynamic limits of one continuous social process.*"[28] This, of course, was his progressive organization of subject matter. Almost foreshadowing Piaget, Dewey states that "children must begin naturally with simple operations, whether in cooking, weaving, woodwork, or whatever."[29] Instead of Piaget's genetic epistemological perspective, of course, he uses a social historical perspective—recapitulation—to describe the genesis of social knowledge in the individual. He continues: "These simple operations agree of necessity in their main features of crude material and simple tools and technique with the operations of men in the less developed, the earlier, periods of social life."[30]

Dewey agrees with Harris about the first theme of our work—the selection and formulation of content from the "experience of the race"—though he differs with Harris's narrow interpretation of culture. But he does not introduce the study of the child as another source of content. Today we might say that Dewey urged study of the child for the second aspect of our work—to produce knowledge that can be used technically—to help make the culture present for or accessible to specific students. The foreshadowing of Piaget is significant. Piaget, looking at hypothetical-deductive and mathematical knowledge in the child, has described the structure of cultural forms in such a way that they become useful or usable for individuals of different ages. Piaget's work does not offer us a new interpretation of culture or of knowledge. Rather, he extends present interpretations into their biological or sensorimotor ground, exploring the hidden form of this knowledge, a form we have taken for granted. In a sense he points to Polanyi's[31] *subsidiary awareness*. Dewey's concern for occupation has somewhat the same quality. He argued that adult forms of social knowledge have their sources in the occupations of "primitive" people; other educational technologies are needed to make them available to children.

I have used these portions of Dewey to support the claim that in our work we must attend to two threads of investigation. The first is the identification of those segments of culture, the "wisdom of the race," that can become the content of the course of study. The second is the identification of the technologies by which this content can be made accessible or made present to particular individuals. The first is describing the what, the second is making it an object of study. That is the core of our work: if "curriculum" has any meaning left today, it is in the identification and the making present of content to persons.

To see how the other diverse interests associated with curriculum since the turn of the century relate to these two aspects of our work, it is necessary to notice something that has clouded our vision, confused our intentions, and distorted our communication and discourse. This is the inherent tension between the interests of the individual and the social interests that have impact upon that individual—the phenomena of social control. Educators are caught in this tension. On the one hand, we proclaim the dignity of the person, speaking of self-realization, individual freedom, or individual potential; on the other hand, we recognize the commitment to a social order—its needs, requirements, and realities. Over the years' this conflict has been resolved in a variety of ways.

In 1901, speaking of the "last two generations of educational history," Dewey expressed the hope that educators were "nearing the close of the time of tentative, blind, empirical experimentation; that we are close to the opportunity of planning our work on the basis of a coherent philosophy of experience and of the relations of school studies to that experience; that we can accordingly take up steadily and wisely the effort of changing school conditions so as to make real the aims that command the assent of intelligence."[32] Thus, Dewey sought to resolve this tension through a unified philosophical position. In the decade of the first world war and in the twenties, the scientific movement in education offered hope that the conflict could be removed by the processes of science. In the forties, some educators hoped it could be resolved through democratic involvement of all parties. In the fifties, Tyler advocated, in effect, a management system to resolve the conflict: priority among the diverse interests could be established by defining objectives and screening them through a "philosophy" of education and an articulated psychology of learning. In the late fifties and early sixties, some hoped that this tension could be resolved by systems analysis or by the powers of new-found technologies. In the late sixties and early seventies, the hope that the conflict could be resolved at all was shattered. Detailed attention to the history of schooling and critical studies of the relation of the school to the social-economic order suggested that the tension was inherent in the process of education. The two most recent critical studies to point out the manifestations of this conflict are Bowles and Gintis's *Schooling in Capitalist America*,[33] and Sharp and Green's fascinating study of English progressive primary, education, *Education and Social Control*.[34]

The interests of the person and the controlling interests of social groups are not to be reconciled in a schema or an interpretation that hides the contradiction or seeks to overcome it. Revealing the essential tension between those with power and those without, if it is not immediately visible to either party, enables the conflict to be used educationally for both. Dialectical thought has this capability when it seeks the historical and socioeconomic sources of current conflict and projects new possibilities for the powerful and the powerless. The practical resolution of the conflict is not to be found in technical or managerial procedures which assume that conflicts can be healed with greater technical sophistication, more specific definitions of learning outcomes, or newly defined educational arts. Too frequently these merely confirm the existing distribution of power, taking the shape of discipline, grades, credentials, and labels, and serve the unquestioned interests of the collective which owns or uses the techniques or arts. If the educator recognizes that conflicts of interest in schools and classrooms are manifestations of underlying socials contradictions, that they have historical and socioeconomic roots, they can be seen to require political rather than educational action. Instead of mediating in any way between the presumed interests of the student and the expressed interest of social groups, we should struggle to keep these inherently contradictory interests distinct and separate.

During the past six decades of this century curriculum lost the vision of its work, in part because it assumed that these contending interests could be reconciled by appropriate educational practices. Considering the literature of this period, let us raise four questions. (1) How have the inherent contradictions been handled between the controlling social interests and the liberating or emanci-pating drives in each person? (2) Have the interested parties provided new in-terpretations of the content of culture? (3) Have new technologies been developed by which content is made present to persons of differing circum-stances? (4) Has our work been confused by too great concern with aspects of education that should be associated with other educational functions? A brief look at the study of the person will illustrate how we may answer.

As observed earlier, Dewey's concern for the child, although he did not so express it, can now be seen as a contribution to the technology of curriculum. In the educational enterprise, child study may be viewed as part of the search for scientifically based technical knowledge. The child-study and child-centered curriculum movement, however, distorted the concern for content and the rein-terpretation of culture by ignoring the contradiction between the child and the established social interests and by romanticizing the child. On the face of it, Kilpatrick was influential in this distortion. Yet if the contradiction is an inher-ent one, in which specific conflicts are to be analyzed dialectically and synthe-sized politically, our making the welfare of the student a curriculum concern weakened both our work and our political task. Interest in the welfare of the stu-dent need not, and should not, be taken over by those who work at identifying and presenting culture as educational content. We show that interest by the way we make content useful to the student. However, the concern with child-centered curriculum earlier in the century had other effects. The child-study movement as-sociated with Prescott's work in the late forties provided an opportunity for teachers and other educators to reflect upon the influence of their behavior on young people; it deepened the self-awareness of the adult. Studying the child became a way of studying oneself. But the interests controlling schooling easily distorted this reflexive quality of child study, as they have done with reinforce-ment theory and behavior modification, with the aim of increasing the possibil-ities for adult control of the student. Works such as deMause's[35] and others, which place in historical perspective the relationship between adults and chil-dren, assist the educator in recalling that self-reflection may be one of the im-portant educational functions of child study.[36]

The child-study movement and the burgeoning child-development literature reveal one interest that properly belongs to our work and two that do not. Direct scientific knowledge of the child can be a technical resource for the reinterpre-tation and presentation of culture—educational content for the child as Piaget's work demonstrates. We are in need of more studies of "genetic culture" paral-leling Piaget's examination of the scientific and logical. Those child-study in-terests which show themselves as care for the child's creativity, power, and self-realization can be fostered more directly by political movements, such as those which recently took the form of child advocacy. The educator who mis-takenly considers love and sensitivity to people a curriculum issue clouds our work and defuses the political struggle for justice. This interest needs to be separated from the traditions of curriculum and associated with other human rights movements. Although knowledge about the child or the young can be used in the more effective "making present" of culture for the student, it can also be used technically for further control and manipulation. The corrective to this tendency is not to assume that the good intentions of the curriculum person and educator, a presumed altruism, will protect the child. We have no strong reason to expect this. In fact, there are those who have claimed that increased national spending for the behavioral sciences is directly or indirectly motivated by the need for social control. The increased specialization of labor in education, which presumably produces more knowledge about the child, in effect increases the number of experts who study children, falsely promises that such expertise will bring liberation, reduces the social demand for fairness and justice in the schools, and probably obstructs the development of those social interest groups which could advocate the child's interest in educational policy. The refusal of some black communities a few years ago to permit further study of their children is a case in point.

Also associated with child study is an interest in self-understanding, which belongs more properly to the humanities than to the curriculum. Any new knowledge is humanistic in that it can promote self-understanding if used reflexively. Child study sheds as much light on the adult world as upon the child's; it informs our philosophies, religions, and sociopolitical orientations, and thus functions as an aspect of liberal—or liberating—education.

Curriculum over the past fifty years has encompassed an interest in aspects of social life as potential educational content, which has broadened our interpretation of content, and consequently of culture. However, the interest in social life has distorted our work in two ways. First, ideological argument has arisen over the function of the school. In specific sociohistorical contexts, this argument is a necessary and critical part of policy making and hence legitimately accompanies the politics of educational governance. However, as discourse about curriculum, this ideological diversion obscures the questions of how social content is to be made present for the student and how it is related to other equally appropriate forms of educational content. Both the policy clarification problem and the technical problem are hidden by ideological components.

The second distortion caused by social content in the curriculum has been a philosophical argument between the perennialist-essentialists and the reconstructionist-experimentalists. This dispute does a disservice to developments in modern philosophy and social thought, as well as impeding our work as educators concerned with content.

Bobbitt called attention to the social as educational content, and attempted to develop a technology by which this content could be made present for students of different circumstances. This technology was not refined until recently, partly because of the ideological and pseudo-philosophical issue. With the advent of systems analysis and video technologies, social content is again being explored, as the diverse competency-based movements indicate. Philosophical support for the interest in the social as "culture"— as content—which was earlier developed on the foundation of Linton's anthropology by Smith, Stanley, and Shores in their valuable and deservedly well-known volume,[37] is today found, for example, in Schutz and Luckmann's *The Structures of the Life-World*,[38] an application of the methods of phenomenology to the social world. Schutz makes the distinction between the knowledge structures of everydayness and those of the sciences and logical systems. If culture is interpreted as the "wisdom of the race," it seems quite evident that that wisdom exists not only in symbolic structures, but also in all sorts of traditions and institutions. Given this awareness, the problem of content is one of asking how diverse traditions are made educationally accessible to persons in differing circumstances. In one sense, then, social content, whether that of conservatives such as Bobbitt or reconstructionists such as Smith, Stanley, and Shores, has added to the reinterpretation of content, and thus of culture. Ignored in Bobbitt's analysis, but present in that of Smith, Stanley, and Shores, is the problem of how culture, in its various manifestations, evolves and changes. The competency-based movement, so similar in some ways to the social-activity analysis of Bobbitt, often ignores this aspect, and thus errs in favor of maintaining the status quo, presumably in the collective interest. Social content requires a distinction similar to that identified for symbolic content by Schwab[39] between the syntax of stable inquiry and the syntax of long-term or fluid inquiry.

The social content made present to the student is frequently something to which he or she must adjust—the syntax of stable inquiry—rather than a field of political possibilities requiring historical and political skills—the long-term syntax of social life. The fact that each person is an historical agent is hidden by the language of socialization and learning. Once again, the inherent contradiction between social interests and the interests of the young, and it's power-based resolution in favor of dominant collectives, has hidden the content problem, which is our work, by framing it as ideological or philosophical.

In the thirties and forties, the concern for curriculum change had significant impact. Caswell's[40] important work in Virginia in the thirties and Miel's excellent *Changing the Curriculum*[41] exemplified this interest, although it can be traced back forty or fifty years earlier. Caswell and Miel, and their many colleagues interested in curriculum change, did much to stimulate the involvement of teachers, laity, and students in the developments of new educational programs. Their work recognized that educational content in schools, and the way it was made present to students, was out of tune with what was known and valued by educators. They addressed themselves to how particular schools and teachers could vitalize the educational program of a school and make it more appropriate to the setting, the time, and the clients. This is an interest that received, and continues to receive, major attention in the literature associated with curriculum. From the perspective of today, informed in part by the post-Sputnik era during which new content was developed by people and groups outside the traditions of curriculum, I would say that the concern for curriculum change, now a major pre-occupation within the field, has drawn us from our work—making content present to students. The interest in curriculum change is more directly related to the way in which institutions maintain vitality, flexibility, and responsiveness. By placing the responsibility for curriculum change—a question of institutional vitality—within the traditions of curriculum rather than of administration, the problems of content have been separated from the problems of budget, personnel, resources, and the logistics of schooling. Those concerned with content had to be concerned with institutional vitality, yet with no responsibility for economic, logistical, or other administrative policies. Policy making became an administrative responsibility, frequently uninformed by the nature of content. Interest in supervision and curriculum development has confused our proper concern for content. Educators thought they were doing curriculum work when they brought about change within a school; but maintaining organizational responsiveness in schools is institutional administration and a function of public policy-making.

The curriculum field of the past one hundred years is not just moribund; for all practical purposes it is dead. It did not die because it depended on theory rather than practice, although its sickness might have been diagnosed sooner if there had been greater correspondence between its rhetoric and its performance. It died because the increasing diversity of interest it tried to carry during those hundred years could no longer be held together by a single focus. There can be no renascence, because the field no longer has unity or integrity A reincarnation might be possible if we cast off some interests that are now autonomous, or can be readily associated with other practical interests, and return to our roots. I believe the roots are in the original meaning of the word "curriculum," but the word may be unimportant. Our work is identifying educational content and finding ways to make it available to young people.

This work requires an awareness of how content is related to culture or traditions, of how the meanings of content and culture have changed as our predecessors attended to new or different content for the schools, and of how they will continue to change. Identifying aspects of culture as potential educational content requires greater precision of language. Since choices of educational content are policy matters, content should be framed with the care that policy debate requires, as Walker[42] suggests.

The second aspect of our work, making content present for or accessible to students, is primarily a matter of educational technology. The various sciences now associated with education, such as learning theory, child development, and cognitive psychology, are most appropriately seen as technical tools for making content available, not for reaching great truths about human being. The technological side of our work has developed greater power and significance during the past twenty years than any other interest associated with the curriculum field. Unfortunately, so-called curriculum people have been quite willing to associate technology with the media and developing system theory, rather than to interpret it as a necessity for giving our work useful form. If the history of the curriculum field were written with a materialistic bias, rather than an idealistic one, the impact of educational technology could more readily be seen. Without adequate clarity about educational content, and about the inherent tensions between the individual and the collective interests, the technical tools now available in method, evaluation, and media are easily co-opted by collectives interested in social control. Educational technology can serve either the interests of the person or the interests of a collective. The specific form this contradiction takes in a specific situation can be used politically. Whether it serves the interests of the person or the interests of the collective depends on the educator's political commitments and his skills of dialectical analysis and political action.

NOTES

[1] Joseph J. Schwab, "The Practical: A Language for the Curriculum," *School Review 78* (November 1969): 1–24. In this 1969 publication of Schwab's essay, the term "mistaken" is absent and does not appear until 1970 when the essay was republished by the National Education Association, Center for the Study of Education. Huebner is referring to one of the later publications. See also Joseph Schwab in *Science Curriculum and Liberal Education: Selected Essays*, eds. Ian Westbury and Neil J. Wilkof (Chicago: University of Chicago Press, 1978). *Ed.*

[2] Ibid., 1.

[3] Ibid., 1.

[4] Joseph J. Schwab, "The Practical: Arts of the Eclectic," *School Review 79* (August 1971): 493–542.

[5] B. Othanel Smith. "Curriculum: The Continuing Revolution," *Educational Leadership 33* (1976): 243–44, p. 243.

[6] Decker F. Walker, "Straining to Lift Ourselves," *Curriculum Theory Network 5*, no. 1 (1975): 3–25.

[7] Ibid., 4.

[8] Ibid., 7.

[9] Franklin J. Bobbitt, *The Curriculum* (Boston: Houghton Mifflin, 1918).

[10] Decker F. Walker, "The Curriculum Field in Formation," *Curriculum Theory Network 4*, no. 4 (1975): 263–80, and D. F. Walker, "Straining to Lift Ourselves."

[11] May Louise Seguel, *The Curriculum Field: Its Formative Years* (New York: Teachers College Press, 1966).

[12] For a discussion of Bobbitt and Charters see Herbert M. Kliebard, "Bureaucracy and Curriculum Theory," in *Freedom, Bureaucracy and Schooling* (Washington, DC: ASCD, 1971), also Kliebard *Forging the American Curriculum: Essays in Curriculum History and Theory* (New York: Routledge, 1992), and Kliebard *The Struggle for the American Curriculum* (New York: Routledge, 1987). *Ed.*

[13]See for instance Lawrence A. Cremin, "Curriculum-making in the United States," *Teachers College Record 73* (December 1971): 207–20, 208–10; and Cremin, *American Education, the Metropolitan Experience 1876–1980* (New York: Harper, 1988). *Ed.*

[14]See Barry Franklin, *Building the American Community: The School Curriculum and the Search for Social Control* (Philadelphia, PA and London, England: Falmer, 1986); and "Whatever Happened to Social Control? The Muting of Coercive Authority in Curriculum Discourse," in *Contemporary Curriculum Discourses*, William F. Pinar, ed., 80–90 (Scottsdale, AZ: Gorsuch Scarisbrick, 1988), *Ed.*

[15]Lawrence A. Cremin, "Curriculum-making in the United States," *Teachers College Record 73* (December 1971): 207–20, 208–10.

[16]Israel Scheffler, *The Language of Education* (Springfield, IL: Charles C. Thomas, 1960), 19–25.

[17]Paul B. Komisar and James E. McClellan, "The Logic of Slogans," in *Language and Concepts of Education*, ed. B. Othanel Smith and Robert H. Ennis, 195–214 (Chicago: Rand McNally, 1961).

[18]According to the Oxford Dictionary, the meaning of the word "curriculum" is derived from a Latin root which refers to the course where chariot or "curricle" races were held. In the middle of the nineteenth century, it took on the meaning of a course of study at a school or university. In many ways, the historical problem would be much easier if this meaning had been retained in educational discourse. To trace the embellishments and uses of the word over the past seventy years would itself be a major task, complicated by the expression "field of curriculum."

[19]John Dewey, *Democracy and Education: An Introduction to the Philosophy of Education* (New York: Macmillan, 1916), 19.

[20]William Torrey Harris, "The Theory of American Education," *In Addresses and Journal of Proceedings of the National Teachers' Associations*, Proceedings of the Tenth Annual Session, 181–2 (Washington, DC: James H. Holmes, 1871). Also published as *The Theory of Education* (Syracuse, NY: C. W. Bardeen, 1893).

[21]William Torrey Harris, "Horace Mann," in *Journal of Proceedings and Addresses of the Thirty-fifth Annual Meeting*, National Educational Association, 52–63 (Chicago: University of Chicago Press, 1896), 60. Also published as *Horace Mann* (Syracuse, NY: C. W. Bardeen, 1896).

[22]William Torrey Harris, "The Kindergarten Methods Contrasted with the Methods of the American Primary School," in *Journal of Proceedings and Addresses of the 1889 Session*, National Educational Association, Kindergarten Department, 448–53 (Topeka, KS: Kansas Publishing House, 1889), 453.

[23]See Talcott Parsons, *Theories of Society: Foundations of Modern Sociological Theory* (New York: Free Press, 1961), and *Talcott Parsons on Institutions and Social Evolution: Selected Writings*, ed. Leon H. Mayhew (Chicago: University of Chicago Press, 1982). *Ed.*

[24]I have chosen the expression "making present" to distinguish between placing content in the presence of the young and expecting that they will somehow master it. Response to "content made present," to culture, can be rejection—or reinterpretation.

[25]Twenty years ago, James Conant called attention to the possible origins of science in the practical empirical interests of artisans and craftsmen. He suggested that science developed as a way to reduce the degree of empiricism in the practical arts. This notion seems supported by education. See James B. Conant, *Modern science and modern man* (New York: Columbia University Press, 1952).

[26]For example, there is a perceptive discussion of the problems of curriculum change in Dewey, "The Situation as Regards the Course of Study," In *Journal of Proceedings and Addresses of the Fortieth Annual Meeting*, National Educational Association, Department of Superintendence, 332–48 (Chicago: University of Chicago Press, 1901).

[27]John Dewey, "Theory of the Course of Study," in *Cyclopedia of Education*, vol. 2, ed. Paul Monroe, 212–22 (New York: Macmillan 1935), 219.

[28]Ibid., 220.

[29]Ibid., 221.

[30]Ibid., 221.

[31]See Michael Polanyi, *Knowing and Being* (Chicago: University of Chicago Press, 1969), also Polanyi, *The Tacit Dimension* (Garden City, NY: Doubleday, 1966). *Ed.*

[32]John Dewey, "The Situation as Regards the Course of Study," 348.

[33]Samuel Bowles and Herbert Gintis, *Schooling in Capitalist America: Educational Reform and the Contradictions of Economic Life* (New York: Basic Books, 1976).

[34]Rachel Sharp and Anthony Greene, *Education and Social Control* (London: Routledge and Kegan Paul, 1975).

[35]Lloyd deMause, "The Evolution of Childhood," in *The History of Childhood*, ed. Lloyd deMause (New York: Psychohistory Press, 1974).

[36]Josiah Royce, "Is There a Science of Education?" *Educational Review* I (1891):15–25.

[37]I am using the word "culture" differently from B. Othanel Smith, William O. Stanley, and Harlan J. Shores, *Fundamentals of Curriculum Development*, rev. ed. (New York: Harcourt, Brace and World, 1957).

[38]Alfred Schutz and Thomas Luckmann, *The Structures of the Life-world*, trans. Richard Zaner and H. Tristram Englehardt, Jr. (Evanston, IL: Northwestern University Press, 1973).

[39]Joseph J. Schwab, "The Structures of the Natural Sciences" In *The Structure of Knowledge and the Curriculum*, ed. G. W. Ford and Lawrence Pugno (Chicago: Rand McNally, 1964).

[40]Hollis Caswell and Doak S. Campbell, *Readings in Curriculum Development* (New York: American Book Company, 1937), 199–201, 611–612, 637. *Ed.*

[41]Alice Miel, *Changing the Curriculum, a Social Process* (New York: D. Appleton-Century, 1946).

[42]Decker F. Walker, "Straining to Lift Ourselves." *Curriculum Theory Network* 5, no. 1 (1975): 3–25.

21

An Educator's Perspective on Language About God

(1977)

Heidegger[1] cautions us that language is our most dangerous possession. It is dangerous because it assumes an "old deluder" quality: it covers or hides at the same time that it uncovers or reveals. Furthermore it is dangerous because we easily fall into the language of the other—which Heidegger calls "idle talk" or the language of "Das Man." Language about language compounds these dangers and even greater caution is required. The danger cannot be prevented. Rather we must stay constantly alert to the danger as we speak, listen and converse and tread our language ground with care. Perhaps you can better stay alert to the dangers of my language if markers of that ground—the sources of my language—are provided.

I am an educator, whose practice has been in elementary schools with children and teachers, and in colleges educating educators. To understand the practice of education I have worked my way through diverse traditions and disciplines, for I have not found the language used by most of my colleagues particularly helpful in the search for understanding. Lately, I have come to recognize that the reasons for this discomfort with the prevailing language of education is the taken-for-granted, and hence unrecognized, positivism or scientism. But to reach this recognition I have had to move from the empirical sciences through the critical social and behavioral studies; from positivism through existentialism, phenomenology, hermeneutics to critical theory and Marxism. Because of this too often taken-for-granted positivism, I have some difficulty accepting and using some of the studies in child development, including language development. The later work of Piaget[2] has value for me because his constructionist orientation tends to be dialectical (cf. Goldmann).[3] My search to understand the practice of education has lead me into theological studies, primarily philosophical and systematic, rather than biblical. My search to understand myself has led me into the Rhineland mystics and related literature. As a consequence of these religious interests, I have been involved for several years with students of religious education, and acknowledge the presence in my speaking of some very fine students of Protestant, Catholic and Jewish education.

As background for this paper, I have read with interest the previous papers prepared for the various consultations on language about God, including "Opening the Door."[4] I have also valued the opportunity to read selections from the increasing volume of literature on sexism and religion and in other facets of our common life. Finally, I have looked again at some of the recent literature on language and language development.

My intention is to gather together some plausible ideas and suggestions about language, sexism and religion which might stimulate reflection, spark conversation and perhaps mobilize action. Throughout, my approach will be that of the educator who is more concerned with general points of view and their significance for educational practice than with the empirical and theoretical warrants of the underlying position. The footnotes and bibliography will provide the entrance to these warrants. The order of presentation, which has a semblance of logic for me, is to begin with the origins of language which I find in the interpersonal dynamics of child and adult. Because of the interpersonal ground I find in interpretation, and its various distortions such as absolutes and reifications as well as other removals of language from the interpersonal, the consideration of origins leads to questions about the nature, structure, or essence of language. To recognize language as an outcome of the interpersonal is to see it as it operates in various forms of life or the various forms of human activity; thus, language which partakes of ritual celebrations has a different form than language which partakes of environmental control or mutual understanding in the conduct of interpersonal life. After the ground and nature of language in its various manifestations are articulated it will be possible to point to the dialectical relationship of language and social relations, as these have been institutionalized into various classes, divisions, or hierarchies including those of sex. With the articulation of these various dimensions of language and its dialectical relationship to forms of activity and forms of social relationships, then it should be easier to see the relationship between language and human formation, and consequently suggest strategies of action for those who are concerned with differing language usages among differing segments of the social world.

THE INTERPERSONAL ORIGINS OF LANGUAGE

Some students of language have attempted to explain the origins of language by the use of anthropological data and methods. However, Piaget has altered our present and future methods and data for studying the origins of any human behavior or institution. His studies of hypothetical-deductive knowledge suggest that adults cannot understand any body of knowledge unless we understand how that knowledge develops in the individual person, which he labels the "epistemic subject." Although his concern has been primarily mathematics, logic and scientific knowledge, I would argue that his method and concern applies to our understanding of all forms of human activity. Whereas he has been concerned with developing what has become known as "genetic epistemology," I believe that we will, in the future, have such fields of study as genetic metaphysics, genetic ontology, genetic axiology, and genetic theology. The warrant for this belief is our increasing awareness of the inherent bias of the adult, who takes the adult world for granted and assumes that the child's task is to be socialized to that adult world. Just as much as we are being forced into a kind of cultural relativism, so Piaget is forcing us into an age relativism, with profound consequences for the way that we look at and are with the young of all ages. Ethnomethodology, a field of study which investigates the mutual construction of meaning, warrants this position, as do the newer studies in the history of childhood.[5] A brief overview of Piaget's major contributions will provide a foundation for a set of assumptions about the origins of language.

Piaget is perhaps best known for the idea of stages of intellectual development. He has contributed to our understanding of how children at particular ages handle certain kinds of data and problems, and has shown the sequence of children's descriptions and explanations of natural phenomena at differing ages.[6] Kohlberg draws upon Piagetian notions as he attempts to describe the stages of moral development. Fowler[7] does the same thing as he attempts to describe faith development. The notion of stages of development is not, however, Piaget's major contribution. The underlying concern through his professional career has been to show or demonstrate the continuity between the biological organism and intellectual functioning. He and his colleagues have established that mathematical and scientific knowledge is grounded in the biological structures and functioning of the organism, and that these biological structures develop and change as a consequence of the organism's interaction with the environment. The process is described as one in which there is a dialectical relationship between the infant and the environment, during which the infant assimilates aspects of the environment into her perceptual and psychomotor structures, while at the same time accommodating these structures to the conditions of the environment. As a consequence of this interaction, the infant builds up "schemas" of assimilation and accommodation which maintain an equilibrium between the infant and the environment, until there are further changes in either the organism or in the environment. The schemas thus undergo change and modification as the equilibration process continues. These schemas permit or direct the operations which link the neophyte and the environment. For Piaget, intelligence consists of these operational structures between the person and the environment. The symbolic operations of adolescent and adult are based upon these basic perceptual-psychomotor schemas. Piaget has established without question that hypothetical-deductive knowledge and logical operations have their origins or ground in the body and the body's activity within the world. Whereas the conception of stage is important, it is, for me, not as significant as the fact that the body-in-the-world is the ground of knowledge. Piaget's method and explanation of the genesis of knowledge urge us to attend to the developmental, and I would prefer to say, dialectical sequencing of events in the formation of the person, starting prior to birth. Our search for understanding of the diverse manifestations of human life must be rooted in the temporality of the person—in that person's emerging biography with others. A dependence upon and acceptance of the idea of stages tends to reify a particular stage so one person sees another as an object in space rather than as a person in time with other people. Conceptions of adulthood are a consequence of this reification, and too easily permit us to look at the child as one who is confronted with the task of adapting to the adult's world. Hence education takes the form of educating the child to the adult world, whereas education is a way of being with other people over time in which a concern for the future or transcendence predominates.

In the study of language, Piaget's commitments to ontogenesis have yet to have their full impact. Much study of developing language in the young is of comparative grammars, in which the syntactical structures of the young person's language are compared with the syntactical structure of adult language. The grounding of language in the body is recognized by Merleau-Ponty,[8] who claims that language is an extension of the body. Within the past few years, the study of mother-infant interaction has been most fruitful and will undoubtedly provide us with new ideas about the development of language as a phenomena between people, confirming the philosophical speculations of Buber about the significance of relationships for defining human life. For instance, Klaus and Kennell have reported that

> there is a sensitive period in the first minutes and hours of life when a mother must have close contact with her infant for later development to be optimal. The doctors have found that when mothers are given their babies shortly after birth, they behave in special ways. Most notably, they speak to them in high-pitched voices as if they knew instinctively that babies are receptive to such tones. The result is "a beautiful linking" of mother and infant in a kind of dance in which, as slow-motion films show, the baby sees, hears, and moves to the rhythm of his [sic] mother's voice.

> Comparing mother-child pairs who had spent hours together immediately after birth with pairs who had only brief contact, the doctors found several differences. At two years after birth, for instance, the long contact mothers asked their children twice as many questions and gave them fewer commands than did the other mothers....[9]

Lewis and Rosenblum have pulled together diverse studies on this parent infant dialectic in *The Effect of the Infant on its Caregiver*.[10] They have shown that the infant has a significant impact upon the caregiver, and that the gestures (vocal, facial, visual) of the infant alter the behavior of the mother. In other words there seems to be increasing evidence to support Macmurray's claim that language does not make communication, but that language is possible only because communication already exists.[11] It seems that a possible inference is that speech is also grounded in the biological schemas of social relations, and that the nature of speech is not simply a function of the nature of language but of the diverse schemas of social relations that the neophyte establishes with people who make up her social environment. We do not have the empirical data to support this position, but I would suggest that the scientific procedures which we now have may be inadequate to the task. The phenomenological investigations of social life which are now embodied in ethnomethodology, which attempts to describe how meanings are constructed between participants of any social action, may be more able to depict the origins of language in social situations. For instance, Merleau-Ponty states, "that we now regard language as the reverberation of my relations with myself and others."[12] Furthermore, he claims that, "speaking and listening not only presuppose thought but—even more essentially it is practically the foundation of thought—the capacity to allow oneself to be pulled down and rebuilt again by the other person, by others who may come along, and in principle by anyone."[13] This vulnerability to the other, which for Merleau-Ponty is crucial for speech, shows itself in the studies of infant-caretaker relations. Hence, the scientific study of others, in which the scientific investigator does not consider her own vulnerability and language limitations, may not be able to detect the origins of language in these basic and foundational relationships of caregiving and care-taking.

Given the established work of Piaget, the developing and fascinating literature of the relationship between the caregiver and the caretaker and the possible language consequences of such interactions, the speculations of Merleau-Ponty, and the philosophical claims of Buber[14] and Macmurray;[15] it seems warranted, at least for the purposes of this paper, to assume that language used by a person with others has its origins in the basic social relationships between the neophyte and the others in her environment. I would not expect to see the impact of these relationships in the grammatical or syntactical forms of the child's language, nor necessarily in the vocabulary, but rather in the way that the child's language is a manifestation of and a vehicle for her relationships with a variety of others in a variety of contexts. In fact, Cazden has pulled together the empirical studies which indicate that language competency is indeed a consequence of the situation within which communication occurs.[16] Further research might indicate that the patterns of discourse or dialogue which are indeed patterns of social relations, might well differentiate among children who come from quite differing social interactive communities. Thus, we might expect to see variation in language functions and functioning as a consequence of early schemas of social relationships. The durability of such functions and functioning is beyond speculation, although there are those psychoanalysts (Shands[17] and Lacan[18]) who interpret some therapy as a reorganizing of the interpersonal, and consequently intrapersonal, modes of discourse.

Obviously, language as it develops between the child and the others in the basic social relationships is informed by the language traditions of the communities to which the adult and, consequently, the child belongs. The distinction that Saussure makes between "langue" and "parole"[19] or what Ricoeur calls "discourse"[20] is helpful here. Ricoeur states that *"Langue* is the code—or set of codes—on the basis of which a particular speaker produces *parole* as a particular message."[21] Ricoeur's interpretation is worth quoting in more detail.

> A message is individual, its code is collective ... A message is intentional; it is meant by someone. A code is anonymous and not intended. In this sense it is unconscious, not in the sense that drives and impulses are unconscious according to Freudian metapsychology, but in the sense of nonlibidinal structural and cultural unconscious. More than anything else, a message is arbitrary and contingent, while a code is systematic and compulsory for a given speaking community.[22]

Ricoeur claims that the systematic aspect of *langue* has leant itself to the scientific study of language and hence in modern linguistic terms *langue* has taken precedence over *parole*. Discourse has been neglected as a field of study, because discourse is *the event* of language, and "events vanish while systems remain."[23] He states further:

> If it is true that only the message has a temporal existence, an existence in duration and succession, the synchronistic aspect of the code putting the system outside of successive time, then this temporal existence of the message testifies to its actuality. The system in fact does not exist. It has only a virtual existence. Only the message gives actuality to language, and discourse grounds the very existence of language since only the discrete and each time unique acts of discourse actualizes the code.[24]

We may safely say then, that language has its origins in the speech or incipient speech events of the young with others—in dialogue, even though that dialogue is primarily gestural rather than linguistic. In the beginning, incipient speech events may be primarily gestural and not-yet-differentiated sounds—primarily body interchanges. The gestures and sound events gradually are disciplined by the collective codes which are carried, usually unconsciously, by the older member of the interaction, and begin to take on the form of the community's language patterns. Whether the discourse between speaker and listener retains its event quality, an exchange of intention and meaning and the consequent experience of "we," or assumes a form of "idle speech" wherein the collective codes or the meanings of only the speaker or the listener dominate the event depends upon whether the power of the older person is used in a caring or controlling way. Obviously, the discourse between the neophytes and the established members of the community, and hence the way language forms between people is, in part, a manifestation of the social relations which exist within a particular community and consequently a manifestation of the way power is distributed within the community. We will take up this theme later in the paper, but before we do, further clarification of the nature of language is necessary.

THE NATURE OF LANGUAGE: EXPRESSION, INTERPRETATION, AND COMMUNICATION COMPETENCE

Merleau-Ponty poses our problem for us. He states that, "The perfection of language lies in its capacity to pass unnoticed."[25] Our use of language easily recedes from our awareness. To call it to focal attention is to drive us to a point of either truisms, or scientific or objective descriptions of others using language which do not seem to fit our own experience. To bring our own experience of language into focal attention is to produce a state of speechlessness, a period of waiting while our language resources seem to reorganize themselves to fill the void—or as Merleau-Ponty states, " ... when the constituted language suddenly off center and out of equilibrium, reorganizes itself to teach the reader—and even the author—what he never knew how to think or say."[26] Obviously, at one level, language is an act of expression. Ricoeur's words are better than mine for describing the phenomena:

> ... Language is the exteriorization thanks to which an impression is transcended and becomes an expression, or in other words the transformation of the psychic into the noetic. Exteriorization and communicability are one and the same thing for they are nothing other than the elevation of a part of our life into the logos of discourse. There the solitude of life is for a moment, anyway, illuminated by the common light of discourse.[27]

And further on he states that:

> ... Language is not a world of its own. It is not even a world. But because we are in the world, because we are affected by situations and because we orient ourselves comprehensively in those situations, we have something to say, we have experience to bring to language.[28]

But exteriorization, or expression via language, is not an event of solitude. It is also a social event. Returning again to the genesis of language within the young child, expression requires, in the first place, one who attempts to express for the child or helps the child express. The question or comments of the parents: "Are you hungry? Did you hurt yourself? Isn't it fun playing with Tommy?" can be seen as an effort of the adult to help the child exteriorize her impressions. The danger of course, is that the expression need not resonate with the child, and hence can be the imposition of someone else's experience onto the child. Douglas Steere, in that wonderful volume, *On Listening to Another*,[29] points out that there is a way of listening to another which will help the other bring to consciousness, clarity, or to articulateness that which has been not yet expressed; and a way of listening, or perhaps non-listening, which impedes, distorts, or even represses expression. And indeed, the therapeutical situation can be seen as reliving not simply the original conflict situations, but the reliving of the never experienced listening situation which was required to give expression to one's impressions and to bring them to the "common light of discourse." As the young person meets others beyond the immediate relationships, other language patterns and their use develop the capability to give greater precision to the exteriorization of internal experience.

But language is never simply expression. If we ground language in discourse and communication, rather than assuming that language makes possible communication and discourse, then it follows that listening and understanding are constitutive of all expression, even though they may not be realized in all situations. Ricoeur, among others, is to the point here. He states that, "The instance of discourse—is the instance of dialogue. Dialogue is an event which connects two events, that of speaking and that of hearing."[30] Merleau-Ponty makes the point in another way, indicating that in the adult or older person the listener may also be the speaker, as those of us who have been taken by surprise by our own expressions have discovered. "In its live and creative state, language is the gesture of renewal and recovery which unites me with myself and others."[31]

Listening and the understanding which accompany or follow it are never simply passive acts of reception; they are active acts of reconstructing or of interpreting. Because words usually have more than one meaning the listener must sort out the various meanings, and in some way or another reflect back to the speaker his interpretation and understanding. In a normal conversation this is simply accomplished by continuing the dialogue, as the speaker acknowledges the appropriateness of the interpretation by the next expression. Ricoeur states that:

> ... mutual understanding does not go without some misunderstanding. Most of our words are polysemic; they have more than one meaning. But it is the contextual function of discourse to screen, so to speak, the polysemy of our words and to reduce the plurality of possible interpretations, the ambiguity of discourse resulting from the unscreened polysemy of the words. And it is the function of dialogue to initiate this screening function of the context. The con-

textual role of dialogue reduces the field of misunderstanding concerning the propositional content and partially succeeds in overcoming the non-communicability of experience.[32]

The interpretive response, or the response based upon interpretation, serves not only to continue the mutuality of the experience, but also serves an educative function for the participants. For to have the speaker's intentions or meanings reflected back, either in the listener's questions or responses, is to inform the speaker of the failure or success of the exteriorization process, of the act or event of expression; and to inform her of other nuance or values in the particular words and propositions. The natural educative consequences of conversation are broken when the power relations between speaker and listener are unequal and when power is used to impose an interpretation, when interpretation is not recognized as a constituent part of language, or when the event of discourse is subservient to some other social act, such as a market exchange, or a ritual or conventional social action. "Idle talk" is not educative.

Again, interpretation, a constitutive part of language, is necessarily grounded in the basic social relationships between caregiver and caretaker and eventually in the social relationship between speaker and listener. Interpretation requires that the speaker recognize that her utterance is not perfectly transparent, and consequently there must be a moment of waiting which is an invitation to the listener to interpret the utterance. Likewise, the listener's stand must be one of self-confidence in the presence of the speaker—a confidence which permits doubt about the meaning of the utterance and a willingness to speak an interpretation. The interpretive act, is thus a social act, not simply a linguistic act; it is grounded in the basic social schema linking speaker to listener.

Interpretation becomes more complex as discourse contains metaphors and/or symbols, for the referential and contextual clues which make interpretation possible in ordinary discourse are no longer sufficient for metaphor and symbol. Again, Ricoeur is most helpful here. Interpretation of metaphor involves the resolution of a contradiction, or to quote Ricoeur ". . . the strategy of discourse by which the metaphoric utterance obtains its result is absurdity. The absurdity is only revealed through the attempt to interpret the utterance literally."[33] Interpretation of metaphor requires a resolution of a conflict in interpretation, thus revealing something new about the context of the participants. Symbol, according to Ricoeur, creates a differing problem of interpretation, for the symbol "brings together two dimensions, we might even say, two universes, of discourse, one linguistic and the other of a non-linguistic order."[34] On the one hand the symbol gives rise to speech, and brings forth a linguistic interpretation. However, the symbol contains a "surplus of meaning" for the linguistic meaning can never be exhausted, because the symbol is grounded in other than the linguistic. "The opacity of symbol is related to rootedness of symbols in areas of our experience that are open to different methods of investigation."[35] For Ricoeur, "Metaphor occurs in the already purified universe of the *logos*, while the symbol hesitates on the dividing line between *bios* and *logos*. It testifies to the primordial rootedness of Discourse in Life. It is born where force and form coincide."[36] This is a remark which supports the grounding of language and discourse in the body and the body's involvements in the world. Ricoeur claims that religious symbols are bound within the sacred universe and hence come to expression as a consequence of the person's experience with the sacred. The interpretation of symbols is, in part, a linguistic interpretation, but also a continual exploration of the sacred, inasmuch as the linguistic component of the symbol has a "surplus of meaning" which is never exhausted because the sacred can never be brought fully into the transparency of discourse.

It is the necessity for interpretation in all acts of discourse which led the linguist Dell Hymes[37] to the notion of communicative competence, based, in part, on Chomsky's distinction between linguistic competence and linguistic performance. Linguistic competence, which is the knowledge of sounds, syntax and meaning, makes possible performance, but does not guarantee it. Performance is a function of context and the ability of the person to use linguistic knowledge in a variety of contexts. Hymes has extended this and refers to communicative competence—the competence to engage in communication in a variety of situations—which enables both speaker and listener to judge the appropriateness of the utterance or series of utterances. Such competence requires the sharing of joint norms of syntax and meaning. The idea of communicative competence has been further elaborated by Habermas,[38] who bases it on an *a priori* ideal speech situation—a significant idea for exploring the relationship between language and social relations.

Distortions of language are derived, in part, from the predominance of the printed or written word and our tendency to understand language as written language. If we stay aware that the genesis of language is in the basic relationship between caregiver and caretaker, and that language is grounded in human dialogue, which implies a speaker and a listener and necessarily requires interpretation; then we approach the written language and its significance in our life from a different perspective. Again, I find Paul Ricoeur most perceptive and helpful here. His argument is rather detailed and I recommend the book to you. A brief summary of his analysis has value for what we are about.

Ricoeur begins with the distinction, made by Saussure, between *parole* and *langue,* and attempts to develop a semantics of discourse. He does so by focusing on parole, and speaks of discourse as the event of language, which as indicated earlier, actualizes the codes of langue. He then identifies the dialectic between event and meaning, and states "if all discourse is actualized as event, all discourse is understood as meaning."[39] By meaning or sense "he designate(s) the propositional content." He recognizes two kinds of meaning, the utterer's meaning and the utterance's meaning. The utterer's meaning is not dependent upon a psychological fact, but is found in the utterance's meaning "thanks to the self reference of discourse to itself as event"[40] which is possible by "shifters" in the sentence—the personal pronouns, tenses of the verbs, adverbs of time and space and the demonstratives. He refers to the utterer's meaning as the subjective meaning and the utterance's meaning as the objective meaning. "The 'objective' side of discourse itself may be taken in two different ways. We may mean the 'what' of discourse or the 'about what' of discourse. The what of discourse is its 'sense' the 'about what' is its 'reference.'"[41] Ricoeur then distinguished speaking from writing. In writing meaning has been detached from the event, leaving what he calls "the semantic autonomy of the text." The dialectic of event and meaning which was found in discourse, is now accentuated in writing. I quote again from Ricoeur.

> ... in spoken discourse the ultimate criterion for the referential scope of what we say is the possibility of showing the thing referred to as a member of a situation common to both speaker and hearer. This situation surrounds the dialogue, and its landmarks can be shown by gesture or pointing a finger.... It is this grounding of reference in the dialogical situation that is shattered by writing.[42]

But this break with the dialogic situation has "tremendous consequences." "Thanks to writing, man and only man [sic] has a world and not just a situation."[43] By world Ricoeur means the totality of references opened up by all texts, of diverse kinds; worlds which open up our possibilities for us, our "project, that is, the outline of a new way of being in the world."[44] For Ricoeur, "hermeneutics begins where dialogue ends."[45] The biblical theologian, it would seem, has a head start in her use of language.

The difficulties we have with language are a consequence of the limitations in our communicative competence. The limitation can merely be incompetence, a consequence of not listening to others, or communication with those insensitive to the interpretive dimensions of language. It can be a result of the mal-distributions of power, in which the objective meanings of one person's expressions are taken as truth rather than as an expression of one's lived experience. The limitation can be a result of individuals who have not learned that reading texts is parallel to listening to discourse, both require the capability and freedom for interpretation. In discourse, the interpretation is facilitated by the interpersonal situation and the common context. In reading, interpretive capabilities too often are inadequately distributed among the differing segments of the social world.

The difficulties that we have with language can also be a result of our propensities to dwell in space but not in time, and our desire to "fix" the world into stable and known practices and expressions. Language easily falls into our structures of inauthenticity and non-dialectical being. Alienation, reification, idolatry are human propensities that show themselves in the way we take language as a given, beyond the possibility of continuous interpretation.

If we are to educate ourselves and each other about sexism in religious language—if we are to transcend the present situation—we must recognize that our problem, in part, stems from viewing language as if it were removed from the interpersonal and as if interpretation were something special, a function of trained hermeneuts, rather than a constituent part of all language. But before this theme is developed, we should at least outline how language—whether in the dialectic of speaking and listening, or writing and reading—assumes different characteristics in different forms of life. Language partakes of life activity, and its form is, in part, a function of the activity of which it partakes. The event character, the meaning, and the nature of the interpretive work reflect these different forms of life.

THE FORMS OF LANGUAGE
AND THE FORMS OF LIFE

In this section, I can do little more than point to an area that needs much more extensive investigation. It need not be done systematically, by trained linguists or trained theologians. It can be done by each of us as we go about our affairs in the world.

One of the more striking aspects of *Language About God "Opening the Door"* is, the ease with which a reader, or at least this reader, infers that language about God is a more or less unitary or single dimensional language; rather than a very complex multi-dimensional language which has differing forms in differing circumstances and many different uses. A reference is made to "our language about God," but the "our" carries with it a universality which may not be warranted, and "our language" a singular possession rather than a diverse set of instruments. There is the reference to theological language, which theological scholars concur "is analogous, symbolical and metaphorical, never univocal, literal, and direct."[46] But is theological language also the language of the laity or the language of children as they talk about their experience of God? There is the reference to biblical language, perhaps the most unquestioned form of religious language, for the inscription fixates and removes the event quality of the discourse. Laity, children, and the professional religious can indeed identify the reference easily. It seems to me that when the expression, "Language about God" is used we must ask who is speaking and listening, who is writing and reading, in what circumstances and perhaps to what end. Unless we can begin to make finer distinctions among the uses of religious language and the circumstances within which that language is used, we will not be able to recognize or challenge why some uses are oppressive and others are not.

My categorization of the forms of religious language is intended to be suggestive, for I have not been able to review the formulations of others, either in the literature or in conversation with others. Because I am not a theologian or a professional religious, I have a certain discomfort about the language of this section, and I welcome conversation, critique and alternative proposals or formulations. It seems to me that the following are situations or circumstances in which religious language is used: religious rituals and liturgies; the addressing of God in prayers of supplication, adoration and thanksgiving; reading the religious writings of others, including sacred texts; writing religious language of various kinds—journals, theologies, devotional materials, testaments, interpretations of events; instruction or education, which is increasingly a doubtful category for me; dialogue or conversation; emancipatory uses of language, whether of therapy or religious formation, or of the search of a collective for transcendence of their present situation as illustrated by this and other consultations about the language of God and sexism. The approach which seems most profitable for our purposes is to elaborate on these forms of religious language and activity in terms of the previously discussed interpersonal foundation and interpretive structure of language.

Unfortunately, I am not acquainted with what must be a vast literature about religious ritual and liturgy. I am somewhat familiar with the religious education literature and presume that the natural adult bias which informs most of that literature extends to the literature of ritual; that is, that adult forms are seen as established and normative and that our task is to find ways to socialize the young into these rituals. This bias hides the need for inquiry into the ontogenesis of ritual. Accepting the Piagetian approach identified earlier, the assumption appears warranted that even very young children have forms of ritual and liturgies that fit their own bodies, their developing psychic structures and their emerging schemes of social relations and that adult ritualistic forms are somehow or another compatible with or extensions of these earlier forms of ritual. In fact, such a genetic inquiry might also provide us with a differing understanding of the significance and form of adult rituals. Furthermore, genetic inquiry of ritual would give us better understanding of our developing relationships with the Divine, for I presume that the ritualistic forms and behaviors of the young serve many interests. The recognition of how the Divine gradually is included in the ritual of the young would be of great value. Rituals are also interpersonal, and such ontogenetic inquiries would enable us to recognize more clearly the interpersonal forms or structures which are foundational to adult rituals.

Ricoeur's[47] analysis of symbol provides a basis for getting at the uses of language in rituals. Ricoeur postulates two dimensions to language, the linguistic component and the non-linguistic component, which in religious symbol is the sacred ground. In ritual, the linguistic symbol is accompanied by symbolic action and perhaps symbolic objects. Nevertheless, the total symbolic component has the qualities of an inscription; that is, the meaning of the symbol has been severed from the dialogical or social event of its origin. There is the autonomy of the ritual which puts it outside of the event or temporal structure of social life. Participating in ritual is, in part, participating in an historical moment. A child's use of ritual carries with it a re-enactment of earlier moments in the personal-social life of the child. In religious ritual, a celebration of an historical moment is also the celebration of our forbearers' experience of the sacred, and opens the possibility of our own encounter with the sacred.

Ricoeur claims that "The symbol ... only gives rise to thought if it first gives rise to speech."[48] The language that surrounds or accompanies that historical moment, whether in the life of the child or the life of a community is the beginning point for the talk about the Divine. Obviously, ritual that is merely enacted, without being followed by conversation among participants or participants and non-participants provides little basis for the conscious formulation of language about God. It would seem, particularly with children, that conversation in which listening and elaborative responses are an essential part, would be crucial for developing appropriate language about the Divine.

Equally obvious, the diversity of ritual form is a necessity in this world because no ritual resonates with all people. Historical moments which are re-enacted in ritual, have different language components associated with them, and thus elicit different speech or language about the Divine. Interpretation necessarily begins with the primary language of the symbol. If the interpretation of this primary language dimension evokes experiences of negation, oppression or pain, these interpretations necessarily must influence discourse about God.

Attention to the origins of ritual is needed to free participants from earlier social moments of oppression or negation. This does not imply doing away with the ritualistic use of negative or expressive language, for the ritual celebration indicates the historical continuity of the community, and the language and symbols of the historical community are not necessarily the language of the contemporary community. But it does imply the need for a sensitivity to the emergence of potentially new rituals and celebrations which can evoke new speech and interpretations about the divine in the celebrants and observers. Furthermore, in the development of the neophyte's language about God, it implies the need to maintain constant opportunities for conversation, in which the linguistic and non-linguistic aspects of the ritual are constantly interpreted and re-interpreted in terms of the experience of the participants. This is particularly true if we accept, with Ricoeur, that there is always a surplus of meaning in symbols, and that this surplus is never totally articulated, but requires repeated and continued interpretations. This means significant interpersonal or communal situations which are truly dialogic—speakers being brought to linguistic clarity or consciousness by caring and courageous listeners who are at the same time sufficiently free to offer their own interpretations.

The language of prayer, to the extent that it is ritual, has the same qualities as that discussed above. Adoration, supplication, thanksgiving and other acknowledgments of the sacred in and beyond human life are moments of human life which occur outside of formal rituals. Better understanding of language about God in these moments requires greater attention to two phenomena. The ontogenetic perspectives of Piaget are crucial. What do we know of the moments in the growth of the individual when experiences of adoration, supplication, thanksgiving, or other experiences of awe or the numinous break through? What are the interpersonal conditions which surround these moments? Is the caretaking-caregiving relationship one which brings appropriate language to the young person at those moments? Is the moment followed by conversation or dialogue which interprets the language and its fit to the experience? Is the young person introduced to the language that other people have used in similar situations and is opportunity provided for that language to be interpreted?

But as we ask these questions about children and look for patterns in the development of the language of adoration, supplication, or thanksgiving in the young, how much do we really know about these moments and their expression in the language of the established community? We know of the formal prayers in rituals, but what of the informal or non-structured uses of the language of prayer? Is the problem of sexism in language about God one which is identified only in the formal life of religious communities, or does it carry over into the personal addresses to the Divine? What is the relationship between the language of private address and public address to the Divine, and how does one inform the other? These are questions, it seems to me, that must be asked and answered in specific religious communities; about all people in the community—the young and the established.

Traditionally, much of the language about God has been associated with writing, primarily, the sacred texts, but with secondary sources also the focus of attention. The literature on translation and biblical interpretation is well informed by the issues which have been raised in this paper. We need not dwell on them further, except to raise the question as to the distribution and public reach of such critical literature, and to call attention to the philosophical problems associated with truth, authority, and the impossible search for a concept of the ineffable, all manifestations of a non-dialectical approach to interpretation.

Of greater concern to me, is the place and functioning of reading of sacred and secular texts in the life of individuals and communities. As has been pointed out by others, the reading act has encouraged the privatizing of experience. Communal reading and communal interpretation appear to be less frequent. Diversity of religious and theological printed materials, combined with joint reading and interpretation would put before the readers the diversity of language and the diversity of interpretations, thus keeping their own language more open to the interpretations of others or to their own conflicting interpretations and to proposed changes in the language about God.

The other concern that I have is the form of language used by children with written materials, a function of the kinds of written and textual materials available for children and young people, but also a function of the social context within which they are used. The production of textual materials for church schools and formal educational contexts, often modeled after secular education, can result in a distortion of the interpretive activity that must accompany all language, and a destruction of the value of print for young people. Books and materials are often written for educational purposes, with too much concern for instructional strategies and too little concern for literary qualities—the qualities that help form the language of the user. The instructional use of written materials with young people also reduces the range of interpretations available to them, for "teaching" is often very directed. Multi-age communal reading, which would require a skill and a patience that few adults have, would increase the value of reading for both young people and adults. Both could be sensitized to others interpretations and begin to place their expressions about experience and their experience of the sacred in a developmental perspective.

The forms of life and language which cluster around print necessarily raise questions about the forms of life and language which cluster around writing. It seems to me that it is important to ask not about the availability of books or printed materials, but to ask questions about whose impressions are being expressed in writing. The demystification of the language of print occurs when one also writes. Those who write and publish also have an opportunity to make public their expressions, their language, and thus increase the possibility of influencing others' use of language. Ann Douglas documents the influence of woman and ministers in the sentimentalization of American Culture after the official disestablishment of the Protestant Church in the United States in 1833. Her introductory overview is worth quoting in some detail:

> What bound the minister and the lady together with the popular writer was their shared preoccupation with the lighter productions of the press; they wrote poetry, fiction, memoirs, sermons, magazine pieces of every kind. What distinguished them from the writer, and made them uniquely central agents in the process of sentimentalization ... is the fact that their consuming interest in literature was relatively new. At the turn of the century, the prominent Edwardian minister, Nathaniel Emmons, returned a novel by Sir Walter Scott lent him by a friend with protestations of genuine horror. A scant fifty years later, serious ministers and orthodox professors of the theology were making secular literature a concern and even an occupation. During the same period woman writers gradually flooded the market with their efforts. While a female author at the beginning of the nineteenth century was consid-

ered by definition an aberration of her sex, by its close she occupied an established if not respected place. The Victorian lady and the minister were
joining, and changing the literary scene.[49]

Literary men of the cloth and middle-class woman writers of the Victorian period knew from first hand experience that literature was functioning more and
more as a form of leisure, a complicated mass dream-life in the busiest, most
wide awake society in the world.... [They] were intent on claiming culture as
their peculiar property ... they sought to gain indirect and compensatory control. Yet they were not insincere, ill-intentioned or simple minded ... they were
Christians reinterpreting their faith as best they could in terms of the needs of
their society.... Whatever their ambiguities of motivation, both believed that
they had a genuine redemptive mission in society: to propagate the potentially matriarchal virtues of nurture, generosity, and acceptance; to create the
"culture of feeling...." It is hardly their fault that their efforts intensified sentimental rather than matriarchial values.[50]

The publishing business has taken control of the printed word. The availability of many inexpensive duplicating devices, the electronic composing and editing machines which make it possible for individuals to publish and circulate
their own newsletters, and the ease of xerography means that writing and publishing can be returned to the average person. Members of a local community
can distribute their writings within the community. The young can give public
form to personal expression. The publication and distribution of religious journals, of interpretative essays, and of theological speculation is available to
more people today, thus increasing significantly the diversity of materials in
print. Writing about God, and religious experience, can now be a prerogative of
the lay person, the neophyte and the established, as well as the professional
writer. Audio and video facilities, including cable television, extend these possibilities beyond print into media that, today, probably make even a stronger
impact on our forms of discourse and conversation. This is a topic that would
require much more extensive exploration, and has potential significance within
religious communities.

The form of life associated with education and instruction, and hence the
forms of language used in education and instruction, create special problems
for us. In secular education today there is increased interest in the language of
education and the language of teaching. This is a language form which has been
largely dominated by instrumental or technical reason, and which manifests the
hierarchal structures in educational institutions and arrangements. One of the
difficulties associated with studies of the language used in education is the failure to problematize the school, or to bring under question the origins and social
functions of educational institutions. Illich has done this in *Deschooling Society*,[51] and Freire has done it indirectly in *Pedagogy of the Oppressed*.[52] Our tendency is to take the school and other educational institutions for granted, and to
assume that their purpose is to educate individuals. When this task becomes dif-

ficult, we tend not to ask about the history and social meaning of these institutions, but to try to define the meaning of education, to define the objectives of the school, or to find the right methodology and the proper means of motivation. Meanwhile we remain blind to the social control functions of the school. The walling off of children from adults and vice versa is hidden by the so-called profession of education, the need to socialize youngsters, and the learning tasks that adults set for youngsters.

At this stage of our educational history it is safer to assume that forms of educational language are derived forms, perhaps even contrived forms. They are derived, in part, from the traditions within which communities dwell. They are derived from the educational institutions and their logistical and bureaucratic structures. They are also derived from the positivistic or scientific studies of children and people, a form of study which produces "knowledge about" and techniques of control; but not necessarily the mutual understanding of self and other required for re-recognizing, sharing, and reinterpreting the traditions within which we dwell.

I prefer, then, at this stage of our educational history, not to claim a form of life and language which is primarily educational or instructional. My reason is to increase our questioning about the existing forms of education, particularly with the school, and to force us to talk about the educational consequences of our life with others as we come up against differences and traditions. This strategy might bring about a more fundamental reorganization of current educational structures, and prevent the language of God from becoming an object of teaching.

Given the importance that I have attached to the interpersonal in language and language development, it seems to me that the most important language form or forms are those of everyday conversation among people. Discussions of hunger, injustice, inequalities, violence, provide opportunities for language about God. How do these discussions become informed by, or include references to the religious dimension of life? Who must be involved in these conversations and discussions, and in what contexts do they occur? Some people have assumed that if people have "concepts" of God then they will bring these concepts to bear in these diverse situations. However, if we recognize concepts as primarily patterns of discourse then the problem is not one of teaching young people about God, but helping them develop the language patterns which include references to the Divine. The crucial problem, then, is the identification of those contexts and those participants where such talk is appropriate; and where all participants have opportunity for interpretation.

Finally, we come to that form of discourse or language use which is exemplified in this consultation and in the work, conversations, writing and reading about sexism and religious language which preceded it. Following Habermas,[53] I identify it as emancipatory discourse. Emancipatory discourse has four moments. Situations and impressions find expression which make us conscious of, that is bring to consciousness in language, present conditions previously taken for granted or below the threshold of public or private awareness. This is followed by inquiry and conversation which asks about the origins of these conditions. Critical and analytical discourse is then necessary to establish the paradoxical qualities of these conditions; their limitations or oppressive qualities and their possibilities or empowering qualities. Finally, new alternatives must be posed and the requirements or changes identified for realizing them. The emancipatory use of language, found interpersonally in education and therapy, and collectively in social criticism and struggle, is for me, inherently religious. Articulating the previously unexpressed is a manifestation of the logos of being, and a manifestation of the Word as I have come to know its mysterious operations in my own life. The search for origins and alternatives is a manifestation of our historical or temporal nature; of our participation in the tension between the immanent and transcendent, created and creator, conditioned and unconditioned, and of our participation in the dynamics of hope. The critical moment, which identifies our freedoms and the forces of domination, is a consequence of the openness to the absolute Other which brings all conditions under judgement. Theology of Liberation is one mode of emancipatory language, pastoral psychology another, and spiritual advising or counseling for religious formation another. Obviously, as this consultation and the work that preceded it indicates, not all four moments are contained in the speech or language work of one person. It is therefore important to have a sense of the collective in which these four moments of the language of emancipation are used. It also seems important to distinguish among those who speak or name the conditions, who seek origins, who identify the boundaries of domination and oppression, and those who pose alternatives. An ontogenetic view is again important. The so-called negative behavior, and the accompanying "no" of two and four year olds, can be interpreted as a form of criticism, which bring the conduct of others under judgement. To say that the child will outgrow these negative strategies is to distract us from listening to the development of the critical capabilities of the child and using them as critical moments in the emancipatory language of the home. These religious moments of emancipatory language also need to be named. They can be named as moments of problem solving, social criticism, or scientific method, thus effectively maintaining the silence about their ultimate source, or they can be named as part of the continuing story of the people of God.

I have presented the position that language is grounded in and continuously partakes of the interpersonal, which determines its expressive and interpretative character or structure, and have suggested some of the possible forms of religious language. We are now ready to ask how the manifestations of sexism in our society interact with this complex of language about God. In doing this, we are acknowledging that our sisters have brought to collective awareness social dominations and limitations of freedom in our past and present. They have created one of the necessary language moments in our mutual emancipation from these limitations and have requested that others join them in the long and difficult completion of this particular work of freedom.

SEXISM, SOCIAL RELATIONS, AND LANGUAGES ABOUT GOD

The task remaining is long and arduous. To this point in the paper only the tools of the needed analysis have been identified. The actual analysis will require much more work with language and in the reorganization of the social relationships which bear upon this language. In the few remaining pages, I can only indicate the general direction that I think this work should take.

Our task is to indicate how the many and diverse manifestations of sexism in our society are dialectically related to the previously identified dimensions of language. However, a strategic error will be made unless we carry the dialectic further and look at the relationships between the manifestations of sexism and the other divisions within society. Our immediate concern springs from the divisions between male and female. But we should not be indifferent to age divisions in our society and the prejudices against the language of children and the language of the aged, sanctioned by our non-dialectical notions of knowledge, truth and education. Likewise the division between the expert and the non-expert, or those in authority and those out of authority, create biases in our investigations and our uses of language. Finally, we must recognize that social relations are, in part, determined by class and cultural groupings, and are obviously related to the economic and political structure of the society. Through this complexity we must work our way with care, remembering that language develops and is sustained in the interpersonal. As the interpersonal is shaped by the institutions and divisions within society, hence by the distribution of power, it follows that language is also shaped by these institutions and divisions. This, too, is a dialectical, not a cause-and-effect, relation. We must identify how the divisions, institutions, and distributions of power influence our language, but we must also use our language to suggest the direction of change within these institutions and divisions. Significantly, language also sustains the interpersonal. Careful use of language with others can alter the mutuality of our experience, creating a fundamental opening into the fabric of social and institutional life and potentially transforming the distribution of power.

How do the social divisions and institutions, the distribution of power, influence language? If language is grounded in the interpersonal, and if the interpersonal is distorted by power or institutionalized relations, the language is also distorted. If expression and interpretation are constitutive of language, and if divisions and the distributions of power impose or inhibit expression and/or interpretations, then language does not realize its potential in human affairs and mutual understanding is never reached. If the forms of language are manifestations of forms of life which are influenced by divisions and distributions of power, then language uses are manifestations of these same divisions and power arrangements. These are the three directions that the remainder of the paper will take.

The first direction requires that we look at the dialectics of sexual divisions and the interpersonal grounding or origins of language. My clue is taken from an extremely provocative book by Dorothy Dinnerstein, *The Mermaid and the Minotaur: Sexual Arrangements and Human Malaise*. She argues that the present sexual-social arrangements in our time, and the problems that arise from them, have their origin in two conditions. First,

> ... our species painful misgivings about enterprise—about free rein for the spirit of mastery and inventiveness and led us to create ourselves in the first place—have not yet been felt through. [54]

And the other condition, more-important for our purpose is

> ... that woman remain almost universally in charge of infant and early child care.... What is important is the effect of predominately female care on the later emotional predilections of the child: The point of crucial consequences is that for virtually every living person it is a woman—usually the mother—who has provided the main initial contact with humanity and with nature.[55]

For our purposes we might add that it is "a woman—usually the mother—who has provided the initial contact" with language and perhaps the language about God. I have been able to find few studies which have factored out this variable in the descriptions of the form and function of early language development of children. If we can tentatively accept some of the dubious conclusions of Robin Lakoff[56] that the spoken language of woman differs from the language of men, then the implication of this early language relationship between young children and women can be important. The differences, if they exist, between the discourse of woman and the discourse of men, are probably class and culture related. We also know little about the transition in language forms and function as the child moves from the primary interpersonal groupings and the language of peers, schools and larger community institutions. Many questions can be asked about how the sexual divisions within the home are related to the origins of language and how the language games of the broader community work their way into the home via the mother, father, siblings, community members, and mass media. Under whose auspices does the young child first begin to hear and participate in talk about religion? If such discourse is limited only to the church and the traditional age, sex and interest divisions within the church, how does such discourse find its way into discourse with the child except through the church school mechanisms? These are questions which are not to be answered in general, but suggest direction for inquiry and study by religious communities concerned with how children use language about God.

Dinnerstein and other writers about woman's liberation point to the obvious linkages between the productive forces in society and the structure of the social relations in the home. The concern is easily traced back to the work of Engels[57] as well as Horkheimer[58] and other neo-Marxists.[59] The continued development of productive forces in our society can lead to changes in the interpersonal dynamics of the family, and hence influence the origins of language in the person. For instance, Dinnerstein suggests that our economy can now support the involvement of woman in the economy and the involvement of men in child rearing. If family roles need no longer be primarily a function of the division of labor wherein women labor in the home and men in the public economy, and if fathers and mothers can spend equal time with the infant and child, then obviously the fathers will be as influential as the mothers in the origins of the child's language. Whether the father's language is more or less apt to assume the forms of religious language is, of course, questionable.

Until such time as these major changes in the economy occur, religious communities can find alternative means by which the caretaker-caregiver language is more reflective of diversity in our language and perhaps more reflective of the religious language. It is crucial that we do not fall into the intellectual trap of assuming a dyadic relationship[60] between caregiver and caretaker. The evidence points to the significance of the social support system for the caregiver: whoever cares for the infant and the child, needs supportive contact with others outside of the home. Language nurses, people who help mothers and other caregivers reflect upon the importance of language responsiveness and develop more effective language relationships, have been suggested by some. Parent groups, perhaps with infants and children, meeting with someone eager and willing to talk about the religious significance of being with and caring for the young might well enrich the religious language in the home. The removal of the sick, the aged, the handicapped, the dying from the home deprives the family of discourse about the limit situations wherein human need and evidence of the sacred are most evident. Again, social and religious support is essential in these limit situations for the language resources of the family could easily be depleted without replenishment.

As pointed out in the psychodynamic literature, the early child-rearing years are also important for developing the basic orientations of the child toward male and female. During these early years, the future interpretative ground for many sex related words are formed. The meaning of "mother," "father," "brother," "sister," "man," "woman" cannot help but take on some significance of these early years. If we follow Dinnerstein's suggestion that both mother and father become equally involved with infant care—the cuddling, cooing, diaper changing, expressions of control and boredom, feeding, playing, frustration and worrying—then the meaning of family terms will be significantly different. Mother will not mean someone who stays home to take care of infant, child and the home, or father the person who disappears into and appears from the outside world. Furthermore, in joint family dwellings, where the tasks of child rearing, housekeeping, and world maintenance and building are not sex related, the meaning of these terms would take on many different meanings.

The final consideration about the caretaker-caregiver relationships, and the social relationships which support them, is that this is the first arena in which impressions are expressed and other expressions interpreted. It is in this arena that sex related terms in religious language can begin to be interpreted, if the various members of the household and the community which supports it provide the opportunity. We must turn, then, to how expression and interpretation are dialectically related to divisions within our society, including those of sex.

Mueller helps us identify the consequences of what he calls "repressive communication," which is a breakdown in expression and/or interpretations:

> On the individual level, any incongruence between inner and outer language, between privatized and externalized meaning, any split in the graphical experience will result not only in distorted communication with oneself, but also in distorted communication with others. This distortion constitutes the repressive nature of communication.

> The common characteristic of repressive communication is that the internalized language system permits neither the articulation of subjectively experienced needs beyond the emotive level nor the realization of maximum individuation, or, thus, implicit autonomy formation. On the psychic level, the language used represses part of one's symbolic biography and inhibits the attainment of consciousness. On the class level the language used results in an incapacity to locate oneself in history and society.[61]

Repressive communication is a consequence of unequal power relationships among language users and those in communication. The problem to which attention must be turned is how the sexual and other divisions within society restrict private and/or public expression and inhibit mutual interpretation of that which is expressed. When and how is power used to prevent and impose expressions and interpretations?

Of interest to us are the ways in which male and female, young and old give language form to their own experiences of the religious; the ways in which these personal expressions of the religious are accepted and interpreted by others; the problems of interpretation when these personal expressions come up against established, accepted and even authoritative expressions of the religious; and finally the way that males and females, the young and old are able to engage in their own interpretations of someone else's expression of the religious, including those in the sacred texts.

Gouldner provides the best tools for identifying those situations wherein the power institutionalized in various social divisions interferes with expression and interpretation. He calls attention to the four elements or conditions needed for an "ideal speech" situation: "(1) no violence; (2) permeable boundaries between public and private speech; (3) allowance of traditional symbols and rules of discourse to be made problematic; and (4) insistence on equal opportunities to speak."[62]

Again, the need is for extended study and action in various religious communities. For instance, when is violence, even symbolic violence or the threat of violence, used to interfere with expression or interpretation of religious language? In the home, young children and the aged are often prevented from giving free form to his/her experiences or interpretations through a variety of fears or projected consequences. In mixed conversation groups, either men or the woman may feel more inhibited. To what extent do males and females, young and old, rich and poor, educated and uneducated feel that the language used to express their private experiences or lack of experiences of the religious are of the same domain as the public speech about God, and hence subject to similar rules of interpretation? Under what circumstances are males and females, young and old, rich and poor, educated and uneducated, allowed to make problematic the "symbols and rules of discourse" about God and religious experience? Do the young, aged, laity, educated and uneducated, and the professional religious have equal opportunities to speak, and in what circumstances? These are the questions that can be asked about discourse in the home, the church, and other settings. The search for answers should help us hear and see how language about God, sexual and other social divisions, and the distribution of power within our society are interconnected.

These lines of inquiry and investigation can be more valuable if we look for differences within the various forms of language identified earlier: ritual, prayer, writing and reading, conversation, instruction, and emancipation. We should identify the control and use of power, consciously or unconsciously, behind the established forms of language about God, in the development of newer public forms of religious expression, in the formal and informal interpretations of ritual, prayers, writings, and over the various moments of emancipatory discourse. Religious language, which is necessarily symbolic, reflects the human dimensions of experience as well as the Divine. If we bring under question the uniformity of religious discourse, then it is appropriate to ask about the human experiences which were the origins of the symbols of the divine. To what extent is the literature expressive of the child's experience of the religious, the elderly's, women's at various stages of their life cycle? How have the skills of writing and of interpretation been deployed in our society so the religious experience of a variety of populations find their way into public discourse? How are the boundaries of institutional life governed so all populations have more or less equal access to making public their private experience of the religious if that seems important, whether in writing, interpretation, conversation, or the moments of emancipatory activity? How do the various media organizations shape and control the religious language which finds its way into print or other public forms? Whose experiences of the religious find their way into new rituals or liturgies, and who controls the selection of rituals for particular communities at particular times?

Religious language, like all forms of language, is dialectically related to the social structures within which it is used. It is this complicated matrix within which we are working, and we have only begun the hard, detailed and necessary work.

SUMMARY: LANGUAGE ABOUT GOD
AND RELIGIOUS FORMATION

The Introduction to *Language About God "Opening the Door"* states

> Our language limits our ability to communicate God's power and love. Words, being of human origin, are restrictive. Therefore, we need to search for more creative ways of expressing our relationship to God.

The danger of the statement is the possible identification of language with words and their restrictiveness, and the assumption that language limits communication. We do indeed need to search "for more creative ways of expressing our relationship with God," but the search is wrongly directed if it is for better and new words, or better and new language. Only, if we recognize that language partakes of the interpersonal and hence of the expressive and the interpretative can our search be sufficiently profound. By grounding language in the interpersonal and in the interpretative, I have tried to get away from the reification of language and have tried to root it in the dialectical processes of which it is a part. Our need is perhaps less new language and words, and more attention to the uses of language among and between people of all ages, sexes, and social conditions. From increased communication among the diverse groups and individuals we might be surprised to find ourselves speaking with greater vitality and less sexual prejudice.

By grounding language in the interpersonal, we can more easily recognize how language use changes as the social and economic conditions within which we live distort the realm of the interpersonal. When individuals or classes of people cannot engage in communication about God, it is not simply that there is a limit to their language, but there is a limit on their relationships with a variety of other people; and this has its origin in infancy and in the social divisions within our society, including the sexual divisions. Thus we can not talk about the limits of communication and language without at the same time talking about the injustices in our life with others. In a sense, then, our language becomes a map of our social relationships, of the way we have granted power and authority to some and impotence and subjugation to others. To study how others speak is to study how they are with others and how others are with them.

Language About God "Opening the Door" also states that "We are convinced that words and concepts form our self-perceptions and our beliefs about God" and asks the question "Why and in what ways is language important in forming concepts of, and relationships to God, self, and society?" I am not convinced that this is the case, for it grants a power to language which does not exist in and of itself. It is only because language is used interpersonally with others, or in significant social situations which may no longer be interpersonal because of the distribution of power, that language seems related to concepts of self and other and seems instrumental in shaping relationships. But if we accept that language is a map of the basic social schemas, then we must look behind language to the interpersonal linkages and their distortions in order to answer the question. And even then the question must be modified, for I doubt if the expression "concepts of God" has any validity at all. We can only talk of the symbols of God and their use.

Our concern it seems to me, is the religious formation of ourselves and those we care for. We must rightfully ask how others, and their language, can participate in the religious formation of someone else. It seems to me that we participate by being with others in such a way that we recognize that language is the expression of someone else's experience, and that its appropriate use is not the search for truth in language, but the listening into awareness of the other, and the participation in the ever necessary interpretation without which language falls into idolatry.

NOTES

[1]Martin Heidegger, "Holderlin and the Essence of Poetry," in *Existence and Being*, trans. Douglas Scott (Chicago: Henry Regnery Co. 1949), 297.
[2]Jean Piaget, *Biology and Knowledge* (Chicago, IL: University of Chicago Press, 1971).

[3]Lucien Goldmann, *Cultural Creation in Modern Society*, trans. Bart Grohl (St. Louis, MO: Telos Press, 1976).

[4]Advisory Council on Discipleship and Worship, United Presbyterian Church of USA, *Language About God "Opening the Door"* (New York, New York, 1975).

[5]Philipp Aries, *Centuries of Childhood: A Social History of Family Life*, trans. Irons R. Baldick (New York: Vintage 1972).

[6]Lawrence Kohlberg, "Stages and Moral Development of a Basis for Moral Development," *Moral Education*, ed. C. Beckow and E. Sullivan (Toronto: University of Toronto Press, 1970).

[7]James Fowler, "Toward a Developmental Perspective on Faith," *Religious Education* vol. 69, 207–219.

[8]Maurice Merleau-Ponty, *The Phenomenology of Perception*, trans. Colin Smith (London: Routledge & Kegan Paul, 1962).

[9]"The Bond of Mother-Baby," Ideas and Trends, *New York Times*, Sunday August 21, 1977.

[10]Michael Lewis and Leonard Rosenblum, *The Effect of the Infant on the Caregiver* (New York: John Wiley and Sons, 1974).

[11]John Macmurray, *Persons in Relation* (New York: Harper and Bros. 1961), Chapter II.

[12]Maurice Merleau-Ponty, *The Prose of the World*, trans. John O'Neill (Evanston, IL: Northwestern University Press, 1973), 20.

[13]Ibid., 20.

[14]Martin Buber, *I and Thou*, trans. Ronald G. Smith (New York: Charles Scribner's Sons, 1937).

[15]Macmurray, *Persons in Relation*.

[16]Courtney Cazden, "The Neglected Situation in Child Language Research and Education," in *Language and Poverty*, ed. Frederick Williams (Chicago: Markham Publishing Company, 1970), Chapter V.

[17]Harley Shands, *Thinking and Psychotherapy* (Cambridge: Harvard University Press, 1960).

[18]Jacques Lacan, *The Language of the Self* (New York: Dell, 1975).

[19]Ferdinand de Saussure, *Course in General Linguistics*, trans. Wade Baskin (New York: McGraw Hill, 1961).

[20]Paul Ricoeur, *Interpretation Theory: Discourse and the Surplus of Meaning* (Fort Worth,TX: The Texas Christian University Press, 1976).

[21]Ibid., 3.

[22]Ibid., 3.

[23]Ibid., 9.

[24]Ibid., 9.

[25]Merleau-Ponty, *Prose of the World*, 10.

[26]Ibid., 14.

[27]Ricoeur, *Interpretation Theory*, 19.

[28]Ibid., 20.

[29]Douglas Steere, *On Listening to Another* (New York: Harper and Row, 1955).

[30]Ricoeur, op. cit., 16.

[31]Merleau-Ponty, op. cit., 17.

[32]Ricoeur, op. cit., 17.

[33]Ibid., 50.

[34]Ibid., 54.

[35]Ibid., 57.

[36]Ibid., 59.

[37]Dell Hymes, *Towards Communicative Competence* (Philadelphia: University of Pennsylvania Press, 1972).

[38]Jürgen Habermas, "Toward a Theory of Communicative Competence," In *Recent Sociology*, No. 2, ed. Hans Peter Dreitzel (New York: Macmillan, 1970), Chapter V.

[39]Ricoeur, op. cit., 12.

[40]Ibid., 13.

[41]Ibid., 19.

[42]Ibid., 34-35.

[43]Ibid., 36.

[44]Ibid., 37.

[45]Ibid., 32.

[46]*Language About God "Opening the Door"*, op. cit.

[47]Ricoeur, op. cit.

[48]Ibid., 55.

[49]Ann Douglas, *The Feminization of American Culture* (New York: Alfred A. Knopf, 1977), 8.

[50]Ibid., 10–11.

[51]Ivan Illich, *Deschooling Society* (New York: Harper and Row,1970).

[52]Paulo Freire, *Pedagogy of the Oppressed*, trans. Myra B. Ramos (New York: Seabury Press, 1970).

[53]Jürgen Habermas, *Knowledge and Human Interests*, trans. Jeremy Shapiro (Boston: Beacon 1971).

[54]Dorothy Dinnerstein, *The Mermaid and The Minotaur: Sexual Arrangements and Human Malaise* (New York: Harper and Row, 1976), 25.

[55]Ibid., 26.

[56]Robin Lakoff, *Language and Woman's Place* (New York: Harper and Row, 1975).

[57]Friedrich Engels, *The Origins of the Family, Private Property and the State*, trans. Ernest Untermann (New York: International Publishers, 1942).

[58]Max Horkheimer, "Authority and the Family," *Critical Essays*, trans. Matthew O'Connor (New York: Herder and Herder, 1972).

[59]cf. Michael Schneider, *Neurosis and Civilization, A Marxist/Freudian Synthesis*, trans. Michael Rologg (New York: Seabury Press, 1975).

[60]From conversations with Dr. Barabra Kenefick.

[61]Klaus Mueller, "Notes on the Repression of Communicative Behavior," in *Recent Sociology*, No. 2, ed. Hans Peter Dreitzel (New York: Macmillan,1970), Chapter IV.

[62]Alvin Gouldner, *The Dialectic of Ideology and Technology* (New York: Seabury Press, 1976), 42.

22

Toward a Political Economy of Curriculum and Human Development

(1977)

The writings of Marx and his followers have too infrequently informed the concerns of the curriculum person and those in related educational fields. The social-political reasons for this under-utilization are obvious, inasmuch as the class analysis of the 1930s and of this recent critical period were often interpreted as being subversive of U.S. political and economic institutions. However, the philosophical-historical reasons are less obvious, and worthy of significant scholarship, for the historical, dialectical, and material content of his writings describe phenomena which can be interpreted as educational. This paper is intended as a pointer to some of the issues and possibilities which might be considered if a curriculum person were to engage in the critical interpretation of the writings of Marx and his followers. I claim no special competency for this task except interest and a home base in this presumed field of curriculum.

The historical task is a major one if we are to understand why the writings of Marx have been ignored by educators of the United States, except those brave few, some of whom have suffered the consequences. I presume that the reason, in part, revolves around two major figures at the turn of the century, plus or minus twenty years or so—Harris and Dewey. The Hegelianism of Harris had no small impact upon the character of schooling in the United States. Cremin[1] credits Harris with establishing the basic paradigm of the curriculum field which prevails today with minor themes and variations. Perhaps even more important is his impact on the organization of the schools and his concern for textbooks as the center of the curriculum, rather than the teacher as the center. Although one American Hegelian, August Willich,[2] was a colleague of Marx and Engels, the Feuerbachian and Marxian critique and surpassing of Hegel did not make much of an impact on the other American Hegelians. Crucial in this historical picture is Dewey's encounter with Hegel by way of G. S. Morris at Johns Hopkins[3] and his turn to pragmatism. I am unfamiliar with whether Dewey's pragmatism is in part founded by a critical reaction to Marx. However, it is fascinating that both Dewey and Marx cut a philosophical eyetooth or two on Hegel. For reasons perhaps best explained by Novak,[4] Dewey's particular pragmatic surpassing of Hegel dominated educational thought to the exclusion of other post-Hegelian philosophies. It seems that the sixty years before the publication of Bobbitt's *Curriculum*[5] might be as important for understanding our intellectual ground as the sixty years following it.

There have been those students of education who have utilized Marx's ideas of *Das Kapital* to analyze the place of schooling in our economic and political structure. In the 1920s and 30s Langford[6] and Slesinger[7] stand out, and in this critical period the works of Mann[8] and Bowles and Gintis[9] are notable. The analysis has been at the macro level. Concepts of class, labor, alienation, commodity, capital accumulation, and imperialism have been used to describe how schools and other structures of education reproduce the labor force and class distinctions within the capitalistic economy and the political and social institutions which accompany it. These macro analyses have called our attention to the controlling functions inherent in institutionalized educational structures, and point out the masking function of much past and present curricular language which proclaims the school's presumed role in "self-realization" and a more perfect "democratic" society.

With few exceptions in this country, the writings of Marx have not been used to explore the micro aspects of education—the interpersonal or intersubjective—the biography of the individual within specific social locations. One of the reasons for this is given by Joel Kovel[10] who writes of the dialectical relationship between Freud and Marx. He suggests that Marx, to accomplish his great achievement, necessarily had to be concerned with only those aspects of human life that could be objectified and hence become a commodity. In effect, Marx had to bracket the subjective in order to explain the objective. Kovel suggests that Freud had to bracket the objective in order to deal with the subjective—the interpersonal and fantasy. Because Marx did not attend to the interpersonal and the subjective, the application of his ideas to the evolving biography of the individual within the prevailing objective structures is difficult, although some neo-Marxists have made the effort.[11] Reich[12] has described the dialectical relation between the economic-political structure and the sexual life of individuals. Horkheimer,[13] in his work on the family, has illustrated how the family mediates between the economic structures and the life of the child. He shows how the relations of production carry into the home, thus producing the individual who fits into the capitalistic structures. Today, I suppose that it would be equally easy to show how the commodity structure and consumerism work their way into the home, not only via the activity of the parents, but by the mass medium of TV, the commodity which carries the image of all other commodities into the bedroom or kitchen. These mediating structures of home and media are surely important vehicles for describing how the forces and relations of production and the market impinge upon the child.

The historical dialectical method of Marx, developed in the mid-19th century, must be interpreted historically and dialectically. The genetic epistemology of Piaget,[14] no matter how flawed or partial, is part of the totality to be considered as the methods and rhetoric of Marx are reinterpreted in the situation of today. The significance which most educators attach to the work of Piaget, namely that he describes the cognitive functioning of the individual during different stages of growth, is, for my purposes, a masking of Piaget's more important contribution. Piaget has described the evolution, in the epistemic subject, of logico-mathematical structures. Piaget's work suggests that the adult decenter. Mathematics is not only what the adult does when computing and operating in science laboratories or in industry. Mathematics is also what the child does when he/she groups objects, orders objects according to various attributes, and engages in a host of other transforming activities in the world. Piaget calls our attention to a different definition of knowledge structures. No longer can we see knowledge as finished form built into the behavior of adults and their tools which must then be "taught" to the child. Piaget has asked us to see knowledge structures as evolving—if you wish, as biographical or historical and as dialectical. Whereas Marx has forced us to see ideologies and social, economic, and political structures within an historical and dialectical focus, Piaget has accomplished the same thing from the perspective of the history of involvement of the individual. Whereas Piaget has attended primarily to the logico-mathematical, and indeed has clearly bracketed out of his consideration metaphysical and ideological knowledge, he makes possible a genetic culture. He brings into our awareness the possibility that all adult forms of knowing and action can be, should be, seen in the perspective of their genesis in the person. No longer should we adults be permitted to see adult forms of knowledge or action as the way to interpret knowledge or action. Just as Marx required that we see them as social phenomena, and interpret them historically and dialectically, so Piaget asks that we now see them genetically (or historically) and dialectically in the individual person.

The Piagetian task confronting Marxism is to identify and describe the forms or structures of a "genetic," Marxism. How does Marxism, as a structure of social action and thought, evolve and become distorted in an individual? It is normally assumed that Marxism is an adult framework for viewing and acting in adult social life, and that the tasks of the Marxist are to develop the class consciousness and political organization of the proletariat to fulfill its historic mission. Given this charge, the Marxist educator must disseminate the political-economic tools for analysis and reconstruction of social life. The use of Marxian tools demystifies the forces of domination, builds political leadership, and develops the class consciousness necessary to mobilize political action of large segments of the people. This is the tack of Bowles and Gintis[15] in education; and indeed it is an important one, whether one shares their political commitments or not.

But if we had a genetic Marxism, the questions of the educator would be different. Assume that Marxian "revolutionary practice" has as its origins biological and social givens and activities of the infant. If the continuities and the discontinuities of this evolving operational structure can be identified, then perhaps we can see how the social and material environment intrudes upon or facilitates the development of so-called mature Marxian thought and action.[16]

This is what I wish to point to in this paper. I do not hope to accomplish the task in the paper, but merely to point to needed and possible intellectual work. If we can move toward this goal of a "genetic" Marxism, then I think that we can also move toward a political economy of the curriculum and of human development itself. We should then depict more precisely the various mediations between the neophyte and the adult world, not with the intent of improving our educational control over the child, but with the possibility of pointing out the educational significance of the child for the adult, and the need to construct more effective means for producing appropriate qualities of life for young and old.

The first task, then, is to map the intellectual tools of Marxism. The function of mapping these tools, these intellectual operations, is to provide a point of origin for genetic analysis. My operation is indeed abstract and conceptual, with the full recognition that the only appropriate method is finally phenomenological and dialectical, which entails bringing to consciousness the child-adult relationship over time—an autobiography of social relations.

The extensiveness, complexity, and detail of Marx's writings make the mapping task almost foolhardy. One is tempted to use already existing maps, such as Ollman's fine work on *Alienation*[17] But a map is a tool, an instrument of production. Even an intellectual tool or means of production one must own, in order that the production has use value for the person. Thus, in my beginning appropriation of Marx's language tools, personal choices are made, with the full recognition that if my production is to have social use value it must become part of the social dialectic, and hence critiqued and negated or surpassed by others.

As a point of origin for this particular activity I would identify the following as significant markers: activity, work, labor, labor power; means of production, property; use-value, exchange-value, commodity; relations of production; alienation, class and class consciousness; surplus value and capital. However, here I shall be concerned only with activity, work, labor, labor power; means of production; and relations of production. My tactic will be to point in the direction that I think a genetic Marxism might take, and to suggest the direction of possible implications for curriculum and the way that we adults might talk about child-adult relations over time.

Marx begins his analysis of Capitalism in Volume I of *Das Kapital*[18] with the commodity and commodity exchange, but central to his analysis is the labor process. Labor is the process by which nature is appropriated for individual and social use and by means of which use-value is produced. The productive process, which is at the same time a process of consumption, requires means of production—the instruments of production and the subject of production: property. Specialization of labor leads gradually to a separation of the laboring process from the ownership of the means of production, hence the selling of one's labor power and the alienation of one's own being from one's labor and the products of this labor. Capital as surplus labor results, and hence the class distinctions between those who own property and have capital and those who have only their labor power as a commodity to exchange for other commodities. Labor, then, is central to any understanding of Marx's writing, and is a key language tool for his economic and political analysis. What are the origins of labor in the person? Or to use Piagetian language, how can genesis of labor be described in the biography of the person and how can its origins be detected in the activity of the young child? Under what circumstances in one's life history does the alienation of labor occur, and when does the person begin to see his/her labor as labor for someone else, as something to be exchanged? Who owns the means of production in the life of the child? How does that ownership contribute to alienation and the loss or increase of power to produce one's own quality of life and to participate willingly in the social production of life?[19]

Marx states that "Labour is, in the first place, a process in which both man and Nature participate, and in which man of his own accord starts, regulates, and controls the material reactions between himself and Nature."[20] In *A Contribution to a Critique of Political Economy* he states that "In the process of production, members of society appropriate (produce, fashion) natural products in accordance with human requirements"[21] and "Production is always appropriation of nature by an individual within and with the help of a definite social organization."[22] For Marx, "The elementary factors of the labor process are (a) the personal activity of man, i.e., work itself; (b) the subject of that work; and (c) its instruments."[23] Within the many writings of Marx, Ollman indicates how Marx gradually shifts from the term "activity" to the term "work." Productive activity is work. Ollman claims that "For Marx, labor is always alienated productive activity."[24]

It is at this point that the specific content of Piaget's writing becomes helpful, not simply his methodology and general commitment to genetic epistemology. There seems to be a striking similarity between Marx and Piaget with respect to significance of activity and the appropriation of nature. You will recall that

Piaget grounds logical-mathematical knowledge in the schemata of action.[25] He claims that knowledge and intelligence are transformations of the world, dependent upon the schemata of assimilation and accommodation. For Piaget, as for Marx, the significant aspect of human life is active interchange with the environment from which Piaget draws his genetic conceptions of knowledge and Marx his historical conceptions of labor, alienation, and capital. The foundation of knowledge for Piaget is the body and the biological determinants of the schemata of assimilation and accommodation. The foundation of the social-economic-political structure for Marx is also the material structure of the body in the world (in fact Marx refers to Nature as "man's inorganic body"[26]) from which develops, historically, our ideologies, knowledge structures, and social relations. The basic "instruments" of activity for Piaget are the schemata which are founded in the biological structures. The instruments of activity for Marx are the means of production, property. Thus, indicating the basic material base upon which they both ground their work.

The obvious hunch at this stage of the interpretation is that Piaget's schemata of action are the subjective correlates of Marx's objective means of production. In fact, Marx, referring to "the factors of the labor process," calls attention to "its objective factors, the means of production, as well as its subjective factors, labor power."[27] The schemata and means of production are not only instruments, but become or are vehicles which support activity, give it direction or intentionality, and increase its power. The use of the word "power" is significant, for Marx refers to "labor-power" as the commodity that the laborer exchanges for wages. Surplus labor-power, the labor-power beyond that needed for the maintenance and reproduction of the laborer himself/herself, is the source of surplus value, the source of capital. Surplus labor power, rather than being consumed for social production or for production of the laborer—going beyond his/her own reproduction to produce new personal qualities of life and activity—is used to produce wealth for someone else.

Marx and Piaget both recognize that activity itself produces the person as well as transforms the world or produces use-value in the social world. Whereas this is readily seen in the works of Piaget, it stands forth less clearly in the more common interpretations of Marx. Marx states quite specifically that the person

opposes himself to Nature as one of her own forces, setting in motion arms and legs, head and hands, the natural forces of his body, in order to appropriate Nature's productions in a form adapted to his own wants. By this acting on the external world and changing it, he at the same time changes his own nature. He develops his slumbering powers and compels them to act in obedience to his sway.[28]

Thus, both Marx and Piaget ground their work in human activity, which is exhibited at birth. Activity is the manifestation of human life and the starting point of our concern. In *The Economic and Philosophic Manuscripts of 1844*, Marx asked "what is life but activity?"[29] We need not dig beneath the surface to infer motive or biological explanations of activity for purposes of understanding education, although clearly such digging is interesting and valuable. The infant exhibits undifferentiated activity. How is that activity gradually differentiated and focused? How does the stuff of the social-material world shape activity and give it power and direction? Under what circumstances does activity cease being activity for one's self and become activity for another, that is, when does it become alienated labor? In thinking through answers to these questions, both Piaget and Marx are helpful; for Piaget attends to the body, specifically to the cognitive, dimensions of some of the answers, whereas Marx attends to the social and property dimensions of some of the answers. Thus we have pointed, so far, to the genetic origins of labor and to the possible significance of the means of production in this genetic labor.

We have also called attention, although much too briefly, to the notion of labor power and the significance of power in human life. As educators, we have been more inclined to talk of the person in terms of needs rather than powers, and we have been inclined to speak of needs assessments or deficiencies rather than how a person uses his/her power. But the focus of labor power suggests that we begin to ask how children use their surplus energy, beyond that needed for self-maintenance. To what extent do they recognize the power to construct, to produce new qualities of life for themselves, and to produce new qualities of life, new environments for others? To what extent is that surplus energy seen as something negative, to be feared, repressed, or sublimated, or used by others; as a source of guilt because it comes up against, and perhaps brings judgments against, the already established which others seek to maintain? In the course of a person's life, when is surplus energy seen as "labor power," a commodity to be exchanged for other commodities? But before these points can be elaborated, we must attend to the social dimension and to the genesis of the relations of production.

Again, Marx is quite clear as to the social dimension in his writings. The significance of social class and class consciousness is the obvious indicator of this social dimension. In the *Grundrisse* he states that: "Each individual's production is dependent on the production of others" and that "private interest is already a socially determined interest."[30] In a sense, then, activity for Marx is always social activity, although the social dimension is often hidden by the alienation of labor and commodities. For Piaget, the social dimension is more opaque. In spite of defining cognition as founded on operations which connect the agent and the environment, he fails to ground his cognition of the child in the operations which exist between himself, the experimenter, and the child. It is interesting that as Piaget speaks of the physicist and physics, he states that "the physicist constantly acts, and the first thing he does is to transform objects and phenomena in order to get at the laws validating these transformations."[31] Yet he appears not to acknowledge his own acts. His very knowledge about cognitive development in the young is a consequence of his action; he has transformed the relationships between the child and his environment by manipulating objects, asking questions, or placing puzzles or tasks before the child. His stages of cognitive development are social, a consequence of his very intervention into the life of the child, and participation in the activity of the child. Piaget's conceptions of the intellectual development of the child are not only conceptions of the intellectual development of the child, but also of the development of the social relationship between the child and the experimenter, in which the social activity of the adult is masked or taken for granted. The correctives against forgetting or masking the activity of the adult are two. First, a phenomenological methodology would help, in which the investigator brackets out his/her own taken-for-granted realities and indeed turns to consciousness of the "thing itself." The thing itself in the Piagetian experiment is not the child and his/her environment, but the child, the material environment, and the social environment consisting of the child and the experimenter, which necessarily includes the language activity between them. The other corrective is the empirical literature which seeks to describe the genesis of the social relationship between the neonate and the caregiver. The role or activity of the experimenter must also be reflected upon in this empirical work.

A speculative overview of the problem is found in Macmurray's *Persons in Relation*,[32] wherein the infant is described as a rational person at birth. A person is not an isolated individual, but can exist only in relation with others. For Macmurray, the child supplies the motives, the caregiver supplies the intentions; the combination of intention and motive means rationality. The infant can live only through or by means of communication; communication does not develop through life with another. Language, then, is a consequence of communication, not vice versa. Social relations are foundational for the continuation of individual life.

An empirical approach to the problem is found in *The Effect of the Infant on Its Caregiver*,[33] edited by Lewis and Rosenblum. The studies which they brought together were intended to support the thesis of the editors that: "Not only is the infant or child influenced by its social, political, economic, and biological world, but in fact the child itself influences its world in turn."[34] The editors demonstrate with empirical findings that which Marx has demonstrated by way of his dialectical materialism and Piaget by his genetic epistemology—that the activity between the person and the world, even the social world, produces the person and transforms the world. In the volume Bell refers to the fact "that both parent and offspring behave so as to produce or maintain the behavior of the other."[35] The various studies point to the mutual significance of facial, vocal, and gaze behaviors in which the infant is often the instigator and terminator of a series of interactions. In a report on the relationship between blind infants and their mothers, Fraiberg describes how the absence of the infant's gaze changes typical mothering reactions, and alters vocalization patterns of mother and infant. Compensation for this lack of visual contact is possible if the mother is helped to respond vocally to the movement cues of the infant, and if tactile replaces visual communication and eye play.[36]

Additional information is provided in *Temperament and Behavior Disorders* by Thomas and others, in which the authors identify temperament as a crucial factor in the development of behavior disorders. They hypothesize that the "behavioral style of the individual child . . . the characteristic tempo, rhythmicity, adaptability, energy expenditure, mood, and focus of attention"[37] of a child is a key factor in understanding the social interactions of the child. I interpret this to mean that the physiological characteristics of the individual organism impact on the evolving social relations between the child and his/her caregivers. It seems reasonable to generalize beyond Piaget here. Piaget claims that the logico-mathematical schemata which serve as "specialized organs of regulation in the control of exchanges with the environment"[38] are founded on the biological structures of the child. It would be reasonable to hypothesize that schemata also evolve which serve as organs of regulation in the control of exchanges with other persons, and that these are grounded in biological structures of the infant, hence the significance of temperament in social relationships and their distortions. However, it does not seem reasonable to use the expression assimilation and accommodation with respect to these presumed schemata of regulation in the exchange with others, unless we add the qualifier "negotiated" assimilation and "negotiated" accommodation, for the mutuality of impact and the mutuality of self-production must be acknowledged.

I have suggested a parallel between environmental interactions and social interactions, using Piaget's formulations of the logico-mathematical as the metaphor. I wish to carry this parallel one step further, in order to get to a potentially more useful handle on the problem of social relations, the relation of production, and the phenomena of consciousness. Piaget states that

> to attribute logic and mathematics to the general coordinates of the subject's action . . . is a recognition of the fact that while the fecundity of the subject's thought process depends on the internal resources of the organism, the efficacy of those processes depends on the fact that the organism is not independent of the environment but can only live, act, or think in interaction with it.[39]

Piaget's overall strategy was to begin with the givenness of mathematics and scientific knowledge and to search for their origins in the child. In so doing he has also, of course, reconstructed our knowledge of these disciplines. But he did not start with general notions of schemata of assimilation and accommodation and then find that they led to logico-mathematical formal structures.

The parallel I would suggest is that the forms of language usage are the coordinates of social relations, and that the clues to the possible schemata of these social relations are to be found in the functions of speech between and among persons in their many relations. The work of Merleau-Ponty, a phenomenologist, supports this parallel. He describes speech as an extension of the body, in a sense affirming that both logico-mathematical operations and speech are founded in biological givens. He states that "language is a manifestation, a revelation of intimate being and of the psychic link which unites us to the world and to our fellow man."[40] Later he claims that,

> There is one particular culture object which is destined to play a crucial role in the perception of other people: language. In dialogue there is constituted between the other person and myself a common ground: my thought and his are woven into a single fabric, my words and those of my interlocutor are called forth by the state of the discussion, and they are inserted into a shared operation of which neither of us is the creator. We have here a dual being, where the other is for me no longer a mere bit of behavior in my transcendental field, nor I in his; we are collaborators for each other in consummate reciprocity.[41]

Paralleling Piaget's reflective abstraction whereby the logico-mathematical structures are constructed, Merleau-Ponty writes that, "It is only retrospectively, when I have withdrawn from the dialogue and am recalling it that I am able to integrate it into my life and make it an episode in my private history."[42]

The work of Kohlberg fails to be informed by the methods of phenomenology and the work of Merleau-Ponty. In fact, he misses the fundamental contribution of Piaget in this respect—that knowledge and formal operations are grounded in action. Kohlberg has merely established stages of potential inauthentic or alienated discourse about moral activity. His failure to ground the evolution of moral discourse in the evolving social relations of individuals, in their coordinates of social action, is a major fault of his work.

The studies of the interaction between infant and caregiver indicate that the infant is born into a social relationship, and indeed partakes in the structuring of the interactive patterns which make up that social relation. Some of the early studies of language development point to the fact that the communicative relationship between caregivers and infant is foundational for the establishment of dialogue and language. We have inferred from this that the functions of speech in dialogue, the forms that language takes between and among individuals, are reflective of the schemata of social relations. Stated from the other side, social relations are constitutive of language functions. That which needs to be traced empirically and phenomenologically is the gradual transition from these social relations of care and communication to the relations of production. Furthermore, if the above hunches are correct it should also be possible to detect the shifts in the language exchanges as these gradually express the language of production. Much of the empirical work probably exists. It is obvious, and indeed the work of Horkheimer[43] and Schneider[44] suggests, that the dynamics of family life begin to assume the shape of the relations of production. Horkheimer has shown how the hierarchy of authority in work-places carries over to the authority structures in family, and hence reproduces in children attitudes and behavior which are required for the work force. The sexual liberation movements of today have also called attention to the penetration of family dynamics by the hierarchical and stereotypical structures in business, industry, and other places of adult occupation. Likewise, it seems rather common knowledge among teachers that the language of the classroom readily and quickly assumes the form of the language of production, with emphasis on production (what one has learned) and external authority. The recent work on communication competence and distorted communication is a possible source of further data and methodologies for exploring the relationships among language functions, social relations, and the relations of production.[45]

The centrality of language in a genetic Marxism is also indicated by the significance of language for consciousness. In *The German Ideology* Marx states that "Language is as old as consciousness, language is practical consciousness .... Consciousness is therefore from the very beginning a social product."[46] Later he claims "that the real intellectual wealth of the individual depends entirely on the wealth of his real connections."[47] I am not certain what he intends by the words "intellectual wealth," but for me it entails consciousness. Again, in education we have been so conditioned to think of the individual and his/her consciousness, his/her language, that we fail to recognize the social and relational aspect of that consciousness and that language. Thus, it is less a matter of changing one's language patterns, of changing his/her consciousness of who he/she is, than of changing his/her relations with others, and broadening this range of relationships. It seems to me that psychotherapy illustrates this, for by working through a significant relationship with the therapist, the client speaks differently about him/herself and others, and has a changed consciousness about him/herself in the world. Hence class consciousness is necessarily a creation of dialectical thinking and awareness. Class consciousness exists when one recognizes those with whom he/she is in relation and those with whom he/she has few or distorted relations, perhaps indeed only relations of production, consumption, or exchange.

Some of the implications of this analysis for curriculum and our "understanding" of human development are easy to generate. If we take seriously the possibility of a genetic Marxism, then further inquiry might produce more useful knowledge about the dialectical relationship between adults, the structures of the adult world, and the child. Central to such inquiry would not be cognition or affect, but the shape of human activity throughout the lifetime of the person, the developing power of the person for self and social production, the evolving social relations of the person, the relationship of self activity to social activity, the evolving functions of language as manifestations of social relations and consciousness, including class consciousness, the functions of production and ownership, and use-value of the materials of production for children, the relationships of these materials to the schemata of assimilation and accommodation of the child, and the relationship of these materials to the productive forces within the society.

Inquiry into such phenomena is part of our problem, for it is a division of labor which produces elites and develops not consciousness, but knowledge, which becomes a commodity to be exchanged for degrees, salary increments, tenure, promotion, royalties, and privilege. As Marx said in his last thesis on Feuerbach "The philosophers have only *interpreted* the world; the point is, to change it."[48]

We really do not need more studies; we need consciousness of our own complicity in the forces of domination, and a critical methodology which will inform and be informed by our practice as educators. That critical methodology, and practice, is social, dialectical, and materialistic. By social I mean only that individuality is only possible because we are, have been, and will be in relation with others; and that our fundamental concern is and must be the quality of that social life. Infants and young children partake of our social being. The unfortunate question as to how they become socialized hides that fact. Only our naive and extreme individualism lets us speak of earning a living so we can raise children, rather than producing a life for ourselves and others. Our activity and that of the young is part of the continuing transformation of energy and material for the sake of our collective life. To have that activity turned into alienated activity, for someone else rather than for the person and the collective which he/she chooses, is the beginning of distortion of the social relations, of domination, and of language which no longer expresses truth and possibility.

By "dialectical" I mean seeing the part in terms of the totality, the present in terms of the past and the future, and recognizing that contradictions are also a mode of relationship which offer as much understanding of the present moment as cause and effect relationships. The child is a part of our whole, a significant part of our past, present, and future, and a source of some of our major contradictions. To speak of adult life without the presence of children is an absurdity, and that absurdity is demonstrated by our efforts to wall them off from our everydayness as adults in schools—public school, preschool, church school, and what have you. Walling them off means that we never have to ask what they mean for us and how much of our productive power should be used for their life.

We only need ask what we mean for them, and what they must learn, how they must be socialized, how they will inherit our wealth. The dialectical method and practice require that we see the life of the child against the lives of the adults, the activity of children in classrooms against the activities of adults in automobile production plants, banana plantations, cocktail lounges at the top of the World Trade Center, the pushers in Harlem, the prisoners and guards in Attica, and in faculty meetings. The contradictions seen and felt will never be reduced by a curriculum, but are the source of consciousness, of class consciousness.

By "materialistic" I intend a concern for the body—the body of the person and the body of the world, and the respect that is due both. Productive interchange between the two is necessary for life. The instruments that have been fashioned to direct this interchange, and to increase life's power, can be respectful or disrespectful of the body of the person and the body of the world, for the instruments that have been fashioned can indeed alienate individuals, increase collective power, or rape the body of the world. The instruments which have become tools of education are often disrespectful of both, used for profit-making, for developing impotence and social weakness, or for producing laborers to do the work of and for others. The schemata of assimilation and accommodation are often for the appropriation of the body of the world for the few; even the public materials for education are often designed for only private gain.

If there is indeed a political economy of the curriculum and of child development, it will not tell us how to educate young people but how the young and the old can live together for mutual benefit and how the current structures of production and consumption intrude upon the social relations among people, young and old, near and far, rich and poor, black and white.

NOTES

[1]Lawrence Cremin, "Curriculum Making in the United States." *Teachers College Record* 64 (1971):196–200.

[2]William H. Goetzman, ed. *The American Hegelians* (New York: Alfred A. Knopf, 1973).

[3]Ibid.

[4]George Novak, *Pragmatism Versus Marxism: An Appraisal of John Dewey's Philosophy* (New York: Pathfinder Press, 1975).

[5]Franklin Bobbitt, *The Curriculum* (Boston: Houghton Mifflin Company, 1918).

[6]Howard Langford, *Education and Social Conflict* (New York: Macmillan, 1935).

[7]Zalmen Slesinger, *Education and the Class Struggle* (New York: Couici-Friedo, 1937).

[8]John S. Mann, "Influences of Marxism on Curriculum Theory." Paper presented to Professors of Curriculum, New Orleans, April 1976.

[9]Samuel Bowles and Herbert Gintis, *Schooling in Capitalist America* (New York: Basic Books, 1975).

[10]Joel Kovel, "The Marxist View of Man and Psychoanalysis." *Social Research* 45 (1976):220–245.

[11]Richard Lichtman, "Marx and Freud." *Socialist Revolution* 30 (1976): 3–56.

[12]Wilhelm Reich, *The Invasion of Compulsory Sex-Morality* (New York: Farrar, Straus and Giroux, 1971).

[13]Max Horkheimer, "Authority and the Family." *Critical Essays*, trans. Matthew O'Connor (New York: Herder & Herder, 1972).

[14]Jean Piaget, *Biology and Knowledge* (Chicago: University of Chicago Press 1971).

[15]Bowles and Gintis, *Schooling in Capitalist America*.

[16]Karl Marx, "Theses on Feuerbach," *The German Ideology* (New York: International, 1947), 195–199.

[17]Bertell Ollman, *Alienation* (Cambridge: Cambridge University Press, 1971).

[18]Karl Marx, *Capital: A Critique of Political Economy. Volume I: The Process: Capitalist Production*, ed. Frederick Engels (New York: International, 1967).

[19]Cf. Lichtman "Marx and Freud" on this point.

[20]Marx, *Capital*, 177.

[21]Karl Marx. *A Contribution to the Critique of Political Economy*, ed. Maurice Dobb (New York: International, 1970), 193.

[22]Ibid., 192.

[23]Marx, Capital, 178.

[24]Ollman, *Alienation*, 171.

[25]Piaget, *Biology and Knowledge*.

[26]Karl Marx, *The Economic and Philosophic Manuscripts of 1844*, ed. Dirk Struik (New York: International, 1964), 110.

[27]Marx, *Capital*, 184.

[28]Ibid., 177.

[29]Marx, *Economic and Philosophic Manuscripts*, 111.

[30]Karl Marx, *Grundrisse*, ed. and trans. David McLellan (New York: Harper and Row, 1971).

[31]Piaget, *Biology and Knowledge*, 338.

[32]John Macmurray, *Persons in Relation* (New York: Harper and Brothers, 1961), Chapter 11.

[33]Michael Lewis and Leonard Rosenblum, ed., *The Effect of the Infant on Its Caregiver* (New York: John Wiley & Sons, 1974).

[34]Ibid., "Introduction," xv.

[35]Richard Bell, "Contributions of Human Infants to Caregiving and Social Interaction," Lewis and Rosenblum, 1–30.

[36]Selma Fraiburg, "Blind Infants and Their Mothers: An Examination of the Sign System," Lewis and Rosenblum, 215–232.

[37]Alexander Thomas, et al., *Temperament and Behavior Disorder in Children* (New York: New York University Press, 1968).

[38]Piaget, *Biology and Knowledge*, 354.

[39]Ibid., 345.

[40]Maurice Merleau-Ponty, *The Phenomenology of Perception*, trans. Colin Smith (London: Routledge & Kegan Paul, 1962).

[41]Ibid., 354.

[42]Ibid.

[43]Horkheimer, "Authority and the Family."

[44]Michael Schneider, *Neurosis and Civilization, A Marxist/Freudian Synthesis*, trans. Michael Roloff (New York: Seabury Press, 1975).

[45]Jürgen Habermas, "Toward a Theory of Communicative Competence." *Recent Sociology*, vol. 2., ed. Hans Peter Dreitzel (New York: Macmillan, 1970) 114–149.

[46]Marx, *German Ideology*, 19

[47]Ibid., 27.

[48]Marx, "Theses on Feuerbach," 199.

23

Developing Teacher Competencies

(1979)

Education during the past quarter of a century has been significantly influenced by the products and activities of the scientific movement which began to take organizational form in the 1920s. It is my contention, however, that the scientific movement and its various intellectual and technical products have had contradictory benefits for teachers and students. Efforts to improve the competencies of teachers and the achievement of students are caught in these contradictions. These contradictions must be faced and transcended. I sincerely doubt that we will significantly improve the quality of our educational enterprises by continuing to do what we have been doing during the past quarter century. The social structures which now support and feed off the problems of teachers and students must be altered.

My basic point is that responsibility for the quality of education rests with local educators and their patrons. They are responsible for locating and solving their problems, although many of the conditions which influence their work are beyond their immediate control. But they cannot assume that responsibility with the present distribution of educational resources and the allocation of time within the total educational community.

The basic problem is that the developing technologies and sciences of education supported people's belief that the locus of control and responsibility for the improvement of educational practice resides in centers of ideas and idea production rather than in centers of educational practice. Thus universities, research centers, and governmental agencies, and the networks of communication and social relations which they dominate, are assumed to be responsible for problem identification and solution. As a consequence we think in terms of innovation and dissemination, of degrees and credentials, of commercial packages and training, and of conferences where practitioners listen to university professors. In a sense, teachers and other educational practitioners are placed in a waiting stance. They execute what others design.

The contradiction is that these idea centers have developed some of the resources and methods crucial for identifying and solving local problems, including those of teacher competence. However, these resources and methods are caught in the social and communication networks dominated by the idea centers. The flow of ideas, information, and resources is constrained. The division of educational labor also allocates socially available time. Members of the university and research community have time to reflect, criticize, and design alternatives. Practitioners barely have time to do all the work allocated to them.

Developing more effective education in local institutions requires reworking the social structures of education. Because administrators often assume responsibility for institutional structures, some of that reworking is their task. More equitable distribution of time for planning, criticism, and finding alternatives is necessary. More democratic distribution of the resources needed to develop better education at the local level is required. I am not simply advocating greater freedom for the local practitioner and a curtailment of freedom of the members of the research and university communities. I am advocating more responsibility for teachers. That they have not assumed greater responsibility for their own teaching effectiveness is not a moral failure or a sign of actual incompetence. It is a structural problem. Increased responsibility can only be attained by changing the social structures which impact upon their work. More openness, and hence more vulnerability, is required. More support is required. Better access to resources and ideas is needed. The norms governing most university and research communities must also be altered with less dependency upon ideas and their warrants and more emphasis upon justice in social relations.

The openness, which is a prerequisite for responsibility, is related to the ideological structures which permeate educational workplaces. By ideological, I mean the intellectual structures, the prevailing ways of thinking and talking about educational problems and possibilities, which are codified in the educational language used by practitioners. Educational language is very standardized. The meanings and interpretations of event and symbol are fairly well controlled by the communication that goes on in academic and research settings, drawing primarily on psychological and other social or behavioral science discourse. As a consequence teachers are often dependent on others for their thinking. The standardized meanings and patterns of talk intrude on the daily activities of the teachers. They are not comfortable voicing their problems in their own language. These ideological structures encourage teachers to think about education in terms of learning. The value questions are too often posed as questions about what the student is to learn; and teachers are encouraged to separate that which is presumed to be cognitive from that which is affective. But behavior and discipline problems, as they are talked about in the teachers' lounge, are not apt to be expressed in those terms.

The standardization of educational talk, and the dominance of psychological and other behavioral discourse, has also had contradictory impact on educational practice. Certainly the sophistication of psychological and other behavioral discourse, has helped educators develop more effective educational materials, more probing diagnostic instruments, and more varied and valuable classroom activities. On the other hand, that very discourse has helped to create the separation between teachers and students, educators and laypeople. I think that this discourse is partly the cause of the increased alienation in some schools and classrooms. Teachers and students frequently do not have much in common. The students are interested in their present life and future. Teachers are interested in what students learn and how they do on achievement tests. Teachers are presumed to be experts, a presumption supported by their knowledge of learning and what must be learned for future effectiveness. Students are caught in the same relationship to teachers that teachers have to the university and academic community. Unfortunately, this discourse of the expert is now very well reinforced by the text and test industries which have equally profound impact upon the classroom. But historically the text and test industries are primarily extensions of the idea centers, with academic norms predominating, not norms of justice and responsiveness.

This distancing of the teacher from the student eases the teacher's conscience as he or she recognizes that perhaps the student is not really being helped. The failure is not the teacher's. It is someone else's. Perhaps it is a failure of the home. Perhaps of the text or course of study. Because the teacher talks one way and the student and parent another, there is no communication or common language. Without common language there can be no community. Without community, responsibility is replaced by scapegoating.

Reworking the ideological structures will take considerable time and effort. At the university and research level, a great deal of critical and historical work is necessary to free educational discourse from the domination of the positivistic sciences and technologies. For instance, we will need a great deal of critical scholarship to trace the relationships between teaching and learning theory and testing. We will also need a great deal of work to free educational practice from the domination of one or two philosophical views and to use current philosophies appropriately, that is, as source of criticism and imagination, not as prescription.

At the local level the domination of a particular form of educational discourse will require opening up the conversations among teachers, students, and parents. We should not expect the professional language of learning and objectives, cognition and affect to be the medium of conversation with students and parents. Nor is it a language which is more truthful or significant than the language of the students or parents. To insist that such language is normative for conversation about education is not to maintain standards of truth, but relationships of power. About thirty years ago, as we talked about student-teacher planning and of community involvement in planning, we were in part of the right track. However, the unfortunate confusion about the content of the curriculum led to confusion about the function of such cooperative planning, and led gradually to the weakening of the curriculum which then came under severe attack in the immediate pre- and post- Sputnik era. In our efforts to tighten up the social and cultural content of the curriculum, we have equated authority with power and hierarchical position. Our present difficulty is in part our imposition of particular meanings and interpretations on students and community, thus curtailing conversation. This is quite distinct from making available social and cultural resources, a legitimate curriculum responsibility, which then can lead to quite distinct and locally significant meanings and interpretations.

It seems to me that as professional educators we might help in this task of reworking ideological structures, and hence opening up teachers to recognize their responsibilities, by increasing our talk about what is happening to individual students. Talk of group scores or scores on achievement tests probably serves a useful institutional or diagnostic function; but such talk hides our concern for Eric and Debbie and other persons with whom we work. Our concern and their concern is their sense of increased power as a result of our educational work with them. Are they more powerful to act in the natural, social, and personal worlds that they inhabit? By focusing on learning and achievement scores, we do not know whether they are more powerful. Do students read and write, participate effectively in the construction of social life, give and receive love, interpret the messages and information that comes to them from so many sources and in different media? Performance criteria should not be performances within schools and on tests, but in their present and future life. Students are concerned with the development of mastery, competence, or power. Parents are concerned with the same. It is this concern for developing and withholding of personal power that brings teachers, students and parents together. It is this that they have in common. It is this which is the basis of communication, community and responsibility for the improvement of education. We will begin to break and rework the ideological structures which distort the teacher's sense of potency and sense of responsibility when we begin to engage teachers, students and parents in discovering reasons why children and young people are not more powerful or competent in their world and their actions. It is important that professional educators not dominate those conversations with their behavioral, psychological and bureaucratic language, but begin to explore their reasons for sensed powerlessness.

Teachers are not skilled in such conversations. One of the reasons for this is that conversations about the failure of schools and teachers to develop the personal power of individual students do not occur frequently in schools. Administrators can take the lead here. They can be more available to explore teaching problems with teachers, students and parents. They can spend more time with groups of teachers talking about their problems and the difficulties that specific students appear to be having. Rather than focusing on the students as a source of the problem, they can focus in on the curriculum and teaching approaches as the source of problems.

But the other reason that teachers do not engage in such conversations with administrators, students and parents is their lack of time for such exploratory talk. The correction of this time lack is not simply a local problem. It is a consequence of how time for exploration of problems is distributed in the wider social order. Because teachers do not have time for such talk and exploration, the solution to these problems of individual students remains outside the control of the teacher. The solution might be in the hands of guidance personnel. But too frequently, guidance personnel see these problems as being rooted in the dynamics of the individual or her family. The creation of the guidance position, and the specialization of labor that goes with it, imply that educators, somewhere in the not too distant past, decided that teachers should continue to be busy with regular teaching activities, and that the time for solving the problems of individuals should be given to other people. The teacher might see the problem of a specific student as a consequence of inappropriate materials or texts, and suggest that curriculum makers and textbook publishers redo their materials. But one reason for this is again the division of labor whereby teachers do not have time to remake materials and are dependent upon other agencies. The teacher might see the problem as inadequate knowledge on his or her part and so return to the university for a course which would shed light on the problems. This return seems a necessity because in the larger social order, time has been so allocated that teachers do not have time for their own knowledge production, whereas university people are specifically provided with time for problem-solving and knowledge production.

But time alone would probably not change the tendency of teachers to see student problems as having their origin outside of their own classroom or own behaviors. The other reason for maintaining this projective defense is that teachers have little or no power over their own behavior and the structure of the school or classroom. Again, this is not a personal deficiency of teachers, but a problem of inadequate social structures and an inadequate and inequitable distribution of resources necessary for producing appropriate classroom behaviors and materials.

These resources now exist. But they exist primarily within the idea centers: the universities, research centers and technological facilities. Their distribution is locked into the network of social relations and communication dominated by the idea centers. These resources are primarily a result of academic efforts to understand and predict teacher effectiveness and the relatively recent efforts to develop theories of teaching. The problem before us is to identify these resources, to break them out of the intellectual structures within which they exist, and then to find or build new social networks to make them usable by teachers.

The academic work to which I refer has its origins in the early work of such educators as Avril Barr[1] and their efforts to predict teacher effectiveness; continued through the work of those who were concerned with classroom climate, such as Flanders;[2] into the work of those, such as, Bellack and Smith,[3] who were concerned with a theory of teaching; and is now found in the work of Gage[4] and Rosenshine,[5] who are seeking to identify process variables that can be related to outcome variables. Efforts to make those lines of research more useful for teachers are to be found in the teacher competency movements of the past six or seven years and more recently in studies which seek to discover how teachers actually plan and think. Both of these are but continuations of the basic problem, which is that solutions are presumed to exist outside of the teacher and must be imposed, either by better training or by a research which turns the teacher into another object so he or she can be better programmed in the future. Both of these moves are anti-democratic in spirit and seek to maintain power in the hands of those who deal in ideas. The contradiction is that these very research efforts have also produced the necessary resources which can be returned to the teacher for identifying and solving their own problems. Again the time problem looms large. Why do those of us in universities have time for critical reflection and productive imagination and why do teachers remain constricted in a time schedule in which they have much too much to do with very limited time resources?

The intellectual structure within which these resources are embedded are the presuppositions of science and the philosophical idealism with which science is often associated. The presumption is that a more or less universal knowledge can be produced which will fit general situations. At one time in education, this led to the hope that we would find a theory of learning that would solve our teaching problems. At another time, we hoped that we would find a theory of teaching that would do the same. Now Gage and others have scaled down their hope to the identification of some relationships among limited process variables and outcome variables. But behind these efforts is the search for some limited universal knowledge which can be used to shape practice. I have reasonable doubts about the success of such enterprises, but even if I am wrong and we can indeed find either such variables or theories, what does the practitioner do in the meantime? Do we simply muddle along until these universal truths have been found? I think not. I think we have our eye on the wrong aspects of these research and theoretical efforts. Rather than look at hoped for and expected results which can inform our teaching, we need to look at the process of search to identify the conditions used to produce knowledge. Even though these conditions might not be able to produce universals, they can be used to help solve local problems. To the extent that conditions are kept or owned by the research community, then the teachers remain subservient to the members of that community and their networks of communication; for they must await the end products. But the democratization of education requires the democratic distribution of the means of production, not one-way communication of products. If knowledge is communicated as a product, it becomes a commodity, and the present distributions of benefits, power, and time are maintained. Therefore, we must recast the social and communicative structures of education. Our social structures, hierarchies, and commnication networks are designed to pass along universals or knowledge. However, we must reorganize to make available the conditions for producing more effective teaching. We must organize to increase the power of teachers to produce their own teaching behaviors and the materials and institutional resources with which they work.

These conditions were developed slowly over the past decades. The first necessary condition shows this historical development perhaps better than the others. For years, supervisors and critic teachers have been considered essential for the development of more effective teaching behaviors. An outsider was crucial because teachers were so busy in the moment-by-moment events that they could not recollect with any clarity the specifics of their behavior or that of the students. Another person could help see the totality and bring before the teacher those events and behaviors that were not part of his or her conscious memory. As researchers began to explore classroom action and tried to describe objectively what was going one, the problem of reliability faced them. At first the problem of reliability was solved by having more than one observer in the classroom. Because this was often inconvenient and because electronic recording was becoming increasingly available, they gradually moved to making audio and video tapes of classroom action. With such records, they could then repeatedly view the same action, and ask others to view it. For the first time in educational history, modern technology has made it possible to look at the same teaching act over and over again. Teaching can become an object, stable rather than fleeting. The value of so objectifying teaching has been hidden behind the knowledge that it presumably makes possible. It is, of course, not a coincidence that the achievements in recording technologies coincide with the research into teaching. It is possible for teachers to observe their own teaching and to study it without the aid of an outsider, whether supervisor, critic teacher or colleague. They can study it at their own leisure with their own questions, and without the intrusion of those with different intentions or responsibilities. They can be independent of their own fallible memories. They can become students and researchers of their own teaching, and gain potential control over future behaviors. For the first time in history they can become an object to themselves. This is no trivial accomplishment. It makes possible, in fact it is a precondition, for the development and improvement of teaching by the teacher. It is not a sufficient condition, however.

Again, the social division of labor, and the time allocations that coincide with those divisions, show themselves as a problem. Researchers have time, not only to view and review teaching, they also have time to analyze it, think about, critique it, and consider alternatives. Teachers have time to teach, to go over student work, to prepare for the next day, and perhaps to have a few conferences or meetings; and then they might have a little time to be normal human beings. But they do not have time for the viewing and reflection and analysis; unless of course we begin to see the agrarian school calendar and the nine months of work and three months of personal re-creation as part of the problem and the solution. The problem of time, however, will not be solved technologically or even by the resources of the universities and research communities. It will require some reorganization of the time allocations within our total educational enterprise.

Given the capability to make teaching an object of self-study by the teacher and the time for doing so, we still face the problem that some teachers might not know how to think about their teaching or how to consider alternatives. Given the self-containment of teaching—behind classroom doors, limited time for interchange, busy-ness which discourages the development or alternatives, and a general restriction of communication with other viewpoints—the teacher, when confronted with his or her own behavior, will often see only what he or she saw teaching. However, my own experience suggests that there is almost always an exclamation of: "Good gosh, did I really do that!" or "Did Pete really do that?" or "I wish I hadn't said that to Amanda." The fact that most teachers are very uncomfortable if others see or hear a tape of their teaching suggests that they recognize much more on the tape than that of which they are conscious when they teach. But generally teachers do not know what to do with that surprise or embarrassment, except to try to protect themselves from the exposure. I think that if we turn to our own experience, this surprise and embarrassment can be placed in perspective, and we can recognize some of the social factors which impede critical reflection and the consideration of alternatives.

My own experience is probably typical. Before I was a college professor, I was an elementary school teacher. I remember my first two years very well, for they were painful years. I hasten to add that I don't think that was unique. They were as troubled and difficult as those of any beginning teacher. I worried. I planned. I schemed. I tried a variety of approaches and techniques. I talked to those in the district who appeared to be of like mind. Knowing the way schools generally operate and the way that I operated, I probably did not talk to those of unlike mind. I felt fragile, doubtful, often incompetent. I had been well trained in the best of institutions, and student-taught in the best of schools with a skillful critic teacher. But the first two years were still years of hard work, frustration, at times despair.

I am convinced that my experience was not atypical. If you remember your own beginning, surely you can remember some of the same feelings. Those feelings are not simply of the past. They are not simply those of a new teacher or of an elementary school teacher. I still have them. Even at the graduate level my stomach still has mulligrubs when I meet a new class. I still have my moments of fragility and frustration, indeed of failure. The major difference is that an error of teaching judgment does not mess up the whole day or whole week, because I meet a class only once a week and time has a healing quality. If I lose a class during the semester, I don't have to work it through because those students will leave me never to bother me again. That doesn't happen in elementary or secondary schools.

That sense of doubt, of possible incompetence, of fragility and tenuousness, of fallibility stays with me. There is a lingering of it whenever I meet a new class or a student on a one-to-one basis. I question whether I am adequate to the task. I know that I am not alone in this. My wife just finished her annual beginnings again as an experienced elementary school teacher. Her first three weeks were as difficult as any that she has had, or that I have had, or that I wager any teacher open to their own feelings has had. I now see those feelings not as personal shortcomings or inadequacies but as a natural feeling by-product of being a teacher. Feelings of doubt, inadequacy, fallibility, possible incompetency are endemic to teaching. I would go so far as to wonder whether a teacher who lacks such doubt can be a good teacher. Why? Because to be a teacher one must be open to others. To meet new young people, people different from those of past years, always raises questions of doubt and competency. It leaves one open. That openness is a source of doubt and fallibility and possible incompetence. Being with others, specifically in a teaching or educational way, is always an exposure to fallibility, doubt, and an invitation to trust and faithfulness. To be closed to others means that mutual understanding cannot be reached and that the possibilities of others cannot be recognized. Understanding can only be imposed and only our own possibilities can be recognized and acted upon.

For Paul Tillich, doubt is a given of human life. It is the source of faith and openness. Paul Ricoeur, a noted French philosopher, speaks of the fundamental fault or fissure, our possible fallibility, an essential for human life. To deny the doubt or the feeling of fallibility is to deny a part of ourselves as human beings.

It seems to be that some teachers, not necessarily on their own, do deny that doubt, that sense of possible incompetence, that fallibility. In a sense they are faithless. They dare not let themselves feel that weakness. Consequently, they cannot see the weakness and fallibility in students. They cannot trust themselves in their doubting and consequently they cannot trust students. They lack faith in themselves to fill the void that comes with those feelings of doubt and incompetence and consequently they lack faith in their students.

Our concern for competency within the present social structures of education encourages teachers to interpret these feelings of doubt and fallibility as personal weakness, to be overcome by individual knowledge, proficiency, and more hard work. If we continue to have them after a few years, then we think that we are misfits in schools. So we cover over our feelings, scale down our aspirations, and conform to the situation as it is. Conformity, loss of aspiration, and hiding feelings are not a sign of personal strength. They are a sign of inadequate social structures. The reason that teachers do not know what to do when they recognize these weaknesses, mistakes, and embarrassments on tapes of their teaching is that they do not work in a social context that recognizes doubt and fallibility as essential—essential to maintain one's humanness and essential as a source of continued growth and development. They protect themselves from this shock of recognition because the social context within which they work does not support doubt and fallibility.

This is a problem of school structure and school organization. Schools are typically organized to cultivate individual teacher guilt for professional difficulties. The alternative is to build a school structure or organization that affirms doubt and feelings of potential incompetency as indicators of possible problems and signs of future professional development. Supportive colleagues, those who can listen with a third ear and who trust and know that specific teaching and curricular problems can be transcended, are absolutely necessary. This is not only a function of time. It is also a function of availability, of listening, of exchange, and exploration. The leadership for the establishment of a human condition within the school must be the administrator. Technical, managerial, and bureaucratic conditions are easily established. But the past quarter of a century indicates that leadership for the more significant human virtues is hard to come by in schools, particularly when the social press is for less significant but more easily measured values.

In a social situation where human fallibility is recognized, and legitimate doubt is seen as a virtue and the beginnings of problem identification, teachers are more apt to be able to face themselves as fallible objects on a tape or in the eyes of a colleague or even a parent. The covering up to protect oneself is not necessary if good teaching is seen as an aspiration rather than an expectation. Why cover up your failings if others use those same failings to help you come closer to your aspirations?

In the midst of such a supportive community, the teacher who is able to face him/herself or to have others face him/her still needs to have ways to assess the value of what he or she is doing within a classroom. Diagnostic or achievement exams do not elucidate process. We need ways of looking at what is going on in the classroom and between teacher and students. We need to be able to describe what is going on and what is not going on. We need to be able to describe alternative actions or alternative processes. Here again, the research community has made a significant contribution, if we can distinguish that contribution from the search for universal knowledge. In their search to describe the regularities of teaching and to identify critical variables in the teaching act, they have come up with a variety of descriptive instruments. There exist multiple ways to look at classroom action. However, these ways of looking are too often interpreted as vehicles for generating reliable facts or generalizations. They are not primarily that. They are different lenses, different views, different ways of criticizing what is going on in a classroom and imagining alternatives. If we want to look critically at the relations between teacher and students, we might use a Flanders interaction analysis. If we want to look at the patterns of discourse, we might use a Bellack analysis. If we want to look at how the ideas in a particular content are developed, we might use a scheme based upon some information processing model. A critical view means that we look at something from another viewpoint; that we try to see other values in that which we take for granted. The variety of instruments produced in various researches on teaching provide these other viewpoints and other valuing systems.

The proliferation of critical viewpoints in the research literature and the rather limited homogeneity of views within schools points to the limited communication networks within which teachers work. With whom do they communicate other than self and spouses or close friends? The limited communication is not of their own making or another sign of moral failure or ignorance. It is an extension of the individualism which spins off from the philosophical idealism which permeates most educational work. The search for principles of teaching and foolproof technology, usable by any able-bodied person are extensions or developments of this idealism, as is the self-contained classroom and closed door mentality governing most schools. Journals for teachers are too often self-help manuals, cast within the very weltanschauung that teachers have. Journals for the educational researchers and university personnel are more apt to report other viewpoints. However, more frequently, these research journals report findings and generalizations rather than the frameworks which generate them. If teachers return to graduate school to broaden out their frameworks for viewing teaching, they frequently do not have access to their own teaching as object so they can see what they were doing or what they might do.

Stated simply, teachers need more than their own viewpoint as they look at their teaching. They need multiple viewpoints, and in many schools today the social situation does not provide other views, particularly if there are different teaching styles within a building. Students and parents provide other views. Sometimes administrators do. For a faculty to sit down together to talk about each other's teaching is a rarity. They may sit down to talk about the behavior of a student, but not their adequate or even inadequate response to that student. To do so would be a significant movement in the development of teaching competency.

The broader problem is one of restructuring the whole range of communicative networks in the educational enterprise. To see this communication problem as one of disseminating information or knowledge is to miss both the needs of teachers and the possibilities of new forms of communication. Teachers need two-way communication with a vast number of other people. Yes, they need to be informed of other ways of viewing teaching and different approaches to organizing and teaching. But they are also the very source of some of these alternatives and viewpoints. They need to be able to look at their own teaching critically, from multiple views. But their own view is a critical perspective for someone else. They need to see other ways of teaching. But their way is already an alternative for someone else. In their knowledge producing activities, university and research personnel flatten out the vast diversity as they look for the "one best system" or the scientific generalization that will help most teachers. So they look at the diversity, the different viewpoints, collapse and synthesize it, and return the simplifications to the teachers. But teachers need banks of critical viewpoints and banks of imaginative alternatives. They need to be able to take their teaching to a variety of other teachers who could respond critically to it. They need to be able to go where they can see many different ways of teaching math or music. There is no reason, given the inexpensive nature of film technologies, why teachers should not be able to go to some place in their own district, say a film library, where they could ask to see how teachers in other parts of the district or province, teach what they teach. The impoverishment of the teacher's imagination is not a function of the teacher's ability, but of the impoverishment of the communication networks of which they are a part and of the fact that they probably have seen few alternatives in their days of teaching. The standardization of teaching is also a standardization of communication. Some teacher centers serve a communication function, for in them teachers can indeed go to exchange views. But I am concerned that this is another extraordinary institution, beyond the work place of the teachers. If we value teacher competency in the work place, then the work place itself should have the necessary resources wherein teachers can criticize their own work and locate alternatives.

But criticism and the discovery of alternatives will not automatically lead to new behaviors. The modification of behavior does indeed require practice. New teaching behaviors frequently require different materials. Again, time is an obstacle. When does a teacher have time to remake his or her skills and remake materials? When is a teacher given support to give up a tried and true way, and encouraged to stumble and muddle through developing more effective ways? It is hard to practice new skills on the job. It is easier for an administrator to find those new skills in a new person; or to hope that summer classes will produce the skills. But universities and colleges are generally ineffective in the production of skilled behavior. Flexibility in staffing and the ability to shift teachers around so they can help and be helped by others provides some of that practice. Micro-teaching with a small group of students is another. Holding everything else steady while one new activity a month is introduced is another way.

The competency of teachers will not be developed by simply more research and more knowledge. We already have far more information and knowledge than we can use. Furthermore, the truths that will significantly improve education are a long time away. Meanwhile, many young people are being deprived of a good education. The improvement of teaching requires a democratization of the work place and a redistribution of those resources that give teachers control over their own destiny as teachers. Those resources are available. They are locked into present hierarchies, present communication networks, and the present allocation of time among different education specialities. They are hidden from view by our expert mentality which is based on our over-confidence in science, the handmaiden of technology and control. The concern for test scores, and minimal competencies of students, encourages teachers to forget the uniqueness of students at either end of those achievement lists; encourages them not to empathize with them. But concern for the failure of the individual student is the source of professional doubt about our competencies as teachers. If that doubt can be supported and used to bring under question our ways of teaching and our materials, and if that questioning can be used to search for alternatives within the school context, then we have some hope for developing teacher competencies. Without acknowledgment of doubt and the democratization of resources, we will go as we have been going. Our present Three Mile Island accidents in education will also not be noticed for several years.

NOTES

[1] See Avril S. Barr, "The Measurement and Prediction of Teaching Efficiency: A Summary of Investigations." *Journal of Experimental Education* 16 (1948):203-283; A. S. Barr et al. "Wisconsin Studies of the Measurement and Prediction of Teacher Effectiveness: A Summary of Investigations." *Journal of Experimental Education* 30 (1961): 1-155. *Ed.*

[2] See Ned A. Flanders work on "interaction analysis" in N. A. Flanders, *Analyzing Teaching Behavior* (Reading, MA: Addison Wesley , 1970); N. A. Flanders and Graham Nuthall, *The Classroom Behavior of Teachers* (Den Haag, Nijhoff, 1972). *Ed.*

[3] Arno Bellack, *Theory and Research in Teaching* (New York: Bureau of Publications, Teachers College, Columbia University, 1963); Bellack, et al. *The Language of the Classroom* (New York: Teachers College Press, 1966).

[4] See N. L. Gage, ed., *Handbook of Research on Teaching* (New York: Rand McNally, 1963). *Ed.*

[5] See B. Rosenshine, "Objectively Measured Behavioral Predictors in Explaining," in *Research into Classroom Processes*, ed. A. Bellack and I. Westbury (New York: Teachers College Press, 1971), 51-98; and B. Rosenshine and N. F. Furst, "Research on Teacher Performance Criteria," in *Research in Teacher Education: A Symposium* (Englewood Cliffs, NJ: Prentice-Hall, 1971), 37-73. *Ed.*

24

Babel: A Reflection
on Confounded Speech

(1985)

All the earth had the same language and the same words. And as men mi-
grated from the east, they came upon a valley in the land of Shinar and settled
there. They said to one another, "Come, let us make bricks and burn them
hard."—Brick served them as stone, and bitumen served them as mor-
tar.—And they said, "Come, let us build us a city, and a tower with its top in the
sky, to make a name for ourselves; else we shall be scattered all over the
world." The Lord came down to look at the city and tower which man had built,
and the Lord said, "If, as one people with one language for all, this is how they
have begun to act, then nothing that they may propose to do will be out of their
reach. Let us, then, go down and confound their speech there, so that they
shall not understand one another's speech." Thus the Lord scattered them
from there over the face of the whole earth; and they stopped building the city.
That is why it is called Babel, because the Lord confounded the speech of the
whole earth; and from there the Lord scattered them over the face of the whole
earth.

—Genesis 11:1- 9

And we are scattered. We cannot build our tower to heaven. That which we propose to do is no longer within our reach. No longer have we the same language
and the same words. We do not understand one another's speech. We cannot protect ourselves from being further scattered. We are dependent upon God.

We appear to have remained in the same place. The stranger, the foreigner, is
the one who appears to have been scattered. We are at home in our language.
That which we propose appears to be within our reach. We can even build towers, intellectual towers, with it. Yet the strangers, the foreigners intrude. Their
language and words are different. Why should those who were dispersed and
driven off in different directions be permitted to confound our language, to interfere with the disciplined laying down of bricks and mortar in the prescribed
patterns of tradition? Why should the building of our city and tower be stopped?

But according to the story, it is not the stranger, the foreigner, who confounds. It is not ignorance, nor a breakdown of control, of discipline, which lead to non-understanding. These appear to be the conditions of humankind. Broken language, broken understanding, broken dreams of towers and cities, scatteredness, keep God before us. They are conditions imposed upon us. It is not our task to build a tower—whether of bricks or of words—to heaven. Scatteredness, failure to understand each other, dwelling with those who do not conform to our language usage—are these the way to heaven?

Though we propose unity, linguistic commonality and mutual understanding, our progress toward it appears Sisyphean. An imposed lingua franca, whether through imperialistic might or media monopolies, merely covers over the "mother" tongue. Might and monopolies do not wipe them out. Indigenous language, part of the body of individuals and of the loving and conflictual patterns of people, cannot be suppressed. It continues to be a vehicle of subversion and potential revolution. And so if we cannot impose a common language, perhaps we can proliferate the easily taught skills of multi-lingualism and multi-language translations for print and media, and simultaneous translations of speech events. Yet, as more and more people seem capable of understanding people of other cultures, other types of strangers and foreigners appear on the scene. The scattering process appears to be constitutive of human kind. As we become unified in some aspects, we become scattered in others. Cultural misunderstandings give way as racial and geographical differences shrink and as the stranger becomes an acquaintance or a trade partner. But these gains, a result of new technologies of communication and transportation, more pervasive bodies of knowledge, and expanding international markets, then lead to new scatterings. Scientists find themselves unable to understand other scientific and technical communities. Nuclear engineers do not easily understand the language of paleontologists and so on through the geographical landscape of new intellectual cultures.

The journey that has shaped my ways of feeling, acting, saying; of worshiping, praying, serving; and the story of that journey differs significantly from the tale of my wife's journey, my mother's journey, the unfolding story of my daughter's and of other women I know and have known. Of course, my tale is also different from that of my father and my brother and my male friends and foes, even though we have some conditions in common. These are temperamental differences, differences of specific historical conditions, and those differences of fate and fortune, of God's grace, that bring about this wonderful diversity among all of us. But the differences with woman are those and much more, for they are based on some commonalities that men and women do not necessarily share. Some of the differences are based upon sexuality, the bearing over against the fathering of children. Some differences are associated with economic and political structures of this society, and the differing opportunities open to men and to women. I was not expected to stay home to take care of my children during their first few months of life. But as they grew I was fortunate that my office was near our home so they could come to be with me after school and my wife could find a place in the public world. Some of the differences are associated with the available cultural symbols which help us imagine our future, describe our present, and re-collect our past. Some of the differences are associated with cultural stereotypes and the way they influence my behavior and expectations and those of the women in my life. How do these differences in the journey lead to an awareness that they have differences with me, which give them commonalities with other women, and hence to their separations, their scattering from me? It comes, the scattering happens, as we begin to tell our tales, or try to tell them. The symbols, images, models that are useful to me are not useful to them, and vice versa. In fact, I know women who cry for a lack of voice, who have been frustrated, angry, and injured because they have not had images to describe, to re-collect, to imagine. And I have known women who have found new power and healing when they finally locate a person who can be a model, or a story that helps them gain perspective on their past, present or future. In my youth, the story telling among women happened over the clothesline and the fence. It happened in the canning and sewing bees, and in the home and foreign missionary society of the local church. The commonness of men's stories were discovered or made up in union meetings, local pubs after work, the locker rooms, or the assembly lines and the offices. But the stories were stories that kept men and women separated in public life, and maintained role distinctions in families and neighborhoods.

At one time the differences between the stories of men and the stories of woman were merely accepted as part of human life and nature. As we all became better informed of different cultures and different times and places, as we became aware of socialization differences in diverse cultures and classes, the differences between the male journey and female journey became more noticeable. These more obvious differences fed the conversations over the laundry line, now the laundromat on the corner, and conversations in dorms, women's Bible study groups and the workplaces of women. These now noticeable differences stoked the mass culture machinery, which further informed the conversations of men and women. The differences and the stories became more public, and behold, the scattering took the form of a social movement in the United States. It was and is a movement that has counter movements, but today one consequence can be seen in political parties of this country.

The term "social movement" merely implies that in the scattering away from others, these people, women, are thrown together to seek common cause. They begin to look for their commonalities and to tell a common story, their history. That common story becomes a platform, a structure, a story line against which the stories of other groups can be seen more clearly, hence criticized and evaluated. In standing together, women can understand themselves differently than they have been understood by others. Likewise, their understanding of others now differs from the way these others understand themselves. In Rorty's terms, no longer do we have a basis for "normal discourse," only for "abnormal discourse."[1] We are forced to move from "epistemology where we understand perfectly well what is happening but want to codify it in order to extend, or strengthen or teach, or 'ground' it" to hermeneutics "where we do not know what is happening but are honest enough to admit it, rather that being blatantly 'Whiggish' about it."[2]

Today's scattering is not identified by geographical territories, but by internal territories, associated with power and oppression and other discriminating features of history and biology. Blacks and whites, once scattered in geographical regions of the world, are brought together by economic interests and physical might. A single language, based on commerce, power and propinquity emerges. But a new scattering occurs as the interior landscapes are exteriorized. The stories, spirituals, biographies, and histories indicate different journeys and scatterings. The presumed common language and presumed understandings are confounded. New, or previously hidden, misunderstandings are new opportunities for struggle, love and creation. The continuing confounding of language that is part of the human condition, prevails over economic and political integration, over the various lingua franca that are imposed, and over the various forms of multi-lingualisms and communication. The continual scattering and confounding of speech, the continual misunderstanding of each other's speech is not something to overcome, a sure sign of human pride. The new scattering and confounding, and the pain, agony and potential joy which accompany giving up control and dominance, are reasons for thanksgiving and rejoicing, a sign of God's action in our not so common life together.

And now, at this time in the history of the people of God, we must thank God for the scattering of women from the presumed commonness, the presumed understandings. As we start to burn our bricks hard for a new vain effort to build a theological tower to prevent further scattering, our speech is again confounded. Again we no longer understand each other. The commonness presumed contains much uncommonness. Again we have been called to stop building our tower and our city in order to attend to God and to the differences and lack of understanding now among us. There is healing work to be done, as there always has been and will be.

Why this scattering of the presumed commonness, from the city and the tower that we thought we were building together? What is this scattering, this separation, this calling attention to differences rather than sameness? In our sameness we are all children of God. In our sameness we share the same covenant. In our sameness we are sinful, alienated from God, in need of confessing this alienation, in need of redemption. In our sameness and in our loving and being loved, we participate in the sinful structures of the world and in the healing work that must be done. We share a common faith that we are part of the new creation, of Christ, in the world. But the stories of our sinfulness, of our redemption, of our pathways and openness to Christ, of our being healed and healing; these stories are not common. These tales differ. They differ because of our maleness and our femaleness, as they differ because of our cultural differences, our differences of wealth and poverty, or power and oppression.

Scattered from previous commonalities (communities?), and thrown together with others who now share aspects of a common journey, they face three tasks. The first is a search for language, for symbols, images, and models that give form and detail to their story. They need, in fact we all do, a form which resonates with their journey and holds it together in a narrative structure. It must help remember their journey, provide detailed awareness of the present, and project a possible and realistic future. They need to be able to describe where they have sinned and been sinned against. They need to name those people, events and times through which they have become aware of the Spirit acting. And they need language to tell how God calls them to the work of Christ in the world, given their different stories of work, love, confession, forgiveness and creation. This poetic work of women eventually leads to language patterns and usages that can be a ground against which the language patterns and usages of others can be seen and criticized more clearly. It is a ground against which all prejudices can be recognized more clearly. Without competing grounds, we remain unaware of our prejudices, which consequently can be a source of problems and evil as well as solutions and the good.[3]

The second task is participation in the reconstruction of the public world, that it might more readily be a space of justice, equality and peace. The public space is not merely the space of those who have something in common. It is the space of and for all.[4] It is not the city or the tower being built by those with the same language and the same words. It is the space for all those who are scattered, with our diversities, different languages and words, different stories and hopes. It is the politically crafted space which, ideally, allows all of us to live with our own sin, our own limits, our own evil, not those imposed by others. Woman have not had equal access to positions of power, prestige and creativity. In like manner, men have not had equal opportunity to participate in the home economy and to share equally in the upbringing of the young, shaping their language and the grammar of personal relationships. The women's movement seeks to redress these inequalities of child rearing, schooling, access to scholarly disciplines, and professions. Hence their effort to be part of the political and economic structures and institutions and to have equal access to various ministries within the church. These efforts entail reworking the home economy, altering access to educational opportunities, revising the rules governing participation in political processes, and accepting or rejecting work on the basis of skill and competence, not stereotypes.

The third task is the recreation of the heritage of symbol and language, to make it a more fitting vehicle for women's stories. Michael Edwards describes language as reflecting the shape or nature of the Christian experience: creation, fall, and recreation; from "greatness" to "wretchedness" to "renewal" and transformation. But let him speak for himself:

> We do have a sense of language in an Edenic condition of efficacy and pleni-
> tude, at one with the world and with ourselves, fulfilling our desires as speak-
> ers and writers, and doing so with ease. We recognize it at times as a quite
> prodigious power. On the other hand, we also know, perhaps more clearly in
> our century than ever before, that language has been subjected, like the hu-
> man and non-human world to which it belongs, to 'vanity' and 'corruption.'
> The Edenic harmonies being lost, our access to it—as to everything else—is
> troubled, and our engagement with it a form of exilic labor. It no longer meets
> the world inwardly, and in our mouths and under our hands it falls short of evi-
> dence and necessity. Languages even die, through disappearing from use,
> and they half-die by altering, and so alienate us from their, and our own,
> pasts.[5]

Edwards claims that it is the writer who brings about the renewal of language and the word, although I would insist upon the inclusion of the teacher in this task of renewal. Language that is publicly available, in the public sphere, does not now provide the wealth of images and models necessary for women to tell their story of creation, of fallenness, of redemption. It provides the grammar, as Paul Holmer[6] would say, but not the images, the details, the models that enable the re-collection and re-membering of the past, that facilitate the description of the thickness of everyday, nor that provide the images of projected hope. Carol Christ in *Diving Deep and Surfacing*[7] depicts the problem in literature and makes some efforts to correct the deficiencies. Carol Gilligan[8] does the same for developmental literature, with specific attention to moral development. The re-creation is not merely criticism of existing forms from a subjective point of view, for the renewal and transformation of language also has its reasons, its disciplines. Language is not, after all, a personal belonging, nor does it belong to some social groups of collectives and not others. Language participates in the mystery of the universe and is related to the sacred cosmos. That it has become part of the fallen world, "seared with trade, bleared, smeared with toil;/And bears man's smudge and shares man's smell,"[9] does not detract from its poten-tial grandeur and its participation in the redemptive structures of the world. To play games with language is to play with the "most dangerous of posses-sions."[10] One would be a fool to tread carelessly into this most dangerous and powerful of human gifts. Poetry and creative writing is one thing, for a work of art requires gifts and talent. A contribution to literary traditions, to the storehouse of story and images, requires profound experience and the capability to anchor that experience in symbols to which others have access. But to tamper with well established literary and historical forms, via translation and interpretation, requires detailed knowledge of the original and its various translations and interpretations, and the arguments for and against any particular translation or interpretation. We might pass lightly over Elizabeth Cady Stanton's *The Woman's Bible*, except as an historical document in the history of woman and Christianity. But we cannot pass over lightly or without serious criticism Elizabeth Schüssler Fiorenza's *In Memory of Her*,[12] Phyllis Trible's *Texts of Terror: Unpreached Stories*,[13] nor Ruether and Keller's two volumes of *Women and Religion in America*.[14]

And what does this imply for issues of inclusive and exclusive language in worship. Really not much except to say that we must proceed with caution and trust on all sides. Of course, we are not concerned with images about God, whether female or male, for the idolatry of images is part of neither the Jewish or Christian traditions. But we are concerned with forms of worship, historically determined and revered by those who do the work of God's people, and with the private images that individuals use in their meditations about God and self. The fact that Christians worship God in such diverse ways must point to the right, freedom, and necessity to find forms of worship that appear true and appropriate for groups and individuals. To change forms of worship, to modify prayer books and hymnals, to even suggest legitimate and warranted changes in the translation of scripture is not to tamper with images. It is, rather to tamper with customs, doctrines, valued practices. These changes require attention to the educational and political processes within specific churches and congregations and to the scholarly bases for such changes; but not to absolute standards of right and wrong.

The problems associated with these proposed changes is not the newness, but the fact that many church people have overlearned certain usages and traditions, and have been removed from a historical dynamic which, unfortunately, too often resides in academia. Changes frequently originate within the scholarly community, because the changes follow from the use of historical/critical, literary, and scientific methods. The average church person, again unfortunately, becomes aware of only the fruits of the methods, not the methods themselves. It is unfortunate that education occurs primarily within the seminary, and not in the church at large. From this perspective, the problems associated with the issues of inclusive language are social organization problems: of education, of access to reasons and warrants, of decision making processes, and of authority.

In such matters of change, we can do no better than attend to the wisdom of Hans Küng as he reflects upon heresy and the Church. He argues that heresies do not exist solely on the basis of error, but that "they draw their strength from part of the truth, often indeed, as closer examination reveals, from a good deal of the truth."[15] Furthermore, he claims that

> Selectivity, which is the essential feature of heresy, does not only lead to error; it can also lead to an impressive degree of concentration in which a single trait, perhaps a vital trait, and even, . . . the real centre of the Christian message, can be brought out in a new way that is all too often neglected by the church."[16]

He asks us to recognize that there is always error in the Church.

When the Church says that it fundamentally preserves all truth, this is primarily a statement of intent, and a good one, indeed the best possible one. Everything will depend upon how this intention is realized. What use are buried talents, undiscovered treasures, unconscious insights, unfulfilled tasks? Moreover, since the Church, as much as heresy, is composed of men, sinful men, the Church's treasure has always been concealed among dross and even dirt, its unknown truths always co-existed with some errors, its unfulfilled tasks with sin and vice.[17]

In answering the question as to why people become heretics, he acknowledges that "light and darkness are not equally distributed between Church and heresy,"[18] and that we must acknowledge the good faith of the heretic. "They wanted the best for the Church," and "they acted in good faith."[19]

Given these condition, Küng states that "Love must be the rule, even in matters of faith" (a rule easily extended to matters of scholarship). Furthermore, understanding is essential.

> True understanding involves working out how people reach their conclusions, finding the punctum veritatis in their viewpoints and establishing points of contact with them; it involves discovering the valid concerns which underlie invalid statements, and measuring discrepancies, not against one's own theology, but against the original message of the Gospel.[20]

> Understanding someone properly involves learning from him, and learning from someone properly involves changing oneself.[21]

Is the confounding of language by the women's movement so different from the confounding of language by the historical/critical movement, or literary movements such as the interests in narrative and story. The scattering of the people of God seems to continue, and with it the confounding of their language so they no longer understand each other. As the rest of us try to accept and understand women's struggles to find language to tell their stories of sin and redemption, of power and oppression; so we must necessarily bring under question our taken-for-granted ways, that we might all serve and worship God better. The confounding of our language could indeed be God's work.

NOTES

[1]Richard Rorty, *Philosophy and the Mirror of Nature* (Princeton: Princeton University Press, 1979), 320.

[2]Ibid., 321.

[3]See Hans-Georg Gadamer, *Truth and Method* (New York: The Seabury Press, 1975), 235ff.

[4]cf. Parker Palmer, *The Company of Strangers* (New York: Crossroads, 1981).

[5]Michael Edwards, *Toward a Christian Poetics* (Grand Rapids: Wm. Eerdmans, 1984), 11.

[6]Paul Holmer, "What Theology Is and Does," *The Grammar of Faith* (San Francisco: Harper and Row, 1978), 1–16.

[7]Carol Christ, *Diving Deep and Surfacing* (Boston: Beacon Press, 1980).

[8]Carol Gilligan, *In a Different Voice* (Cambridge: Harvard University Press, 1982).

[9]Gerard Manley Hopkins, "God's Grandeur," in *The Oxford Book of English Mystical Verse*, Chosen by D. H. S. Nicholson and A. H. E. Lee (Oxford: Clarendon Press, 1921), 355.

[10]From a letter by Hölderlin, quoted by Martin Heidegger in "Hölderlin and the Essence of Poetry," *An Introduction to Metaphysics*, Trans. Ralph Manheim (Garden City, NY: Doubleday, 1961).

[11]Elizabeth Cady Stanton, ed., *The Original Feminist Attack on the Bible: The Woman's Bible* (Facsimile edition, New York: Arno Press, 1974).

[12]Elizabeth Schüssler Fiorenza, *In Memory of Her* (New York: Crossroads, 1983).

[13]Phyllis Trible, *Texts of Terror: Unpreached Stories* (Yale Divinity School, The Beecher Lectures, 1982).

[14]Rosemary Ruether and Rosemary Keller, eds., *Women in America* (San Francisco, Harper & Row, 1981).

[15]Hans Küng. *The Church* (Garden City, NY: Image Books, 1967), 318.

[16]Ibid., 318–319.

[17]Ibid., 319.

[18]Ibid., 318.

[19]Ibid., 318.

[20]Ibid., 329–330.

[21]Ibid., 330.

25

Education in Congregation
and Seminary

(1985)

Basing recommendations for seminary education on actual or ideal characteristics of education in the local church is like carrying coals to Newcastle. At
this late stage of their development, these institutions appear to be more or less
independent. However, they have common roots, as Lynn has emphasized.

> The genius of the American people in the years from 1815 to 1860 was not so
> much located in persons as in institutions. After the War of 1812-14, a remark-
> able array of institutions came into being.
>
> At the heart of this educational ecology was the Revival. Around this center
> clustered a host of varied enterprises, propelled into existence by the evan-
> gelical spirit of the revival. One of the first offshoots of the revival was the
> Sunday School. Next came the nineteenth century denominational college
> .... Another institution created on the American shores was the seminary.
> Making up the ecology of that period—an ecology which persists to this
> day—were others: the system of public schools that were beginning to take
> form; the various mission agencies of the churches, foreign and domestic;
> and a variety of reform movements, such as abolition of slavery, peace, tem-
> perance, education and the like. Meanwhile, numerous religious journals
> kept church people informed about the work of each one of these educa-
> tional ventures.
>
> That basic pattern is still evident, though often in a feeble and disorderly
> state. The problems of the contemporary Sunday School are not simply
> those of one institution, but rather a reflection of a large systematic confusion
> within the enterprise as a whole. But whenever the ecology remains intact
> and the evangelical spirit is strong, there one will discover latter day remind-
> ers of the Sunday School in its hey day.[1]

Given this ecology, "seminary" could be substituted for "Sunday School"
and his statement could read: "The problems of the contemporary" seminary

"are not simply those of one institution, but rather a reflection of a large systematic confusion within the enterprise as a whole." Likewise, given this common ecology, probably few possibilities for the reformation of theological education will be found in the present practice of or discourse about education in the congregation.

Whereas the common rootedness makes us pause, that origin suggests another reason for pessimism about finding clues for seminary education. According to Lynn, and others, the Sunday school was founded as a lay movement and expanded as a consequence of lay leadership. Education within the twentieth century American Protestant congregation has seldom been a major function of the clergy. Education has happened through preaching and other leadership activities of the clergy, often unintentionally or without any reflection about the educational consequences. Glen has spoken to this problem in his *The Recovery of the Teaching Ministry*. He states

> If now we ... recognize that the subordination of the teaching ministry pertains not only to the classroom but to the pulpit, we should proceed to recognize that it pertains to the total conception of the ministry itself. This will mean a recognition of how the teaching ministry is subordinated in the various roles a minister is expected to play in the practical work of the congregation ... the fact of subordination is conspicuous in the optional nature of his teaching role in comparison with other roles. He may chose to teach or not to teach. If he does not teach, no one will call him into question. If he does teach, his action may even be regarded as exceptional. But he has no such liberty of choice in respect to other roles. He must conduct public worship. He must preach. He must provide the sacraments. He must engage in pastoral work. He must devote himself to church organization. All of these are compulsory in a way in which the teaching role is not.[2]

He goes on to say that the congregation will readily think of the clergy person as preacher, celebrant, pastor, administrator, but that "they will seldom think of him as the teacher."[3]

In some traditions, of course, the cleric has assumed responsibility for adult classes and for confirmation, with various degrees of enthusiasm and success. Although we lack firm documentation about the comparative involvement of clergy and laity in education within the church, it nevertheless appears to be outside of the daily responsibilities of the clergy. This is obviously true in terms of number, given the sheer magnitude of the church education establishment, but it is also probably true in terms of leadership. Establishing the reasons for this would require considerable historical research. Repeatedly, clergy have been urged to be more involved in educational activity of the local congregation. For instance, in 1908 Faunce stated:

> Here, then, is the unrivaled opportunity of the modern pastor. He finds close at hand a sword already fashioned, but rusty and sticking to its scabbard. He

has not to begin the work of religious education—it was begun in the Sunday School more than a century ago. He has not to induce his church to organize a school, to appoint teachers, to set apart some time for instruction. The machinery is at hand, though antiquated and creaking, and sometimes a mass of revolving wheels that achieve no output. To take this mechanism, remodel it to suit present need, to harness it now to new sources of power, and put it in charge of the most vital and forceful personalities of the community—that is the pastor's imperative task.[4]

An indication that the pattern of minimal clergy involvement continues is illustrated by the traditions in geographical areas surrounding some seminaries. The tasks of youth education, confirmation classes, and some adult education are given to seminarians (or in other geographical areas to the young junior pastor) as good experience for the neophyte. That these same people look forward to the time when they can delegate such labor to other seminarians (or new junior pastors) indicates the depth of the problem.

About the same time that Faunce was making his plea, the Religious Education Association was forming. William Rainey Harper, one of the leaders in that formation, was interested in fostering critical study of the Scripture in settings beyond the university and the seminary. He saw the REA as a vehicle for fostering this study. However, he died in the early days of that organization, and his interest was replaced by interests of the other leaders. The rapidly developing study and professionalization of education, a consequence of the emerging fields of psychology and administration, proved too much of a lure for them. Religious educators forsook affiliation with Biblical Scholars and joined hands with secular educators. The efforts of secular educators to understand the educational process and to make teaching and instructional resources more effective, as well as their interest in the potential expansion of the educational system and the need for administrative efficiency, was enticing. To use the words of Coe, the "Democracy of God" was a possibility on earth, and religious educators needed the problem solving techniques and the know-how of the secular educators. Learning theory, curriculum building, resource development, teacher training, supervision and administration, research—these were possible tools and structures to further their ends of education within the congregation. The short term future of education in the Protestant church became tied to the secular study and practice of education and reflected the vast changes that occurred in schools during the next half century. The uniform lesson plan, an effort to tidy up Biblical Studies in the church under the laity, was replaced by the graded lesson plan, a reflection of the impact of developmental studies on church education. As curriculum packages and materials for secular education changed, so, too, did the curriculum packages for religious education. One consequence of this affiliation then, was the centering of power in publishing houses and the national denominational offices where persons with more knowledge of the psychology of learning and development and its implications for writing curriculum materials might be found. The social gospel fit well with Dewey's impact upon education and Coe and his progressive colleagues had a profound influence on the shaping of the discourse about religious education. One consequence was an increased interest in personality and character development. For instance in 1929 Coe wrote

> What constitutes Christian education is an unsolved problem. Through many centuries, to be sure, the churches have taught the people, but is teaching the same as education? Moreover, though any teaching by the churches is in a proper sense Christian teaching, the question remains, to what extent is the effect thereof upon the personality of pupils a genuinely Christian effect? In respect to both these question marks—education(?) and Christian(?)—the churches are at sea.[5]

> The Protestant churches of the United States never have had an inclusive plan for the development of Christian character.

> If they had such a plan it would be manifest in the curriculum of the seminaries that prepare leaders for the church. But, until recently, only the faintest traces of the problem of Christian education could be discerned in the courses of study for prospective pastors, and even now, after twenty-five years of agitation for real religious education, in only a seminary or two can one find any considerable information about the dynamics of human growth. Something is being said, to be sure, about the church's care of the young, but, just as missions have endeavored to insert Christian education into a secular school framework, so the leaders at home are laboring to develop church schools within an ecclesiastical framework that is unadapted to them. Wherever, in theory or in practice, Christian education begins to reveal the depth and the breadth of its problems immediately a gap appears between it and theological ideas and church customs that are taken for granted. The theological and ecclesiastical mind is not at home in the sphere of education.[6]

The interest in professionalization recommended by Coe and others did not change the status of the laity so much as place the professional in a position to coordinate lay efforts, and be directly subordinate to or parallel with the clergy. The cleric had an expert to do what she or he was not educated to do, either formally or traditionally. The symbiotic relationship with secular education was another by-pass of the clergy.

Smith warned about this connection with secular, progressive education in 1941.[7] After Smart's work on the Presbyterian curriculum in the late forties and early fifties he also tried to re-establish the centrality of Biblical studies in the education of the congregation.[8] And about the same time, Miller suggested that we had to return to the theological roots of Christian Education.[9] Yet, their alerts did not seem to shift the dynamic of leadership for Christian education into the mainstreams of theological education. Seminaries recognized the necessity and importance of Christian Education by making faculty appointments in that area. But church education has been so determined by the lay roots and influenced by its graft of secular educational resources, techniques, and language that seminaries experienced difficulties finding points of leverage. They frequently succumbed to practical concerns, the educational dogmas of secular education or maintained their academic respectability. Negotiating among these diverse concerns has been an extremely difficult task. Professors of Christian education organized their own courses to develop perspectives and competencies for the educational work of the church, worked cooperatively with colleagues who shared their orientation and concern, wrote books and journal articles, and did the other things that university professors do to impact upon the world. Within that body of educational literature can be found a host of solutions to the problems of education within the church. For various reasons, the same problems continue today.

The origin of twentieth century Protestant Church education, the nineteenth century Sunday School movement, was primarily a lay movement. The transition from the nineteenth century to the twentieth century was not accompanied by a movement from laity to clergy, but a movement from laity to professional. It was a professionalism largely defined by the emergence of education as a field of study, an educational technology, administrative structures, and professional organizations. The efforts, since the 1950s, to make church education more directly a component of theological education and a responsibility of the clergy has not met with much success. The remnants of its lay origins, and the social and intellectual structures of professional education, appear as barriers to clergy leadership and involvement.

But the barrier is mere appearance. The lay remnant is a given—a necessary foundation for education in the congregation. The theological competencies of the clergy—their interests in Scripture, theology, and the history and life of the church—are absolutely essential for education in the congregation. The limits of the social and intellectual structures of professional education now can be seen more clearly inasmuch as they have not produced the expected solutions for education within the church. These limits must be articulated.

Education in the church, and to a large extent in society at large, is associated with children and youth. In part this is because education has become associated with schooling, and schools are the socially constructed place where children, youth, and young adults who are not yet in the work force, spend their time, presumably being educated. If adults are lucky, or in need, they can return to school. Recent talk of learning being a life long affair is the self-legitimating talk of educators, specifically those who have made a career out of adult education, for it is obvious that education is a natural consequence of living in an unpredictable, unknown and evolving world. That such talk is necessary suggests how easily education has become equated with schooling. To equate education with schooling is obviously an error. To associate education with children and young people is an error of the same kind.

The consequence of these errors is that thought about education tends to use the intellectual paraphernalia generated around schooling during the past century. In the United States the great expansion in common schooling occurred between the Civil War and the World War I, with expansion in secondary and higher education continuing until World War II. It was an expansion of social institutions and expectations accompanied by elaborate intellectual structures supporting education within schools. The newly emerging field of psychology migrated from the laboratories of Wundt in Germany into the academic laboratories of United States, in part because of possibilities and needs associated with the expanded business of schooling. G. Stanley Hall's study of adolescence prepared the way for the years of infant and child study that were to follow. Thorndike's studies of animal learning were followed by intensive study of human learning, and the emergence of testing, a formidable educational technology that has profoundly shaped educational practice. By the 1920s Freud's work was becoming known in the United States, influencing thinking about education and the practices in some progressive schools. Increasingly, thought about education took the form of thought about schooling. Schooling thought easily became thought about children and youth. And thought about children and youth increasingly came under the domination of the language flowing out of the centers of child study, psychological investigation, and therapeutic settings. Through the publications and activities of the REA, religious educators and their leaders came under the influence of these schooling practices and the language that accompanied them.

We have this fascinating situation then. Education in the church is and has been primarily a lay activity. Leaders within the field (although not necessarily within the local congregation) come under the heavy dominance of the prevailing educational discourse and may be affiliated with the professional educators. If this professionalization does not show in the behavior and language of the church leader it probably shows within most of the curriculum materials used by the church. The cleric, formally educated away from the language of the laity and the professional educator, has a different set of discourse relationships with both, governed by the sacramental, preaching, pastoring, counseling, and administrative roles. Frequently, then, the cleric is in an "ecstatic" relationship with laity and the professional educator, standing outside of their discourse structures—waiting to be the profound preacher, the knowledgeable Scriptural authority, the expertly wise counselor.

In a typical church educational situation with children or young people a variety of forces can be at work. The lay educator's traditional patterns of interaction and discourse with the people to be educated get messed up by the professional language of the instructional material or the orientation of the professional educator. The relationships between adult and child, mediated in other situations by more or less traditional patterns of community and family are now mediated by thought and language of laboratories and institutions of higher education, therapeutic settings, or curriculum production centers. Increasingly, teaching becomes a technical skill requiring some familiarity with these forms of thought about children and youth. The teacher depends less and less upon his or her own skills of being with children and youth, and is encouraged into dependency upon the curriculum materials and teacher guidebooks.

The consequences of the development is the distancing of the educator from the person to be educated, a displacement from the everydayness of being together. It is accompanied by the fabrication of a technical process (education), and the fabrication of a being to be educated (child or youth) about which one has to have knowledge that is different in kind from the knowledge of one's self or personal acquaintances. The existence of specialized knowledge gives the holder advantages, or depending upon one's point of view, disadvantages. It reduces the risks of meeting and increases power over the other person. Consequently the quality of the meeting between the two and their perceptions of education are changed.

The teacher meets the other person as one who is more or less predictable, one who can be known and hence taught. Schooling and the language that it has spawned legitimates calling the other person "child" or "youth." The educational and technical knowledge covers over the fact that the meeting of the teacher is with another human being, a person fundamentally unknowable, a stranger. As Marcel points out, knowing another person is a gift from that person, a willing disclosure, not something that can be forced by intellectual operations. To overcome being a stranger is to share and/or construct intersubjective structures of language, meaning, and ways to be together—a set of common understandings and experience, in other words to be part of a community. This is one reason that children and youth are strangers. They are not yet full members of the community because they do not yet share some of the intersubjective structures. Parts of the community are not yet a part of them, nor are they part of the community.

We tend not to see the young as strangers, because of our language and our schooling habits. We label them as ours and see them as children or youth. We do not recognize that they are not really part of the community, because they are our children and dwell among us. (The scales fall from our eyes when adolescents respond with unsettling energy to the enticing possibilities of the surrounding pluralism.) Given the habits of education, habits in the form of schools and teachers, habits which institutionalize the power relationship between the younger and older people, we do not recognize readily the gaps in the intersubjective structures. We see a deficiency in the young rather than a gap in our relationships. It is a deficiency to be filled by teaching, an activity which does not acknowledge the possibility of our transformation by the presence of the stranger in our midst. It is a deficiency that raises educational questions: "What should we teach?" "What are they to learn?" "What do they need to know?" We tend to answer these question too quickly by looking through curriculum materials for an appropriate curriculum. The necessary content is somewhere "out there." Furthermore, the language of the curriculum materials, and consequently of the lay teacher who uses them, is often a language not rooted in the community. The curricular materials and language of the professional educator usually by-pass the laity and ignore the theological competencies of the local clergy, thus canceling an inherent educational opportunity within the congregation. Education has become a thing, a process removed from the ordinary ways of living in community. Lost is the awareness that education is the dialectic between individual and community. Lost is the awareness that educational content is an aspect of community life. Also lost is an awareness that education is a consequence of having strangers in our midst. Education is not a phenomena that centers around the young. It is the phenomena that hovers around the stranger in our midst.

The stranger is someone who is not at home with us, someone who does not share our ways, our language, our images and worldview. The stranger is someone with whom we lack the interpersonal structures that permit and encourage easy exchange and mutual availability. Concern with our power produces stereotyping or the desire to teach. Concern with the stranger's power produces withdrawal or defensiveness. If we are not enamored with power, the stranger constantly brings us under question and vice versa. The stranger calls us outside of ourselves and our own closed interests. Thus the stranger can be a mirror. If we are hopeful, have confidence in the mirror, and ignore our propensity to penetrate the reflective surface then we can recognize our values, our traditions, our world view in our reflected image. If we are open, the stranger can relativize our socially constructed self and our socially constructed world. Through this relativizing we become aware of who we are and what our world is.

When the members of a congregation are aware of who they are and what their world is—when they are aware of congregation as Church—then they can meet the stranger educationally, for education is the dialectic between the stranger and the community. Hence the importance of the historical roots of church education. As a lay movement, grounded in the life and interests of the local church, church education expressed the religious awareness of the people in the community. To the extent that education within the congregation is grounded in methods and materials of the distant professional, it is removed from that awareness of the people. If the work of professionals has value it gives form and voice to the consciousness and intentions of the congregation, not alternatives or substitutes for them. We must turn, then, to how the congregation gives objective form to its self awareness as Church to find clues for education within the congregation and hence clues for theological education. Education is not a special work of the congregation. Rather, as Nelson[10] points out, all work of the congregation is educational. Education is possible when the congregation makes explicit in its forms of life that it chooses to be the Church of Jesus Christ and makes public its awareness of what it means to be that Church. Education happens when the stranger is invited into the forms of life of the congregation and into its awareness as Church.

If education is possible when the stranger is invited into the forms of life of the congregation as Church, then those forms need to be identified. For the purposes of this paper, the following description is proposed as a heuristic device to move the analysis. It is not intended as an engagement with the literature on the church, a very necessary and needed part of theological education.

1. The Church is a people who acknowledge and seek God's presence.
2. The Church is a people who worship God.
3. The Church, as the Body of Christ, is a servant people.
4. The Church is a people who study the Bible as the Word of God.
5. The Church is a community, a fellowship of love and mutual care.
6. The Church is a people with a public vision and memory of being the people of God.

The claim is that the congregation, as the Church, has forms of life, or of activity. Obviously they are interdependent. Attending to only one or the other, rather than all, makes the congregation less than Church. For instance, viewing the congregation primarily as a worshiping community is a problem within the society at large, perhaps within the congregation, and could be a problem within seminaries. Worshiping does not complete one's commitment to be Church. Being active in more than worship does not make one super-religious or pietistic. To consider only one or two forms of life of the religious community distorts theological education. Students are educated as leaders of worship, and perhaps as leaders of community through pastoral work. They are not often educated to engage the community in the study of scripture—which is seen as a function of the leader rather than a function of the congregation as Church. The leader is educated to study scripture, not educated to lead the congregation in the study of scripture. Preaching the Gospel, however, does not replace teaching the Gospel, nor vice versa. The leader may be educated to preach servanthood, not necessarily to lead the congregation as a servant people. If servanthood is viewed by the congregation as a social activity, rather than as form of life of the Church, then questions can be raised about how that congregation's vision and memory is continually formed and reformed by Biblical study.

The same kind of analysis can be made of how the congregation recognizes that it is a people who acknowledge and seek God's presence. The privatism of

religious belief in the West intrudes here. Acknowledgment and seeking are often assumed to be pre-conditions for baptism, confirmation or membership. To
question the assumption suggests an invasion of that privatism. These assumptions might be explored in the pastoral counseling work of the cleric. But again,
pastoral competency is too often recognized as a clerical competency, not a
competency of the congregation as Church. Prayer, meditation, retreats and
other forms of spiritual disciplines are a recognition of this form of life of the
church. Yet, because these activities are not viewed as central in the life of the
congregation as Church, they are given minor attention within the curriculum,
often limited to merely one of the many concerns within a course in practical
theology or in field experience. The view of the congregation as Church is often
restricted to the obvious and safe form—worship, that form of life which requires minimal witnessing and congregational competence.

    If education is the dialectic between the stranger and the congregation as
Church, then the congregation as Church must be a focus of study. Again, attention is called to the lay foundations of education within the church, for if education is that dialectic between the stranger and the forms of life of the
congregation, then we must ask how these forms of life are embodied within the
congregation, not merely within the clergy. The problem is illustrated negatively in the language associated with teaching "church school." The scarcity of
teachers is identified as a problem of recruiting and training teachers. This language dismisses the real problem, which is how the forms of life of Church are
embodied within the congregation itself. To speak of recruitment is to speak of
jobs and work, not the way that a congregation lives out its call to be the Church.

    The student needs to develop the competencies to do historical analyses of
congregation as a manifestation of the Church. This must be a study which
combines an historical analysis with a sociological one. If leadership of a congregation is building up the Body of Christ within the world, then one competency is the ability to assess how the present congregation embodies that
Church. What does it do and what does it not do as Church? At what point in its
past, with what constellations of leadership and events, did the present forms
evolve or atrophy? With such awareness the leader can consciously guide the
congregation into a recognition of their participation in the historical Church.
Seminary courses and experiences are offered in the history of the Church, usually from an academic perspective. The seminarian is helped to understand the
polity of the local church, frequently as an historical form imposed upon the local situation. The seminarian is also given help in understanding the local
church in field experiences. More often than not these are experienced as opportunities to develop the skills needed to operate within that situation, and the
broader implications of such study are ignored.

    Are seminarians educated to be maintenance people? Do they maintain the
local church as a social institution because they tend to think in organizational

and social language? Do they have a vision of what it means to be an instrument for building the Body of Christ, or is their vision primarily ministerial and pastoral. If the seminarian had such vision, then education of the congregation would not be a replication of the education that goes on in the seminary, with an emphasis on learning. Rather education would happen because the congregation was aware of its history and seeking to be an embodiment of the Church. To be this embodiment means living out the various forms of life that are the Church. And to do this would require, in part, helping the congregation become aware of itself as an historical entity, shaped by the leadership and events of the time, but in dialogue with those events and traditions that are the Church.

The forms of consciousness which pervade the Protestant liberal church would seem to interfere with developing this consciousness. The cultural focus upon individual spirituality, personal faith and piety, and the privacy of belief has fostered and supported the current directions of education within the parish. If religious education is assumed to be a matter of educating individuals for their own private vision and experience of faith, then the forms of education in the church can model secular education, which is often a commercial form. Packages of educational stuff and activity are available, often sold, to those who express a need, and have the where-with-all. Such commercialism covers the view that education does not merely happen in, to and for the individual. It happens in the in-between-ness of person and community. It is a dialectic between person and community.

It is for these reasons that education for the strangers, known as children and youth, falls short. Often they are not invited to participate in the forms of life of the congregation. They are asked to develop knowledge, information, and other forms of "learning" as prerequisites for participation, perhaps like skills to be sold on the labor market. In an earlier time they were expected to develop certain kinds of personality or character. Today, they are expected to develop moral and spiritual values. These are abstractions from community, not participation in the life of the congregation.

Education within the congregation is a function of the vitality of its life, its commitment to be the Church of Jesus Christ in the world. Education, then is a function of the awareness that the congregation has of what that commitment means. The congregation faces difficulties when it seeks to make public its collective awareness of what it intends to be as the Church of Jesus Christ. The individuals who make up the community are caught in structures of consciousness which reflect the non-Church, the secular structures. Berger has expressed the problem as well as anyone:

> An individual's existence takes place under certain external conditions—in this case, under the conditions brought about by certain technological, certain economic and political arrangements, and so forth ... there is an internal-

ization of at least some of these conditions—in this case, conditions that can be summed up by saying that a contemporary individual finds himself afflicted or blessed by the aggregate of psychological and cognitive structures commonly called modern consciousness.[11]

Modern consciousness is part and parcel of the situation in which the contemporary individual finds himself. Put differently, anyone today is not only situated in the modern world but is also situated within the structures of modern consciousness. Thus modern consciousness is given, is a datum, for contemporary thought. It is, if one prefers, an empirical a priori.

But now something else must be added immediately, to avoid a fatal misunderstanding: To say that modern consciousness is an individual's situation is not to say that this experience and thought must irrevocably remain within the boundaries of this situation.[12]

Modern man finds himself confronted not only by multiple options of possible courses of action but also by multiple options of possible ways of thinking about the world. In the fully modernized situation (of which contemporary America may be taken as the paradigm thus far) this means that the individual may choose his Weltanschauung much as he chooses most other aspects of his private existence.[13]

A religious worldview, just like any other body of interpretations of reality, is dependent upon social support.[14]

The awareness of the congregation as Church is apt to be articulated in the languages of modernity, or one of the many variants, unless that articulation is guided and disciplined by the traditions which the Church is. The traditions are not abstractions or historical narratives. They are embodied in individuals who carry them in and through the various confrontations with aspects of the evolving world. The confrontations transform the person, the world, and the traditions. These transformations are not arbitrary, but have a rationality of sorts. Toulmin's efforts to understand the evolution of cognitive and institutional structures supports this point:

The existence of regular procedures for criticizing the consequences of social or political institutions, and for advocating changes in social or political practice, is what makes the conduct of political affairs a "rational" matter, rather than a mere exercise of arbitrary authority or contest for power. In politics, as in science, the "rationality" of our present institutions requires the existence of accepted procedures for the self-transformation of social and political institutions . . . the overall "rationality" of the existing procedures or institutions depends on the scope that exists for criticizing and changing them from within the enterprise itself.[15]

Canon in scripture would appear to be a manifestation of a rationality of this sort. It would appear, then, that the guiding and disciplining of the articulation of awareness of congregation as Church must be done by someone who does not merely embody the traditions as they exist, but one who embodies the "rationalities" guiding their transformations—one who is familiar with the structure of their canonicity. Such guiding and disciplining must originate with those within the community who have had the necessary support for developing these "rationalities" of the Church and, to use Berger's term, have been in the necessary "plausibility structures."[16] Those socially fortunate enough to have been well educated in the various traditions of the Church, and their transformational rationalites, could provide this discipline. In most cases this is the ordained leader, and the support or plausibility structure is the seminary and the networks associated with them.

There is a caveat associated with this claim, however. That is that the seminary, as a support system and a plausibility structure, can not be an academic factory that retools the consciousness of the student, merely replacing the structures of "modernity" with those of a religious consciousness. Such educational experiences leave the student feeling that the seminary has been all "theory," not preparation for life in the parish. The theory-practice distinction, in this case, is an artifact of pedagogical style, not an epistemological distinction. Such pedagogy carries over into the work with the congregation, and hinders guiding and disciplining the congregation's self awareness into an awareness of congregation as Church. The graduate, unable to mediate between the congregation's present understanding of itself as a social organization and its potential collective awareness as Church, imposes a clerical awareness and suppresses conflicts of consciousness, or operates within the congregation's present understanding as a social organization or fixed historical reality.

The limited ability to guide and discipline the congregation's self understanding may be a consequence of a substitution of consciousness on the part of the student rather than a transition in consciousness. Conflicts in consciousness, world views, and disciplines are ignored. Transition from one state to another are assumed to be discontinuous, perhaps similar to conversion. Such discontinuities ignore the support mechanisms and the differing plausibility structures within which consciousness exists. They ignore the student's change in social location. They ignore how conflicts were resolved and the shift in rationalities that undergird these resolutions.

The educational processes of the seminary need to lift into awareness these student conflicts and the processes though which resolution and transformation occur. This means, in part, monitoring the social context and the norms governing conversation and intellectual work. Thus, the seminary must be a place where the norms and plausibility structures of neither the Church nor of variants of modern consciousness have priority. The adjudication of competing claims is necessary if the seminary graduate is to offer leadership in the articulation of congregational awareness, for that is the process that will occur within the congregation. The seminary can not be a place of withdrawal from the various structures of modern consciousness, nor a place where the traditions of the Church exist in isolation from the rest of the world. It is the supporting context for the student's work of embodying the rationalities that mediate the encounter of the traditions—the Church—with other forms and styles of consciousness. The disciplines necessary for working with lay people are, in part, disciplines developed by monitoring one's own transformations, the transformations of colleagues and the transformations of the traditions as they are worked through the bodies of other members of the Church.

By awareness, I mean the way the congregation gives public expression, through language and other symbols, to this way of life. In terms of the earlier comments from Berger, it is a matter of the consciousness of the stranger gradually being transformed by participation in these various forms of the congregation's life and reflection upon them. As Berger pointed out, such reflection does not happen in the privacy of one's mind. It is a consequence of the plausibility structures—the other people who inhabit that way, the conversations that go on, and the mechanisms that limit divergency. Thus reflection is also an activity, a function of the congregation in dialogue and conversation. Reflection is not theology as it is known in the academic world of the seminary. In fact, Kavanagh refers to academic theology as secondary theology and claims that primary theology is what happens when people reflect upon the encounter of God in worship.

> The liturgical assembly is thus a theological corporation and each of its members is a theologian. But the assembly's members are, as such, not secondary theologians, nor is their theological discourse second order language. Their theological capacity and discourse are nonetheless real for all this, and both lie closer to reality than does the theological ability and discourse of those who practice analysis by concept and proposition in a scientific manner. Mrs. Murphy and her pastor do not fail to be theologians at the point where the seminary professor who taught the pastor succeeds in being one. The professor is a secondary theologian. Mrs. Murphy and her pastor are the primary theologians whose discourse in faith is carried on not by concepts and propositions nearly so much as in the vastly complex vocabulary of experiences had, prayers said, smells smelled, words said and heard and responded to, emotions controlled and released, sins committed and repented, children born and loved ones buried, and in many other ways no one can count or always account for.[17]

I believe that Kavanagh is correct. The primary theologians are the members of the congregation, including the clergy, who carry on their discourse "in the vastly complex vocabulary of experiences had." Thus, the primary means of attending to the developing awareness of the congregation is by attending to the opportunities for discourse. And it is my assumption that this discourse is about the forms of life of the church discourse about worship, about being servants, about the Bible, about the fellowship and the pastoring that is part of that fellowship, about prayer and other efforts to be open to God's presence, and about the individual and public visions of the future and memories of the past. In one way, we can say that formal and informal educational opportunities make such discourse possible. But so does the work of the church—the planning and committee meetings, pastoral work of clergy and laity, the deliberations about social policy and ethical issues of business and medicine, possibly even the social hours after or before worship.

Under no circumstances is the clergy leader a passive facilitator of conversation among other members of the congregation. For the leader educated within the seminary is not concerned with the mere expression and evolution of awareness, but with the disciplining of that awareness by the traditions of the Church, including the traditions of the Church that now reside in seminaries. This discipline is not the imposition of authoritarian control. Rather, it places the conversation in an appropriate historical context, and identifies the rationalities needed to help the congregation resolve conflict and handle the needed transformations as it comes in contact with the newness of the world. The clergy leader is an instrument for the building up of the church in the world. Needed is a perspective of the specific historical location of that church, and of the Church in general. Hence the clergy leader needs a vision of that congregation's past and emerging awareness, which means a vision of the discourse structures within the congregation. As the congregation is able to reflect more and more about it's forms of life as Church, as it has more conversational networks for such reflection, then it can bring into public awareness how the life forms of that congregation are a manifestation of the Church of Jesus Christ.

As the congregation invites the stranger into its forms of life and into its awareness as Church, it also invites newness into its body. It risks bringing itself under question. Its constructed awareness of itself and its ways of living together are relativized. Although threatening, relativizing is also a gift. It, too, requires disciplining. Being relativized raises questions about origins and futures, about the continuities and discontinuities between these times. The stranger, the relativizer, offers an opportunity to rethink the taken for granted of the congregation, and perhaps a new beginning. Without discipline, these possibilities would be lost, and the future would be but a continuation of the present.

The disciplines required to use the relativizing effect of the stranger are not primarily of the traditions which are the Church, although these continue to be useful. They are the unrecognized and underdeveloped disciplines of education. Underdeveloped because they are the late-comers to the discourse about education. Unrecognized because educators are still triumphant about their power, and do not yet realize that imperialism, even intellectual imperialism, is dead. The modern roots of these disciplines are the sociology of knowledge, however one cares to locate its origins, and the genetic epistemology of Piaget.

It must be recognized that these are but the roots, not the current or future shape of the disciplines. They point to the needed discipline, they do not necessarily give it precise form or method. Both disciplines do the same thing. They mandate that the observer hesitate and be reflexive before describing the observed. They force the question: "How can you be certain that you are not reading yourself into the description of the observed?"

The sociologist of knowledge grants the validity of the other person's descriptions and truth claims, and suggests that the observer's descriptions and truth claims must be held in abeyance, perhaps even questioned. For instance, in *The Heretical Imperative*, Berger claims that the confrontation of Western Christianity with the religions of the East will open up the West's understanding of the religious experience, in ways that it could not be opened up by the contestation between Christianity and modernity.[18] In the same manner, the meeting of the individual Christian with the individual Muslim or Hindu, puts the Christian world view into a different light so that it can be better understood. By attempting to dwell in the perspective of the stranger, our own perspective is better understood. Hence, the significance of the stranger sociologically. By forgoing the desire to teach, and by trying to dwell in the perspective of the other person, we can better understand our own world view, our own forms of life. As we come to understand our own view and the view of the stranger, we are in a much better position to dialogue, to mutually construct a new reality, and less inclined to bring the other into harmony with us.

The tradition of the sociology of knowledge disciplines us to be patient, to ask what there is within our tradition that might be changed and what there is in the traditions of the stranger that might become ours. To invite strangers into the forms of life and awareness of the congregation is not to expect them to take on the traditions and understandings of the congregation and to forsake their own, but to participate in the construction of new structures owned by the both. To see education merely as teaching is to miss the mutuality of transformation and participating in social creation.

The discipline of the sociology of knowledge protects us from absolutizing our ground as we meet the stranger in space. The disciplines derived from genetic epistemology protect us from absolutizing our history as we meet the stranger in time. The work of Piaget, for instance, in mathematics, enables us to recognize basic structures of mathematics so their early forms can be recognized in the actions of the young. The older person cannot say that the young does not know mathematics, only that they do not know it in the same form as the older. Furthermore, the older are encouraged to retrieve the memory of those earlier forms so conversations with the young stranger can be more gratifying to both. Such conversations have a two way benefit. In the old the young can see possibilities. In the young the old can see possibilities missed, distorted, or forgotten—socialized out of awareness by the plausibility structures that could not embrace novelty.

The reflexivity associated with Piaget, and its subsequent dialectical psychology, has profound implications for the congregation's collective understandings of its forms of life as Church. Fowler[19] has pointed the way but left an immense fog over that way by encompassing his many concerns under the rubric of faith and by modeling Kohlberg. His work is strongest when he makes reference to the symbolization of meanings, rather like a developmental or genetic theology. What he points to, as did Montessori for worship in the twenties, is the way the young relativize the congregation's awareness of its forms of life. Do the young acknowledge and seek God's presence as do the old? Do the young worship God in the same way as the old? Do the young serve and reconcile in the same way as the old? Do the young encounter the Gospel, whether written or oral in the same way as the old? Are the visions and memories of the young the same as the old? The structures of the religious life are not unitary, but several; hence there are probably several dimension to depict. To speak of the stages of faith is to assume a single dimensionality which covers over the multi-dimensionality of the forms of life of the congregation as Church.

Fowler's work also points in a mis-direction by the emphasis on stages, rather than the emphasis on the dialogue which is the occasion for telling one's religious story. This is not his error, for his work is legitimate psychological inquiry. The error is grounded in the way in which religious education became attached to psychology, and tried to optimize effectiveness in the educational work. Consequently, his work contributes to the stereotyping of the stranger as a child at certain stages of growth. Covered over is the reflexive value of his work. It provides a scaffold for conversing with the young stranger based upon the memory of one's own earlier forms of religious life. Such conversation provides confidence that these forms will be transformed through other experiences. Stage theory encourages us to forget our transformations and contributes to the distancing between the old and the young. In many ways, his interview schedule has greater value for the work of congregations than does his depiction of stages. The process of interviewing places activity back into the hands of the laity, whereas stage theory reinforces the leadership of professionals.

To invite the young stranger into the forms of life and awareness of the congregation does not require educating that stranger into established forms of life of the congregation. That forces the young to postpone participation, and brings forth the urge to teach. In this case, teaching is a substitute for invitation and a justification for amnesia. To invite the young stranger to participate in the life of the congregation is to be hospitable, to make room for joint activity and joint meanings, and to jointly construct ways of being community, worshiping God, confronting the Bible, serving others, and articulating memories and visions.

The invitation to the stranger to participate in the forms of life and awareness of the congregation, suggests needed educational disciplines in the seminary. The relativizing capability of the stranger is lost unless these disciplines can be developed by the congregational leader. That leader needs to be able to attend to the forms of consciousness and the forms of religious activities of the "foreign" stranger and the "young" stranger. Through that acknowledgment, the congregation can modify its own awareness and forms of religious life to be more hospitable to the stranger. This does not require abandoning the traditions of the congregation, but being aware of them, their past, their present, and their future; and being aware of their inclusivity and exclusivity. Consequently, the educational work will become less oppressive and self-righteous, less dependent upon technique and more dependent upon participation in the continual creation of the congregation's life.

The implication of all this for theological education is to reduce the dependency upon professional education and to return the educational task to the congregation. To do its work educationally, the congregation needs to be conscious of itself as Church. Collective awareness of its forms of life and meanings entails developing the discourse networks, the conversational possibilities, within the congregation, and disciplining these conversations by and through the traditions of the Church. The disciplining is facilitated by historical and sociological perspective of the congregation, and its location within the history of the Church. Education is possible when the congregation is aware of its forms of life and their meanings as Church. Education will happen when the congregation invites strangers to participate in the forms of life of the congregation and its awareness as Church. The invitation brings the congregation under threat, for the stranger has the capability of relativizing those forms of life and the collective awareness. The threat is turned into gift when the congregation is disciplined to entertain that relativizing consciously, which leads to further understanding of its self and the conscious ability to make room for the stranger—to be hospitable to the stranger. When the stranger becomes part of the congregation, its collective memories are enlarged and enriched and the images of reconciliation renewed. Education happens when a congregation gives serious attention to itself as Church and to the strangers in its midst.

NOTES

[1] Robert W. Lynn, "The Last of the Great Religious Movements," *The Duke Divinity School Review* 40, no. 3 (1975):153.

[2] J. Stanley Glen, *The Recovery of the Teaching Ministry* (Philadelphia: Westminster Press, 1960), 14–15.

[3] Ibid., 15.

[4] William P. Faunce, *The Educational Ideal in the Ministry*, The Beecher Lectures of 1908 (New York: Macmillan, 1908), 199–201.

[5]George A. Coe, *What is Christian Education?* (New York: Charles Scribner' Sons, 1929), 3.

[6]Ibid., 14.

[7]H. Shelton Smith, *Faith and Nature* (New York: Charles Scribner's Sons, 1941).

[8]James D. Smart, *The Teaching Ministry of the Church: An Examination of the Basic Principles of Christian Education* (Philadelphia:The Westminister Press, 1954).

[9]Randolph Crump Miller, *The Clue to Christian Education* (New York: Charles Scribner's Sons, 1950).

[10]C. Ellis Nelson, *Where Faith Begins* (Richmond, VA: John Knox Press, 1967).

[11]Peter L. Berger, *The Heretical Imperative: Contemporary Possibilities of Religious Affirmation* (Garden City, NY: Anchor Press, 1980), 5.

[12]Ibid., 6–7.

[13]Ibid., 15.

[14]Ibid., 24.

[15]Stephen Toulmin, *Human Understanding*, vol. 1 (Princeton: Princeton University Press, 1972), 168.

[16]Berger analyzes a plausibility structure in terms of "the specific human beings that, inhabit it, the conversational network by which these 'inhabitants' keep the reality in question going, the therapeutic practices and rituals, and the legitimations that go with them." Peter Berger, *A Rumor of Angels: Modern Society and the Rediscovery of the Supernatural* (Garden City, NY: Anchor Press, 1970), 36.

[17]Aidan Kavanagh, *On Liturgical Theology* (New York: Pueblo Publishing Company, 1984), 146–147.

[18]Peter L. Berger, *The Heretical Imperative*.

[19]James W. Fowler, *Stages of Faith: The Psychology of Human Development and the Quest for Meaning* (San Francisco: Harper and Row, 1981).

26

Spirituality and Knowing

(1985)

A chapter entitled "Spirituality and Knowing" in a National Society for the Study of Education Yearbook suggests a new direction in the continuing dialogue between traditions of education and traditions of religion in the United States. For several decades educators in the United States have made efforts to distance their work from its origins in Christian, primarily Protestant, traditions. For instance, the McGuffey and New England readers were replaced by reading textbooks informed by the newly developing psychology of learning. Thus began the merger of the traditions of education and those of the scientific and technical enterprises, culminating in the symbiotic relationship of the testing industry and the traditions of schooling.

The merger of the scientific and educational traditions did not dampen questions of values and ends. It merely altered the rhetoric. In the early decades of this century, these questions were questions of what is best for the person. The emerging developmental literature within psychology became the idiom for framing the questions. In the 1930s and 1940s, questions of value were questions of the good society and were often framed in the language of sociology and anthropology. After the Second World War the value question turned to problems of prejudice and intergroup relations, using social-psychological language. But the language of value increasingly was dominated by formal and technical concerns, particularly for the teaching educator. Questions of value became questions of objectives, and behavioral language became the most desirable idiom. The historical questions about the meaning and significance of life gave way to technical questions of control and behavior. The distancing of education from the religious traditions was complete. In spite of the fact that questions of life's meaning and significance loom large within the religious traditions, the dependency of education upon those traditions appeared to yield to dependency upon the traditions of science, often narrowly defined as scientistic by the educator. However, questions of value could not be suppressed.

340

During the past two decades questions of value have resurfaced, frequently cloaked in scientific and developmental language. The cognitive emphasis of the post-Sputnik era influenced this in two ways. By emphasizing individual intellectual achievement, the social and historical fabric of human life became an easily forgotten and often neglected background. A corrective for blatant individualism was a renewal of interest in personal responsibility for maintaining social standards and hence a concern for values and ethics. Attention to a disembodied mind led quickly to an awareness of a feeling body and an interest in moral and spiritual values to discipline the body and its passions. The social fabric could be held together by the threads of personal morality and spirituality. Kohlberg assumed a pivotal place in the rhetoric of moral values. Using the currency of developmental theory, he neatly used the educator's attachment to scientific traditions to raise age-old concerns for the moral dimensions of education. Simon's[1] concern for value clarification used the educator's commitment to the technology of method to do the same for the teaching educator.

These concerns for moral and spiritual values managed to maintain the separation of the religious and educational traditions. They did so by subsuming value questions under the scientific inquiry that undergirded education, and by identifying them as necessary components of a democratic culture. The links of education with science and with the political-economic-social structures obviously are extremely necessary and vital. But the long-standing dialogue between the traditions of education and religion is not thereby overcome or replaced. The dialogue is merely displaced to new and different questions and concerns. On the one hand, there has been increased interest in parochial schooling since the civil rights debates and struggles, particularly within Protestant traditions. On the other hand, individuals who recognized the importance of the separation of religious and educational traditions also recognized how diverse religious traditions informed cultures, societies, and persons; hence education. Examples of this are the increased interest in Eastern religions in the West since World War II and the renewed interest in Native American religious traditions since the new ecological awakening. As a result, comparative religions and the objective study of religion have found places in some school curricula. These interests in diverse religions help make and maintain a distinction between religion as a significant historical phenomenon influencing every culture, and religion as personal meaning with the very real problem of internalization and ownership of the tradition. At issue, of course, is the possibility of objectivity, particularly of teachers and materials, in dealing with religious traditions and the obverse possibility of indoctrination or conversion.

As of this writing, the relationship between schooling and specific religious traditions is being publicly debated as Congress considers the place of silent and spoken prayer in schools. The hard-earned separation of religious practices from public schools, the gradual shifting of attention to appropriate and more difficult issues (for example, values), the place of the home and religious community in the education of persons, and the significance of religious traditions in the history of particular cultures are being eroded by a simplistic political solution to a profound historical problem.

By phrasing the relationship between religion and education in new and different ways, the editors of this yearbook contribute to the more difficult dialogue. Suggesting relationships between knowing and spirituality does not raise new questions historically, but brings into the educational community possibilities for new dialogue with those within religious traditions. Concern for the spiritual provides other perspectives for considering issues of values, the comparative objective study of religion, and even the place of prayer and meditation in education.

How Shall the Words "Spirit" and "Spiritual" be Used?

Are the words "spirit" and "spiritual" restricted to the domains of religious language? Does their use in education imply an intrusion of religious traditions into the educational enterprise? Certainly the words have had a dominant place in religious discourse, and their usage has been primarily within religious contexts. This is less so of the word "spirit" than of "spiritual." "Spirit" is not owned by religious traditions nor is its use limited to religious contexts. A person or team may be described as having "spirit," suggesting drive, optimism, hope, enthusiasm, acceptance of one's condition. Animals also are often described as "spirited." A person who lives with and overcomes handicaps with courage and acceptance is spoken of as a person who has "spirit." Political and social movements are sometimes spoken of as being a manifestation of the "spirit" of the times or age. One can be considered to be "out of spirits," depressed for various reasons internally or externally. A creative person is often spoken of as being "inspired." The word sometimes refers to intentions such as the "spirit" rather than the "letter" of the law. The word also refers to alcohol, and its consumption often results in "high spirits" as well as the "low spirits" of the afterglow. The word is also associated with the strange and the ethereal—fairies, sprites, and other beings of strange and different worlds, whether romantic or demonic. This usage leads easily into the occult and the dimensions of spiritism and spiritualism, to disembodied "souls," evil "spirits," and the ability to be in contact with "forces" and "spirits" outside the human world known by most persons.

However the words "spirit" and "spiritualism" are associated primarily with diverse religious traditions. The religions of East and West—of Buddhism, Hinduism, Islam, Judaism, Christianity, of Native Americans and the peoples of Africa—all acknowledge the spiritual as an integral aspect of human life. For all of these religious traditions, human beings participate in a spiritual dimension of existence, something more than the material, the sensory, and the quantitative. To speak of the "spirit" and the "spiritual" is not to speak of something "other" than humankind, merely "more" than humankind as it is lived and known.

One who uses these words, then, need not fall unintentionally into a religious domain, and hence into the metaphysics and ontologies that are part and parcel of great religious traditions. However, the use of these words does require careful attention, lest the conversation bring forth connotations of superstition or uncritical and unwarranted religious positions. The untangling of these diverse uses would be a major study in itself, clearly a needed work. Required would be a major study of the contexts and uses of the words over the centuries and among different cultures. Such a study would map the uses of these words in various contexts and determine their boundness to and freedom from various traditions. Such studies are not readily available, nor is that the function of this chapter.

Available today, however, are movements that question today's prevalent culture and point to other dimensions of reality not usually associated with the empirical and materialistic structures of the West. The interests of the 1950s and 1960s in higher, or deeper consciousness, such as Zen Buddhism or transcendental meditation, point to popular concerns, perhaps even needs, to acknowledge the supra-sensory. A variety of scholarly and popular works supported those concerns or needs. For instance Suzuki compared the meditative and mystical traditions of East and West.[2] In *Beyond the Post-Modern Mind*, Huston Smith called attention to the increasing body of scientific and philosophical literature that questions today's prevailing mind-set.[3] He critiqued the dependency upon the quantitative that hides qualitative dimensions, and acknowledged a sacred consciousness or spirit, a less difficult task after the unmasking of modern consciousness by Marx, Freud, and Jung.

Are there ways of talking about spirit and spiritual that do not reflect particular religious traditions—ways that point to or suggest how these aspects of human life have been experienced and acknowledged by others within and without religious traditions? One beginning is the dictionary. The Oxford English Dictionary indicates that "spirit" is derived from the Latin word for breath and breathing. "Spirit" refers to "the animating or vital principle in Man (and animals); that which gives life to the physical organism, in contrast to the purely material elements." Spirit refers to that which gives vitality, that which gives life, not merely to the forms of life. It indicates that life is more, or can be more, than the forms in which it is currently lived. The expression "that a person has spirit" suggests that one has gone beyond the forms and norms of everyday life that might pull one down. To be "inspired" by someone else is to be encouraged to go beyond the usual. To "have spirit" is to be in touch with forces or aspects of life that make possible something new and give hope and expectations. Spirit refers to the possible and the unimagined—to the possibility of new ways, new knowledge, new relationships, new awareness. Spirit refers to that which makes it possible to acknowledge that present forms of life—the institutions, relationships, symbols, language, habits—cannot contain the human being. That quality of life, that participation in the deeper hidden dimensions of life made possible these forms. They provide the vehicle wherein the everydayness of life can be lived with reasonable comfort and reasonable freedom from anxiety and unpredictability. These forms do not contain life, although they can box it in for one who lacks "spirit." Rather, life contains these forms. They are a part of life, life is not a part of them. They are a manifestation of life, not vice versa. This going beyond, this "moreness" of life, this transcendent dimension is the usual meaning of "spirit" and "spiritual."

Talk of the "spirit" and the "spiritual" in education need not, then, be God talk, even though the traditions wherein "spiritual" is used most frequently are religious traditions. Rather the talk is about lived reality, about experience and the possibility of experiencing. Another sphere of being is not being referred to. The "spiritual" is of this world, not of another world; of this life, not of another life. But the spiritual is not necessarily contained, nor even acknowledged, in the way that we presently know and live in this world.

Nevertheless, within the various religious traditions are veins of language about the spiritual. They should be mined for the educator. They contain centuries of experience and experiencing of the supra-sensory, the qualitative, the transcendent—experiences that are stored in histories, stories, myths, and poems. Interpreting them requires more hermeneutical skill than reading textbooks, newspapers, scientific reports, behavioral science descriptions, or histories based upon more tangible traces. With sufficient care, usages and meanings can be located to inform and enlighten the understanding of knowing in its diverse modes, and hence inform and enlighten the understanding of education. No single religious tradition should be consulted or ignored. If a particular religious tradition shows forth too strongly, the appropriate response is not a cry of prejudice but argument and discussion that would further inform and enlighten.

What are these histories, stories, myths and poems? They are symbols of moreness, of otherness, of the transcendent—symbols that life as lived can be different. The otherness, moreness, the transcendent is demonstrated in creativity. It shows forth in insight and new understanding, and is anticipated in hope for the future. The symbols may be stories of relationships—of struggle, conflict, forgiveness, love—during which something new is produced: new life, new relationships, new understandings, new forms of power and political control. There are symbols of wholeness and unity: of the body and mind, of self and others, of the human and natural world, of past, present, and future. There are symbols of at-one-ness when the inchoate and disturbing cohere in new meanings. There are symbols of liberation, of exodus from various forms of enslavement and domination: personal, interpersonal, or social. They are symbols of more than the present; more than current forms for life. These are the symbols of the spirit and the spiritual and how life as lived is, and can be, informed, reformed, and transformed.

The symbols of the religious traditions point to dimensions of human experience. They are descriptions of how particular people have encountered or acknowledged the spiritual. The presence of these symbols points to the fact that encountering, experiencing, and acknowledging the spiritual are possible. Everyone experiences, and continues to have the possibility of experiencing the transcending of present forms of life, of finding that life is more than is presently known or lived. This is what education is about. Education is only possible because the human being is a being that can transcend itself.

The condition for experiencing the spiritual is openness and receptivity. This experience requires acknowledging one's fundamental vulnerability and accepting that one can be overpowered and transformed. This openness and receptivity is a fissure, a "fault" in our knowledge and current forms of life. Doubt is one such fissure. It is an awareness that what we are and what we know can never completely contain what we might be or what we might know. It is epitomized by science, a human activity that at its best keeps looking for negative proofs, for novelty, newness and data that upset and overthrow current theories and paradigms. Siu, who brings together in one person the traditions of Eastern spirituality and the traditions of scientific research speaks of this dwelling in as "no-knowledge."[4] This is a state of vulnerability and openness, not a condition of ignorance. Ignorance is associated with embarrassment, fear and trepidation, impotency from the inability to control or predict. The vulnerability and openness of the spiritual are accompanied by hope, by patience and forbearance, by sensitivity to the otherness of the world, and by love. With these qualities, existing forms of knowledge can be used without idolatry, brought under question, and new forms invented or created.

Are There Spiritual Modes of Knowing?

The questions guiding this undertaking now can be posed and answered. Are there spiritual forms of knowing? Is it possible to know spiritually? Are there particular forms of understanding that can be identified as spiritual? Is there any particular kind of understanding that is secured within a dimension of life called the spiritual? Can spirit, which gives vitality, force, and transcending capability to human life, be known? These questions have only one answer: No.

That "no," however, is a consequence of the way the questions are asked. Of primary interest to the educator is the relationship between knowing and the spiritual. Questions should explore that relationship. It does not have to be expressed as "knowing the spiritual" or "spiritual modes of knowing." These two do not exhaust the possible relationships among these two words.

Three dimensions can be explored. The first is the relationship between knowing and the experience of the spiritual. When one has an experience that appears to be associated with the spiritual, does that necessarily imply that the person "knows" the spiritual or that the experience leads to knowledge of the "spiritual"? The second dimension concerns the publicly stored or symbolized records, traces, or memories of others who "experience the spiritual." Should these stored traces—histories, stories, myths, poetry, or other symbolic forms—be considered knowledge of the spiritual? The third dimension is the relationships of the spiritual to all modes of knowing. How are various forms of knowing or knowledge related to the spiritual? These questions raise necessary and crucial epistemological issues. They can be considered here only very superficially.

The claim has been made that people experience moments when present forms of behavior are somehow transcended. These moments might be explained or depicted as growth, education, insight, intuition, power. They could be a result of struggle and work, of suffering and pain, of ecstasy and joy. They could be a consequence of something or someone new breaking into their present form of life, of being loved and cared for by someone. A spiritual reality is not claimed, only the possibility of transcending oneself. The vitality or power of life that makes this possible has been commonly labeled "spiritual." The experience itself is important; not the source, the reason that explains, nor the label that names. People need not reach behind or beyond the experience to know something hidden or elusive. As these experiences continue throughout life, individuals begin to recognize patterns within their own lives. They can identify commonalities in these moments. They can offer a variety of explanations for these experiences. Patterns of availability, openness, and vulnerability can be detected, often linked to relationships with others. From these experiences an awareness of being vulnerable, open, and available for others and the new is developed. What is known from personal experience is not the spiritual, but the story of one's life, its many transforming and transcending moments, and the qualities or attributes needed or associated with such moments. Knowledge of one's self accompanies and follows from these experiences, not knowledge of the spiritual. To anchor this awareness in consciousness, a social fabric, a speaking and symbolic community, is required.

The need for this social fabric, this language or symbol world, points to the second dimension: histories, stories, myths, poetry, or other symbols. These are the records of those who have been transformed, or have experienced transcending moments, individually or communally. They are traditions that conserve and make available the language and the social fabric to anchor personal experience into a broader historical matrix.

The claim here is that throughout human history other individuals, and groups of individuals, have also experienced transforming and transcending moments and that these moments have been stored within the various traditions of these people. The fact that these stored traces assume the status of what Tracy calls "religious classics"[5] speaks to the importance of these records, these texts. They provide a language, a symbolic world within which one can project and understand one's own possibilities. If that textual language enters into the thinking and speaking language of the person, then the tradition becomes part of the person and the person becomes part of the tradition.[6] Consequently, this experience is brought into a usable consciousness, capable of being made public and integrated, or at odds, with the community's story. Those stored memories—histories, stories, myths, poetry, and other symbolic forms—are usually maintained and honored within specific religious traditions, often being labeled "sacred." They are one part of the religious tradition connecting personal experience of individuals to the experiences of the historic community.

Can it be said that these provide knowledge of the "spiritual"? That claim might be made within the religious community. A more limited claim, appropriate within this context, is that the texts make possible knowledge of other people. They are not modes of knowing the spiritual, but ways to know others, and consequently also ways to know one's self. The knowledge that comes from these histories, stories, myths, and poems can claim only as much truth as similar symbolic materials. Their sacredness does nor reside in the knowing that comes from encountering them or even in what they reveal. The sacredness resides in the community's allegiance to them and the place that they have in the life and history of the community. As narrative, historical, poetic, and mythical structures, they provide ways to think and talk about one's self, with others, from birth to death. They provide possibilities, to be chosen or rejected. The choice is not only a function of the text and the personal experience of the reader, but of the community that is the context of both.

The religious traditions store these transforming and transcending moments in their religious classics, and they also store them in various disciplines. Within these traditions they are sometimes known as spiritual disciplines. These are the disciplines of worship, prayer and meditation, text study, and disciplines of action in, and sometimes withdrawal from, the world. These are disciplines by which persons keep themselves open, available, and vulnerable so that they can be transformed and participate in experiences of transcendence. These are not knowledge-producing disciplines. In fact, one fourteenth-century writer referred to them as disciplines that enabled one to be in the "cloud of unknowing."[7] They are disciplines for staying open and hopeful. Again, these are not necessarily privileged modes of access to openness. For instance, Parker Palmer refers to the disciplines necessary for the spiritual formation of the teacher.[8] He refers to the traditional disciplines of his own religious community. But he also calls attention to disciplines within academia that also keep one at risk, open, and available. These are studying outside one's own discipline, teaching in a new field, becoming someone else's student, and the discipline of trying to get inside someone else's skin.

The claim has been made that there are no modes of knowing the spiritual. There are modes of knowing self, others, and their traditions. Through personal experience the self can be known as vulnerable, open to the world, and capable of being transformed or capable of transcending one's current forms of life. The openness, vulnerability, and experiences of transformation of others can be known through their histories, stories, myths, poetry, and other symbols. These others have also handed down disciplines that enabled them to stay open and to hope for or expect moments of being transcended. These disciplines can be known, in the sense of being able to use them and to make them part of one's habits. "Knowing the spiritual," then, refers to knowing one's self and others and their traditions.

The claim also has been made that there are no spiritual modes of knowing. To claim spiritual modes of knowing is to assume privileged access to realms of experience, knowing that would be free from the rules and warrants governing forms of knowing. The work of centuries to free various forms of knowing from the dogmas of particular religious traditions would be compromised if this claim were to be accepted. However, an active dialectic between religious traditions and the many and diverse modes of knowing must be maintained. Religious traditions should not dominate any particular mode of knowing, nor should the various modes of knowing dominate religious traditions. Religious traditions not open to developments in the various fields of knowledge become closed, sometimes idolatrous, and their proponents unnecessarily defensive. The study of sacred texts has been significantly altered and facilitated by developments in historical-critical methods, and more recently by the developments in literary criticism. Theology always finds new expression in developing philosophical idioms. The understanding of religious traditions is usually enriched by new developments in the various fields of knowledge. The reverse is also true. To the extent that various modes of knowing are separated from religious traditions they become closed in upon themselves and lose their vitality, their "spirit," their creativity, and the possibility of being transcended. Phenix states that "study and teaching in each discipline, in depth, thus constitutes de facto acts of religious devotion, even though conventional religious symbols and concepts may not be employed."[9]

The point of this essay, however, is not to explore this dialectic, but to indicate how various modes of knowing are suffused with the spiritual. That this suffusion is not commonly recognized is a consequence of enlightenment tendencies, now increasingly brought under question by philosophers of science and other epistemologists.[10] These enlightenment values have been more or less assumed by educators, hiding from view how the qualities associated with the spiritual are foundational in every mode of knowing. Space does nor permit attending to each mode of knowing, as Phenix does in *Education and the Worship of God*, but a general framework for beginning that hard work of analysis can be suggested.

Every mode of knowing is a mode of being open, vulnerable, and available to the internal and external world. The form of a human being is complete and fixed only at death. Aspects of the self and most of the external world always remain beyond the structures and schemes of knowing. Present forms of knowing are always incomplete, always fallible. Behind every confidence and certainty is residual doubt. As scientists have pointed out, the only thing known for certain is what is not true, what has been disproved. There is always a better way of being in the world, more complete prediction, more perfect expression of experience and feeling, more just meetings with others, better techniques and instrumentalities. Heidegger speaks of truth as openness to being.[11] Truth acknowledges the incompleteness and expects to uncover something else. This is the fissure in human knowing, the openness that is part of the spiritual. If it is blocked from consciousness, truth is weakened, the person falls into a state of hubris, into patterns of oppressive authority, into increasing alienation from the sensory and interpersonal world, and perhaps into psychotic states. In children and scientists, openness takes the form of curiosity and inquiry. In the arts, openness is indicated by the search for new and different experiences. In the practical, openness takes the form of problems—unresolved and "problematic" situations. Identification with those who are broken, marginal, or clearly different from self is a manifestation of being open in interpersonal modes of knowing.

Every mode of knowing is also a mode of being in relationship. It is a relationship of mutual care and love, often distorted into mere attentiveness and sometimes distorted into control and oppression. When vulnerable one must either recognize and accept the other and the necessity of care or love, or one must seek control of the other, who is both threat and possibility. As those who live close to and in harmony with the land know, and as the modern ecology movement suggests, the land, also a threat, will care for those who care for it. The knowledge between two people—parent and child, or two in love—points to this dialectic between knowing and loving. The dialectic is also suggested by the Biblical Hebrew word for "to know," which also means sexual union. Often the scientist comes to care for that which becomes known and in the caring process comes to know even more. By letting one's self be in the care of a part of the world one is informed by it. The distortion of this relationship occurs only when caring is for the self and knowing becomes an act of control, often an act of violence. The significance of the relationship of caring and knowing is reflected in the increasing interest in communication transactions and dialogue within the social sciences. The primary influence in this awareness of the dialogic structures is, of course, the seminal work of Martin Buber,[12] although today the importance of Habermas[13] and diverse other scholars must also be acknowledged.[14]

Every mode of knowing is also a mode of waiting—of hoping and expectancy. Knowledge is not produced by a process of accretion of additional parts, as things are produced on production lines. All who have tried their hand at creative writing, or the arts, or even speaking something other than the tired talk of gossip are aware of the importance, and the risk, of waiting. The pause is important in speech, the incubation period in creative work. A body full of jumbled and partial ideas, formless intuitions, and vague inarticulate feelings often requires changed focus, perhaps even sleep, before form emerges or takes over. Hard work and preparation are insufficient. Bringing previous structures and forms under question, stumbling around in the muck and mire of problems, filling the head with sensations and data are necessary. These discomforting and unsettling actions are possible because of hope and expectation. If hope gives way to despair or is prohibited by time pressures, the formless is filled with premature form, accompanied by nagging doubt and dissatisfaction. The various modes of knowing are grounded in the possibility of a different future. To wait actively and expectantly for that different future is a manifestation that modes of knowing are grounded in more than merely present forms of knowing. They are grounded in and depend upon hope.

Every mode of knowing is participation in the continual creation of the universe—of one's self, of others, of the dwelling places of the world. It is co-creation. If knowing is in language forms, then the events between self and the other create new language forms.[15] If knowing is in visual and plastic forms, then co-creation is change in the qualitative and sensory aspects of the world. If knowing is practical and technical, it modifies the forms of the ever present but changing relationship between the human and the other than human. If it is knowing of the other, it is the creation of new relationships—of exclusion or inclusion, of love or enmity, of dialogue or control.

Every mode of knowing witnesses to the transcending possibilities of which human life is a part. All knowing requires openness and vulnerability. This means that present forms of knowledge, which relate the person to the vast otherness in the world and which hold together past, present, and future, must be acknowledged as limited, fallible, insufficient. To have new forms emerge, old forms must give way to relationship: love takes priority over knowledge. Love and care, however, provide not certainty but hope. Hope makes possible patience and peaceful waiting in the midst of turmoil and unsettledness. With openness, love, and hope, new creation is possible. Old forms can be transcended. New containers for the overpowering vitality of life emerge for the time being, and the cycle begins again. The cycle is not new. Openness, love, hope—this is the story of human life as celebrated in religious traditions—the traditions that keep the spiritual acknowledged in collective and individual consciousness.

The problem, of course, is that schools and other institutions of education are not places of knowing, but places of knowledge. Knowledge is the fallout from the knowing process. Knowledge is form separated from life. It stands by itself, removed from the vitality and dynamics of life, from the spirit. It becomes part of life only when it is brought once again into the knowing process of an individual. Until then it is dead. To bring knowledge to life, to enliven it, it must be brought into the living form of the human being, into the form that is a form of the transcendent. If the student is brought into the deadness of inert knowledge, the student is also deadened, alienated from the vitality that co-creates the worlds of self and others. By enlivening knowledge, the student is also empowered. To enliven knowledge is to accept it with doubt and to place it back into the eternal cycle of openness, love, and hope. Knowledge that falls out from the modes of knowing, that becomes alienated from openness, love, and hope, risks becoming idolatrous.

But Tennyson said it better:

Flower in the crannied wall,
I pluck you out of the crannies—
Hold you here, root and all, in my hand,
Little flower—but
if I could understand
What you are, root and all, and all in all,
I should know what God and man is.
(Lord Alfred Tennyson, "Flower in the Crannied Wall")

NOTES

[1] See Howard Kirschenbaum and Sidney B. Simon, ed., *Readings in Values Clarification* (Minneapolis, MN: Winston, 1973). *Ed.*

[2] Daisetz T. Suzuki, *Mysticism: Christian and Buddhist* (New York: Harper and Brothers, 1957).

[3] Huston Smith, *Beyond the Post-Modern Mind* (New York: Crossroad Publishing, 1982).

[4] Ralph G. Siu, *Tao of Science: An Essay on Western Knowledge and Eastern Wisdom* (Cambridge, MA: M.I.T. Press, 1958).

[5] David Tracy, *The Analogical Imagination* (New York: Crossroad Publishing, 1981).

[6] Paul Ricouer, *Interpretation Theory* (Fort Worth, Texas: Texas Christian University Press, 1976).

[7] Ira Progoff, trans., *The Cloud of Unknowing* (New York: Julien Press, 1957).

[8] Parker J. Palmer, *To Know as We Are Known: A Spirituality of Education* (San Francisco: Harper and Row, 1983).

[9] Philip H. Phenix, *Education and the Worship of God* (Philadelphia: Westminster Press, 1966).

[10] Michael Polanyi, *Personal Knowledge: Toward a Post-Critical Philosophy* (Chicago: University of Chicago Press, 1962); David Bohm, *Wholeness and the Implicate Order* (London: Routledge and Kegan Paul, 1980).

[11]Martin Heidegger, *Being and Time*, trans. John Macquarrie and Edward Robinson (London: SCM Press, 1962).

[12]Martin Buber, *Between Man and Man* (London: Collins, 1961).

[13]Jürgen Habermas, *Communication and the Evolution of Society*, trans. Thomas McCarthy (Boston: Beacon Press, 1979).

[14]Richard J. Bernstein, *Beyond Objectivism and Relativism: Science, Hermeneutics, and Practice* (Philadelphia: University of Pennsylvania Press, 1983).

[15]Paul Ricouer, "Structure, Word, Event," in *The Philosophy of Paul Ricouer*, ed. Charles Reagan and David Stewart (Boston: Beacon Press, 1978), chapter. 8.

27

The Redemption of Schooling: The Work of James Macdonald

(1985)

Jim loved life. He threw himself into it with gusto. My image of that gusto is a memory of Jim on a warm summer day at the University of Wisconsin. He and Sue were walking from the education building to her dorm. The day was inviting, Lake Mendota was inviting. With no hesitation and great delight he jumped from the pier into the lake. He didn't bother with a swimming suit nor a birthday suit. That was the way Jim saw people and events. If they looked inviting, if they offered a way to become more deeply immersed in the world, then he jumped in without a second thought. Jim did this with people. He threw himself into their midst without fear, without hesitation, without bothering to change his persona, or to strip from one set of clothes to another.

Because he loved life, he knew what was important. His hierarchy of values for education was clear. Schools were important to Jim. He believed that they could be improved. But he recognized that teachers were more important than schools. Schools could be improved only if others had confidence in teachers. However, in the final analysis, education was about children and young people.

Jim loved children. That is one of several reasons he became an elementary school teacher. It was this love that made him aware of the limits of the curriculum, the limits of teachers, and the limits of schooling. He loved kids enough not to give up on teachers, curriculum, or schools. He spent his life redeeming them—bringing teachers, curriculum, and schools to the point where they would serve children rather than entrap them. This was his work.

The well-being of children and youth took priority over the welfare of teachers. The well-being of children and youth took priority over the present structures of schools. He knew that educators must be clear about their values.

Children, youth, and teachers are more valuable than technical details and institutional structures. If educators knew that, and acted accordingly, then schools could be redeemed. They could become places of education in the best sense of that word.

Jim's commitment to the redemption of schools surpassed that of most of his colleagues. That commitment governed his work—his work with students, teachers, colleagues, and his intellectual work.

Because of that commitment he gave freely of his time. The moist eyes and choked voices of all of us who worked with him during these past thirty years attest to that. He gave willingly and graciously to the many students with whom he worked, helping them clarify their ideas and their values. He gave his time willingly to teachers and school staffs. Being out in the world of schools was a source of joy for him. He brought his faith and confidence to bear to the work, frustrations, and problems of teachers and other educators. His commitments energized ASCD, AERA, and local and state groups. He knew that if others shared his faith in schools and in teachers, then the young people in this world would have a better deal. If others cared, as he cared, young people would recognize and realize more of their potential. After all, that is what schools and teachers were all about.

He enjoyed giving his time to his intellectual work. In the eyes of our future colleagues, it is this work that will be remembered as his effort to redeem schooling. Early in his academic career, Jim made a fundamental decision. Although trained as a researcher and an empiricist, able to work with observation data and statistics, he recognized that the process of SEARCH took priority over the process of RE-SEARCH. Research made no sense unless the underlying ideas and assumptions had power and legitimacy. It did not take him long in his academic career to recognize the limitations of existing empirical work in education. He noticed the blindness of many educators to the ideas in other disciplines and other domains of life. These informed the world beyond schools. Why shouldn't they inform and shape schools? So Jim threw himself into the world of ideas in much the same way that he threw himself into Lake Mendota—with gusto, enthusiasm, with the love of thrashing about, and the joy of doing it with others.

To understand Jim's intellectual work, we must understand the period during which he started his professional career. Jim began his work before interest developed in the history of curriculum. In fact, it was the next generation of curricular scholars, the students of Jim and of his colleagues and peers, who attended to the history of the field. They did so, in part because of the questions that Jim was asking. His work might have taken a different tack if the historical work had started seriously before the 1950s. Theory, not history, was the spirit of his time. Jim's professional career began in an historical situation in which optimism reigned. The desire was to find a technology, or some other means, by which that optimism could shape educational programs. Because optimism shaped our efforts, our search for understanding was a search for vehicles that provided prediction and control. Jim's contributions must be seen against that backdrop. Fortunately, his intellectual interests and competencies were equal to his concern for children and schools. His concern for children could not be contained within the existing taken-for-granted understandings. He, too, ran up against the limits of current ways of doing and thinking in his teaching. He knew that the limitations of schools were not simply the breakdown in good will or know-how. The limits were there, in part because school people had taken hold of only a limited portion of the great intellectual traditions which have and could shape our consciousness. Educators were acting out of a very limited bank of the cultural wealth of the world. His work must be seen as an effort to bring together curriculum workers and teachers and these rich traditions of reflection, imagination, and criticism. In a sense, all of us are here because Jim helped open the door of the curriculum workers' room. Because of him the rest of the world and its riches would flood our work room with light. Our work could be illumined by the light that shines from the intellectual and critical imaginative work of others. That we are free to explore, to search rather than re-search, is a result of Jim's courage, of his commitment to the redemption of schooling.

To understand Jim's intellectual work, it is necessary to understand the nature of theory, as, I think, he understood it. One who engages in theory is one who stands back to look at something. It is to be a spectator, one who can remove himself from the course of events to see what is going on. This is not an act of alienation and removal from the fight. It is an act of love. One cannot commit oneself to another, to people or institutions, if one is in bondage to other institutions or people. To have a view of the world which is derived from other people in other times can be a bondage to those times and people. Jim knew that from the bottom of his heart. Much curriculum theorizing before Jim's time was technical or rule-governing material. It was derived from those who sought control and power. It was created to enable educators to act, to build programs of education and instruction. It was not necessarily created to see more clearly, to love more dearly. Jim, sensing problems with what was going on, felt it necessary to see practice in a broader perspective. He stood back and looked in order to see the ground within which practice occurred, to identify our bondage. In so doing, he generated alternatives for action, to further our commitments to children and youth. Of course, others also did this. Yet their work appeared more entangled in the ground, rather than rising above it so we could see more clearly what we valued.

Jim's contribution was to help all of us see more clearly, by suggesting other perspectives from which to view our work and our commitments. In an early paper, "Structures in Curriculum," Jim stated that theory "is based upon the assumption that there is a set of phenomena in curriculum which may be similar but is not identical to any other set of known phenomena, and that these phenomena can be identified, described, and related to each other."[1] From such theory, such spectator positions, the curriculum worker obtains power to recognize limitations and possibilities of particular places. By his reflective work, Jim sought to provide curriculum workers with descriptions of what they do, to propose alternatives and thus more power to embody their values in the world. It was this need for curriculum workers to be more self conscious about their work in our society which led to his interest in theory, and hence to our interest in theory. Theory was not merely an escape into the esoteric. It was part of the necessary work for the redemption of schools.

His standing back started much of the current explorations within curriculum. Perhaps some of us fell into the trap of esoteric theorizing removed from the work of redeeming schools. Jim kept his eye on the educational ball. His exploring (his re-SEARCHING) was always two-dimensional. He kept before us the educational work to be done, while he searched other disciplines. He kept in better tension than most of us, the commitment to young people, teachers and schools, and his excitement and enjoyment of the intellectual search.

In one of the papers near the end of his career, he stated clearly his position about theory. He used Whitehead's distinction between simple-minded and muddle-headed people. He admitted that he was more muddle-headed, like Whitehead. He recognized that his work was metaphorical in intent. He did not see himself providing a map of reality so it could be followed to get to some predetermined place. He was more meditative in his intent, more contemplative. He wanted to deal with the whole, the unity, not parts that could be separated and put back together. This did not mean that he was less concerned with practice. The relationship between theory and practice was not one of applying theory to practice. Theory was a mirror for one's self as a practitioner, a magic mirror. Theory is not a mirror that reflects back what you are, but what you might be and how you might see the world anew with deeper penetration of its structures and qualities. For him, the theory-practice relationship is a hermeneutical process. Theorizing is an act of creation—creating oneself and thereby eventually recreating the world. As Jim said, " ... there is a mystery to be probed, curiosity to be satisfied, confusion and ambiguity to be faced and lived with."[2]

In the long run, then, theorizing was a religious activity for Jim. It was an act of faith that kept one in touch with the sources of life. Five years earlier, he made explicit this grounding. In his "Values Bases and Issues for Curriculum," he argued that all curriculum workers should make explicit their values concerning the good life, which was the base of all of their proposals anyway. As you may recall he argued that curriculum work was extremely important, and that under no circumstances was it moribund. He claimed that the school was a microcosm of the rest of the world. To give up on schools and the curriculum was to give up on the rest of the world. Obviously he would not do that for he enjoyed the world too much. Nor would he expect or want his friends or colleagues to do so. He stated in that paper that the ground of his work, and for him the ground of the school and curricular activity, was a religious ground, for "religious impulse and spirit ... pervades human history and activity."[3] A similar concern and interest appeared three years before as he used Jung and James to explore the possibilities of a "Transcendental Developmental Education."[4] His concern for the internal dialectic and wholeness acknowledged that the person is more than can be known. Faith in that internal unknown, whether unconscious or preconscious, is a necessary part of the educational venture.

Jim's love of life and of those who peopled this world with him has left us a heritage of work, and a tradition that shines forth on schools. The light of his work and of the tradition that many of you carry on shows the schools as they are, but also as they might be. Jim knew that they could be redeemed, made right. And they can be if our images are embedded in hope, carried with courage, made public with poetic power, and given freely and gracefully to young people, their parents, and their teachers. Can we carry on Jim's work?

NOTES

[1] James B. Macdonald, "Structures in Curriculum," in *Conference on Curriculum Leadership*, ed. Frank M. Himmelman (Wisconsin Department of Public Instruction, 1966).

[2] — "How Literal is Curriculum Theory?" *Theory Into Practice* Vol. XXI, No. 1 Winter 1982.

[3] — "Values Bases and Issues for Curriculum," in *Curriculum Theory*, ed. Alex Molnar and John A. Zahonk (Washington: ASCD, 1977).

[4] — "A Transcendental Developmental Ideology of Education," in *Heightened Consciousness, Cultural Revolution, and Curriculum Theory*, ed. William F. Pinar (Berkeley, CA: McCutchan, 1974). See also Bradley J. Macdonald, *Theory as a Prayerful Act: The Collected Essays of James B. Macdonald* (New York: Peter Lang, 1995), *Ed*.

28

Religious Metaphors in the Language of Education

(1985)

The use of metaphor is a way of shedding new light on an already existing phenomenon, by looking at and speaking about that phenomenon from a totally different perspective. In this way we obtain a transfer of meaning, and thus an opening up of awareness.

Religious language could be used as metaphor to look at and speak about educational events and phenomena. This assumes that religion and education are more or less independent realms, and that language usages can be transferred that will enable us to see the already familiar educational events and phenomena as strange or different and hence see them anew. But this work is not of that kind. In fact that very process of transferring religious language to education strikes me as being foreign to what I am about, and in part would distort the story of my own life as an educator.

Perhaps a brief aside to describe what I think I have been about will provide a perspective for interpreting my comments. Most of my professional career has been a search for more adequate and powerful ways to describe education—as it occurs in various places and as we try to think about it critically and creatively. That search has taken me through the language of psychology, sociology, and other behavioral sciences. It has also taken me into diverse schools of philosophy—analytic, existential, phenomenological, critical theory, Marxism, structuralism and those schools now drawing upon the new hermeneutics. That search has also lead me into theology and other religious languages of the west and of the east. Over the years I have been led more and more directly into studies of and work in theological and religious education. My own faith community commitments are Christian, although I have worked with many students and some colleagues who are educators within the Jewish tradition. This <u>work</u> with students and colleagues within the Jewish and Christian faith communities has gradually shifted my perspective, and it is that perspective which I will try to place in coherent public form here.

I accept Whitehead's statement that "the essence of education is that it be religious"[1] My acceptance of that position carries with it profound consequences. The search which engages us is not for metaphors. If "the essence of education is that it be religious" then the natural language for talking about education is religious language or language which articulates religious experience. Our problem is not to locate metaphors within the language traditions of the faith communities that might illuminate educational experiences and events. The problem is to recognize that the language now used to talk about education is already metaphorical. The habitual use of these metaphors blocks our ability to recognize more appropriate language to describe our work as educators. Herb Kliebard's [2] work, identifying some of the metaphors in educational discourse is only part of the needed unmasking or de-metaphoring. Metaphors of growth, production, agriculture system, political control, and socialization hide from us what we are really about when we educate. Even the language of learning is metaphorically carried over from that human activity of studying animals, including the human being as an object. It is not descriptive of what we do when we educate.

Let me return to Whitehead and flesh out his statement. We too often stop at his one sentence and do not read the paragraph that follows in the first chapter of *The Aims of Education.*

> A religious education is an education which inculcates duty and reverence. Duty arises from our potential control over the course of events. Where attainable knowledge could have changed the issue, ignorance has the guilt of vice. And the foundation of reverence is this perception, that the present holds within itself the complete sum of existence, backwards and forwards, the whole amplitude of time, which is eternity.[3]

The roots of Whitehead's statements could be found in the sacred books of a variety of religions but for reasons of familiarity I choose to find the roots within the biblical traditions of the Jews and Christians. We can see in Whitehead's "duty" reflections of the first creation story in Genesis 1:

> So God created man in his own image, in the image of God created he them, male and female he created them. And God blessed them and God said unto them, be fruitful and multiply, and fill the earth and subdue it, and have dominion over the fish of the sea, over the fowl of the heaven, and over the beasts, over all of the earth.

Whitehead's use of the term "control" suggests subduing and dominion. In this day of ecological consciousness, we might advise Whitehead not to focus on the Genesis 1 creation story, but the Genesis 2 creation story, wherein subduing and dominion over the world is replaced by the charge to "serve" and "keep" the Garden of Eden. But we need not engage in such fine points here. That concern for duty, however, is not simply for the earth, but for the people of the earth as it is expressed in the second great commandment found in Leviticus 19:18: "Love your neighbor as yourself" and in Leviticus 19:33-34:

> When a stranger resides in your land you shall not wrong him. The stranger who resides with you shall be as one of your citizens; you shall love him as yourself, for you were strangers in the land of Egypt.

My interpretation of Whitehead's concern for education as duty is that it is a response to, indeed a response-ability for, the earth—the flora and fauna—and those of us—neighbors and strangers, friends and foes—who people it. Thus education is a call from the other that we may reach out beyond ourselves and enter into life with the life around us. Duty is that dimension of education which leads to the identification, elaboration, and presentation of content.

Whitehead proposes reverence as the other dimension of education that makes it religious. The foundation of reverence "is the perception that the present holds within itself ... eternity." In the present is the past *and* the future. In the present is the sum of all existence. In the words of the mystics, the present is the eternal present or the presence of the Eternal. In the traditions of the Jewish and Christian faith communities, in the present dwells God—beyond comprehension, beyond knowing except for the glimmerings and the hints that shine forth in acts of love, dwell in the awesome appearances of beauty and overwhelm us at the gift of life in birth and the loss of life in death. For me, reverence is spoken in the first great commandment announced in Deuteronomy 6:4-5:

> Hear, O Israel! The Lord is our God, the Lord alone. You shall love the Lord your God with all your heart and with all your soul and with all your might.

The otherness that informs and accompanies education is the absolute Otherness, the transcendent Other, however we name that which goes beyond all appearances and all conditions. Education is the lure of the transcendent—that which we seem is not what we are for we could always be other. Education is the openness to a future that is beyond all futures. Education is the protest against present forms that they may be reformed and transformed. Education is the consciousness that we live in time, pulled by the inexorable Otherness that brings judgment and hope to the forms of life which are but the vessels of present experience. To interpret the changingness of human life as "learning" and to reign in destiny by "objectives" is a paltry response to humankind's participation in the Divine or the Eternal.

The source of education is the presence of the transcendent in us and in our midst. We can transcend ourselves, go beyond ourselves, become what we are not, because we participate in the life which is transcendent and transcending. If we do not "love the Lord your God with all your heart and with all your soul and with all your might" then our education comes to an end for we cannot get beyond ourselves and we are no longer open to that which is new. We can be drawn out of our present self and present forms, we can be educated, only if we recognize the possibility of the transcendent in us. "Motivation" seems a meager expression and distortion of the first great commandment.

How then can we speak of education? Education is not something that we do to others, although it can only happen in community. Education happens to us. If we accept the Latin etymology as significant (from ducare—meaning "to lead;" and the prefix e—meaning "out"), then education is indeed a leading out. But the leading out is not as a horse is led out of the stall by a would-be rider, it is a leading out by the Otherness that is the source of our transcendence. It is a component of being a human being. The reason, it seems to me, that Whitehead emphasizes the necessity or importance of reverence, is that if we forget the transcendent foundation of education and assume that it is a consequence of human agency, then we lose the possibility for continued education and assume a maturity that presumably completes education. Forgetting the Shema and substituting human agency for the absolute Otherness, means that we fall into idolatry and away from the source of our education. To prevent the fall we are instructed to impress these commandments upon our children and to recite them "when you stay at home and when you are away, when you lie down and when you get up."

But education is not only a leading out from that which I am, it is also a leading toward that which I am not. Thus the significance of the second commandment which calls our attention to our neighbor, to the stranger in our midst, and even to our enemy. My recent thinking about this dimension of education has been greatly influenced by my colleague, Parker Palmer,[4] who in his book *The Company of Strangers* clearly depicts the educational significance of the stranger in our midst. In a similar fashion, Hans Küng[5] in his book *The Church* speaks of the educational significance of the heretic, the alien in our midst. The stranger, the alien, the enemy—anyone who is different than I am—poses an unspoken question to me, in fact to both of us. The question is why am I as I am, and why is she as she is? Her life is a possibility for me as mine is for her. And in the meeting of the two of us is a new possibility for both of us. The difference and perhaps the tension between us is an opening into new possibilities for us. Differences are manifestations of Otherness. They are openings in the fabric of everydayness. They are invitations to be led out, to be educated. We fail to recognize the invitation when we forget the source of education. We cannot recognize the invitation if we look at the other as a mirror image or extension of our own self. We reject the invitation if we pass judgment on the other and ourself, and assume that we know either.

When we speak of the stranger, the neighbor, the alien, we appear to refer to dimensions of experience that are not part of our normal ways of thinking about education. That appearance is a result of our taking for granted metaphors which now describe, and in part obscure, education. The language of learning, of systems, of production, of goals and objectives seems to make familiar that which is unfamiliar. However, ask a student about the stranger, the strangeness of content. When does one feel at home with a new content area? When it is no longer strange and alien and when one shares a new life form. To speak of the stranger, the neighbor, the alien is to speak of content which is necessary for any educational experience. The opening of possibility requires the presence of otherness.

Content is otherness. The presence of other life in this world, life of which I am not yet a part, is the content of my future education. That life is the comings and goings of other people. In their comings and goings—their journeys and pilgrimages—they house themselves, construct tools and equipment, negotiate institutions, engage and interact with flora and fauna. And when they rest and relax from the struggles of life and have time to contemplate and converse, they tell stories of where they have been and where they are going, they sing and dance and paint and build and write so they will not forget what they have endured and experienced and hoped for. They ex-press so their past will not op-press and their hopes and dreams will not be re-pressed by fatigue and failure.

We have fallen into the language habit of saying that we teach content. This doesn't work if the stranger and her comings and goings are the content. We do not teach the stranger, the alien, and neighbor; nor do we teach about them. Our task is to bring the stranger, and the fruits of her comings and goings, into the presence of the person to be educated—to be led forth. How do we make present the stranger? To the young child, the stranger is almost everyone. To one who has become accustomed to almost everyone, the task is to call attention to those who have been ignored or are outside the field of attention. Communication and transportation systems are vehicles for this. Much educational material can be appropriately spoken of as a means of communication. To those who appear to have made everything and everyone familiar and known, the task is to make strange that which seems familiar or hidden from view. Within ourselves we have the stranger lurking, in the sexuality and anger that is suppressed, the hurts and disturbing feelings that have been repressed. Within our social world the stranger lurks in the stereotypes and roles that we use for social convenience. Here the task is not one of communication or transportation, but the educational use of weakness and power in the intersubjective relationship.

I have been dwelling on the educational significance of our participation in the transcendent and of the stranger as a manifestation of the Otherness that confronts us. If education is the "lure of the transcendent," "openness to the future," "a protest against present form," a "consciousness which brings judgment and hope" then education carries with it the possibility of the unknown. If education requires giving up that which we are so we may have more life, then it carries with it participation in death as we willingly or perhaps forcefully give up part of ourselves. If education demands or requires acknowledging the stranger and alien in our present, it also requires that we acknowledge the possibility that the stranger or alien will overpower us rather than empower us. To give up that which we know or are for that which we do not know or are not yet is threatening. The lure of the transcendent must be present for education to happen, but that lure is threatening.

How can we face the threat of the unknown and the threat of the stranger outside of us and inside of us? It is not easy. We need the assurance that we will not be destroyed, that life will indeed be enhanced rather than destroyed. Love is that assurance. We can face the threat of the unknown and of the stranger if we are not alone; if we are in the presence of love which affirms life.

Love is a sticky wicket in educational circles. The word appears to be verboten in education as if it conjures up images of softness, privatization and indulgence. Too bad. We owe it to ourselves to explore the distortion of that word, its misuse and hence our hesitation to use it. Unfortunately, I have neither the time nor the expertness to engage in such retrieval. Rather, I shall draw upon my understanding of that word as I have encountered it and reflected upon it from within the Christian faith community. The first reflection concerns the locus of love. The second concerns its healing quality, love as reconciliation or as a concern for wholeness. These are educational concerns whether consciously recognized or not.

The religious community, as I understand it from within the Christian tradition, is one that embodies love as the norm. Love among people is possible because faith communities have carried the tradition of love through the centuries and across generations. We love one another because we have been loved and because we know, from our tradition, that life without love is empty and perhaps meaningless. Thus, the tradition instructs us to care for the hungry, the poor, the ill, the broken, the powerless, the children, the foreigners in our midst. To ignore the least of these is to break with the tradition that guides and shapes our community. The community of faith is a community that makes manifest that love. In words that are perhaps less loaded with specific religious affiliation, we could speak of the structures of care in our world society—who cares for whom and for what reasons. If we do not care for someone, why should we participate in their education—in their being led out to find new forms of life? We often assume that the only structure of care in our society is the home. That appears to be an unwarranted assumption. The usual loving relationship between mother and infant does not continue naturally and evenly through infancy and childhood, let alone adolescence and adulthood. Sometimes it does not exist even in the first few months of infancy. The intrusion of "careless" social structures occurs early, quickly, and forcefully in many homes or domiciles. As the past several years have indicated, the schools cannot be depended upon as structures of care in this society. As schools are tied more tightly to the dominant forms of technology and social-political control, competency and discipline have replaced care. Teaching has been construed to mean helping someone learn. The "careless" structures of our society appear to have become dominant in schools and other formal places of education.

Those who claim to be educators must care for, indeed love, those whom they would presume to educate. The source and renewal of that love is primarily within the faith communities, for they are the primary keepers of the traditions of love and care. Even the faith communities however, frequently, come under the domination of social forces that are "careless"—management, public relations, media, self-righteousness. If education is to happen in other places and locations within society, then the vitality of these faith communities must be maintained. Their traditions must be remembered and celebrated. The distortions of that love, whether by institution, knowledge, or social habits, need to be identified so they can be a focal point of critical and creative struggle within the public domain.

What does love do in education? When faced with the new, the possibility of loss or destruction as we reach beyond ourselves, love provides the assurance that we will not be destroyed, that we can be whole again. The power of love can acknowledge weakness. Love heals the differences within us. It reconciles the new tensions and divergences in our life. There are three forms of healing that love assures.

First, the presence and acknowledgement of the stranger in our life upsets the desired unity of thought, feeling, and action that we struggle to establish over time. Confronted by something new, forced to give up a part of our self, that unity is disrupted by new thoughts, new feelings, or new actions. Trust, patience and conversation provided by one who cares or loves provides the time, support, and language necessary to bring discordant feelings, thoughts and actions into new unity. A relationship of love and care is a relationship of assurance—assurance that you will not be overcome by the stranger, and that you will still be loved even though you are no longer what you were but have taken on new life and new memberships in the world.

The encounter with the stranger also tears apart the integral relationship between past, present, and future. Encounters with the new and giving up of part of what we are means that past memories may now seem inappropriate, dreams of the future may be altered, or that forms of present life have been transformed. Being with another who cares, listens, celebrates and hopes with you, provides the occasion for recollecting that which had been forgotten or ignored. Being with another who cares is an invitation to rework dreams and hopes. Being with another who cares makes possible the reconstruction of new forms of present life. Love is reconciliation. The parts of me that got out of whack by the acknowledgement of and response to the stranger are reconciled one to another. The disruptions that could tear me apart are healed and brought into wholeness.

Finally, the presence and response to the stranger upsets the fabric of social relationship established through time. The birth of a second child disrupts the existing social fabric of the home. The presence of a foreigner at dinner disrupts the normal patterns of conversation. The presence of a new white person in a congregation of blacks or vice versa changes the dynamics of exchange. The presence of a non-English speaking person in a classroom changes the expectations within that classroom. The presence of a new idea in the structure of understanding that binds two or more people together upsets that common understanding. Love and care, as reconciliation, provide the patience, trust, collective memories and hopes, and conversation to heal the social body—to bring wholeness to the family, class, organization, or gathering which appeared to be disrupted by the newness. Love and care provide the assurance that the family or social gathering will not be destroyed if it gives up some of what it has come to value, but will find new life and new meaning.

What of Whitehead's concern for knowledge and ignorance: ignorance as possible vice and knowledge as related to duty? Because ignorance and knowledge are major educational concerns we cannot pass over them lightly. The traditions which inform our use of these two words are so extensive that any discussion here must be limited and perhaps distorting.

Earlier I suggested that Whitehead's concern for education as duty could be understood as a response-ability for the earth and those of us who people it. Knowledge is related to our ability to respond to the neighbor or stranger. It is an acknowledgement of the presence of otherness in our life.

Knowing is a relationship between the person and the other, as indicated by the biblical use of "to know," to describe sexual relations. The work of Piaget affirms this in one sense, for hypothetical-deductive knowledge consists of schemas of interaction between the person and environmental phenomena.

Ignored by Piaget, but recognized by Schutz and others of similar intersubjective persuasion, knowledge is also a schema of intersubjective or interpersonal relations. Knowledge as a symbolic structure is a structure of personal relation. Thus knowledge, as a referential system, as a symbolic system that points to something beyond those using it, is a twofold relationship. It depicts our love, or lack thereof, for the earth and those of us who people it. Thus, knowledge is also a manifestation of duty and of reverence for the stranger and the transcendent. It is a manifestation of love and its distortions.

Knowledge is often understood as a pre-existent structure. Because it has been produced elsewhere, we see our task merely to reproduce it. We forget that knowledge came into being through someone, that it was created by other people. We forget the origins of knowledge, and thus forget our own involvements in history. Hence knowledge is seen as fixed, as reified. Knowledge appears removed from the interactions that link person to environment or person to person. We fail to recognize it as an invitation to join hands with someone else in their involvements with the earth. We fail to recognize it as an invitation to establish a relationship of care and being cared for—a relationship of duty, love, and reverence. In forgetting this history and these invitations, knowledge becomes a vehicle of power and oppression.

It is important to remember that knowledge is, first of all, a relationship with something that was, at one time, strange. Thus knowledge is a consequence of our being called forth by the otherness of the world. In play and in science, in just messing around and in systematic inquiry, we circle the stranger, poke and pinch it, ask it questions by a variety of "if ... then ... " manipulations until we presumably know it in its comings and goings. Bridgeman and a variety of philosophers of science have pointed out that knowledge does not describe merely an object. It describes our operations on, our interactions with, or perhaps more appropriately our dancing with, the object.

As that knowledge, that set of interactions and intersubjective relations, is moved from the scientific community to the technical community—as it becomes technical knowledge rather than scientific knowledge—we shift our relationship with the phenomena to which the knowledge points. As technical people with technical interests, we make the objects of the world care for us. We harness these objects, their qualities and characteristics, to our needs and wants, frequently destroying them, and gradually the earth, so they can serve us. The mutuality of love and reverence is broken in technical communities, for we no longer care for that which cares for us. The lore of Native Americans and the concerns of the emerging ecologically conscious communities remind us of the significance of love and reverence in the structure of knowledge.

The scientist lives, in her own special field of inquiry, with reverence, whereas the technician forgets the reverence and duty which is the source of his power. The scientist is, presumably, always open to the other which is the object of her work. Even the theory which presumably describes the dance between the scientist and the phenomena of inquiry is a tentative theory. The evolution of science requires the search for negative evidence or proof. Existing theories must be capable of being overthrown or displaced by negative proofs as the phenomenon shows new dimensions of its being and as the scientist awaits the call of the transcendent other. To be otherwise is to form idols and to participate in the structures of idolatry. Thus the creation of scientific knowledge requires participation in the transcendent and a responsiveness of the other. In one sense, the one who is a scientist is one who lets the object, the phenomenon which is other, love her. She is one who gives up her present ways that she may be formed anew by that strangeness, that otherness before and beyond her. The scientist accepts this incomplete relationship with the world and gives of herself to be drawn out, to be educated or transformed by that which is before her.

Scientific knowledge, a symbol system which describes a dance of love with other phenomena, is also a conversation, a dialogue, with human beings. It is a consequence of meeting someone else and of saying, "this is the way I dance with the world. Is it also the way you dance with it? If so can we dance together?" But the other may dance differently, and the conversation leads to new meanings of what it is to do in the world. Knowledge, as social meaning, is always constructed with the other. Knowledge is a social construction, not an individual construction. New knowledge, that which comes from others, is a description of their comings and goings in the world. Hence knowledge which comes from others must always be interpreted. We must always engage in conversation with those who construct and give it. That interpretation is also a manifestation of transcendence and love, of being open to and responsible for the other.

Knowledge is a gift from the stranger and may be considered from two points of view. My present way of being with others in the world and the conjoint symbolization of that can be described as a system of meaning. The meanings of others, that is their knowledge, is legitimately a source of criticism of our ways—in that it brings our ways under question and doubt. However, a knowledge or meaning system is also an invitation to new meanings, new ways of being in the world. The meaning systems of others, their knowledge, is also a source of creativity for us—an invitation to be part of other life forms. Hence, education as communication of knowledge or meaning system is criticism and re-creation. It is threat and possibility. It is the stranger in symbol, and hence must be made present in a community that assures new life. New knowledge, as a symbol of the stranger, must be made present in a community of care and love.

If knowledge is not seen within the fabric of a faith community, if it is separated from the pull of the transcendent, and the duty and responsibilities of love, then we risk idolatry. We risk falling into the struggles among the principalities and powers which appear to be overpowering and oppressing those of us who people this earth—in schools, homes, governments, through activities of production and communication, and in developing, underdeveloped, and overdeveloped lands. Idolatry exists where knowledge is presented as if it is removed from those who construct it and use it. Idolatry exists when knowledge is not part of the story of a particular people with their particular faith commitment. Idolatry exists when interpretations and meanings are standardized by textbooks or standardized evaluation forms. Idolatry exists when teachers present knowledge, forms, symbols, as if interpretation and conversation are frills rather than duties informed by love and responsibility.

We have no choice but to take a stand as individuals if we want to participate in the happening of education—in this openness to the transcendent and to the stranger who shares this earth with us. Professional knowledge and professional organization have been shown to be caught in the struggles among the principalities and powers. They are outside of the communities of care—the communities of faith which are a safeguard against oppression. But even communities of faith fall prey to these principalities and powers.

As we know, not all strangers in this world call us forth to live a new life. Some invite us to live their restricted life, closed to the possibilities of their own transcendence, broken off from communities of love and care. They would educate, but not be educated. They would use knowledge as a manifestation of power, not as a manifestation of reverence and duty.

Within one faith community, we are urged to give unto Caesar that which is Caesar's. Other faith communities have other memories which recall the struggles with these principalities and powers. Those of us who choose to help in the happening, which is education, are constantly faced with the difficult task of discerning the siren call of these principalities and powers from the call of the transcendent. We are faced with the choice to be a part of the community of care or the community of idolatry. We are faced with the hard decision to give to Caesar only that which is Caesar's—and to be certain that we give no more.

If we recognize that education is a response to the otherness of the world, that the stranger of the world will not destroy us if we meet him or her in the reconciling communities of care and love, and if we see in the structure of knowledge the manifestation of otherness and love; then perhaps we can be more certain that Caesar will get only his share. These difficult tasks are easier if they occur among people who participate in communities of faith, no matter what their specific tradition.

NOTES

[1] Alfred North Whitehead, *The Aims of Education and other Essays* (New York: Macmillan, 1957, 1929), 14.
[2] Arno A. Bellack and Herbert M. Kliebard, eds., *Curriculum and Evaluation* (Berkeley, CA: McCutchan, 1977).
[3] Whitehead, *Aims of Education*, 14.
[4] Parker Palmer, *The Company of Strangers* (New York: Crossroads, 1981).
[5] Hans Küng, *The Church* (Garden City, NJ: Doubleday, 1976).

29

Christian Growth in Faith

(1985)

I

The title "Christian Growth in Faith" requires explanation and some unpacking before an argument can be developed. I have chosen not to write about faith in some universal terms, for I believe that faith can best be explored from within specific religious traditions. I make no claim that the Christian tradition offers a better entrance into the problems of faith than, say, Judaism. However, I must write within the tradition that I know, hoping that those of other traditions will do the same. From such comparative explorations we might have a better basis for any universal statements about faith.

"Christian" points to that tradition of religious life which has its origin in the life, death, and resurrection of Jesus. It points to a covenant that God made with humankind through Christ, adding to the covenant with Abraham and the tribes of Israel. Given the different Christian traditions and the different reading of the scriptures, we may differ in how we see those covenants and the significance of Jesus' life, death and resurrection. We may weigh differently the various stories and interpretations of those covenants during the past two thousand years. Although we may differ about the precise meaning and implication of the word "Christian," we have common scriptural grounds to clarify the differences and commonalities.

The words "growth" and "faith" should not be accepted with quite the same degree of anticipated common understanding. An exploration of how these two words are related makes inroads into our understandings and misunderstandings of faithful growing and growing faithfully. For it is the relationships between growth and faith that need exploration, not merely a concern for the growth in faith.

Since the turn of the century, many ways to understand the processes of human growth have been given to us. Most of them come from diverse developments in psychology. These many ways are in addition to the common folklore and old wives', and indeed old husbands', tales of how people grow. As a father of two teen age daughters, I am not sure how one puts together folklore and psychological language to make sense, conceptually or in action. Human growth, ultimately, is mysterious. I am constantly surprised by what happens to me, to the members of my family, and to the people that I know intimately and casually. Perhaps, surprise is the only event we can know with assurance.

For me, the mysteriousness of human growth is another way of referring to God's grace, as it breaks into our life. It does so in a variety of ways. It breaks in through these bodies of ours—bodies that we take for granted and think we understand. The human body is one of God's truly miraculous creations. We are often surprised by some new aspect of that body. Our understanding, itself a manifestation of the body, always lags behind what is happening to us. The gift of speech often stuns us in the poetry that arises from within us. The gift of sexuality overwhelms us with its fearful power, the joyful comfort of its delights, and the awesome demands of its consequences. The power and manipulative capability of the hand—enlarged, transformed and extended by the images and rationality of our brain—have transformed the face of the earth. The gift of forgetting overcomes the gift of remembering, and we fail to remember that the changes in the earth are our doing, that these instruments of destruction are extensions of our hands. Even the gifts of aging body parts and mechanisms remind us of how God's grace calls us outside and beyond ourselves and into new ways of being in the world.

The mystery of human growth happens through our bodies. It also happens through the stranger and the strangeness of the world. God's grace keeps breaking into our lives, fracturing and breaking us through the strangers that we meet. The parable of the Good Samaritan is an example of that grace. The stranger may be the foreigner, a friend, lover, or foe. It may be the person next door, whom we can't stand, the hurting folk in Africa, our neighbors in Central and South America. The stranger is our own child whom we think we know, but who surprises us, disturbs us, brings new joys and awareness to us. Finally, the stranger is also that part of me that I would prefer not to acknowledge to myself, let alone to anyone else. God's grace pulls us out of our self rootedness to attend to that which we are not, and thus calls our attention to the fact that we were not created to be self sufficient individuals, but created as children of God. Our plans are always thwarted by that unknown sibling, the sisters and brothers we would prefer to ignore.

Human beings distort this inbreaking of God, for good and for evil. Potentially, we are all channels for God's grace. But as our Christian story tells us, we are also fallen creatures, and hence potential channels for evil and sin. Through our human love, we mediate God's love for the other person. Through our propensity to create, maintain, and worship idols, we also deflect God's grace.

What is the place of the other human being in the growth process? As stranger, the other person draws us out of ourself, or may throw us back, defensively into ourself. But this is adult language speaking of more or less adult relationships. What we must do is return to that period of our life when our identity, our individuality, was totally dependent upon the other person. To understand how faith and growth go together or are related, we must take a page from Piaget's books and decenter from our adult perspective.

II

The place to begin our exploration of faith and growth is with the relationship of infant and caregiver, hopefully infant and parent. John Macmurray, in a very helpful work entitled *Persons in Relation*,[1] states that an infant is a person at birth. This is not a mere definition, but follows from the fact that the infant could not live without the intentionality of another person. The infant is born into a personal world, a world of others who care, who give intention and reason to the undirected, unfocused motives and drives of the newcomer. Without the love and care of another person, the infant would cease to exist, would die. The infant is not distinct, an individual. The infant is a person because the infant must be in relationship with other persons. All of us are. It is merely our language and living habits that permit us to forget this fact, and to presume, unthinkingly and unthankingly, that we are individuals, and that as we grow older and more self sufficient, we negotiate contractual relationships of interdependency. But again, this is adult talk. The fabric that makes infants persons is the fabric of love. If, as those within the Christian story say, God is Love, then the fabric that makes persons persons is God.

But human love is not God's love. At best it is a poor representation of it—flawed, filled with self-interest, distorted by alienation from the very Source of that love. But that is the way God acts among us—through the broken, distorted, alienated beings that we are. Fortunately, the Story of the Good News helps us know that brokenness and alienation are not permanent. We are brought back into a right relationship with God through God's love lived out for us in the life, death, and resurrection of Christ. According to our Story, God's forgiveness requires only that we acknowledge our brokenness, our alienation. It requires our repentance.

The infant experiences God's love through the fragility and tenuousness of human love. The infant has more chance to know it as God's love if the caregiver acknowledges it as God's love. The infant also experiences our brokenness, our alienation, our idolatry. Whether the infant also experiences and knows God's forgiveness is also dependent upon whether the caregiver acknowledges God's love as forgiveness. Here we must begin the hard work of speaking of faith.

James Fowler[2] has led us to think that faith grows through stages. I think that he is in error. I do not think that faith grows. It is present through God's grace, although we may choose to disregard that presence. Fowler has used Piagetian structuralism to speak of faith. Piaget's project has been of immense significance. He has tried to explicate how the structures and forms of knowledge, grounded in the body's interaction with the environment, evolve. They do so as a consequence of the history of those interactions and as a consequence of changes in the body. For me, there is no question but that we change—in form, structure, complexity, and relationships—with time and experience. It is appropriate to ask, and try to answer, how faith is related to these changes and emerging structures. That doesn't mean, however, that faith itself grows. Rather it becomes more and more a part of the complex evolving structures that involve us in the rest of the universe.

In Matthew's Gospel, Jesus acknowledges the "little faith" of the disciples, and the faith of the centurion, the hemorrhaging woman, the friends of the paralytic, and the Syrophoenician woman. Recognizing their faith in them, he grants that it need be no more than the grain of a mustard seed. It is, however, a faith that must be acted upon—used. Or as our Story proclaims "Ask (as the Syrophoenician woman did) and it will be given to you; seek (as the hemorrhaging woman did) and you will find; knock (as the paralytic's friends did with boldness) and it will be opened to you."

The mustard seed image is one image for speaking of faith. It has value because faith need not be some overpowering quantitative thing. It can be as tiny as a mustard seed. But there is also a negative aspect to that image. When a seed is planted, it grows and changes in form and structure. In so growing it takes up more and more space. It displaces that which is already there. As an image for faith, this one doesn't work for me. I do not see faith replacing other schemas and structures of our being, but infusing them, transforming them, sanctifying them. If I were to use biological images, I would prefer that of yeast. A single yeast cell divides, reproduces itself, generates carbon dioxide and thus transforms the dough into a different texture, but not into a different substance. It doesn't replace the dough. It doesn't destroy it or replace it. It modifies its quality.

I prefer a non-biological image. It is of a clearing in the midst of the busy-ness of life, in the jungle of our doings, concerns and worries. It is not mere emptiness. It is a clearing for God's presence, the Spirit. Jesus instructs those of little faith to "Seek first God's kingdom and God's righteousness." The image is of a clearing in the midst of our everydayness wherein God is sought, waited for, acknowledged, depended upon. Faith is an awareness of God's presence. God is easily forgotten during the busy-ness of the everydayness. Faith is remembering God.

How are growth and faith related? We need to reflect first upon faith in growth, not growth in faith. By this I do not mean having faith in the phenomena of growth, but acknowledging the presence and necessity of God's grace for growth. Growth is mostly beyond our control and ken. To grow is one thing, to be conscious of that growth is another. Its mysteriousness is a manifestation of God's grace. If the mystery and grace are acknowledged, then, faith can be connected with growth. (Is faith, then, an intentional activity, related to consciousness?) The problem of faithlessness arises when we describe, depict, offer explanations, or think about growth. In such thinking activities, we usually fail to acknowledge the presence of God's gifts or God's grace. Growth "happens"; explanations and understandings are socially constructed. Growth is a consequence of God's grace; explanations and understanding are presumed to be under the control of the person. Forgotten, in the rush to understand, is an acknowledgement of grace in the projects of explanation and understandings.

This is what I mean by faith as a clearing in our everydayness, a place for acknowledging God. Growth is a manifestation of God's presence. It is a continuation of God's creating and creation. But in our explanations and understandings we do not remember and acknowledge that grace. We have not created a clearing for God in these understandings and explanations. Faith, a clearing for remembering God, is too often not present in our understandings of human growth. Consequently, we must be thankful that growth is, in large matter, not a consequence of our understandings. Fortunately, understanding comes after the fact, rather than before the fact. The presence of grace in growth requires a response of thanksgiving. The presence of faith in our understanding leads to thanksgiving. Hence our understanding needs the clearing which is faith.

God acts in our life through our bodies and through the otherness of the world. As we begin to construct our human world and our understanding of ourselves in that world, we fail to save clearings for remembering and praising God and for seeking God's presence. In building our human world and our understanding we, in effect, construct idols that detract us from memory, praise, and hope.

This shows most clearly in the relationship between infant and parent/caregiver. The love and concern which make the infant a person is named human love and the Source of that love is forgotten. The intrusion of anger, disregard, selfishness in the relationship is brokenness or sin, unacknowledged as such. Because it isn't acknowledged the broken relationship is not healed through repentance and the gift of forgiveness. The clearings of faith, in which the presence of God is acknowledged and sought, are preempted by idols and the preoccupations which they produce. The infant, in growing with a cluttered adult and without the necessary clearings for remembering, thanking, and seeking God, constructs or takes on idols, not clearings of faith. The structures of receptivity—of hearing, seeing, feeling—are cluttered and faithless, because the consciousness of the adult is cluttered and faithless. So also are the structures of action—of reaching out and doing, of relating to others. And finally, so are the structures of thinking and symbolizing.

The clearings for God, if they are part of culture and the human world, can become part of the person's understanding and mind, for these are socially constructed in the processes of growth from infancy through adulthood. This, then, is what I mean by faith in growth. God's love, the divine "culture" in which human growth occurs, is mediated, in part, through the imperfections of human love. Human love, manifest through human care, makes the infant a person. But care is not always, or even usually, an unconscious activity. It is guided by intention, by understanding, and by consciousness. If that consciousness does not have, somewhere, a clearing which is faith, then faith will be missing in the growth of that person who goes from infancy into childhood and beyond. Obviously, that doesn't mean that growth is without God's grace. Thankfully, grace has infinite channels into human life and is not dependent upon the frailties of human love. If the clearing which is faith is present then faith can also be part of the growing child.

III

Finally, can one legitimately, speak of growing in faith? If you accept that faith does not change form, structure, complexity, then the obvious answer is no. Faith is the openness to God, which is itself a gift of God. It does not grow. The clearing for God in our understanding and our human world may be only a tiny clearing, no bigger than a mustard seed. "How do we make it grow?" is not the question. It is more appropriate to ask "Where faith—the clearing in which we acknowledge, seek, and thank God—is located in that part of us that is socially constructed?" and "How it can be located in other aspects of our being?"

How can we look at persons to identify regions wherein faith can be found? It is convenient to look at four aspects or qualities that we have or are as human beings. First, there is that part of us that receives the world. We take in food. We also take in qualities and information with our senses. We notice things through our eyes, ears, olfactory organs, touch. Second, we act. We do things with the musculature of our body and get engaged with the thingness of people and the world. Third, we are made up in such a way that much goes on inside of us. We think, dream, imagine, feel, and many more things. Finally, we are our relations with other people. These relations, of course, require the taking in, the acting, and the thinking and feeling, but they are much more than that.

When we ask of faith, we must ask where faith is located in us. For instance, most of us have provided a tiny clearing in our actions. We are willing to go to church for at least an hour a week, maybe more. In this small action, we acknowledge, to different degrees and in different ways, the presence of God. Some who are church goers may not personally acknowledge God, but go because others go. Yet, even this small action is a gift of grace, a tiny seed of faith. It is a clearing for God in the everydayness of doing.

The appropriate question is not how that tiny seed can grow, but rather how that clearing, which is faith, can become part of the other parts of our doing self? How can it become a part of our receiving self? Our acting self? How it can become a part of that internal self of images, thinking, feeling, judging. Finally, how it can become part of our relations with others?

These questions can be answered if we begin to ask how the person is involved in community and how the community is involved in the person. How do two or more gather in God's name? We must attend to the church. How do the people of the new covenant, as a historic people, keep the faith? How do they keep the clearings necessary for acknowledging, thanking, worshiping, and seeking God? How is the kingdom of God, which is both present and not yet, lived out within the church, among the people? These are questions about the rule of life which guides the church, about the disciplines necessary to keep free of the idols we so easily construct, and to construct the clearings for God.

These are questions about the past as well as a question about the now. They are questions about the church in its totality, not about one of its specific historic forms. Walter Brueggemann, in his fascinating little volume, *The Prophetic Imagination*,[3] warns us of the danger of a royal consciousness wherein God is presumably domesticated and at the beck and call of the people. This happens when tradition is unthinkingly lived out in such a way that God is no longer the God beyond—pushing, pulling, calling us out of ourselves. All communities are apt to fall into that royal consciousness. The presence of diversity within the church universal helps us be aware of the propensity to domesticate, rather than be domesticated by God. Faith, those clearings, are lived out differently in different traditions, thanks be to God.

The people of the new covenant are a worshiping people. The clearings of individual persons are influenced by the way a people worship. The diversity is instructive and necessary. The silent meditative worship of the Quaker, the rich intellectual worship of the preaching churches, the overflowing dramatic and aesthetic worship of the Orthodox—all of these keep a clearing in different parts of us. To go, at times, from the liturgy and eucharist of the Episcopal church to the quiet of the Quaker meetings, is to be touched and opened up differently. My daughter is an acolyte in the Episcopal church, but in the evening worships and studies Bible with the Baptists. Her clearings, her faith, are in different parts of her being compared to her friends who are only Episcopal or only Baptist. Worship touches us in different parts of our living and being. It helps keep faith—the clearing for God—in various parts of our language, our images, our relations with others. It is unfortunate when religious education is seen as merely an indoctrination into or understanding of only one form of worship. Young people need different parts of their being opened, cleared of idols, for God. During their formative years worshiping God in various ways can better do this.

The people of the New Covenant are a people of Scripture. Who we are, collectively, is influenced by how we use the Bible. The rich diversity of our unity again suggests how Scripture keeps us free from our own idolatrous interpretations and frees us to hear the word afresh in our encounters with the text. In the so-called liberal, university related, seminaries, the encounters with Scripture inform and are informed by all the facets of the intellectual life of the university. In the literal fundamentalists churches, a detailed literal knowledge of the text informs daily life. In the preaching churches, the texts inform the communities' discourse about personal and social concerns. In the meditative traditions, the Bible informs, shapes, and reconstructs the images of consciousness. To compare how the different faith communities keep open and responsive to the Word of God in Scripture is to be informed about how different parts of our being, of our consciousness, can be opened up, cleared—can be faithful. Growth in faith is not through teaching the Bible, but by making the Scripture part of the various and many facets of our life.

The people of the New Covenant are a people of prayer. Again, our rich diversity is informing of how the clearing, which is faith, can be attached to different parts of our being. The open, expressive prayer of the Baptists, the formal, disciplined prayer of the Anglicans, the private meditative prayer of the Quakers, the public prayers of the Methodists, the private evening prayer of the family at dinner time—all of these traditions inform different parts of our being, and inform the community in different ways.

The people of God are a servant people, called forth into the world to feed the poor, heal the sick, and free the prisoners. By serving others—the strangers in our midst (and today by way of TV and transportation people everywhere—in South Africa, in Central and South America, in China and Russia—are in our midst) we are forced to see the world differently. We are forced into new relations and pulled into new actions. The rich diversity of the historic churches suggests our possibilities. There are those who minister, primarily, to their own. Sometimes they wall off those who are different with stereotypes. Others have work projects and missions to the poor or witness as peace keepers on the strife laden borders of Central America. Some serve by collecting money for missions, others people the soup and bread lines. Some seek connections and direct conversations with those behind the political curtains that divide our troubled world. Others seek only one way communication, recognizing the possibility of evangelizing but not of being evangelized. Our diversity again informs us of how service opens clearings in our being of perceptions, of thought and feeling, of actions of relations. The Mennonite youth on a peace mission, the suburban folk who go into the inner city, the work camp adolescent who go to Appalachia or the hills of Maine and New Hampshire—all have new ways of looking at the world, and new ways of feeling about it—new clearings for God's presence. By experiencing how others pull us out of ourselves, we can express how God's grace is part of our human growth. These meanings can stay with us throughout our lives.

Also, the people of the New Covenant are a reflective people—a people who try to understand their faithfulness. In academic language, we are a theologizing people. This merely means that we try to bring more and more of our understanding under the sway of God and that we take our meager understanding of what it means to be faithful into the rigorous and not so rigorous encounters with other ideas—philosophy, politics, arts, the behavioral sciences and what have you. In his fascinating book, *Liturgical Theology*,[4] Aiden Kavanagh claims that Mrs. Murphy, his favorite Catholic layperson, does theology when she leaves the Mass to reflect on the vicissitudes of her everyday life. He claims that her theologizing is primary theology, and those in academia do secondary theology.

Faith seeking understanding is complimented by understanding seeking faith. The theological task, for the people of God, is to bring under the purview of God as much of our language, our consciousness, as possible. Diverse traditions of the church keep before us how different parts of our intellect, our relations, our seeing-hearing, and our actions can be opened up, cleared of idols, and cleared for God. Thank God, that no one tradition can be normative. Some of us can respond to Richard J. Neuhaus,[5] others to the liberation theologians of South America.[6] We witness differently in our language, which is a sign of our theologizing. Hence the importance of discussions about sex and God; about war and God; about anger and God—and so on throughout all the spheres of one's life. Hence the value of adults and youth talking together about the problems and joys of growing up and being responsive and responsible. Hence the importance of grandparents and older adults telling their journeys of faith to children. Hence the importance of engaging many in planning for social action, worship, and even for the church budget.

What does it mean, then, to grow in faith. Faith is not refined, made pure and perfect. It does not change its structure through growth. It means that more and more parts of us, how we are in the world, are cleared of idols and for God—so God's work can be done through us, through our relations with others, through our minds, through our bodies. Newcomers to a faithful community, whether born into it, or accepted into it as a stranger, will be sustained through the imperfect, fallible love of the people. The love of God can be recognized ever so unsurely, and then only dimly, in the way we try to live in the kingdom which is now and not yet.

NOTES

[1]John Macmurray, *Persons in Relation* (New York: Harper and Brothers, 1961).

[2]James Fowler, *Stages of Faith* (San Francisco: Harper and Row, Publishers, 1981).

[3]Walter Brueggemann, *The Prophetic Imagination* (Philadelphia: Fortress Press, 1978).

[4]Aiden Kavanagh, *Liturgical Theology* (New York: Pueblo Publishing Co. 1984).

[5]Richard John Neuhaus, *The Naked Public Square: Religion and Democracy in America* (Grand Rapids, MI: W. B. Erdmans, 1984). *Ed.*

[6]Gustavo Gutiérrez, *A Theology of Liberation: History, Politics, and Salvation*, trans. Sister Caridad Inda and John Eagleson (Maryknoll, N.Y: Orbis Books, 1988, 1973)

30

Teaching as a Vocation

(1987)

I have a rather simple thesis. If teaching is to be improved we must attend to the teacher—not to the teacher's income and benefits or the other resources available for teaching. Rather, we must attend to how the teacher's work influences the teacher's life. My thesis is that teaching is a vocation, not a profession or a job with long vacations and inadequate pay. Nor is teaching a technology dependent upon science.

The Latin root of "vocation" refers to a call or summons. Within a religious context "vocation" is often interpreted as a call from God. Whereas a religious perspective can illuminate all forms of work,[1] my intent is not to engage in religious reflection about teaching and teachers. After many years of working with teachers, I like to think that they do indeed see their work as a calling. For many, teaching is something that they have wanted to do for years. Perhaps it is because they like children and youth, or because their interests have significant value for other people, or they want to make a difference in the quality of human life. I am quite certain that few, if any, teachers respond to a call for money or a particular style of life. The living that can be produced with a teacher's income is not much of a life by today's standards, but the living that is teaching is as rich and as meaningful, and as socially valuable, as any can be.

A call to be a teacher often wears thin. But disillusionment after two or three years, or "burnout" after fifteen, does not mean that the call—the vocation of teaching—is over. It means that the school is not designed to support the living that teaching is. Teaching is a consuming activity in the sense of transforming, not merely wasting away. It is also, under the appropriate circumstances, renewing and life forming. If this is to happen, schools must be socially constructed and there must be people who recognize that the activity of teaching is meaning making for teachers as well as students. I think that this is not so because schools are not planned on the basis of an image of teaching as a vocation.

Imaging The Schools

Some schools are designed with the image of teaching as a job, like any factory job. Teachers are replaceable: anyone given the right tools and training can achieve goals the "experts" have selected. Other schools are designed with an image of teaching as a profession, based upon warranted scientific knowledge. University and research personnel produce knowledge about child development, learning and cognition, and theories and methods which teachers can acquire in order to practice the profession. As a consequence, schools are the arms of establishments that produce knowledge, while teachers are but the hands and fingers of those arms. Today the image for some schools is a communication center. Ideas and skills are gathered and organized to be communicated by teachers to young people. In each of these cases teachers become subservient to an institution that reflects a particular image of teaching, an image that constrains, restricts, and perhaps distorts the teaching process.

I would propose an alternative image for the school: a place where those who are called to be teachers come together to live out their vocations. Schools could be shaped by that image rather than teachers and teaching being shaped and pummeled by forms of schooling. These places and the people in them would support teachers in their continuing development and realization of meaning. A vocation is living life intentionally and openly, not routinely. It means to be prepared to accept newness and surprise, pain and happiness; for these are dimensions of the world that make us rethink, almost daily, who and what we are. Such a life cannot be lived in isolation or privacy. The closed classroom door can be deceptive and illusory; it only hides the inherent communal nature of teaching.

Moreover, a vocation is not simply being called forth; it is also being called by. We are not called merely to be something other than we are, nor are we called by some mysterious force beyond us. To accept the vocation of a teacher is to answer the call of children and young people. Sometimes their call is suppressed by those in charge of schools or by others with power over young. The voices of the powerful frequently dominate the channels of communication, noisily covering over the voices of the young. These activities of the powerful cause some of the frustration in the work and life of the teacher. Yet, it is precisely this frustration that encourages the teacher with a vocation to journey outward beyond current meanings and values.

If teaching is seen merely as a job, then frustration can be accepted as part of the wear and tear of factory labor. If teaching is only a technology and method, then better methods or techniques are the answer to frustration. Conflicts lead to new research projects on the part of gurus, to develop better knowledge to guide our professional activity. But from the point of view of vocation, in which teaching is our life, frustrations indicate that we are not yet whole, at one with our work. Living intentionally, that is, always in search of new integrating meanings and values, requires that we read the conflict between children's voices and the dominating noise of the powerful as a new question about emerging structures of justice and freedom. Of course, what we hear today from young people and the powerful is not what we heard when we were first called to teaching: the old methods no longer fit; the kids are not what they were. These changes are indicators that the world has changed and that meanings and values we forged in the past must be transformed once again. To be teachers means re-shaping our values as we ourselves are being re-shaped by the newness of this changing world. What we fight for or against continues to change as struggles and conflicts of the world unfold in our place of call and response.

Tradition Calls

In addition to the call of youth we are called by the traditions we serve and which serve us. Traditions are the communal recollections and hopes which give structure, meaning, and value to individual and collective life. These traditions have become identified as content, that which is to be taught. But the habits of schooling have intruded here, too. The limits on what to teach, the domination of technical language, of behavioral objectives and evaluation cloud the understanding: understanding of self, of our work, of young people, and of the traditions themselves. Whereas we tend to see these traditions as having a life of their own, they are carried and embodied in people and communities.[2] An example is the use of language: speaking and listening, writing and reading. From these derive the traditions of literature in its many forms and critical reflections and the changing traditions of print: script, type, and now word processing.

Teachers are called to be trustees of ways of life that would decay and be forgotten were it not for them. Moreover, the call of traditions engages us in struggles of value and meaning, another indicator that teaching is a way of living. Struggles over the control of language in listening and speaking, freedom of expression in writing, and access to ideas in media go on constantly in our vocation. We are called to participate in these struggles. If teaching becomes routinized and we do not help to maintain the life-enhancing qualities of tradition—sources of beauty, truth, and freedom—then we are no longer constructively partaking in the unfolding, and making of human history. That is when we become bored and dull, tired and unresponsive.

Journey Into Story

To be called by other individuals and by traditions is to be called forth into the journey of life. Teaching as vocation means we participate intentionally in the unfolding, or perhaps the collapse, of this social world. This vocation does not permit fixed meanings or values or a final complete "self-understanding" on the part of the teacher. Emerging in the philosophical literature, and to a limited extent in the psychological, are other ways of talking about human beings, more useful than "self-understanding."[3] Human life is a journey with a narrative structure that is best expressed in story form. We tell our own story, and come to know that of others. A story begins before birth and ends usually at death. How do we give language form to that story? Developmental theory cannot help us recollect and shape our experiences into patterns which can be remembered and used to map our future journeys with others. Nor can a theory of teaching compose these experiences with young people and traditions so they continue to make sense rather than becoming repressed burdens. But being able to tell our story to others and listen to the narratives of teachers who take their calling seriously may give us a picture, a moving picture, of where we have been, where we are, and where we are going.

The vocation of teaching offers adventure, an invitation to remain open and vulnerable, and occasions to re-shape and re-compose the story of our life. What dramatic turns, maybe even reversals, has the story of our teaching undergone as we try to hear the calls of children and youth amidst the siren call of drugs, the voyeuristic invitations of TV, and the profit call of the industries of war which consume to destroy? These increasing complexities are not a sign of the decay of teaching, but an invitation to think and feel again what is of value and what we are called to do and be.

Narrating our own personal journeys can help us think about the others with whom we work. If the frameworks of developmental theory are inadequate to help us understand our own story and journey, how can we know that they will be sufficient to compose the events, activities, and moods of the young people before us? Can we look at students as we look at ourselves: on a journey, responding to that which calls them into the world? How have other persons, events, places influenced their story? How do we help them have a sense of who they are, where they are, and who they might be? Teaching as vocation is to find one's life and work participating in the formation of another's story, and vice-versa. Bringing journey into story form, however, is possible only when a person is invited to be fully present. Any part of the self that remains hidden or suppressed because of threat, shame, or possible ridicule cannot be incorporated into a person's story line, for it distorts other aspects of the narrative. The teacher, like host or hostess, helps the student be comfortable, totally present and able to be open to others. In an environment that invites and supports presence and openness, the noise of prevailing powers is reduced, and the teacher can hear more clearly and respond more directly to a young person's call. The stories of both can be more fully told.

Tradition And Language

Another dimension of the teachers' calling is to make available the tradition which they value. A clearly articulated tradition provides a ground against which the figure and story of the young person stands out more distinctly. Against this background, the young person can more easily envision a future which integrates present and past, and empowers future growth. Such images of possibility and hope become a part of a young person's story, serving as a beacon into a vague land. Unfortunately, this imagining of the future in one's story has been neglected or distorted. In the technical-bureaucratic terminology which dominates schooling, the future is expressed in watered-down language as objectives or goals. Image or vision, in contrast, is necessarily poetic and in large measure personal. Goals or objectives—distorted images of the meeting between young persons and tradition—are shaped by the language of school, curriculum materials and evaluation instruments. This language of school people cannot be owned by the young person. It cannot therefore become part of the young person's story.

Yet this conflict of languages becomes part of the story of the teacher who is caught between the dominant language of the school and commitment to the tradition, and the story of the young person. Because consciousness is often dominated by school language, frequently this dilemma may not be brought into the teacher's conscious story as part of the vocational struggle. Still, the teacher is a mediator between the young person and the tradition. A teacher at home in the tradition represents it in many different ways, so that it can become a factor in the young person's narrative. On the other hand, the teacher can bring to the surface those dimensions of the young person's past and present which have some bearing on the tradition. Thus a student, silenced by school language, is encouraged by a gracious host or hostess to bring feelings, memories and hopes to the present in a personal story.

Finally the teacher, to participate in a young person's emerging or unfolding story, must be an able listener, one who "listens" the young person into an articulate consciousness,[4] and a narrator who has the necessary language to fit an episode into the young person's story line. This narrative function has been left to instruments of evaluation, the language of which is severely limited, restrictive and often distracting. These instruments do answer the question, "Where are you?" but the answers which come back in terms of impersonal groups or structures cannot inter-relate the young person's past, present, and future. In contrast, the language of the person who is called to teach can become poetry in Heidegger's sense—naming "what is" in new ways.[5] This poetry can recollect old life, redirect it and renew it for the future.

Vulnerability

We teachers, if our work is a vocation, cannot expect our skills, meanings, methods, values, and our story to carry us fixed and finished into each new teaching moment. We are inherently vulnerable, not because we are teachers, but because teaching is our way of living. Paul Ricoeur speaks of an inherent "fault" or "fissure" (as in a geological formation), meaning an openness to the other-ness and the newness in the world. To accept teaching as a vocation is to acknowledge a fundamental fallibility, hence a fragility and insecurity. And we know it in the pit of our stomach every time we start a new class. Our competence as teachers is continuously brought into question by the newness of the young people who call us farther into our journey of selfhood. It is brought into question still more by changes and growth in the traditions that we value and by the conflicts when principalities and powers struggle for dominance.

Our fallibility and insecurity have been concealed by the various images of teaching we have outlined. Emphasizing method or technology carries with it the false promise that better methods can reduce teachers' insecurities. Teaching seen as profession is a knowledge-based activity, with teachers sufficiently well educated to cope with its problems. Knowledge becomes a protection against insecurity and fallibility. From another perspective, the schooling image, the teacher's vulnerability is a sign of weakness or is denied. It is thought to be overcome by bureaucratic routines such as finding a replacement teacher, getting new texts, demanding conformity to the syllabus, discipline, or other school-generated techniques. But these are misunderstandings of vulnerability. Actually it is a prerequisite for, as well as a consequence of, a journey through life. We are required to be comfortable with reasonable doubt, openness, and unsure-ness, if we are to respond afresh to that which is given afresh. But it is this very openness and doubt that is the source of the insecurity and fallibility of teachers. Insecurity is neither a consequence of ignorance nor a sign of incompetence.

We cannot take on a calling without risk. Rather than seeking ways to overcome fallibility, vulnerability, and insecurity—which is how we have misused our knowledge, methods, materials, and organizations—we need to find ways to live without being overpowered or overcome by newness and novelty. This does not deny the significance and importance of inquiry, research, and additional knowledge for the continuous improvement of teaching. The point is that they cannot do away with or cover over the built-in vulnerability. If that should happen, we simply turn teaching into a productive technical enterprise, unresponsive to people and surroundings. Too often knowledge-makers and researchers are interested in problems and insecurities only in order to market their wares, to design more research, or to search for grants. They are not interested in teachers who respond, however inadequately, to the newness and otherness of the world.

Teachers In Community

Teachers must act in an imperfect world. To postpone action until the makers of knowledge and technique establish the educational millennium is sheer irresponsibility, based upon illusions of progress. We have no choice but to risk ourselves. The choice is whether to risk privately, or to build a community that accepts vulnerability and shares the risk. Vulnerability can be endured in a community of care and support, one in which members take time for telling and listening to the stories of each other's journeys.

To teach because we are called is to feel a need for colleagues, companions, friends with whom we can communicate and search for new values and meanings. Obviously, this is not the environment of many schools. We need people who listen and share conversation about what we are doing, how the young people of this year differ from those of past years, about the developments in our traditions, about the conflicts between the young people and the traditions, and between students and school rules. People who listen to us and to whom we listen can help in telling our story, so that we can more readily recognize our own changing values and meanings. We need to become intentional about our surroundings, creating new coalitions and building suitable communities.

We must ask who belongs to the teaching community and how time is used there. The schools' learning periods are obviously not structured or organized to facilitate the needed conversation, and teachers are not often available to each other for community building (one of the side benefits of team teaching). Part of the reason for our lack of time is the division of labor in the total educational enterprise. It is classroom teachers who have problems, while college and university personnel have time. The problems are taken up by the latter, who mull them over, research them, and write and lecture about them. Teachers become dependent upon their theories and methods and return to summer school or read their books to find solutions.

It is also obvious that administrators do not necessarily take their titles seriously. To administer is to minister to, to serve. Organization, management, and policy interests often preclude concern for the teacher as education's primary ingredient. Administrators are apt to see teachers as problems. I am inclined to reverse judgment and propose that the chief problems in schools are administrators who have been educated to control rather than to serve and minister to teachers. What is meant by an administrator ministering to teachers? One who ministers is concerned about the life of the other and recognizes that the work, the calling, of that person is significant and meaningful. The work of the administrator, therefore, is to "listen" someone else into consciousness, to accept teaching problems as occasions for new growth and development, to explore the social and personal significance of changing characteristics of young people. It is to search for new structures or communities which can reflect the changing values of the members, and it is to mediate between the principalities and powers and the people of the school.

Under present arrangements, the school is a false or forced community, one of control rather than of collegiality. Those who are its members by virtue of their control over it often do not share face-to-face contact. They remain out of sight, embedded in their materials, evaluation instruments, and methods. Few people are fortunate enough to be part of a teaching community where vocation is the norm and the guiding metaphor: a listening/speaking community where personal story is talked and "listened into being," and values and meanings are assessed and reconstituted. Too often teachers have been isolated, vocationally, from community. Silence about their working life inhibits community formation and may explain why we tend to think about education in individualistic and privatistic ways.

Perhaps, besides other teachers, our real partners in this vocation are those who call us to serve them. Young people and their families, though they could be in coalition with teachers, too often are seen as opponents, or problems. If we respond to their calls, participate in their journeys, open up futures for them, reconcile their past and presents, participate in the narration of their lives, are they not tied closely to our story and our own search for what is of value and has meaning? While young people and their parents cannot minister to us in the same way we serve them, they could be part of our support matrix in the same way that we could be part of theirs. Open communication between teachers and students and the sharing of our journeys encourages the intertwining of our stories. We have more in common than we usually acknowledge when we recognize that young people also work and live, make meaning and establish values in the classroom situation.

Teaching is loaded with value considerations. In fact it is one of the dominant forms in the creation and maintenance of values. Yet today, moral and spiritual values have been introduced as something special, detached from the everyday life of teachers and young people. Why was this not a concern thirty years ago? Can it be that the recent interest in teaching values in places of education is a consequence of a collective breakdown in educational communities? The fact that we must now attend to the teaching of values in relative isolation from the rest of life suggests that our frameworks for thinking about and doing education have been concealing the value considerations that inhere in all teaching.

If we live our values and reflect responsibly on our life together, what need have we to teach values? When we are called to teach, the community that is the school becomes the part of the world which is our responsibility and the place where we live out our values and meanings. We can then give life in classrooms the attention it deserves. When we regard teaching as vocation, acknowledging that it is a way of living and not a way of making a living, and if we attend to the meanings and value making of the teacher, we will rebuild our educational communities so that we live more truthfully, justly, openly and beautifully in the classroom.

NOTES

[1]Douglas Steere, *Work and Contemplation* (New York: Harper and Brothers, 1957).

[2]See Arthur R. King and John A. Brownell, *The Curriculum and the Disciplines of Knowledge* (New York: John Wiley a Sons, 1966) for an exploration or the educational consequences of such communities. Michael Polanyi, *Personal Knowledge: Toward a Post-Critical Philosophy* (Chicago: University of Chicago Press, 1958) and Hans-Georg Gadamer *Truth and Method* (New York: The Seabury Press, 1975), offer philosophical explorations.

[3]Paul Ricoeur, *Time and Narrative* (Chicago: University of Chicago Press, 1984).

[4]Douglas Steere, *On Listening to Another* (New York: Harper and Row, 1964).

[5]Martin Heidegger speaks of poetry as the originative naming of what is, in "Hölderlin and the Essence of Poetry," *Existence and Being* (Chicago: Henry Regnery Co. 1949), 291–315.

31

Religious Education: Practicing the Presence of God

(1987)

I

Brother Lawrence, the barefoot lay brother who worked in the kitchen of the Carmelites in the 1600s, wrote that he could not "imagine how the religious person can live satisfied without the practice of the presence of God."[1] If he were alive today imagining that would be no problem. The practice of the presence of God is, for most, restricted to moments of prayer and worship. But for Brother Lawrence, "Times set aside for prayer were not different from the other times ... because his greatest business did not divert him from God."[2] For some of us, given our socialness and spiritual dryness, God is even missing in those moments. Most of our business seems to divert us from God. The world is, indeed, too much with us. God's presence is displaced by our social structures symbols and material goods—by our idols.

In the minds of some, religious education is a time set aside. It has become a place, such as Sunday school; or an activity with others, such as teaching; or special materials, such as a curriculum or study materials. However, it need not be time, activity, materials set aside or different, no more than prayer was for Brother Lawrence. Religious education can be a way of practicing the presence of God.

How can that be? To be religious is to be with God in the world with others. How we are with God depends, of course, upon our traditions and our own experiences. It may be an awareness of God's grace, discipline, redemption, or gifts; a commitment to God's ways, laws, and love; a celebration of God's covenants and mighty deeds; or merely a sense of God's presence and our faithful response. Practicing that presence requires more or less constant awareness of, or reference to God in our life. Paradoxically, an awareness of God's absence or our distance or separation from God can be a practice of God's presence.

To be in the world in an educational way is to be conscious of how the present is shaped and reshaped by the past and the future—our own past and future, and the past and future of those who share (have shared and will share) life with us on this planet and perhaps in this universe. To participate in education, or to be educated, is to work at integrating the personal and collective past into our lives, such that the new life that we are revitalizes and transforms the personal and collective past. To participate in education is to image the future, and to make some effort to shape that future in terms of how we value the personal and collective past.

The expression, "religious education," then, is not only a pointer to places, times, techniques, materials, organizations or activities. It is also a pointer to a way of thinking about what we do and how we are with God and others in this world. All of us think, in some way, about how we are in this world. Some of us may regularly think about how we are in this world with God. Not all of us think in religious educational ways about these matters. It is that to which I wish to call attention.

II

But we have some thinking habits that must be overcome if we are to think in religious educational ways—habits of thinking deeply embedded in our consciousness and ways of living. These habits revolve around the idea that we are individuals, and that we can abstract an individual from his or her context. We have established patterns of speaking that idolize individualism. We speak of learning, of being socialized to a community, of stages of individual growth and development. As patterns of speech associated with scientific modes of social inquiry, they invite further inquiry. As patterns of speech embedded in and giving form to our everyday life with others and God in this world, they stereotype and deform that life.

If we are individuals at any time in this life it is at that time of absolute individuation, death, when we give leave to our companions of this life and speak of our being with God. But until that absolute moment we are not monads merely bumping into other monads. We are of a fabric, a fabric of life, and we have no meaning, indeed no life, outside of that fabric. This we forget because of a brain that enables us to abstract, and a language that gives a sense of reality to those abstractions. It is easy to abstract ourselves from that fabric in our thinking, but not in our life. But the abstraction of our individualism is an illusion; an illusion converted into a way of life by our economic and cultural systems. And because of these habits of language, economy, and culture, we tend to think of individual faith, and the growth of that faith. To focus upon the fabric of life is to call attention to God's realm, to biblical metaphors of the kingdom of heaven or of God. Through God's covenants with us, we dwell in this realm with others. We do not speak of ourselves as a person of God; rather we acknowledge that we are a people of God.

We are our relationships. Our so-called personalities and habits of language and thinking are the fabric of yesterday—the way we are in relationship with the people of our past. Our present feelings are often the conflicts or compatibilities between the fabric of yesterday and the fabric of today. Our hopes are the images of the fabric of tomorrow. The tension between our hopes and our present is a consequence of fabrics that do not match perfectly. To sew them together is to risk tears. Reweaving is necessary, not merely sewing together different fabrics.

Of the relatively recent depictions of this fact, that we are our relationships, one of the best is found in the 1954 Gifford lectures of John Macmurray.[3] He claims that we do not grow to become persons, but that we are persons at birth. The reason for this claim is that persons are always persons in relation. The drives and unfocused activity of the new born infant take on focus and meaning through the intentions of the parent. The infant cannot live without those intentions, and hence human life is impossible without the other person. This fact, that our life is possible only because of others, is soon forgotten. Our language patterns and our memory, aided and abetted by cultural traditions, easily discards the significance of other persons in our lives.

Piaget indirectly supports this claim through his understanding of knowledge as relationship. Operational knowledge is a schema of relationship. Given our propensity for abstractions, we remove the schemas from the interactive context and see them only as physiological structures embedded in the body of the "individual." The Old Testament use of "knowing" as a way of speaking of sexual relationships is compatible with Piaget's language. To "know" some one sexually is to be in an intimate relationship with that person. In Piagetian language, to know something of the world, is to be in interaction, in relationship, with that something. Our memory, reinforced by our language, hides the relationship. Our memory pulls the other person or the something of the known world into our interior, and our language exteriorizes the abstraction rather than the relationship.

In religious language Buber calls attention to the fact that the Spirit, God, is between people, not in an individual. John's Gospel states that God is love. Love, God, is the interlocking weave that holds together the fabric of which we are a part. In forgetting the centrality of love, of God, we forget the fabric. We think that love is something that we do to build relationships between and among these individuals that we have let ourselves become. We think that love is an intentional act, something that we learn. We forget that it is a given. The forgetting of the given and the presumed need to learn to love is, perhaps, a manifestation of sin, of our alienation from and forgetting of God. The language of religious education must be a way of speaking of our relationship as a given, one of God's gifts. It must be a way of speaking that enables us to see our individualism and our separation from each other as a breakdown in our acknowledgement of God's grace, of the love that binds us to each other in and through God.

The fabric of relationships is of two different weaves, intermingled, and not always separately identifiable. The first is the relationships of intimacy, in which we are linked and respond to the innerness of each other—needs, feelings and other so- called subjective or inner aspects of life. The second is the relationships of community, wherein we join hands and voices to do something in and of the world. Two levels of intimacy, and three kinds of community can be identified.

In relationships of birth, the intimacy is of parent and child. Parents involve themselves in the internal life of the infant, and bring that new subjectivity into the family fabric. The needs, temperament, wishes, pains, desires of the infant are woven into the family fabric through the intentions and awareness of the parents. The infant/child is given care by the parent; that is, the family fabric is rewoven to welcome and support the new being. In the early weeks and months this is a one sided intimacy, although recent studies of parent-infant relationships indicate that the child also influences the internal life of the parent. That is, the family fabric is also rewoven by the infant/child. Other members of the family begin to take on a different texture and design as a result of the new thread in, and weaver of the family fabric.

There comes a time, however, when parent intimacy with the child is insufficient and child intimacy with the parent intrusive. The family fabric is no longer adequate to contain and support all of the life of the child, no more than it can contain and support the life of the adults. The child, noticing life outside of the family, reaches out to become part of other life forms and fabrics. The lives and fabrics of other people offer new possibilities to the child/youth, new supports, new responses to one's subjectivity and new jointly woven fabrics. The family begins to reinforce those parts of the fabric tested as the child/youth weaves fabrics of intimacy with those beyond the family. If family fabrics cannot be reinforced, the erupting tears are rewoven. The young person gradually establishes new relationships of intimacy, of shared innerness, which eventually reach the most transforming depths of human love and sexuality wherein new being is again created.

Not all relationships are intimate, wherein the inner depths of needs, feelings, memories, and hopes are shared. Our community fabrics lack the rich depth of intimacy. They weave us into the external worlds of others—the worlds of work, of re-creation and celebration, and or worship.

The worlds of work fabricate and maintain those traditions which make the world a dwelling place for people, wherein they are sheltered, sustained, and cared for. This is the world that people have built so laboriously over the centuries, with its various centers of powers, conflicts and many imperfections.

The worlds of celebration and re-creation are those traditions in which we stand back from our work and rejoice in the creation and our creations. Thereby we are renewed, re-created, and can say, in the verbal image of God: Behold, it and we are good! Rejoice and be glad!

The worlds of worship are those traditions in which we stay open to the transforming power of God. Through praise, repentance, participation in sacred rites and reflection upon God's words and deeds in and through human history, we open ourselves to the sources of life and love and become what we can be, but are not because of our fallenness.

As adults, we are all woven into various communities and their worlds of work, re-creation, and worship; no matter how deficiently and imperfectly. And because of the family fabrics that weave adults and the young together, the young are also partially woven into the same communities.

III

Here, then, is our agenda for religious education. It is one of scrutinizing the fabrics of relationships that we have, those of intimacy and those of community, and of asking how God is present or absent in those relationships. And then, with the help of our religious traditions, imagining how we can practice the presence of God in these relationships of intimacy and community. From that act of imagination, informed by the resources of our religious traditions, we need to transform our present relationships to include God's presence. This is more a problem of remembering and recollecting than it is one of weaving new fabrics. For if God is love, the Master Weaver of the fabrics of which we are a part, then it isn't a matter of reweaving new fabrics with God's presence, but of noticing how we have ignored or failed to notice that presence. In large measure, this is a matter of reconstituting our habits of thinking, which means, primarily, reconstituting our language habits to acknowledge God's presence in those times and places where we have forgotten God.

In the fabrics of intimacy, the educational task seems easy, yet, because of our present language habits, is very difficult. We need to begin with an exploration of human love as a manifestation and, usually, a distortion of God's love. As Love, God is in the love relationship of parent and infant, but because of our idols, our selfishness and needs, and the injustices of our social and economic systems, God, as the source of that love, is forgotten. The religious traditions of which we are a part need to be brought to bear here. The worshiping community can acknowledge that God is present in the family fabric by recollecting that we are all fallen creatures, and that human love aspires to God's love, but fails. The failure, the permanent human fault that keeps us open to God's grace, is spoken of and witnessed to by acts of repentance, and forgiveness; wherein we acknowledge our humanness and our dependency upon God's forgiveness and God's grace. In our impatience, selfish willfulness, arguments, anger, and other imperfections of family life, God is present if we can acknowledge the limits of our ability to love, God's forgiveness and acceptance, and God's promise that human love can be improved.

But human love within the family can be refined and improved only through our own repentance, and our ability to forgive and to accept forgiveness. In the language habits of the family, then, we must begin to use the language of repentance and forgiveness. In the necessary, humbling, and life giving struggles between wife and husband, parent and child, we must find a place for the language of God's love. We must acknowledge to each other that we are fallen, that we have our personal and collective idols, that we can forgive and accept forgiveness because God is a forgiving and accepting God. The language that is part of the family fabric must incorporate, then, the language of our sacred texts and the language of our public worship services. If children have a fabric of family intimacy where fault, limit, repentance, and forgiveness are expressed as manifestations of God's love, then the failure of human love in the family leads not to neurotic distortions but to an awareness of our need for God's presence in the midst of the complexity, conflict, and mystery of family life. With this primary fabric of intimacy, wherein God is part of the weave and the Master Weaver, then, as the young weave their own new fabrics of intimacy, God's presence can be acknowledged and celebrated.

A special time and place to teach about the practice of the presence of God in the family is not needed. Rather we must find ways to talk about our intimate relationships, acknowledging God's presence and involvement in those relationships. In our intimate relationships we need to acknowledge God's grace, God's acceptance of our fallenness and tendency toward idolatry and forgetfulness, God's forgiving love, and God's promise that we can approach that love in our own life of relationship. No one place is more appropriate for this religious education than any other. It can occur during sermons, pastoral work and in the many occasions when marital and family life is the topic of conversation, whether in the home, the church, or elsewhere.

As the child/youth reaches beyond the family fabric to establish his or her own fabrics of intimacy, our religious educational task is to help explore the meaning of intimacy as a manifestation of God's love, and to place sexuality within that fabric of intimacy, rather than intimacy within the fabric of sexuality. The worshiping community is again the locus of such language and awareness. The religious traditions that affirm the goodness of creation, (such as the Song of Solomon), the sanctity of human life, the significance of love as giving and receiving, our own fallenness and forgiveness, and the joys and struggles of marriage and family as a form of discipline[4] are means to bring God's presence into our thinking and acting as we help others weave new structures of intimacy.

As we move beyond the relationships of intimacy to the relationships of community, the educational task is somewhat the same. The fabrics of community are perhaps less well defined or visible than the fabrics of intimacy, for we hide the community under our idols of individualism. We do indeed work to make money to support our family or to provide a way of life. We do indeed have leisure time to do as we want and to relax from pressure. We do indeed worship to be renewed spiritually. But we fail to see the larger fabrics of which we are a part because of our self-centeredness. Our educational task is to assess the traditional baggage we carry from our past that covers over God's presence and to find ways to affirm that personal and collective past which acknowledges God's presence. It is true that we work to make money for self and family support. It is also true that working is participating in the life God has given us, one of stewardship and caring for the world around us that it might nourish and support us as we nourish and support it. It is true that we have leisure time for refreshment, but it is equally true that recreation is re-creation—time when we stand back to be refreshed by acknowledging that God's creation, including ourself, is indeed good. And even when we stand back to notice its fallenness, the presence of God can be recognized by noticing the need for redemption and reconciliation. Recreation is participating, through grace, in the goodness of God's work. It is true that worship is a time for spiritual nourishment and renewal. But it is equally true that worshiping is a time to be with others who have accepted the covenant that God has established with us, and where we, collectively, not individually, are enabled to be transformed by participating in that covenantal relationship with God. We are protected from the idolatry of individuality by the fact that discernment is inherently a community activity, requiring encounter with sacred texts, sacred traditions, and others in covenant with the worshiping community. We are protected from the idolizing of self, by worshiping in community with others, by reading sacred texts with others, and by joining at the table with others.

Educationally, the movement that needs to be observed and attended to is the movement from the family fabric of intimacy to other fabrics of relationship. The movement to broaden out one's participation in the complexity and mystery of life has no particular universal form. Intimate relationships, beyond the family of birth, probably develop out of community relationships of work, re-creation, or worship. In the middle class society of today, the first community fabric is probably that of re-creation rather than work or worship. In the time when schooling and work had more valence for young people, the work community was probably the major transitional community. The claim could be made that the worshiping community is the major transitional community; but today the worshiping community is not necessarily a religious community, or one in which the monotheistic God is acknowledged, worshiped and celebrated. The significance of this claim, besides setting an agenda for observation and inquiry, is an agenda of priority, making certain that the community that worships God also helps those woven into that fabric recognize that re-creation and work are forms of responsiveness to God's presence. The educational task of the worshiping community is to help those woven into that fabric to find God's presence, or absence, in their communities of re-creation and work.

The religious part of the religious educational work before us is to help ourselves and others practice the presence of God in all of our doings in this world. The educational part of the religious educational work before us is to overcome those habits—whether they are habits of mind, of language, of social convention—that substitute our diverse idols for God's presence in our midst, and to establish new habits more adequately grounded in God's realm and God's covenant with us.

NOTES

[1]Brother Lawrence, *The Practice of The Presence of God* (NewYork: Fleming H. Revell, 1895), 46.

[2]Ibid., 19.

[3]John Macmurray, *Persons in Relation* (New York: Harper and Brothers, 1961).

[4]e. g., Mike Mason, *The Mystery of Marriage* (Portland, OR: Multnomah Press, 1985); and Ernest Boyer, Jr. *A Way in the World: Family Life as Spiritual Discipline* (San Francisco, CA: Harper and Row, 1984).

32

Educational Activity and Prophetic Criticism

(1991)

But you are not to be called rabbi, for you have one teacher, and you are all students ... Nor are you to be called instructors, for you have one instructor, the Messiah.

—(Matthew 23: 8 - 10, NRSV)

Education has been practiced and thought about as if it were a human enterprise. Is it not, however, God's enterprise—part of God's creative work?

Human activity associated with education often gets in the way of God's WAY, distorts God's creative work, and clutters God's Kingdom. In serving humankind, rather than God, the human activity associated with education frequently increases our alienation from God, legitimates and covers over our golden calves, maintains the structures of bondage to human powers, restricts or limits our freedom as God's children, and inhibits our ability to participate in God's healing love. By claiming education as something that human beings do, we fail to recognize the educational significance of prophetic criticism, of exorcism and forgiveness, and of love.

How can the claim be supported that education is God's work?

Education happens because human beings participate in the transcendent. Education—the "going beyond" of what we are at any moment—indicates that we are in, but not of, the world. Participation in the transcendent is not recognized because adult human beings ground educational ends in human standards and expectations. Augustine's vision "Lord, you have made us for yourself, and our hearts are restless until they find their rest in you" is dusted over and dirtied by images of human progress and achievement. But the dust is blown away by the winds of human failure and the dirt is washed away by the tears of pain—whether of sickness, separation, or death.

Education happens because we are confronted by the other—an image of what we are not, but can be. Sometimes, the other is an image of our future self, a narcissistic reflection of an enhanced present. Sometimes it is an image that others have of us, societal narcissism. But isn't education, in part, a dying to oneself that we may find ourselves? A losing of our life, so we can find it? Confrontation with the other brings us under question and enables us to shed the idolatrous self into which we have poured ourself and which now contains us.

Education happens because we are loved. Being loved, we are able to give up our present self, to flounder in the unformed or in that process of being re-formed. We know, intuitively and through relationship, that our anxiety of possible loss, of being splintered and reshaped, will not result in permanent fragmentation, dismemberment, or multiple personalities because we are loved in our wholeness (a wholeness anticipated rather than felt) and by One who can help us withstand the fragmenting pulls of the world's otherness. Love holds together that which appears separate and distinct. Love maintains the unity within the diversity of the world.

Education happens because God attends to our healing—to the re-integration, re-membering, re-collection of who we are in God's image. Tensions among feelings, thoughts, actions, relationships, memories and hopes constantly prod us to hope and pray for wholeness, atonement, to be in tune with all that we are, hope to be, and can be. Fragmentation and internal hemorrhaging prepare us to reach out to touch the garment of the One who saves. Our audible, even silent, cries can be heard over the crowd by the One who restores sight. The turmoil caused by that foreign part in us, unintegrated and perhaps even rejected, makes us recoil from the truth, and secretly hope that the demons within, whom we cannot love, will be cast into the herd of swine.

Education happens because creation is still happening, in and through us—individually and collectively. Our gifts and talents invite and push us to find new ways to be in and for the world, while still not of it. The uniqueness which we are leaves new marks in the world to which others respond. The curiosities that we bring into the world unveil what would have remained hidden without us. The stories and memories of others and otherness we leave behind become signs of the Holy, joining the signs of other witnesses.

If education is God's enterprise, then how do we participate with God in that enterprise, rather than claim it as our own? How can we prepare the Way, rather than get in the way? The questions seem monumental, because the human educational edifice (which is crumbling under the weight of the humanly constructed educational mainframe) is so monstrously cumbersome. Actually, the questions are not monumental. We know their answers. They have been given time and time again in human history. They comes in many forms.

The two great commandants are one answer: "*You shall love the Lord your God with all your heart, and with all your soul, and with all your mind.*" And a second is like it: "*You shall love your neighbor as yourself.*"

The difficulty, of course, is that we have too much human junk and debris cluttering the human world—junk that gets in the way of seeing clearly the radiance in our midst. Our educational work is not to set goals, prepare the learning environment, develop new curriculum materials, or train teachers. We participate with God in God's educational enterprise by clearing away the clutter and debris. Our task, as of old, is to name and own up to our idols, to call ourselves and our friends to repent of the habits which separate us from God, and to praise God's mighty works in our midst. In other words, our educational work is not to construct more effective learning environments and educational theories, but to *de-* struct that which gets in the way of acknowledging and praising God. If education is God's enterprise, then we must empty ourselves so God can work.

We don't like that answer. We have built education as a human activity, and we want to maintain control. But that's our problem. In taking control of education, we have discarded God for something known, rather than letting God be. We take control because many people interpret "get out of God's way" as "we don't have to do a thing, for it is all in God's hands."

But it isn't yet. It is still in our hands. But the hands have been too grasping and clutching, holding on for dear life—our dear life. The hands of praise—the open palm, not the clutching fist—are required. But that is hard work. Why? Because we have constructed our home on earth as if it is ours, to have and to hold, to clutch and to hang on to. We must be willing and able to see all of this as possible folly. Even better we must see what we have constructed as symbolic of God's creation. We are but stewards of the temples we have constructed, where glimmers of God's Kingdom shimmer through.

To participate with God in the educational enterprise, is to be critical and worshipful. It is to be able to say boldly and loudly—"Hallowed be *Thy* name. *Thy Kingdom* come, *Thy will* be done. Forgive us our sins, as we forgive others."

It is hard work to remove ourselves and our society from center stage, which most educators prefer. It is hard work to stay aware that God's creation and creativity is in and behind that which we do and make. It is hard work to keep God's word or God's images before us in this noisy and image-filled century. It is hard work to love the self made in God's image, whether our's, our neighbors, or our enemy's. It is hard work to accept hope rather than progress, for a future shaped by hope is murky at best. It is hard work to get out of our children and let God be in them.

That we trust ourselves more than we trust God, with respect to our children, is sad. Is the world too filled with us and our things, and not filled enough with the "Grandeur of God"? Are we perhaps afraid that God will indeed "flame out, like shining shook foil" and sear us, whereas we are already "seared with trade; bleared, smeared with toil." It takes work to remember, that

... nature is never spent;

There lives the dearest freshness deep down things;

And though the last lights from the black West went,

Oh, morning, at the brown brink eastward, springs—

Because the Holy Ghost over the bent

World broods with warm breast and with ah! bright wings.

(Gerard Manley Hopkins, "God's Grandeur")

If we and our world get in the way of God's educational enterprise, our task is the one of old. That which we have constructed and in which we think, live, and have our being, must be severely criticized, brought under question, and God's presence proclaimed through and over our junk. We are responsible if God's educational work is bottled up. Our task is to remove the logs from our own eyes so we can see our clutter, remove it, and then see the Way more clearly. This is the task of prophetic criticism. This is our educational work as we participate with God in the educational enterprise.

Educators need to be followers of John the Baptist, crying out into our cultural wilderness "Prepare the way of the Lord, make God's path straight." This is not an easy task, for we must be both proclaimer and the hearer. Frequently, because we sit in Moses' seat, we are more accustomed to talking than listening.

For too long those who claim to be educators have thought that they could by-pass the idols and sinfulness of the world by educating children and the next generation. We couldn't improve this world, but our children and young people could if we educated them properly. It hasn't worked.

"Do whatever they teach you and follow it; but do not do as they do, for they do not practice what they teach." We thought that was directed to someone else, but it is directed to us. Unfortunately, there is no mirror facing Moses' seat. We tied heavy burdens on children and youth, in the form of catechisms, boring classes, text books. We loved to have the places of honor, to be greeted with respect in the market place, and to be called teacher.

Children and young people don't recognize their participation in transcendence, and hence can't celebrate it. They don't rejoice at the strangers around them. They don't feel the comfort of love so they hang on for dear life rather than the dear death that brings new life. Unfortunately, their cries of pain are relieved by hearing that someday they too will be adults.

The task is not to educate children and young people. It is to hear the cries of the St. Johns of today in our many wildernesses, pointing out our caughtness, our idols, the absence of God in our midst. We participate in God's enterprise of education by cleaning up our own act, so children, young people, and the strangers in our presence, can feel the comforting warmth of the Holy spirit, can see the radiance of God shining through our work, and can hear the Word in our language.

God educates. We don't. But God can educate only if we hearken to John's call "Prepare ye the Way!" We participate in God's educational work by bringing under criticism our self made world, and by proclaiming God's presence. " ... for you have one teacher." We are but the Teacher's servants.

33

Education and Spirituality

(1993)

How can one talk about the education, specifically, curriculum, and also talk about the spiritual? The problem is one of language and of the images that are both a source and consequence of that language. With what language tools and images (metaphors, ideas) do we describe, envision, and think critically about education? Thanks to Macdonald, Pinar, Apple, and a variety of other curriculum writers who stand on their shoulders, we no longer have the horrendous hegemony of technical language (drawing primarily on learning theory and ends/means structures) usurping discussion of education. Nevertheless, that language orientation is strongly established, embodied in educational architecture, materials, methods, organizations, and teacher education. Breaking out of that language is difficult, however, for the structures and processes which shape education—themselves derivatives of that language—force conversation into that technical mode. Our very locations and practices are framed by the language tools and images we would like to overcome.

We depend upon the language, practices, and materials as if they were the givens with which we have to work. We have forgotten, or suppressed, that imagination is a foundation of our so-called "givens." Our languages, practices, and resources are merely the embodied or materialized images in which we choose to dwell. Other images, in which we could dwell, are currently unembodied in worldly structures and abandoned. But embodied images are no more a reality than are unembodied images a mere figment of an "unreality." Embodied, or materialized images, and the language patterns associated with them, are more directly related to our sensory systems and our relations with powerful people. However, our sensory systems, and our social/political systems, are in touch with but a small part of the reality of the universe. The complicated and expensive technologies of modern physics take us into the strange world of electromagnetic frequencies, matter and anti-matter, particles and waves that several years ago were far beyond our wildest dreams, rooted only in

401

the imaginations of science fiction writers. The mysterious crop circles throughout the globe also indicate the limited contact of our sensory systems, and their congruent language resources, with a larger, more encompassing reality. Religious and meditative communities point to other limitations of our sensory systems, and to alternative social/political structures.[1]

Can education be re-imagined? This does not mean inventing new language, new practice, and new resources, new buildings. It means having a different view of people, of our educational spaces and resources, of what we do and what we say—a view that will enable us to critique the embodied images, see obstacles, and recognize alternatives.

My vocational history indicates how one person became aware of the problem and tried to solve it—a move from secular to religious education. I recall my first year or two of teaching in elementary schools. Piaget had not yet influenced educational language—although the research on concept development was underway. Aware of that beginning research, I wishfully thought that I could do a better job of planning and teaching if I knew what was going on in the heads of my students. I wanted to discover what was going on inside heads, through my own research or that of others. Several years later I began to question the educator's dependency on the research enterprise, and realized the absurdity of my wishful thinking. It had the same quality as the question, "What do you do until a cure is found for the disease that we have?" Do you stop living and working and wait until there is more knowledge? Can action be postponed until more is known? If so, we have an infinite regress of waiting as new problems emerge. Is empirically based knowledge necessary before one can teach? Is there wisdom independent of research, yet open to that research? People have been teaching for centuries without research based knowledge. Obviously, they have not been without wisdom.

What do we do until a cure is discovered? We live and work, talk and play, laugh and cry, love and hate with our friends and neighbors. Our students share with us the human condition. They are our neighbors, if not our friends. The language of teacher/student—specifically the language of teacher/learner—hides that neighborliness, and the student's strangeness. We and our students are part and parcel of the same mysterious universe.

It is a universe in which we know more than we can say, and often say more than we know, to quote Polanyi. It is much fuller, deeper, stranger, more complex, mysterious than I, and I am bold to say, than we, can ever hope to know. I know that

The world is charged with the grandeur of God.

It will flame out, like shining from shook foil;

It gathers to a greatness, like the ooze of oil

Crushed. Why do men then now not reck His rod?

Generations have trod, have trod, have trod;

   And all is seared with trade; bleared, smeared with toil;

   And wears man's smudge and shares man's smell: the soil

Is bare now, nor can foot feel being shod.

And for all this, nature is never spent;

   There lives the dearest freshness deep down things;

And though the last lights from the black West went,

   Oh, morning, at the brown brink eastward, springs—

Because the Holy Ghost over the bent

   World broods with warm breast and with ah! bright wings.[2]

We may differ in our choice of words. Hopkins writes from within the Christian tradition, and feels comfortable with the word "God" and the words "Holy Ghost." Others may not or do not, and for me, in this paper, it matters not.

There is more than we know, can know, will ever know. It is a "moreness" that takes us by surprise when we are at the edge and end of our knowing. There is a comfort in that "moreness" that takes over in our weakness, our ignorance, at our limits or end. It is a comfort that cannot be anticipated, a "peace that passeth all understanding." Call it what you will. Hopkins calls it the Holy Ghost. One knows of that presence, that "moreness," when known resources fail and somehow we go beyond what we were and are and become something different, somehow new. There is also judgment in that "moreness," particularly when we smugly assume that we know what "it" is all about and end up in the dark or on our behinds. It is this very "moreness," that can be identified with the "spirit" and the "spiritual." In fact Kovel defines "spirit" as what "happens to us as the boundaries of the self give way."[3] Spirit is that which transcends the known, the expected, even the ego and the self. It is the source of hope. It is manifested through love and the waiting expectation that accompanies love. It overcomes us, as judgment, in our doubts, and in the uncomfortable looks of those with whom we disagree, particularly those with whom we disagree religiously. One whose imagination acknowledges that "moreness" can be said to dwell faithfully in the world.

If one dwells "faithfully" in the world, what images of education, specifically curriculum, are possible? I speak as one who tries to dwell as a Christian, because that is my religious tradition, and because I am more familiar with its many qualities, quirks, and its language than I am that of other traditions. Those in other traditions are invited to attempt the same, thereby enriching the ensuing conversation.

I use the word image in the sense of a view of a landscape. I assume that there is an educational landscape that may be envisioned (or imaged) in many ways. Different images of the same landscape enable us to see different possibilities, different relationships, and perhaps enable us to imagine new phenomena in that educational landscape.

A new image must be articulated or described so others can move within the landscape as they did in the past, but with greater freedom and new awareness of their choices and limitations. The current images of the educational land-scape provide the comfort of the already known, even old familiar problems. A different image must not disorient those who feel that comfort. An image of the educational landscape that makes room for, or includes the spiritual, cannot be too alienating. It must welcome the experienced educator and the stranger. An image that lets the spiritual show needs to use most of the current categories of education. However, once inside that image, the educational landscape should appear differently, showing limitations in current educational practices and perhaps opening up new options for action. Traditional curriculum concerns need to be addressed—namely the goal or meaning of education, the social and political structures of education, content, teaching, and evaluation. However, an image of education that permits the spiritual to show will depict these dimen-sions differently. An image that acknowledges the spiritual shows other prob-lems and tasks more clearly, such as moral and spiritual values, and the need for spiritual or religious disciplines for the teacher.

THE GOAL OF EDUCATION

The bewitching language of psychology and the behavioral sciences has skewed our view of education. The language of ends and objectives, which guides educational practice and decision making, is used to depict a future state of affairs. The process whereby an individual moves from one state of be-ing to another and develops new capacities or competencies is identified as "learning"—a term so much a part of the coin of the realm that it blocks the imagination. We ask how "learning occurs," thus hiding the fact that we dwell in a near infinite world, that our possibilities are always more than we realize, and that life is movement, change, or journey. "Learning" too quickly explains and simplifies that movement or journey.

The "moreness" in the world, spirit, is a moreness that infuses each human being. Not only do we know more than we say, we "are" more than we "cur-rently are." That is, the human being dwells in the transcendent, or more appro-priately, the transcendent dwells in the human being. To use more direct religious imagery, the spirit dwells in us. Our possibilities are always before us. Our life is never a closed book, until death. In the Judeo-Christian tradition, there is no better image than Augustine's "our hearts are restless until they repose in Thee."[4] Kovel defines spirit as "connoting a relation between the person and the universe; while soul is the more self-referential term, connoting the kind of person who undergoes that relation. In a sense, soul cuts even closer home than spirit, because while spirits can be—and are—seen everywhere, soul refers to who we are, and necessarily, to what we make of ourselves. We may define soul, therefore, as the spiritual form taken by the self."[5]

What has this to do with education? The fact that we partake of the transcendent means that we are never complete, until death. We can always be more then we are. Within the Christian tradition, we are always open to a "turning;" to forgiveness, redemption and the new being which results. The future is before us as open and new if we are willing to turn away from what we are and have, if we are willing to let the past in us (the self) die. Life is a journey of constantly encountering the moreness and constantly letting aspects of us die that the new may be born within us. It is not necessarily a comfortable journey, and moments of rest and peace are often more infrequent than we might want.

"Learning" is a trivial way of speaking of the journey of the self. The language of growth and development is a rather mundane way of talking about the mystery of participating in the transcendent, or in uniquely Christian language, the mystery of incarnation, death and resurrection.[6] We do not need "learning theory" or "developmental theory" to explain human change. We need them to explain our fixations and neuroses, our limits, whether imposed by self or others. The question that educators need to ask is not how people learn and develop, but what gets in the way of the great journey—the journey of the self or soul. Education is a way of attending to and caring for that journey.

Educators and students are blinded by social and cultural systems and do not recognize their participation in the transcendent, in their ever open future. The journey of the self is short circuited or derailed by those who define the ends of life and education in less than ultimate terms. We are always caught in our proximate goals (our idols) or in the limitations imposed by others (our enslavements). Infrequently do we look beyond these limits or notice how life has been restricted by the social/cultural context. We are reminded of unrealized possibilities through social criticism, through art that points to other ways of seeing and being, through the stranger in our midst who illustrates that we too could be different, through worship and confession, and perhaps by divine discontent.

Our caughtness in systems that restrict our ultimate journey points to the fact that the journey is never a solitary one. In spite of this culture's bias toward privacy and individualism, we cannot be human beings without others.[7] We journey with others. Some precede us, some accompany us, some follow us. Consequently, we have paths, maps, models, scouts, and co-journeyers. We must be thankful for and wary of these co-journeyers. They show us the way, and lead us astray. Life with others is never a substitute for the individuation required of us. Others cannot take our journey. Yet being with others on the journey is a source of hope, comfort, and love—all manifestations of the transcendent. It is also the source of the ever present possibility of domination. Given this existential fact, it is essential that our image of the educational landscape show the social/political structures of education.

The image of journey also shows the possibility of falling off the trail, deviating from the journey, being caught in byways and dead ends. In the Biblical tradition this is known as sin, a word much distorted in some circles, but which means falling away from God or off the path toward God. This risk in the educational landscape is best noticed when the problems of content come into view.

THE SOCIAL/POLITICAL STRUCTURE
OF EDUCATION

An image of the educational landscape that allows the spiritual to be noticed points to the ultimate goal of education—the journey of the soul. The question that needs answering is why human beings try to derail that journey for their own purposes? Why do we try to shape the journey of others to fit cultural molds—whether of class, race, economic setting? Why do we try to shape the journey of others to maintain the present distribution of power, subjugating some people to the whims and fancies of others? Once we have in view the ultimate aim of education, then the misuses of power in the human world, and in education, are clearly seen. In the social/political context—e.g., the ordinary context of life—the journey of life is predefined for many, severely restricted for others, and the ultimate journey to God encouraged for only a few.

What must the image of the educational landscape contain to enable us to think about the constraints within which we work as teachers and educators? Joel Kovel's *History and Spirit* helps explore this as he renews the language of spirit in this culture, removing it from the restrictions of any one religious tradition.[8] Walter Wink's *Engaging the Powers*,[9] is most helpful in thinking about this problem from within a Christian perspective. In Biblical language, the journey and the corresponding commitment to God, is restrained, redirected, and derailed by the principalities and powers—the forces that no longer serve God, but serve false gods and human beings. The principalities and powers bring us into their spheres of interest, where we serve their ends, rather than the ultimate end. Bob Dylan's "You Gotta Serve Someone," depicts the problem. The pursuit of our journey to God is short-circuited by the pursuit of lesser ends or outcomes, which are manifestations of the principalities and powers. They restrict and impede the religious journey, condition human life to the mundane world, or fixate human life before the journey is completed. Fortunately, educators now have ample depictions of the restrictive forces operating in education,[10] and ideas to think about those restrictions. References to "education as liberation" or "education as self realization" acknowledge and seek to overcome these principalities and powers in the ordinary structures of education. The idea of liberal education, which frees one from the limits of a particular culture and society in order to take on the awesome responsibility of freedom, also acknowledges and seeks to overcome the restrictions of the principalities and powers. However, the articulation of these ideas is often merely another political claim, albeit liberal or progressive, rather than a religious claim, and hence often another effort to restrict the journey.

Wink calls attention to the domination systems of this world, and speaks of a world free from domination, obviously a utopian ideal, but also a central religious image in Christianity and other religious traditions. In the world controlled by domination systems redemption is through violence. Wink calls this the "myth of redemptive violence," which is implicit in almost all of the images of mass media and popular culture (Popeye, Superman, Robocop, etc.), as well as in the military systems that, by the threat of violence, keep peace in the world (and sell their excess arms to nations of the third world). In a domination free world the redemptive myth is that of redemptive love. According to Wink the myth of redemptive violence is deeply ingrained in each of us—we have internalized the principalities and powers, or as Pogo said many years ago, "We have met the enemy, and they are us." Because the myth of redemptive love, (in the Christian tradition, the "story" of redemptive love) is not deeply ingrained in our characters (a major failure of religious traditions), our educational system short circuits the journey of the self or leads it to dead ends.

The organization of the school, the selection of content, and teaching itself clearly illustrate this. The school is the one social institution constructed with children and youth in mind, yet they are often alienated in and from that institution. Others dwell in it and make it their own. Schools are a major institution of the principalities and powers, and a major source for teaching the myth of redemptive violence—that the world can be corrected and redeemed through power (including the power of knowledge) and might, but not through love. This criticism has been common enough in educational circles since the sixties, and I need not dwell on it. The influence of the principalities and powers in education is seen more clearly, as problems of curricular content are brought into focus.

THE CONTENT OF EDUCATION

In current images of the educational landscape teachers and curriculum people ask what is to be taught. The question is asked prematurely, for there is a prior realm of thinking and imagining, which if by-passed, ignores a crucial starting point. Even the prior thinking of epistemology brackets questions of spirituality.[11]

Where do we start to think about the content of education? The religious journey, the process of being educated, is always a consequence of encountering something that is strange and different,[12] something that is not me. That which is "other" and strange can be part of the I. In the infant the "other" is the hands, the sounds made, the feet that move; in childhood it might be feelings; in adolescence sexuality. The internal "otherness" continues throughout life as shadow, as thoughts, dreams, yearnings and desires that frighten, shock or stir us. Usually we think of the "other" as something in the external environment that is unknown, strange, new. Hovering always is the absolute "other," Spirit, that overwhelms us in moments of awe, terror, tragedy, beauty, and peace. Content is the "other." Knowing is the process of being in relationship with that "other." Knowledge is an abstraction from that process.

When the world no longer appears as "other," no longer seems strange, or has no strangeness, education appears to come to an end. Woe is that day, of course, for the power of knowledge has become prejudice, and the power of influence has become ownership, bringing all "otherness" into a relationship of domination. The whole world still seems new and strange to the young child, and education happens easily and naturally. This is curiosity. With age, less and less seems new or strange, and education appears less natural and frequent. Curiosity seems to end. The problem is not that education is just for the young, or that curiosity is a phenomenon of children and youth. The problem is that our controlling tendencies result in the hermetic environment, self or socially constructed, and we fail to recognize, or we forget, our relationship with and indebtedness to the absolute "Other" often manifested through the neighbor and the strange. The cause is not the decay of curiosity. It is idolatry and slavery. Educators, and people still being educated by the otherness of the world, easily slip into conditions of idolatry and slavery. The protection against this, of course, is criticism—calling attention to how our attention and our journey have become fixated or overpowered, a theme addressed later.

This image of the educational landscape helps us notice our traps, our limits, our idols, our slaveries. How does it help us plan? How can we use the image of the "other," the stranger, to design environments that educate? The topic is too vast for this paper, and I can only call attention to a few characteristics. First of all, it is crucial not to reify educational content, the otherness of the world, as if it were merely stuff made by human beings. To forget that knowledge and objects of culture are manifestations of and outcroppings from the creativity of the human species is a disastrous mistake. Priority must be given to human beings and the natural order. Then we can see more clearly how human kind participates in the continual creation of the world. We can also see how the "creations" of human kind sometimes bring us closer to extinction. Hopefully, then, our students can see, more easily, their own journey as a participation in the continual creation (or destruction) of the world.

Content is, first of all, "other" human beings. Others see the world differently, talk differently, act differently. Therefore, they are possibilities for me.

They point to a different future for me, another state on my journey. I could be like them. By being different they bring my particular self under criticism. What I am, I do not have to be. What they are, I could be. Other people call attention to a future that is not just a continuation of me, but a possible transformation of me. Through the presence of the "other" my participation in the transcendent becomes visible—the future is open if I will give up the self that is the current me and become other than I am. As content, other people are sources of criticism and new possibility.

Beside criticism and possibility, the "other" as content provides an opportunity to listen and speak with a stranger. Not only are the visions of my own journey shifted, perhaps reformed or transformed, but my party of co-journeyers is also enlarged. Strangers become neighbors. I have others to listen me into consciousness of self and the world. I have the gift of other stories of the great journey. Through conversation, I have a chance to refine my way of talking about the world, and to participate in the refinement of theirs. Through the caring act of listening and speaking, I have a chance to participate in the mystery of language. In listening and speaking the transcendent is present as newness comes forth, as forgiveness is given and received, and as the poetic shaping of the world happens.

Whereas I have referred to the "otherness" primarily in terms of human beings, it is crucial to give the same credibility and respect to nature. Our habits do not include thinking about how the possibilities of the natural world intertwine with ours, or how we might carry on "conversations" with non-human "others." Hence the increased destruction of the natural world. The religious response to the ecological crisis, the interest in how other cultures (Native Americans for instance) respect the land and its occupants, and the emerging paradigms of the new physics and other sciences indicate how the world view is gradually shifting to see nature and human beings as part of the same creation. The thinking of educators has not kept pace with these changes, in part because of dominant economic interests that view nature as resource and commodity.

When we shift our focus from the content which is "other" people, to the content which is the outcropping of their creativity and actions—symbols, bodies of knowledge, works of art, institutions, technologies, products, and practices—we face problems too numerous for an essay. The strangeness persists, the "otherness" is still there. These are parts of the world still "other" to the student. How does the presence of this cultural object bring me under criticism? What new possibilities does it offer me? How can my life be different because of it? What new paths, maps, scouts and co-journeyers are before me? What new conversations can I enter? What new stories of the great journey are available? But ownership also exists, in that these outcroppings of human creativity are usually in the possession of other people or other communities. These outcroppings are available as gifts, or they may be stolen or purchased. The teacher should be a gift giver. However, there are segments of the educational community, particularly at the graduate level, where one has to purchase the symbolic "other," perhaps by paying dues for belonging to that community of cultural ownership.

Wink suggests that all human constructions (institutions, structures of knowledge, etc.) have vocations and spiritual dimensions. They serve God. They can also serve Caesar or mammon. They have the possibility to free people for their journey, or to tie them into structures of idolatry or slavery. All content areas of the curriculum need to be looked at with this in view, a task much too complicated for this essay. Phenix does this in some ways in *Realms of Meaning*.[13] Foshay looked at the spiritual in mathematics.[14] Noddings and Shore explore aspects of this in their work on intuition.[15]

From within this image, planning appears different. The question is not what does this "other" mean to the student, for meaning is an operation from within the current self. Rather, the question is how will the student be different because of this "other." For people already captivated by idols, or fixated to other aspects of self and world, the question is, what must be given up, or in Christian language, what part of oneself must die so new life becomes possible? Those familiar with the Christian Gospels, may recall that in Mark the followers of Jesus exclaimed, after an exorcism, "What is this? A new teaching—with authority! He commands even the unclean spirits, and they obey him."[16] Teaching is, in part, a form of exorcism, the casting out of the "unclean spirit" so new vitality and life is possible. But we must be exceedingly careful, for the power to destroy seems easier than the power to give. Too frequently teachers ask "How do we motivate?" or "What threats (such as grades and testing) can we use?" More appropriate questions are—"How can this student see himself or herself anew in this content?" and "How can one be supported while one gives up one's old self to become a new self?" The first question must be answered esthetically, for it requires attention to the presentation of the "other" in a way that "grips" the student. The answer to the second question is of a "pastoral" nature because dying to one's self, giving up a part of one's self or past, entails grief work, and requires a community of life wherein one can die and know that life will not be lost, but found.

The second step in the planning process is that of displaying the fascination and structure of the "other." The student is invited in and begins to recognize new power and pleasure of self. "Playing with" is the image, because play is nonthreatening and gradually introduces one into the rules, habits, and forms of the content. This should be a "playing with" that gradually introduces the student to more complexity, and to the feeling of more power or more pleasure. Many of the achievements of the post-Sputnik period with respect to math and science were of this kind—displaying structure as an invitation to "come and play" so the student could feel enhanced. This is not to imply that education is never work. However, the word "work," in school and in society, has come to mean a form of losing self for others, of alienation, not of finding myself, my power, my future and my journey. Similarly, the significance of the word "study" has been destroyed. Students study to do what someone else requires, not for their own transformation, a way of "working" on their own journey, or their struggle with spirit, the otherness beyond them. Just as therapy is work, hard work, but important for the loosening of old bonds and discovering the new self, so too should education as study be seen as a form of that kind of work.

TEACHING

Teaching has been seen as a set of skills, as particular kinds of action. Teachers are not replaceable cogs in an educational machine, nor is teaching carrying out a set of tactics and strategies owned by others. Teaching does require skills, and hence depends, at times, on reproducible knowledge. However, if teaching is restricted to that image, there are few ways of thinking about the spiritual aspects of teaching and the teacher. Teaching needs to be grounded in a life. It is not a way of making a living, but a way of making a life. The spiritual dimensions of teaching are recognized by acknowledging that teaching is a vocation.[17] When that is acknowledged other dimensions of teaching will also be seen more clearly.

A vocation is a call. In the religious traditions it is a call from God, or a call to serve God. But the religious meaning need not be invoked here. A teacher is called to a particular way of living. Three voices call, or three demands are made on the teacher. Hence the life that is teaching is inherently a conflicted way of living. The teacher is called by the students, by the content and its communities, and by the institution within which the teacher lives. Depending upon the institution, teachers feel this conflict differently. For elementary school teachers the call of the students is probably more dominant. College and university teachers hear the call of content, and its communities, as primary. Of course, given the institutional binds that teachers feel, few ever feel called by the institution. But it is there, if only fully responded to by those aspiring to administrative posts. Each of these calls place demands or obligations on the one who would live the life of a teacher.

That part of the teaching life that is a response to the call of the student results in the work of love; to the call of content, the work of truth; to the call of the institution, the work of justice. As in all vocations, these works are easily distorted by the principalities and powers. Spiritual warfare is inherent in all vocations.

The work of love is obvious. The teacher listens to the student, and speaks with great care, that the gift of language, jointly shared, may reassure and disclose a world filled with truth and beauty, joy and suffering, mystery and grace.

The teacher makes promises to the student. The journey of the student is filled with hope, rather than despair; more life, rather than less. The teacher introduces the student to the "otherness" of the world, to that which is strange, and assures the student that the strangeness will not overpower but empower. If the encounter with the "other" requires that old ways of knowing, relating, feeling, be given up, the teacher assures the student that during the resulting vulnerability no harm will come and that the grief will be shared. If the student is temporally disabled by the loss, the teacher may step in to fill the void. If some dying of the self happens, the past will not be forgotten, but celebrated and integrated as useful memory. If idols are given up, the teacher promises the security of the spirit that is the source of all transcendence. If the security of slavery is thrown overboard, the teacher will help the student find new communities in which power is shared. These positive images, derived in part from the redemptive myth of love, disclose the negative power of the social/political context wherein the life that is teaching is lived.

The work of truth is a work of stewardship. Responding to a particular discipline or content area the teacher is called to keep it truthful and useful. The language and other symbols of the content are easily distorted, tarnished and stained by the principalities and powers. They lose their luminosity—their power to disclose. They hide more than they reveal. They become idolatrous, ends in themselves, and no longer point to the spirit that enlivens human beings. The teacher's work of truth is to keep vitality and signs of transcendence in the language and symbols. The content that makes up the curriculum is part of creation and a source for its continuance. Thus the deadness must be rooted out, and those parts that have become idols, criticized and renewed or placed in the museum of the past—to be beheld as that which once gave and celebrated life. To be called to the work of truth is to recognize that the "other" also has a vocation of honoring spirit and participates in the transcendent. Thus that part of the "other" by which it is criticized, transformed, improved, made more serviceable, must also be available for the student. In science, this is done by making accessible not only the outcroppings of the scientists, the theories and technologies, but also the methods, procedures, and communities through which a science renews itself.

The work of justice is the third call, the call of the institution within which the teaching life is lived. The institution of the schools is the meeting ground of conflicting interests. It is not and cannot be a neutral place. The teacher lives and works in an almost unbearable conflict zone among those competing interests. The present form of the institution is shaped by the balance of interests. To assume that the present order and structure are givens is to yield unthinkingly to the principalities and powers of the past.

The school as an institution also has a vocation. It serves students, the communities with interest in the curriculum content, the teachers, and those who support it economically. Its vocations become tainted when justice does not prevail among these competing interests, and one or more of the interests, or some other power, gets control. Justice, which is never an absolute value, always requires the adjudication of competing claims.

Teaching is a vulnerable form of life, for the teacher works among these competing interests. Teachers often fall away from the vocation of teaching and become mere functionaries as they do the work demanded by others in workbooks, schedules, exams, grading and what have you. It is often easier to deny the vulnerability, the competing interests, and to fall into the form demanded by the principalities and powers, those in control. Teachers lose hope, accept idols and enslavement, and burn out. Teachers give up teaching as part of their own spiritual journey, to pick up the journey at the end of the school day, the beginning of summer, or the end of their career.

The work of justice requires acknowledging the impotency of the isolated individual, and the danger of the closed classroom door. Teachers called to the work of justice need alliances and coalitions of those called to the same vocation. The struggle for justice in schools requires sensitivity to pain and unfairness. Such sensitivity brings under question curriculum materials, teachers' skills, and institutional practices like grading, grouping. The pain of teachers, unable to respond to the call of some students, is often too much, and they seek relief by hardening their hearts.

CRITICISM

The fourth rubric in traditional curriculum planning, after goals, content, and teaching, is evaluation. The process involves stepping back and asking how we are all doing in this educational enterprise. Students and teacher are evaluated, because they are the weakest politically, and most at the mercy of the principalities and powers. Students move on. Teachers can be replaced. Thus they are the scapegoats in the domination system. The school's procedure, materials, and basic organization have longer lives.

An image of the educational landscape that makes room for the spiritual suggests other ways of thinking about evaluation. In *The Protestant Era*[18] Tillich calls attention to the necessity for continuous protest against form. Form gradually loses its vocation, becomes idolatrous, and no longer points to the transcendent. Continual protest against form is necessary for reformation and renewal of vocation. Others speak of the necessary dialectic of creation and criticism. Forms created by human beings soon become idols or enslave others. Criticism calls attention to what is still beautiful, truthful, transparent for God, filled with the possibilities of transcendence and the promise of life. It also calls attention to the breakdown of vocation and the fading of luminosity.

The dialectic of criticism and creation is hidden by the idea of evaluation. Evaluation is the act of those already in power to determine the effectiveness of their power. Some forms of evaluation are used appropriately in the instructional process for diagnostic purposes. This is criticism of instructional materials and techniques, based upon teacher and student sensitivity to their failure to serve students. Such evaluation should result in different materials or procedures, a reforming of method to fit the student.

However, the power of existing evaluation instruments points to the impotency of other participants in the schooling process to criticize and reform education. In some ways, the discipline problems of students are forms of criticism; the lunch room, coffee break, and after school conversations among teachers are forms of criticism; parent complaints can be forms of criticism. However, the possibilities to reform schools and classrooms are not in the hands of those who live there, for a variety of reasons. Hence criticism is removed as part of the creative process and becomes merely carping and blowing off steam. This is a denial of the spirit in those who work in the educational landscape, for criticism is also part of the creative power of the spirit.

CONCLUSION

I have briefly sketched an alternative image of some of the basic principles of curriculum and instruction, drawing upon sources and images that make room for the spiritual aspects of human life. Much more needs to be done. Two problem areas can be seen more clearly through this image.

First, recent discourse about moral and spiritual values in the classroom is incorrectly focused. That discourse assumes that there is something special that can be identified as moral or spiritual. This assumption is false. Everything that is done in schools, and in preparation for school activity, is already infused with the spiritual. All activity in school has moral consequences. The very highlighting of the need to teach moral and spiritual values in schools implies a breakdown not in the spirituality and morality of the student, but a breakdown in the moral activity and spirituality of the school itself, and of the people in control of the school. Those in control of the schools cover over their own complicity in the domination system by urging the teaching of moral and spiritual values. They do not urge that the moral and spiritual climate of the schools, which they control, be changed. That teachers do not feel the freedom to be critical and creative is a sign of their enslavement to other principalities and powers. The need is not to see moral and spiritual values as something outside the normal curriculum and school activity, but to probe deeper into the educational landscape to reveal how the spiritual and moral is being denied in everything. The problem of the schools is not that kids are not being taught moral and spiritual values, the problem is—the schools are not places where the moral and spiritual life is lived with any kind of intentionality.

It is also quite clear to me that it is futile to hope that teachers can be aware of the spiritual in education unless they maintain some form of spiritual discipline. This needs to be of two kinds. Given the inherent conflicts involved in teaching, and the inherent vulnerability of their vocation, teachers need to seek out communities of faith, love, and hope. Teachers can deal with conflict and vulnerability if they are in the presence of others who radiate faith and hope and power. To be in the company of co-journeyers is to be enabled to identify personal and collective idols, to name oppression, and to undergo the continuing transformation necessary in the vocation of teaching. The second discipline is a disciplining of the mind, not in the sense of staying on top of all the educational research and literature, but in the sense of developing an imagination that has room for the spiritual. When teachers examine the educational landscape we should see what is there and hear the call to respond with love, truth and justice. We should also see the principalities and powers, the idols and the spiritual possibilities hidden behind all of the forms and events that are taken for granted. Teachers should be able to see that nature is never spent;

There lives the dearest freshness deep down things;

And though the last lights from the black West went

Oh, morning, at the brown brink eastward, springs—

Because the Holy Ghost over the bent

World broods with warm breast and with ah! bright wings.

NOTES

[1]For example in the Christian traditions see Stanley Hauerwas and William H. Willimon, *Resident Aliens* (Nashville: Abingdon Press, 1989); and Dietrich Bonhoeffer, *Life Together*, trans. John W. Doberstein (New York: Harper and Row, 1954).

[2]Gerard Manley Hopkins, "God's Grandeur," in *The Oxford Book of English Mystical Verse*, Chosen by D. H. S. Nicholson and A. H. E. Lee (Oxford: Clarendon Press, 1921), 355.

[3]Joel Kovel, *History and Spirit: An Inquiry into the Philosophy of Liberation* (Boston: Beacon Press, 1991).

[4]*The Confessions of St. Augustine, Book One*, trans. J. Sheed (New York: Sheed and Ward, 1943).

[5]Kovel, *History and Spirit*, 33.

[6]Other religions have other ways of talking about this mystery. The work of Ken Wilber has been the most helpful in bringing together the multitude of religious and psychological perspectives. See "The Spectrum of Development" in *Transformations of Consciousness*, ed. Ken Wilber, Jack Engler, and Daniel Brown (Boston: New Science Library, 1986), 65–106.

[7]See John Macmurray, *Persons in Relation* (New York: Harper, 1961).

[8]Kovel, *History and Spirit*.

[9]Walter Wink, *Engaging the Powers* (Philadelphia: Fortress Press, 1992).

[10]See, among others, the works of Michael Apple.

[11]I explored this in two previous essays. See Dwayne Huebner, "Spirituality and Knowing," in *Learning and Teaching The Ways of Knowing* (Chicago: National Society for the Study of Education, 1985), 159–173; and "Religious Metaphors in the Language of Education," *Phenomenology & Pedagogy: A Human Science Journal* 2, no. 2 (1984), also in *Religious Education* 80, no. 3 (1985): 460–472. See Chapters 26 and 28, *Ed.*

[12]The best psychological analysis of this process is Robert Kegan, *The Evolving Self* (Cambridge: Harvard University Press, 1982).

[13]Phillip Phenix, *Realms of Meaning* (New York: McGrawHill Book Co., 1964).

[14]Arthur W. Foshay, "The Curriculum Matrix: Transcendence and Mathematics," *Journal of Curriculum and Supervision* 6, no.4 (1991): 277–293.

[15]Nel Noddings and Paul J. Shore, *Awakening the Inner Eye: Intuition in Education* (New York: Teachers College Press, 1984).

[16]Mark 1:27

[17]See Dwayne Huebner, "Teaching as a Vocation" in *Teacher Renewal: Professional Studies, Personal Choices* (New York: Teachers College Press, 1987). A revised form is available in The Auburn News, Fall 1987 (New York: Auburn Theological Seminary). See Chapter 30.

[18]Paul Tillich, *The Protestant Era* (Chicago: University of Chicago Press, 1948).

34

Can Theological
Education
be Church Education?

(1993)

In the last several years, Edward Farley, Professor of Theology at the Divinity School, Vanderbilt University, has contributed significantly to the contemporary shake-up of theological education through his historical and idealogical critiques of this discipline.[1] In one influential essay[2] Farley explored "the mystery of why the ideal of an educated clergy is found alongside a complacency over uneducated believers in the life of the church."[3] He proposed that a "cumulative, rigorous educational process ... will have to be introduced into church education."[4] The essay calls attention to significant issues in church and theological education. However, his proposal ultimately fails because he did not attend to several significant issues which shaped church education. This essay addresses those issues.

FARLEY'S CASE

The gulf between educated clergy and uneducated believers raised historical questions which, for Farley, went far beyond the history of church education. He identified two "formative presuppositions that effected and now maintain the gulf."[5] The first was "the ambivalence the Christian movement has always felt about the importance of learning, knowledge, and the sciences."[6] The second was "the social structure of earlier Western societies which restricts learning to the elite classes," and which "reinforced the gulf between educated clergy and uneducated believers."[7] In spite of the democratization of education and the development of public education, "the church continues on the assumption that ordered learning with respect to matters of religion, its texts, history, beliefs, and practices is not possible for the believer."[8]

Farley identified three themes that "help open up the mystery of the gulf: the professionalization of theology, the homiletic paradigm of the way faith occurs, and the generalizing of the meaning of education."[9] These three themes left their mark on theological schools, preaching practices, and the religious education movement.

The first, explored historically in *Theologia*,[10] involved changes in the use of the word "theology." The original use of the word implied wisdom—a predisposition of the believer, common to laity and clergy. However, with the rise of the university in Europe, and the move of theology into the university as a science, theology came to refer to doctrines and systems of belief. It became "an umbrella for the clusters of sciences and disciplines organizing" the education of clergy.[11] Eventually, "theology was lost even to the clergy, the ordained leaders, and came to be restricted to teacher-scholars who presided over clergy education … "[12] Consequently, "Whatever education in the church is, it cannot be theological education, since that is what the clergy study in schools designed for their training."[13] Church education must be something different. Over the years it carved out something for itself other than the disciplined study of the seminary or university, and distinct from wisdom. According to Farley, the movement which understood theology as a highly disciplined set of scholarly enterprises, not as wisdom available to all believers, widened the gulf between educated clergy and uneducated believers.

Farley's second explanation for the gulf between educated clergy and uneducated believers was acceptance of the paradigm that "faith is formed and nurtured primarily in the weekly liturgical event,"[14] which in the Protestant tradition "centers on proclamation and the sermon … the sermonic liturgical event is the primary resource for the believers' knowledge of tradition and for their interpretation of situations."[15] Farley acknowledged that this "is inadequate as a comprehensive paradigm of the way the believer's existence in the world before God is shaped and disciplined."[16] Nevertheless, he postulated that the acceptance of this paradigm discouraged church leaders from asking other questions about faith formation and nurture.

His third explanation for the gulf was the church's understanding of education as it attempted to overcome the limitations of the homiletic paradigm. He claimed that the various attempts to understand education in the church led to an undervaluing of "ordered learning,"—"subject matters with their attending methods and modes of thought; cumulative, sequential stages of learning; rigorous disciplines"[17]—and an over valuing of the view that all forms of community life educate.

In conclusion, Farley claimed that if church education is ever to be theological education then the following conditions will have to be established:

A cumulative, rigorous educational process and post-Enlightenment tools of analysis and interpretation ... will have to be introduced into church education. A very different kind of church teacher will be called for. Directors of religious education will have to be more than administrators of church programs. The educator on the church staff will have to be a theologian-teacher. But for that the church will have to reassess the axiom that it takes for granted: that church education cannot be theological education.[18]

Farley made a significant contribution to thought about the education of clergy, and raised important questions about the education of the laity. In *Theologia* his suggestions for the needed restructuring of theological education of the clergy were well grounded in the history of that education. In *Fragility*, he attended carefully and creatively to the epistemological foundations of such study, foundations equally applicable to the education of laity. His analysis of the conditions and quality of church education are essentially correct. It is highly desirable that "a cumulative, rigorous educational process and post-Enlightenment tools of analysis and interpretation ... be introduced into church education."[19] However, contrary to his prescriptions for theological education of clergy, his prescriptions for education of the laity are based upon an inadequate mastery of critical historical detail.

He failed to depict the church school as grounded, historically, in the laity, and ignored previous efforts to upgrade the quality of church education through institutionalized means. Furthermore, he ignored the twentieth century struggle to define education in the church and the subsequent development of religious education as a speciality. And finally he failed to test, historically, his claim that there was a homiletic paradigm that explained the formation and nurture of faith. Before his proposed solutions for church education can be addressed, these historical errors must be corrected.

THE CHURCH'S EDUCATIONAL PAST

Three closely intertwined conditions have influenced church education today. They are: the lay origin of the church school in the United States, the establishment of publishing houses for church education materials, and the formation of the Religious Education Association and the subsequent "professionalization" of religious education. No current historical account of religious education combines these three into a unified history, yet each has influenced the other.[20]

The lay origin of Protestant church education continues as a major influence. From its beginnings in the urban centers of the east coast, through the establishment of church schools and libraries in the opening west, lay leaders exerted major influence. Their influence continued through the formation of the Sunday School Union and the establishment of Sunday School conventions and teacher institutes in the middle of the nineteenth century. Lay religious education committees and lay Sunday school superintendents continue as major sources of power in many churches throughout the country. The recruitment of lay teachers was, and continues to be, a way to involve lay persons, including adolescents, in church "ministries." This historic lay tradition has stymied attempts to upgrade the "ordered learning" quality of church school education.

Another influence was the early establishment of the publishing houses for Sunday school material. In the early part of the nineteenth century, the American Sunday School Union established and distributed materials for Sunday schools, and church and community libraries. Shortly thereafter, publishing houses were established by the Episcopalians, the Methodists, Baptists, and Presbyterians.[21] The history of these ventures has not been told in a single story, although Dykstra and Wigger[22] explored the development and problems of various Presbyterian series over the last century. Three major problems associated with this publishing venture can be identified.

The tension between interdenominational interests and the particular doctrinal interests of specific denominations continued over the years. In the early part of the nineteenth century the American Sunday School Union provided interdenominational materials, thus covering over theological differences among the denominations. In response, the various denominations set about producing and distributing their own materials. In 1872, during the third national convention of Sunday school workers, the uniform lesson plan was hatched, which provided common Biblical lessons, but enabled denominations to embellish in appropriate ways. The founding of the International Council of Religious Education, in 1922, led to the development of the graded lesson plan, which incorporated developmental and educational insights of the newly involved professional educators and educational psychologists.[23] And again, denominational interests drew upon the developmental insights and went their own way. One hundred years later, several Protestant denominations joined efforts (JED - Joint Educational Development project) to produce "Christian Education: Shared Approaches" which offered four different approaches to curriculum, one of which continued the uniform, now graded, approach. After a few years denominational interests again took precedent and JED collapsed.

In later years, conflicts also developed between curriculum writers (frequently seminary educated, often ordained, and sometimes with secular educational planning backgrounds), and lay consumers of the materials (Sunday school teachers). These differences led to the rejection of the materials by local churches. Dykstra and Wigger[24] and Kennedy[25] explore this problem with respect to the Presbyterian materials. The Episcopal Church encountered similar conflicts between lay consumers and professional producers with "The Seabury Series."

Conflict between publishers and church consumers indicates the third problem. Publishing houses became market driven, and lost their mission focus. Lay control over Sunday School content extended to the control over the agendas of publishing house by virtue of the laity's ability to vote with church budgets. The historical evidence seems to indicate that efforts of seminary educated curriculum developers to develop more rigorous church school materials failed because the need for church schools materials is driven by the interests of the laity.

Another effort to upgrade the quality and substance of church education was the formation of the Religious Education Association in the first few years of this century. William Rainey Harper, George Coe, and others were interested in harnessing the newly emerging studies of education, psychology, and human development for religious education. According to Schmidt, "Coe and Harper represented a growing group of modern intellectuals who wished to reform the Sunday School while not losing the faith of the past."[26] The formation of a professional organization of "religionists" and "educators" led to the gradual professionalization of religious education, and to a major role for the emerging educational specialists and researchers in religious education. Several institutional programs in religious education had their origin about that time, including Union Seminary/Teachers College, Yale Divinity School, and the Presbyterian School of Christian Education. In subsequent years, church educational programs were significantly influenced by graduates of these programs.

Dykstra and Wigger[27] explored the intermeshing of these three streams of historical influence. Denominational educational boards and publishing houses worked with the newly formed professional religious educators, as well as with secular educational specialists, to prepare church school materials for lay church teachers. Efforts to increase either the religious or educational sophistication of the materials created problems for lay teachers, and were doomed to eventual failure.

Protestant involvement in the founding of the public schools also shaped church education. Given the cultural hegemony of the Protestant establishment in the founding and development of the United States, the first public schools were seen by some people as an extension of the church. The early public school curriculum included resources to encourage moral and religious development. Catholics and other immigrants discovered that the Protestant hegemony interfered with the religious formation of their own children and they built parochial schools. As fundamentalism and other religious groups continued to take issue with public school practices and built parochial schools, many Protestant religious educators turned their attention to the larger issue of how the church can help shape the public.[28] Coe and other leaders of the Religious Education movement signaled this concern in the early part of this century. The interest in public education became increasingly important as religious educators realized that the Sunday school was being expected to carry a role much too heavy given its meager time, limited resources, volunteer teachers, and the vanishing Protestant ethos in the society at large. For many religious educators, then, the task of religious education was not "ordered learning" within the church, but the formation of Christian or religious citizens.

Finally, Farley is not alone in suggesting that the qualities of church education should be improved. In 1960, Glen claimed that "In spite of the traditional emphasis the church has placed on catechetical instruction and the education of its ministry ... a strange subordination of the teaching function prevades its life, work, worship, and proclamation."[29] He argued, with little long term effect, that church education required more attention to the problems of "truth" and "teaching." He pointed to the paucity of the educational resources in contrast to the support for the church's other ministries. In 1991 Williamson and Allen argued that "all clergy, regardless of whether they are appointed as parish clergy, as judicatory executives, or whatever, should understand themselves primarily as teachers of the Christian faith."[30] The pleas of a variety of seminary academicians have echoed the same need—Why can't education in the church be more rigorous?[31]

Farley's proposal to bring "ordered learning" to the church school ultimately fails. He raised a significant content issue—the place of "ordered learning." But earlier efforts to improve the content of church education through curriculum materials and professional leadership had very limited success. The lack of attention to structural issues of church leadership is one explanation for the repeated failure. Farley did not bring into view the historical significance of the laity, the development of the professional religious educator, or the failure of the ordained leadership to assume educational leadership within the congregation. He continued the very "gulf" to which he objects. By continuing to talk "church teacher," "directors of religious education," and "educator on the church staff," Farley failed to name the central issue in church education, namely the role of the clergy person.

The religious education movement and the presence of the professional religious educator further altered the gulf between the "educated clergy" and the "uneducated laity" by inserting another functionary in the gulf—the religious educator. In churches with good working partnerships within the staff, and between the staff and the laity, the professional religious educator, or the DRE (director of religious education) did reduce the size of the gulf. As the DRE shared educational skills with clergy, both could work with the volunteer teachers, and attend to the development of a religious community which was also an educational community. However, in many cases the gulf was no longer merely between the lay person and the clergy, it became a three way gulf: between the educated clergy and laity, between the educated professional educators and the laity, and between two differently educated church professionals. Farley's proposal uncritically accepted the presence of the religious educator and assumed that the professional educator must be more of a theologian. However, his analysis did not bring under question the absence of the ordained clergy from positions of educational leadership. Thus he failed to bring under question the relationship between the other ministries of the church and the educational ministry, depicting such linkages as distortions of "real" education. To improve church education, merely improve the education of the professional religious educator.

However, the very existence of the religious educator in Protestant churches interferes with the fulfillment of Farley's intentions. The clergy person is the most immediate bridge between the "ordered learning" of the seminary and the church. "Ordered learning" in the church is more probable if the clergy person is preacher and educator. To think that someone else will attend to the education of the church community is a dysfunctional luxury. The division of responsibility discourages integrative thinking about the various aspects of church life. Imaginative and provocative preaching is a prerequisite for excellent teaching and provides necessary perspective for other ministries.

How the seminary uses "ordered learning" in the preparation of persons for congregational leadership has direct impact on the quality of "ordered learning" in the church. The question is not, "Can church education be theological education?" but, "Can theological education be church education?"

An answer to this question requires a further exploration of the "homiletic paradigm" and theological education. Whereas the paradigm entails notions of faith formation and nurture, it hides the many complex relationships among preaching, today's culture, faith formation and nurture of the laity, and the education of clergy.

THE HOMILETIC PARADIGM REVISITED

Farley's homiletic "paradigm" assumed that "faith is formed and nurtured" primarily through proclamation in worship, and that because of the paradigm church leaders did not seek other means to form and mature faith. Farley acknowledged the paradigm's inadequacy. However, its inadequacy is less significant than its more questionable "truthfulness," or at least "usefulness," as an explanatory paradigm today.

In the minds of clergy and laity of colonial New England that paradigm appeared workable. Stout claimed that the "topical range and social influence" of the New England sermon "were so powerful in shaping cultural values, meanings, and a sense of corporate purpose that even television pales in comparison."[32] However, the source of its power was the compatibility of message with the cultural milieux in which it was delivered. Stout claimed that as "the only event in public assembly that regularly brought the entire community together, it [the sermon] also represented the central ritual of social order and control."[33] Because there were no competing voices for influence, the sermon "became as important for social meaning as for spiritual insight."[34] However, the authority of preaching did not continue through the following years. The uniformity of community life declined, and with it the authority of preaching and the preacher.

McClure traced the changes in that authority in the twentieth century Presbyterian church. In the early years of this century, the "authority [of preaching] was traditional for the Presbyterian church. It was assumed largely as part of the preacher's institutional and social role. Preachers "filled pulpits'."[35] However, given the social ministry emphasis during the early years of this century that authority was directed toward social or ecclesial programs, not faith formation and nurture. McClure pointed out that as "specialized ministries developed to meet the urban social situation and needs of the large suburban churches" the "idea that 'great preaching' was the central feature of ministry began to change."[36] Preaching today does not have the same unambiguous place in worship that it had during the founding of this country, nor that it had in seventeenth century England.[37] The "noise" of the social/cultural context within which a sermon is preached interferes with how it is heard, perhaps with it even being heard. The compatibility of church context and social/cultural context does not exist as it did during the settling of New England or in seventeenth century England. The development of historical/critical exegetical skills for Scripture was not accompanied by the development of equally powerful skills for the exegesis of the cultural context of the laity. Consequently, preachers lost the skill of making contact between Scripture and the culturally seasoned minds of the laity, a necessary connection if the sermon is to have educational value. The hypothesis of a homiletic paradigm hides the fact that the cultural context significantly influences the impact of the sermon as an educational event, and is itself a significant factor in the faith formation of the laity. Today's cultural pluralism and flood of images offer severe competition for the images necessary for Christian faithfulness.

Probably seminarians and church people today do not have paradigms relating sermons, cultural complexity, and faith formation and nurturance; Seminarians aspire to church leadership positions where they can minister through preaching, pastoral care, social outreach, administration, and perhaps teaching. Churches seek preachers, pastoral care givers, community leaders and administrators with financial competencies. It is an unusual church which adds to this roster of competencies "educational leadership" or "teaching competencies." Multi-staff churches often look for a religious educator or a junior clergy person who will cut eye teeth working with youth groups, but whose ultimate desire is a position where the "real" ministries of preaching, pastoral care, community leadership and administration can be practiced. Even in single clergy churches the clergy person inherits an established church school and education committee with well established customs.

The significance of the sermon is not articulated in terms of the faith formation and nurturance of the laity. In the seminary curriculum of today its significance is acknowledged, although its incompatibility with the cultural context might not be. The cultural noise is frequently ignored. In the current cultural context the lay person likely endures the sermon as a part of an hour long worship service, not recognizing its potential as an imaginative or educational event standing out from the surrounding hegemonic images of the culture. The imagery of the sermon seems anemic against the power of these cultural images. Yet scriptural images, proclaimed imaginatively in the sermon, are crucial for the formation and nurture of faith.

If homiletics is not the context for reflecting on faith formation and nurturing, where does such reflection occur? Seminarians may take for granted that a successful church leads to faith formation and nurture, but where do they look systematically at how that happens today? On what occasions do they reflect on how what they do helps form or nurture the faith of the lay person?

The predominate location for thinking about faith formation and nurture is the context of pastoral care, where problems of human life, usually induced by the cultural complexity and the abundance of secular images, are worked on. Courses in pastoral counseling, and the clinical pastoral experience, contribute to this reflection. In both cases the reflection takes a clinical form, with a heavy emphasis on the personal and interpersonal, for pastoral care is primarily a one to one relationship. Holifield describes how this conversation, and reflection, became increasingly influenced by psychological discourse.[38] Fowler's *Stages of Faith*[39] also contributes to possible reflection. However, the pastoral and developmental approaches do not encourage reflection about how the events of the church, or the images and press of the culture, form and nurture faith. A competency that the religious educator brings to education in the church, other than knowledge of material, curriculum and teaching, is an awareness of how the formation of faith is influenced by developmental and environmental conditions; how people of different ages and in different places require different nurturance. However, that very speciality is a hindrance today, for it presumes privileged or specialized knowledge. The presumption licenses others to ignore their own history, the narrative of their religious journey, and the struggles with self, others and the principalities and powers of the world.

In an institution devoted to education, to "ordered learning," it is unfortunate that student reflection about faith formation and nurture is demarcated from the ordinary course of educational events and assigned to experiences associated with pastoral care. The narrative of their religious journey and their struggles with self, others, and the principalities and powers in the world of knowledge and teaching, is not brought into focal attention, and reflected on, as an aspect of faith formation and nurture. Consequently, access to the heritage of the faith is not integrated into their personal journey as gift, but as a "rite of initiation" preceding ordination. "Ordered learning" in the seminary appears to serve a different purpose than "ordered learning" in the church. It is little wonder that clergy have a difficult time making connections between what happens to them, educationally, in the seminary and what happens to the laity in the church. By its teaching and curriculum, the seminary often demonstrates that formal educational experience, organized around disciplines, is unrelated to the formation and nurture of faith—this under the guise of scholarship or academic excellence.

"ORDERED LEARNING" AND FAITH FORMATION AND NURTURE

Farley acknowledges the problem, but his resolution is incomplete. Appropriately, much of *Fragility* is devoted to an exploration of the "corruption and redemption" of knowledge in theological study. Theological education is viewed as reflective interpretation of five types: of situations, vocation, tradition, truth of gospel, and praxis. Ordered learning "disciplines and rigorizes reflective interpretation."[40] He proposes that the aim of theological study is "to communicate and discipline basic modes of interpretation already at work in the believer's situation."[41]

However, a basic mode "of interpretation already at work in the believer's situation" is neglected by Farley. Its neglect is strange given that his earlier work, *Ecclesial Man*,[42] prepared the way for such interpretation. Faith formation and nurture requires more than attention to moments of conversion. The forces which impede faithfulness and the struggles to overcome those forces, the encounters with sin and redemption, also require attention. Farley acknowledged this in his description of "Disrupted Historical Existence" and "Redemptive Existence."[43] When these struggles are conceptualized as requiring pastoral work they are ignored as invitations to religious education. Everyone, not merely those who hurt in crisis, experiences such struggles, including seminarians in their education. That journey of the personal life, not merely the vocational part of it, also must be brought under critical interpretation. Call it what you will, it is the journey of the soul, the spiritual quest recounted by the mystics and writers of religious autobiographies, detailed in traditions of spiritual direction, depicted in rudimentary structural terms by Fowler,[44] but in more interesting form by Wilber.[45] It is the interpretative mode neglected by Farley. Through reflection on the religious or spiritual journey—the encounters with idols and flight, freedom and obligation—seminarians and clergy begin to understand their educational experiences, in seminary and out, as part of their struggle to be faithful. These include the struggles with the unveiling and idolatrous knowledge of academe and the flight from that knowledge which questions their taken for granted faith realities. They also include the struggles with idolatrous images in the dominant culture, and with the pull of self-serving communities. Through these struggles they begin to recognize that some educational experiences free them from the restraints of the past and impose new obligations as faithful people. The journey also includes encounters with sermons that informed their faith, the many sermons forgotten because of imaginative emptiness, and the encounters with other persons and communities that also influenced their faith. These too can be recollected, brought under disciplined reflection, and used to think educationally about their educational ministry with others.

Enlarging a stock of knowledge is not enough. Seminarians and clergy need, as a normal part of their interpretative repertoire, the ability to reflect on how the variety of educational experiences formed, informed, transformed and nurtured their faith. This is not an esoteric reflective competency. It is the basic reflection necessary for thinking about education—how the formation and nurture of faith can be helped by clergy. It is a neglected competency because reflection about education has been taken over by specialists, turned into educational theorizing with heavy psychological overtones, and removed from the educational consciousness of those being educated. Seminarians and clergy generally lack this reflective capability as it pertains to their own lives and religious journeys, hence imagining participation in the education of others is difficult. Given this lack, they look for educational gimmicks, prepared materials, notes from lectures, or "educational specialists." Forgotten struggles with sin and redemption as adolescents, and forgotten encounters with teachers and others who helped and hindered them in that struggle, contribute to worry and fear as they contemplate teaching youth. The consequence is a hesitancy to work with youth, and ritualized youth group activity rather than significant educational encounters between clergy and youth. Failure to reflect on how academic experience has formed, informed, transformed or nurtured their faith, restricts their ability to teach the curious and the non-curious about Scripture, theology or church history. The result is the presentation of content, not the education of the laity by significant interpretative encounters with Scripture, tradition, praxis, vocation, and situations.

HOW CAN THEOLOGICAL EDUCATION
BE CHURCH EDUCATION?

Farley would resolve the problems of church education by making it theological education—a "cumulative, rigorous educational process and post-Enlightenment tools of analysis and interpretation"[46] brought into church education. Different types of church teachers and church educators would be required. He proposed remediation in the church, whereas remediation in the seminary is required. But then, proposals are always easier when directed at the institutions of others.

It is crucial in this multi-institutional world of education, however, to improve the institutions wherein we dwell. It is important because the reform of the world, even the educational world, begins with us, not with others. Farley has attended carefully and thoughtfully to the reform of the theological curriculum, a curriculum that does requires reform. Reflection on how education (teaching and study) forms, reforms and nurtures the faith of all does not require curriculum change, although some change would help. Nor is the problem one of religious formation, for the seminary is not a church or religious community, but an educational community. The problem is in the teaching—the failure to recognize that teaching is a vocation, and that a vocation places demands on one who is chosen to be a teacher.

One who is chosen to be a teacher is called to assume responsibility for three phenomena—often in conflict with one another. The first is the tradition which the teacher professes, the second is the student, and the third is the institution which is the meeting ground of teacher, student and tradition.

The tradition is that part of the world for which the teacher assumes responsibility; seeing to it that the tradition remains truthful (however that claim is adjudicated) and serviceable. Scholarship is the activity of maintaining the truthfulness of the tradition, of preventing the tradition from becoming merely an idol standing for itself and the human beings who founded it, rather than pointing beyond itself. Teaching is the activity of maintaining the serviceability of the tradition. The teacher promises that renewing and enlivening truth is available. That truth is not something precious locked among the possessions of the teacher, and from which she makes a living. It is a gift which the teacher renews through the giving. The teacher keeps the tradition alive and renewed through teaching. Through teaching the teacher witnesses to God's glory and to our participation in creation, alienation and redemption. Acknowledging teaching as a vocation means that the teacher accepts the call of the tradition, that it be cared for and ever renewed in human life so that it may continue as a witness to the truth.

Acknowledging teaching as a vocation also means that the teacher accepts the call of the student who would study with her, a call often distorted by admissions policies, grading systems, degree requirements and other institutional demands. The teacher, as one who cares for the tradition that it might not be lost but ever renewed, makes a gift of it to the student, and at the same time entrusts the tradition to the student. The tradition is renewed through the life of the student and the student's life is renewed through the truthfulness of the tradition. The tension between the two responsibilities—toward student and toward tradition—is a tension that can only be lived in, not overcome. A serviceable tradition entails a promise of new life. The truth of the tradition opens to the student a way of being in the world that shows new possibilities of loving, serving and honoring. To lay before the student the promise without attention to its fulfillment is a breakdown in the vocation of teaching.

It is as this point that reflection on the journey of the self is necessary. By attending to how the gift of the teacher stands over against the student's past and present life, the student can begin to know how education frees one from constraints, redeems the past, and forms and transforms faith. The student needs to know promises of newness and to know how the past is brought under judgement and either transformed or celebrated. This knowing is not a solitary act of the student. It requires disciplined awareness of how the journey of the soul is ever caught in the images and confines of an alienated world; how it is always promised a truth that frees it and binds it again to new obligations. One of the obligations is to maintain and renew that tradition of truth by teaching others, by giving the gift of truth to others. With this disciplined reflection, the student will begin to sense the meaning and processes of education, and will be ready to accept the call to be teacher as well as preacher in the church community.

When teaching in the seminary is seriously accepted as a vocation, by teachers and students, teaching in the church will also be renewed. When the traditions of ordered learning in the seminary are taught truthfully and with serviceability in mind, then ordered learning in the church will become a possibility. Educational experts are not required if all can reflect critically and carefully on how education is but part of the journey of the self toward God.

NOTES

[1]Others who have contributed to this shake-up include Joe Hough, Barbara Wheeler, David Kelsey, and John Cobb.

[2]Edward Farley, "Can Church Education be Theological Education, *Theology Today* 42 (1985): 158–171. Reprinted in *The Fragility Of Knowledge: Theological Education in The Church and The University* (Philadelphia: Fortress Press, 1988), 85–102.

[3]Edward Farley, "Can Church Education be Theological Education," *The Fragility Of Knowledge: Theological Education In The Church And The University* (Philadelphia: Fortress Press, 1988), 92.

[4]Farley, "Can Church Education," 99.

[5]Farley, "Can Church Education," 93.

[6]Farley, "Can Church Education," 93.

[7]Farley, "Can Church Education," 94.

[8]Farley, "Can Church Education," 94.

[9]Farley, "Can Church Education," 94.

[10]Edward Farley, *Theologia: The Fragmentation and Unity of Theological Education* (Philadelphia: Fortress Press, 1983).

[11]Farley, *Theologia*, 95.

[12]Farley, *Theologia*, 95.

[13]Farley, *Theologia*, 95.

[14]Farley, *Theologia*, 96.

[15]Farley, *Theologia*, 96.

[16]Farley, *Theologia*, 96.

[17]Farley, *Theologia*, 99.

[18]Farley, *Theologia*, 99–100.

[19]Farley, "Can Church Education," 99.

[20]The most inclusive histories are Anne M. Boylan, *Sunday School: The Formation of an American Institution, 1790–1880* (New Haven: Yale University Press, 1988); and Robert W. Lynn and Elliot Wright, *The Big Little School: Two Hundred Years of the Sunday School*. (New York: Harper & Row, 1971).

[21]Boylan, *Sunday School*, 77.

[22]Craig Dykstra and J. Bradley Wigger, "A Brief History of a Genre Problem: Presbyterian Educational Resource Materials," in *The Pluralistic Vision: Presbyterians and Mainstream Protestant Education and Leadership*, ed. Milton J. Coatlet, John M. Mulder and Louis B. Weeks (Louisville: Westminster/John Knox Press, 1992), 180–204.

[23]See Lynn and Wright, "Old Time School vs. New Time School," in *The Pluralistic Vision*, chapter 5, 77–99.

[24]Dykstra and Wigger, "A Brief History," 108–204.

[25]William Bean Kennedy, "The Genesis and Development of the Christian Faith and Life Series," (Ph.D. Dissertation, Yale University, 1957). See also his "Neo-Orthodoxy Goes to Sunday School," *Journal of Presbyterian History* 58, no. 4 (1980): 326–370.

[26]Stephen A. Schmidt, *A History of the Religious Education Association* (Birmingham: Religious Education Press, 1983), 19. See Lynn and Wright, "Old Time School," 77–99.

[27]Dykstra and Wigger, "A Brief History," 108–204.

[28]See Robert W. Lynn, *Protestant Strategies in Education* (New York: Association Press, 1964); and Jack Seymour, Robert T. O'Gorman and Charles R. Foster, *The Church in the Education of The Public: Refocusing the Task of Religious Education* (Nashville: Abingdon Press, 1984).

[29]J. Stanley Glen, *The Recovery of the Teaching Ministry* (Philadelphia: Westminister Press, 1960), 9.

[30]Clark M. Williamson and Ronald J. Allen, *The Teaching Ministry* (Louisville: Westminster/John Knox Press, 1991).

[31]e.g., James D. Smart, *The Teaching Ministry of the Church* (Philadelphia: Westminster Press, 1954).

[32]Harry S. Stout, *The New England Soul: Preaching and Religious Culture in Colonial New England* (New York: Oxford University Press, 1986), 3.

[33]Stout, *The New England Soul*, 3.

[34]Stout, *The New England Soul*, 23.

[35]John McClure, "Changes in the Authority, Method, and Message of Presbyterian" (UPCUSA) "Preaching in the Twentieth Century," in *The Confessional Mosaic: Presbyterians and Twentieth Century Theology*, ed. Milton J. Coalter, John M. Mulder and Louis B. Weeks (Louisville: Westminster/John Knox Press, 1990), 86.

[36]McClure, "Changes," 88.

[37] See Ellen Davis, "Holy Preaching: Ethical Interpretation and the Practical Imagination" in *Reclaiming Faith: Essays on Orthodoxy in the Episcopal Church and the Baltimore Declaration*, ed. Ephraim Radner and George Sumner (Grand Rapids: W. B. Eerdmans, 1993), 197–224.

[38] E. Brooks Holifield, *A History of Pastoral Care in America: From Salvation to Self-Realization* (Nashville: Abingdon Press, 1983).

[39] James Fowler, *Stages of Faith: The Psychology of Human Development and the Quest for Meaning* (New York: Harper and Row, 1981).

[40] Farley, *Theologia*, 135.

[41] Farley, *Theologia*, 143.

[42] Edward Farley, *Ecclesial Man: a Social Phenomenology of Faith and Reality* (Philadelphia: Fortress Press, 1975).

[43] Farley, *Ecclesial Man*, chapter 6.

[44] James W. Fowler, *Stages of Faith: The Psychology of Human Development and the Quest for Meaning* (San Francisco: Harper and Row, 1981).

[45] Ken Wilber, "The Spectrum of Development" in *Transformations of Consciousness*, ed. Ken Wilber, Jack Engler and Daniel Brown (Boston: Knew Science Library, 1986), 65–106.

[46] Farley, *Fragility*, 99–100.

35

Challenges Bequeathed

(1996)

The story line of how my thinking developed over nearly fifty years seems much less important than my current awareness of the challenges faced by educators. I do not seek to explain the pathways that led me to recognize and articulate these challenges, although a perusal of the previous chapters may provide clues to those pathways. Nor will I endeavor to convince others that I see truly. Inasmuch as I no longer gain much pleasure from reading current curriculum literature, I plead ignorance about whether these challenges are being worked on or even sensed by others. My intent is merely to bequeath five challenges to those interested in my earlier work. They are to:

— Surpass the technical foundations of education.

— Affirm the significance of the imagination.

— Use the world's intellectual traditions and achievements.

— Engage in public discourse about education.

— Speak out for children and youth.

SURPASS THE TECHNICAL FOUNDATIONS OF EDUCATION

The positivistic and technical aspects of education have been frequently criticized by me and a host of others. Testing, textbooks, programmed materials, media, competency based teaching, as well as the undergirding intellectual structures such as learning theory and some developmental theories, have all been grist for the mills of criticism. Some of the criticism has been unwarranted, and suggests mere frustration or irresponsibility. Much has been well deserved. To attend to the appropriateness or inappropriateness of criticism, however, hides the more significant factor—that criticism is an important aspect of our work. Marcuse calls attention to this by his valuing of negation. Tillich argues that protest against form is necessary for the continual creation of the human world. But Hegel is the primary source with his articulation of the dialectic of thesis, antithesis, and synthesis. To surpass does not mean to discard, but to identify significant achievements and their accompanying new problems, and to move to a different level of human life. In education this means recognizing achievements and losses that accompany the research of the past seven decades, acknowledging new problems and identifying their possible resolutions. It means being about the next stage in the history of intentional education. To participate responsibly in history one must criticize *and* create. To surpass the technical foundations of education, then, requires historical awareness of where we once were, sensitivity to present problems, resistances and binds, and openness to future possibilities. To label any particular development a "movement" is to hide the historical continuity and the dialectical processes which led to that development, a substitute for hard historical work. Labeling undermines awareness of the historical relationships among thesis, antithesis, and synthesis. We need to better understand such things as the following:

— how testing became such a significant influence in educational decisions, practices and thought, and the reasons for the overwhelming acceptance of the work of Thorndike and his followers.

— why William Torrey Harris made more of an impact on schooling and its administration than Dewey.

— how the work of Bobbitt, Charters, and Tyler and their lineage became so instrumental in curriculum.

— how the growth of AERA from about a thousand or so in the early nineteen fifties to about twenty-three thousand now has influenced educational thought and practice.

Specifically, what is to be surpassed with respect to the use of the technical achievements of the past fifty years and the positivistic modes of reflection accompanying them? First, as many have pointed out, these practices and modes of thought do not depict the complexity, or even begin to approach the mystery, of the human condition. The beauty and tragedy of the new human being's journey with others and their prejudices, cultural accouterments, and power is glossed over. Technical views of persons need to be surpassed. Progress has been and continues to be made on this problem. The educational process (an aspect of that mystery) and educational institutions (manifestations of the prejudices, cultural accouterments, and power) can never be encompassed by a single intellectual form or structural arrangement.

Next, the technical fall out from the scientific movements of the past seven decades has contributed significantly to the creation of educational environments, which Dewey[1] identified in 1916 as central to education. We surpass that achievement when the power to build environments is gratefully acknowledged and its various ramifications explored. To compare the classrooms of today with those of the first thirty years of this century, or the wealth of educational resources today with the limited resources that accompanied the McGuffey readers, is to glimpse and appreciate that power. Learning theories have reshaped educational materials and teacher behaviors. Cognitive theories and the explorations of knowledge structures have sharpened educational purposes, improved the sequencing of educational materials and led to the construction of diagnostic instruments. Information processing knowledge and its instruments, (computers and communication tools) have altered the relationships among people and their use of language and symbols. The power to fabricate educational environments has increased many fold in the past fifty years. This is a wonderful and significant achievement.

However, the technical must become a subsidiary language for educators, a tool that helps build educational environments. A more inclusive language net is required if more consequential questions and problems are to be entertained. It should call attention to the variety of fabricated environments available in this culture and ask about their relative worth and larger social function. The environments available for children and youth should be contrasted with other environments in a culture. In the large cities of Chicago, New York and Washington, D.C., and elsewhere, run down schools come to mind. Parks, alleys, rooftops, crowded one room apartments, stoops and streets, and perhaps playgrounds are other spaces used by children and youth. The environments built for or available to children and youth illustrate the poverty of our culture. Schools are often in poor physical shape. They often lack aesthetic qualities. But more significantly they lack the qualities that permit morally gratifying relationships among people. Compare the environments created for children and youth with the environments created for the corporate elite. Today's corporate headquarters are some of the most exquisite architectural spaces created in this country—spaces designed with sensitivity to the work needs and ease of social relationships of the people they house, and enhanced with works of art. They illustrate the wealth of our culture. Schools are usually designed for functional efficiency, without much sensitivity to the work needs or social relationships of teachers and students and without aesthetic qualities. Corporate headquarters are often designed as symbols—representative of the values of the corporation and the culture. Who asks about the symbolic function or the aesthetic quality of the buildings known as schools? The architectural creativity financed by corporations is a business expense, using pre-taxed dollars of the corporations (although the resulting building and facilities are taxed per the local property tax codes with tax abatement to entice them to build one place rather than another). Imagine what could be achieved if the expenses of building new corporate headquarters were taxed to help finance the creation of spaces for children and youth. A small percentage of the wealth used to build symbolic and beautiful structures for the corporate elites could be used to provide beauty and morally redeeming space for the young of this society, the future corporate leaders and the producers and consumers of their products and services.

Another contrast is of the poverty of the symbolic world of the schools with the wealth (not necessarily the beauty) of the symbolic worlds of the mass media. Businesses spend millions of dollars educating consumers to purchase their goods and services, via the media, a pre-tax expenditure. This educational form is known as advertising. Advertising attempts to shape desire and value. So do schools, usually with meager resources. What would happen if all advertising was taxed to provide new educational resources for children and youth? If but a portion of the money spent to educate people via media was spent for the cultural social and moral education of children and youth the schools would be vastly different cultural spaces.

Third, these technical developments have led to significant shifts in power, both within the educational establishment and in the relationship between the educational establishment and the larger social order. The technologies of textbook making and test construction have resulted in powerful new industries that influence local decision makers and school teachers. The information processing industries have become another powerful group in the political mix, as TV, computer and information highway people seek income and influence by educating children and youth. The rhetoric associated with these industries shapes public discourse and influences public thinking about education. For instance the rhetoric of tests and test scores has become an extremely powerful vehicle for talking about schools, hiding or covering other markers that also depict school quality. Talk about linking every classroom to the information highway displaces other kinds of talk about schools—school libraries, the quality of educational materials, the moral qualities of classroom action. Rhetoric shaped by technical interests rather than educational interests influences public perception about the nature of education and thus grants undue power to people with technical interests who sway the minds and affections of young people. To truly surpass the technical foundations of education demands that these shifts in power be understood and confronted.

These are the kinds of questions that result from the efforts to surpass the present technical modes of thought and practice that now dominate education. Other questions can be asked if the technical is seen as auxiliary, rather than primary, and if other phenomena of the social world are juxtaposed against the formal and informal structures that educate children and youth.

AFFIRM THE SIGNIFICANCE
OF THE IMAGINATION

The need to surpass the technical foundations points to the undervaluing of imagination in the educational enterprise. A causal relationship may exist between the educators dependency upon the technical and the undervaluing of the imagination. Mary Warnock suggests as much when she states that "*The greatest enemy of the imagination is to be locked in the present*,"[2] It is to the present that the technical calls attention. The technical foundation of education tends to emphasize the need for clarity about what is to be achieved, or next steps, as if the future can be known and controlled by human reason. Shaping educational processes around the known diminishes the need for the imagination, for then the future is no longer a field of imagined possibilities. The imagination makes connections between present and future, present and past, and future and past. With connections already known and no need to imagine those connections, the imagination takes on a minor role. It merely serves to shape emotional expression and stimulates the expressive arts.

Imagination plays a much more significant role in human life. It is central to all aspects of human life and is at the core of educational phenomena. It is not an add on to the educational project. It undergirds everything that the educator thinks and does.

Imagination is a manifestation of human freedom—a cultural birthright. Persons participate in the necessities passed on down through cultural forms and social relationships, but they also participate in a freedom that transcends these necessities. Of course, the imagination can also be hooked into those necessities—distorted, turned into mere fancy, or an instrument of escapism from the necessities in which we dwell. Imagination is the storehouse of human possibility—ethical, intellectual, political. It shapes the possibilities from which the choices for perceiving, knowing and acting are selected. Perceiving, knowing and acting not grounded in the imagination reek of pride and incline toward idolatry. To focus only on the formation of the young person's intellect, values, and actions diminishes freedom. By encouraging the imagination, freedom is affirmed. It is protected by disciplining that imagination with the outpourings of the imagination throughout human history of East and West, North and South.

Mary Warnock states that "*imagination ... should be central in any curriculum decision*,"[3] and it has not been ignored by educators. It has been an off and on concern for years. Rugg's interests in the imagination took published form in 1963.[4] During the 1960s that interest was manifested in frequent writings about creativity. Today the work of Sloan,[5] Eisner,[6] and Egan[7] are probably only the tip of an iceberg, the whole of which is more clearly seen by those swimming in the icy waters of the curriculum field. But it deserves even more careful and sustained attention, and significant intellectual effort. Warnock warns that "In addressing the topic of Imagination, (one enters) ... a field that is not only very ancient, but increasingly well trodden."[8] Kearney, much concerned about the potential decline of the imagination today, states that "The story of imagination needs to be told. Like all species under threat of extinction, the imagination requires to be recorded in terms of its genealogy: its conceptual genesis and mutations."[9] For the next two decades or so imagination should receive the volume and quality of attention that learning received during the first half of this century.

Increased attention to the role of imagination in the life of the young and in education needs to be paralleled by increased attention to how the imagination is being shaped, perverted, and diminished by the easy commerce in symbols and images of the mass media. This is also an arena receiving considerable attention, but with few consequences within the educational enterprises. The problems of reading achievement are still seen by the public as a problem of reading scores in the third and sixth grades, not as a problem of the distribution of and access to word images and visual and sound images. Appropriate concern is still being given to the skills of writing, but too little given to the skills of other tools of the imagination. The cultural dominance of media experts cannot be confronted by people who remain unaware of how their imagination—the foundation of their knowing, acting, valuing, and freedom—has been and is being shaped or formed.

USE THE WORLD'S INTELLECTUAL TRADITIONS AND ACHIEVEMENTS

A major achievement within the curriculum field over the past forty years has been its emerging openness to a host of intellectual enterprises. Pinar's[10] most recent volume is a witness to that achievement. The isolation of educational thought from the wealth of the intellectual life of the world no longer exists. The monopoly of certain discourse systems has been broken. But warranted depictions of how those monopolies became established, and broken, do not yet exist. How did psychological thought become so powerful? Why did it take so long for the exciting post World War II developments in European philosophy to make an impact on the study and practice of education?[11]

One reason for the failure to embrace a wide variety of intellectual systems earlier was the early separation of the study of education from the main centers of intellectual life—the universities. A case in point was the establishment of two year teacher training schools. Many of these eventually became four year teachers colleges, then liberal arts colleges, and finally universities as the need for universal higher education became greater. However, even in universities where the study of education was legitimated by the establishment of departments or schools of education, the separation continued. University schools of education developed their own mini-university, with departments in which the faculty of education taught educational psychology, educational philosophy, educational sociology, educational history. The history of Teachers College, Columbia University, is an illustration of that unfolding story. It established its own departments of educational foundations. Not until after the mid-twentieth century did it establish substantial working relationships with the academic departments at Columbia University and some joint appointments. The historical and structural reasons for the separation of the study and practice of education from the centers of intellectual vitality deserve to be exhumed. Pinar's volume celebrates these achievements of increased openness, but it does not explore the conditions that brought about the intellectual monopolies. The volume is not to be faulted for that, however, for his basic intent—to picture the variety of current approaches to the study of education—was achieved.

He argued, correctly, that a separation between practice and reflection about practice is needed if important intellectual work is to be achieved. Ortega y Gasset[12] and Macmurray[13] both refer to the importance of the rhythm of withdrawal from and return to action. The university is the premier place for withdrawal for developing the critical and imaginative resources needed by society. To be completely tied to and responsible for practice decreases the quality of the critical and imaginative work required for the renewal and continued development of cultural forms and social institutions. Pinar forcefully acknowledges this.

Once the monopoly of educational thought was broken, a few educators engaged in a virtual orgy with other university based disciplines and fields of inquiry. The educational tower of Babel was destroyed, and as Pinar has suggested, people in the "field" now find it difficult to communicate with each other. The "scattered people of curriculum" are now brought into a new tent where the various discourse systems and texts can be acknowledged and where people can be helped with the difficult task of interpretation. However, he points to, or suggests, a potential new monopoly: "The next stage will involve a relative movement away from sources, although historically informed students will not forget them, and the establishment of a conceptually autonomous discipline of curriculum theory."[14] The prediction seems unwise and unwarranted. Pinar's philosophical idealism or foundationalism breaks through his own commitments to post modernism and the significance of university dialogue. The significant development has been the commerce with other departments of the university. Better historical and analytic studies should temper any hope for a new monopoly, even if theoretical, and reinforce the importance of dialogue within the university.

But this privileged status of the university, as a location of criticism and imagination, is a fragile social arrangement, and cannot be guaranteed by a mere commitment to "truth." It is guaranteed by wealth, by the commitment of some members of society to make provisions for those who would critique and imagine. There is no reason to believe that such freedom will continue in universities supported by public funds, unless the redeeming social value of critique and imagination are demonstrated over a period of years. Pinar is correct, at this moment in time, that

> ... curriculum theorists must still offer friendship and colleagueship to teachers; we must offer teachers our expertise as they request .... We can offer politicians and policy makers that expertise but we ought not be surprised, and certainly not deflated, when they decline to employ it. After all, their interests in the schools are not necessarily educational, rather political and economic. We curriculum theorists must be firm that we are not responsible for the ills of the public schools, especially given that our advice ... has been and is so consistently ignored.[15]

> ... Like physics or art, curriculum as a field cannot progress unless some segment of the field explores phenomena and ideas that perhaps few will comprehend and appreciate, certainly not at first and perhaps never.[16]

However, it needs to be pointed out that much of this theoretical activity is taking place in state supported universities, and that few well endowed universities have supported such educational activity. Yale abolished a department of education in the 1950s, and there has been no effort to re-instate it. This is only to suggest that imagination and critique must be seen as having redeeming social value by other than the theorists themselves. And as the struggle at the University of Minnesota between the faculty and the trustees indicate, tenure is no longer an assured status. Therefore, questions remain about how the recent intellectual excitement about education relates to current educational structures and problems.

The opening to other discourse systems, important as it is, does not clarify how these different discourse systems can be related to educators and educational structures. The university is the locus of social/cultural critique and imagination. The whole university is the source of potential discourse about education, not just a department or school of education. The problem is how these different voices within the university reflect on educational matters. The establishment of a "conceptually autonomous discipline of curriculum theory" co-ops the rest of the university. Looked at another way, the educational experience and the institutions and arrangements that influence it partake of the profundity and mystery of the human condition. To think, even for an instant, that there will be a time when that profundity and mystery can be contained by any single discourse system reflects that quality that shapes so much human tragedy and comedy—hubris.

We are left with the task of asking how the great diversity of intellectual systems of critique and imagination can be related to the human enterprise of education. The self-contained departments of educational psychology, philosophy, history, sociology, were a solution of the forties through the seventies. Pinar's focus on curriculum discourses and texts is a solution for the nineties. What historical patterns will next come into being as current intellectual sorties are replaced by new explorations of education? The need is great for significant historical studies of this problem and its solution over the years.

One way to begin to sort some of this out is to look at different aspects of the educational process, rather than lumping everything under the label "curriculum." For instance, understandings of the journey of individuals as they pass through their allotted time are needed. Learning theories, developmental theories, therapeutic theories, autobiography, narrative, currere—these are different ways of speaking about that process or aspects of that process, each shaped by the intellectual milieu and fashion of the times. Where in the university is this phenomena addressed? Where should it be addressed? Will there ever be a time when the educator has something unique to say to which the philosopher or psychologist will have to listen? A history of the structures of those conversations between the educators and others in these privileged social locations of imagination and critique might uncover patterns of conversations that need to continue, perhaps with some modification.[17] Other illustrations would be to consider how the school as a structured place of education has changed over the years, how reflection about teachers has changed, or as I pleaded earlier, to limit the study of curriculum to the study of content[18]—the factors that influence its selection and structure. Attention to educational domains or phenomena, acknowledging that they too will change with different intellectual fashions, might make it easier to see how the forms of critique and imagination in the universities have influenced educational thought and practice. The next stage in the work before us is again historical, exploring how the problems and domains of education have been identified, critiqued, and imaginatively confronted.

ENGAGE IN PUBLIC DISCOURSE
ABOUT EDUCATION

Other discourse systems, not part of the university, are equally important in education and to the educator. These are the "text" of public discourse about education: the texts in various media—TV, newspapers and journals, and books for the non-specialist; the talk of parents; and of course, the talk of young people. Each significantly influences the practices of and thinking about education. Typically, the educator does not participate in these public discourses. They are not usually considered "texts" that must be consulted, studied, interpreted or mastered by the educator.

But the phenomena of education is not esoteric, in spite of the educator's professional language. Education "happens" to everyone through informal and formal activity. Some try to articulate that experience, but find professional language a barrier. It tends to mask the educational experience rather than open it up. Hence, the conditions which foster education cannot be clearly perceived, understood, and critiqued by those who are being educated. The problem probably originated in the first half of this century, although few (or no) studies exist that chart or depict the changing patterns of everyday talk about educational experience. Educational language became increasingly distant from the experience of people as the study of education became a scholarly activity. Eager to better understand and control educational activity, educators developed or took on a specialized language, forsaking the language of those who endure the educational process. Perhaps the problem emerged as educators became more dependent on psychological language, or as the language became more technical and farther removed from the everyday speech of children, parents, and teachers. This problem also deserves significant historical attention.

Three problems are created by the separation of educational language from public discourse. First, those who use current intellectual fashions to understand educational phenomena need to understand the changing fashions of everyday discourse about education. What has influenced the evolving forms of public discourse about education in various media? How have the various media influenced the way that parents and community members talk about education? How did the fashion of using test scores become so firmly embedded in public parlance about education? Are there studies of how people, in various contexts, use different idioms to talk and write about education?

Next, the university educator needs to participate in that larger discourse. Educators tend to write for and to each other. Writing for public consumption is usually done by professional journalists, or by individuals with an ideological axe to grind, with specific suggestions for schools (e.g., Sizer, Bennett), or with trenchant criticisms of the lives of children in schools (e.g., Kozol). Educators either lack interest or know-how to participate in the dialogue. Both are unfortunate and unnecessary. The professional educator needs to master and participate in the public discourse about education, and not be content to merely engage colleagues. Such activity could easily be a project for teacher education and the advanced study of education.

Third, educators have given insufficient attention to the educational discourse of students and parents. Students are often at a loss to describe their own education and how it has happened. The language of educators is not descriptive of their own educational experiences, in or out of school. Young people either lack words to describe these experiences or lapse into school language—covering texts, passing tests, getting grades, passing the grade or course, graduating, or being prepared for work. The educational language of the university classrooms is not a language they can use. Technical and psychological language, and the language of tests and grades, mystifies their educational experience, fails to correspond to their feelings, and displaces their talk. Reflective and critical thought about their own experiences is difficult or impossible. Consequently, when they become parents they have difficulty talking about education with their children. They lack the ability to reflect in their own language on their experiences of education, and are often rooted in the outdated school language of their own school days. The need is for the educator to talk about educational experience in such a way that those outside the professional community can gain personal insight into how education is happening to them. This means that teachers, and other educators, need the ability to converse with them about education, without imposing the mystifying language of educators.

Educators must forsake their imperialistic language and enter into public discourse, the discourse of young people, and the discourse of parents. As the language of these three publics critique the language of educators, so must the language of educators critique theirs. Ways of talking about education must be found and fostered that resonate with the experience of young people and their parents, that can be used in the mass media without being captured by ideological positions, and that can displace or replace the slogans used to shape political judgments about education.

SPEAK OUT FOR CHILDREN AND YOUTH

Tyler, in his significant contribution to the curriculum field,[19] suggested three sources for objectives: studies of the learners, studies of contemporary life, and suggestions from subject specialists. For years arguments raged about the appropriate focus of the school. Should it be the student? The social order? Or subject matter? Dewey, of course, offered a profound philosophical resolution to that problem, showing how the three were connected. Tyler removed the ground for argument. He claimed that all three should be sources of objectives, and that final objectives would be identified by screening them through a philosophy of education and a psychology of learning. The attention to the focus of the school gave way to objectives of the school.

The great debate gave way to a concern for identifying objectives within a pre-scribed methodology. Philosophy became another tool in the calculus of defining objectives. One of the unacknowledged consequences of that great synthesis was to dampen major arguments or ideological positions.

Lost in this methodological synthesis was concern for the student. Knowledge of the student, as a source of objectives, replaced concern for the student as a person. Of course, Tyler's synthesis didn't end interest in the student. His framework merely fed into the cultural stream that saw the school as only a place where children and young people learn, not as a place where they also live a good share of their young life. Another negative influence was the establishment of the guidance counselor, first in secondary schools, and then in elementary schools. Teachers should teach. The personal life of the student would be the guidance person's concern. But this specialization of interest also gave way as the guidance person increasingly served the school; or served the larger educational complex by helping students think about the next stages in their journey through educational institutions, rather than their journey through life.

Teachers have become increasingly removed from concern for the uniqueness and individuality of the student qua person. The educational task has been so strongly focused by the need for the teacher to teach and the student to learn, that neither has time to think about how that which is taught influences the life of the student—his own unfolding journey through a difficult time in history. Educators no longer speak for the students they educate. That is a task left to someone else, and consequently to no one else. This development feeds the current interest in parental rights and the "hands off" values concern that is part of current popular educational rhetoric. The concern has sufficient truth to warrant it, yet given the complexity of this particular epoch, a non-family friendly voice might be of help to the student, and to the parent. But the current rhetoric encourages the separation of this work from acts of teaching.

Who in this culture speaks for children and youth? For the most part, they remain essentially voiceless. A few find their voices in the counter-cultural activities of youth. More find them in the great cultural chorus which celebrates this era without reflection or criticism

The school is the only institution in this culture built specifically for children and youth to live in. The old argument about the role of the school—for children, for society, for content—need to be exhumed from its burial by the grand synthesis that saw all as sources of objectives. The argument needs to be kept alive. The competing interests among these three should not be permitted to be folded into any technical or other grand synthesis. The vitality of the argument can feed the lives of teachers and students if the tension is lived in productively. The three foci should critique each other. Today, the social critique of both subject matter and the student seems uppermost. The critique of society seems beyond the pale, as major social and economic forces tend to silence most criticism. But the student, inherently the element of newness required for social renewal, also brings under criticism content and the social order. Students are graded against the backdrop of content and society, but the reverse is not true.

The significant need today is to include the interest of the young person in the ongoing and needed debate about the place of children and young people, not only in the school but in the society. Who is more able to do that than the educators? Who know the hurts, pains, pressure points of children and young people as well as teachers and educators. By becoming captive of a particular educational ideology, the educator cannot voice the irritations produced by the friction between the society (as it is embodied in the school) and the student. The irritations can not, indeed, should not be removed. They can be a pearl producing irritant for individual and social creativity. Nor does speaking for children and youth turn the school into the old child centered school of the twenties through the fifties. The competition of voices should never be silenced by any group in a position of dominance. Educators too busy trying to understand the educational process may fail to hear and respond to the muffled sounds of those caught in the system. Please, please speak for the children and youth, those persons who give meaning to all educational endeavor and thought.

NOTES

[1]John Dewey, " ... the only way in which adults consciously control the kind of education which the immature get is by controlling the environment in which they act ... We never educate directly, but indirectly by means of the environment" *Democracy and Education* (New York: The Macmillan Company, 1961, first published in 1916), 19.

[2]Warnock, *Imagination & Time* (Oxford: Blackwell, 1994), 174.

[3]Ibid., 173.

[4]Harold Rugg, *Imagination* (New York: Harper & Row, 1963).

[5]Douglas Sloan, *Insight-Imagination: The Emancipation of Thought and the Modern World* (Westport, CT: Greenwood Press, 1983).

[6]Elliot Eisner, *The Educational Imagination: On the Design and Evaluation of School Programs* (New York: Macmillan, 1979, 1985).

[7]Kieran Egan, *Imagination in Teaching and Learning* (Chicago: University of Chicago Press, 1992).

[8]Warnock, *Imagination and Time*, 1.

[9]Richard Kearney, *The Wake of Imagination: Ideas of Creativity in Western Culture* (London: Hutchinson, 1988).

[10]William F. Pinar, William M. Reynolds, Patrick Slattery and Peter M. Taubman, *Understanding Curriculum: An Introduction to the Study of Historical and Contemporary Curriculum Discourses* (New York: Peter Lang, 1995).

[11]Obviously the commitment to Dewey's pragmatism was one factor.

[12]José Ortega y Gasset, "The Self and the Other," In *The Dehumanization of Art; and Other Writings on Art, Culture and Literature* (Garden City, NY: Doubleday & Company, 1956), 152.

[13]John Macmurray, *The Self as Agent* (New York: Harper and Brothers, 1957), 181.

[14]Pinar et al., *Understanding Curriculum*, xvii.

[15]Ibid., 851.

[16]Ibid., 852.

[17]For an example in another field see Brooks Holifield, *A History of Pastoral Care in America: From Salvation to Self Realization* (Nashville: Abingdon Press, 1983).

[18]Dwayne Huebner, "The Moribund Curriculum Field: Its Wake and Our Work," *Curriculum Inquiry 6*, no. 2 (1976): 153–167; Chapter 20.

[19]Ralph Tyler, *Basic Principles of Curriculum and Instruction* (Chicago: The University of Chicago Press, 1949).

Autobiographical Statement[1]

(1975)

I am a child of working class parents and of the depression who found first time educational success and a potential career in the physical sciences in high school. Having met a great high school chemistry and physics teacher, I started by majoring in chemistry and served as a lab assistant in the local junior college. From there the armed services took over and I ended up in a program in electrical engineering at Texas A & M. It seemed natural to put my two interests together and to go into nuclear physics.

That idea lost its hold as I became more and more disillusioned with my own education and the education of some of the people around me. I was also becoming less excited by the intellectual challenges of the physical sciences.

To better understand my own poor education and to see if I could improve the education of others, I chose to study teaching. It seemed logical to start where formal education begins so I decided to major in elementary education. The University of Chicago and Teachers College, Columbia University seemed likely places because of the well-known educators associated with both places and the early influences of the two institutions. Chicago accepted my application and I entered an elementary education program in the division of the social sciences. With my background in the physical sciences and mathematics, and the corresponding lack of background in the humanities, history, and the social and behavioral sciences, I struggled with the demands to use language rather than numbers and to be with people rather than with apparatus. I did it with reasonable, if unglowing, success. I taught elementary school for two years, long enough to know that I knew very little about teaching and education.

---

[1]Originally published in *Curriculum Theorizing: The Reconceptualists*, ed. William F. Pinar, 213-215 (Berkeley, CA: McCutchan, 1975).

While at Chicago, besides coming under the influence of some of their notables, I had the good fortune to come to know Paul Eberman and Virgil Herrick. Herrick and Tyler had had their conference on curriculum theory while I was there, and Eberman was completing his doctorate at Chicago and was an instructor in the elementary education program. Herrick left Chicago to begin a new program in elementary education at Wisconsin, and Eberman was invited to join the new program (where he stayed until accepting the deanship at Temple). With the sensitivity of a fine human being and an excellent educator, Eberman invited me to continue graduate studies at Wisconsin with the promise of research assistantships. I stopped teaching in elementary schools to undertake three full years of doctoral work in education and sociology to overcome my ignorance. The work was primarily positivistic—empirical and statistical and good. Wisconsin required a minor for the Ph.D. and we got to know students and staff in other departments throughout the university. In my third year I participated in an experimental program for a dozen doctoral students from diverse departments of the university who lived in an old mansion and held weekly seminars on their various disciplines—my first face to face contact with interdisciplinary work. My research assistantships involved the study of handwriting and classroom interaction using a Q-sort technique. With the completion of my course work and the beginning of the dissertation, I began to sense that my statistical and empirical competencies far outweighed my conceptual competencies. My last year in the university was spent in the library and in a seminar with Hans Gerth in advanced social psychology. My philosophical interests were starting to develop. Of major formative value at that time were Talcott Parsons, Donald Hebb, Susanne Langer, Ernst Cassirer and Bertrand Russell. From that point on the intellectual development was strange, rather subconsciously self-directing, and increasingly alienating from my colleagues in education. As I began my college teaching career in a preservice program I found myself turning to the mystics of the East and West including Meister Eckhart and other Rhineland mystics and some Buddhists. The religious dimension of this took me into Tillich's three volumes of his systematic theology and gradually into the writing of other theologians. By the time I left undergraduate teaching to join the staff of Teachers College, I had stopped reading in the positivistic sciences, whether sociology or psychology, and was into existentialism by way of Marcel, Merleau-Ponty, Jaspers, Sartre and others. My interest in theology led to advising in the joint program between Teachers College and Union Theological Seminary and very rewarding contacts with diverse theologians, including a short time as a visiting scholar with the Episcopal Theological Seminary of the Southwest.

Throughout this contact with the diverse philosophical and theological traditions, the basic operating assumptions of curriculum thought bothered me. How could one plan educational futures via behavior objectives when the mystical literature emphasized the present moment and the need to let the future care for itself? The thread that ran through my questions and my searching was an intuition that an understanding of the nature of time was essential for understanding the nature of education. This intuition turned me to the literature on time and the criticism of learning theory as only one way of conceptualizing man's temporality. Heidegger's basic work *Being and Time* kept coming before me, and when the Macquarrie translation of it became available I bought it, to remain on the shelf for a year until I had the time to get into his language. Reading Heidegger was as freeing as reading Parsons and Shils in my early sociological days, or Hebb in my early psychological days, or Langer in philosophy or Tillich in theology. New ways of thinking became available—new questions, new modes of speech. With the cracking of my native scientific bent by Heidegger, and the preparation for that crack by Langer, Tillich, and others, I found it possible to reconceptualize the educational process and to begin intentionally to weed out the work of others which would fill in bits and pieces. And so the progress to hermeneutics via Ricouer and Palmer, and to critical theory via Marcuse and Habermas. The journey has been lonely at times, but the direction feels right even though the destination seems veiled in a "Cloud of Unknowing." I am convinced that the curriculum person's dependency on scientific thought patterns, even though these have not yet found their way into practice as they should, has broken his linkage with other very great and important intellectual traditions of East and West which have profound bearing on the talking about the practice of education.

Chronology of Events

Date of birth: October 16, 1923
Education:
1943: Grand Rapids Junior College (Michigan)
1945: Texas A & M
1949: M.A., University of Chicago
1959: Ph.D., University of Wisconsin-Madison.

APPOINTMENTS

1994 Horace Bushnell Professor Emeritus of Christian Nurture
1990-1993 Associate Dean of Academic Affairs, The Divinity School, Yale University.
1992- Horace Bushnell Professor of Christian Nurture
1985- Professor of Christian Education, The Divinity School, Yale University
1982-1985 Visiting Professor of Christian Education, The Divinity School, Yale University
1981- Adjunct Faculty and Consultant, Auburn Theological Seminary
1979-1982 Chairman, Department of Curriculum and Teaching, Teachers College, Columbia University
1970-1975 Lecturer, Union Theological Seminary
1964-1966 Principal Agnes Russell School, Teachers College, Columbia University
1957-1982 Assistant, Associate, and Professor, Teachers College, Columbia University
1954-1957 Assistant Professor, Northern Illinois University
1949-1951 Elementary schoolteacher, Michigan.

Author Index

Subject Index

A

Administrators, *see also* Supervisors
  power of, 238
  role of, 385–386
  teachers' discourse with, 302–303
Aesthetic experiences, 60–63
  heightens sensitivity to sensory data,
    59–60
Aesthetic valuing of educational activity,
    dimensions of
  psychical distance, 109
  symbolic meaning, 109–110
  wholeness and design, 109
Aloneness, 76
Artistic skill, 58–59
Artists, 23–24, 88
  teachers as
    appreciation of and sensitivity to
      others' art, 29–30
    crafts of, 32–33
    emotional responsiveness of, 28–29
    molding "cage" of creation, 31–32
    standing at hub of things, 27–28
    turning inward to compose, 30–31
Artist-teachers, 29–30
Art(s), 37, 62, 63, 148, 436, *see also*
    Teaching, art of
  exploration and expression in, 58
  nature of, 23–24, 26–33
ASCD, 233, 234, 238, 239
Authoritarianism, 237
Autobiography, 381–382, 440
  of social relations, 288
Awe, 3, 5, 6–8, 124, 408, *see also* Wonder

B

Being-in-the-world, 137–140, 143–144
  language and, 147–149
Behavioral sciences, 2–3, 7, 131, 168, 170,
  discourse of, 215–217, 404,
  and teachers 301
  education in the church 176–177
Biography, 135, 185, 226, 286–287
Breath, spirit as, 343
Burnout, teacher, 379, 413

C

Care, 156, 187–188, 189, 349–350,
    363–366, 374
Caregiver, 261, 266, 278, 292–294
Challenge-routine, 70–71
Change 381–382
Change and innovation, 118–119, 135,
    310, 405
  and responsiveness, 119–124
  rhythms of, 141
Chaos, ordering of, 23, 114–115
Child advocacy, 443–445
Child rights, 200, 202
Child-study movement, 250–251
Christian education, 321–325, *see also* Re-
    ligious education
Christian growth in faith, 369–377
Christianity, 317, 369–372, 375, 403
Church, 318–319, 424, *see also* Clergy;
    Congregation
  education and, 175–183

D

E

462

SUBJECT INDEX

as work, xxiii
goals of, 404–406
meanings, xxi
need to rethink, 175–177
presence of new being, 187–189, 195, 197
sociopolitical structure, spirituality and, 406–407, 414–415
theoretical perspectives, 198–206
Educational activity, 105, *see also* Curricular thought, valuing and
esthetic valuing of, 114–117
ethical valuing
forgiveness and, 114, 126
knowledge an instrument of promise, 113
response-ability and, 112–113
speech and conversation and, 112–113
goals, purposes, and objectives, 132–133, 141
noninstrumentality of, *see* Psychical distance
political, 108
prophetic criticism and, 396–400
role of influence in, 111–112
Educational conditions, 160–161
economic realities, 161–164
fabrication of, 165–166
historical realities, 163–164
political realities, 164–165
Educational content, 205, *see also* Curriculum content
spirituality and, 407–411
"thingness" of, 198
from learning to, 199–206
traditional conceptions and, 206–209
as stranger, 361–362, 408
Educational environment(s), 160–161, 404, 406, 434
aspects of, 221–222
curricular practice as, 221–223
designing, 166–168, 170, 172–173
problems in, 167
values reflected in, 167
history, 223–224
impact on education, 160–161
reality of human situation and, 168–169
sources of environmental components, 224
Educational ideologies, 17, 19–20, 164–165, 251, 301–302
Educational process

dimensions, 440
sources for thinking about, 2–3
Educational technology, 253–254
"Educative," 205
Educators
conflict of interest between students and, 200, 203
failure to speak for children, 443
responsibility for quality of education, 299–300
Elementary curriculum, inadequate design of, 10–13
Elites, educational, 17, 19, 21
power of, 17, 19, 20
Encounters, *see* "Dialogical encounter"; Social encounter
Environmental design, xix
Epistemology, 54–56, *see also* Knowing
Esthetics, *see* Aesthetics
Ethical value systems, *see also* Educational activity, ethical valuing of
curricular thought and, 110–114
Evaluation, 413–414
Existentialism, 5, 88–91, 136–139, 146, *see also* Temporality; Time
educational implications, 3, 7
Explanatory language, 215–216

F

Faith, 307, 334
communities, 368
human growth and, 369–377
Farley, Edward
homiletic paradigm, 423, 425
"ordered learning," nurture, and formation of faith, 423, 425–427
theological and church education and, 417–419, 422–423
Forgiveness, 114, 126
God's, 371–373, 393
Freedom, 76, 91
learning process and, 6

G

Gender, language and, xiii, 268, 269, 271, 275–280
Gender roles and gender discrimination, 314–316
"Genetic epistemology," Piaget and, 259
Goals and objectives, language of, 132–133, 383